Research Methods for
Environmental Psychology

"The chapters in this volume offer a broad-gauged, in-depth overview of diverse research methods for studying and improving people's relationships with their everyday surroundings. This book will be an invaluable resource for scholars and practitioners working in the interdisciplinary fields of environmental psychology, urban planning, and environmental design research."

Daniel Stokols, Ph.D., Chancellor's Professor Emeritus,
School of Social Ecology, University of California,
Irvine, USA

"A highly accessible and long overdue book which sets the methods in context by starting with the problems environmental psychologists are trying to solve; it reflects what we tell our students to do – start with the problem and then explore the most appropriate methodology, not vice versa. An interesting choice of research methods have been selected that go beyond the normal suspects."

David Uzzell, Professor of Environmental Psychology,
University of Surrey, UK

"This is not only a volume on research methods, but an invaluable book showing the incredible richness and potential of the still growing field of environmental psychology."

Mirilia Bonnes, Professor of Social and
Environmental Psychology, Sapienza
University of Rome, Italy

"As economic and global climate changes press human health and the human spirit, insights about how to study the role of the physical environment in human behavior are more critical than ever. This volume provides up-to-date overviews of multiple methodological approaches to studying human–environment relations. The collective wisdom and experiences of the chapter authors reflect well on environmental psychology. Professionals, scholars, and advanced students interested in people and the environment will repeatedly rely on this volume."

Gary W. Evans, Elizabeth Lee Vincent
Professor of Human Ecology,
Cornell University, USA

"In this much-needed book research methods are introduced in a fun way without overly simplifying the topics, which should appeal to both students and teachers. The uniquely broad coverage of different research methods in environmental psychology will be very useful for academic courses."

Tommy Gärling, Emeritus Professor of Psychology,
University of Gothenburg, Sweden

Research Methods for Environmental Psychology

Edited by
Robert Gifford

WILEY Blackwell

This edition first published 2016
© 2016 John Wiley & Sons, Ltd

Registered Office
John Wiley & Sons, Ltd, The Atrium, Southern Gate, Chichester, West Sussex, PO19 8SQ, UK

Editorial Offices
350 Main Street, Malden, MA 02148-5020, USA
9600 Garsington Road, Oxford, OX4 2DQ, UK
The Atrium, Southern Gate, Chichester, West Sussex, PO19 8SQ, UK

For details of our global editorial offices, for customer services, and for information about how to apply for permission to reuse the copyright material in this book please see our website at www.wiley.com/wiley-blackwell.

Library of Congress Cataloging-in-Publication Data

Names: Gifford, Robert, editor.
Title: Research methods for environmental psychology / edited by Robert Gifford.
Description: Hoboken : Wiley, 2015. | Includes bibliographical references and index.
Identifiers: LCCN 2015031981 (print) | LCCN 2015039975 (ebook) |
    ISBN 9781118795330 (cloth) | ISBN 9781118795385 (pbk.) |
    ISBN 9781118795415 (pdf) | ISBN 9781118795453 (epub)
Subjects: LCSH: Environmental psychology–Research.
Classification: LCC BF353.R46 2015 (print) | LCC BF353 (ebook) | DDC 155.9072/1–dc23
LC record available at http://lccn.loc.gov/2015031981

A catalogue record for this book is available from the British Library.

Cover image: © fotoVoyager/iStockphoto

Set in 9.5/11.5pt Galliard by SPi Global, Pondicherry, India
Printed and bound in Malaysia by Vivar Printing Sdn Bhd

1   2016

Contents

Contributors

Wokje Abrahamse   Victoria University of Wellington, New Zealand

Paul A. Bell   Colorado State University, CO, United States

Navjot Bhullar   University of New England, NSW, Australia

David Canter   University of Huddersfield, United Kingdom

Angel Chen   University of Victoria, BC, Canada

Victor Corral-Verdugo   Universidad de Sonora, Mexico

Valeria Cortés   University of Victoria, BC, Canada

Thomas Doherty   Lewis and Clark Graduate School, OR, United States

Jay Farbstein   Jay Farbstein & Associates, Los Angeles, CA, United States

Martha Frias-Armenta   Universidad de Sonora, Mexico

E. Scott Geller   Virginia Polytechnic Institute and State University, VA, United States

Robert Gifford   University of Victoria, BC, Canada

Harneet K. Gill   Victoria University of Wellington, New Zealand

Branda Guan   University of Victoria, BC, Canada

Donald W. Hine   University of New England, NSW, Australia

Christine Kormos   University of Victoria, BC, Canada

Anthony D. G. Marks   University of New England, NSW, Australia

Mark Martin   Optimal Environments, Inc., FL, United States

Lindsay J. McCunn   University of Victoria, BC, Canada

Amanda McIntyre   University of Victoria, BC, Canada

Taciano L. Milfont   Victoria University of Wellington, New Zealand

Daniel R. Montello   University of California, Santa Barbara, CA, United States

Cheuk Fan Ng   Athabasca University, AB, Canada

P. Wesley Schultz   California State University, San Marcos, CA, United States

David Seamon   Kansas State University, KS, United States

Jennifer Senick   Rutgers University, NJ, United States

Arthur E. Stamps III   Institute of Environmental Quality, San Francisco, CA, United States

Linda Steg   University of Groningen, The Netherlands

Robert Sommer   University of California, Davis, CA, United States

Reuven Sussman   University of Victoria, BC, Canada

Richard E. Wener   New York University, NY, United States

John Zeisel   Hearthstone Alzheimer Care, United States

1

Introduction
Environmental Psychology and its Methods

Robert Gifford
University of Victoria, BC, Canada

How did we get here? I don't mean biologically; I mean to the point where we are sharing a book about how to do research in environmental psychology. You will have your story; here is mine. Like many others, I was initially drawn to psychology because of its potential to help people with emotional and cognitive difficulties. I entered graduate school as a student in clinical psychology, even though I had worked as an undergraduate assistant for a professor (Robert Sommer) who was curious about such things as how people tended to space themselves from others and whether one's choice of study areas influenced academic performance. These studies were driven partly by pure curiosity about how humans operate in their daily environments, and partly by the goal of informing environmental design from the person outward rather than from the building inward. Put another way, these studies sought to discover fundamental *principles* of human behavior, which could then be translated into *practice* by talented designers, who would create people-centered optimal environments.

I slowly realized that I was more suited and more interested in these questions and goals than I was in being a clinical psychologist. At about the same time, in the late 1960s, what we had been doing acquired a name, environmental psychology.[1] In some senses, having a name makes something real, or at least more real. Activity becomes legitimized, recognized, and organized. After dropping out of graduate school (I also dropped out of kindergarten, but that is another story) and contemplating my future in a cabin on a remote island that had no electricity or running water, or even any furniture, I knew I had to be engaged in discovering the principles and aiding the practice as an environmental psychologist. I went back to graduate school, and here I am, 45 years later.

Why this personal story? Frankly, it is an attempt to connect with you, the reader, who also probably did not enter your post-secondary education with a ringing declaration that "I want to be an environmental psychologist!" Your story undoubtedly

Research Methods for Environmental Psychology, First Edition. Edited by Robert Gifford.

differs from mine in its details, but I suspect that in broad terms it is the same. At some point you discovered environmental psychology, you were intrigued, and here *you* are.

So, where is it exactly that you are? You may well have entered this big house through a variety of doors. Do you want to conduct fundamental research, that is to learn how humans interact with their physical environments (without any particular or immediate application to saving the planet or designing better buildings)? If so, welcome to the big house; this book has chapters for you. Do you want to understand how the physical environment impacts people in negative and positive ways? We have space in the big house for you, too. I know … you want to learn how and why people are damaging the only planet we have available to live on. Yes, of course, this big house has space for you, as well. All this book's editor expects is that you respect and tolerate others in the house who have different goals.

Environmental psychology needs all of you, just as medicine needs fundamental biochemistry, knowledge about pathogens and paths to health, those whose practice focuses on the usual but important run of flu and fractures, and activist physicians who are willing to put their lives on the line by going to the front lines of the latest dangerous epidemic or war.

That is why the book has four protagonists, whom you will meet at the beginning of each chapter. I hope you will see a bit or a lot of yourself in one of these characters. They are all just now entering graduate school. Maria, Ethan, Gabriel, and Annabelle share a house and are friends who met through school or work. All four happen to be dedicated to environmental psychology, but they vary in their interests within the field and in their backgrounds.

Maria has a undergraduate degree in psychology, with a minor in neuroscience. She believes that knowledge advances best when strong and clear scientific methods are employed. She feels most comfortable in the laboratory, but she is willing to leave the lab to work on problems as long as the issue can be worked on with scientific methods. Privately, she is skeptical about the validity of field studies.

Ethan also has an undergraduate degree in psychology, but his minor was in sociology. He prefers to study environmental issues in the community, through surveys, interviews, and talking to community members. He believes that lab studies have their place, but ecological validity trumps the value of the confined laboratory. He is not so private about his belief that you can't be sure of any finding that isn't verified in the community. He belongs to three activist organizations.

Gabriel's undergraduate degree was in geography. He spent a year in architecture school before realizing that he was more interested in the human dimensions of the built environment. Currently, he has a co-op position with the regional government; he is taking a term off from graduate school, but will return next term. Every day he hears from co-workers about how academics are OK, but they take far too long to conduct studies, and are unrealistic about policy, politics, and the application of research to the real world. Although he is a scientist at heart, he largely agrees with them. He is trying hard to bridge the science–policy gap.

Annabelle did her undergraduate degree in psychology, but she took as many courses about people with problems as she could; if she were not primarily interested in environmental psychology, she would be a clinical psychologist or social worker. Her minor was in environmental studies and she gets out into nature almost every weekend.

Annabelle sees research more as a way to solve immediate problems for people. She is most comfortable with qualitative approaches, with research that has an immediate impact, and with research that sooner or later will help people overcome their personal difficulties.

As another way to connect the graduate student experience with this book, I invited some of my own advanced students to co-write the chapters with established, senior, well-published co-authors. The goal was to maximize the chances that each chapter reflected (a) the ways and means that people who are just entering environmental psychology understand it, and (b) the great experience that the senior authors possess. I hope that comes through as you read the chapters.

Which chapters? I thought you never would ask! OK, here is the preview. We cannot be a credible force in the world, even as activists, if we do not have a firm foundation in basic research. Without it we are simply ... I was going to use a common phrase that involves "... the wind," but let's change that to "an ignored voice, devoid of authority." So Chapter 2, by Reuven Sussman, describes what I call Step One: observing what actually occurs in an environmental context. We should "just watch" first, then try to figure out what is going on and how to change it. But "just watching" requires more special skills than one might think. So Reuven informally calls it "You Can Observe A Lot Just by Watching," a cute title with an important theme. Whether you are studying how the built environment affects the behavior of its occupants or whether people recycle resources into the correct receptacles, a very important first step is to simply watch people, without trying to change or influence them. The design and execution of an intervention to change people or the environment can be greatly successful and useful (or not!), depending on observations about what people are actually doing now. Haste in conducting an intervention might, for example, involve much effort at changing a behavior that is already common (but you did not know that), or changing one that is so resistant to change that the planned intervention simply will not be effective. Just watching people will help to shape the nature of your study, and help to avoid you wasting much time and effort on a research design that is doomed to failure because you assumed what was going on in the setting but, sadly, you were wrong.

Chapter 3, by Cheuk Fan Ng, focuses on three special kinds of watching. Behavior mapping is about "adding up" the paths and activities of many people who use or visit a particular setting. Behavior tracking is doing the same for specific individuals in the setting, often those who have a special relationship with that setting. Observing physical traces is the "archeological" form of observation in environmental psychology. After many people have used a setting, they collectively leave traces: the wear on the floor, the impromptu signs put up, the path across the grass between buildings. This tells much about how the setting is being used.

Wokje Abrahamse, Linda Steg, and Wes Schultz contributed Chapter 4, all about the basics of moving beyond observation to actually conducting research in environmental psychology, with an emphasis on understanding human failings in our treatment of the environment. Some aspects and methods of research in environmental psychology are similar to those in other areas of psychology, but they focus on topics of interest in this big house. If you have taken a course called Research Methods in Psychology, these will be ... let's not say redundant; let's say they will be refreshers. Who remembers everything about random assignment and statistics anyway? So Chapter 4 is like that. The basics, applied to environmental psychology.

Chapter 5, by Donald Hine, Christine Kormos, and Anthony Marks, reverts to the "often used in other fields" category. However, their topic, Survey and Interview Techniques, is highly customized for this big house, and includes some ideas and techniques that are not found or used in those other fields.

Chapter 6, by Amanda McIntyre and Taciano Milfont, is the book's big-house take on the most commonly used method in all of psychology. However, no other area of psychology uses *these* measures, which have been developed over the lifetime of environmental psychology specifically to learn how people think about the physical environment. Need a tool for that? McIntyre and Milfont describe and discuss a whole toolbox of instruments for measuring each particular kind of attitude toward the environment ... and if you think there is just one, you will be surprised. Selecting the most appropriate attitude measure for the hypothesis you wish to test is just as important as selecting the correct wrench for loosening a nut.

Not all methods use "objective" methods (actually, perhaps no method is fully objective anyway, but you know what I mean). In Chapter 7, David Seamon and Harneet Gill explain how to use qualitative approaches in environment-behavior research. The great value of this approach is that "the people speak, and in their own tongue." What I mean by this is that in experiments, we researchers *impose* conditions on participants and then observe how they respond. Usually we don't know what is going on in the "black box" of their minds, and that is a crucial part of learning about any person–environment interaction. Even if we conduct a survey or an interview, most of the time the person is restricted to answering the questions we ask; what if the important aspects of the person's interaction with the environment is not among the questions we ask? We should often or even always try to "learn what is going on" before we rush into experiments and interventions. What are people in a particular environment of interest thinking and experiencing, in their own words, before we impose our own frames on that experience by asking questions of our own choice, or pressing them from our external positions without knowing how they experience their environments?

I vividly remember a study that Donald Hine and I conducted in which we asked participants to "think aloud" *as* they made decisions about allocating natural resources in a microworld (see below for a chapter on microworlds). We were quite surprised at some of the rationales we heard: in the whole history of experiments in that area, no researcher had thought to investigate *these* rationales, which were important to the people in our study who were making decisions. Without a qualitative approach, some of these rationales may never have come to light.

Chapter 8, by David Canter, explores the question: "how do different places fit together – or not – in people's minds?" Which aspects of, say, restaurants or schools or cities, make them similar to or different from us? Canter explains several methods for assessing place constructs.

In Chapter 9, Daniel Montello will take you into the world of finding our way around environments. Cognition is a core psychological process, often studied in other areas of the discipline, but *spatial* cognition is a specialty of environmental psychology. Where would we be without it? Constantly lost, is where, which is why spatial cognition is so important. Because studying cognition itself is very difficult,

Montello focuses on the observables: our behavior that reflects what we must be thinking as we navigate real and virtual spaces. Spatial cognition research spans our twin themes of principles and practice: just how it works (or not) is fascinating, but what we learn about it can have huge effects on the wayfinding success (or failure) of every person who tries to find any destination, in terms of helpful (or useless) signage or building design.

Chapter 10, by Angel Chen and Paul Bell, is about microworlds, that is, computer programs that simulate natural resources and the decisions that people make about using them. We know that people often (but not always) do a poor job of managing the bounty that Earth offers, but what is it that leads us to make more or less sustainable choices? One may choose to study a real-world commons (i.e., any shared limited, potentially renewable natural resource from which a number of harvesters may remove resources, such as a fishery or shared grazing land). However, as in any real-world context, identifying the causes of a person's choices is difficult or even impossible because researchers usually are unable control the influences or factors that drive that person's choices. Thus, causal relations cannot be known in field studies. To learn about the causes, for decades environmental psychologists have been creating simulated resource dilemmas called microworlds to do just that. Chen and Bell review the main methods and microworlds that can be used to supply answers to this crucial question.

How do we understand, perceive, or comprehend the built environment? If we could see them before they are built, might we avoid bad design or create more beautiful designs? Chapter 11, by Arthur Stamps, explicates the methods and challenges involved in simulating built environments. Again we have a topic (perception) that is traditional in psychology, but is unique in its emphasis on the built environment. Again we have a topic that spans principles and practice: Simulations may be employed to discover the fundamental science of human perceptual tendencies but also to inform the design of built environments that are actually to be (or already are) constructed or renovated.

This logically leads to the subject of Chapter 12, about planning the built environment through programming, contributed by Jay Farbstein, Richard Wener, and Lindsay McCunn. When any new building is contemplated, one might leave its design to the architect's imagination, or one might work with the architect to design the building from its future users outward. That is, one might (environmental psychologists say *should*) begin with the needs and desires of those who will use the new building when it is being designed. Some may foolishly believe that these needs and desires are known or obvious; much experience of environmental psychologists says they are not. Programming is the systematic, user-centered method for creating building designs that will optimally serve those who will work, study, live, or visit it.

In turn, this leads to Chapter 13, by Richard Wener, Lindsay McCunn, and Jennifer Senick, on post-occupancy evaluation. After the building has been constructed, does it work for those who use it? Whether the "plan" was merely in a designer's head (without any programming as in Chapter 12) or even if it was carefully planned with well-conducted programming, is the real structure, as built, working for those who use it? Programs may be thought of as a kind of hypothesis, and hypotheses should be tested. Wener, McCunn, and Senick describe the methods we use to test the hypothesis that the formal programming (or "based on my experience" guesses when programming was not done) worked to deliver what it promised, whether that is client satisfaction, or work efficiency, or optimal social relations, or anything else.

In Chapter 14, on action research, Valeria Cortés and Robert Sommer describe how to make a difference in the real world while conducting scientific research at the same time. Most environmental psychologists either conduct research to discover the principles of person–environment relations, or work to implement those principles in some real-world setting. Action research fuses the search for principles *with* their application to practice. For some, this is the dream or epitome of environmental psychology: doing both at the same time. Cortés and Sommer explain how to carry off this important two-for-one goal. Action research has its own special methods, ways to achieve both objectives without falling into a number of potential pitfalls.

Action researchers often focus on the built environment. In Chapters 15 and 16, we move to improving sustainability in one context or another. In Chapter 15, Wokje Abrahamse emphasizes the various strategies and research designs that can be used to create science-oriented change in real-world behavior. In Chapter 16, Scott Geller with Wokje Abrahamse, Reuven Sussman, and Branda Guan outline the specific approach to interventions called applied behavioral science (ABS). Although ABS and the approaches in Chapter 15 share the same goals, they offer a choice of philosophies about how to achieve those goals.

In Chapter 17, on ecotherapy, by Thomas Doherty and Angel Chen, the focus moves from improving the environment with human scientific efforts to improving people with environmental efforts. Nature is know to be a healing force (when it is not destroying people and places!). In the Hindu Shaivism tradition, the god Shiva is the creator, destroyer, and preserver – the very (spiritual) embodiment of what nature does for us and to us. Doherty and Chen document how nature can be harnessed, when it is being nice, to improve human functioning.

Not everyone has the same capabilities, and in Chapter 18, John Zeisel, Mark Martin, Lindsay McCunn, and I discuss some methods and concerns that are required in researching special populations. Disabilities come in many forms, each requiring somewhat different methods depending on which ability has been reduced, so we obviously cannot describe methods for every disability, but we thought as much as we could of the sorts of considerations that might be general as we wrote about designing for persons with Alzheimer's (more of a cognitive problem) and multiple sclerosis (more of a physical problem).

Chapter 19, by Donald Hine, Victor Corral-Verdugo, Navjot Bhullar, and Martha Frias-Armenta, gets serious about numbers. Quantitative empirical science measures things. Measurement results in numbers. Numbers must be analyzed to decide whether those numbers are meaningful. Policymakers ignore numbers that are not meaningful (yes, policymakers also sometimes ignore meaningful numbers, but if the results are not statistically meaningful, they have very little chance of their meaning being moved toward policy). So, environmental psychology must include ways of deciding whether the numbers that emerge from our studies are meaningful. This book assumes that its readers already have some knowledge of statistics, including such basics as correlations, t-tests, analysis of variance, multiple regression, and perhaps factor analysis. Hine et al. describe the more interesting, useful, advanced, and newer forms of deciding whether the numbers are meaningful, that is, multi-level modeling and structural equation modeling. These words may well sound scary to anyone new to them, but the authors explain them in nice, clear prose, without too many formulae and subscripts, so that even the neophyte will come away from Chapter 19 at least well informed about what these modern techniques have to offer.

Finally, we must recognize that every individual study is limited in its sample population, the measures used, and the influences considered. Therefore no study "proves" any general principle. So, research is useless? Not at all. I like to compare the research we do to the work ants do, although that may sound unflattering (whether to researchers or to ants depends on one's point of view). Each study, like each grain of sand laboriously carried to the anthill and carefully placed there, is a valuable contribution to a larger whole. How do we create our "anthill" in science? We must somehow combine the results of studies. We can either do that by "eye-balling" the published studies (i.e., subjectively decide what all the "grains of sand" amount to, and write a narrative about them), or by combining them in a scientific (and therefore more objective) way. In Chapter 20, Christine Kormos shows just how to do that through meta-analysis.

The starry galaxy of authors of these chapters and I sincerely hope that you find our explications of environmental psychology's research methods useful.

Note

1   Let's get one thing out of the way right now: the name thing. Since the 1960s, several other names for the field have been proposed. Among these are *environment and behavior*, *ecopsychology*, and *conservation psychology*. In fact, the very first conferences that focused on these topics, in the mid-1960s, used the name *architectural psychology*. Quickly, however, those involved realized that the field included questions and answers that went beyond buildings to broader concerns with the environment itself, and *environmental psychology* was chosen as the most appropriate name. This name covers the whole field, from fundamental psychological processes such as perception and cognition of the built and natural environment to the use of everyday space by people, the design of physical settings of all kinds, understanding the impacts on people and by people on natural resources both living and not, and the climate-related behavior and attitudes. I suppose you can call it what you want to, but I believe that each of the other names represent pieces of the whole. *Environment and behavior*, by its very name, excludes such constructs as attitudes, values, and norms (although the journal of that name does publish studies involving these mental constructs). *Ecopsychology* focuses on clinical or therapeutic experiences. *Conservation psychology*, a name inspired by, and parallel to, conservation biology, originally focused on human–animal relations, although some have tried to broaden its scope to include the conservation of nature and natural resources, which was already being investigated by environmental psychologists. Perhaps it is natural that over time some researchers within a broader field specialize and prefer a narrower name for their work. I do not mean at all that the topics studied under these banners are not valuable, and so I have invited chapters on what would fit under these names in this book. However, environmental psychologists as a group unfortunately are so far a mere drop in the bucket of psychology as a whole. The membership of Division 34, the home of APA's members with these interests, is less than one-third of one percent the size of APA's total membership. This very clearly signals to

me that we should use the inclusive name environmental psychology for all who are interested, regardless of our personal research interests, partly because it is the most accurate and inclusive umbrella terms of all these topics, and partly to avoid the field splintering into even smaller factions, which likely would be followed by oblivion. Only through having an inclusive, widely accepted "brand" will universities continue to fund professorships in this field, and professors are the essential institutional foundation for training future researchers like you, who, of course, represent the future of the field. Creating and promoting even smaller groups could lead to the disappearance of the field through the attrition of university professors and programs with the inclusive name.

2

Observational Methods
The First Step in Science

Reuven Sussman
University of Victoria, BC, Canada

"Great show last night, Gabe!" exclaims Maria, referring to Gabriel's band's show the night before at Clinton's. "Really, because I thought the show went much better last month at Sneeky Dees," answers Gabriel. "Don't you remember, everyone was dancing and singing along … And they even demanded two encores!"

The conversation reawakens a question in Gabriel's mind that he had been secretly pondering for some time. Why were the shows at some bars more fun for the audience than others? Last month they played almost the same songs, to a similar audience, who drank (according to the bar tab) nearly the same amount of alcohol; and yet there was far more audience engagement at the first show than at the second. After two years of playing in just about every bar in the city, Gabriel thinks he might have an idea – the physical environment is playing a role in helping the audience engage with the band.

Gabriel decides to put his architectural research skills to use and, for the next few weeks, meticulously records detailed information about every show he attends (as an audience member). He notes all of the physical aspects of the space (such as lighting and the placement of tables and bar stools), as well as the number of people, the alcohol consumed, the weather outside and, of course, the amount of audience participation. Despite Maria's incessant complaining ("this is useless, you can't learn anything without controlling all the variables!"), he enlists her help, and after each show they compare notes to see how much they agree in their observations.

Eventually, a pattern seems to emerge – smaller bars with lower light levels and less seating appear to have more audience members closer to the stage, dancing and singing along.[1] Maria is impressed, but unconvinced. "This doesn't prove anything, Gabe," she points out, "there are too many possible explanations. Maybe the best bands play at certain bars, or maybe people go to those bars because they know that they'll have a good time there."

Gabriel knows Maria has a point. So he asks a friend of his who owns a local bar if he could systematically change certain aspects of the stage and dancing area to see if they have an effect on audience participation. His friend agrees, and over

Research Methods for Environmental Psychology, First Edition. Edited by Robert Gifford.
© 2016 John Wiley & Sons, Ltd. Published 2016 by John Wiley & Sons, Ltd.

the next few weeks, Gabriel changes the lighting levels, size of the dance floor, and other aspects of the physical environment while several friends independently record observations of audience responses. With the same bands playing every week and similar audiences attending the shows, Gabriel and his team are able to empirically demonstrate that his theory is correct – the physical environment indeed plays a role in audience involvement!

Although Maria isn't impressed at his methods, she can't deny that she had witnessed a real change in behavior as a result of Gabriel's suggestions to the bar owner. Gabriel now knows the secret to picking the best venues for his band and is able to earn a little extra cash as design consultant for bars and restaurants!

With such an emphasis today on survey methods in behavioral sciences, one might easily forget that **observation** is the true foundation of the scientific method. Indeed, "simple observation" was the tool by which Babylonians pioneered the earliest forms of astronomy. Later, the formation of empiricism in ancient Greece required a movement away from purely philosophical and (often) supernatural explanations of causes to more concrete approaches founded on observation and induction.

With the establishment of psychology and other behavioral sciences, observational research continued to play a role, but its importance has waxed and waned over the years. In the early years, psychologists were keen to demonstrate that their field was a true "science" and thus that it, like other scientific fields, relied heavily on physical, observable evidence. Later, psychology shifted its focus to Freudian principles and internal states, only to later shift back to behaviorism and observable actions. In recent years, however, with the rise of cognitivism and diminished interest in behavioral approaches, the field has once again moved to measures of internal states and self-reported behavior, as evidenced by the gradual shift from observation to self-reports in both of the major environment–behavior research journals: *Journal of Environmental Psychology* and *Environment and Behavior* (Giuliani & Scopelliti, 2009).

Perhaps the focus of behavioral research now relies too heavily on survey methods and theory testing without real behavioral observation. Many commonly held beliefs can often be overturned by simple observation; for example, Underhill and his colleagues (Underhill, 2000) learned that, contrary to popular belief, the best selling location for store items is *not* right by the entrance. Despite every customer passing this area, it is almost always ignored; customers do not actually begin shopping or looking for items until they are a minimum of several feet inside the door. This type of insight is easily and clearly established by waiting, watching, and recording.

The rest of this chapter will be devoted to: (1) defining observational research and when it is appropriate for use, (2) describing general approaches and specific methods for observation (along with their ethical considerations), and (3) discussing the intricacies of **coding** and inter-observer reliability.

What is Observational Research and Why do it?

In its simplest form, observation can be defined as receiving information through one of the five human senses. By this definition, however, nearly every study of behavior within an environment involves observation. Certainly, watching people explore a space or use a recycling bin is a form of observation, but so too would be viewing the results of cortisol tests or listening to answers from an interview. Given that topics such as interviewing, participant observation, and surveying will be covered elsewhere in this book (mainly Chapter 5), this chapter will focus solely on research methods pertaining to direct observation.

Indirect observation, another important tool for the study of environment–behavior relationships, involves methods such as personal diaries, informants, or **trace measures**. These will not be examined in depth here, only to say that they can be quite effective. For example, the Rochester Interaction Record (Wheeler & Nezlek, 1977), and related Social Behavior Inventory (Moskowitz, 1994), standardized **event-contingent reporting** methods (diary methods) are reliable and valid ways to learn about participants' daily interactions from their own notes. In addition, trace measures (or a lack thereof) caused by erosion, leftovers, adaptations, repairs, or personalizations to a space (Zeisel, 1984) can also be "observed" for information about how the physical environment is used. For example, the wear on a door can be a good indication of where a handle should be situated (Chang & Drury, 2007). This type of indirect measure will also not be elaborated upon in this chapter given that it is particularly useful in the programming and post-occupancy evaluations of buildings (see Chapters 12 and 13), and is thus discussed at greater length in those chapters.

Direct observation, on the other hand, involves researchers learning about human–environment interactions using any or all of the five senses. To understand the effects of a restaurant on its diners, for instance, a researcher should smell the air, eat the food, feel the temperature in the room, listen to the background music, and watch how people respond to the whole experience. Certainly, our senses and abilities to record information could be enhanced with a variety of tools, but *just watching* (or *listening, smelling*, etc.) can provide a great deal of information as well. Arguably, although sense-enhancing technologies, such as microscopes, are vital for advancing science, the naked eye provides information in *human-sized* units that are at least equally important for the understanding of human–environment interaction as are other "enhanced" measures. Many ground-breaking studies make use of audio or video recordings and these methods will be discussed later in this chapter.

Finally, observational research methods can (and are) used for the study of both humans *and* the physical environment. Despite a focus on direct observation of *human behavior*, most of the observational methods discussed below are also applicable to environmental observation. Specifically, recording attributes of the physical environment also requires multiple observers, systematic procedures, and replicability. Sometimes researchers observe physical aspects of environment as possible predictive variables for human behavior. In addition to the fictitious example at the start of this chapter, Wachs (1990) noted the physical aspects of infants' homes and tested whether they predicted the infants' future development. In these cases, principles of observation, coding, and inter-observer reliability (as described later) continue to be important.

Why use observational research? There are two primary reasons why researchers choose to directly observe individuals within their environments: **measurement accuracy** and **preliminary investigation**. In some cases, direct observation may be more accurate or useful than other forms of measurement. As a method of data collection, direct observation is more immediate and objective than self-reports which rely on participants' abilities to remember events and recall them without bias. Research on human memory and cognition demonstrates that, despite their best efforts, participants often forget details or recall them based on their current knowledge and frame of mind. In addition, participants are often motivated to describe their behavior in the best possible light or to tell the researcher what they think he or she wants to hear. Therefore, even if participants accurately remember their behavior, they may present it in an inaccurate (but socially desirable) manner. In a meta-analysis (Kormos & Gifford, 2014), self-reported behavior was found to strongly, but not perfectly, predict actual behavior ($r = .46$). Given that self-reported behavior rates often differ from actual behavior, some researchers use direct behavioral observation to validate questionnaires or as part of a multi-method approach. For example, Bator, Bryan, and Schultz (2011) combined direct observation of littering behavior with subsequent follow-up interviews of those individuals.

Measurement accuracy is also an important consideration when studying populations of individuals who are incapable of self-reporting their behavior or when studying behavior that is difficult to self-report. In one study of infant development cited earlier (Wachs, 1990), for example, observed aspects of "play" were the dependent variables in a contrived situation. In another study, nonverbal (and verbal) expressions of aggression in fifth graders were observed to determine whether or not crowding was associated with increased aggression (Ginsburg, Pollman, Wauson, & Hope, 1977). In general, studies of special populations (see Chapter 18), such as babies or individuals with Alzheimer's disease, as well as studies of reactive, context-dependent or nonverbal behavior are strengthened by some form of observational research.

Observational measures of behavior, especially if collected in the field (rather than the lab), increase a study's **external validity** and generalizability. In particular, they address each of Brewer's "three Rs" of external validity (Brewer, 2000): robustness, representativeness, and relevance. These principles are particularly important for person–environment research in which applicability is paramount and external validity is important to establish.

The second primary reason for employing observation as part of environment–behavior research is to gain preliminary data for hypothesis generation or design ideas. As described at the beginning of this chapter and, later, in the chapter on programming (Chapter 12), observation can be used to form the basis for future research or building design ideas. In this case, a researcher may start by engaging in **casual observation**, followed by in-depth systematic observation. He or she may consider creating an **ethogram** by carefully noting all aspects of a situation and behavior without a hypothesis or pre-determined idea of what may occur; these types of logs, when combined together, may then reveal a pattern that can be addressed in a more experimental approach. This, and other approaches to observation, will be discussed next.

General and Specific Methods for Observation

General methods

Researchers can take up to three basic approaches to direct observation: casual, passive, or active. Commonly, as Gabriel demonstrates in this chapter's opening story – and as depicted in Figure 2.1 – a program of research may progress from

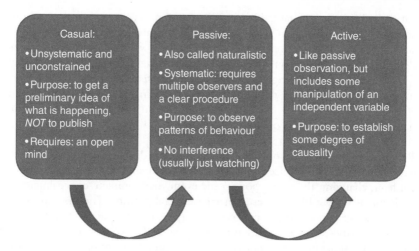

Figure 2.1 Sequence of observational research approaches for studying human–environment interactions.

casual to passive (or naturalistic) to active. That is, a scientist may begin formulating ideas based on simple, unsystematic observations (a casual approach). Then, if these ideas require more in-depth analysis and explanation (or publication), the scientist may move to a more rigorous and systematic observation technique where multiple observers record information (without interfering) and compare their degree of agreement (a passive or naturalistic observation approach). If patterns of behavior are found using this technique, and the researcher would like to establish some degree of causality to explain it, he or she may then shift to an experimental or quasi-experimental design where aspects of the environment are systematically manipulated (an **active observation** approach). A more detailed explanation of each major approach is provided below, with particular emphasis placed on passive observational methods.

Casual observation Casual observation is unsystematic and unconstrained. The purpose of this type of observation is not to determine a cause of behavior or publish a report. Instead, the purpose is merely to get a sense of what is happening in a given situation by putting one's self in the situation, keeping an open mind and brainstorming. Sometimes casual observation occurs in response to a request (e.g., a client asking an architect to redesign their building), and sometimes it can occur in response to a personal experience (e.g., Gabriel's performances). In any event, the purpose of casual observation is to inform the direction of a possible future study and, as such, may not entail physically recording data. This type of observation can last anywhere from an hour to several months.

Passive observation Passive or naturalistic observation does not involve changing the environment or interfering with behavior, but does require reliable and systematic data recording. Typically, passive observation consists of watching people within a space doing certain activities. Data can be recorded quantitatively (e.g., frequency or duration behavior) or qualitatively (e.g., verbatim account of entire situations, followed by an examination of the data for commonalities). Passive observation tends to produce information that has high external validity (because it occurs in real-world environments), but care should also be taken to maximize internal validity. For this reason, **sampling and observation consistency** are vital. In order for an observational study to be replicable, the sample being observed should be representative of the population that is being studied and **inter-observer agreement** should be established (two or more observers should independently record notes about the behavior and then compare them).

Researchers should attempt to remain concealed when conducting passive observation in order to reduce **reactivity** from those being observed and to prevent them from changing their behavior. In the event that complete concealment from participants is impossible, the researcher has several options. The first option is to "blend in" as well as possible or conceal the purpose of observation. For instance, in one study conducted on a restaurant patio by the author of this chapter, observers recorded trash separation behavior by customers on a sheet of paper, but appeared to other diners as students working on a school assignment, as seen in Figure 2.2 (Sussman & Gifford, 2013). Similarly, a recent study of zoo animal exhibitions

Figure 2.2 Observing trash separation behavior at a local fast food restaurant.

employed "plain clothes" observers to unobtrusively record the drawing and holding power of certain animal exhibits (Moss & Esson, 2010). If participants know they are being observed, but think that there is an unrelated reason, then observations may also remain accurate; for example, if the observer's goal is to note customer service agents' performance under low lighting conditions, they could be told that interactions with customers are being watched to understand what questions the customer is asking. In extreme cases, participants may be told that they are *not* being observed when, in fact, they are. However, deception should be avoided at all costs, and should only be used in labs or other situations where a thorough debriefing is possible. In these cases, participants should also be given the option to have their data excluded from the study after they learn of the deception. This debriefing process and other ethical considerations will be discussed later in this chapter.

Should the researcher choose to conduct an open observational study without concealment or deception, then the observees should be given time to acclimatize to the situation before recording begins. For instance, a study of social interaction taking place in a lab setting with a video camera in the room will produce unusual interactions for some time before participants habituate to the camera and behave normally. Generally, therefore, researchers should discard the first several minutes of observations in this sort of study. The more concealed the observer (or observing device), the faster actual observations may begin.

A second major consideration for observational research is what to observe. One strategy is to record an ethogram. That is, to record *everything* about a behavior or situation, without censorship, to later look for patterns in the data. **Spot sampling**, an anthropological method of observation used to record individuals' behavior at random times in a given location, has been used, for example, to examine the shopping behavior of adults with children in supermarkets (O'Dougherty, Story, & Stang, 2006). After watching many child–parent pairs walk through the store aisles, the researcher found that several parent purchase behaviors were influenced by their children.

But is recording everything in an uncensored and unbiased way actually possible? At some point a decision must be made on what to record, where to point the camera, when to turn on the audio recorder, etc. These decisions (and related decisions about how to code data) are affected by culture and shared social under-standings that may be impossible to escape. Therefore, researchers should not pretend that they are completely objective (which is impossible) and, instead, acknowledge their biases, deciding what to observe and code based on theoretical frameworks. Sometimes, coding decisions are based on the data themselves (rather than theory) and, in this case, the exploratory nature of the codes should be declared to readers.

Cultural and social biases can enter into observation decisions (i.e., what to observe) by affecting the definition of the behavior or the size of the **behavioral unit**. That is, some behavior may be noteworthy in certain cultures but not others. For example, in India people commonly use a head wiggle (side-to-side head tilting) as a gesture of agreeing with a speaker, whereas the same gesture does not exist in North America. Therefore, a study of nonverbal agreement behavior in different environments might have vastly varying results depending on the background and experience of the observer (and location of observation). Similarly, decisions of what behavioral unit to measure can be affected by social or cultural biases.

Behavioral units refer to the *scale* of observation. For example, a molecular unit of observation may include small movements of the face, hands or legs, whereas molar units of analysis may include larger scale behaviors such as "walking to school" or "recycling." Generally, molecular units require less interpretation and are, therefore, more reliable, but molar units are more meaningful. In choosing which level of behavioral unit to observe, researchers should recognize their own possible biases, acknowledge them, and present compelling reasons for their decisions.

Frequency and timing of observations is another consideration that can be important in planning an observational study. Based on preliminary observations, previous research, and the researchers' objectives, observations can be noted at various intervals. Primarily, the two options are **event sampling** (recording information whenever a certain event occurs) and **time sampling** (recording information at regular or random intervals). Regardless of which sampling method is used, observers should strictly adhere to their procedures in order to avoid biasing their results. This can occur, for instance, if observers only note the easiest or most frequent examples, or if they change the timing and duration of observations.

Finally, blinding observers may sound counter-productive if they are asked to watch behavior (!), but blinding them to certain aspects of the study may be important. **Experimenter bias**, or the preponderance for experimenters to obtain the results that they expect, can have a dramatic effect on observational research. Therefore, blinding observers to the purposes of the study, the hypotheses of the study, and the experimental condition of participants is an asset, when possible. However, observational studies pose particular problems in this respect. Quite often, the two or more experimental conditions in which participants are placed are difficult to hide from observers (who are watching the participants' reactions to those conditions). To minimize observer bias in this type of situation, one solution could be to give observers video or audio clips to analyze out of context (rather than live observations), or to employ larger numbers of observers with final ratings being the mean, median, or modal observation among them. Following the end of all data recording and coding, observers should be interviewed to determine if they were, in fact, blinded to the purpose and hypothesis of the study. At this time inter-observer reliability should also be calculated.

Active observation   Active observation requires all of the same considerations as passive observation described above, with the additional requirements of establishing a degree of causality. As before, observations should be replicable and valid measures of behavior and the environment, but researchers should also think about how they may demonstrate a causal link between the changed environment and resultant behavior. Ideally, causality would be established using a true experimental design with participants randomly chosen from a population and then randomly assigned to a comparison or experimental group. However, observational research (especially in the field rather than in the lab) rarely permits this degree of control. Instead, researchers will probably use some form of quasi-experimental design to demonstrate support for a causal link between dependent and independent variables, without establishing a definite causal relationship. Typically, an active observational study involves watching individuals in an environment with or without a small change to it (e.g., watching park users in a sign or no-sign condition to see if they smoke less when there is a no-smoking sign near the park entrance). However, passive observation can also be used in a quasi-experimental design; for example, upkeep behavior in two different neighborhoods can be observed without changing any aspect of the two environments. Chapter 4 describes the pros and cons of a variety of experimental designs that establish different degrees of causality. This chapter will be particularly useful for planning field studies of human–environment interactions.

Whereas most passive observation takes place in natural field settings, active observational research can occur in the lab or the field. Personal space, for example, has been studied in both settings. In one field study, privacy and distance between individuals was measured in a queue for an automated teller (Kaya & Erkíp, 1999); whereas in a lab study, preferred personal distance was measured by observing the experimental "waiting room" for changes in seat preference (Holland, Roeder, van Baaren, Brandt, & Hannover, 2004). These are just two examples from a large body of literature on personal space.

Active observational research requires creativity, patience, and effort but can produce reliable and convincing evidence. Many examples of this type of research exist in person–environment research. Some examples include: observing the littering behavior of individuals as they walk through a littered or clean environment, or as they see others littering or not (Reno, Cialdini, & Kallgren, 1993); watching the behavior and purchase decisions of shoppers in a cafeteria to determine if playing different musical genres affects sales (North & Hargreaves, 1998); noting whether diners who see other (confederate) diners compost are more likely to compost as well (Sussman, Greeno, Gifford, & Scannell, 2013); recording user decisions to walk up stairs rather than travel in an elevator in response to an incrementally increased delay in the time it takes for the door to open and close (Van Houten, Nau, & Merrigan, 1981); experimentally manipulating the population density of a street corner to determine if it affects the rates of helping a confederate who drops her groceries (hypothetical example); and observing the frequency of social interactions in a workplace under different levels of noise (hypothetical example). Other examples of active observational research can be found in Chapters 15 and 16 on interventions toward sustainability.

Specific tools

Regardless of the approach, both passive and active observational research requires systematically recording information. Observers may either translate what they see (or hear) into codes immediately (on site) or produce video or audio recordings that are coded later. This section will first discuss tools that may be used on site for either recording or coding, and then discuss more detailed coding and inter-observer reliability issues.

The simplest and most foolproof method for recording observed data is the **paper-and-pencil method**. Here, observers watch an area or population of interest and note observations by jotting them down on a paper using either codes (for efficiency) or extensive notes (for detail). This method is cheap (unless a great deal of photocopying is required), easy to transport, discreet, unlikely to malfunction, and does not require batteries or some other power source. Using a real piece of paper also allows for easy modifications and creative note taking such as drawing pictures or writing in the margins. To improve efficiency, researchers often create templates (charts) that can be easily completed while observing behavior with relatively little effort. For many years, this was the primary method of data recording and thus several standardized templates have been created for use in environment–behavior research.

Behavioral mapping, noting where behaviors occur within a space, is an important tool for environment–behavior research and is still largely conducted with a paper-and-pencil approach (although this may be usurped in the near future by small handheld electronic devices). To create a behavioral map, Ittelson and colleagues (1970) suggest first designing a template that contains a drawn to scale map of an area that allows for a mark to be made each time a specific behavior occurs within the mapped area. Figure 2.3 shows a hypothetical example of a behavior map indicating where diners sat in a shopping mall food court. In this example, different

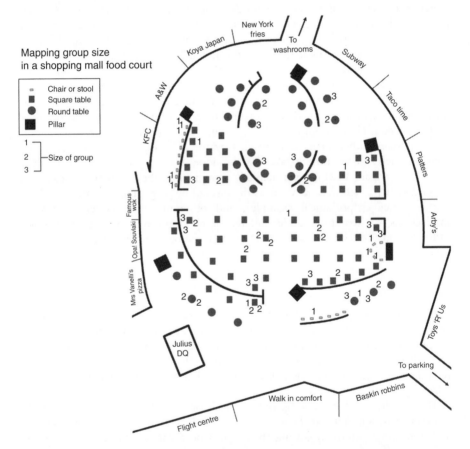

Figure 2.3 A sample behavior map used to describe seating preferences for groups of people in a shopping mall food court. On this type of map, the researcher marks a number (1, 2, or 3) to indicate the size of the group eating at each location on the map.

symbols were drawn on the map each time a group of one, two, or three people sat together in the food court. Behavior maps may also take the form of charts with check-boxes for potential behaviors (for an example see Figure 1-4 in Bechtel & Zeisel, 1987). Behavior could be mapped whenever it occurs (event-contingent) or during pre-determined intervals (time-contingent). Ittelson et al. (1970) postulate five necessary elements for effective behavior maps: the graphic or physical map itself; the definitions, codes, and categories of behavior being noted; the schedule of observation; the systematic procedure; and the counting or coding system being used. Determining which behavior to record and how to code it requires significant pre-testing and inter-observer reliability. Behavioral maps are frequently used for programming of buildings and post-occupancy evaluations and, thus, are discussed in greater detail in Chapter 3 and elsewhere.

Behavioral mapping, along with other paper-and-pencil approaches (such as **proxemics**, the study of body postures, and **kinesics**, the study of small body movements), usually involve a sophisticated note-taking "short hand" that is specific to each research group or study. Learning these methods and sharing raw data among researchers can therefore be challenging. Edward Hall (1974) and Ray Birdwhistell (1970), among others, have developed standardized methods for recording information in proxemics and kinesics studies, but Roger Bakeman has proposed a more generalizable tool (Bakeman & Quera, 1995). The **Sequential Data Interchange Standard (SDIS)** has four data forms (event, state, timed event, and interval sequence) that can describe most any type of observation. However, standardization and sharing of data using SDIS (as with any type of data) is easiest when the information is digitized and, therefore, the SDIS is designed to be used with a computer program called Generalized Sequential Querier (Bakeman & Quera, 1995).

The downside to using paper-and-pencil for recording observations is that, although recording is easy, analysis is difficult. Given that nearly all data analysis is conducted using computer programs, all paper-and-pencil observations will have to be manually entered into a computer database of some sort. This will more than negate any time saved during the observation recording phase of the study and may result in more error as well (if notes are not entered accurately). Therefore, if a paper-and-pencil approach is used for recording observations, researchers should double-check (and ideally double-enter) some or all of their data before beginning any analysis.

Computer-assisted note taking can be a simple and easy way to both efficiently record observations and avoid the hardships of later data entry. Computer technology is now portable enough that observers can discreetly enter data directly into a laptop computer or handheld device and later import the data into a statistical analysis program or share it electronically with other members of the research team. In some ways, digital data entry can also be easier and faster than paper-and-pencil methods. Instead of drawing a symbol or writing a note, some computer programs can permit observers to hit a specific keyboard key or pick an option from a drop-down menu when they see a behavior occur. Computer programs, such as the Interactive Shared Education Environment (ISEE), have been designed to make coding video content easier; in this case, by linking observers' notes directly with the original video content using hyperlinks (Mu, 2010).

Other, less common, apparatuses have also been used to record observational data. Some of the more creative examples are videos, audio recordings, internet-enabled cameras, automatic voice recorders, motion- or sound-activated video, time-lapse video or photography, and cell-phone photography (in response to text messages). In one study of kitchen water use, researchers installed webcams above volunteers' sinks to observe their dishwashing behavior, and also asked them to take digital photos of their dishwasher loads before turning them on (Richter, 2011). In this way they were able to determine that dishwashers used, on average, less water per item than hand washing.

The **Electronically Activated Recorder (EAR)** is another device that has been used to study people in their natural environments. This is a small recording device attached to volunteers' clothes that turn on at set (or random) intervals throughout the day. It has been used, for example, to study teenagers' discourses across various contexts (Mehl & Pennebaker, 2003). Motion-activated video, such as the EthoVision system, may also prove useful for recording human activity (such as the speed at which people travel through different types of spaces). Thus far, it has only been used to record the activity of nonhuman animals (e.g., Walton, Branham, Gash, & Grondin, 2006), but this technology holds potential for person–environment research.

As a general rule of thumb for video or audio recording, researchers should strive to retain as much information as possible in a well-indexed manner. Unnecessary extra information can be ignored during the coding process, but one never knows if or when that extra information may be useful in future! That is when a good indexing system will pay off (and the extra effort early on will have been worthwhile).

Technology is now emerging that will allow computers to fully automate video or audio coding and eliminate the need for human observation. As one example, facial or voice recognition software may, in the near future, be able to identify different human emotions (e.g., identify a smile or the sound of laughter), and this type of technology may facilitate studies linking workspace design with worker happiness. Yet, despite these technologies being currently available in some form, the complexities involved in adapting and using them make their application infrequent, especially in environment–behavior research. At the time of writing this chapter, fully automated observation procedures remain relatively uncommon in environment–behavior research. One reason for this is that humans have an innate ability to recognize patterns and make use of contextual cues – a process that is still rather complicated for computer programs.

A Word on Ethics

Observational studies require special ethical consideration. One of the primary advantages of observation is that it provides a window into real-world, naturally occurring behavior. Observations are therefore invalid if observees are actively aware that they are being watched or listened to; hence, asking participants to provide consent prior to being observed can be problematic. If consent can be obtained without evoking reactance from the observee, then it should certainly be requested. If, for example, the observation period is long or nonspecific (e.g., observing a social interaction in a lab for an hour, or observing dishwashing behavior every day for a month), then consent should be obtained prior to beginning the study. However, if reactivity could be an issue, such as when participants are observed in a natural setting from a distance (e.g., in a park), or for a short, specific behavior (e.g., to determine a choice of seat in a waiting room), then explicit consent may change the findings.

Ethically, researchers' first choice should be to obtain explicit consent prior to beginning observation if possible. If not possible (as is often the case), the second choice should be to debrief participants after observation has taken place, and to offer participants the option of withdrawing their information if they wish. As a third and final option, researchers may conduct studies in which participants are completely unaware that they were ever observed. Most casual and passive observation can take place without ethics board review, and many active observation studies, although requiring ethics board review, can be conducted without explicit consent or debriefing. Thus, in general, observing individuals in public areas, where observees have reasonable expectations of being watched, may be done without human research ethics board approval.

If, however, the participants' environments will be altered (i.e., active observation), then ethics board approval should be obtained (along with *consent of the establishment* in which the observation will be conducted). Furthermore, if participants' behavior will be recorded (photographed or video/audio recorded), then *participant consent* may also be required. Observing behavior in private areas (e.g., hand washing in the washroom) can pose additional ethical considerations, and each study's ethical issues should be considered on an individual basis. Human ethics review boards should be consulted prior to beginning any observational study, even if approval may not be required.

Coding and Inter-observer Reliability

Coding

Coding observations involves categorizing what is observed. It can occur as part of data collection (i.e., on site) or later, from a record or transcript. Systematic data coding is an important part of what makes observational studies replicable and scientific. Therefore, data code development and implementation requires effort and care.

Typically, observation codes are categorical, mutually exclusive, and exhaustive; that is, each behavior of interest (or other type of data point) receives a single, unique code that defines it. Although not necessary, this approach facilitates later data analysis. In this way, a study of civic engagement might, for example, code for petition signing, volunteering, and donating money with dichotomous yes–no variables for each behavior. Alternatively, some codes may be best represented by continuous variables, such as ratings. For example, observers rating the quality of social interactions in two different parks might use a Likert-type scale ranging from 1 (uninvolved) to 7 (extremely involved).

Given that defining data codes involves the critical act of deciding what information should be included and disregarded, this process should be taken seriously. Observation codes, or behavior categories, should be defined clearly and specifically.

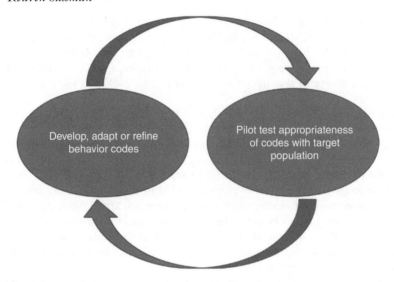

Figure 2.4   The process of developing behavior codes for observational research.

Each should have a dictionary-type definition and elaboration, followed by borderline and excluded examples of the behavior. Ideally, the first step in developing behavior codes should be to find what has already been used in similar research in order to adapt it for the purposes of the current study.

Whether the codes have been used before, or are being developed for the first time, researchers should engage in extensive pre-testing (with the target population) and refining of the measures prior to beginning their study. As Figure 2.4 depicts, the cycle of development, pilot testing, and redevelopment should be repeated until a reliable and robust system of coding has been established. This will save considerable future effort (and potential disappointment) as the study progresses.

Deciding on which behaviors to code and which to exclude can be challenging. Generally, codes should be chosen based on a theoretical framework, the research question being posed, and the actual behavior that is observed. When in doubt, researchers should code more behaviors rather than less, with the possible intention of later combining codes into more meaningful units. When behaviors occur infrequently (i.e., less than five times), categorical data analysis may be difficult and collapsing categories together may be necessary for statistical purposes. When creating or collapsing categories, researchers should keep in mind their study question and whether they can accurately answer it with the information they have.

Inter-observer agreement

Coding observations requires a degree of subjectivity, and therefore, is susceptible to observer bias. To circumvent this problem, multiple observers should independently code their observations so that their degree of agreement can be used as a test of the reliability of the measure. If inter-observer agreement (commonly known as **inter-rater reliability**) is high, then the behavior (or other type of observation) is likely to be clear and easy to interpret. However, if inter-observer agreement is low, then the behavior may be difficult to identify or susceptible to observer bias, in which case the researcher may be unable to use the measure and should consider excluding it from statistical analysis. Given the amount of effort required to code and record all of the information, this can be an unfortunate situation indeed! To avoid the problem, researchers are advised to spend considerable time and effort training observers to accurately code behaviors of interest, and to provide the most favorable conditions for observation. That is, try to use multiple observers in situations with long observation periods (to allow breaks) and provide viewing or listening locations that permit the best (and most consistent) possible observation perspective.

The degree of inter-observer agreement should be calculated prior to conducting any other statistics. In general, observational studies should include at least two observers with a minimum 50% overlapping observations (although this is an arbitrary rule of thumb that may be modified depending on the specific situation). When using categorical data, one should avoid simply reporting the percentage of agreement between observers because this statistic does not account for observations in which observers agree by chance alone (which is especially problematic when there are few possible levels of the behavior, such as "yes or no" variables). Instead, agreement should be calculated using Cohen's Kappa (for two observers) or Fleiss's Kappa (for more than two observers), and intra-class correlations may be used for assessing agreement between observers on continuous variables. Depending on the variable being observed, the degree of agreement that has been reported in the past, and several other factors, acceptable Kappa levels can vary greatly. In cases where observers code data at multiple time points, a repeated-measures ANOVA may be used to test differences in observers' ratings from one time to the next. However, Kappa levels are usually convincing enough for study reviewers and readers.

A final note of caution: Inter-observer agreement is necessary, but not sufficient for demonstrating a measure's appropriateness. When multiple observers agree on an observation, that observation is likely to be precise and reliable (the observers are seeing and noting the same thing), but that observation is not necessarily valid. All of the observers may, for example, share the same biases and, consequently, agree on their (possibly) incorrect observations. This is another reason why the behavior being observed should be clearly defined, and why observers should be "blinded" whenever possible. The onus is on the researcher to convince readers that observations are indeed valid, as well as reliable.

Observing by Watching: Final Thoughts

Observation is one of the founding principles of the scientific method, and can be a very effective tool for studying human–environment interactions. Using casual, passive, and active observation, a researcher can build convincing cases for real-world phenomena in ways that surveys and other indirect measures do not permit. Given that observation can be used both in lab or field studies with a variety of experimental or quasi-experimental designs, these methods can also provide some evidence of causality. But in order for observational research to be scientific and replicable, researchers should pay extra attention to issues of reliability and validity. Issues of validity should be addressed by clearly articulating what behaviors will be observed and coded, and issues of reliability should be addressed by using multiple observers (who are blinded to the objective and hypotheses of the study). Researchers should also pre-test observational measures and train observers extensively prior to beginning a study, and strive to be as systematic and unobtrusive as possible during the study. Although requiring considerable effort, the external validity of observational research makes this type of method a valuable addition to the researcher's toolbox.

Glossary

Active observation   An observational method in which people are observed in environments that are systematically changed. This allows experimenters to infer whether the environment has some influence on behavior.

Behavioral mapping   Noting where behaviors occur within a space.

Behavioral unit   The scale of behavior that is observed. For example, a *molecular* unit of observation may include small movements of the face, hands or legs, whereas *molar* units of analysis may include larger scale behaviors such as "walking to school" or "recycling."

Casual observation   A method of observation that is unsystematic and unconstrained. The purpose of casual observation is to inform the direction of a possible future study and, as such, may not entail physically recording data.

Coding   Categorizing observations made as part of data collection for a study.

Ethogram   A qualitative observation method in which the observer notes all aspects of a situation and behavior without a hypothesis or pre-determined idea of what may occur. Notes are then examined to reveal behavior patterns.

Electronically Activated Recorder (EAR)   A small recording device attached to volunteers' clothes that turns on at set (or random) intervals throughout the day.

Event-contingent reporting   Standardized methods for learning about participants' daily interactions from their own notes, often using personal diaries.

Event sampling   Recording information whenever a certain event occurs.

Experimenter bias   The preponderance for experimenters to obtain the results that they expect.

External validity   The extent to which the results of a study can be generalized to other situations or people.

Inter-observer agreement   Two or more observers independently record notes and determine the degree of similarity between them (also called inter-rater reliability).

Inter-rater reliability   *See* inter-observer agreement.

Kinesics   The study of small body movements.

Measurement accuracy   Observational research may be better than other methods for getting *true* descriptions of behavior and its antecedents.

Observation   Receiving information through one of the five human senses.

Paper-and-pencil method   A method of recording behavior in which observers watch an area or population of interest and note observations by jotting them down on a paper using either codes or extensive notes.

Passive observation Passive or naturalistic observation does not involve changing the environment or interfering with behavior, but does require reliable and systematic data recording; usually using multiple observers or coders.

Preliminary investigation Observational research may be a good way to develop a theory or hypothesis about human behavior before designing a structured experiment.

Proxemics The study of body postures.

Reactivity The phenomenon in which people who believe they are being observed change their behavior.

Sampling and observation consistency The population being observed should be representative of the population that is being studied and inter-observer agreement should be established.

Sequential Data Interchange Standard (SDIS) A standardized form of measurement for proxemics and kinesics studies for use with a computer program called Generalized Sequential Querier.

Spot sampling An anthropological method of observation used to record individuals' behavior at random times in a given location.

Time sampling Recording information at regular or random intervals.

Trace measures Indirect indicators of how a space is used, such as erosion, leftovers, adaptations, repairs, or personalizations to a space.

Note

1 This is not an actual study and these findings are speculative. They were invented for the purpose of this fictitious introductory story.

References

Bakeman, R., & Quera, V. (1995). *Analyzing interaction: Sequential analysis with SDIS & GSEQ*. New York, NY: Cambridge University Press.

Bator, R. J., Bryan, A. D., & Schultz, P. W. (2011). Who gives a hoot? Intercept surveys of litterers and disposers. *Environment and Behavior, 43*, 295–315. doi:10.1177/0013916509356884

Bechtel, R. B., & Zeisel, J. (1987). Observation: The world under a glass. In R. B. Bechtel, R. W. Marans & W. Michelson (Eds.), *Methods in environmental and behavioral research* (pp. 11–40). New York, NY: Van Nostrand Reinhold.

Birdwhistell, R. L. (1970). *Kinesics and context: Essays on body motion communication*. Philadelphia, PA: University of Pennsylvania Press.

Brewer, M. B. (2000). Research design and issues of validity. In H. T. Reis & C. M. Judd (Eds.), *Handbook of research methods in social and personality psychology* (pp. 3–16). New York, NY: Cambridge University Press.

Chang, S., & Drury, C. G. (2007). Task demands and human capabilities in door use. *Applied Ergonomics, 38*, 325–335. doi:10.1016/j.apergo.2006.04.023

Ginsburg, H. J., Pollman, V. A., Wauson, M. S., & Hope, M. L. (1977). Variation of aggressive interaction among male elementary school children as a function of changes in spatial density. *Environmental Psychology & Nonverbal Behavior, 2*, 67–75. doi:10.1007/BF01145822

Giuliani, M. V., & Scopelliti, M. (2009). Empirical research in environmental psychology: Past, present, and future. *Journal of Environmental Psychology, 29,* 375–386. doi:10.1016/j.jenvp.2008.11.008

Hall, E. T. (1974). *Handbook for proxemic research.* Washington, DC: Society for the Anthropology of Visual Communication.

Holland, R. W., Roeder, U., van Baaren, R. B., Brandt, A. C., & Hannover, B. (2004). Don't stand so close to me: The effects of self-construal on interpersonal closeness. *Psychological Science, 15,* 237–242. doi:10.1111/j.0956-7976.2004.00658.x

Ittelson, W. H., Rivlin, L. G., & Proshansky, H. M. (1970). The use of behavioral maps in environmental psychology. In H. M. Proshansky, W. H. Ittelson & L. G. Rivlin (Eds.), *Environmental psychology* (pp. 658–668). New York, NY: Holt, Rinehart, & Winston.

Kaya, N., & Erkíp, F. (1999). Invasion of personal space under the condition of short-term crowding: A case study on an automatic teller machine. *Journal of Environmental Psychology, 19,* 183–189. doi:10.1006/jevp.1999.0125

Kormos, C., & Gifford, R. (2014). The validity of self-report measures of proenvironmental behavior: A meta-analytic review. *Journal of Environmental Psychology, 40,* 359–371.

Mehl, M. R., & Pennebaker, J. W. (2003). The sounds of social life: A psychometric analysis of students' daily social environments and natural conversations. *Journal of Personality and Social Psychology, 84,* 857–870. doi:10.1037/0022-3514.84.4.857

Moskowitz, D. S. (1994). Cross-situational generality and the interpersonal circumplex. *Journal of Personality and Social Psychology, 66,* 921–933. doi:10.1037/0022-3514.66.5.921

Moss, A., & Esson, M. (2010). Visitor interest in zoo animals and the implications for collection planning and zoo education programmes. *Zoo Biology, 29,* 715–731. doi:10.1002/zoo.20316

Mu, X. (2010). Towards effective video annotation: An approach to automatically link notes with video content. *Computers & Education, 55,* 1752–1763. doi:10.1016/j.compedu.2010.07.021

North, A. C., & Hargreaves, D. J. (1998). The effect of music on atmosphere and purchase intentions in a cafeteria. *Journal of Applied Social Psychology, 28,* 2254–2273. doi:10.1111/j.1559-1816.1998.tb01370.x

O'Dougherty, M., Story, M., & Stang, J. (2006). Observations of parent–child co-shoppers in supermarkets: Children's involvement in food selections, parental yielding, and refusal strategies. *Journal of Nutrition Education and Behavior, 38,* 183–188. doi:10.1016/j.jneb.2005.11.034

Reno, R. R., Cialdini, R. B., & Kallgren, C. A. (1993). The transsituational influence of social norms. *Journal of Personality and Social Psychology, 64,* 104–112. doi:10.1037/0022-3514.64.1.104

Richter, C. P. (2011). Usage of dishwashers: Observation of consumer habits in the domestic environment. *International Journal of Consumer Studies, 35,* 180–186. doi:10.1111/j.1470-6431.2010.00973.x

Sussman, R., & Gifford, R. (2013). Be the change you want to see: Modeling food composting in public places. *Environment and Behavior, 45,* 323–343. doi:10.1177/0013916511431274

Sussman, R., Greeno, M., Gifford, R., & Scannell, L. (2013). The effectiveness of models and prompts on waste diversion: A field experiment on composting by cafeteria patrons. *Journal of Applied Social Psychology, 43,* 24–34.

Underhill, P. (2000). *Why we buy: The science of shopping.* New York, NY: Simon & Schuster.

Van Houten, R., Nau, P. A., & Merrigan, M. (1981). Reducing elevator energy use: A comparison of posted feedback and reduced elevator convenience. *Journal of Applied Behavior Analysis, 14,* 377–387. doi:10.1901/jaba.1981.14-377

Wachs, T. D. (1990). Must the physical environment be mediated by the social environment in order to influence development? A further test. *Journal of Applied Developmental Psychology, 11,* 163–178. doi:10.1016/0193-3973(90)90003-3

Walton, A., Branham, A., Gash, D. M., & Grondin, R. (2006). Automated video analysis of age-related motor deficits in monkeys using EthoVision. *Neurobiology of Aging, 27,* 1477–1483. doi:10.1016/j.neurobiolaging.2005.08.003

Wheeler, L., & Nezlek, J. (1977). Sex differences in social participation. *Journal of Personality and Social Psychology, 35,* 742–754. doi:10.1037/0022-3514.35.10.742

Zeisel, J. (1984). *Inquiry by design: Tools for environment–behavior research.* Cambridge, UK: Cambridge University Press.

Suggested Readings

Reis, H. T., & Judd, C. M. (2000). *Handbook of research methods in social and personality psychology.* New York, NY: Cambridge University Press.

Zeisel, J. (1984). *Inquiry by design: Tools for environment–behavior research.* Cambridge, UK: Cambridge University Press.

3

Behavioral Mapping and Tracking

Cheuk Fan Ng
Athabasca University, AB, Canada

"Oh my God, that black truck almost hit that old lady crossing the street! She is lying on the road," screamed Maria, as she looked out of the window of their apartment.

Gabriel, Ethan, and Annabelle rushed to the window to watch what is happening. "Those crosswalks don't allow much time for pedestrians. We young people can make it through, but anyone who is older or has some physical problems would have trouble making it across," said Annabelle.

"Drivers are impatient. They have to wait for all the pedestrians to finish crossing before they can make that left turn onto Busy Street. I wonder if moving the crosswalk a few meters south would help. Then drivers making a left turn wouldn't need to wait for the pedestrians," Gabriel added.

Now that Gabriel has convinced Maria how useful behavioral observation can be for understanding environment–behavior interactions (see Chapter 2), Gabriel comes up with an idea. "Why don't we make some systematic observations of what people are doing on our street? If we use behavioral mapping and tracking, we would be able to identify patterns of behaviors. We could then present our findings to the City's Planning Department and improve our street," Gabriel proposed.

The housemates gathered around their dinner table, and worked out a preliminary sampling plan, behavioral categories, and observation procedure. Gabriel drew a plan of their street. Soon they noticed a pattern of jaywalking, pedestrians who are texting or talking on their phones running into garbage bins and lamp posts, parents pushing strollers having trouble negotiating the snow-covered sidewalks, and other problems.

They decided to write a formal proposal to the Planning Department for funding to continue their observations.

Research Methods for Environmental Psychology, First Edition. Edited by Robert Gifford.
© 2016 John Wiley & Sons, Ltd. Published 2016 by John Wiley & Sons, Ltd.

This chapter focuses on three specific observation techniques: direct observation using **behavioral mapping** and **behavioral tracking**, and indirect observation using **physical traces**.

Behavioral Mapping

I first describe what behavioral mapping is, its purposes and importance as an observation tool, and a brief history. Next, I provide recommended procedures for conducting behavioral mapping, illustrating with examples of studies conducted in various physical settings and a case study. Finally, I discuss the challenges and limitations of this research technique.

What it is

Behavioral mapping is a technique used in environmental psychology and related fields for recording people's behaviors and movements systematically as these behaviors occur in particular locations (Bechtel & Zeisel, 1987). A behavioral map is basically a record of where people are, what they actually do, and how their behaviors are distributed in a space. Sommer and Sommer (2002) distinguish two forms of behavioral maps: place-centered or individual-centered. A place-centered map shows the locations of people in a particular setting at a particular time engaging in various activities. Place-centered mapping is appropriate when the goal is to assess the usage of a particular area or location, such as a cafeteria. In contrast, an individual-centered map is a record of a person's movements and activities in a setting or settings over time. Individual-centered mapping is appropriate when the goal is to learn about a person or a group's activities in relation to location and time, for example, where and how teenagers spend their time after school. Place-centered mapping can be used in combination with individual-centered mapping, as in the case study described at the end of this chapter.

Why this technique is important

As reviewed in Chapter 2, behavioral observation in general has several advantages over self-reporting of behaviors. First, for social desirability reasons, people may not provide honest answers to questions about what they do in their daily lives, or where and how they carry out certain activities, particularly if the activity in question is illegal or against the social norm. Second, people may not remember accurately whether they have done something or not, or how often they have done something, particularly regarding routine activities. Third, people may not be consciously aware of their own behaviors.

In addition to recording objectively what actually occurs, behavioral mapping as an observation tool has the advantage of recording behavior in its context. According to Roger Barker's ecological psychology theory (1968), every behavior setting (e.g., homes, classrooms) is associated with certain physical characteristics and a consistent pattern of behavior. Behavioral mapping allows researchers to relate various observed behaviors to particular locations (i.e., where an activity occurs), physical environmental features (i.e., what feature is used), type of users (e.g., children), and over time (e.g., in a week).

Purposes

Behavioral mapping is used in architectural programming (see Chapter 12), post-occupancy evaluation (see Chapter 13), and behavioral research. Ittelson, Rivlin, and Proshansky (1970) identified four general uses. The first use is for describing the distribution of behaviors throughout a particular space. The second use is for comparing two different situations or conditions, such as usage by men and by women. The third use is to identify general patterns in the use of space in a variety of settings, such as when usage peaks. Finally, behavioral maps can be used to provide quantitative predictions of distribution of behaviors in a new facility before the facility is constructed or occupied, mainly in architectural programming (Chapter 12). Behavioral maps can be a useful tool for checking if the assumptions behind the design of spaces and facilities are accurate, in post-occupancy evaluation (Chapter 13). A record of customer or visitor locations and behaviors, and traffic flow patterns can allow managers and space designers to identify any problems, take remedial and prospective actions to improve services or the use of space (Burke, 2006; Given & Leckie, 2003; Yalowitz & Bronnenkant, 2009).

Apart from its use in descriptive research, behavioral mapping can be used in correlational research. In a study of public squares or plazas, Zacharias, Stathopoulos, and Wu (2004) examined the relationships between user distribution over locations in the square and microclimate within the square (e.g., sunny vs. shady areas, temperature), and users' behaviors (sitting, standing, smoking).

Behavioral mapping is also used in experimental research. In a study of human navigation in a supermarket, participants' search behaviors and their locations were recorded and compared in three experimental conditions, in which items belonging to different categories were placed in different shelf locations (Kalff & Strube, 2009).

Behavioral mapping is often used with young children who may have difficulty verbalizing their thoughts, feelings, and behaviors and those elderly who have cognitive impairment. For example, the spatial movements outdoors, measured with behavioral tracking, were correlated with psychosocial variables in Oswald et al.'s (2010) study of elderly residents with dementia.

A brief history

It is generally recognized that William Ittelson, Leanne Rivlin, and Harold Proshansky of the City University of New York first introduced behavioral mapping to environmental psychology. They defined behavioral maps as "a technique for studying the relationships between behavior and the physical space in which it occurs" (Ittelson et al., 1970, p. 349). Behavioral maps include descriptions of behavior, participants, and statements about the relationships between the behavior and design features in the physical setting. Using behavioral mapping, these early environmental psychologists observed – somewhat obtrusively – and documented the behaviors of adult patients in two psychiatric wards in a large, urban hospital (Ittelson et al., 1970), a children's psychiatric ward (Rivlin & Wolfe, 1972), and children in open classrooms (Rivlin & Rothenberg, 1976). A precursor to this technique was demonstrated in a series of studies in college libraries in the 1960s, in which Robert Sommer and his colleagues observed systematically how seats at a table in college libraries and study halls were occupied (e.g., Sommer, 1966).

According to Hill (1984), behavioral tracking (or individual-centered mapping in Sommer & Sommer's terminology) was first used to study pedestrian movement by Weiss and Boutourline (1962). They accompanied visitors to a World's Fair, observed (obtrusively) and recorded as trip logs visitors' movements and locations and when each movement took place. Weiss and Boutourline (1962, as cited in Hill, 1984) proposed that an *obtrusive observer* did not affect the behavior of the observed. Bechtel disagreed, and demonstrated in his study possible "observer effects," that is, museum visitors who knew they were being observed had different movement behaviors than those who were unaware that they were being observed (Bechtel, 1967).

Unobtrusive observation then became an important criterion. In an effort to develop a photographic simulation for testing visitors' behaviors in the laboratory, Winkel and Sasanoff (1966) tracked visitors' movements unobtrusively through a museum in Seattle by observing at an appropriate distance. Tracking involved recording the visitor's movements by drawing a line on a base map that corresponded with the visitor's movements in the actual gallery. Using the same tracking technique, Hill (1984) observed and recorded pedestrians' movements unobtrusively through urban areas. To reduce obtrusiveness, Garbrecht (1971) observed pedestrians' trips through a parking lot from an office building in Boston.

Bechtel (1967) was the first to use "machine observers" to replace human observers in behavioral mapping. A hodometer was used to record automatically the number and location of footsteps across the floor of a museum. The device "consists of a cluster of electric switch mats covering on entire floor space with each mat connected to an electric counter" (p. 54). The use of the hodometer allowed the researcher to measure the area covered by a visitor, the number of footsteps, and the time the visitor spent in the exhibit room.

Since then, researchers have used both human observers and machine observers to record behaviors in various spaces. Two well-known projects are used to illustrate such use. In the Street Life Project, described in the book *The Social Life of Small Urban Spaces* (1980), a team of researchers led by William Whyte used both human observers and time-lapse photography to record how the spaces in New York City parks, plazas, and other public spaces were actually used. Where possible, the researchers took photographs at regular intervals from a tall building overlooking the public space. Based on these objective records of diagrams and photographs, Whyte was able to identify several important factors in the success of small urban plazas. Their findings helped to improve the design of parks and plazas throughout the world. In a 25-year project conducted by Envirosell, a marketing research consultant company, Paco Underhill used a combination of video and human observers – trackers – to do behavioral mapping in a systematic and unobtrusive way in a variety of stores. Very detailed and useful, though sometimes surprising, results for retailers are summarized in Underhill's book, *Why We Buy: The Science of Shopping* (1999, updated 2009).

The use of behavioral mapping and tracking waned as researchers relied more and more on self-reported methods of data collection, perhaps because of the intensive time and resource commitment and the stringent ethics requirements for unobtrusive observation (to be discussed later in the chapter). Page (2000) lamented that the lack of unobtrusive observation studies had jeopardized the ecological validity and relevance of knowledge to real-life situations. Giuliani and Scopelliti (2009) observed the decline of observational studies in environmental psychology since the 1980s. There have been a small number of studies conducted in a variety of settings over the years. More studies have been reported by researchers and professionals in environmental design at recent conferences (e.g., Khasawneh, Kato, & Mori, 2013; Zamani, 2012).

Advances in computing and communication technologies in recent years have facilitated automatic observation, recording, data entry, data analysis, and data visualization. The use of portable or handheld devices, radio frequency identification (RFID), global positioning system (GPS), and geographic information system (GIS) have become increasingly common in behavioral research. At the same time, the use of such technologies for mapping and tracking people's behaviors has raised new ethical issues for researchers. More will be discussed later in this chapter.

Procedure

Ittelson et al. (1970) identified five elements of behavioral mapping: (1) a base map identifying the essential physical features of interest; (2) behavioral categories with their definitions and codes; (3) a schedule of observation; (4) a systematic procedure of observation; and (5) a system of coding and counting (yes/no, or frequency). Based on these elements, I recommend the following steps in conducting place-centered behavioral mapping.

Step 1: Create a base map The first step is to create a base map, a scale drawing of the physical space, identifying each area with the kinds of behavior expected to occur there (e.g., eating in a living room) and any salient environmental features that may affect the behaviors of interest to the researcher (e.g., windows). The architect's blueprint can be used as a guide, but these floor plans may not be up to date and may not include the portable features of the space, such as chairs and direction signs (Sommer & Sommer, 2002). The recording document can be in forms other than a map; a table in which rows representing physical locations and columns representing behavior would suffice (Bechtel & Zeisel, 1987). Researchers can use an established scale for measuring the physical or architectural features of a particular setting (e.g., residential care facility).

Step 2: Define behavioral categories and their codes/symbols, and develop a system of coding The next step is to define the behavioral categories that are relevant to the research problem under investigation. These behavioral categories must be explicit, precise, and relatively narrow. The development of behavioral categories involves three sub-steps: cataloging observed behaviors, generalizing the behaviors into categories for observation, and combining observational categories into analytic categories. Cataloging the behavior involves having observers record all specific examples of a particular behavior over a period of time, then eliminating any duplicate, trivial, or idiosyncratic observations to form a list of summary observational categories.

Trained judges divide the list of behaviors into observational categories that are similar within the group and different among the groups. The observational categories can be combined further into analytic categories that address the particular problems being studied (Ittelson et al., 1970). Special scoring symbols are then used to represent each behavior (e.g., Eat = eating, Wri = writing). Develop a system of coding and counting (e.g., yes/no, frequency of occurrence, or ratings of intensity).

Step 3: Develop a schedule of observation   Behavioral observation can be either event-contingent or time-contingent at either fixed intervals (e.g., every 15 minutes) or random intervals. Mapping should take place at all possible times that the area is used, just in case observation may reveal the occurrence of unexpected events or behaviors. To reduce the likelihood of observing the same people engaging in the same activities, spread out the sessions throughout the day (Sommer & Sommer, 2002).

Step 4: Develop an observation procedure   Scan the physical spaces of the site systematically (e.g., following a pre-determined path in a clockwise direction). Observation can be on an "instantaneous" basis by having enough observers to complete all areas in as short a time as possible. Observations can be recorded on data sheets that include such information as the location and time of observation, the number and type of users engaged in each category of activities (Ittelson et al., 1970). Well-trained observers will spend considerable time on site to become familiar with the behaviors of the users. The users may be aware of the presence of the observer but observers should avoid direct involvement in the activities of the users (Ittelson et al., 1970). An individual's location in space can be recorded using time-lapse photography, video tape, and prepared diagrams (Sommer & Sommer, 2002), and newer technologies (see elsewhere here and in other chapters).

Step 5: Training of observers and pre-testing   Train observers so as to ensure there is good agreement in the coding of the environmental features of the setting, behavioral categories, and observation procedure. Pre-testing helps to identify any problems that need to be rectified before the actual study is conducted. It can also identify how much time is needed to scan the setting.

Behavioral Tracking (Individual-centered Mapping)

Researchers can follow the steps below to conduct individual-centered mapping.

Step 1   As in place-centered behavioral mapping, a map of the observation area is drawn. A rectangular grid of the area could help with identifying specific locations within an area (Sommer & Sommer, 2002).

Step 2   Define behavioral categories and their codes or symbols, and develop a system of coding, as in place-centered mapping.

Step 3   The next step is to identity the sampling strategies and the sample. As this procedure can gather detailed information about the movement and activities of individuals, a much smaller number of individuals are involved than in place-centered mapping (Sommer & Sommer, 2002). An individual with specific characteristics may be selected for tracking, or an individual can be selected at random by picking the third person, for example, who enters a setting. Follow a sampling plan that ensures coverage of all days and times.

Step 4: Develop an observation procedure The observer needs to obtain the individual's cooperation, and perhaps consent, to be followed. The researcher may need to observe the individual in stages to allow for habituation to the observer's presence. The researcher can observe the same individual continuously over a period of time (e.g., a work day) or periodically at intervals throughout the day (e.g., for 10 minutes in every hour). More than one individual could be observed when time sampling is used. The researcher could shift to observing a second individual when further observation would not provide any new information (Sommer & Sommer, 2002).

Track and record the movement of the individual through the space by drawing a line on the plan with arrows showing direction of movement. If the individual being observed stops at a location, the line is drawn up to the location and the time spent at that point recorded. The observer may record other behaviors and information such as sex, estimated age, and alone or with a group. At all times the tracker should try to remain inconspicuous by observing at an appropriate distance (Winkel & Sasanoff, 1966).

Step 5: Training of observers and pre-testing As in place-centered mapping, training of observers and pre-testing of the study are important steps. Pre-testing may help identify how likely people are aware of being observed and what the reactions of those being followed are. Strategies need to be devised to deal with such situations, taking into consideration the ethical issues to be discussed later in the chapter.

Data Analysis and Presentation

In most studies, the results of place-centered behavioral mapping are presented in simple, descriptive statistics such as number and percentage of observations at a certain location in tables, charts, or figures. Often, tabulations of activity by location, type of people by location, type of people by activity, and occasionally location or activity over time are presented. When observations are recorded on a map, a series of maps that represent behaviors at intervals can be combined into a single composite map to show the usage for all time periods (Sommer & Sommer, 2002). Data can also be aggregated and presented in visual form, using number of dots or people to represent the frequency or percentage of occupants present at a particular time, as in Ledingham and Chappus's (1986) study of playgrounds.

Ittelson et al. (1970) suggested that behavioral mapping can help identify several general principles in the use of space. Peaking indicates that certain areas are consistently used primarily for a single type of activity. Constancy indicates that certain behaviors tend to remain constant over many different conditions. Reciprocity refers to spaces where an increase in behavior in one space is associated with a decrease in that behavior in another space.

Sanoff (1971) proposed three ways of analyzing behavioral maps: (1) behavioral density refers to the total frequency of all types of activities at a place; (2) activity profile refers to the frequency of specific types of activities occurring at a place; and (3) behavioral range refers to the range of different activities occurring at a place, indicating the degree to which the setting is a diffuse setting. For example, the behavioral density for each behavioral category and the total behavioral densities for each square of the grid were calculated in Ledingham and Chappus's (1986) study of children in playgrounds.

In individual-centered mapping, the maps can be summarized in tables showing the percentage of time spent in various locations and activities. The person's journey each day can also be recorded as a single line, which becomes thicker with more frequent travel (Sommer & Sommer, 2002). Separate tracking maps can be converted into composite maps, which give an overview of the paths taken by the individuals. Breakdowns of the composite maps according to the path behavior of the sample can be made (e.g., men vs. women). However, the composite maps alone do not tell why people take different paths (Winkel & Sasanoff, 1966). One technique is to calculate the behavior range, that is, the number of different settings that the person enters during a given time period (Sommer & Sommer, 2002).

Needless to say, how data are analyzed is dependent on the purpose of study. In a study of primary and secondary school classes, Martin (2002) measured mobility within the classroom as the percentage of total area of the room covered by the teacher and degree of centeredness as the time spent at specific locations as a percentage of the total lesson time. The combined tracking data showed the route taken by the teacher within the room and the total area covered by the teacher during the lesson. She found that some teachers tended to circulate throughout the classroom, while other teachers remained close to their desks throughout the school day. Various behaviors were related to the flexibility in the layout of the classroom, calculated as the total area of the room where changes could be made.

Behavioral mapping data have also been analyzed using multi-regression analysis to predict spatial behaviors such as standing and sitting as a function of temperature, sunny or shaded areas, and seating (Zacharias et al., 2004).

Examples

Behavioral mapping and tracking have been used in studies of a variety of settings: playground and schoolyard, classroom, library, psychiatric ward, long-term care facilities, urban neighborhood, retail setting, aquarium and museums, public squares, and university plaza. A few examples of such studies are provided below.

Public squares

Hampton, Livio, and Goulet (2010) used a combination of place-centered and individual-centered behavioral mapping to record behaviors and locations of wi-fi users in seven public squares in the United States and Canada in 2007. Between place-centered observations, they selected one Internet user (and accompanying group) at random for tracking for 30 minutes. The researchers observed that the wi-fi users were largely white, male young adults who were alone. The majority of them used their wireless Internet connection to communicate with people who were not physically present. Users spread out evenly throughout the square, and their locations were influenced by the presence of power outlets, comfortable seating, or relative privacy. They observed that a limited number of wi-fi users in one of the parks were there to work – busy shuffling papers and scribbling notes – and did not socialize with either any strangers or their companions. Working was facilitated by the abundance of small tables and chairs with desk attachments, which provided limited space for any companions.

Playground and schoolyard

Ledingham and Chappus (1986) used behavioral mapping to study the importance of the physical and social environment for social play among 32 children with behavior problems. To evaluate the extent of localization of behaviors and the effects of social density, they calculated the behavioral densities for each observational category and the total behavioral densities for each square of the grid. They reported that cooperative play, rough and tumble play, and games play alone tended to be concentrated in open areas whereas individualistic behaviors tended to be at the play structure. The results have important implications for the design of playgrounds. Fjortoft, Kristoffersen, and Sageie (2009) used portable GPS units and GIS to track 71 six-year-old children's movements and locations within two schoolyards in a study in Norway. They reported that even though the two schoolyards provided different space and qualities of outdoor environment for the children, the physical activity level as measured in heart rate did not differ when playing in these schoolyards.

Aquarium

In a review of visitor tracking studies, Yalowitz and Bronnenkant (2009) conclude that there are distinct patterns of visitor behavior in museums, zoos, and aquariums. For example, Yalowitz and Ferguson (2006) observed unobtrusively 155 visitors at Monterey Bay Aquarium to see what visitors attended to and for how long. They reported that large live animal tanks were attended to by the highest percentage of visitors (90%; staying 77 seconds), followed by hands-on or interactive exhibits, and the lowest among text-only exhibits. These findings helped exhibit personnel to set realistic expectations for particular types of exhibits, to arrange exhibits in a way that would lessen visitor crowding and maximize circulation, and to assess how changes to the exhibits may influence patterns of visitor behavior.

Residential care setting

Milke, Beck, Danes, and Leask (2009) investigated the activity patterns of 184 elderly residents with Alzheimer's disease and the staff in five similarly designed residential care facilities. Assessments of general architectural design features and the overall environmental quality using established scales revealed no significant differences between the two 12-resident facilities and the three 20-resident facilities. The researchers collected samples of behaviors systematically in 1998 using place-centered behavioral mapping. At every hour over 14 hours on each of two days at each site, observers followed a pre-planned path through the buildings and recorded quickly on copies of floor plans individuals present at a public space and the type, time, and location of their activities.

Trained on-site staff followed instructions in a procedure manual that specified standardized use of behavioral categories with comprehensive definitions, floor-plan notation, ethogramatic checklists, and time-locked sampling. General activity categories included just sitting, activities of daily living, light housekeeping, leisure, disruptive behavior, walking, watching, and other behaviors. The results of behavioral mapping revealed that residents' activities did not conform to the architects' expectations. In practice, more use of the common spaces for activities was seen in the 12-resident house design whereas more activities were held within the house in the 20-resident house design. Behavior was affected by the house design and by the way that staff chose to organize activities.

Library

Given and Leckie (2003) used a place-centered behavioral mapping technique they called "seating sweeps" to observe patrons' behaviors in two larger public libraries three times daily for a six-day period, Monday through Saturday. Their results showed that most patrons were male and were younger than 60 years old. The busiest time of day was mid-afternoon. The most popular location was the study carrels or work tables, followed by computer workstations, and the food court or indoor street area. Library patrons had with them most frequently books, carrying cases, and some had food and drinks even though these items were not allowed in the libraries. Not surprisingly, reading was the most prominent activity. Talking to other patrons was fairly common even though talking was discouraged in the libraries.

Simpson (2007) studied patrons' behaviors in relation to locations within a small library in a university. Data were entered into an Excel spreadsheet on a personal digital assistant (PDA), and then analyzed and visualized using GIS software ArcGIS (Environmental Systems Research Institute, 2006). The results of behavioral mapping showed the lack of use of the stacks, the need for more space for group study and for the use of laptops, and conflicting needs for space for quiet reading and for talking.

Retail setting

Sorensen (2003) used a real-time tracking system to record the location and paths of shopping carts and baskets, as proxies for shoppers. The tracking system consists of a small tag mounted under the shopping cart that emits a uniquely coded signal; antennae around the perimeter of the store to pick up the signals from each shopping cart; a locate processor system that locates the tags; and a software system that integrates location data, purchase transaction data, and planogram data to produce marketing data.

The most important finding was that the average shopping trip only covers about 25% of the store; this led to the suggestion of pushing the products shoppers are interested in onto their path rather than having shoppers come to the products. Sorensen also suggests setting up "anchor departments" to attract shoppers to certain locations. In the same study, Larson, Bradlow, and Fader (2005) used a multivariate clustering algorithm to analyze the data sets, taking into account spatial constraints such as location of aisles and other inaccessible areas of the store. They observed that shoppers tend to travel only to select aisles or to take short excursions into and out of the aisle, and that short trips tend to be to the perimeter and convenience store areas.

Challenges and Limitations

Despite its usefulness, behavioral mapping has its limitations and poses several challenges for researchers.

Intrusiveness and reactivity

Place-centered mapping can be intrusive, and individual-centered mapping can be even more intrusive. Except in crowded places such as a busy store or shopping mall (Underhill, 1999), an observer following someone around will have difficulty not being noticed by the person observed and others (Hill, 1984; Sommer & Sommer, 2002). Observers should try to blend in as much as possible with the surroundings (Given & Leckie, 2003), or observe from tall buildings or other fixed spots high above (Hill, 1984). Using a handheld device is likely less noticeable than using a clipboard to record data.

Reactivity can be a problem when people are aware that they are being observed in a setting, as demonstrated in Bechtel's (1967) study of museum visitors. In research using multiple methods, researchers should complete mapping (the less reactive procedure) before interviewing or photographing (the more reactive procedures) (Sommer & Sommer, 2002).

Ethical issues

As behavioral mapping and tracking involve unobtrusive observation, researchers need to address several major ethical issues: informed consent, and privacy and confidentiality. Current *Tri-Council Policy Statement: Ethical Conduct for Research Involving Humans* (2010) stipulates that research involving naturalistic observation of people in public places where specific individuals cannot be identified does not require review by research ethics boards (Article 2.3). However, in some jurisdictions, publication of an image of an identifiable individual taken in a public place may be considered an invasion of privacy in civil law (Article 10.3).

Take caution that some "public places" such as a shopping mall are not in fact public. When in doubt, seek approval from institutional ethics review boards and any appropriate jurisdictions and organizations where the study is to be conducted. As in any research involving human participants, it is the responsibility of the researcher to weigh the potential social benefits against the social costs of the research.

Researchers have taken several measures to alleviate these ethical concerns. First, to respect the privacy of the individuals, make sure that the individuals being observed are not identified by name (Burke, 2006; Given & Leckie, 2003; Milke et al., 2009;

Sommer & Sommer, 2002). Typically, the results of the behavioral maps are reported in aggregated form. Securing the privacy of individuals is particularly important in individual-centered mapping or behavioral tracking. Anything seen or heard by the observer must be kept confidential. In a small sample, it may be very difficult to conceal the identity of an individual; in which case, it may be necessary to broaden the description of the individual's activities to maintain the privacy of that individual (Sommer & Sommer, 2002).

To address the issue of lack of informed consent, researchers can let potential subjects know that a research study is being undertaken, and that they may be observed. For example, visitors to public places such as a museum or a public library can be informed directly before they are being observed, or at the least indirectly with a sign posted. The observer must explain what is occurring and what the purpose of the study is, perhaps by handing out an information sheet explaining the study, if an unobtrusively observed individual suspects that he or she is being observed. If behavioral tracking is to be followed by an interview, the individual should be informed at the beginning (Given & Leckie, 2003; Yalowitz & Bronnenkant, 2009).

The increasing feasibility of researchers using new technologies to record behaviors in natural settings has raised additional ethical concerns. Goodwin, Velicer, and Intille (2008) suggest that to address the issues of privacy and confidentiality, data can be encrypted and indicators be in place to inform participants that they are being sensed or recorded. Researchers must also ensure that research participants understand what data are being collected, what the data could be used to infer, and how they can stop the collection of their information if they wish. Particularly disconcerting is the increasing use of electronic surveillance to track the mobility patterns of the elderly with dementia, who are unable to give informed consent and yet their privacy is invaded during such surveillance (Shoval et al., 2008).

Reliability and validity

As discussed in Chapter 2, inter-observer reliability can be established by having two observers report behaviors at the same setting at the same time independently (Ittelson et al., 1970). Observers must be trained to record behavior in a systematic and reliable manner through repeated practice and feedback. Where reliability for a specific behavior is low, that behavior may be removed from the data analysis (Sommer & Sommer, 2002).

To establish convergent validity, the results of behavioral mapping and tracking can be compared with data obtained in other ways (e.g., interview). To establish discriminant validity, verify any expected differences in behaviors between two conditions (e.g., weekdays vs. weekends) (Ittelson et al., 1970).

Data analysis

Techniques for analyzing behavioral maps are not yet well developed. Combining behavioral maps from several individuals observed at various times can make interpretation difficult (Sommer & Sommer, 2002). A combined place-centered behavioral map of 10 observational sessions in a schoolyard may show 10 dots at a specific location. These 10 dots may represent one child observed at that location 10 times or 10 children on one occasion. Is the number of different users important or not? Or is the percentage of time that a particular location or a particular environmental feature is used more important than the number of users? Answering temporal and context-dependent questions may require appropriate statistical techniques for modeling longitudinal data both within and across individuals (Goodwin et al., 2008).

Explanations for behavior

Although behavioral mapping data can reveal environmental choices made by individuals, the data do not explain why these choices are made. The maps must be supplemented with interviews or other data in order for researchers to understand the motivation behind these choices (Sommer & Sommer, 2002).

Labor intensive

Behavioral mapping and tracking with pencil and paper are labor intensive and time consuming. Transferring data from paper to a database is also time consuming and subject to human error. New technologies can help.

Use of Technology

New mobile computing and telecommunication technologies have become available to facilitate observation, recording, data entry, analysis, and visualization of behavioral mapping and tracking data. Compared with the paper-and-pencil technique, electronic behavioral coding and analysis systems can be more accurate (Hecht, 1997), permit separate times recording for concurrent behaviors, eliminate data entry, and are less intrusive.

In the last two decades or so, researchers have used handheld devices such as personal digital assistants (PDAs) to record behavioral mapping data in the field (e.g., Lulham & Tietjen, 2004; Simpson, 2007; Wener, 2002). Wener (2002) used BMAP software on Psion, and Lulham and Tietjen (2004) used the "Track" program from the field of biology on a Palm Pilot. A number of other software programs have been developed, such as Pocket Observer 3.0 and Outdoor Explorer for recording behavioral mapping data, and WayTracer for behavioral tracking. For a comparison of the functionality of these software programs, refer to Dalton, Dalton, Holscher, and Kuhnmunch (2012). The PeopleWatcher App, being developed to run on the iPad, can be used for behavioral mapping and tracking, and is particularly suitable for wayfinding and navigation tasks (Dalton et al., 2012; see Chapter 9).

The use of GPS in tracking movements is becoming popular in the area of dementia care. Such technology can allow the caregiver to monitor the location of a person with dementia when outdoors. The external tracking device that can be worn on clothing or part of the body sends GPS position coordinates to a secured website. The caregiver can then look up on a map the actual position of the person with dementia and the route the person took (Pot, Willemse, & Horjus, 2011; Shoval et al., 2008). Various measures such as walking speed, time spent in different places, trip length, or change of direction can be monitored (Oswald et al., 2010).

The main drawback of using GPS in tracking is that any kind of obstruction, such as buildings, will produce an inaccurate reading. Its main advantage is that it virtually spans the globe (Shoval et al., 2008).

Land-based tracking systems consist of antenna stations distributed throughout a local area and the end unit does not have to be exposed directly to the antenna stations (Shoval et al., 2008). Wearable computing and ubiquitous computing technologies have made it possible to embed various sensors in clothing or accessories, and in objects in our physical environment (Goodwin et al., 2008)

Still photography and video photography can provide useful data regarding people's use of space and their movement. However, normal video cameras cannot track visitors over larger spaces, at least not with a single video camera (Burke, 2006; Yalowitz & Bronnenkant, 2009). New technologies that use specialized cameras or multiple overlapping camera views have been developed to allow behavioral tracking of people automatically and non-intrusively (Spink, Locke, van de As, & Noldus, 2013). And of course, security surveillance video cameras that are now installed at road intersections, retail stores, public buildings, and just about everywhere can store an enormous amount of data. In a novel way, Hipp, Adlakha, Eyler, Chang, and Pless (2013) were able to access existing public data feeds from the Archive of Many Outdoor Scenes (AMOS) images from public webcams in order to assess the effects of introducing protected bike lanes at a road interaction had on transportation mode usage.

Retail stores can now use a combination of RFID, GPS, and video-based camera systems to track shoppers' navigation. One such system recently developed is TrackLab by Noldus Information Technology that incorporates tracking technologies (GPS where satellite reception is possible, ultra-wideband sensors and tags for indoors, stereo cameras) to track behaviors of customers in retail environments and to provide visual presentation of the data. Such a system can be used in other settings as well (Spink et al., 2013).

GIS is becoming more commonly used as a visualization tool to help analyze behavioral mapping and tracking data (e.g., Fjortoft et al., 2009; Simpson, 2007).

The increasing popularity of smartphones has made it economically feasible for their users and behavioral scientists to record and log their users' daily activities. Data collection is unobtrusive in that data logging runs reliably in the background of the smartphone.

Perhaps the most promising feature of the smartphone for behavioral mapping and tracking is its sensing ability that allows for automatic gathering of location data, currently at a crude level. More accurate location data can be collected when integrated with a GPS device, although the need to carry an external device is likely to increase reactivity of measurement. Other sensors can be integrated to allow gathering of physiological data (e.g., heart rate), or activity data (e.g., accelerometers). The smartphone also allows for self-documentation of experiences, feelings, and thoughts with its audio and text, still images, and video functions. No doubt technological advances in the future will overcome the current limitations (Miller, 2012; Raento, Oulasvirta, & Eagle, 2009). Newer systems that might integrate information from GPS, motion, infra-red light, and perhaps ambient sound sensors will likely be developed (Intille, 2012). Technologies are changing so fast that behavioral scientists will need to keep abreast of any new developments constantly.

Case Study: Behavioral Mapping and Tracking in a Small Public Library

Let me illustrate the process and challenges of using behavioral mapping and tracking in a post-occupancy evaluation of a small public library. Although the study was completed by myself and the editor of this volume many years ago, the principles remain much the same. Suffice to say, various technologies could now help with data recording, entry, and analysis. Nevertheless, similarly small projects are feasible for a senior undergraduate or a graduate student to complete in a semester or a year, and at low cost.

The plan to relocate a small public branch library in Esquimalt, British Columbia, Canada provided us with an opportunity to study the use of space and to assess the effectiveness of the physical design from the library user's perspective. Two of the goals stated explicitly in the building program for the new library included: (1) adequate seating for study and leisure reading for adults and children, and (2) provision for expansion and relocation of shelves and counters.

The new library occupied the main floor of a two-story building on a busy road near a small shopping mall. It had a usable floor area of 6300 square feet, including a multipurpose room for community activities. At the time of data collection, the library had been open to the public for three months. The library served adults, youths, and children and had books, magazines, audio records for loan, and reference material.

Three data-collection techniques were used in this study: a questionnaire survey, behavioral mapping, and behavioral tracking. The study was approved by the Greater Victoria Public Library Board and the Ethics Review Committee at the University of Victoria. We addressed the librarians' concerns by posting a sign that said the University of Victoria was conducting a study on the physical features of the library, minimizing following patrons, observing before questionnaires were handed out, voluntary participation from questionnaire respondents, and interviewing employees.

Before data collection, the four observers met to ensure agreement on the behavioral categories. The questionnaire and the observation procedure were pretested. Data were collected on two weekdays (10 a.m. to 9 p.m.) and on Saturday (10 a.m. to 6 p.m.) for three consecutive weeks.

Behavioral mapping provided information about the distribution of user behaviors in various locations throughout the library. At 15-minute intervals, the observer made the rounds of the library and marked on a floor plan the location and activity of each patron in the library. It usually took the observer one to two minutes to complete each observation and recording. In 133 observation periods, 1342 behavioral mapping observations were made. No observation of behaviors was made during periods when questionnaires were distributed. This eliminated the possibility of recording questionnaire-related behaviors, which of course were not typical library activities.

Behavioral tracking served to identify sequences of users' activities during library visits, and the duration of these activities. A trained observer positioned herself so that as much of the library as possible was visible. She then randomly selected the first library patron who entered the library, and recorded the patron's activities, locations, and time spent on each activity in a sequence using a stopwatch. At times, it was necessary for the observer to move around in order to keep the patron in sight. The observer experienced no difficulty blending in with other patrons so as not to be intrusive. After the patron had left the library, the next patron who entered the library was observed. Figure 3.1 shows the recording sheet.

The behavioral mapping data show that there were, on average, 9 to 10 patrons in the library at any time. The stacks (except those in the youth area) were used most intensively and about equally. The longest visits were made to the sitting area near

Time Diary

Subject No._____ Sex _____ Age _____ Brief description_____

Date _____ Day of the week _____ Weather _____ Observer_____

Activity Code

Browsing B

Study/work SW

Check out/return Bo

Talking T

Playing PL

Waiting (standing) WST

Parenting PA

Waiting (sitting) WSI

Reading R

Walking W

Searching S

Writing WR

Sitting SI

Location Code

Circulation C

Entrance E

Information I

Office OF

Sitting lounge 1-5 L1-L5

Stacks 1-5 ST1-ST5

Activity No.	Activity	Starting time	Finishing time	Amount of time	Alone	With friends/family	With patron	With staff	Location	Remarks
1										
2										
3										
4										
5										
6										
7										

Figure 3.1 Behavioral tracking recording sheet.

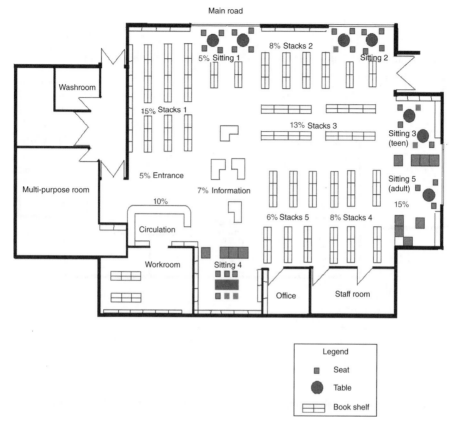

Figure 3.2 A composite behavioral map showing the percentage of total observations of patrons present at each location.

the adult magazine section (average 13.5 minutes). Of the five sitting areas, the one at the magazine section was the most intensively used (15% of the patrons at a given time) (see Figure 3.2). Reading at this corner of the library comprised 12% of the observations. The sitting area in the youth section was used the least (1%).

Behavioral tracking of 93 patrons showed that they spent, on average, about 13 minutes in the library. The longest stay was one hour. As expected, reading was the activity on which patrons spent the most time (an average of 16.5 minutes), followed by browsing (11.5 minutes). Analysis of traffic patterns showed that 38% of the patrons who were tracked stayed close to the library entrance. The activities involved were either checking out or returning library materials, or making photocopies. Most patrons (63%) visited only one or two sections of the library. A small percentage of patrons (7%) seemed to wander about the library aimlessly. Figure 3.3 shows the paths taken by two library patrons.

The results of the study showed that library patrons were generally pleased with the physical design of the library. Our observational data indicated that tables and seats were substantially underused (an average of 3 of the 42 seats occupied at any

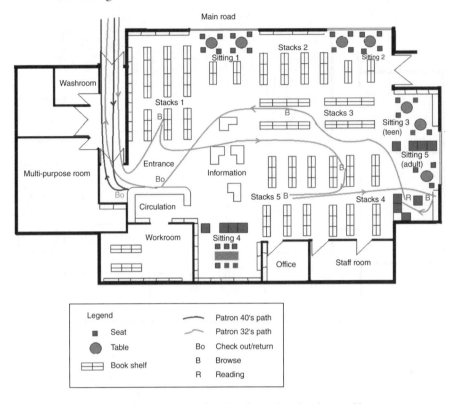

Figure 3.3   A behavioral tracking map showing the paths taken by two library patrons.

given time). Yet one-third of the respondents in the questionnaire survey complained that the tables were too small and that there were not enough tables and seats. This conflict in the findings suggested that the tables and seats were not located where patrons wanted them. As the adult sitting area at the magazine section was the most heavily used area, future expansion of library services may consider adding magazines, newspapers, and reading and study areas.

This evaluation demonstrated that behavioral mapping and tracking techniques, when used together with a questionnaire survey, can provide a more comprehensive picture of patrons' satisfaction with the library and their space use pattern than any one technique alone (Ng & Gifford, 1986).

Physical Traces

In addition to observing behaviors as they are occurring, behavioral researchers can use physical traces to infer people's behaviors. Physical traces are physical evidence of people's past behaviors or their interactions with the physical environment. Trace measures are of two general forms: accretion and erosion (Sommer & Sommer,

2002; Webb, Campbell, Schwartz, & Sechrest, 2000); additional trace measures include adaptations and repairs to a space, and personal and public messages displayed in a space (Zeisel, 2006). **Accretion** refers to physical evidence of people's past behaviors or their interactions with the physical environment; for example, empty beer bottles and litter left after a party, graffiti on walls in washrooms, and dirty footprints on the carpet. **Erosion** refers to deterioration of the physical environment that results from use; for example, bare spots on a lawn or footprints in the snow suggest a shortcut from one building to another. Signs of wear and tear in floor tiles are another example.

The collection of physical traces is unobtrusive because the researcher is seldom present at the scene where the behaviors occurred. Physical traces are often collected indirectly, after the people whose behaviors are being measured have left the scene, which makes the measurement of physical traces non-reactive.

Researchers can use physical traces in creative ways to test hypotheses about behaviors and preferences. These measures can be used to assess the validity of verbal reports. Consider, for example, the posters of pop music stars on the walls of a teenager's room, which may be used to assess the validity of that teenager's expressed liking for his or her favorite stars.

The use of physical traces as measures of past behaviors has its limitations. Measures of physical traces can be imprecise as they do not indicate who, when, and for how long deposits or wear and tear are made. However, systematic monitoring of these physical traces can improve precision of these measures (Sommer & Sommer, 2002). Other factors can influence the deposit or erosion of physical traces, so it is important that physical trace measures not be used alone. The researcher must consider alternative hypotheses or explanations, and then collect data from other sources to refute these alternative hypotheses. For example, are the empty beer bottles left by one person or many persons, and is this the result of janitors on strike? The best approach is to use multiple methods to collect data to test the same hypothesis. If different methods lead to the same conclusion, then the researcher has increased confidence in the hypothesis.

Summary and Conclusions

Behavioral mapping is a research tool used to observe and record behaviors in a particular setting at a particular time. Behavioral mapping can be either place-based or individual-based, depending on whether the focus of the observation is to identify locational or temporal patterns of behaviors. Behavioral mapping can be used in descriptive, correlational, or experimental research, and is used in architectural programming and in post-occupancy evaluation. Behavioral mapping follows several steps, including preparing a floor plan of the setting, identifying behavioral categories and their coding, developing a sampling plan and standardized observation procedure, training observers, and pre-testing. In addition to being a more objective measure of behaviors than self-reports, behavioral mapping facilitates the study of behaviors in their physical and social contexts. However, it has several challenges, including ethical issues, intrusiveness and reactivity, difficulty in data analysis, intense time and labor commitment, and the inability to infer individuals' motivation behind their behaviors. Advances in technologies have, and will no doubt continue to, lessen time and labor commitment. When combined with other methods of data collection, behavioral mapping can be a useful tool for environment–behavior research.

Glossary

Behavioral mapping   An observational technique used to record people's behaviors and movements systematically as these behaviors occur in particular locations at a particular time.

Behavioral tracking   An observational technique used to record a person's movements and activities in a setting or settings over time.

Physical traces   Physical evidence of people's past behaviors or their interactions with the physical environment.

Accretion   Deposition of material on the physical environment as a result of people's past behaviors or their interactions with the physical environment.

Erosion   Deterioration of the physical environment that results from use.

References

Barker, R. G. (1968). *Ecological psychology: Concepts and methods for studying the environment of human behavior*. Stanford, CA: Stanford University Press.

Bechtel, R. (1967). The study of man: Human movement and architecture. *Trans-action, 16*, 53–56.

Bechtel, R., & Zeisel, J. (1987). Observation: The world under a glass. In R. B. Bechtel, R. W. Marans, & W. Michelson (Eds.), *Methods in environmental and behavioral research* (pp. 11–40). New York, NY: Van Nostrand Reinhold.

Burke, R. R. (2006). The third wave of marketing intelligence. In M. Drafft & M. Mantrala (Eds.), *Retailing in the 21st century: Current and future trends* (pp. 113–125). New York, NY: Springer.

Canadian Institutes of Health Research, Natural Sciences and Engineering Research Council of Canada, & Social Sciences and Humanities Research Council of Canada. (2010). *Tri-council policy statement: Ethical conduct for research involving humans* (2nd ed.). Retrieved from http://www.pre.ethics.gc.ca/pdf/eng/tcps2/TCPS_2_FINAL_Web.pdf

Dalton, N. S., Dalton, R. C., Holscher, C., & Kuhnmunch, G. (2012). An iPad app for recording movement paths and associated spatial behaviors. In C. Stachniss, K. Schill, & D. Uttal (Eds.), *Spatial cognition, LNAI 7463* (pp. 431–450). Berlin, Germany: Springer-Verlag.

Environmental Systems Research Institute (ESRI) website (2006). *Desktop GIS*. http://www.esri.com/software/arcgis/about/desktop.html

Fjortoft, I., Kristoffersen, B., & Sageie, J. (2009). Children in schoolyards: Tracking movement patterns and physical activity in schoolyards using global positioning system and heart rate monitoring. *Landscape and Urban Planning, 93*, 210–217. doi:10.1016/j.landurbplan.2009.07.008

Garbrecht, D. (1971). Pedestrian paths through a uniform environment. *Town Planning Review, 4*, 71–84.

Given, L. M., & Leckie, G. (2003). "Sweeping" the library: Mapping the social activity space of the public library. *Library and Information Science Research, 25*, 365–385. doi:10.1016/S0740-8188(03)00049-5

Giuliani, M. V., & Scopelliti, M. (2009). Empirical research in environmental psychology: Past, present, and future. *Journal of Environmental Psychology, 29*, 375–386. doi:10.1016/j.jenvp.2008.11.008

Goodwin, M. S., Velicer, W. F., & Intille, S. S. (2008). Telemetric monitoring in the behavior sciences. *Behavior Research Methods, 40*, 328–341. doi:10.3758/BRM.40.1.328

Hampton, K. N., Livio, O., & Goulet, L. S. (2010). The social life of wireless urban spaces: Internet use, social networks, and the public realm. *Journal of Communication, 60*, 701–722.

Hecht, J. B. (1997). Using a PDA for field data collection. ERIC document ED433369.

Hill, M. R. (1984). Stalking the urban pedestrian: A comparison of questionnaire and tracking methodologies for behavioral mapping in large-scale environments. *Environment and Behavior, 16*, 539–550.

Hipp, J. A., Adlakha, D., Eyler, A. A., Chang, B., & Pless, R. (2013). Emerging technologies: Webcams and crowd sourcing to identify active transportation. *American Journal of Preventive Medicine, 44*, 96–97.

Intille, S. S. (2012). Emerging technology for studying daily life. In M. R. Mehl & T. S. Conner (Eds.), *Handbook of research methods for studying daily life* (pp. 267–282). New York, NY: Guilford.

Ittelson, W. H., Rivlin, L. G., & Proshansky, H. M. (1970). The use of behavioral maps in environmental psychology. In H. M. Proshansky, W. H. Ittelson, & L. G. Rivlin (Eds.), *Environmental psychology: People and their physical setting* (2nd ed.) (pp. 340–351). New York, NY: Holt, Rinehart & Winston.

Kalff, C., & Strube, G. (2009). Background knowledge in human navigation: A study in a supermarket. *Cognitive Processing, 10*, S225–S228. doi:10.1007/s10339-009-0287-6

Khasawneh, F. A., Kato, A., & Mori, S. (2013). Changing campus learning space design to correspond with adopting problem based learning: Student collaboration, prominent activities, and its relationship to learning style. *Proceedings of the 44th annual conference of the Environmental Design Research Association (EDRA)*, Providence, Rhode Island, USA.

Larson, J. S., Bradlow, E. T., & Fader, P. S. (2005). An exploratory look at supermarket shopping paths. *International Journal of Research in Marketing, 22*, 395–414. doi:10.1016/j.ijresmar.2005.09.005

Ledingham, J. E., & Chappus, F. T. (1986). Behavioral mapping of children's social interactions: The impact of the play environment. *Canadian Journal of Research in Early Childhood Education, 1*, 137–148.

Lulham, R. & Tietjen, B. (2004). Behavioral map or behavioral mess: A computer tool for clean behavioral mapping? *Proceedings of the 35th annual conference of the Environmental Design Research Association (EDRA)*, Albuquerque, New Mexico, USA.

Martin, S. H. (2002). The classroom environment and its effects on the practice of teachers. *Journal of Environmental Psychology, 22*, 139–156. doi:10.1006/jevp.2001.0239

Milke, D. L., Beck, C. H., Danes, S., & Leask, J. (2009). Behavior mapping of residents' activity in five residential style care centers for elderly persons diagnosed with dementia: Small differences in sites can affect behaviors. *Journal of Housing for the Elderly, 23*, 335–367. doi:10.1080/02763890903327135

Miller, G. (2012). The smartphone psychology manifesto. *Perspectives on Psychological Science, 7*, 221–237. doi:10.1177/1745691612441215

Ng, C. F., & Gifford, R. (1986). *Use of multiple techniques in post-occupancy evaluations.* Paper presented at the Annual Convention of the Canadian Psychological Association, Toronto.

Oswald, F., Wahl, H.-W., Voss, E., Schilling, O., Freytag, T., Auslander, G., Shoval, N., Heinik, J., & Landau, R. (2010). The use of tracking technologies for the analysis of outdoor mobility in the face of dementia: First steps into a project and some illustrative findings from Germany. *Journal of Housing for the Elderly, 24*, 55–73. doi:10.1080/02763890903327481

Page, S. (2000). Community research: The lost art of unobtrusive methods. *Journal of Applied Social Psychology, 30*, 2126–2136.

Pot, A. M., Willemse, B. M., & Horjus, S. (2011). A pilot study on the use of tracking technology: Feasibility, acceptability, and benefits for people in early stages of dementia and their informal caregivers. *Aging and Mental Health*, 1-8. doi:10.1080/13607863. 2011.596810

Raento, M., Oulasvirta, A., & Eagle, N. (2009). Smartphones: An emerging tool for social scientists. *Sociological Methods and Research, 37*, 426–454. doi:10.1177/0049124108330005

Rivlin, L. G., & Rothenberg, M. (1976). The use of space in open classrooms. In H. M. Proshansky, W. H. Ittelson, & L. G. Rivlin (Eds.), *Environmental psychology: People and their physical setting* (2nd ed.) (pp. 479–489). New York, NY: Holt, Rinehart, & Winston.

Rivlin, L. G., & Wolfe, M. (1972). The early history of a psychiatric hospital for children: Expectations and reality. In H. M. Proshansky, W. H. Ittelson, & L. G. Rivlin (Eds.), *Environmental psychology: People and their physical setting* (2nd ed.) (pp. 459–479). New York, NY: Holt, Rinehart, & Winston.

Sanoff, H. (1971). Behavior settings in residential environments: A research strategy for determining what happens in the designed environment. *Journal of Architectural Education, 15*, 95–97.

Shoval, N., Auslander, G. K., Freytag, T., Landau, R., Oswald, F., Seidl, U., Wahl, H.-W., Werner, S., & Hienik, J. (2008). The use of advanced tracking technologies for the analysis of mobility in Alzheimer's disease and related cognitive diseases. *BMC Geriatrics, 8*. doi:10.1186/1471-2318-8-7. Retrieved from http://www.biomedcentral. com/1471-2318/8/7

Simpson, H. (2007). Mapping users' activities and space preferences in the academic business library (Unpublished master's thesis). University of Alberta, Canada.

Sommer, R. (1966). The ecology of privacy. *Library Quarterly, 36*, 234–248.

Sommer, R., & Sommer, B. (2002). Mapping and trace measures. In *A practical guide to behavioral research: Tools and techniques* (5th ed.) (pp. 63–81). New York: Oxford University Press.

Sorensen, H. (2003). The science of shopping. *Marketing Research, 15*, 30–35.

Spink, A., Locke, B., van de As, N., & Noldus, L. (2013, September). TrackLab – An innovative system for location sensing, customer flow analysis and persuasive information presentation. *UbiComp'13 Adjunct*. Zurich, Switzerland.

Underhill, P. (1999, updated 2009). *Why we buy: The science of shopping*. New York, NY: Simon & Schuster.

Webb, E. J., Campbell, D. T., Schwartz, R. D., & Sechrest, L. (2002). *Nonreactive measures* (rev. ed.). Thousand Oaks, CA: Sage.

Wener, R. (2002). BMAP 3.0: Handheld software to support behavior observations. *Presentation at the 33rd annual conference of the Environmental Design Research Association*, Philadelphia, PA, USA.

Whyte, W. H. (1980). *The social life of small urban spaces*. New York, NY: The Conservation Foundation.

Winkel, G., & Sasanoff, R. (1966). An approach to an objective analysis of behavior in architectural space. In H. M. Proshansky, W. H. Ittelson, & L. G. Rivlin (Eds.), *Environmental psychology: People and their physical setting* (2nd ed.) (pp. 351–363). New York, NY: Holt, Rinehart & Winston.

Yalowitz, S. S., & Bronnenkant, K. (2009). Timing and tracking: Unlocking visitor behavior. *Visitor Studies, 12*, 47–64. doi:10.1080/10645570902769134

Yalowitz, S. S., & Ferguson, A. (2006). *Myth and mystery: Summative evaluation*. Monterey Bay Aquarium. Retrieved from http://informalscience.org/images/evaluation/ report_227.PDF

Zacharias, J., Stathopoulos, T., & Wu, H. (2004). Spatial behavior in San Francisco's plazas: The effects of microclimate, other people, and environmental design. *Environment and Behavior, 36,* 638–658. doi: 10.1177/0013916503262545

Zamani, Z. (2012). The comparison of cognitive plan affordances within natural and manufactured preschool settings. In R. Awwad-Rafferty & L. Manzo (Eds.), *Proceedings of the 43rd annual conference of the Environmental Design Research Association (EDRA),* New Orleans, Atlanta, USA.

Zeisel, J. (2006). *Inquiry by design: Environment/behavior/neuroscience in architecture, interiors, landscapes, and planning* (Revised ed.). New York, NY: W.W. Norton.

Suggested Readings

Ittelson, W. H., Rivlin, L. G., & Proshansky, H. M. (1970). The use of behavioral maps in environmental psychology. In H. M. Proshansky, W. H. Ittelson, & L. G. Rivlin (Eds.), *Environmental psychology: People and their physical setting* (2nd ed.) (pp. 340–351). New York, NY: Holt, Rinehart & Winston.

Milke, D. L., Beck, C. H., Danes, S., & Leask, J. (2009). Behavior mapping of residents' activity in five residential style care centers for elderly persons diagnosed with dementia: Small differences in sites can affect behaviors. *Journal of Housing for the Elderly, 23,* 335–367. doi:10.1080/02763890903327135

Miller, G. (2012). The smartphone psychology manifesto. *Perspectives on Psychological Science, 7,* 221–237. doi:10.1177/1745691612441215

Sommer, R., & Sommer, B. (2002). Mapping and trace measures. In *A practical guide to behavioral research: Tools and techniques* (5th ed.) (pp. 63–81). New York, NY: Oxford University Press.

Webb, E. J., Campbell, D. T., Schwartz, R. D., & Sechrest, L. (2002). *Nonreactive measures* (rev. ed.). Thousand Oaks, CA: Sage.

4

Research Designs for Environmental Issues

Wokje Abrahamse[1], P. Wesley Schultz[2], and Linda Steg[3]

[1] *Victoria University of Wellington, New Zealand*
[2] *California State University, San Marcos, CA, United States*
[3] *University of Groningen, The Netherlands*

"Hey, guys, listen to this!" Ethan and Gabriel look up from their bowls of cereal. Maria is scanning the morning headlines. "Green space linked to obesity in city dwellers." Ethan has a sip of coffee and ponders this for a moment. "That doesn't make any sense," he says. "You'd expect it to be the exact opposite, green space linked to slim waists in city dwellers." Gabriel just grunts. He's not fully awake yet.

Maria continues reading: "The researchers collected data on more than 10,000 people living within walking distance of a park and found unexpectedly high levels of obesity." "Did they compare this to people living further away from a park?" asks Ethan. "The article doesn't say," Maria responds. "Well, there you have it. No comparison group." "Hang on a minute." Gabriel's coffee has finally kicked in. "Surely there are other factors that play a role in the prevalence of obesity. In my social influence class, our prof was telling us about the role of social networks in the spread of obesity. If your friend is obese, your likelihood of also being obese significantly increases. This could help explain the results."

"Either way," Maria says "the results are based on correlational data, so there is no way they can claim cause and effect. They cannot rule out the possibility that another variable is influencing both obesity and walking distance to green space." "Maybe that's just the headline though. You know how the media loves sound bites. Is this FOX News?" Maria nods. "My point exactly."

Environmental psychology is an empirical science. This means that the discipline is grounded in research in which hypotheses are tested using observations. Research questions and theories are used to guide predictions about human beliefs, emotions, behavior, or performance, and these predictions are tested through various research designs and measurement techniques. Research studies in environmental psychology are guided by diverse research questions. For example, why do people

Research Methods for Environmental Psychology, First Edition. Edited by Robert Gifford.
© 2016 John Wiley & Sons, Ltd. Published 2016 by John Wiley & Sons, Ltd.

buy environmentally friendly products? How do we reduce littering behavior in public places? Or, what is the best way to reduce household electricity consumption? Some studies focus on demonstrating relationships between variables, such as the relationship between environmental values and preference for green products. Other studies manipulate one or more variables in an effort to identify the causes of beliefs or behavior, such as whether the provision of information about climate change causes a change in attitudes toward climate change.

In the first part of this chapter, we describe the defining features of three main research designs used in environmental psychology, namely experimental, quasi-experimental, and correlational studies (for related chapters on survey research, see Chapter 5; for field studies, see Chapters 15 and 16). We highlight some of the main advantages and disadvantages of each design. At the end of the chapter, we discuss some general issues in conducting research, including measurements of variables, mediator and moderator variables, validity, and replication.

Choosing a Research Design

An **experimental design** includes the systematic variation of one or more independent variables, and is characterized by random assignment of participants to conditions, or groups. In a **quasi-experimental design**, one or more independent variables are systematically varied, but random assignment of participants to condition does not occur. A study using a **correlational design** describes the relationship between independent and dependent variables, without systematic variation of these variables or random assignment of participants (see also Pelham & Blanton, 2007). In research on human–environment issues, researchers typically use correlational and quasi-experimental designs to examine their research questions (see, e.g., De Groot & Steg, 2008). Increasingly, however, experimental studies are being conducted to examine environmental issues (e.g., Griskevicius, Tybur, & Van den Bergh, 2010).

Experimental designs

Experimental designs are **true experiments** that address research questions that aim to find out the cause of a particular phenomenon (see also Pelham & Blanton, 2007). Experimental designs share three important characteristics: manipulation of relevant variables, random assignment to treatments; and the use of comparison groups to eliminate the effects of other variables. **Manipulation** of variables occurs when one or more variables is systematically varied, while holding the other variables constant.

For example, consider an experiment designed to determine whether exposing people to environmental concepts affects people's preferences for green products. The researcher may ask one group of participants to complete a word association task that contains environmental words (e.g., green, conservation), while another group of participants (the control group) is asked to fill out a word association task that consists of neutral words (e.g., desk, shoe), before completing the same product preference task. **Random assignment** of participants to groups occurs when the researcher arbitrarily assigns participants to experimental and control groups. This way, each participant has an equal chance of ending up in either group (e.g., exposure to environmental words or exposure to neutral words). Any difference between groups in the outcome measure (e.g., preference for green products) is very likely attributable to the manipulation (e.g., activation of environmental concepts), not to group differences in other characteristics.

In experimental designs, the variable that is systematically varied is referred to as the **independent variable** and the outcome measure is referred to as the **dependent variable**. The group of participants that is not exposed to the manipulation is generally referred to as a **control group** or a comparison group. A control group consists of individuals who complete a similar task or activity to the manipulated variable, while a comparison group often does not engage in any activity.

Experimental designs have a number of advantages and disadvantages (see also Creswell, 2009; Pelham & Blanton, 2007). Experimental designs are generally high in **internal validity**, which refers to the ability to infer causal relationships between independent and dependent variables. In lab studies, the researcher has a great deal of control over what happens, such as which variables are varied and which variables are held constant. Because participants are randomly assigned to groups, any differences between groups on the outcome measure may be attributed to the treatment or the manipulation. It is less likely that group differences are attributable to systematic differences between groups.

Further, in experimental designs, the researcher can minimize the effect of confounding variables. A confounding variable is an additional variable that is correlated with the independent variable and affects the dependent variable. An **operational confound** occurs when a measure designed to assess a particular construct also measures something else. For example, if a researcher measures people's product preferences with a choice task, this may also gauge people's decision-making abilities. It is important to carefully select the dependent and independent measures. This can be done for example by pre-testing a measure in a pilot study. A **procedural confound** occurs when the researcher inadvertently varies more than one independent variable.

Imagine, for example, that all sessions of one experimental condition (e.g., control condition) were run in the same week, in which it happened to be raining every day and that the other sessions (e.g., exposure to environmental concepts) were run the week after, in which it happened to be sunny every day. Perhaps the good weather put people in a good mood, which made them more likely to choose environmentally friendly concepts. The researcher would not be able to draw a causal conclusion between the independent variable (exposure to environmental concepts) and the dependent variable (preference for green products) because of a confounding factor (the weather). Obviously, one cannot control the weather, but the researcher does have a great deal of control over procedures (e.g., time of day, day of the week, location, training of research assistants) to ensure that there is no systematic variation between groups as a result of how the research is set up.

A **person confound** refers to an individual difference variable among participants in the study, which may affect the outcome measure. For example, people may differ in their preference for green products, or people may have different levels of environmental concern from the outset. Because experimental designs use random assignment of participants to conditions, they are generally protected against this type of confound, as normally these individual differences would be equally distributed across conditions and not vary systematically with the outcome measure.

An experimental design also allows for the test of **interaction** effects. Interaction effects indicate that the effect of an independent variable on the dependent variable depends on another independent variable. This type of design, where two independent variables are systematically varied to assess interaction effects, is called a factorial design. For example, a researcher could examine the effect of exposure to environmental concepts and social influence on people's preference for green products, whereby both exposure to environmental concepts and social influence are systematically varied. The researcher may find, for example, that the effect of exposure to environmental concepts on people's preference for green products depends on whether or not participants have been told that a majority of other people prefer green products. Interactions can help in providing insight into the conditions under which a hypothesized relationship does and does not apply. For example, as a general theory, exposure to environmental concepts can be said to increase people's preference for green products, but only when people are told that a majority of other people also prefer green products.

A disadvantage of experimental designs is that they generally have low **external validity**, which refers to the ability to generalize findings from a study to different situations or populations of individuals. Lab studies are conducted in artificial situations that are unlikely to occur in everyday settings. While experimental studies provide an opportunity to examine one or two variables in isolation, this is not representative of real-life situations. One possible solution is to make the lab setting as realistic as possible, or alternatively, to conduct a study in a naturally occurring setting which allows a similar level of control over variables.

Yet another possibility is to replicate the findings using other research designs (see also the section on replication at the end of the chapter). Experimental studies often make use of convenience samples (e.g., undergraduate psychology students). The use of such samples is practical (e.g., labs are usually situated on campus, ease of recruitment of students). Another advantage of convenience samples is that the sample is relatively homogeneous, because variables such as gender, age, and education are held constant. However, this limits the possibility to generalize the findings to other populations. A possible solution to this problem is to conduct follow-up studies with different samples to examine whether the findings are generalizable to other populations.

Quasi-experimental designs

Quasi-experimental designs can be described as holding the middle ground between true experiments and correlational designs. While quasi-experimental designs are generally characterized by a relatively high level of control over variables, manipulation and random assignment are often not possible.

Many different types of quasi-experimental designs are known (see Campbell & Stanley, 1963). The most commonly used design is the **person-by-treatment quasi-experiment**. In this design, one independent variable is systematically varied and the other independent variable is measured. For example, a quasi-experimental

Box 4.1   Example of a true experiment.

Griskevicius et al. (2010) examined why people purchase green products, given that green products are often more expensive than conventional products. They argued that a higher price may be associated with a higher status and that buying a more costly, green product reflects positively on one's social status.

To examine this, Griskevicius and colleagues set up an experiment in which they systematically varied status motivations. They examined whether activating a desire for social status among participants affected their choice of green versus conventional products. One hundred and eighty undergraduate students were recruited and randomly assigned to one of two conditions. In one condition, the students read a scenario that was aimed to elicit a desire for social status. As part of this scenario, participants were asked to imagine graduating from college, landing their first job, with immediate possibilities for promotion, and the potential of moving up in social status relative to their peers. In a control condition, a neutral scenario was presented. Participants then completed an (ostensibly unrelated) product preference task. For each product, participants were asked to choose between a green or a conventional (more luxurious) product.

The results provided support for the study's main hypothesis. In the control group, the non-green products were chosen more often than the green products, but when a desire for social status was activated, participants were more likely to choose a green product. This study found that activating status motives increased the likelihood that people choose a green product over a non-green (but more luxurious) product. In their second experiment, they examined how status motives affected preference for green products when people considered shopping in a public setting (a store) or a private setting (online at home). This study used the same manipulation of status motive as in study 1. Then, participants were asked to choose between green and non-green items, but one group of participants were asked to imagine they were online shopping at home alone and another group of participants were asked to imagine they were out shopping at a store. The researchers found a significant interaction effect between status manipulation and shopping in the public or private sphere. Activating status motives encouraged people to choose green products more often, in particular when shopping in public (see Figure 4.1).

design can be set up to address the question of whether the effect of information provision about the environmental benefits of eating organic food is different for people with different environmental values. In this case, one of the independent variables is manipulated (environmental information or neutral information) and one of the independent variables is measured (environmental values).

Imagine a study in which all participants fill out a survey to measure environmental values. Then, one group of participants watches a video with information

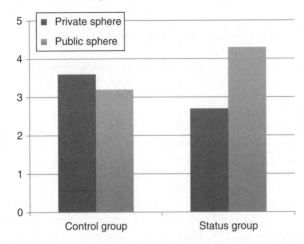

Figure 4.1   Preference for green products versus non-green products (*y*-axis) in the control group and the status group. The dark gray bar indicates the choice was made in the private sphere (at home, online), the light gray bar indicates the choice was made in the public sphere (in a store).

about organic food, while another group watches a video on an unrelated topic. This study may find that the provision of information about environmental benefits of organic food is effective in encouraging organic food choices, but that this effect depends on the extent to which people endorse environmental values. For example, environmental information may only be effective when people already have relatively strong environmental values, but when they have weak environmental values, the information does not affect their choices.

A drawback of quasi-experimental designs is that random assignment to conditions often does not occur, which may introduce systematic differences between the groups. However, researchers are able to include **covariates**, which allow them to examine the relationship between the dependent and independent variables of interest, while controlling for other relevant variables. In our example, the researchers might consider including covariates such as gender, income, or scores on an environmental knowledge test. By including these covariates, the researcher can examine whether the difference in preference for organic foods are indeed related to the variable of interest (information provision). By statistically eliminating the effect of other, relevant variables, one can be more certain of the existence of a relationship between the independent and dependent variables.

One of the main advantages of quasi-experimental designs is that they allow researchers to include variables that are difficult to mimic in experimental lab studies, which makes them very suitable for examining applied, real-life issues, such as environmental issues. Also, in quasi-experimental designs, researchers have a relatively large amount of control over the variables they wish to include. By including covariates, it can help make alternative explanations less plausible. Of course, one would need to know beforehand which covariates to include (based, e.g., on previous research), and sometimes not all potential covariates are known. Research in environmental psychology often makes use of quasi-experimental designs (see Box 4.2).

Box 4.2   Example of a quasi-experiment.

Verplanken and Holland (2002) examined whether the activation of environmental values would affect environmental decision making. They were interested to know whether this effect depended on how central or important environmental values were for participants. To measure the centrality of environmental values, the researchers used the Schwartz Values Inventory. To activate environmental values, participants were given a description of a person and they were asked to form an impression of this person. In one condition, the person was described in terms of values related to the environment (e.g., concerned about nature), and in the control condition, the values that described this person were unrelated to the environment (e.g., perfectionism). Then, participants were asked to complete an (ostensibly unrelated) consumer choice task. Participants were asked to choose between 20 television sets. Some television sets scored very well on environmental aspects (e.g., efficient use of electricity) while other television sets scored poorly on environmental aspects.

The results provided support for the environmental value activation hypothesis. That is, when environmental values were activated, participants were more likely to choose a television set that scored more favorably on environmental aspects, compared to when environmental values were not activated. In addition, this effect was stronger for participants for whom environmental values were more important. These results are important in that they suggest that making environmental values salient (e.g., in an information campaign) will be more effective in encouraging environmentally related choices among people for whom environmental values are important, compared to people for whom environmental values are less important.

Correlational designs

Correlational research examines the relationship between two or more variables in a naturally occurring setting (Pelham & Blanton, 2007). For example, a researcher may be interested in the relationship between people's level of physical activity and level of access to green spaces. Correlational studies do not involve a form of manipulation of variables as is the case in lab studies; rather, all variables are assessed as they occur, for example, by means of a survey (see Chapter 5) or observation (see Chapter 2). The **correlation coefficient** gives an indication of the strength and the direction of the association between two variables, ranging from −1 to +1. The strength of the association is represented by the value of the correlation, the higher the number the stronger the two variables are related to one another. The sign indicates the direction of the association: a negative correlation suggests that an increase in one variable is associated with a decrease in the other variable; a positive correlation indicates that an increase in one variable is associated with an increase in the other variable.

The main advantage of correlational designs is that they possess relatively high external validity. Correlational studies are often conducted in real-life settings among representative groups of the population and they measure (rather than manipulate) variables. These features of correlational studies contribute to a greater degree of generalizability of the findings to other situations, compared to experimental studies. In addition, when the study is conducted among representative samples of participants, the study findings may be more readily generalizable to other people.

Correlational studies have a number of important drawbacks. In correlational studies researchers have much less experimental control over the variables, which means that these studies can only infer correlation and not causality. One of the main issues related to correlational studies is **reverse causality.** Reverse causality refers to the fact that there are different ways of interpreting the same correlation. For example, a significant positive correlation between people's environmental concern and their engagement in environmentally friendly behavior may signify that because people have a higher environmental concern, they are more likely to engage in environmentally friendly behavior. But it may also be that because people engage in environmentally friendly behavior, they develop a stronger environmental concern. In other words, the direction of the relationship may be reversed.

Another disadvantage of correlational studies is the potential presence of a third variable which affects both variables. The **third-variable problem** refers to the

---

Box 4.3   Example of a correlational study.

What requires more energy: transporting goods via airplanes, or via trucks? What requires more energy: making a glass bottle or an aluminum can? Attari, DeKay, Davidson, and de Bruin (2010) examined the accuracy of people's perceptions of the energy use of several appliances and activities. They conducted an online survey among 505 participants in seven US metropolitan areas (New York, Philadelphia, Washington DC, Houston, Dallas, Denver, and Los Angeles). Participants were asked to estimate the energy requirements of a number of devices and appliances and the energy saved by several household activities (the energy used by a 100-watt incandescent light bulb in one hour was provided as a reference point). The results indicate that participants' estimates of energy use and savings were not always accurate (see Figure 4.2). Note that in most cases the estimates fall below the accurate-estimate line, indicating that people tend to underestimate the amount of energy required by different devices or saved through behavior changes. For example, participants incorrectly reported that making a glass bottle required less energy than making an aluminum can (the reverse is true). However, participants did correctly indicate that transporting goods via airplanes required more energy compared with other modes of transportation. The study also examined individual differences in these estimates and found that people with more positive environmental attitudes (measured by the New Environmental Paradigm; see also Chapter 6) had more accurate estimates. The study reported a positive correlation between environmental concern and accuracy of estimates, $r = .38$.

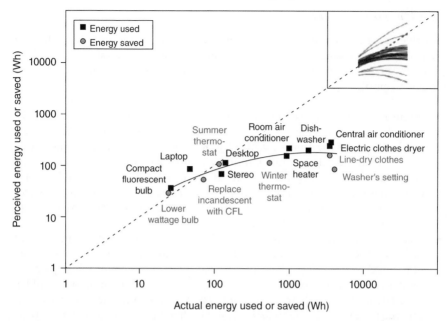

Figure 4.2 Mean perceptions of energy used or saved in relation to actual energy use or saved. The diagonal line represents accurate estimates. Note that in most cases the estimates fall below the accurate-estimate line, indicating that people tend to underestimate the amount of energy required by different devices or saved through behavior changes. (Source: Attari et al., 2010.)

existence of a third variable (not included in the study), which relates to both variables involved, that better explains their relationship. Consider the finding that city dwellers living in areas with little greenery are more likely to be obese than those living in pleasant areas with lots of greenery. This may also be explained by other features of these areas (other than lack of greenery, such as lack of walking trails, or access to fast food places). So-called third variables are not included in a particular study, but they may account for the observed effects.

Measurement

Measurement is at the heart of research. In the research process, once the hypotheses are formalized, the researcher must operationalize them. This involves providing clear definitions of the constructs implicated in the hypotheses, and specifying how these constructs can be measured in the research process. While measurement typically focuses on the dependent variable, measured variables can be used in a variety of other ways, including as non-manipulated independent variables in quasi-experimental and correlational studies. We discuss a number of issues related to measurement, including the four primary levels of measurement, different types of measures, and the uses of measured variables in the research process.

Levels of measurement

Variables can be measured on a variety of levels, and in a variety of ways. Measured variables can be classified into four levels: nominal, ordinal, interval, and ratio. These four levels range from the most basic level of measurement (nominal), to the most complex (ratio).

- **Nominal**: Measures that involve the categorization of observed events. For example, coding whether or not a person recycles a beverage container, where "yes" is coded as the numeric value of 1, and "no" is coded as the numeric value of "0." Note that the designation of 1 and 0 is arbitrary, and the observations could have just as easily been coded as the reverse. Nominal variables can be dichotomous, as in the above example, or polytomous, with many categories. For example, the different types of material recycled might include paper, plastic, glass, and organics, coded from 1 to 4 respectively.
- **Ordinal**: Measures that assign numeric values to observed events, and the order of these values is meaningful. For example, a researcher staffing a household waste collection event on a Saturday might count the sequence of residents who come to the event. The first resident to show up would be coded 1, the second 2, and so on until the last resident. These numbers indicate the time when residents arrived, and higher scores indicating later arrivals. But note that the distance between the scores is not meaningful. It could be that in the morning, only a few residents arrived, whereas the afternoon was crowded. This distance between residents would not be represented in the ordinal level measure.
- **Interval**: Measures in which the interval between the units is meaningful, but where 0 does not indicate the complete absence of the construct. For example, a researcher studying environmental concern might ask participants in a survey to rate their level of agreement with a statement from 1 = strongly disagree to 5 = strongly agree. These Likert-style measures allow researchers to quantify psychological constructs like "environmental concern," and to create scales that allow for comparisons across individuals. But note that 0 does not indicate the absence of concern.
- **Ratio**: Measures in which the interval between units is meaningful, and where 0 indicates the complete absence of the construct. For example, a researcher studying recycling by businesses might quantify the behavior by weighing the amount of materials collected each week in kilograms. Other ratio-level measures include physical properties like distance, length, mass, speed, and volume.

A large amount of the work involved in scientific research focuses on measurement. Studies are designed to use a specific measurement protocol, using specific tools, and to obtain observations from a sample of the target population on a specific level. Where possible, researchers strive for ratio-level measures. These measures contain the maximum amount of information, and most parametric statistical techniques were developed for analyzing ratio-level data. In contrast to ratio-level measures, ordinal and nominal levels may restrict which analyses one can conduct.

Types of measures

Measures can be obtained in a variety of ways, and environmental psychologists are often quite creative in developing their measurement protocols. Observational data are obtained by coding an event that is personally witnessed. For example, measuring whether or not a walker in a park sits on a bench, which would be coded using a nominal-level measure (1 = yes, 0 = no). The researcher could have also opted for a ratio-level measure, recording the number of seconds that each walker in the park spent sitting on a bench (from 0 to a defined maximum value).

A second type of measure in environmental psychology involves asking individuals to answer questions. These questions can be asked in a structured interview, using paper and pencil, a webpage, or on a mobile electronic device like an iPad. The questions can be asked using an open-ended format (see also Chapter 7 on qualitative measures), in which respondents elaborate in their own words, or closed ended in which respondents use a specified response scale. Note that self-report data can be obtained on any of the four measurement levels. For example, asking a person to report the amount of their last utility bill (in dollars) would provide a ratio-level measure, whereas asking a participant if they paid their last utility bill (1 = yes, 0 = no) would provide nominal-level data.

A third type of measure in environmental psychology involves the coding of residual data. In this type of measure, the researcher codes the residual evidence of a past behavior. For example, a researcher might count the number of littered items in a park as a measure of littering behavior. The researcher did not directly observe the littering, so the residual evidence is used as a proxy for the behavior, and measured at a ratio level. As with the other types of measures, residual data can be quantified at any of the four levels. Other examples of residual data include, for example, utility meter readings or annual mileage.

Psychometrics

Measured variables differ in their quality, and some measures are better than others. In assessing the quality of a measure, researchers consider the reliability and validity. *Reliability* refers to the likelihood that if the same measure was applied to the same event, it would yield the same score. Every measure has some level of unreliability, but the goal in developing good measures is to maximize the reliability. The reliability of a measure is typically quantified as the strength of the relationship between two independent assessments of the same construct.

This can be done in a variety of ways, depending on the type of measure. With observational data, estimates for reliability are often obtained by having two or more coders record the same event – a procedure called inter-rater reliability. With self-report data, researchers often use multiple questions to measure the same construct, and then calculate the strength of the relationship among the items. This is referred to as the internal consistency of a measure and often quantified using Cronbach's alpha (which ranges from 0 to 1, with 1 indicating perfect reliability).

Reliable measures are critical for any area of research, and researchers often spend considerable time refining their measures. In the case of inter-rater reliability, it is important to provide coders with very specific guidelines for recording their observations. Researchers typically develop and refine their measurement protocols over many days and weeks, coding, discussing, and assessing reliability until a satisfactory level is achieved.

With self-report data, researchers typically utilize existing measures that have been shown to provide good levels of internal consistency in previous research. Note that in utilizing existing measures, it is important to use the full set of items that have been previously tested. While it is tempting to pick and choose items that appear most relevant to the current project, any change to the items can undermine the scale's reliability. It is not always possible to use existing scales and for more information about creating your own scale, see Chapter 3.

Validity refers to a measure that accurately reflects the construct of interest. Consider the case where a researcher conducts a survey asking residents about the degree to which they support a 10-cent deposit on beverage containers, using a Likert-style response scale. Because the researcher has a basic understanding of research design, she asks a series of questions about support and opposition for bottle bills in order to establish that the measure is reliable. But she then (mistakenly) concludes that higher scores on the scale indicates a respondent's level of environmental concern. While environmental concern might be correlated with support for bottle bills, the two constructs are different and obtaining self-report data about bottle bills is not a valid measure of environmental concern.

Typically, the validity of a measure is established in prior research. (Again, note the importance of utilizing measures developed and tested in prior studies.) The validity of a measure can be assessed by examining its correlation with measures of similar constructs. This approach is called convergent validity, and in establishing the validity of a measure it is important that it correlates with other similar measures. For example, in the previous example of attitudes toward bottle deposits, a researcher might ask residents to sign a petition supporting a new law. This behavior (signing the petition) should be correlated with their expressed attitudes toward the policy. In addition, a valid measure should also possess divergent validity. That is, the measure should *not* correlate with unrelated measures. Continuing the previous example, attitudes toward bottle deposits should not be strongly related to support for increasing property taxes to provide better schools in the local area. In establishing a new measure, researchers must show both divergent and convergent validity.

Uses of measured variables

As discussed in the opening section of this chapter, measured variables can serve as independent or dependent variables in a study. While these are the primary uses of measured variables, contemporary research in environmental psychology has used measured variables in other notable ways.

Moderator variables are those that affect the relation between an independent and dependent variable. Consider an experiment in which residents are provided with real-time information about the costs of electricity consumption through an in-home display mounted on the kitchen counter. The display shows the current hourly cost at their given rate of consumption, along with the total amount accumulated over the billing cycle. In this experiment, households are randomly assigned to receive the in-home display, or not, and the average daily consumption in kilowatts is measured. The independent variable is the presence or absence of the display (a nominal measure), and the dependent variable is the daily amount of electricity consumed (a ratio-level measure of a residual type). The results show that households receiving financial information use less electricity over the next month than do households without a display.

In the energy study described above, there are a number of potential moderators that could affect the impact of the in-home displays. One potential moderator is household income, and it is likely that households with higher incomes will be less affected by the display than low-income households. Other potential moderators might include home ownership, presence of children in the home, or hours spent working outside the home. Such moderators are typically indicated as interactions, whereby the independent variable "interacts" with the moderator variable (see also interaction effects in experimental designs section above).

Mediator variables explain why an effect occurs. Like moderators, mediators are third variables that are measured as part of the research process, but mediators are the generative mechanism by which the independent variable affects the dependent variable. Consider the case of the energy study described above. As a starting point, the research has shown that the presence of the in-home display reduces the amount of electricity consumed per day. But why? One possibility is that residents in the home engage in specific behaviors, such as turning off lights when they leave the room. To identify the mediating mechanism for the effect of the in-home displays, the researcher must measure the behavior (e.g., turning off the lights), establish that the behavior changed as a result of the independent variable (e.g., the display), and finally show that the change in behavior accounted for the reduction in electricity consumption.

A third use of a measured variable is to account for confounding. Confounding occurs when the independent variable co-varies with one or more other measured variables. In the case of an experiment where participants are randomly assigned to condition, confounding is not a concern because random assignment generally removes the possibility for systematic co-variation. However, in the case of quasi-experiments or correlational studies, confounding is an ever-present concern. Consider a research example testing whether employees at a large company who drive a personal car to work are more likely to eat organic food for lunch, compared with employees who take public transport. The independent variable (transportation mode) and the dependent variable (eating organic food) are measured variables and neither is manipulated. One potential confounding variable is income: it is likely that employees who drive to work are more affluent and therefore more likely to purchase organic food. In this case, transportation mode and income are confounded. By measuring income, the researcher can test the possibility that income is confounding the results and address it as a limitation in the study.

General Issues

In this final section, we discuss some general issues that are relevant when conducting scientific research. We first discuss the added value of combining multiple research designs as a key way to secure internal and external validity of research.

Next, we discuss the value of replication and meta-analyses. Finally, we elaborate on possible threats to scientific progress, including the file drawer problem, voodoo correlations, and selective reporting.

Internal and external validity

As described above, internal and external validity of findings are of key importance in scientific research. Internal validity implies that we understand which variables cause certain effects, while external validity implies that results of a specific study can be generalized to other situations or to the population at large. Yet, enhancing internal validity often involves a loss of external validity, and the other way around. One way of securing both internal and external validity is by combining multiple research designs in a series of studies examining the same issues.

Consider a study that is aimed at understanding whether environmental knowledge encourages pro-environmental actions. This could be examined with a questionnaire study among a representative sample of the population, including questions on environmental knowledge and pro-environmental behavior, and study the correlation between both constructs. The external validity of this study would be rather high, given that the reliability and validity of the measures are high. This implies that results can probably be generalized to different populations or different situations (e.g., you are likely to find similar correlations when you conduct the study again one year later, in a comparable sample). Yet, internal validity is likely to be low, because it is not clear whether environmental knowledge caused pro-environmental actions (or the other way around), or whether a third variable may have accounted for the observed correlation. For example, environmental concern may have increased both environmental knowledge and pro-environmental behavior.

To address these concerns, you could run an experimental study among university students in which you manipulate environmental knowledge (e.g., by presenting information on environmental problems via a documentary or a leaflet), and examine its effect on pro-environmental behavior. If you find that the experimental group (who received the information) scores better on a subsequent knowledge test (which serves as a manipulation check) and more often engages in subsequent pro-environmental behavior than a control group who received unrelated information (e.g., on university policies), you would be reasonably sure that environmental knowledge caused pro-environmental actions. In this case, internal validity would be high, while external validity would be low. Yet, by combining both studies, it is possible to compensate for the weakness of one research design with the strength of another design.

Replication and meta-analysis

Next to combining research methods, replication of research is another important way to increase confidence in and validity of research outcomes. Replication involves finding consistent support for certain findings by running similar studies in other settings. By doing so, one can rule out the possibility that the findings occurred by chance because the researcher just happened to create a particular set of conditions that yielded the effects. Typically, replication studies imply a test of basic ideas or findings in a different way. This may involve the use of a different sample, or the use of slightly different operationalizations of key constructs included in the study. For example, the manipulation of the independent variables may be changed, or different items to measure a construct can be included.

Additionally, replication may involve running a similar study in a different lab, in order to rule out the possibility that results are due to specific conditions in a lab that have not been reported by the researcher or that occurred outside the awareness of the researcher. For this reason, it is important that researchers report their research method in sufficient detail, so that others are able to follow the same procedure and use the same (or at least similar) measures. This is also important in identifying possible confounds. For example, it may be that a researcher gave some additional instructions or delivered additional interventions that were deemed to be unrelated to the task, but were crucial to find the effects.

Another important way to study consistency and validity of research findings is by conducting a *meta-analysis* (see also Chapter 20). Meta-analysis refers to using statistical techniques to analyze the results of a group of studies to establish the relative strength of observed effects, the variability in effect sizes (reflecting whether effects are similar or different across studies), and the conditions under which effects were particularly small or large.

An important issue for researchers conducting meta-analysis is that studies yielding non-significant results tend to be underreported in the literature (and may hence not have been included in the meta-analysis). This is referred to as the *file drawer problem* (Rosenthal, 1979): a bias toward publishing positive results (supporting the hypotheses), while negative results (supporting the null hypothesis) are less likely to be published. This may be because researchers themselves decide not to publish their null results, or because journal editors (and reviewers) prefer publishing significant results rather than null results.

Publication bias is a serious problem, as it may result in concluding that some effects are significant and important, while in fact the majority of (unpublished) studies clearly suggest otherwise. Therefore, it is of great importance to also make null results available. In fact, there are a number of websites that collect non-significant findings to make these available in the public domain (see Spellman, 2012).

Researcher degrees of freedom

The overrepresentation of significant effects in the literature may not only be influenced by publication bias and file drawer problems, but can also be caused by the publication of inflated effects. That is, researchers may be motivated by finding significant effects, and adjust their research until effects become significant (e.g., McGuire, 1973). This may result in developing and selecting very specific stimuli, task settings, instructions, dependent and independent variables, treatment levels, mediators, moderators, and favorable boundary conditions that are most likely to yield the expected effects (Fiedler, 2011). By doing so, a researcher capitalizes on chance in model testing. This will likely result in so-called *voodoo correlations*, that is, inflated correlations in which the effects of phenomena are overestimated as they only occur in very specific conditions that have not been specified. This again demonstrates the need for replicating research in different conditions and trying to find convergent evidence for an effect across different methods and situations.

Another possible bias in publication lies in selective or inaccurate reporting of the research methods or results. For example, researchers may decide to only report the results of manipulations that yielded significant results. This is related to the file drawer problem, but in this case it implies that researchers only publish part of their research, and leave out unfavorable parts. Yet, the result of this practice is very similar: inflated effects.

Conclusion and Summary

In environmental psychology, research questions and theories are used to make predictions about human behavior in relation to environmental issues, and various research designs and measurement techniques are used to test these hypotheses. Each of these has advantages and disadvantages. One important difference is that internal and external validity can differ greatly across research designs. Internal validity implies that we understand which variables cause certain effects, while external validity implies that results of a specific study can be generalized to other situations or to the population at large.

Experimental studies have high experimental control and therefore high internal validity, but the findings are more difficult to generalize to other people and other situations. Quasi-experimental studies have less control over the variables, but the findings are typically better generalizable to other people. Correlational studies do not involve a form of manipulation of variables as is the case in lab studies and therefore have low internal validity. But because the variables are assessed as they occur naturally, the results can be more easily generalized to other situations. To measure any changes in the variables of interest, environmental psychologists might use observational data (personally witnessing an event, such as people littering in a park), self-report data (asking questions such as "how often did you recycle in the past month?"), or collect residual data (e.g., counting the number of littered items in a park). Researchers can assess the reliability and validity of each of these types of measures to ensure quality of measurement. Combining research methods (e.g., first a lab study, then a correlational study, or vice versa) and replication of research findings (e.g., testing the same hypothesis among a sample of students and a sample of employees) are important steps to help increase confidence in the research outcomes.

Glossary

Confound   An additional variable that affects the dependent variable and varies systematically with the independent variable(s).

Control group   A group of participants in a study that are not exposed to the manipulation.

Correlation coefficient   A statistic used to represent the association between two variables, ranges from −1 to +1.

Correlational design   A design that describes the relationship between independent and dependent variables, without systematic variation of these variables or random assignment of participants.

Correlational research A study in which the investigator measures naturally occurring variables and the relations between these variables.

Covariate A variable that is related to both dependent and independent variables.

Dependent variable A variable in an experiment that is measured.

Experimental design The systematic variation of one or more independent variables, characterized by random assignment of participants to conditions, or groups.

External validity The ability to generalize findings from a study to different situations or populations of individuals.

Independent variable A variable in an experiment that is systematically varied by the researcher.

Interaction The effect of an independent variable on the dependent variable depends on another independent variable.

Internal validity The ability to infer causal relationships between independent and dependent variables.

Manipulation Occurs when one or more variables is systematically varied, while holding the other variables constant.

Operational confound This occurs when a measure designed to assess a particular construct also measures something else.

Person confound An individual difference variable among participants in the study, which may affect the outcome measure.

Person-by-treatment quasi-experiment A design in which one independent variable is systematically varied and the other independent variable is measured.

Procedural confound This occurs when a researcher inadvertently varies more than one independent variable.

Quasi-experimental design A design in which one or more independent variables are systematically varied, but random assignment does not occur.

Random assignment Used to ensure that every study participant has the same chance of being assigned to the experimental or control conditions.

Reverse causality The observation that when two variables are related, it is not possible to tell whether variable 1 caused variable 2, or the other way around.

Third-variable problem When two variables are related, this may be because a third variable that was not included in the study is in fact related to the two variables.

True experiment A study characterized by random assignment and systematic variation of variables of interest.

References

Attari, S. Z., DeKay, M. L., Davidson, C. I., & de Bruin, W. B. (2010). Public perceptions of energy consumption and savings. *Proceedings of the National Academy of Sciences, 107*, 16054–16059.

Campbell, D. T., & Stanley, J. C. (1963). *Experimental and quasi-experimental designs for research.* Chicago, IL: Rand McNally.

Creswell, J. W. (2009). *Research design: Qualitative, quantitative, and mixed methods approaches.* (3rd ed.). Thousand Oaks, CA: Sage.

De Groot, J. I., & Steg, L. (2008). Value orientations to explain beliefs related to environmental significant behavior: How to measure egoistic, altruistic, and biospheric value orientations. *Environment and Behavior, 40*, 330–354.

Fiedler, K. (2011). Voodoo correlations are everywhere – Not only in neuroscience. *Psychological Science, 6,* 163–171.

Griskevicius, V., Tybur, J. M., & Van den Bergh, B. (2010). Going green to be seen: Status, reputation, and conspicuous conservation. *Journal of Personality and Social Psychology, 98,* 392–404.

McGuire, W. J. (1973). The yin and yang of progress in social psychology: Seven koan. *Journal of Personality and Social Psychology, 26,* 446–456.

Pelham, B. W., & Blanton, T. (2007). *Conducting research in psychology: Measuring the weight of smoke* (3rd ed.). Belmont, CA: Wadsworth/Thomson Learning.

Rosenthal, R. (1979). The file drawer problem and tolerance for null results. *Psychological Bulletin, 86,* 638–641.

Spellman, B. A. (2012). Data, data, everywhere … especially in my file drawer. *Perspectives on Psychological Science, 7,* 58–59.

Verplanken, B., & Holland, R. W. (2002). Motivated decision making: Eeffects of activation and self-centrality of values on choices and behavior. *Journal of Personality and Social Psychology, 82,* 434.

Suggested Readings

Creswell, J. W. (2009). *Research design: Qualitative, quantitative, and mixed methods approaches* (3rd ed.). Thousand Oaks, CA: Sage.

Pelham, B. W., & Blanton, T. (2007). *Conducting research in psychology: Measuring the weight of smoke* (3rd ed.). Belmont, CA: Wadsworth/Thomson Learning.

5

Agree to Disagree
A Practical Guide to Conducting Survey Research in Environmental Psychology

Donald W. Hine[1], Christine Kormos[2], and Anthony D. G. Marks[1]

[1] University of New England, NSW, Australia
[2] University of Victoria, BC, Canada

Maria and Ethan are having dinner together one evening. As they polish off dessert and remove the cork from their third bottle of red, the discussion turns to whether or not fear appeals are an effective strategy for getting people to take action against climate change.

"Well, it's obvious that the simplest, and most accurate, way to answer this question," starts Maria, "would be to just run a laboratory study where you randomly assign undergraduate students to two experimental conditions: one in which they receive a big scary message about climate change, and the other where they receive a control message on a bland topic, like – I don't know – maybe something about ballet or Canadian politics. Then – just outside the lab, you could set up a table with Greenpeace volunteers collecting donations for their latest climate change campaign."

"You've got to be kidding?" says Ethan shaking his head. "You're going to base your conclusions on whether a small group of psychology undergraduates donate money to Greenpeace? You won't be able to say anything about how 'normal people' in the community respond to fear appeals based on those findings."

"Okay then – if you're so smart, what do you suggest?" Maria responds, not trying particularly hard to disguise her contempt.

"To get really good data, you need to use a community sample – there's just no way around it. It's worth sacrificing the control of the lab for the ecological validity gained in the field." He continues, "I would create a survey that assesses people's past exposure to fear messages, along with questions about their involvement in a wide range of climate change-relevant behaviors. Then I'd collect data

Research Methods for Environmental Psychology, First Edition. Edited by Robert Gifford.
© 2016 John Wiley & Sons, Ltd. Published 2016 by John Wiley & Sons, Ltd.

from a random sample of households in our city." He smiles triumphantly, and gulps down the rest of his wine.

"OK," says Maria, "I'll admit that your community survey strategy is probably going to generate a more representative sample, and I also like your idea of measuring a range of pro-environmental behaviors rather than just focusing on donations to Greenpeace. But, I still think you have a couple of problems. First of all, you have no experimental manipulation. So, maybe you can demonstrate that exposure to fear messaging is correlated with climate change action, but, unlike my experimental study, you can't say that exposure to the messages caused the behaviors to occur. Your second problem is that your behavioral measures are all self-report. At least with my donation dependent variable, we would be assessing 'actual behavior'."

"Wait a second," responds Ethan, "I think all this wine has caused me to develop powers of 'super-intelligence.' What if we could design a study that incorporated the strengths of both experimental and survey research?" He excitedly continues, "I just read this great report on online surveys, and it's amazing what the latest technology can do. We could incorporate your experimental manipulation into the online survey – randomly assigning our respondents to either view the very scary climate change video or the control one. Then, using my idea about the community survey, we could administer the online survey to a random sample of city residents. This would help to ensure that our results generalize beyond our sample."

Maria jumps in. "And then in a few weeks' time, we could send our respondents a second survey where they would report on the climate change activities they had engaged in following the experimental manipulation. We could send them email requests to donate time and money to various environmental causes. This would give us the best of both worlds in that we would have an experimental design, a representative sample, and a good mix of self-report and behavioral measures." An uncomfortable silence descends over the room, as Maria and Ethan realize that this is the first time they have ever agreed about anything.

Surveys are a popular method of collecting self-report data on individuals' values, attitudes, beliefs, and behaviors. They are commonly used by politicians to guide campaign strategies, by governments to set policy agendas and evaluate program effectiveness, and by marketeers to identify markets for new or existing products. Surveys are also an important research tool in many areas of psychology, including environmental psychology. Indeed, a quick perusal of recent articles in the *Journal of Environmental Psychology* and *Environment and Behavior*, the two flagship journals of the discipline, suggests that environmental psychologists are embracing survey methodology like never before.

This chapter is intended as a practical guide to survey research for advanced students and researchers working in the area of environmental psychology. We take the reader, step by step, through the process of survey design, development, analysis, and reporting. Throughout the chapter, we make recommendations about best practice, highlight common pitfalls, and identify useful supplementary resources.

Designing Survey Research

Research design

Survey research can take a variety of forms. Researchers may study a single group of respondents at one point in time (**cross-sectional design**), different respondents at different points in time (**repeated cross-sectional design**), or the same respondents at different points in time (**panel design**). There is no one correct design – each approach has its own distinct uses and limitations (see Table 5.1), and researchers should select the design that best matches their research objectives. For example, for a study investigating which socio-demographic factors correlate with an individual's concern about biodiversity, a cross-sectional survey design would be suitable. On the other hand, if the aim of the study is to better understand the processes by which Australians' biodiversity concerns evolve over time, a repeated cross-sectional survey or panel survey design would be more appropriate.

Although surveys are most often used for descriptive purposes or to explore correlations among variables, it is worth noting that surveys and experimental research methods are not mutually exclusive and, in fact, these techniques are quite complementary. For example, Villar and Krosnick (2011) embedded experiments in a set of surveys to explore whether wording choices (such as climate change versus global warming, and higher taxes versus higher prices) affected public risk perceptions about climate change and support for mitigation policies, noting that wording choices are important but do not appear to have a uniform effect across the population.

Survey development

In this section, we outline several points to keep in mind when selecting and developing items to include in surveys. We begin by discussing fundamental measurement issues related to reliability and validity, and then address several practical matters related to the use of closed- versus open-ended questions, the ordering of questions and responses, selecting a rating scale response format, social desirability, and memory fallibility.

The importance of reliability and validity When designing a survey, researchers should aim to use measures that are both reliable and valid. **Reliability** refers to the extent to which a measure is accurate, consistent, and stable. It represents the extent to which an instrument is free of measurement error. **Validity**, on the other hand, refers to the extent to which a measure assesses the construct that it is intended to assess. Reliability and validity are often (but not always) positively correlated – as the reliability of an instrument decreases, its validity also tends to decrease.

The use of unreliable and invalid measures in a survey can seriously undermine the interpretability of research findings. One way to avoid this problem is to use existing measures that have been previously demonstrated to be reliable and valid. Chapter 6 in this volume outlines some measures most commonly employed within environmental psychology to assess environmental attitudes and concern. Of course, using an existing measure is not always possible. Thus, in cases where an appropriate scale

Table 5.1 Common study designs for survey research.

	Description	Common uses	Limitations
Cross-sectional	Data are collected from a single group of respondents (sample) at a single point in time	Used to document the prevalence of values, attitudes, beliefs, and/or behaviors in a population, compare these variables across subgroups, and/or investigate the associations between these variables	Cross-sectional data can be used to demonstrate that variables are correlated with each other, but in the absence of random assignment to experimental conditions, or multiple time points, causal inferences are not possible
Repeated cross-sectional	Independent samples are drawn from the same population during at least two points in time	Used to assess whether changes across time in one variable (e.g., state of the economy) within a population are associated with changes in other variables (e.g., environmental concern)	Provides slightly stronger evidence for causal effects given that one can establish that change in one variable co-occurs with change in another, but lack of random assignment precludes strong causal inferences
Panel	Data collected from the same individuals during at least two points in time	Used to assess how respondents change over time, and whether changes in certain variables are associated with changes in other variables (e.g., are changes in respondents' beliefs correlated with changes in behavior?) Can also be used to determine whether individual or situational factors present during Wave 1 of the survey (e.g., pro-environmental values or economic conditions) predict change in other variables (e.g., energy use behaviors) across time	Respondents may drop out of the study across multiple waves of data collection. This reduces statistical power and may undermine the representativeness of the sample Completing the initial survey may sensitize respondents to the purpose of the study, changing the phenomena under investigation Respondents' desire to appear consistent may mask actual changes in beliefs, behaviors, etc. over time Although temporal sequencing of measurements can provide stronger evidence for causality, in the absence of random assignment, strong casual inferences are not possible
Experimental	Respondents are randomly assigned to experimental treatment manipulations embedded within the survey or to a control group	Used to assess the causal impact of the manipulated variables on one or more outcome variables Can be applied to all the study designs described above	Surveys often lack level of control and precision available in laboratory-based experiments. This can increase error variance and decrease statistical power

has not yet been developed, researchers may need to either modify an existing scale or to create an entirely new scale, and then demonstrate that the new measure is psychometrically sound (i.e., has acceptable levels of reliability and validity).

When using existing measures, standard practice is to provide evidence from past studies of their adequate reliability and validity. Whether a new measure is being developed, or an existing one adapted, the results of reliability and validity analyses should be reported.

Closed- versus open-ended questions   Researchers often wonder whether it is better to include closed- or open-ended survey items. **Closed-ended questions** provide the respondent with two or more pre-determined alternatives from which to choose (e.g., "*Disagree*," "*Agree*," or "*Don't know*"), whereas **open-ended questions** place few constraints on responding. Most psychological researchers use closed-ended items, given they are typically easier to analyse, less demanding on both participants and interviewers, and facilitate comparisons across individuals (Bradburn, Sudman & Wansink, 2004). If open-ended questions are to be subjected to a formal analysis (either quantitative or qualitative), they must first be coded into discrete categories. This can be a time-consuming and costly task, particularly for studies involving large samples and questions that generate highly variable responses. Such coding also introduces another potential source of error into survey data, given that even the most conscientious of coders can make mistakes.

Despite these challenges, open-ended questions have several distinct advantages over closed-ended questions, including the fact that interviews provide useful opportunities to increase rapport between the respondent and researcher, elicit richer and more nuanced responses, and create the possibility for unexpected but theoretically important answers of which the researcher would otherwise be unaware (Bradburn et al., 2004). Evidence also suggests that, in some situations, open-ended questions may produce more reliable and valid data than closed-ended questions (Krosnick, 1999).

Given that closed- and open-ended items have complementary strengths, one attractive option involves the use of hybrid scales that provide a fixed set of closed-ended items with one or more open-ended responses at the end of the scale. For example, if researchers were interested in farmers' risk perceptions related to shale gas fracking on agricultural land, they could include a fixed list of perceived risks for respondents to evaluate, followed by one or more open-ended questions in which respondents could either mention additional risks or provide additional comments to supplement their earlier responses.

Question wording   The wording of questions should be carefully considered, as item characteristics can contribute to response errors and biases (Bradburn et al., 2004). Items should be clearly written using well-known words to ensure consistent understanding across respondents with a broad range of backgrounds and abilities. In addition, questions should not be double-barreled. For example, a question that simultaneously addresses two distinct issues (e.g., "To what extent do you believe professors *and* students have made efforts to switch to sustainable modes of transportation in recent years?") does not provide the opportunity for respondents to answer differently for each issue (i.e., about both professors and students). Finally, it is important to avoid biased wording or leading questions that convey the attitudes of the researcher. For instance, a question such as "How often do you engage in wasteful water consumption behavior?" conveys that the researcher disapproves of excessive water use, and thus may elicit socially desirable or reactive responses from respondents.

Ordering questions and response options within questions   According to Visser, Krosnick, and Lavrakas (2000, p. 241), one key goal when determining question order is to "establish a respondent's comfort and motivation to provide high quality data." The first few survey questions help establish trust and rapport with the respondent, and so it is useful to lead with questions that are easily understood and unlikely to be controversial. Within the survey, questions should be organized into conceptually related groups (e.g., topics). However, because initial questions in a sequence may influence responses to later questions, it can be useful to vary the order of questions across respondents to assess, and control for, potential order effects. As we discuss shortly, one advantage of online survey technology is that question order can be easily randomized within sections, and section orders can also be randomized within surveys, such that each respondent is provided with his or her own unique form of the survey.

The order of response options within questions should also be given careful consideration. Answers to closed-ended survey items are sometimes influenced by the order in which response alternatives are listed. Visser et al. (2000) note, that in self-administered questionnaires, respondents often choose options listed nearer the top of the list of possible responses in self-administered questionnaires. However, when these categorical responses are read aloud to respondents (as in an interview situation), respondents tend to select responses offered last. These effects are particularly strong among respondents with low cognitive ability and when questions are challenging. This suggests that, where possible, researchers should strive to present questions in an easy-to-understand format and to randomize the order of response options across respondents.

Choosing a rating scale response format   Many closed-ended questions in environmental psychology employ a **rating scale response format** in which respondents choose a point on the scale that best reflects their beliefs or behaviors. As such, survey designers commonly ask, "How many points should I include on my rating scale?" Thankfully, sound empirical evidence, summarized by Visser et al. (2000), helps to guide these types of decisions. Reliability and validity for bipolar scales (e.g., scales that run from negative through neutral to positive) tends to be highest for 7 points whereas, for unipolar scales, the optimal number appears to be closer to 5 points (e.g., those that run from "*Not at all important*" to "*Very important*"). Visser et al. (2000) also note that scales with a large, or infinite, number of points (e.g., magnitude scaling) are not recommended because they tend to generate less psychometrically sound data. Last, they recommend that all scale points should be labeled with words, and that researchers should choose verbal labels that divide the scale points into roughly equal units (e.g., "*Negative, Neutral, Positive*," as opposed to "*Negative, Neutral, Very positive*"). Vagias (2006) provides a useful table of common response labels for a variety of 5- and 7-point scales.

Controlling for socially desirable responding Survey respondents sometimes feel compelled to present themselves in a favorable light and in line with valued societal norms. For instance, when asked about their environmental values and attitudes, many individuals espouse a strong commitment to environmentalism, even when these responses are at odds with observed behavior. This can lead to **socially desirable responding**, such that socially desirable behaviors are overreported in surveys, and socially undesirable behaviors are underreported. These distorted responses can arise either from self-deception or a desire to appear in a positive light, both of which are forms of impression management. The latter is generally easier for researchers to address given that they can control situational factors (e.g., promising anonymity or confidentiality), which may decrease the perceived need for impression management.

Two strategies are commonly employed in surveys to control for social desirability bias. First, measures such as the Marlowe-Crowne scale (Crowne & Marlowe, 1960) or the Balanced Inventory of Desirable Responding (BIDR, Paulhus, 1991) can be included to assess the participants' propensity for socially desirable responding. Researchers can subsequently either drop respondents with high social desirability scores from the sample, or they can use these values to statistically adjust respondents' scores on the other variables of interest, such as by using a covariance analysis. Of these two options, dropping respondents is less desirable given that this reduces the representativeness of the sample and there is no universally agreed cut-off for classifying data as "contaminated." If one decides to statistically control for social desirability effects, the BIDR is probably a better choice than the Marlowe-Crowne because the BIDR has subscales to assess both impression management and self-deception, whereas the Marlowe-Crowne assesses impression management only.

Controlling for memory fallibility In many surveys, respondents are asked to provide information about how often they have engaged in different types of pro-environmental behaviors, such as purchasing green products, water and energy conservation, and environmental activism. However, people often forget specific details and combine similar events into a single generalized memory, and thus recall of such events is sometimes unreliable because of memory fallibility (Bradburn, Rips, & Shevell, 1987). Bradburn et al. (2004) recommend several strategies to facilitate accurate recall. First, they recommend that questions include a specific time period to frame the response (e.g., "How many times have you engaged in behavior X during the past week?"). The specified time period should be related to the salience or personal significance of the topic under investigation because personally salient events are less likely to be forgotten than less salient events; thus, asking respondents to report on major events (such as the birth of child, installation of solar panels, or the purchase of an energy efficient car) that occurred over a year ago will generally produce reasonably accurate recall. However, periods of a month or less should be used when asking about the prevalence of more mundane types of day-to-day behaviors, such as recycling or walking to work. Bradburn et al. (2004) also recommend that respondents should be encouraged to use secondary records, such as power or water bills, as memory aids to corroborate or enhance the accuracy of their responses.

Survey Administration

When conducting survey research, several key decisions must be made regarding the development and implementation of an appropriate delivery strategy. In this section, we focus on three main components of the survey administration process: sampling, mode of survey administration, and pre-testing.

The initial step in the survey administration process involves defining the **population of interest** (i.e., specifying the broad group of individuals you wish to study) and selecting an appropriate sampling method. With small, well-defined populations, it is sometimes possible to collect data from all members of a population. However, if populations are large or geographically diffuse, this is often not feasible. Thus, in such situations, researchers generally conduct their research on a **sample**, a smaller group of respondents selected from the population.

Probability and non-probability sampling

Sampling methods can be divided into two general classes: probability sampling and non-probability sampling. Tables 5.2 and 5.3 provide a description of some common types of probability and non-probability sampling techniques used in psychological research, along with their respective strengths and weaknesses.

In **probability sampling**, every member of the population has a chance of being selected to participate in the study, and this likelihood is known. With **non-probability sampling**, on the other hand, some members of the population have no chance of being selected or the probability of their selection cannot be determined. Probability samples are generally regarded as superior to non-probability samples because, if done correctly, they reflect the characteristics of the target population, meaning that the results derived from the sample can be used to draw conclusions about the population. Probability sampling also enables researchers to estimate the variance attributable to sampling error and to compute confidence intervals around population parameter estimates, both of which are useful to establish the precision of a survey's findings.

Perhaps the most common problem associated with survey research in environmental (and other areas of) psychology is an over-reliance on non-probability samples. The main problem with non-probability sampling is that it almost invariably fails to provide data that are representative of a clearly specified population. In other words, descriptive statistics and correlations found in a sample may have little resemblance to the actual parameters within the population. In addition, non-probability sampling provides us with no mechanism to precisely determine the magnitude of this difference.

Clearly, if resources permit, probability sampling is the preferred option. However, the reality of research (e.g., time, effort, and funding) sometimes makes trade-offs necessary. In certain instances it may be preferable to conduct a less than methodologically ideal study, particularly when the flaws are presented in a transparent manner to readers, as opposed to conducting no study at all. Often the primary aim of a study is to determine whether or not a psychological phenomenon occurs, to better understand the underlying processes or causal mechanisms, and/ or to identify situational or individual factors that strengthen or attenuate the effect.

Table 5.2 Types of probability sampling: strengths and weaknesses.

Type	Description	Strengths	Weaknesses
Probability sampling	Class of techniques where respondents are randomly and independently selected from the population so that each respondent has a known, non-zero probability of being selected	Respondents are selected by chance, which removes bias from the selection process and ensures a representative sample. Thus, these sampling techniques allow for the estimation of variance attributable to sampling error and the establishment of confidence intervals around parameter estimates which, in turn, allows findings to be generalized beyond immediate respondents	Given the difficulty inherent in knowing all possible members of the population, these techniques are often too difficult, costly, or impossible to implement. In practice, true probability sampling techniques are rarely used, except in the case of small populations
1. Simple random	All individuals in the population are identified and assigned a numerical value, and then the sample is selected using a random number generator. Therefore, all elements have the same chance of being selected	See general strengths above	See general weaknesses above
2. Systematic	All individuals in the population are identified and enumerated, and then an interval is selected based on the population size and the desired sample size. For instance, for a population of 2000 individuals, and assuming a desired sample size of 100, every 20th respondent would be selected, starting with a random start number	See general strengths above	See general weaknesses above. To avoid potential selection bias related to "periodicity," the order of the respondents within the population should be randomized prior to sampling

(continued)

Table 5.2 (continued)

Type	Description	Strengths	Weaknesses
3. Random stratified	The population is divided into homogeneous groups based on a shared characteristic (e.g., age, sex, region). Then a separate sample is selected within each group using simple random sampling	See general strengths above Helps ensure that all important groups in the populations are adequately represented in the sample	See general weaknesses above Appropriate strata are sometimes difficult to identify. More difficult to implement than simple random sampling
4. Cluster	Selection occurs within "clusters" instead of one by one. Rather than compiling a list of all households in a city, for example, a researcher can first select a sample of neighborhoods and then sample either all or a portion of individuals in those neighborhoods, using a combination of sampling techniques, referred to as *multi-stage sampling*	See general strengths above By creating localized groups of respondents, cluster sampling can facilitate data collection (e.g., objective data about neighborhood crime rates) in that one objective rating can be applied to all in the same neighborhood. Thus, cluster sampling can save time and money	See general weaknesses above Cluster sampling also can increase sampling error, given that those within a cluster are likely to be more similar to one another on various dimensions than would those selected by a simple random sample. Thus clustered samples violate the "independent observations" assumption required for many parametric statistical tests, and often require more sophisticated data analytic strategies (e.g., see Chapter 19 on multilevel modeling)

Table 5.3 Types of non-probability sampling: strengths and weaknesses.

Type	Description	Strengths	Weaknesses
Non-probability sampling	A class of techniques where respondent selection procedures are not random, so that some respondents have an unknown or zero probability of being selected	Can save the researcher considerable time, money, and effort. Although probability sampling techniques are the only means to guarantee representativeness, balanced samples (presumed to be roughly representative) can be obtained through careful use of non-probability sampling methods	These techniques are prone to bias given their reliance on researcher judgment. For example, often large numbers of the population have a zero probability of being selected, which makes it difficult to establish the representativeness of the samples and to estimate sampling error or confidence intervals for the point estimates
1. Judgmental	Individuals thought to be "good" respondents are sought for inclusion in the study	See general strengths above	See general weaknesses above
2. Convenience	Individuals who are most easily accessible are selected	See general strengths above	See general weaknesses above Furthermore, sampled individuals may be qualitatively different from other members of the population who are less accessible. For example, undergraduate students are commonly used in university research. Yet these respondents – typically drawn from Western, Educated, Industrialized, Rich, and Democratic (WEIRD) societies – are unusual compared to other populations of people (Henrich, Heine, & Norenzayan, 2010)

(continued)

Table 5.3 (continued)

Type	Description	Strengths	Weaknesses
3. Quota	A pre-determined number of members of different subgroups in the population are recruited and assembled into a sample, which is intended to represent the socio-demographic characteristics of the target population (e.g., gender, age, education)	See general strengths above	See general weaknesses above Quota sampling also can generate an illusion of generalizability, even though the obtained sample can vary considerably from a simple random sample. Furthermore, ensuring that a sample is demographically similar to a population does not necessarily ensure that sample scores will be similar to true scores in the population
4. Snowball	Some members of a subpopulation are identified, invited to participate, and then asked to recommend others whom the researcher may contact	See general strengths above	See general weaknesses above Snowball sampling also violates the "independent observations" required for many parametric statistical tests, and thus necessitates more sophisticated analytic techniques (e.g., see Chapter 19 on multilevel modeling)

Although these types of studies do not enable us to draw inferences about populations, they may still provide useful information about how a phenomenon operates within the specific group of individuals studied. If several studies investigating the same phenomenon are conducted across a diverse set of non-probability samples, we can draw conclusions about the generalizability of an effect by examining the pattern of results across multiple studies, using quantitative review techniques such as meta-analysis (see Chapter 20). Thus, a series of studies, each employing less than optimal sampling procedures, when considered together, may provide potentially useful information about a population.

A final note about samples: the basic principles of sampling can also apply to any group of objects, events, or locations. For example, environmental psychologists can draw samples from non-human groups ("populations") such as geographic locations, building types, and even levels within experimental manipulations (e.g., randomly sampling different noise levels from a pre-specified population to administer in an auditory experiment). In fact, sampling across multiple elements within a study is a key feature of what Egon Brunswik (1956) referred to as **representative design**. Representative design helps ensure that study findings generalize not only across individuals but also across settings. If a research team is interested in how children interact with nature to restore cognitive capacity, for instance, a representative design consisting of random samples of children in a particular country and random samples of natural environments would enable the researchers to generalize their findings to both a population of individuals and also a population of settings.

Minimizing sampling and non-response error

In an ideal world, probability sampling would always produce samples that are representative of the population. However, in practice this rarely occurs, due to two factors: sampling error and non-response error. **Sampling error** refers to the difference between sample data and the actual values in the population due to random variation in the sampling process. The magnitude of sampling error in a study is determined, in turn, by the following three factors:

1. *Sample size.* As sample size increases, sampling error decreases (although this relationship is not linear). As noted by Visser et al. (2000, p. 232–233), "Moving from a small to moderate sample size produces a substantial decrease in sampling error, but further increases in sample size produced smaller and smaller decrements in sampling error."
2. *Variability in measured variables.* Variables with high variances produce more sampling error than variables with low variances. In a study in which variables have large variances, the sample size can be increased to ensure that sampling error remains at an acceptable level. For studies in which population variances are low (e.g., brain imaging), smaller sample sizes are often adequate.
3. *Type of sampling strategy.* Stratified sampling produces less sampling error than simple random samples, whereas cluster sampling tends to yield greater error (Visser et al., 2000). See Table 5.2 for an explanation of these sampling strategies.

Non-response error represents a second important cause of non-representative samples in probability sampling. Even if a probability sample is drawn from a well-defined population, obtaining responses from all members of that population is unlikely. Researchers may reasonably ask, "Why go to the trouble of selecting a probability sample if a substantial proportion of those selected will not respond?" It is important to note that non-responses will only produce biased results if individuals who respond to the questionnaire systematically differ from those who do not respond on the variables being assessed. If responders and non-responders are similar on the variables of interest, the results will not be biased, even if a relatively large proportion of the sample does not complete the survey.

Approaches to reduce non-response error generally take one of two forms. The first approach involves strategies designed to increase the probability that potential respondents complete the survey, although specific strategies to increase response rates vary somewhat depending on whether one is conducting telephone, mail, or online surveys. For telephone surveys, Fowler (2009) recommends ensuring interviewers have flexible schedules so that they can make appointments that are convenient for respondents, making repeated attempts to contact difficult-to-reach respondents, having well-trained interviewers who can build rapport and trust, and, when necessary, replacing ineffective interviewers who have poor response rates. For mail and online surveys, Dillman (2007) presents an extensive array of tried and tested strategies for increasing response rates, including distributing advance letters to alert prospective participants that they will soon be invited to complete the survey, applying attractive formatting to the survey, using incentives (e.g., payments or prizes), and sending out personalized reminder postcards to participants who have yet to respond.

A second general approach to reduce non-response bias involves making statistical adjustments to repair imbalances in key subgroups by weighing responses from some groups more heavily than others, which ensures that the sample is a proportionate representation of the population. This issue is further discussed in the data analysis section later in the chapter.

Selecting a mode of survey administration

The range of options for survey delivery has expanded over the past few decades along with technological advances, from face-to-face interviews, to printed and mailed questionnaires, to the faster and cheaper telephone interviews, to Internet-based online surveys. All of these methods are still used, to some degree, and researchers should therefore decide which mode of administration is best given the trade-off between survey requirements, the likelihood of attaining unbiased coverage, and cost restraints (Groves et al., 2009). Face-to-face and telephone interviews both afford the opportunity to build rapport with respondents, to clarify questions, and to probe more detailed responses. Print and online surveys lack these interpersonal attributes, but are substantially less expensive to administer.

Online administration. The past decade has witnessed unprecedented growth in worldwide availability of the Internet which has, understandably, enhanced the attractiveness of online surveys compared to their historical predecessors – telephone interviews and pen-and-paper questionnaires. The expanding online community represents a much more accessible population, with potentially global reach. Furthermore, invitations to participate may be individualized in a controlled sampling protocol. Where this method is used, the demographic characteristics of the entire sample are known, and thus researchers are able to contrast the attributes of respondents versus non-respondents. Participants may also be recruited using bulk invitations by email, or via links or pop-ups embedded in web pages and social media sites.

Online surveys have also become attractive to researchers because of the savings in administration costs, compared to pen-and-paper questionnaires (Evans & Mathur, 2005). In terms of survey development, the ready availability of user-friendly survey software packages has substantially reduced programming costs and, in terms of survey delivery, the printing and mailing costs associated with paper surveys have been totally eliminated. In addition, evidence suggests that measures exhibit similar psychometric properties when presented online or in hardcopy format (Miller et al., 2002; Riva, Teruzzi, & Anolli, 2003), although other evidence suggests that response rates to online surveys appear to be more sensitive to the nature of the topics and the characteristics of the sample (Evans & Mathur, 2005). Respondents, it seems, are more likely to complete online surveys that are subjectively interesting, brief, and user friendly.

One major criticism directed at online surveys, however, is the lack of representativeness of the Internet population. Yet, as Scholl, Mulders, and Drent (2002) observed, these population biases are rapidly disappearing as society increasingly embraces Internet use and becomes more technologically savvy. In spite of this, researchers who recruit from the online community should be aware of the demographic biases that remain in the Internet population. According to a recent United States Census report (2009), the American online population is underrepresented in terms of older adults, the unemployed, and those with less education.

The power of online surveys: much more than merely asking questions. A key benefit of online surveys is the ability to present stimuli, ask questions, and elicit responses in a wide variety of formats. For example, the survey company Qualtrics™ promotes the availability of over 100 different question types at its website (www.qualtrics.com). Question types include:

- multiple choice, single or multiple response, vertical or horizontal format;
- Likert-type scales;
- bipolar (semantic differential) questions;
- open-ended text responses;
- rank order in text or drag and drop format;
- constant sum – where numerical responses sum to a total;
- heat map – where respondents click on attractive/unattractive parts of an image; and
- dragable slider bars.

In addition, researchers can embed audio and video media into survey questions, time respondents' actions, allow respondents to upload files, save response data and "pipe" (integrate) it to other questions, randomize question delivery and even randomly assign participants to experimental conditions. Programmable logic can also be incorporated, so as to withhold questions that become redundant or irrelevant due to a previous response or to selectively display questions based on previous answers.

Online surveys provide demonstrable advantages in the efficiency and accuracy of data analysis because the error-prone coding and data entry from paper surveys is removed. In addition, most survey software packages provide real-time graphic analysis of response sets, plus the capability for direct download of data to spreadsheets and/or statistical packages.

Online survey companies (such as Qualtrics™) are also able to provide access to panels of survey respondents, given specific demographic specifications. For example, for a prescribed fee for each survey completion, a researcher may order a specified sample of Australian residents who are representative of the population on age, sex, state of residence, and so on. However, it is important to note that although panel samples may match a population on key demographic components, they may differ from the population in other important ways that could potentially influence the outcome of one's study. Indeed one could reasonably argue that the *professional survey takers* that comprise some online panels are a unique breed, and very different than the average person on the street.

Pre-testing Surveys

Pre-testing is an important part of the preparation phase in the research process. Researchers can recruit a small sample (even one known to be biased) to evaluate their proposed scales and method; specifically, this sample can be used to establish the optimal timing of experimental trials (e.g., in reaction time experiments), evaluate respondent comprehension of the instructions, identify ambiguous items or misinterpretations, and estimate response rate, cost, and timeframe of data collection. This preliminary phase is essential to identify, and subsequently fine-tune, any problems that need to be addressed before the main data collection process.

Pre-testing is particularly important when the data are collected through self-administered questionnaires, given that the questionnaire has to be easily comprehensible because an interviewer will not be present to answer questions. Yet it is especially difficult with this type of questionnaire, because issues related to item understanding are less evident than with interview-based questionnaires. Pre-testing with self-administered questionnaires may be done by asking respondents to complete the self-administered questionnaire as they normally would and then interviewing them afterwards (see Visser et al., 2000). This process can help to clarify the interpretation of items and question wording, as well as to generally improve the ease of completion.

Data Analysis and Reporting Data Analysis

Several excellent textbooks are available that provide detailed accounts about how to select and apply the myriad of data analytic strategies available to survey researchers (e.g., Field, 2013; Tabachnick & Fidell, 2013). In this section we focus on two data analysis issues which, based on our experience, are underutilized and perhaps not fully understood by environment–behavior researchers: (1) statistical adjustments for non-representative sampling, and (2) dealing with missing data.

Statistical adjustments for non-representative samples

As noted earlier, when researchers use probability sampling techniques, they often fail to obtain responses from all individuals in their intended sample. One common strategy for dealing with this problem is to attempt to quantify how your sample differs from the list of potential respondents from which the sample was drawn. For example, it is common for researchers to compare how respondents in their sample differ from the general population on demographic factors that may have been previously collected as part of a census. If they determine that certain population subgroups are underrepresented in the sample, they can "weight" responses to make the sample data more similar to the population. For example, if the ratio of males to females in one's sample is 1:2 (i.e., two females for every male), but the actual ratio in the population is closer to 1:1, responses from males in the survey will be underrepresented relative to the population. To correct this underrepresentation problem, a researcher may choose to weight each male's response in the sample by two.

Although survey organizations and researchers commonly apply such weighting, it is important to note that not all survey analysts support this solution, given that it is based on the largely untestable assumption that those responding from a specific subgroup (in this case, males) are similar to those who did not respond. If respondents are not similar to non-respondents, weighting may actually lead to greater distortions in the sample data (Fowler, 2009). For those who wish to learn more about how to apply adjustment weightings to survey data, Has-Vaughn (2005) has written a good primer on the subject.

Missing data occur at the item level when respondents complete some, but not all, questions on a survey. This problem can be caused by a variety of factors such as the inclusion of socially sensitive questions, carelessness, or attrition (respondents decide to drop out from the study after completing part of the survey). Perhaps the most common strategy for dealing with missing data involves dropping individuals who do not provide information for a given item for analyses involving that item. This approach is known as **listwise deletion** and generally provides reasonably unbiased results when the amount of missing data is low ($<5\%$, Fowler, 2009). When missing data are more substantial, deleting cases can produce more bias and also substantial losses in statistical power, undermining the ability to find statistically significant effects in the sample, even if "real effects" exist in the population. To overcome this problem, survey researchers often use **data imputation**, which involves building a statistical model to generate predictions about how each non-respondent would have likely answered the question. Most statistical software packages now include sophisticated "missing values" algorithms that generate these "best guess" predictions based on patterns of responses across the data set. Importantly, imputation techniques should not be blindly applied without first understanding the nature of the missing value problem; different missing value patterns require different solutions. Allison (2002) provides an accessible introduction to the main issues that should be understood and evaluated prior to imputing missing data.

Writing up survey research findings

The final stage in the survey process involves generating a report that effectively conveys the conclusions and recommendations derived from your research project. For survey projects, it is essential to report: the sampling strategy employed; response rates, an estimate of sampling error (if probability sampling is used); a description of the measures used along with supporting evidence for their validity and reliability; a description of the survey procedure including information about participant recruitment, survey format (e.g., online, telephone), and interviewer training; and the statistical methods used for data analysis, including information about statistical adjustments for sampling deficiencies and strategies for managing missing data. In many instances, it is expected that a copy of the survey instrument be included with the report, along with more detailed information about sampling methodology and statistics.

For more general advice about writing research reports, we recommend Bem's (2002) excellent chapter "Writing the Empirical Journal Article." Field (2013) as well as Tabachnick and Fidell (2013) provide examples of how to write up results associated with a wide range of statistical analyses, and Meltzoff (1998, p. 164) includes a useful checklist for critiquing psychological research reports, which can also be used as a writing guide. Finally, the *Publication Manual of the American Psychological Association* (2010) is the definitive guide to formatting, presentation, and style in research reports in psychology.

Summary and Conclusions

Surveys are an invaluable methodological tool for environment–behavior researchers and their merits are reflected by their increasing popularity. They are an efficient means by which to collect large amounts of data and, when appropriate sampling and analysis strategies are used, they can provide valuable insights into the broader population. However, like all research methods, surveys can provide misleading and incorrect information if safeguards are not in place to prevent biased data collection and analysis. In this chapter, we have identified common challenges confronting survey researchers and outlined some strategies to help avoid these pitfalls. We have also introduced several new developments related to online data collection that we believe have the potential to revolutionize survey research. We hope that you, like our protagonists Maria and Ethan, use this information in your future projects to achieve the best possible outcomes in your chosen areas of research.

Glossary

Cross-sectional design   A type of research design in which researchers study a single group of respondents at one point in time.

Closed-ended question   A type of question in which respondents are provided with two or more pre-determined alternatives from which to choose (e.g., "*Disagree,*" "*Agree,*" or "*Don't know*").

Data imputation Replacing missing data with predictions about how each non-respondent would have likely answered the question based on patterns of responses across the data set.

Listwise deletion The most common strategy for dealing with missing data. Involves excluding individuals from an analysis if they did not provide responses for one of more variables involved in the analysis. This approach generally provides reasonably unbiased results when the amount of missing data is low (<5%).

Non-probability sampling A type of sampling in which all individuals in the population do not have an equal likelihood of being selected.

Non-response error A situation that arises when a probability sample is drawn from a well-defined population, but some members of that population do not respond. The degree of non-response error is an important potential cause of non-representative samples in probability sampling.

Open-ended question A type of question in which few constraints are placed on participants' responding, and, unlike multiple-choice questions, possible answers are not presented. Responses to open-ended questions are often analyzed using qualitative analysis.

Panel design A type of research design in which researchers study the same respondents at different points in time.

Population of interest The broad group of individuals that a researcher wishes to study.

Probability sampling A type of sampling procedure in which every member of the population has a chance of being selected to participate in the study, and this likelihood of being selected is known by the researcher. Probability samples are generally regarded as superior to non-probability samples because, if done correctly, the results derived from the sample can be used to draw conclusions about the population.

Rating scale response format The format of closed-ended questions, whereby respondents are asked to choose a point on the scale that best reflects their response to the item. For instance, rating scales often range from 5 points to 7 points, and may assess degree of agreement with certain beliefs or likelihood of engaging in certain behaviors.

Reliability The extent to which a measure is accurate (i.e., free of measurement error), consistent, and stable.

Repeated cross-sectional design A type of research design in which researchers study different respondents at different points in time.

Representative design A type of research design that involves sampling across multiple elements within a study, such as both human and non-human populations (e.g., building types or geographic locations). Representative design helps ensure that study findings generalize not only across individuals but also across settings.

Sample The small group of respondents selected (i.e., sampled) from the population.

Sampling error The difference between sample data and the actual values in the population due to random variation in the sampling process.

Socially desirable responding The potential tendency for respondents to overreport socially desirable behaviors and underreport socially undesirable behaviors due to either self-deception or a desire to appear in a positive light.

Validity The extent to which a measure assesses the construct that it is intended to assess.

References

Allison, P. D. (2002). *Missing data*. Sage University Papers Series on Quantitative Applications in the Social Sciences, Thousand Oaks, CA: Sage.

American Psychological Association (2010). *Publication manual of the American Psychological Association* (6th ed.). Washington, DC: American Psychological Association.

Bem, D. J. (2002). Writing the empirical journal article. In J. Darley, M. P. Zanna, & H. L. Roediger III (Eds.), *The compleat academic: A career guide*. Washington, DC: American Psychological Association.

Bradburn, N. M., Rips, L. J., & Shevell, S. K. (1987). Answering autobiographical questions: The impact of memory and inference on surveys. *Science, 10,* 157–161.

Bradburn, N. M., Sudman, S., & Wansink, B. (2004). *Asking questions: The definitive guide to questionnaire design – For market research, political polls, and social and health questionnaires* (revised edition). Hoboken, NJ: Wiley.

Brunswik, E. (1956). *Perception and the representative design of psychological experiments* (2nd ed.). Berkeley, CA: University of California Press.

Crowne, D. P., & Marlowe, D. (1960). A new scale of social desirability independent of psychopathology. *Journal of Consulting Psychology, 24,* 349–354.

Dillman, D. A. (2007). *Mail and Internet surveys: The tailored design method* (2nd ed.). Hoboken, NJ: Wiley.

Evans, J. R., & Mathur, A. (2005). The value of online surveys. *Internet Research, 15,* 195–219.

Field, A. (2013). *Discovering statistics using IBM SPSS Statistics* (4th ed.). Los Angeles, CA: Sage.

Fowler, F. J. (2009). *Survey research methods* (4th ed.). Thousand Oaks, CA: Sage.

Groves, R. M., Fowler, F. J., Couper, M. P., Lepkowski, J. M., Singer, E., & Tourangeau, R. (2009). *Survey methodology* (2nd ed.). Hoboken, NJ: Wiley.

Has-Vaughn, D. L. (2005). A primer for using and understanding weights with national datasets. *Journal of Experimental Education, 73,* 221–248.

Henrich, J., Heine, S. J., & Norenzayan, A. (2010). The weirdest people in the world? *Behavioral and Brain Sciences, 33,* 61–135.

Krosnick, J. A. (1999). Survey research. *Annual Review of Psychology, 50,* 537–567.

Meltzoff, J. (1998). *Critical thinking about research: Psychology and related fields.* Washington, DC: American Psychological Association.

Miller, E. T., Neal, D. J., Roberts, L. J., Baer, J. S., Cressler, S. O., Metrik, J., & Marlatt, A. G. (2002). Test–retest reliability of alcohol measures: Is there a difference between Internet-based assessment and traditional methods? *Psychology of Addictive Behaviors, 16,* 56–63.

Paulhus, D. L. (1991). Measurement and control of response bias. In J. P. Robinson, P. R. Shaver, & L. S. Wrightsman (Eds.), *Measures of personality and social psychological attitudes* (pp. 17–59). New York, NY: Academic Press.

Riva, G., Teruzzi, T., & Anolli, L. (2003). The use of the Internet in psychological research: Comparison of online and offline questionnaires. *CyberPsychology & Behavior, 6,* 73–80.

Scholl, N., Mulders, S., & Drent, R. (2002). Online qualitative market research: Interviewing the world at a fingertip. *Qualitative Market Research, 5,* 210–223.

Tabachnick, B. G., & Fidell, L. S. (2013). *Using multivariate statistics* (6th ed.). Boston, MA: Allyn & Bacon.

U.S. Census Bureau (2009). *Internet use in the United States: 2009*. Retrieved from http://www.census.gov/hhes/computer/

Vagias, W. M. (2006). *Likert-type scale response anchors*. Clemson International Institute for Tourism & Research Development, Department of Parks, Recreation and Tourism Management. Clemson University, SC.

Villar, A., & Krosnick, J. A. (2011). Global warming vs. climate change, taxes vs. prices: Does word choice matter? *Climatic Change, 105,* 1–12.

Visser, P. S., Krosnick, J. A., & Lavrakas, P. J. (2000). Survey research. In H. T. Reis & C. M. Judd (Eds.), *Handbook of research methods in social and personality psychology* (pp. 223–252). Cambridge, UK: Cambridge University Press.

Suggested Readings

Bradburn, N. M., Sudman, S., & Wansink, B. (2004). *Asking questions: The definitive guide to questionnaire design – For market research, political polls, and social and health questionnaires* (revised edition). Hoboken, NJ: Wiley.

Fowler, F. J. (2009). *Survey research methods* (4th ed.). Thousand Oaks, CA: Sage.

Visser, P. S., Krosnick, J. A., & Lavrakas, P. J. (2000). Survey research. In H. T. Reis & C. M. Judd (Eds.), *Handbook of research methods in social and personality psychology* (pp. 223–252). Cambridge, UK: Cambridge University Press.

6

Who Cares? Measuring Environmental Attitudes*

Amanda McIntyre[1] and Taciano L. Milfont[2]

[1] *University of Victoria, BC, Canada*
[2] *Victoria University of Wellington, New Zealand*

As part of a research project, Ethan has been asked by his lab coordinator to attend community events in three different neighborhoods and gather data from each group of community members. He wants to know if their thoughts, feelings, and behavioral intentions regarding the natural environment predict their acceptance and use of a new curbside composting pick-up program that has been implemented by city officials. Because he will be surveying a large number of people and wants to easily compare scores across the neighborhoods as well as with existing published research, he would prefer to use a simple standardized measure of environmental attitudes. Looking back over the literature, he realizes that there are many published measures of environmental attitudes and concern. He wonders how all the measures differ from one another and which one is best to use in his own research.

Information in the following chapter will help Ethan to answer his questions, and will also help you (the reader) in choosing a measure of environmental attitudes.

This chapter will provide readers with a definition of environmental attitudes and discussion of why it is useful to measure them. It will also provide a brief description of many of the well-established measures of environmental attitudes as well as some guidelines for how to choose and use an appropriate measure in your research. Finally, some current trends and suggestions for the future will be outlined. Information provided in this chapter along with information provided in Chapter 5 in this volume on survey techniques will help guide your research on environmental attitudes.

---

*Preparation of this chapter was supported in part by a Marsden Fast Start grant from The Royal Society of New Zealand (Te Putea Rangahau a Marsden) awarded to Taciano L. Milfont.

Research Methods for Environmental Psychology, First Edition. Edited by Robert Gifford.
© 2016 John Wiley & Sons, Ltd. Published 2016 by John Wiley & Sons, Ltd.

Definition of Environmental Attitudes

What constitutes an attitude toward the environment? As highlighted by Heberlein (1981), "any object outside of self exists in the individual's environment, so all attitudes except those beliefs about self could be correctly called environmental attitudes" (p. 243). The word "environment" typically refers to both built and non-human environments. Hence, using this all-encompassing definition, environmental attitudes may refer to attitudes toward all external objects of one's reality (Milfont, 2012). Although such a broad definition is reasonable, researchers have preferred to focus on more specific, parsimonious definitions.

To start with, researchers have distinguished between **environmental attitudes (EA)** and **environmental concern**, with many distinct definitions proposed for both constructs. EA have been described as "the collection of beliefs, affect, and behavioral intentions a person holds regarding environmentally related activities or issues" (Schultz, Shriver, Tabanico, & Khazian, 2004, p. 31); as "people's orientations toward environmentally related objects, including environmental problems themselves and problem-solving actions, and [divided] into three types: cognitive, affective, and evaluative environmental orientations" (Yin, 1999, p. 63); or as "perceptions of or beliefs regarding the physical environment, including factors affecting its quality (e.g., overpopulation, pollution)" (Gallagher, 2004, p. 97). In contrast, environmental concern has been defined as "the degree to which people are aware of problems regarding the environment and support efforts to solve them and/or indicate a willingness to contribute personally to their solution" (Dunlap & Michelson, 2002, p. 485); or as "the affect (i.e., worry) associated with beliefs about environmental problems" (Schultz et al., 2004, p. 31).

Despite these multiple and distinct definitions, EA and environmental concern are often used interchangeably. Since environmental concern is now generally considered to be one aspect of EA (Bamberg, 2003) and "environmental attitudes" is also the psychological index term frequently used (Gallagher, 2004), it can be asserted that EA is the preferable term in psychological research. Drawing from contemporary attitude research, Milfont (2007, 2012) has provided an EA definition, which has been expanded for use in the present chapter:

> Environmental attitudes are a psychological tendency to evaluate the natural and built environments, and factors affecting their quality, with some degree of favor or disfavor.

Why Measure Environmental Attitudes?

Many view environmental problems as resulting from maladaptive human behavior (Maloney & Ward, 1973), and thus having an anthropogenic origin (Stern, 1992; Takala, 1991). Due to its disciplinary focus on studying behavior, psychology can play an important role in the amelioration of environmental issues by fostering pro-ecological behavior. The study of individual difference variables (such as EA) is one way psychology can help because these variables may underlie individuals' behavior in preserving or damaging natural resources. With regards to the built environment, it is important to understand how individuals perceive and are influenced by their physical environment as well as how they are impacted by environmental stressors, design, risk, and so on. Chapters 12 and 13 in this volume focus more on the importance of assessing individuals' relations with the built environment, while the present chapter addresses mainly the natural environment. For a continued discussion of measuring attitudes toward the natural environment, read on.

Broadly speaking, the measurement of EA follows the well-established tradition of differential psychology. Research on individual differences typically focuses on two main questions: (1) whether individuals are more similar to themselves over time and across situations than they are to others; and, (2) whether variations for a single person across time and situations are smaller than the variations between two or more individuals (Revelle, 2000).

The extent to which particular individual difference variables – including personality traits, basic values, and time perspectives – affect behavioral predispositions to preserve or damage the environment at large is well studied by environmental psychologists. The underlying questions these researchers are trying to solve are why some individuals are more disposed toward environmental protection than others, and what the personological roots of pro-environmental protection are. In particular, the assessment of attitudes is important because individuals are more likely to intend to engage in a particular behavior if positive attitudes toward that behavior are held. Often, research focuses on the relationships between broader, upstream personality dispositions (e.g., values, traits) and more specific, downstream attitude and behavioral dispositions (e.g., Milfont, Duckitt, & Wagner, 2010).

In sum, when measuring EA, the underlying goal is to identify individuals' perceptions and beliefs regarding the environment, how these perceptions and beliefs can be operationalized in terms of dimensions (or more specific psychological constructs), and how these dimensions can be measured by means of survey questionnaires or other methods. By conceptualizing, developing, and validating tools to measure EA, reliably indexing individual differences in preference for preservation or damage of environmental surroundings is possible.

Measuring Environmental Attitudes

EA are typically measured using direct self-report methods such as interviews and questionnaires (i.e., **explicit measures**). Less frequently, **implicit measures** and techniques are used, such as unobtrusive behavioral observations, physiological measures, and response latency measures (e.g., Corral-Verdugo, 1997; Schultz et al., 2004, 2013). Although this chapter will introduce you to many of the existing explicit self-report measures of EA, the field would greatly benefit from further development of implicit techniques to assess individuals' EA.

At present, there is no one ideal measure of EA. Researchers often create specific measures in the context of a particular study, or adapt well-known, published measures. Because these measures are not consistently altered, interpreting the outcomes of studies that use altered measures is challenging (e.g., Hawcroft &

Milfont, 2010). And, without consistent methodological practices or systematic knowledge-building approaches in place when measuring EA, it is difficult to integrate the literature. As a result, the systematic assessment of the degree to which EA indeed influence behavioral intentions and dispositions toward the environment gets trickier to achieve.

This lack of consistency has resulted in the creation of a vast number of EA measures, with over 700 reported in the literature (for a review, see Dunlap & Jones, 2002). In an attempt to provide some integration of the existing measures, Dunlap and Jones (2002) have proposed a four-fold typology of EA measures. They suggest measures to be categorized based on the number of environmental issues addressed (e.g., air pollution, climate change, population growth) and number of expressions measured (e.g., beliefs, concern, attitudes, intentions, and behaviors related to environmental issues). This typology is depicted in Figure 6.1.

Despite the existence of hundreds of EA measures, no "gold standard" measure has emerged. Additionally, only a few measures have been consistently and widely used, and many have not had their psychometric properties adequately assessed so that they may be used with confidence (Dunlap & Jones, 2003; Fransson & Gärling, 1999). In the next section some of the more widely used measures will be presented, with notes on their content and specific uses (see Table 6.1 for a comprehensive list of all the measures included in this chapter). Going forward, researchers and practitioners should attempt to utilize existing measures where appropriate, rather than create new measures that may lack sufficient validation and theoretical underpinning.

	Multiple-topic	Single-topic
Multiple-expression	Instruments that focus on both multiple environmental issues and multiple expressions of concern	Instruments that focus on a single environmental issue and multiple expressions of concern
Single-expression	Instruments that focus on multiple environmental issues and a single expression of concern	Instruments that focus on a single environmental issue and a single expression of concern

Figure 6.1   Classification of EA measures (based on Dunlap & Jones, 2002).

Table 6.1 List of EA measures reviewed in this chapter.

Measure	Original publication	Intended for use with	Country of origin/ original sample	Number of items	Number of subscales	Response format
Measurement of Ecological Attitudes and Knowledge Scale (MEAK)	Maloney & Ward, 1973	Adults	United States	130	4	True or false and multiple choice
Measurement of Ecological Attitudes and Knowledge Scale-Revised (MEAK-R)	Maloney, Ward, & Braught, 1975	Adults	United States	45	4	True or false and multiple choice
Environmental Concern Scale (ECS)	Weigel & Weigel, 1978	Adults	United States	16	n/a	5-point Likert-type agreement scale
New Environmental Paradigm Scale (NEP)	Dunlap & Van Liere, 1978	Adults	United States	12	3	4-point Likert-type agreement scale
Revised New Ecological Paradigm Scale (NEP-R)	Dunlap, Van Liere, Mertig, & Jones, 2000	Adults	United States	15	5	5-point Likert-type agreement scale
Ecocentric and Anthropocentric Attitudes Toward the Environment Scale	Thompson & Barton, 1994	Adults	United States	33	3	5-point Likert-type agreement scale
Environmental Attitudes Inventory (EAI)	Milfont & Duckitt, 2010	Adults	New Zealand (also Brazil and South Africa)	120 (72- and 24-item short forms available)	12, reflecting two higher order factors	7-point Likert-type agreement scale
Environmental Motives Scale (EMS)	Schultz, 2000	Adults	United States	12	3	7-point Likert-type scale rating level of concern
New Ecological Paradigm for Children Scale	Manoli, Johnson, & Dunlap, 2007	Children aged 10–12	United States	10	3	5-point Likert-type agreement scale

(continued)

Table 6.1 (continued)

Measure	Original publication	Intended for use with	Country of origin/ original sample	Number of items	Number of subscales	Response format
Children's Environmental Attitudes and Knowledge Scale (CHEAKS)	Leeming, Bracken, & Dwyer, 1995	Elementary school aged children	United States	66	2	5-point Likert-type True or false and multiple choice
Children's Attitudes Toward the Environment Scale (CATES)	Musser & Malkus, 1994	Elementary/ middle school aged children	United States	25	5	Non-numerical response format for use with children
Children's Attitudes Toward the Environment Scale Preschool Version (CATES-PV)	Musser & Diamond, 1999	Preschool aged children	United States	15	n/a	Non-numerical response format for use with children
Children's Environmental Motives Scale (ChEMS)	Bruni, Chance & Schultz, 2012	Adolescents ages 10–18	United States	12	3	7-point Likert-type level of importance scale
Environmental (2-MEV) Scale	Bogner & Wilhelm, 1996	Adolescents and children ages 9–12	European countries	19	5 underlying factors	5-point Likert-type agreement scale
Scale of Perceived Environmental Annoyances in Urban Settings (SPEAUS)	Robin, Matheau-Police, & Couty, 2007	Adults	France	51	7	5-point Likert-type level of disturbance scale
Environmental Preference Questionnaire (EPQ)	Kaplan, 1977	Adults	United States	64	7	6-point Likert-type scale
Environmental Response Inventory (ERI)	McKechnie, 1974	Adults	United States	184	8	5-point Likert-type agreement scale
Environmental Appraisal Inventory	Schmidt & Gifford, 1989	Adults	Canada	24	3	7-point Likert-type level of perceived threat scale

Self-report measures of EA for use with adult populations

Measurement of Ecological Attitudes and Knowledge Scale   The Measurement of Ecological Attitudes and Knowledge Scale (MEAK; Maloney & Ward, 1973) was designed to measure individuals' verbal commitment, reported behaviors, and feelings toward ecological issues, as well as specific knowledge regarding ecological problems. The measure consists of 130 items divided into four multi-item subscales: *verbal commitment, actual commitment, affect,* and *knowledge*. The verbal commitment subscale measures what an individual says he or she is willing to do and has 36 items (e.g., "I'd be willing to ride a bicycle or take the bus to work in order to reduce air pollution"). The actual commitment subscale also has 36 items (e.g., "I save some waste materials for recycling") and it measures what a person actually does with regards to environmental issues. The affect subscale measures an individual's emotionality toward certain environmental problems and has 34 items (e.g., "I get depressed on smoggy days"). The knowledge subscale measures individual's factual knowledge in relation to environmental issues and has 24 items (e.g., "Which of the following materials usually takes longest to decompose: tin, iron, aluminum, copper, or steel?"). Maloney and colleagues (1975) have also developed a revised short-form version of this scale, consisting of 45 balanced items measuring the same four subscales: 10 items for each of the verbal commitment, actual commitment and affect subscales, and 15 items for the knowledge subscale. (If you are wondering what "balanced items" or "**balanced scales**" mean, check out Box 6.1.)

Although widely used, the MEAK Scale includes items tapping specific environmental topics that have become dated as new issues emerge, such as ozone depletion (Dunlap & Jones, 2002, 2003). Thus, without sufficient revision of the measure to update its content, other measures may be more favorable, such as those that touch on more general environmental issues, or ones that measure the overall relationship between humans and the environment.

Environmental Concern Scale   The Environmental Concern Scale (ECS: Weigel & Weigel, 1978) seeks to gauge an individual's concern for the environment by measuring their cognitions, evaluations, and intentions as they relate to a range of environmental topics (e.g., pollution). The ECS is a balanced scale with 16 items (e.g., "I'd be willing to make personal sacrifices for the sake of slowing down pollution even though the immediate results may not seem significant," "Even if public transportation was more efficient than it is, I would prefer to drive my car to work"). Similar to the MEAK Scale, the ECS includes dated topics that may no longer be relevant, and thus efforts should be taken to adequately revise the measure or a different measure should be selected.

New Environmental Paradigm Scale   The New Environmental Paradigm (NEP) Scale (Dunlap & Van Liere, 1978), also known as the New Ecological Paradigm Scale (Dunlap et al., 2000), is the most widely used measure of EA (Dunlap & Jones, 2003; Stern, Dietz, & Guagnano, 1995). The NEP Scale measures "ecological world-view," which reflects the degree to which an individual believes humans are a part of nature rather than being independent from and superior to nature. The NEP items

Box 6.1   Understanding balanced scales.

The majority of EA measures employ a Likert-type scale in which respondents are given a set of response options to indicate their level of agreement to each of the EA items. A common format is the 5-point Likert scale: 1 = Strongly Disagree, 2 = Disagree, 3 = Undecided (or Neutral), 4 = Agree, 5 = Strongly Agree. Self-reported measures are particularly prone to be affected by biases in individuals' responses to Likert-type scales, notably acquiescence bias and extremity bias – the section "Other Important Issues" below discusses these biases.

Methodologists recommend that self-reported measures should be "balanced" by including positively keyed and negatively keyed items. Balanced scales reduce the effects of individual differences in scale usage, yielding more reliable results.

Positively keyed items are those items phrased so that agreement or endorsement indicates a high level of the psychological attribute being measured. For example, the item "Humans are severely abusing the environment" is a positively keyed item on the New Environmental Paradigm (NEP) Scale. Someone answering 4 (Agree) or 5 (Strongly Agree) indicates a relatively high level of endorsement of the item, and thus to the attribute measured by the NEP Scale, while someone answering 1 (Strongly Disagree) or 2 (Disagree) reflects lower endorsement of the item/NEP.

In contrast, negatively keyed items are those items phrased so that agreement or endorsement indicates a low level of the psychological attribute being assessed. The item "Humans have the right to modify the natural environment to suit their needs" is a negatively keyed item on the NEP Scale, so that agreement (someone answering 4 or 5) reflects a low level of endorsement of NEP.

Responses to negatively keyed items must be reversed before computing total scores on the measure. To reverse-code the negatively keyed items we need to transform or reflect their values: $5 \rightarrow 1, 4 \rightarrow 2, 3 = 3$ (the neutral point stays the same), $2 \rightarrow 4, 1 \rightarrow 5$. Reverse-coding all of the relevant items ensures that all items of the scale are consistent with each other in terms of the response format (i.e., what an "agree" or "disagree" implies).

do not refer to obsolete environmental problems, and therefore the Scale has not become dated like some other early measures.

The original scale comprised 12 items, but has been revised and now includes 15 items (Dunlap, et al., 2000), with three items reflecting each of five hypothesized components of an ecological worldview. These five facets are: *the reality of limits to growth* (e.g., "We are approaching the limit of the number of people the earth can support"); *antianthropocentrism* (e.g., "Plants and animals have as much right as humans to exist"); *the fragility of nature's balance* (e.g., "When humans interfere with nature it often produces disastrous consequences"); *rejection of exemptionalism* (e.g., "Despite our special abilities humans are still subject to the laws of nature"); and *the possibility of an eco-crisis* (e.g., "Humans are severely abusing the environment"). Despite presenting these five facets, researchers typically sum/average all 15 NEP items (after reverse-coding the negatively keyed items, see Box 6.1) to give a single overall score.

Ecocentric and Anthropocentric Attitudes toward the Environment Scale The Ecocentric and Anthropocentric Attitudes toward the Environment scale (Thompson & Barton, 1994) consists of 33 items and measures *ecocentrism, anthropocentrism,* and *apathy* toward environmental issues. The ecocentrism subscale measures the degree to which individuals believe that nature has inherent value in its own right and consists of 12 items (e.g., "I can enjoy spending time in natural settings just for the sake of being out in nature"). The anthropocentrism subscale measures the degree to which individuals believe in the instrumental value of nature; that is, nature is valuable insofar as it benefit humans. This subscale consists of 11 items (e.g., "We need to preserve resources to maintain a high quality of life"). The third subscale measures overall apathy or a general lack of interest or concern regarding environmental problems, using 9 items (e.g., "I don't care about environmental problems").

Environmental Attitudes Inventory The Environmental Attitudes Inventory (EAI; Milfont & Duckitt, 2010) assesses a broad range of beliefs regarding the natural environment. The measure was created based on an attempt to integrate past measures and was specifically developed to capture the multidimensional and hierarchical nature of EA (Milfont & Duckitt, 2004). The scale measures 12 dimensions of EA: Enjoyment of Nature, Support for Interventionist Conservation Policies, Environmental Movement Activism, Environmental Fragility, Personal Conservation Behavior, Ecocentric Concern, Support for Population Growth Policies, Altering Nature, Conservation Motivated by Anthropocentric Concern, Confidence in Science and Technology, Human Dominance over Nature, and Human Utilization of Nature.

These dimensions reflect two higher order factors of *Preservation* and *Utilization*. Preservation reflects an overall viewpoint that the natural environment should be preserved and protected from further human destruction and alteration. Conversely, Utilization reflects the utilitarian stand point which suggests that humans have the right to make use of the natural environment for human gain. The full version of the EAI has 120 items, but shorter versions of the scale with 72 and 24 items are also proposed (Milfont & Duckitt, 2010). Some sample Preservation items include "Being out in nature is a great stress reducer for me," "I think spending time in nature is boring" (reversed), "When humans interfere with nature it often produces disastrous consequences," and "I do not believe that the environment has been severely abused by humans" (reversed). Some sample Utilization items include "The idea that natural areas should be maintained exactly as they are is silly, wasteful, and wrong," "Turning new unused land over to cultivation and agricultural development should be stopped" (reversed), "Humans were meant to rule over the rest of nature," and "Plants and animals have as much right as humans to exist" (reversed).

Environmental Motives Scale   The Environmental Motives Scale (EMS; Schultz, 2000) is a measure of environmental concern and is consistent with the tripartite theory of environmental concern proposed by Stern, Dietz, and Kalof (1993). This measure asks individuals to rate their level of environmental concern stemming from perceived consequences for 12 "value objects." The measure consists of three subscales with four objects each, reflecting three possible types of environmental concern: *egoistic* or concern for the self (e.g., "my health"); *altruistic* or concern for others (e.g., "all people"); and *biospheric* or concern beyond humans to include all living things (e.g., "animals").

Self-report measures of EA for use with children and adolescents

New Ecological Paradigm for Children Scale   The NEP Scale has been adapted for use with children to measure children's environmental worldview (Manoli, Johnson, & Dunlap, 2007). It consists of 10 items, five fewer than the original NEP Scale, and the wording has been made appropriate for use with children ages 10 to 12 years. Typically, an overall score is calculated for this measure, however, three subscales exist. The *Human Exemptionalism* subscale reflects the degree to which children believe that humans are not subject to the constraints of nature (e.g., "People are clever enough to keep from ruining earth"). The *Eco-Crisis* subscale reflects the degree to which children believe that an environmental crisis is possible (e.g., "If things don't change, we will have a big disaster in the environment soon"). Finally, the *Rights of Nature* subscale reflects the degree to which children believe that nature has intrinsic value (e.g., "Plants and animals have as much right as people to live"). This scale has not yet been widely used in published research, therefore further attempts to establish the validity of the scale may be necessary.

Children's Environmental Attitudes and Knowledge Scale   The Children's Environmental Attitudes and Knowledge Scale (CHEAKS; Leeming, Bracken, & Dwyer, 1995) is based on the Measurement of Ecological Attitudes and Knowledge Scale (Maloney & Ward, 1973) for adults. The scale measures school-aged (grades 1 to 7) children's general attitudes toward the environment as well as their knowledge about the environment. The measure consists of 66 items. The *Attitude* subscale consists of 36 items and measures children's verbal commitment, actual commitment, and affect with regards to six environmental domains (i.e., animals, energy, pollution, recycling, water, and general issues). Some sample items include: "I would be willing to stop buying some products to save animals' lives," "To save water, I would be willing to use less water when I bathe," "I would not give $15 of my own money to help the environment." The second subscale, *Knowledge*, includes 30 items that measure children's knowledge across the same six domains using a multiple choice format of response (e.g., "Burning coal for energy is a problem because it: a. Releases carbon dioxide and other pollutants into the air, b. Decreases needed acid rain, c. Reduces the amount of ozone in the stratosphere, d. Is too expensive, e. Pollutes the water aquifers"). The authors suggest that the knowledge portion of the scale may be too difficult for younger children, and thus does not reflect children's knowledge but rather their guessing.

Children's Attitudes Toward the Environment Scale The Children's Attitudes Toward the Environment Scale (CATES; Musser & Malkus, 1994) is a measure of children's general environmental attitudes. This 25-item scale is intended for use with middle school aged children (specifically grades 3 through 5). The items consist of "child-tested" words and use a unique, non-numeric response format. The measure includes five subscales which seek to measure children's beliefs, affect, and behaviors in relation to the following topics: *Recycling, Conservation, Animal Rights and Protection, Nature Appreciation*, and *Pollution*. An example of a recycling item reads as follows: "Some kids don't sort trash, but other kids sort their trash and recycle it." Children are asked to indicate which groups of children they are "most like." Additionally, a version of this scale has been created for use with pre-school aged children and uses pictures alongside the written items to make them more appropriate for this age group (Musser & Diamond, 1999). Both versions of this measure would benefit from additional validation before further use.

Children's Environmental Motives Scale The Children's Environmental Motives Scale (ChEMS: Bruni, Chance, & Schultz, 2012) is an adapted version of the EMS scale described earlier. The scale still seeks to measure a tripartite classification of environmental concern but has been modified for use with children and adolescents, aged 10 to 18 years. Its format is similar to that of the original version but some wording has changed so that the topic of environmental degradation is introduced in a more concrete manner. The measure distinguishes between *egoistic, altruistic*, and *biospheric* concern and consists of 12 items, with four items reflecting each of the three types of concern.

Environmental (2-MEV) scale The Environmental (2-MEV) scale (Bogner & Wilhelm, 1996) seeks to tap into adolescents' environmental perceptions, by measuring various attitudinal and behavioral indicators. It has been greatly revised since it was first introduced, and currently consists of 19 items (Bogner, 2000, 2002; Bogner, Brengelmann, & Wiseman, 2000; Bogner & Wiseman, 2002a, 2002b). Five underlying primary factors have emerged which are labeled: *Care with Resources* (e.g., "I always switch the light off when I don't need it any more"), *Intent of Support* (e.g., "Environmental protection costs a lot of money. I am prepared to help out in a fund-raising effort"), *Enjoyment of Nature* (e.g., "I especially love the soft rustling of leaves when the wind blows through the treetops"), *Human Dominance* (e.g., "In order to feed human beings, nature must be cleared, so that, for example, grain can be grown"), and *Altering Nature* (e.g., "A real nature fan brings home beautiful and rare plants when he/she has been out in the countryside").

These five primary factors reflect two higher order factors, with the first three reflecting *Preservation* (i.e., a biospheric orientation that emphasizes conservation and protection of nature) and the later two reflecting *Utilization* (i.e., an anthropocentric orientation that emphasizes the dominance of humans over nature and the right to use natural resources for human gain). These dimensions form the basis for the Theory of Ecological Attitude Scale (Wiseman & Bogner, 2003; see also Milfont, 2012; Milfont & Duckitt, 2004). The scale was originally created and validated using various European samples, but has also been modified for use with American children aged 9 to 12 (Johnson & Manoli, 2011).

Self-report measures of EA toward built environments

The measures that have been presented so far all focus on evaluations of the natural environment. However, a few measures have been published that measure attitudes and perceptions regarding only the built environment, or both the built and natural environment. For more information on measuring individuals' attitudes and use of built environments beyond the self-report measures presented here, see the chapters in this volume on planning the built environment (Chapter 12) and post-occupancy evaluation (Chapter 13).

Scale of Perceived Environmental Annoyances in Urban Settings   The Scale of Perceived Environmental Annoyances in Urban Settings (SPEAUS; Robin, Matheau-Police, & Couty, 2007) measures the degree to which individuals are bothered by potentially adverse factors and situations encountered within a large urban setting. These factors/situations include social, physical, and functional elements of the urban environment. The measure consists of 51 items, each of which describing a factor/situation, and asks the participant to indicate how personally disturbed they are by it. The measure consists of seven subscales described below.

The *Feelings of Insecurity* subscale measures perceptions of interpersonal threat and potential victimization in an urban environment (e.g., "Thinking that one might be a victim of assault in a public place"). The *Inconveniences Associated with Using Public Transport* subscale measures feelings of physical discomfort and powerlessness with regards to using public transport (e.g., "Public transport which is not frequent enough"). The subscale of *Environmental Annoyances and Global Environmental Concerns* measures individuals' perceptions of noise, pollution, poverty, and lack of green space (e.g., "The increase in industrial pollution"). The *Lack of Control Over Time Due to the Use of Cars* subscale measures individuals' feelings with regards to traffic and time spent commuting (e.g., "Driving around for an hour looking for a parking space"). The *Incivilities Encountered in the Shared Use of Public Spaces* subscale measures perceptions of aggression or lack of respect among different groups of people who are all navigating or occupying public spaces (e.g., "Drivers of cars who don't respect pedestrians and cyclists"). The *Loss of Efficiency Related to the Population Density* subscale measures frustration with regards to inconveniences associated with a high population density (e.g., "Crowds in the supermarkets on busy days and at certain hours of the day"). The last subscale, *An Insecure and Run-Down Local Environment*, reflects individuals' dissatisfaction with the maintenance of their residential environment and neighborhood (e.g., "Blocks of flats that are poorly maintained in my neighborhood"). The SPEAUS was constructed within the social-cultural context of France, and would therefore need to be adapted to reflect differing urban environments and validated to be used in other contexts. Because this measure has not been widely used, further validation effort is necessary.

Environmental Preference Questionnaire   The Environmental Preference Questionnaire (EPQ; Kaplan, 1977) measures individuals' satisfaction and preference in relation to various built and natural environmental contexts. The measure includes 64 items and consists of seven subscales that reflect specific environmental settings: *City, Nature,*

Modern Development, Suburbs, Social, Passive Reaction to Stress, and *Romantic Escape.* The City subscale measures the degree to which individuals enjoy urban settings, whereas the Nature subscale measures preference for the wilderness, such as forests and lakes. The Modern Development subscale measures preference for modern housing developments, industrialized settings, and related issues. The Suburbs subscale measures preference for suburban lifestyles and related topics. The Social subscale measures individuals' preferences for a social environment, such as parties, or interactions that include large groups of people. The Passive Reaction to Stress subscale measures individuals' preference for relaxing, undemanding settings, and activities when feeling stressed. Finally, the Romantic Escape subscale measures individuals' preference for rustic, isolated environments (e.g., the "backwoods"), which is in part reflective of a distaste for socially dominating settings such as the suburbs. Because this measure has not been widely used, further validation effort is required.

Environmental Response Inventory The Environmental Response Inventory (ERI; McKechnie, 1974, 1977) measures individuals' attitudes toward and interactions with various natural and built environmental contexts. The ERI consists of 184 statements which reflect eight different subscales (*Pastoralism, Urbanism, Environmental Adaptation, Stimulus Seeking, Environmental Trust, Antiquarianism, Need for Privacy,* and *Mechanical Orientation*) and one scale which measures the test taker's attentiveness (*Communality*).

Pastoralism measures attitudes toward environmental conservation, touching on many facets of this issue including preservation of natural lands and resources, and enjoyment of natural spaces (e.g., "Our national forests should be preserved in their natural state, with roads and buildings prohibited"). The Urbanism subscale measures enjoyment of fast-paced, high-density living that typically characterizes large urban settings (e.g., "I like the variety of stimulation one finds in the city"). The subscale Environmental Adaption measures the degree to which individuals believe that humans should be able to modify the environment to suit their needs without regulation, and that environmental crises will be solved by advances in technology (e.g., "Fertilizers improve the quality of food"). The Stimulus Seeking subscale measures the degree to which an individual engages in travel to unique places and exploration of unusual or foreign environments (e.g., "I enjoy being in dangerous places"). The Environmental Trust subscale measures individuals' comfort and openness when navigating an environment as well as their feelings toward being alone and isolated (e.g., "I'd be afraid to live in a place where there were no people nearby"). Antiquarianism reflects individuals' enjoyment of antiquated and historical structures, places, and objects (e.g., "I would enjoy living in a historic house"). The Need for Privacy subscale measures preference and enjoyment of isolated and secluded spaces, and need for freedom from interruption (e.g., "There is too little emphasis on privacy in our society"). Lastly, the Mechanical Orientation subscale reflects kinesthetic ability and proficiency with science and technology (e.g., "I can repair just about anything around the house").

Environmental Appraisal Inventory The Environmental Appraisal Inventory (Schmidt & Gifford, 1989) measures three dimensions of environmental appraisal (i.e., *Perceived Environmental Threats to Self, Threat to the Environment,* and *Perceived Control over Environmental Hazards*) in the face of hazards and disasters. The measure lists 24 threats (e.g., acid rain, noise, earthquakes) and respondents indicate the degree to which each hazard is (a) a threat to the self, (b) a threat to the environment, and (c) controllable by themselves, should the threat become salient. This results in three subscales (i.e., *Self, Environment,* and *Control*). This scale, originally developed using a Canadian sample, has been validated in samples from other countries: United States (Fridgen, 1994), Irish (Walsh-Daneshmandi & MacLachlan, 2000), Japanese (e.g. Sako & Gifford, 1999; Sako, Hirata, & Gifford, 2002) and Chinese (Lai, Brennan, Chan, & Tao, 2003) samples.

Choosing and Using a Measure of EA

Given the broad range of EA measures available, selecting the appropriate measure for your research is imperative. The appropriate measure will be one that reflects the construct you are trying to measure, relating back to your research question. If you are hoping to measure only one specific aspect of environmental attitudes, ensure your measure reflects only that aspect and not another. For example, if you are planning to measure individuals' thoughts about the environment, make sure you use a measure that reflects cognition, rather than affect or behavioral intentions.

The quality of your chosen measurement will influence your results (i.e., replicability, level of statistical significance, and observed effect sizes), as well as your ability to infer meaningful and valid conclusions. Ideally, scales that intend to measure important psychological variables are developed through a rigorous process emphasizing psychometric properties. If a measure is ambiguous, or psychometric properties are not well established, then it may not accurately reflect the psychological construct you have chosen to measure (which in the present context is EA, but this is true of any concept or variable you are interested in measuring). However, if a measure has clear meaning with respect to the chosen construct, and is able to consistently capture that meaning, then you can interpret your results using that measure with confidence and make valid psychological inferences. This chapter primarily includes measures that have been validated psychometrically, and notes have been made if further validation is necessary before the measure can be used confidently.

For the above reasons, it is important when conducting research to select a measure with good psychometric properties. More specifically, this means that the measure has been assessed in terms of reliability (i.e., how consistent the measure is) and validity (i.e., does it measure what it purports to measure). For more information on the different types of reliability and validity, see the chapter in this volume on survey techniques (Chapter 5). Additionally, the psychometric properties of the data you collect using the measure should be assessed before you can confidently interpret the results. For example, a scale that is reliable within one sample (e.g., undergraduates) may not generalize to all samples (e.g., adolescents, adults). The equivalence of a particular measure in terms of its psychometric properties across different groups should also be considered (see more on this topic below). Selecting psychometrically sound measures and assessing their performance within your own sample are both necessary if you want to be able to draw meaningful conclusions. The following sections will briefly outline some of the general aspects to consider when choosing or using a measure of EA. We also encourage the reader to access more specialized publications on questionnaire design and attitude measurement (e.g., Furr, 2011; Krosnick & Fabrigar, 2006; Krosnick, Judd, & Wittenbrink, 2005)

Reliability and Validity

Every time you use a measure, the psychometric properties of the measure regarding your data should be examined before you interpret the results. This includes examining both **reliability** (i.e., how consistent a measure is performing) and **validity** (i.e., how accurately a measure is capturing the intended construct). Researchers should provide evidence demonstrating that the used measure has accepted levels of reliability and proves to be valid. This fundamental psychometric information should be included in the written research report. When looking at your data, ask yourself whether the scale is performing well in the sample. Does the scale seem to truly reflect what it is attempting to measure? The strength of your statistical analyses may also be influenced by the performance of your measures. Thus, you want to make sure the measure is performing well before you attempt to analyze your data.

Dimensionality

Dimensionality (or factor structure) refers to the number and nature of variables assessed by items/questions in a measure. Some measures are proposed to be unidimensional, with items reflecting a single construct (e.g., the ECS; Weigel & Weigel, 1978), while others are multidimensional, with sets of items reflecting different components or dimensions (e.g., the EAI; Milfont & Duckitt, 2010). Dimensionality influences how one scores a measure and its meaning. If a scale includes two or more *independent* dimensions, the items should be scored accordingly, otherwise the scores produced may not truly reflect the proposed underlying construct, and thus scores may be meaningless. When you use a measure, you should determine if the originally reported dimensions or factors emerge in your own data. Also make sure that your measure is scored according to the number of subscales or factors originally intended for the scale.

Modifying scales

If you wish to modify an existing scale (e.g., shortening a measure, adding additional questions), be aware that the measure may not have the same psychometric properties as the original. Typically the more a measure is modified the less likely it will have the same properties as the original. Also be aware that this practice hinders the development of the field because results from different versions of a given measure are not easily comparable. If you do modify a measure, make sure to re-evaluate the psychometric properties, including reliability, validity, and the dimensionality, and to report the findings. This information will help the accumulation and progress of scientific knowledge in the area by means of meta-analysis (e.g., Hawcroft & Milfont, 2010).

Scale length

As you may have noticed, scales vary in length from brief measures to extensive inventories. Using scales with fewer items, or even a single item, may seem appealing. However, shorter measures might lead to psychometric issues and domain underrepresentation. On the other hand, if a measure is too lengthy you may have to worry about participant inattention, fatigue, or attrition. You may also need to consider any time restrictions you have when administering measures, as this may influence which measure you choose. Fortunately, short-form versions have been validated for some measures, and thus may be appropriate to use when length is a factor.

Measurement across groups

Researchers should not assume that a measure's psychometric properties generalize across different samples or groups (e.g., from adults to children, across cultures). A measure or scale may be valid in one population, but not another. If you wish to use a measure with a group that differs from the group with which the measure has originally been created and validated, you should take extra precautions to ensure that the measure remains reliable and valid. Psychometric properties should be examined within each new group, and psychometric differences should be examined, understood, and rectified before scores are used in those groups. If possible, more stringent tests examining the extent to which the measure is equivalent across groups should be employed (Milfont & Fischer, 2010). Some reasons why divergence may be observed are group differences in the understanding and interpretation of words or questions used, the scale may not represent the same latent construct, or the construct may psychologically differ across various groups.

Other important issues

Explicit measures, such as self-report questionnaires, are more susceptive to response bias than implicit measures. There are three main biases affecting individuals' responses to questionnaires that researchers should be aware of (Paulhus, 1991): socially desirable responding (tendency to give answers in questionnaires that make participant look good); acquiescence bias (tendency to agree or disagree with all or most of the questions asked); and extremity bias (tendency to choose extreme ratings in response-scale formats). Most recent measures of EA are balanced scales with positively keyed and negatively keyed items. Balanced scales help minimize the issue of acquiescence bias (see Box 6.1). Inspection of response distribution and descriptive statistics (e.g., mean, median, mode, range, and standard deviation) can provide useful information regarding extremity bias and even indication of outlier cases. Because items or text that come before or after a measure can have a considerable effect on the way individuals respond to a scale (Schwarz, 1999), you should also counterbalance the EA measure you selected with other measures/stimuli, when appropriate, and statistically check for order effects.

Participants may consciously or unconsciously respond to the questions they are asked in socially desirable ways. That is, they respond in a way thought to be viewed as favorable by others. Moreover, when completing explicit measures participants may give responses that they *think* the researcher and others want to hear or that they think are the right answers. In order to avoid such response bias, attempt to disguise the purpose of your study or your own expectations as a researcher if possible. You may also wish to reassure participants that you are looking for a variety of opinions with regards to your topic and that there is no right or wrong answer. There is evidence that social desirability does not exert a strong influence on self-reported measures of both pro-environmental attitudes and behavior (Milfont, 2009). But it seems obvious that participants would be more prone to admit interest in environmental protection than admit disinterest or anti-environmental stands. Therefore, the issue of social desirability influence on EA is an issue worthy of further exploration in future research.

New Trends in the Area

Overreliance on explicit measures can be seen as a negative trend in the area. The measures presented in this chapter are all explicit, self-report measures of EA. These types of measures are more prone to the biases previously discussed. They are also limited in that they only serve to measure what the participant is aware of, or what they are capable of expressing. This is why in the future more implicit measures of EA should be developed. One could tentatively say that use of implicit measurement techniques is a new trend in the area. Indeed, in measuring pro-environmental attitudes and behaviors many (somewhat) recent studies have used implicit techniques such as unobtrusive behavioral observation and response latency measures (e.g., Corral-Verdugo, 1997; Schultz et al., 2004, 2013).

Another important trend is a recent quest to properly conceptualize EA, with a resulting positive influence on the development of more sound measures and theory building. One may look, for example, to the Theory of Ecological Attitude Scale (Wiseman & Bogner, 2003). As stated earlier, Bogner and colleagues presented a model in which EA are organized into the two broad dimensions of Preservation and Utilization. After the publication of the model, a number of publications have provided refinement both in terms of measurement and theory (see, e.g., Milfont & Duckitt, 2004, 2010).

Perhaps another important new trend is the increasing number of meta-analyses in the field (See Chapter 20 in this volume for a detailed discussion). Because meta-analysis is a methodology that systematically summarizes a body of quantitative research (Rosenthal & DiMatteo, 2001), this methodology contributes to the accumulation and development of scientific knowledge. An early meta-analysis in the field was conducted by Hines et al. (1987), who reviewed findings about the relationship between EA and ecological behavior. Three recent meta-analyses (Bamberg & Möser, 2007; Hawcroft & Milfont, 2010; Osbaldiston & Schott, 2012) have also addressed this relationship. Additional meta-analyses on this topic and other topics in environmental psychology would also be of use.

Summary and Conclusions

This chapter focuses on the measurement of environmental attitudes (EA). It provides a brief overview of the conceptual definition of EA, the importance of their measurement, and ways EA have been measured. Within the chapter, several self-report measures of EA are described, including six that can be used with adults and five that can be used with children and adolescents, as well as four measures that focus on the evaluation of the built environment (or a combination of built and natural environment). Practical and methodological issues regarding the selection and use of EA measures are also discussed. The chapter concludes by focusing on three trends that will ideally continue in this research area: less reliance on explicit measures of EA (especially self-reports); more theory building in conceptualization and measurement of EA; and use of meta-analytical approaches to summarize and move the field forward. In conclusion, researchers interested in measuring individuals' EA should consider the information presented in this chapter before deciding how to proceed. Ideally, an established measure with good psychometric properties that is consistent with one's research goals should be used to measure EA.

Glossary

Balanced scale   A measured scale that has both positively keyed and negatively keyed items. See Box 6.1.

Environmental attitude   A psychological tendency to evaluate the natural and built environments, and factors affecting their quality, with some degree of favor or disfavor.

Environmental concern   Often previously used interchangeably with the term environmental attitude, environmental concern is now typically considered to be just one component of environmental attitudes, particularly an affective component.

Explicit measure   A technique or measurement that relies on an individual's own self-reports on questionnaire or in an interview to ascertain the individual's attitude toward a subject.

Implicit measure   A technique or measurement tool that does not rely on an individual's own report of his/her conscious awareness of a topic, but instead relies on the measurement of unobtrusive behavioral observations, physiological measures, or response latency measures (e.g., "implicit association task") to ascertain the individual's attitude toward a subject.

Reliability   The overall consistency of a measure. Reliability is an important psychometric property and is often measured by means of Cronbach's alpha coefficients.

Validity   The degree to which a measure actually reflects what it is supposed to measure. Validity is also an important psychometric property and there are multiple types of validity that can be assessed (See Chapter 5 for a detailed discussion).

References

Bamberg, S. (2003). How does environmental concern influence specific environmentally related behaviours? A new answer to an old question. *Journal of Environmental Psychology*, *23*, 21–32.

Bamberg, S., & Möser, G. (2007). Twenty years after Hines, Hungerford, and Tomera: A new meta-analysis of psycho-social determinants of pro-environmental behaviour. *Journal of Environmental Psychology*, *27*, 14–25.

Bogner, F. X. (2000). Environmental perceptions of Italian and some European non-Mediterranean pupil populations. *Fresenius Environmental Bulletin*, *9*, 570–581.

Bogner, F. X. (2002). The influence of a residential outdoor programme to pupils' environmental perception. *European Journal of Psychology of Education*, *17*, 19–34.

Bogner, F. X., Brengelmann, J. C., & Wiseman, M. (2000). Risk-taking and environmental perception. *The Environmentalist*, *20*, 49–62.

Bogner, F. X., & Wilhelm, M. G. (1996). Environmental perception of pupils: Development of an attitude and behaviour scale. *The Environmentalist*, *16*, 95–110.

Bogner, F. X., & Wiseman, M. (2002a). Environmental perception: Factor profiles of extreme groups. *European Psychologist*, *7*, 225–237.

Bogner, F. X., & Wiseman, M. (2002b). Environmental perception of French and some Western European secondary school students. *European Journal of Psychology of Education*, *17*, 3–18.

Bruni, C., Chance, R., & Schultz, P. W. (2012). Measuring value-based environmental concerns in children: An environmental motives scale. *Journal of Environmental Education*, *43*, 1–15.

Corral-Verdugo, V. (1997). Dual "realities" of conservation behavior: Self-reports vs. observations of re-use and recycling behavior. *Journal of Environmental Psychology*, *17*, 135–145.

Dunlap, R. E., & Jones, R. E. (2002). Environmental concern: Conceptual and measurement issues. In R. E. Dunlap & W. Michelson (Eds.), *Handbook of environmental sociology* (pp. 482–524). Westport, CT: Greenwood Press.

Dunlap, R. E., & Jones, R. E. (2003). Environmental attitudes and values. In R. Fernández-Ballesteros (Ed.), *Encyclopedia of psychological assessment* (Vol. *1*, pp. 364–369). London, UK: Sage.

Dunlap, R. E., & Michelson, W. (Eds.). (2002). *Handbook of environmental sociology*. Westport, CT: Greenwood Press.

Dunlap, R. E., & Van Liere, K. D. (1978). The new environmental paradigm. *Journal of Environmental Education*, *9*, 10–19.

Dunlap, R. E., Van Liere, K. D., Mertig, A., & Jones, R. E. (2000). Measuring endorsement of the new ecological paradigm: A revised NEP scale. *Journal of Social Issues*, *56*, 425–442.

Fransson, N., & Gärling, T. (1999). Environmental concern: Conceptual definitions, measurement methods, and research findings. *Journal of Environmental Psychology*, *19*, 369–382.

Fridgen, C. (1994). Human disposition toward hazards: Testing the environmental appraisal inventory. *Journal of Environmental Psychology*, *14*, 101–111.

Furr, R. M. (2011). *Scale construction and psychometrics for social and personality psychology*. London, UK: Sage.

Gallagher, L. A. (Ed.). (2004). *Thesaurus of psychological index terms* (10th ed.). Washington, DC: American Psychological Association.

Hawcroft, L. J., & Milfont, T. L. (2010). The use (and abuse) of the new environmental paradigm scale over the last 30 years: A meta-analysis. *Journal of Environmental Psychology*, *30*, 143–158.

Heberlein, T. A. (1981). Environmental attitudes. *Zeitschrift für Umweltpolitik, 4*, 241–270.

Hines, J. M., Hungerford, H. R., & Tomera, A. N. (1987). Analysis and synthesis of research on responsible environmental behavior: A meta-analysis. *Journal of Environmental Education, 18*(2), 1–8.

Johnson, B., & Manoli, C. C. (2011). The 2-MEV Scale in the United States: A measure of children's environmental attitudes based on the theory of ecological attitude. *Journal of Environmental Education, 42*, 84–97.

Kaplan, R. (1977). Patterns of environmental preference. *Environment and Behavior, 9*, 195–216.

Krosnick, J. A., & Fabrigar, L. R. (2006). *The handbook of questionnaire design.* New York, NY: Oxford University Press.

Krosnick, J. A., Judd, C. M., & Wittenbrink, B. (2005). The measurement of attitudes. In D. Albarracín, B. T. Johnson & M. P. Zanna (Eds.), *The handbook of attitudes* (pp. 21–76). Mahwah, NJ: Lawrence Erlbaum.

Lai, C. J., Brennan, A., Chan, H., & Tao, J. (2003). Disposition toward environmental hazards in Hong Kong Chinese: Validation of a Chinese version of the environmental appraisal inventory (EAI-C). *Journal of Environmental Psychology, 23*, 369–384.

Leeming, F. C., Bracken, B. A., & Dwyer, W. O. (1995). Children's environmental attitude and knowledge scale: Construction and validation. *Journal of Environmental Education, 26*, 22–33.

Maloney, M. P., & Ward, M. P. (1973). Ecology: Let's hear it from the people. An objective scale for measurement of ecological attitudes and knowledge. *American Psychologist, 28*, 583–586.

Maloney, M. P., Ward, M. P., & Braucht, G. N. (1975). Psychology in action: A revised scale for the measurement of ecological attitudes and knowledge. *American Psychologist, 30*, 787–790.

Manoli, C. C., Johnson, B., & Dunlap, R. E. (2007). Assessing children's environmental worldviews: Modifying and validating the new ecological paradigm scale for use with children. *Journal of Environmental Education, 38*, 3–13.

McKechnie, G. E. (1974). *Manual for the environmental response inventory.* Palo Alto, CA: Consulting Psychologist's Press.

McKechnie, G. E. (1977). The environmental response inventory in application. *Environment and Behavior, 9*, 255–276.

Milfont, T. L. (2007). *Psychology of environmental attitudes: A cross-cultural study of their content and structure.* Unpublished doctoral dissertation, University of Auckland, New Zealand.

Milfont, T. L. (2009). The effects of social desirability on self-reported environmental attitudes and ecological behaviour. *The Environmentalist, 29*, 263–269.

Milfont, T. L. (2012). The psychology of environmental attitudes: Conceptual and empirical insights from New Zealand. *Ecopsychology, 4*, 269–276.

Milfont, T. L., & Duckitt, J. (2004). The structure of environmental attitudes: First- and second-order confirmatory factor analysis. *Journal of Environmental Psychology, 24*, 289–303.

Milfont, T. L., & Duckitt, J. (2010). The environmental attitudes inventory: A valid and reliable measure to assess the structure of environmental attitudes. *Journal of Environmental Psychology, 30*, 80–94.

Milfont, T. L., Duckitt, J., & Wagner, C. (2010). A cross-cultural test of the value–attitude–behaviour hierarchy. *Journal of Applied Social Psychology, 40*, 2791–2813.

Milfont, T. L., & Fischer, R. (2010). Testing measurement invariance across groups: Applications in cross-cultural research. *International Journal of Psychological Research, 3*, 112–131.

Musser, L., & Diamond, K. E. (1999). The children's attitudes toward the environment scale for preschool children. *Journal of Environmental Education, 30*, 23–31.

Musser, L., & Malkus, A. (1994). The children's attitudes toward the environment scale. *Journal of Environmental Education, 25,* 22–26.

Osbaldiston, R., & Schott, J. P. (2012) Environmental sustainability and behavioral science: Meta-analysis of proenvironmental behavior experiments. *Environment and Behavior, 44,* 257–299.

Paulhus, D. L. (1991). Measurement and control of response bias. In J. P. Robinson, P. R. Shaver, & L. S. Wrightsman (Eds.), *Measurement of personality and social psychological attitudes* (pp. 17–59). San Diego, CA: Academic Press.

Revelle, W. (2000). *Individual differences.* In A. Kazdin (Ed.), *Encyclopedia of psychology* (Vol. 4, pp. 249–253). Oxford, UK: Oxford University Press.

Robin, M., Matheau-Police, A., & Couty, C. (2007). Development of a scale of perceived environmental annoyances in urban settings. *Journal of Environmental Psychology, 27,* 55–68.

Rosenthal, R., & DiMatteo, M. R. (2001). Meta-analysis: Recent developments in quantitative methods for literature reviews. *Annual Review of Psychology, 52,* 59–82.

Sako, T., & Gifford, R. (1999). Principal factors of environmental awareness: A study of the construct validity of the environmental appraisal inventory. *MERA Journal, 5,* 9–14.

Sako, T., Hirata, S., & Gifford, R. (2002). Measurement of attitudes toward environmental problems: An examination of the Japanese version of the environmental appraisal inventory. *Environmental Education, 11,* 3–14.

Schmidt, F. N., & Gifford, R. (1989). A dispositional approach to hazard perception: Preliminary development of the environmental appraisal inventory. *Journal of Environmental Psychology, 9,* 57–67.

Schultz, P. W. (2000). Empathizing with nature: The effects of perspective taking on concern for environmental issues. *Journal of Social Issues, 56,* 391–406.

Schultz, P. W., Bator, R. J., Large, L. B., Bruni, C. M., & Tabanico, J. J. (2013). Littering in context: Personal and environmental predictors of littering behavior. *Environment and Behavior, 45,* 35–59.

Schultz, P. W., Shriver, C., Tabanico, J. J., & Khazian, A. M. (2004). Implicit connections with nature. *Journal of Environmental Psychology, 24,* 31–42.

Schwarz, N. (1999). Self-reports: How the questions shape the answers. *American Psychologist, 54,* 93–105.

Stern, P. C. (1992). Psychological dimensions of global environmental change. *Annual Review of Psychology, 43,* 269–302.

Stern, P. C., Dietz, T., & Guagnano, G. A. (1995). The new ecological paradigm in social-psychological context. *Environment and Behavior, 27,* 723–743.

Stern, P. C., Dietz, T., & Kalof, L. (1993). Value orientations, gender, and environmental concern. *Environment and Behavior, 25,* 322–348.

Takala, M. (1991). Environmental awareness and human activity. *International Journal of Psychology, 26,* 585–597.

Thompson, S. C. G., & Barton, M. A. (1994). Ecocentric and anthropocentric attitudes toward the environment. *Journal of Environmental Psychology, 14,* 149–157.

Walsh-Daneshmandi, A., & MacLachlan, M. (2000). Environmental risk to the self: Factor analysis and development of subscales for the environmental appraisal inventory (EAI) with an Irish sample. *Journal of Environmental Psychology, 20,* 141–149.

Weigel, R., & Weigel, J. (1978). Environmental concern: The development of a measure. *Environment and Behavior, 10,* 3–15.

Wiseman, M., & Bogner, F. X. (2003). A higher-order model of ecological values and its relationship to personality. *Personality and Individual Differences, 34,* 783–794.

Yin, J. (1999). Elite opinion and media diffusion: Exploring environmental attitudes. *The Harvard International Journal of Press/Politics, 4,* 62–86.

Suggested Readings

Hawcroft, L. J., & Milfont, T. L. (2010). The use (and abuse) of the new environmental paradigm scale over the last 30 years: A meta-analysis. *Journal of Environmental Psychology, 30,* 143–158.

Van Liere, K. D., & Dunlap, R. E. (1981). Environmental concern: Does it make a difference how it's measured? *Environment and Behavior, 13,* 651–676.

7

Qualitative Approaches to Environment–Behavior Research
Understanding Environmental and Place Experiences, Meanings, and Actions

David Seamon[1] and Harneet K. Gill[2]

[1] *Kansas State University, KS, United States*
[2] *Victoria University of Wellington, New Zealand*

As Annabelle drove to her morning appointment with a real estate developer, she thought about arguments that might convince him to modify a townhouse project to include public access to the river on which it will be built. Because of her interest in solving environmental problems, she has taken an internship with "Save Our Rivers," a non-profit organization that works to protect and restore Canadian streams and rivers in the region around Vancouver. Annabelle is an avid hiker and knows firsthand the emotional and aesthetic pleasure that natural and historically significant places offer.

Three years ago in the town where she grew up, she became involved in a community effort to save eight handsome nineteenth-century buildings that town officials sought to demolish and replace with a huge, nondescript big-box town hall set far back from the town's main street and surrounded by a large parking lot. After a lengthy law suit and a contentious ad hoc campaign to harness supportive public opinion, Annabelle's volunteer "Save the Main Street Buildings" group was able to rescue three of the eight buildings and to convince town officials to accept a modified town-hall design that blended in with the surrounding nineteenth-century architecture and connected directly to the sidewalk and street.

Out of this trying experience, Annabelle came to realize first-hand that different individuals and groups often understand the same environment or place in considerably different ways. This recognition led to her internship efforts to facilitate dialogue and compromise among opposing parties that see the same environmental problem or project differently. One body of research she has found useful for her work is "qualitative approaches," which provide conceptual and applied ways for better understanding people's real-world dealings with places and environments, whether natural or human-made.

Research Methods for Environmental Psychology, First Edition. Edited by Robert Gifford.
© 2016 John Wiley & Sons, Ltd. Published 2016 by John Wiley & Sons, Ltd.

Qualitative research relates to a broad range of conceptual and methodological approaches that examine the lives and situations of real people in real times and places. Qualitative research is *inductive* in that it draws on the richness and complexity of human situations and meanings to generate descriptive generalizations and theories grounded in experience. This openness to human worlds is considerably different, conceptually and methodologically, from quantitative methods, which typically establish a limited number of pre-defined, deductive categories by which the complexity of human life can be reduced to standardized measures and analyzed statistically.

The qualitative researcher is not constrained by pre-determined concepts, data, or measurements. Through examining human experiences, meanings, and events directly, the qualitative researcher works to draw accurate descriptions, discover unnoticed interconnections, and identify practical understandings that might be of human and environmental benefit. The information used by qualitative researchers is primarily (although not exclusively) non-quantitative and may include interview transcripts, field notes, video recordings, reports from focus groups, autobiographical accounts, descriptions from participant observation, and material texts such as drawings, photographs, paintings, films, architecture, imaginative literature, and historical documents.

Having to regularly deal in her "Save Our Rivers" internship with individuals and groups that understand the same environmental situation or problem in different ways, Annabelle is drawn to qualitative approaches because she realizes that they provide a conceptual and practical way to clarify why environmental and place experiences and meanings can vary so widely. This chapter draws on Annabelle's interest in place experience and environmental meaning to describe qualitative research broadly and to suggest how different philosophical starting points lead to different ways of doing empirical research.

Commonalities Among, and Differences Between, Qualitative Approaches

In examining environmental and place studies involving qualitative approaches, Annabelle has come to understand that there are several common features that include: (1) describing people's real-world experiences, places, situations, and meanings; (2) using these descriptions inductively to facilitate a more comprehensive and integrated portrait of those experiences, places, situations, and meanings; (3) drawing on this generalized portrait as a springboard for identifying broader principles and theories; (4) recognizing that, throughout the research process, it is the dedicated enthusiasm, skill, and insight of the researcher (rather than any specific research instruments) that are the primary engine for the relative empathy, accuracy, and comprehensiveness of a qualitative study (Creswell, 2007; Groat & Wang, 2013; van Manen, 2014).

In spite of these similarities among qualitative approaches, Annabelle realizes that there are also important differences, most of which involve contrasting conceptual assumptions and understandings. "Where she begins is where she ends up" may be a cliché, but Annabelle recognizes that it points toward a foundational principle in all research, whether quantitative or qualitative: That the philosophical stance one assumes in relation to the nature of reality and the nature of knowledge largely determines how the researcher conducts research, what he or she considers as legitimate research evidence, and what the nature of the research results turn out to be. Annabelle understands that the conventional scientific approach emphasizing deductive theory and quantitative measurement is only one pathway to understanding. In fact, there are many different ways to examine and understand the same phenomenon and, thus, it becomes important for researchers to familiarize themselves with these contrasting approaches to decide which they feel most comfortable with personally and professionally.

Ontologies and Epistemologies

In studying the various approaches to qualitative research, Annabelle has come to recognize that one important concern is **ontology** – in other words, what she as a researcher assumes the nature of reality to be. For example, is there a single, unitary, true reality for which the researcher can gradually delineate a trustworthy and thorough portrait? Or are there as many realities as there are individuals and groups? If one supposes there are only multiple realities, does this assumption mean that all research results are incomplete and that researchers can only produce partial, tentative, relativist accounts of phenomena?

In turn, Annabelle has come to realize that, as a researcher, she always assumes a particular stance in regard to **epistemology** – what, in other words, does she consider to be legitimate knowledge in research? Are researchable entities only to be known empirically – that is, as material, identifiable things that can be understood and recorded sensuously and thus counted, measured, and correlated quantitatively? Or are researchable entities also knowable as intangible, inner phenomena such as feelings, intuitions, and attitudes; or as intangible inner/outer phenomena like "sense of place," "feeling at home," or "epiphanies with nature"? Should researchers be interested in imprecise, immaterial phenomena like these and, if so, what are legitimate criteria for making sure they accurately locate, describe, and understand these phenomena?

There are also epistemological questions in regard to how knowledge comes into being. Does the world of experience reveal meaning, or is meaning constituted through human language and discourse? In other words, does knowledge appear or is it constructed? What is to be a trustworthy research apparatus for identifying and explicating knowledge? Must knowledge be objective in the sense that it can only be collected through the use of pre-defined theory and concepts operationalized through data-collection devices (e.g., lie detectors, surveys, or structured questionnaires) that guarantee that data collected is empirical, measurable, and therefore equivalent in representativeness, content, and quantity? Or can knowledge be *lived* in the sense that research evidence might include descriptive accounts of the researcher's own experience or narrative accounts provided by respondents through interviews or focus groups. In short, what constitutes reliable research data and evidence?

Three Philosophical Positions

In studying the various conceptual approaches drawn upon in qualitative research, Annabelle has identified three broad philosophical positions that together consolidate many of the differences in regard to ontology and epistemology: (1) *realism*; (2) *critical realism*; and (3) *social constructionism* (Sullivan, 2010, pp. 21–37). **Realism** is associated with conventional scientific-quantitative research and assumes that entities unequivocally pre-exist and give rise to any secondhand representation (whether a mathematical measurement or descriptive account). In assuming a realist position on the world, the researcher works to generate an accurate secondhand representation of reality. Data are the means by which representations can be compared with reality to establish which representations of reality are most correct. Realists assume that researchers can successfully distinguish between entities and representations of those entities, thereby establishing which representations are more accurate and thus more trustworthy.

A philosophical opposite of the realist position is **social constructionism**, which argues that all representations of reality presuppose humanly constructed discourse and are not necessarily an accurate understanding of that reality. Social constructionists contend that, because of diverse values, preferences, beliefs, and world views, researchers cannot establish clear-cut procedures to identify a unitary truth or to evaluate which modes of knowledge are more accurate or "better" than others. The social-constructionist position assumes that the most appropriate means by which to represent and understand the world is discourse and language, which become a main focus of research. If truths are multiple and only exist in the form of varying representations, then the researcher must give these representations direct research attention and recognize their dependence on language and discourse. In the end, there are no immutable facts or solid truths; rather human understanding of the world continually shifts, and all knowledge is thus tentative, partial, and relative.

In an effort to overcome extreme realist and relativist stances, some researchers have sought a middle position identified as **critical realism**. This perspective assumes that phenomena are not completely relativist representations but correspond at least in part to real entities and processes. This assumption means that researchers can gain access, although it may be incomplete, to a reality beyond representation that is at least partly describable in representational fashion. With the social constructionists, critical realists recognize that knowledge is always culturally and historically specific and, thus, research methods and findings can never be completely accurate and truthful because of the ever-present partialities of the values and world views of researchers and research participants.

In addition, language needs to be understood not only as a potentially truthful reflection of reality but also as an impulse for establishing our conceptions of what is real. Knowledge of reality will always be distorted by world views, culture, and societal power, whether social, political, economic, religious, or the like. Critical realists contend, however, that, in spite of these potential distortions, truth claims can be evaluated in terms of real-world evidence, and thus some measure of knowledge and understanding is possible.

Three Conceptual Approaches Used in Qualitative Research

Figure 7.1 summarizes some key ontological and epistemological assumptions of realism, critical realism, and social constructionism. Annabelle is most attracted to critical realism because, on the one hand, it accepts the possibility of underlying, more or less stable structures and patterns in the world yet, on the other hand, recognizes that they will always be incomplete, tentative, and at least partially determined by the individual researcher's personal and professional voice and world view. In practice, contrasting ontological, epistemological, and ideological understandings and starting points have generated a wide range of specific qualitative approaches, a partial list of which is provided in Table 7.1. Annabelle is particularly interested in three of these approaches because they offer a range of ways to think about environmental and place meanings. These three approaches are: (1) *grounded theory*; (2) *phenomenology*; and (3) *discourse analysis*. Here, each approach is described broadly and then illustrated by a research example dealing with a specific place.

Grounded theory

First developed by sociologists Barney Glaser and Anselm Strauss in the late 1960s, **grounded theory** draws on specific real-world experiences and situations as they are

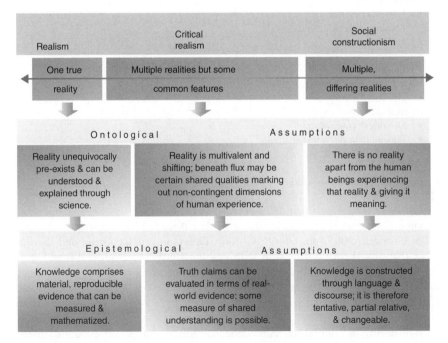

Figure 7.1   Some Key ontological and epistemological assumptions of realism, critical realism, and social constructionism (based partly on Sullivan, 2010, pp. 21–37).

Table 7.1 Qualitative approaches, loosely arranged from more knowledge-oriented to more advocacy-oriented perspectives (based on categorizations from Creswell, 2007; DeLyser et al., 2010; Denzin & Lincoln, 2005; Forrester, 2010; Groat & Wang, 2013; Hay, 2000; Smith, 2008; Wertz et al., 2011).

The range of qualitative approaches

- Pragmatism
- Grounded theory (realist, critical-realist, and social-constructionist modes)
- Symbolic interactionism
- Narrative research
- Conversation analysis
- Phenomenology
  - First-person
  - Third-person
  - Hermeneutic
  - Interpretive phenomenological analysis (IPA)
- Ethnomethodology
- Intuitive inquiry
- Performative research
- Non-representational research
- Affect-based research
- Ethnography and autoethnography (critical-realist and social-constructionist modes)
- Social constructionism
- Critical theory
  - Neo-Marxist theory
  - Feminist theory
  - Cultural theory
  - Critical race theory
  - Queer theory
  - Postcolonial/Subaltern theory
  - Disability theory
- Discourse analysis
  - Discursive psychology
  - Foucauldian discourse analysis
  - Billigian discourse analysis
- Action research
- Advocacy/participation studies

a source for broader theoretical concepts, structures, and frameworks (Charmaz, 2008; Creswell, 2007, pp. 64–68; Gordon-Finlayson, 2010). Grounded theorists argue that any theory must begin with empirical evidence from real-world situations. Thus, the aim is to draw on narrative accounts from research participants to generate a general explanation of some experience, event, or activity. Grounded theory is useful in research situations where no theory is available for explicating the topic of concern.

In reviewing the literature, Annabelle has found that some grounded-theory researchers assume a critical-realist position and contend that the relative "structuredness" of human life can lead to a fair amount of theoretical order (Strauss & Corbin, 1998). In contrast, other researchers have reinterpreted grounded theory through a social-constructionist perspective and emphasize the lived "messiness" of human life and theoretical concepts and structures that are multivalent and tentative (Charmaz, 2008). Although some grounded theorists (e.g., Charmaz, 2008) have laid out detailed steps and stages in doing research, Creswell (2007, p. 64) summarizes the method as a "zigzag" process in which the researcher gathers data in field work, analyzes the data, returns to the field for additional data to clarify uncertainties that arose in analysis, uses that new data for more analysis, and so forth, until he or she has generated a clear conceptual understanding of the topic of study. One important methodological technique in grounded theory is **theoretical sampling**, by which additional study participants are progressively selected to further examine patterns and themes pointed to in the data already analyzed. This incremental addition of research participants continues to a point of **theoretical saturation**, a stage where the researcher feels confident that he or she has gathered sufficient information from an adequate number of research participants to justify finalized concepts and theoretical structures (Gordon-Finlayson, 2010, pp. 156–157).

An example of grounded-theory research: Heat wave in Chicago   One example of grounded-theory research relevant to environmental and place concerns is sociologist Eric Klinenberg's *Heat Wave*, a book-length study of why some 700 Chicago residents, most of them elderly or poor, died in a five-day heat wave in 1995 (Klinenberg, 2002). Annabelle particularly appreciates the book's third chapter, in which Klinenberg explored how environmental and human features of two contrasting Chicago neighborhoods – North Lawndale and South Lawndale – "imperiled or protected residents during the extreme summer climate" (Klinenberg, 2002, p. 85). Klinenberg selected these two residential neighborhoods because, even though they are adjacent to one another, they had dramatically different heat-wave mortality rates. Klinenberg worked to understand this difference through intensive field work and in-depth interviews with local residents, public officials, and media representatives.

Through a "zigzag" process in which he moved back and forth between field data and analytic efforts to make sense of that data conceptually, Klinenberg came to realize that contrasting place characteristics and practices were a key to understanding the contrasting mortality rates. Neighborhood differences included "the ways in which residents use sidewalks and public spaces, the role of commercial outlets in stimulating social contact, the strategies through which residents protect themselves from local dangers, and the role of community organizations and institutions in providing social protection" (Klinenberg, 2002, p. 86). Significantly, Klinenberg knew of few of these factors when he first began his research and only gradually identified them as he exposed himself to the people, activities, and situations of the two Chicago neighborhoods.

In "zigzag" fashion, he analyzed what he saw, returned to the two neighborhoods for further evidence, and so forth, until he had a clear understanding that North Lawndale had many more deaths than South Lawndale because the latter was a place of lively streets, much commercial activity, residential concentration, and a relatively low crime rate that promoted a sense of community especially important to older people, who are more likely to leave home when nearby amenities are available.

In contrast, North Lawndale was a neighborhood of violent crime, devolving commerce, abandoned buildings, empty streets, and lower density, all of which undermined the viability of public life, setting the stage for fearful older people who rarely left their dwellings. During the heat wave, these dramatically contrasting place situations undermined or sustained "the possibilities for social contact that helped vulnerable Chicagoans survive" (Klinenberg, 2002, p. 91).

In his introduction, Klinenberg explained that his research involved some six months of almost daily neighborhood observations and more than 40 formal and informal interviews with residents, merchants, civic officials, and others (Klinenberg, 2002, p. 34). Ultimately, however, Klinenberg's aim was not simply an ideographic place ethnography of the two neighborhoods but a broad, multi-dimensioned understanding of how and why the heat wave caused so many deaths. Klinenberg accomplished this larger aim by gathering as much information as possible about heat-wave victims. He conducted interviews with friends, neighbors, and family members of decedents; visited apartment houses and transient hotels where people had died; examined death certificates, police reports, and public health records; read news articles; watched television news casts of the event, and so forth. Ultimately, Klinenberg concluded that the many heat-wave deaths were the result of "extreme forms of vulnerability, isolation, and deprivation" (Klinenberg, 2002, p. 36). Annabelle admires this study because it demonstrates quite powerfully how the grounded-theory method of an extended, intensive, back-and-forth dialogue between data and analysis can lead to valuable theoretical and practical understandings.

Phenomenology

Another approach to qualitative research is **phenomenology**, which Annabelle has come to appreciate because of its effort to describe human experiences, situations, and meanings as thoroughly and as accurately as possible. A major aim of phenomenology is to identify and understand broader, underlying patterns – for example, the lived importance of place – that give order and coherence to the richness and "chaos" of human experience as it is lived in everyday life.

Although she has learned that, like grounded theory, phenomenology incorporates different conceptual styles and methodological approaches (Giorgi & Giorgi, 2008; Smith, 2008; Willig, 2001), she has become most interested in **existential phenomenology**, a way of knowing that seeks to describe the underlying, essential qualities of human experience and the world in which that experience happens (Finlay, 2011; Seamon, 2000, 2013, forthcoming; van Manen, 2014). The research focus is on **phenomena**, things or experiences as human beings experience those things or experiences, for example, the experience of place, environmental embodiment, at-homeness, out-of-placeness, or heightened encounter with nature.

Phenomenological approaches include: (1) **first-person phenomenological research**, in which the researcher uses his or her own firsthand experience of the phenomenon as a basis for examining its specific characteristics and qualities (e.g., Toombs, 2001); and (2) **third-person phenomenological research**, which explores phenomena through descriptions of experiences and situations garnered by interviews, questionnaires, and other texts from third-person parties (e.g., Finlay, 2011;

Giorgi & Giorgi 2008). Annabelle notes that phenomenological researchers often highlight three procedural steps when analyzing descriptive accounts phenomenologically: First, identifying the phenomenon in which the phenomenologist is interested; second, gathering descriptive accounts of the phenomenon; and, third, carefully studying these accounts with the aim of identifying any underlying commonalities and patterns (Finlay, 2011, pp. 125–138; Seamon, 2000, p. 166).

Annabelle recognizes that phenomenology and grounded theory are similar in that they both work inductively with experiential evidence to draw broader generalizations, but she also realizes that there are substantial conceptual and methodological differences, particularly in the way that phenomenological work is typically more interested in understanding broad experiential qualities and structures (e.g., concepts like "being-in-the-world," "lifeworld," "lived body," and "place") that arise from but conceptually move beyond specific, grounded experiences and situations and therefore speak to the human situation more broadly (Finlay, 2011).

In contrast, grounded theorists remain much closer to the real-world experiences and events that have generated their data. Any resulting theory remains "grounded" in those specific situations. In his heat-wave study, for example, Klinenberg largely limits his focus to the two Chicago neighborhoods and the underlying reasons for the many heat-related deaths; he is not concerned with the phenomenological question of how his two Chicago neighborhoods point to broader phenomena such as place, displacement, out-of-placeness, environmental embodiment, and so forth.

An example of phenomenological research: An African-American neighborhood   One example of phenomenological work relevant to environmental and place concerns is psychologist Eva-Maria Simms's study of children's lived spaces in Pittsburgh's African-American Hill District (Simms, 2008). Making use of in-depth interviews and participants' map drawings, Simms asked 12 adults (24 to 84 years old) to remember important neighborhood experiences, activities, and events that transpired when the adult was around 10 years old. Methodologically, Simms adapted a procedure she called "narrative mapping," which involved a combination of drawings and in-depth, open-ended, biographical interviews (Simms, 2008, pp. 75–76).

Participants were asked to describe, in words and pictures, their remembered "childhood roaming space." They were encouraged to draw a rough map of the neighborhood and then to talk about places and situations highlighted cartographically. At the start, the interviewer asked only clarifying questions but, as discussion continued, inquired into "play places, paths taken by children, the way to school, the presence of adults and other children, communal activities, and finally the participants' sense of how the neighborhood had changed since their childhood" (Simms, 2008, p. 76).

Simms analyzed the interviews by identifying specific localized activities and comparing them across interviews. She interpreted the place descriptions at two levels: first, separately, by generation; second, as a way to understand underlying lived qualities and processes that have led to the Hill District's shifting sense of place. In regard to the first theme, she determined that participant descriptions pointed to three distinct periods in the Hill's history: first, 1930–1960, a time when the Hill had a strong sense of community; second, 1960–1980, a time when much of the original neighborhood was replaced by barrack-style public housing and the Hill's sense of community began to disintegrate economically and socially; and, third, 1980–2004, a time when the Hill became much more unsettled socially and less safe for children as extended families faced deep economic and social stress.

Simms then used these contrasting neighborhood experiences as a way to identify broad lived changes in the Hill District's sense of place and community. For example, the first generation remembered a powerful situatedness that sustained a sense of identity and belonging, whereas the two later generations more often spoke about their neighborhood in terms of displacement, with families moving frequently, the use and sale of drugs increasing, and "turf war" among gangs becoming a major threat to everyday life and a stable sense of community and place.

Most broadly, Simms's thematic interpretation indicated that childhood places were marked by political and social changes: each generation of 10 year olds lived in the same neighborhood but experienced life there in dramatically contrasting ways. Annabelle appreciates Simms's study because it used remembered experiences of an actual neighborhood to draw helpful generalizations as to why places are important in human life and how social, economic, and societal changes can undermine a vibrant urban neighborhood (which is what the Hill District originally was, according to the oldest participants' accounts). In addition, Simms indicated the broader significance of her work by pointing to practical implications for environmental design and policy – for example, bringing forward the question of how one might design buildings and other environmental elements that encourage neighborly exchange and allow for child-friendly public spaces (Simms, 2008, pp. 87–88).

Discourse analysis

A third methodological approach that interests Annabelle is **discourse analysis**, which, in accepting a social-constructionist perspective, argues that language does not passively reflect the facts of the world but, instead, produces an active construction of a specific version of reality (Sullivan, 2010; Wiggins & Riley, 2010). Discourse, in this sense, refers to any sort of talking or text, including bodily gestures, voice inflections, visual signs, artistic works, written documents, digital media, and so forth. Discourse is considered to be formative and thus the world can be interpreted in an unlimited number of ways constructed through language.

Whereas many grounded theorists and most phenomenologists typically assume that language is a transparent medium through which "reality" is accurately expressed, researchers involved in discourse analysis argue that language and discourse do not neutrally describe the world but formulate it actively. This claim means that there are multiple realities and thus multiple ways, rather than one correct way, of understanding. One can ask why individuals or groups make use of one version of reality rather than another and what the consequences of using one version rather than another mean psychologically, socially, and politically.

As with grounded theory and phenomenology, there are several different approaches to discourse analysis (Wiggins & Riley, 2010). Annabelle is particularly interested in **Foucauldian discourse analysis**, named after the French political philosopher Michel Foucault. This mode of discourse analysis focuses largely on discourse and texts as they shape the reality of social life. A central research concern is societal power relationships as expressed through language (Scheurich & Bell McKenzie, 2005; Willig, 2001). One begins with a **discursive object**, a thing or event as interpreted by various discourses, which are often different and thus in competition or conflict. For example, Annabelle is interested in how people living in the same place talk about that place, and what these various place discourses mean in terms of who decides through what power relationships what happens to that place politically and economically. The researcher would interview a range of individuals who play major roles in shaping the place and also study situations and events where major decisions regarding the place are rendered (e.g., town council meetings, statements and actions by advocacy groups, newspaper accounts, and so forth).

These various accounts would be analyzed to identify how and why the discursive object is understood in different ways by different power players. The aim is to identify the range of discursive constructions, including associated narratives, metaphors, and attitudes. Next, the researcher looks for differences among the contrasting discourses with the aim of clarifying how they reflect and sustain various **subject positions**, the taken-for-granted positions of power and aims that individuals and groups associated with the discourses take up in terms of themselves and others whom they support or oppose.

An example of research in discourse analysis: A contested public space in Barcelona Annabelle recognizes that the specific methods and stages of discourse analysis depend considerably on the nature of the discursive object. One study that she feels illustrates well the value of discourse analysis for place research was conducted by Andrés Di Masso, John Dixon, and Enric Pol (2011). These three psychologists examined a contested public space in Barcelona, Spain, known either as the "Hole of Shame" or "Figuera's Well," depending on two different, competing interpretations: on the one hand, that of local residents who illegally occupied the site; or, on the other hand, that of corporate businesspeople and governmental officials who sought to transform the dilapidated, working-class neighborhood into a district of gentrified housing and high-end shops and eateries that would appeal to tourists (Di Masso et al., 2011).

To examine the two groups' conflicting discursive understandings and actions in regard to this public space, Di Masso et al. conducted a discursive analysis of two "texts": first, 186 media reports that included two widely read city newspapers as well as alternative publications produced by the various advocacy groups sympathetic to the occupation of the public space; and, second, 16 interviews conducted with the various parties involved in the conflict, including members of five groups defending the occupation; members of four neighborhood groups against the occupation; a public-relations spokesperson representing the private realty company that would redevelop the space; two district councilors elected from the neighborhood; and two urban planners.

Interviews consisted of open-ended questions, beginning with broad queries about the current state of the open space and then moving to more specific questions regarding users, uses, management, and future of the space. Interviews were transcribed and then analyzed to identify "broad strategies of argumentation" (Di Masso et al., 2011, p. 236). The aim was not only to delineate attitudinal commonalities and differences among the various parties contesting the open space but also to show

"how, when, and to what effect, such views are expressly designed to undermine plausible alternatives" (Di Masso et al., 2011, p. 233).

Methodologically, this analysis involved several stages. First, the researchers studied the media reports and interview transcripts to identify recurring arguments the various parties used to justify their claims and plans in regard to the open space. Second, the researchers examined how each account was organized to counter contrary claims and to engage with wider ideological controversies in Barcelona regarding the development of other urban open spaces. Last, the researchers analyzed how the accounts worked to either support or to undermine particular forms of political action.

As the analysis proceeded, the researchers were able to locate three types of discursive arguments: Those relating to: (1) the identity of the contested open space; (2) the categories of people who use or have the right to use the space; and (3) various oppositional meanings of the space – for example, the space as it was said to be accessible to everyone vs. the space as it was said to be accessible to only particular groups; or the space as understood as public good vs. the space as understood as a profit-generating commodity.

Having encountered a similar controversial situation in her personal struggle to save the eight old buildings in her hometown, Annabelle appreciates this study because it clarified the role of social and political power and conflict in establishing and shifting place meanings and values. Di Masso et al. demonstrated that place making is at least partly discursive in that the power structure of a place contributes to facilitating and normalizing a particular version of that place while dismissing other versions.

In the case of the Barcelona's open space, the researchers determined that social and political conflict "reflects underlying dynamics of political inequality, which are expressed, for example, through struggles to impose and resist normative definitions of who belongs in a given place and what activities are deemed appropriate and acceptable there" (Di Masso et al., 2011, p. 242). Although Annabelle's hometown struggle to save the nineteenth-century buildings involved a considerably different cultural and political context, she recognizes that many of the discursive arguments and justifications for the Barcelona space have thematic parallels with her hometown experience and with her more recent internship experiences with "Save Our Rivers."

Interviewing as a Qualitative Method

As the list in Table 7.2 illustrates, there is a wide range of specific research methods used in qualitative research relating to environmental and place concerns. The considerable methodological range of this list reflects the complex, multi-faceted nature of human beings' interactions with environments and places. On one hand, some of these methods – for example, interpretations of actual landscapes or artistic media portraying landscapes – focus the researcher's attention more on physical features of the environment or place itself. On the other hand, other methods – for example, the observation of user behaviors – bring attention to environmental and place actions and events. Yet again, methods like surveys and

Table 7.2 Some major methods used by qualitative researchers (drawn from Creswell, 2007; Denzin & Lincoln, 2005; Hay, 2000; Groat & Wang, 2013; Sommer & Sommer, 2002; Zeisel, 2006).

Some major qualitative methods

Methods to elicit information from individuals and groups:
- Surveys and questionnaires
  - Structured
  - Semi-structured
  - Open-ended
- In-depth interviews
  - Structured
  - Semi-structured
  - Unstructured
  - Group interviews
- Focus groups
- Case studies
- Cooperative inquiry
- Biography
  - Autobiography
  - Oral history
  - Life history

Methods to observe people and place:
- Place and environmental observation
  - Impressionist descriptions, whether verbal or graphic
  - Pure objective descriptions, whether verbal, graphic, or numerical
  - Counting users
  - Mapping users
  - Recording user movements
  - Filming and time-lapse photography
  - Observing physical traces
- Participant observation
  - Observer-as-participant
  - Participant-as-observer
  - Complete participation
- Ethnography (realist, phenomenological, and social-constructionist modes)
- Case studies
- Photography, drawing, and mapping

Methods to analyze and interpret texts:
- Content analysis
- Conversational analysis
- Reading places, landscapes, and buildings as texts (includes semiotic, post-structural, deconstructionist, and hermeneutic modes)
- Hermeneutics of landscapes, places, and artifactual texts (buildings, art works, tools, decorative objects, etc.)
- Interpreting artistic media (paintings, drawings, film, imaginative literature, etc.)
- Interpreting historical documents (archival research)
- Arts-based inquiry
- Interpreting media (newspapers, television newscasts, internet news sites, etc.)

---

interviews provide a research vehicle for eliciting information from individuals and groups who use or are otherwise associated with a place or environment (for discussion of these research methods, see Groat & Wang, 2013; Hay, 2000; Sommer & Sommer, 2002; Zeisel, 2006).

Because interviewing is one of the most commonly used methods in qualitative studies, it is overviewed here. Annabelle appreciates interviewing as a research method because it involves a direct interaction between researcher and participant, whether face to face or at a distance (e.g., via telephone or video conference). This immediacy provides the researcher with a window into the research participant's life and experiences. In qualitative research, this information can be primary data for analysis or a means to corroborate participants' understandings with other data sources (McDowell, 2010). Dunn (2000, p. 52) identified four main reasons for using interviews: (1) to collect information that other research methods (e.g., observations of a place) cannot provide; (2) to examine complex motivations, situations, and behaviors; (3) to gather a diversity of experiences and perspectives; and (4) to offer a method that "shows respect for and empowers those people who provide the data."

The information generated through interviewing is most often qualitative and includes descriptions relating to experiences, meanings, events, and situations from the perspective of the interviewee (Hermanns, 2010). Perhaps the most significant value of interviews is their potential for generating data relating to context and meaning (Seidman, 2006, p. 10). Observational research provides information about behaviors but does not generate insight into associated meanings often necessary to understand human–environment interactions. As a complementary method, interviewing can provide contextual information relating to environmental behaviors and interactions, including why they occur in the manner they do and how people understand them (Seidman, 2006, p. 10.).

Structured, semi-structured, and unstructured interviews

Interviews range from fully structured and non-interactive to open-ended and generated through give-and-take between interviewer and interviewee. **Structured interviews** are similar to questionnaires and consist of predetermined questions that are used as a script from which there is little deviation (Willig, 2001). Structured interviews are useful for collecting standardized information that can be corroborated and compared. They can provide useful information about context, but they restrict the researcher's ability to probe more deeply or elicit unexpected responses.

In contrast, semi-structured and unstructured interviews emphasize *in-depth discussion* of the topic under study and offer more flexibility in the direction and outcomes of questions (Willig, 2001, p. 24). In **semi-structured interviews**, the interviewer devises beforehand a general plan, which might incorporate several open-ended questions. In contrast, an **unstructured interview** is guided primarily by the unfolding discussion between interviewee and interviewer. Although the researcher identifies some broad aims of the interview, he or she provides minimal direction so that the interviewee's comments are as spontaneous and free-ranging as possible.

Whether semi-structured or unstructured, an interview is a joint production of knowledge because the resulting data depends not only on the participant's responses but also on the interviewer's queries and prompts (Willig, 2001, p. 25). What and how the interviewer chooses to probe largely determines the interview outcome (Hugh-Jones, 2010, p. 83). Because it involves a good amount of unplanned spontaneity, an in-depth interview can never be replicated exactly, even with the same interviewer and interviewee.

Group interviews and focus groups

Group interviews elicit data from multiple participants through group discussion (Hesse-Biber & Leavy, 2010, p. 166). Group interviews include two or more participants, although the ideal number is said to be between three and eight. Too few participants may hinder a free-flowing discussion, whereas too many participants may inhibit some group members from speaking. Because discussion requires more time in a group context, the design of a group interview should be kept simple, with only a few questions or topics for discussion. Group interviews can work in several different ways: (1) as an exploratory tool before more focused research begins; (2) as a way to evaluate ideas and interpretations; (3) as a means to provide a safe space for individuals who feel stigmatized or marginalized in some way (Hesse-Biber & Leavy, 2010, pp. 165).

One variation on group interviews is the **focus group**, which involves a small gathering of interested individuals who discuss a theme or topic identified by the researcher, who acts as moderator (Cameron, 2000, p. 84). This method can be a useful source of data and provides a means to shift the balance of power away from the researcher toward the participants and thus allow for constructive, supportive encounters (Seamon, 1979). As Cameron (2000, p. 84) explains, focus groups are "generally characterized by dynamism and energy as people respond to the contributions of others." In this sense, participants have more authority and control over how their comments are expressed, compared, and considered (Hesse-Biber & Leavy, 2010, p. 167).

Validity and Qualitative Research

A major concern that all qualitative research must address is **validity**, the trustworthiness of the particular qualitative interpretation. Annabelle has come to realize that, in qualitative research, validity most broadly relates to **interpretive appropriateness**, the degree to which there is a reasoned, well-demonstrated fit between real-world data, its summary description, and any conceptual interpretation (Seamon, 2000, pp. 169–170). Annabelle feels that the three studies highlighted above successfully illustrate interpretive appropriateness because each depicts real-world situations convincingly and provides perceptive theoretical formulations, although from contrasting conceptual perspectives.

In her study of qualitative approaches, Annabelle has discovered that some researchers have worked to pinpoint specific criteria for evaluating the relative validity of qualitative studies (Creswell, 2007; Willig, 2001; Yardley, 2008). In an effort to synthesize these various perspectives, Annabelle has found the following criteria useful:

- *Demonstrating sensitivity and empathy*, whereby the study illustrates convincingly that its descriptive and conceptual patterns, structures, and meanings have accurately emerged from the real world and are not cerebrally contrived or arbitrarily imposed (Yardley, 2008, pp. 246–247). The study offers satisfying evidence that it is grounded in penetrating, extended observation and engagement with the study site, with the research participants, with the sources of data, and with the ongoing process of interpreting that data.
- *Making use of triangulation*, whereby the researcher draws on multiple data sources, methods, evaluators, and conceptual approaches as a means to identify different lived perspectives and to corroborate evidence from different data sources (Creswell, 2007, p. 208; Yardley 2008, pp. 239–240). Examples of triangulation include: drawing on a combination of interviews, field observations, historical documents, and other sources to understand a particular place or environmental experience; identifying contrasting experiences of different user groups to gather a more comprehensive understanding of a situation or place; having different reviewers analyze and interpret the same data.
- *Incorporating negative case analysis*, whereby the researcher shifts and refines his or her interpretations and conceptual understandings as unexpected or contradictory evidence comes to light (Creswell, 2007, p. 208; Willig, 2001, p. 142). The researcher progressively revises his or her theoretical account of the situation until all or most of the data have a fitting place in any wider generalizations.
- *Striving for coherence*, whereby the researcher works to provide analyses and interpretations that are effectively shaped and ordered, whether through a story line, interrelated aspects of the phenomenon, or coherent conceptual structure. The aim is for the study to comprise an integrated whole in which the descriptive and conceptual parts all have a place that "makes sense" (Willig, 2001, p. 142; Yardley, 2008, pp. 248–249).

In thinking about the three qualitative studies highlighted above, Annabelle realizes that they do not accommodate all of these criteria for validity. She believes, however, that this lack is not intentional oversight but points to the complex nature of qualitative research and the recognition that each particular study has its own unique set of subject matter, methods, and modes of evidence and proof. Whereas in quantitative studies, the researcher has available a wide range of theoretical and methodological devices to demonstrate and verify measurement, equivalence, and relationship, the qualitative researcher must depend on his or her personal integrity, dedication, persistence, and creativity as the major grounding and engine for accurate, persuasive research. On one hand, the potential weakness of qualitative research is shallow, contrived, inaccurate interpretations that misinterpret the real-world individuals and situations that the research claims to represent. On the other hand, the potential strength of qualitative research is its facilitating creative, heartfelt, persuasive interpretations in tune with real-world sources and perhaps helping those sources to understand themselves better and to improve their lot.

Summary and Conclusions

Qualitative researchers generate descriptions, generalizations, concepts, and theories grounded in real-world experiences, behaviors, and meanings. Qualitative research methods include interviews, careful observation and description, participant observation, thoughtful interpretation of texts, and other research vehicles that allow the researcher to empathize with the phenomenon and understand it in a fair, comprehensive way. Throughout the research process, the researcher works to stay attuned to the phenomenon studied. He or she continuously confirms that any broader claims arise from and are in accurate contact with the phenomenon. Though there are many different conceptual approaches to qualitative research, an important methodological commonality is allowing concepts, patterns, and meanings to emerge in their own manner and connectedness. In this sense, qualitative approaches allow the researcher to locate unexpected possibilities and to generate fresh understandings.

In qualitative research, the researcher is the research instrument. Accuracy, thoroughness, and validity hinge on the researcher's skill, resourcefulness, sensitivity, and devotion to the phenomenon. Qualitative research places difficult responsibilities and demands on its practitioners, but its successful accomplishment offers much personal and professional satisfaction as well as innovative perspectives on human experience, meaning, and life.

Glossary

Critical realism   A philosophical perspective that assumes reality corresponds at least in part to real entities and processes; in spite of potential distortions, truth claims can be evaluated in terms of real-world evidence, and thus some measure of understanding is possible. See **realism** and **social constructionism**.

Discourse analysis   A research tradition that assumes language produces an active construction of a specific version of reality; language and all forms of discourse (spoken, written, artistic, or digital) are understood as a form of social practice that shapes and is shaped by human society and culture.

Discursive object   In discourse analysis, the thing or event as interpreted by various discourses, which are often different and thus in competition or conflict; the meaning of these objects is said to be constructed through language and, thus, their significance can vary from individual to individual and from group to group. See **discourse analysis**.

Epistemology   The study of the nature of knowledge; what is it to know and what research evidence constitutes reliable knowledge? *See* **ontology**.

Existential phenomenology   One tradition in phenomenological research that grounds description and interpretation in the *lifeworld* – the tacit unfolding and tenor of daily life to which normally people give no reflective attention; the research aim is to make the lifeworld an object of scholarly attention and thereby locate and describe underlying experiential patterns and structures.

First-person phenomenological research   A mode of phenomenological inquiry in which the researcher uses his or her own firsthand experience as a basis for examining its specific characteristics and qualities. See **third-person phenomeno-logical research**.

Focus group   A research method that uses a small group of interested individuals who discuss a theme or topic identified by the researcher, who acts as moderator; the method provides a means to shift the balance of power away from the researcher toward the participants and thus allows for constructive, supportive encounters.

Foucauldian discourse analysis   Arising from the work of French political philos-opher Michel Foucault (1926–1984) and a mode of discourse analysis that emphasizes societal power relationships as expressed through language; a key focus is how social and political power are expressed and actualized in talk and text. See **discourse analysis**.

Grounded theory   A research tradition that draws on specific real-world experi-ences and situations as they are a source for broader theoretical concepts, struc-tures, and frameworks; assumes that any theory must be grounded in life and, thus, the aim is to draw on narrative accounts from study participants to generate a general explanation of some experience, event, or activity.

Group interviews   Interviews that elicit data from multiple participants through group discussion; assumes that discussion among a group of individuals from the same social world may provide more comprehensive information than interview-ing those individuals separately.

Interpretive appropriateness   The degree to which a qualitative study provides a reasoned, well-demonstrated fit between conceptual claims and real-world situa-tions and events. Does the research provide an accurate correspondence between experience and language and between what we know as individuals in our own lives versus how that knowledge is placed interpretively and theoretically?

Ontology   The study of the nature of reality and of being. Is there a single, unitary true reality that the researcher can fully identify and represent, or are there as many realities as there are individuals and groups in the world? See **epistemology**.

Phenomenology   A research tradition that describes and interprets human experi-ence and consciousness; the phenomenologist examines human actions, meanings, situations, and events with the research aim of locating and clarifying broader expe-riential patterns and structures – for example, the significance of place in human life.

Phenomena   The central focus of phenomenological research and referring to things or experiences as human beings experience those things or experiences – for example, the experience of home and at-homeness; or the experience of heightened encounter with nature.

Qualitative research   The broad range of conceptual and methodological approaches that examine the lives and situations of real people in real times and places; incorporates an *inductive* method in that these approaches draw on the richness and complexity of human situations and meanings to generate descriptive generalizations and theories grounded in human experience.

Realism   A philosophical perspective that assumes reality unequivocally pre-exists and can be understood through science; the world examined by science is the real world, independent of what we might take it to be otherwise. See **critical realism** and **social constructionism**.

Semi-structured interviews   Interviews in which the interviewer devises before-hand a general plan, which might incorporate several open-ended questions; the direction of questioning is established broadly, and at least a few questions allow for some degree of free-ranging response. See **structured** and **unstructured interviews**.

Social constructionism   The philosophical perspective that assumes all representations of reality presuppose humanly constructed discourse and are not necessarily accurate portrayals of that reality. Knowledge is constructed through language and discourse; it is therefore tentative, partial, and relative; there are no unitary truths or knowledge systems. See **critical realism** and **realism**.

Structured interviews   Interviews using pre-determined questions as a script from which there is little deviation; helpful for collecting standardized information that can be corroborated and compared. See **semi-structured** and **unstructured interviews**.

Subject positions   In discourse analysis, the taken-for-granted positions of power and aims that individuals and groups take up in terms of themselves and others whom they support or oppose. See **discourse analysis**.

Theoretical sampling   A methodological technique in grounded theory by which additional study participants are progressively selected to further examine patterns and themes pointed to in data already analyzed; guided by and helps to guarantee the "theoretical sensitivity" central to grounded theory and other qualitative approaches. See **grounded theory** and **theoretical saturation**.

Theoretical saturation   A research stage in grounded theory when the researcher feels confident that he or she has gathered sufficient information from an adequate number of research participants to justify finalized conceptual concepts and theoretical structures. See **grounded theory** and **theoretical sampling**.

Third-person phenomenological research   A mode of phenomenological research in which the basis for generalization is the specific experiences of individuals and groups involved in actual situations and places; descriptions are garnered through interviews, focus groups, and other texts elicited from users or others associated with the situation or place.

Unstructured interviews   Interviews guided primarily by the unfolding dialogue between interviewer and interviewee; interviewer provides minimal direction so that the interviewee's comments can be as spontaneous and free-ranging as possible. See **structured** and **semi-structured interviews**.

Validity   A term referring to the reliability and trustworthiness of a particular research approach or method; for quantitative research, validity is grounded in clearly definable variables measured and correlated mathematically; for qualitative research, validity is much more difficult to establish and is typically grounded in convincing and comprehensive description and interpretation. See **interpretive appropriateness**.

References

Cameron, J. (2000). Focussing on the focus group. In I. Hay (Ed.), *Qualitative research methods in human geography* (pp. 83–102). Oxford, UK: Oxford University Press.

Charmaz, K. (2008). Grounded theory. In J. A. Smith (Ed.), *Qualitative psychology* (pp. 80–120). Thousand Oaks, CA: Sage.

Creswell, J. W. (2007). *Qualitative inquiry & research design*. Thousand Oaks, CA: Sage.

DeLyser, D., Herbert, S., Aitken, S., Crang, M., & McDowell, L. (Eds.). (2010). *The Sage handbook of qualitative geography*. Thousand Oaks, CA: Sage.

Denzin, N. K., & Lincoln, Y. S. (Eds.). (2005). *The Sage handbook of qualitative research* (3rd ed.). Thousand Oaks, CA: Sage.

Di Masso, A., Dixon, J., & Pol, E. (2011). On the contested nature of place: "Figuera's Well," "The Hole of Shame" and the ideological struggle over public space in Barcelona. *Journal of Environmental Psychology, 31*, 231–244.

Dunn, K. (2000). Interviewing. In I. Hay (Ed.), *Qualitative research methods in human geography* (pp. 50–82). Oxford, UK: Oxford University Press.

Finlay, L. (2011). *Phenomenology for therapists*. London, UK: Wiley-Blackwell.

Forrester, M. (Ed.). (2010). *Doing qualitative research in psychology*. Thousand Oaks, CA: Sage.

Giorgi, A., & Giorgi, B. (2008). Phenomenology. In J. A. Smith (Ed.), *Qualitative psychology* (pp. 26–80). Thousand Oaks, CA: Sage.

Gordon-Finlayson, A. (2010). Grounded theory. In M. Forrester (Ed.), *Doing qualitative research in psychology* (pp. 154–176). Thousand Oaks, CA: Sage.

Groat, L. N., & Wang, D. (2013). *Architectural research methods* (2nd ed.). New York, NY: Wiley.

Hay, I. (Ed.). (2000). *Qualitative research methods in human geography*. Oxford, UK: Oxford University Press.

Hermanns, H. (2010). Interviewing as an activity. In U. Flick, E. Von Kardorff, & I. Steinke (Eds.), *A companion to qualitative research* (pp. 209–213). Thousand Oaks, CA: Sage.

Hesse-Biber, S. N., & Leavy, P. (2010). Focus group interviews. In S. N. Hesse-Biber & P. Leavy (Eds.), *The practice of qualitative research* (2nd ed., pp. 163–175). Thousand Oaks, CA: Sage.

Hugh-Jones, S. (2010). The interview in qualitative research. In M. Forrester (Ed.), *Doing qualitative research in psychology* (pp. 77–97). Thousand Oaks, CA: Sage.

Klinenberg, E. (2002). *Heat wave: A social autopsy of disaster in Chicago*. Chicago, IL: University of Chicago Press.

McDowell, L. (2010). Interviewing. In D. DeLyser, S. Herbert, S. Aitken, M. Crang, & L. McDowell (Eds.), *The Sage handbook of qualitative geography* (pp. 156–171). Thousand Oaks, CA: Sage.

Scheurich, J. J., & Bell McKenzie, K. (2005). Foucault's methodologies. In N. K. Denzin & Y. S. Lincoln (Eds.), *The Sage handbook of qualitative research* (3rd ed., pp. 841–868). Thousand Oaks, CA: Sage.

Seamon, D. (1979). *A geography of the lifeworld*. New York, NY: St. Martin's.

Seamon, D. (2000). Phenomenology in environment-behavior research. In S. Wapner, J. Demick, T. Yamamoto, & H. Minami (Eds.), *Theoretical perspectives in environment-behavior research* (pp. 157–178). New York, NY: Plenum.

Seamon, D. (2013). Lived bodies, place, and phenomenology: Implications for human rights and environmental justice, *Journal of Human Rights and the Environment, 4* (2), 143–166.

Seamon, D. (forthcoming). A phenomenological and hermeneutic reading of Rem Koolhaas's Seattle Central Library: Buildings as lifeworlds and architectural texts. In R. Dalton & C. Hölscher (Eds.), *Take one building: Interdisciplinary research perspectives on the Seattle Central Library*. Farnham, UK: Ashgate.

Seidman, I. (2006). *Interviewing as qualitative research*. New York, NY: Teachers College Press.

Simms, E.-M. (2008). Children's lived spaces in the inner city. *Humanistic Psychologist, 36*, 72–89.

Smith, J. A. (Ed.). (2008). *Qualitative psychology* (2nd ed.). Thousand Oaks, CA: Sage.

Sommer, R., & Sommer, B. (2002). *A practical guide to behavioral research* (5th ed.). New York, NY: Oxford University Press.

Strauss, A. L., & Corbin, J. M. (1998). *Basics of qualitative research* (2nd ed.). Los Angeles, CA: Sage.

Sullivan, C. (2010). Theory and method in qualitative research. In M. Forrester (Ed.), *Doing qualitative research in psychology* (pp. 15–38). Los Angeles, CA: Sage.

Toombs, S. K. (2001). Reflections on bodily change. In S. K. Toombs (Ed.), *Handbook of phenomenology and illness* (pp. 247–262). Dordrecht, Netherlands: Kluwer.

van Manen, M. (2014). *The phenomenology of practice*. Walnut Creek, CA: Left Coast Press.

Wertz, F. J., Charmaz, K., McMullen, L. M., Josselson, R., McSpadden, E., & Anderson, R. (2011). *Five ways of doing qualitative analysis*. New York, NY: Guilford.

Wiggins, S., & Riley, S. (2010). Discourse analysis. In M. Forrester (Ed.), *Doing qualitative research in psychology* (pp. 135–153). Thousand Oaks, CA: Sage.

Willig, C. (2001). *Introducing qualitative research in psychology*. Philadelphia, PA: Open University Press.

Yardley, L. (2008). Demonstrating validity in qualitative psychology. In J. A. Smith (Ed.), *Qualitative psychology* (2nd ed., pp. 235–251). Thousand Oaks, CA: Sage.

Zeisel, J. (2006). *Inquiry by design* (Rev. ed.). New York, NY: Norton.

Suggested Readings

Creswell, J. W. (2007). *Qualitative inquiry and research design*. Thousand Oaks, CA: Sage.

Dalton, R., & Hölscher, C. (Eds.). (Forthcoming). *Take one building: Interdisciplinary research perspectives on the Seattle Central Library*. Farnham, UK: Ashgate.

DeLyser, D., Herbert, S., Aitken, S., Crang, M., & McDowell, L. (Eds.). (2010). *The Sage handbook of qualitative geography*. Thousand Oaks, CA: Sage.

Denzin, N. K., & Lincoln, Y. S. (Eds.). (2005). *The Sage handbook of qualitative research* (3rd ed.). Thousand Oaks, CA: Sage.

Forrester, M. (Ed.). (2010b). *Doing qualitative research in psychology*. Thousand Oaks, CA: Sage.

Groat, L. N., & Wang, D. (2013). *Architectural research methods* (2nd ed.). New York, NY: Wiley.

Sommer, R., & Sommer, B. (2002). *A practical guide to behavioral research* (5th ed.). New York, NY: Oxford University Press.

van Manen, M. (2014). *The phenomenology of practice*. Walnut Creek, CA: Left Coast Press.

Willig, C. (2001). *Introducing qualitative research in psychology*. Philadelphia, PA: Open University Press.

Zeisel, J. (2006). *Inquiry by design* (Rev. ed.). New York, NY: Norton.

8

Revealing the Conceptual Systems of Places

David Canter

University of Huddersfield, United Kingdom

The conflict between good science and effective influence on policy troubles Gabriel in his current internship with regional government. The people he works with want answers now but he knows good research takes time. So he is always on the look out for efficient procedures that will give him a useful answer that he can defend as scientifically valid. An opportunity to explore this came when a demand emerged to find outdoor recreational space for a new housing development without encroaching on protected wilderness.[1]

In his undergraduate degree Gabriel was very taken with the insights from human geography that places take their significance not only from their physical characteristics but also from the way their users think about them and the sorts of activities that they support. Canter's (1977) The Psychology of Place, although published before Gabriel was born still seemed to encapsulate the simple, but powerful idea that places have psychological, behavioral, and physical components which all need to be explored if the meanings, use, and design of those places are to be effective. Many publications since then have developed this idea but the central recognition of the importance of how people conceptualize places has become a fundamental idea in environmental psychology.

Therefore when faced with the need to explore the opportunities for outdoor recreation in a limited area around a proposed major housing development, it seemed natural to Gabriel to start by considering how potential users would make sense of the possibilities for outdoor recreation within reach of their homes.

Gabriel's insight that people have ways of thinking about the world and their interactions with it, and that these concepts can be explored and related together to form a more or less coherent system, has deep roots in psychology. Such conceptual systems are composed of ways of distinguishing between different entities. These distinctions may be called "concepts" or "categories."

The idea of such differentiation being fundamental to thought can be traced back to Aristotle. However, over the years many psychologists have emphasized that the ability to function in the world relates closely to the ability to form

Research Methods for Environmental Psychology, First Edition. Edited by Robert Gifford.

categories and to construct systems of classification by which non-identical stimuli can be treated as equivalent (e.g., Bruner, Goodnow, & Austin, 1956; Miller, 1956; Rosch, 1977). As Smith and Medin (1981) reiterated, if we had to deal with objects, issues, behavior, or feelings on the basis of each unique example, then the effort involved would make intelligent existence virtually impossible. Thus, an understanding of the categories people use and how they assign concepts to those categories is one of the central clues to the understanding of human behavior. As a consequence, an important question for many investigations is the nature and organization of the concepts that people have, specific to the issues being explored.

There are many methods for exploring the categories and systems of classification that people use in any given context. A particularly useful one is the *multiple sorting procedure*. This allows a flexible exploration of conceptual systems either at the individual or the group level. In considering this procedure though, an important distinction must be made between the underlying categorization processes and the "ordinary" explanations that people give for their actions. The methods being considered here work with the words people themselves use in order to reveal the underlying psychological issues.

In Britain, at least, the concern with understanding the personal conceptual systems of individuals was spurred on by the writings of the US psychologist George Kelly (1955) and helped along by the prolific enthusiasm of Fransella and Bannister (e.g., Fransella & Bannister, 1977). Yet, the view that each individual had a unique way of construing the world was not alien to William James many years earlier (1890) and was emphasized in some of Allport's writings (1937). He argued for the value of an idiographic approach, studying each individual in their own terms, rather than using standard responses that were the same for everyone as happens with multiple-choice questionnaires.

Anthropologists and sociologists, especially those with a structuralist orientation, have also emphasized throughout the last century the importance of understanding individuals' systems of meaning (cf. Douglas, 1977). Furthermore, social psychologists, in studying the role of situations in human behavior, have established the importance of the interpretations people make of those situations in which they find themselves (Argyle, Furnham, & Graham, 1981).

Restrictive Explorations

The brief review above reveals that there are two common themes in many disparate writings on psychology. One is the need to explore the view of the world as understood by the respondents in any inquiry. The second is the recognition that their world view is built around the categorization schemes people employ in their daily lives. Yet, unfortunately, psychologists have been influenced by a further consideration, which has tended to dilute the impact of these two themes: the desire for quantitative, preferably computer analyzable, results. Most computing procedures have limitations that are so fundamental that they are taken for granted and rarely challenged, thus influencing the data-collection procedures in ways so subtle that researchers are unaware of them.

A self-structuring cycle is then set in motion. Data are collected in a form that fits known methods of analysis. Standard analytical procedures gain in popularity and are easy to use because they fit the usual data. Data are then commonly collected in the form appropriate to the standard procedures. Thus the existing capabilities of readily available computing procedures help to generate standard forms of data collection, even if those computing procedures are inappropriate for the psychological issues being studied. Without going into a lot of technical detail, a number of restrictions imposed by conventional, widely used, statistical procedures can be summarized:

1. The most commonly used statistics tend to limit data to those having a strong, clear, linear order. Categorical data are seen as being difficult to accommodate. Thus, rating scales (e.g., 7-point) are much preferred to qualitative categories.
2. The procedures limit the structure of the set of variables, so that there is the same number for each respondent. Furthermore, the number of divisions into which each variable is coded is constrained, so that it is the same for all people. Analysis is limited to the manipulation of arithmetic means and correlations over large groups, but this requires that the actual organization of the data for each respondent is identical.
3. Because of their computational efficiency and mathematical elegance, statistical models have tended to be restricted to those that are based on assumptions of underlying linear dimensions and that consequently generate dimensional explanatory models. Qualitative models, although increasing in popularity, are still rare in psychology, although much more prevalent in other social sciences.

These constraints on the analysis of data have become more apparent with the increasing availability of other computing procedures that do not have these limitations and with the strengthening of the idiographic perspective. Indeed, it is being recognized that the popularity of procedures such as the semantic differential, still in use over half a century since it was first proposed (Osgood, Suci, & Tanenbaum, 1957), is due to the ease of data analysis rather than any conviction that they are measuring important aspects of human experience. The semantic differential with its 7-point scales, standard set of items, and factor analysis of results, has been shown to be insensitive to differences between cultures (Osgood, 1962), and, although this may be of interest to cross-cultural psychologists, it does not suggest itself as a technique that will reveal important differences between individuals.

In effect, the semantic differential constrains the concepts people can reveal by providing them with a set of terms to which to respond and by giving precise instructions as to how that response can be structured. Procedures that allow some possibility for the respondent to frame his/her own answers are essential if the essence of any given individual's conceptual system is to be established. Thus, open-ended procedures, especially those built around the interaction possibilities provided by the one-to-one interview, recommend themselves to the students of conceptual systems.

Many researchers (unaware of the range of analyses now available) are fearful of embracing open-ended procedures because they are concerned that their results will be difficult to interpret and the report or the publication they seek will be difficult to structure. Thus, even when they are interested in their respondents' understanding of the world, they explore it through multiple-choice questions or very constrained rating procedures. Yet, serious researchers will still insist on what is usually termed "good pilot research" or what is often couched in terms of "grounded theory" (Glaser and Strauss, 1967).

This involves talking to people in a relaxed, open-ended way and learning from them about the concepts they use in a particular context. It is often at this stage that the real objectives, and in effect the major findings, of the research emerge. Subsequent research frequently only clarifies a little, or provides numerical support for, the insights gained at this "pilot" stage. This is a curious state of affairs when data comes from one part of the research activity and insights from another. Research would be more effective if procedures allowed the interviewees to express their own view of the issues at hand, in their own way, while still providing information that is structured enough for systematic analysis and reporting.

The Repertory Grid

The interview, with its potential for subtle interactions and its concern with the interviewee's understandings, is a fruitful context in which to explore people's concepts. Over the past 30 years a number of procedures have emerged for generating and examining people's conceptual systems within that context. One of the most popular is George Kelly's Repertory Grid (Kelly, 1955). Kelly emphasized that people have personal **constructs** that relate to each other to form a "construct system."

It is worth repeating that Kelly's ideas are part of a general perspective in cognitive psychology that the human ability to function effectively requires the formation of systems of classification in which non-identical phenomena can be treated as equivalent. Around the time Kelly was writing, influential psychologists such as Miller (1956) and Bruner, Goodnow and Austin(1956) were making similar more general points about cognitive processes. These formed the basis of what became known as cognitive psychology, moving away from the fundamentalist, behaviorist tradition that dominated at the time.

Repertory Grid procedure

Kelly (1955) created a structured interview procedure known as the Repertory Grid that is still used today, often in relation to environmental matters (e.g., Hankinson, 2004). It consists of three components:

- the entities to be conceptualized, known as "**elements**," for example, places, people, activities;
- the ways in which those places (elements) are distinguished from each other, known as "constructs";
- the ratings or ranking of the elements on the constructs. For instance, as in the example illustrated in Figure 8.1, each element is rated from 1 to 5 on each construct. This generates a "grid" with elements as columns and constructs as rows and the ratings or ranking in the cells of the grid.

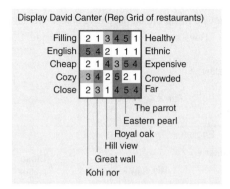

Figure 8.1 An example of a Repertory Grid of restaurants.

The original Kelly Grid was derived by asking respondents who the significant others are in their lives. It was therefore called the "Role Repertory Grid" because it worked from significant roles, such as mother, father, teacher, and so on. However, since the 1970s people studying places have found it interesting to use by substituting places or activities for the elements (see Honikman, 1974 and Stringer, 1974 for early examples). These can be presented as labels, or photographs, or in any other way that can be readily shown to people.

A very simple example of a Repertory Grid is illustrated in Figure 8.1 in which the places (restaurants I was thinking of) are the elements and the descriptions are the constructs. Typically grids contain a dozen or more elements and a similar number of constructs. Much larger grids take a long time to complete and are more difficult to make sense of. This grid is as summarized by WebGrid 5, an excellent Repertory Grid analysis software system freely available at http://gigi. cpsc.ucalgary.ca:2000/.

An important aspect of the Repertory Grid is that the constructs are derived by what is known as the **method of triads**. This consists of presenting the respondent with three of the elements and asking "in what way are any two of these similar to each other and different from the third?" This procedure is continued with different combinations of elements until an exhaustive set of constructs is developed. The process generates bipolar constructs on the assumption that all constructs consist of two opposite poles as shown in Figure 8.1.

The point to keep in mind is that this is produced by one respondent. It is a *personal* construct system being explored. It is possible to create composite grids from a number of people and also to explore aspects of grids across a sample of respondents. But I won't go into those possibilities here because there are so many of them. Over the past 50 and more years since the Repertory Grid was first developed there have been hundreds of developments in its use. Aficionados even refer to the whole approach, drawing on Kelly's ideas, as "Personal Construct Psychology," rather than just a limited theory. In other words, they see it as a whole way of doing psychology, not just a limited theory and method. The mention here is therefore only a taster to hint at the possibilities.

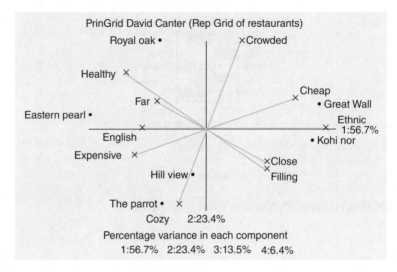

Figure 8.2   Output from WebGrid 5 showing the main dimensions of the grid illustrated in Figure 8.1.

As I have emphasized, the constructs and their poles are the personal decision of the respondent. For example in Figure 8.1 the respondent (me in this case) thinks of the opposite to a restaurant that is cozy not as "uncomfortable" but as "crowded." Also the rather unusual construct of "healthy – filling" may not be one that many other people would apply to a restaurant.

The Repertory Grid can be analyzed in many different ways:

- The nature of the elements can be examined. In this case the range of restaurants I have selected as significant to me could well tell you something about my experience of them. Putting them on a map could also tell you about my activities.
- The actual constructs I use are also of interest because they tell you something about how I conceptualize these places.
- The structure of the grid is also of great psychological interest. What are its underlying components? How complex is it? What dominates it? There is now a lot of software freely available for revealing this. But as I indicated above one particularly powerful approach is to carry out a principal component analysis to reveal the dominant dimensions and how much each contributes to the overall framework. WebGrid 5 gives different ways of doing this, but the one I find clearest and most interesting is given in Figure 8.2.

The six restaurants are represented in a two-dimensional space defined by the constructs. This shows how the constructs relate to each other and how they in turn relate to the elements. There is also an indication of the proportion of the variance accounted for by each of the major dimensions. The more evenly spread the variance across the components (in this case four components have been derived) the more complex the construct system.

Figure 8.2 shows that I am revealing one dominant dimension that accounts for nearly 60 percent of the variance. This is strongly defined by the distinction between "English" and "Ethnic" restaurants (possibly influenced by my university days in Liverpool, where Indian and Chinese restaurants are the haunts of students). But it can also be seen that for me English restaurants are typically "expensive" and "far" and probably regarded as "healthy."

The second component, which accounts for less than a quarter of the variance, is defined by the distinction between "cozy" and "crowded." So we now have a reduction of my five constructs into two dominant dimensions. This can be used to understand the choices I make and for comparing me with other individuals. The distilled components can also be summarized across a number of individuals to give some composite account of how people are conceptualizing places.

The complexity of the conceptual system can be measured in many different ways as well as looking at the proportions of the variance. Personal Construct theory and many other explorations of **cognitive complexity** argue that it is an important aspect of personality. It can indicate how open to change a person's construct system is. Generally the more complex the more readily can new constructs be incorporated. It also can indicate levels of sophistication in dealing with the elements being construed.

One interesting point here is that cognitive complexity is not a general aspect of a person but related to the particular domain you are studying. For example a wine buff may be able to distinguish the taste of "New World" wines from European wines, but someone who is not expert could only distinguish sweet from dry. (Note by the way the polar opposite in wine for "sweet" is not "sour" but "dry," showing that constructs have what Kelly called a "range of convenience." They are relevant for particular contexts but may be inappropriate for others.)

From pilot work some sort of standard grid could be developed so that the same framework can be used by all respondents, making aggregate analysis much easier.

Problems with the Repertory Grid

As many authors have noted (e.g., Adams-Weber, 1979; Bonarius, Holland, & Rosenberg, 1981; Fransella & Bannister, 1977), the Repertory Grid, deriving as it does from a theory of people that puts emphasis on their conceptual systems, does have much to recommend it; yet the Role Repertory Test, which has evolved from Kelly's original proposals, is often used with less sympathy for Kelly's personal construct theory than might be expected. Furthermore, the forms of statistical analysis known to Kelly limited the forms of development in grid analysis procedures, which has had direct consequences for the forms of grid which he and his followers have developed.

Fransella and Bannister (1977) comment on many of these weaknesses of the grid as used; they point out:

1. The grid "has been turned into a technology which generates its own problems and then solves these problems. Such problems do not necessarily relate to any attempt to understand the meaning which the person attaches to his universe" (p. 113).

2. Grid use has been limited by the "requirement that the subject present his judgements in handy grid statistical format before we can analyse pattern" (p. 116).
3. It is a fair guess that it is the mathematical ingenuity of the grid which has attracted psychologists rather than its possibilities as a way of changing the relationship between "psychologist" and "subject" (p. 117).

Developments in computing procedures of the years have weakened some of these criticisms, especially interactive online computing, which allows a much more flexible exploration of construct systems (cf. Shaw, 1982 and WebGrid5 mentioned above), but the main point made by Fransella and Bannister, that the grid technology as such has masked other possibilities for exploring personal constructs, still remains.

The Repertory Grid technique is neither as unique in its contribution nor as definitively special to personal construct theory as its users often claim. Kelly himself traces the origins of the grid to the sorting procedures used by Vygotsky (1934) and others, and thus puts his grid technique firmly in the realm of the exploration of categories and concepts. He writes:

Methodologically the Repertory Test is an application of the familiar concept formation test procedure. It uses as "objects" those persons with whom the subject has had to deal in his daily living. Instead of sorting *Vygotsky blocks*, a procedure in which people are asked to assign blocks of different sizes shapes and colors to different categories of their choice, the subject sorts people. The technique bears some resemblance to the sorting employed in the Horowitz Faces Test. It is also somewhat similar to Hartley's later procedure in which he used pictures in a sorting test. Rotter and Lessor have also experimented tentatively with the formation of "social concepts" in the sorting of paper dolls of the Make-a-Picture-Story (MAPS) Test. (Kelly, 1955, Vol. 1, pp. 219–220).

The Repertory Grid instead of Q-sorts and paired comparisons

The Q-sort technique was, like the Repertory Grid, developed as a way of examining the critical concepts people hold about role figures or events of significance to them (Stephenson, 1953). But, while this method enables people to assign elements to categories, the categories themselves are specified, usually as increments of an adjectival scale. Moreover, the Q-sort is typically used in a form whereby the interviewee is required to assign elements to the categories in a specified (almost always an approximately normal) distribution (Pitt & Zube, 1979).

The use of an enforced distribution is defended, in part, on the grounds that the procedure provides data that are more conveniently processed (Block, 1961), and eliminates the problem, inherent in rating scale procedures, of different individuals calibrating the scale in different ways (Palmer, 1978). These restrictions on the interviewee's sorting behavior thus make the Q-sort more akin to the semantic differential technique and Likert scales in general, than to the intensive one-to-one interview procedure I am advocating.

Other highly restrictive sorting procedures have also been developed as an alternative to paired-comparison judgments of similarity. For example, Ward (1977) and Ward and Russell (1981) have used sorting procedures in which both the sorting criteria and the number of categories are specified, as a means of generating similarity matrices. Although Ward argues that the process of sorting is probably more "natural" for the interviewee than similarity judgments, the key argument for its use seems to be that it is less time consuming than paired comparisons while at the same time providing equivalent similarity data that is suitable for multidimensional scaling procedures.

Indeed, the development of multidimensional scaling procedures grew out of the analysis of similarity judgments of pairs of stimuli. Schiffman, Reynolds, and Young (1981) see similarity judgments as "the *primary* means for recovering the underlying structure of relationships among a group of stimuli" (p. 19). They go on to state that they think that similarity judgments are to be preferred to verbal descriptors because such descriptors are "highly subjective and often conceptually incomplete" (p. 20). However, while there may be some validity to this contention in the experimental study of perceptual stimuli, to which Schiffman and her colleagues repeatedly make reference, such a view of all human conceptualizations is unnecessarily restrictive and has not been defended with any theoretical strength.

Perceived similarity is a more complex phenomenon than can accurately be described by a single rating. Perceived similarity may, in fact, be defined by a set of multiple categorizations based on a wide variety of criteria. In many cases it is the overall patterns that emerge as a result of the concepts people themselves naturally apply to the objects or elements that are of psychological concern. Even when people are unable to put words on their categorization of elements, it is the structure they impose on the world that should be the starting point for the psychologist, rather than any general mathematical theory.

Although interview-based sorting procedures do have a long history, the full possibilities of this approach are increasingly becoming apparent. These possibilities attempt to avoid the limitations of earlier procedures. The multiple sorting procedure, to be described, does not impose a view of the likely structure and content of an individual's conceptual system on the interviewee. It minimizes the "technique for its own sake" syndrome by allowing the exploration of both the nature and the organization of concepts about any issue, maintaining the freedom and open-ended qualities considered so essential by many researchers, yet still providing for systematic analysis of individuals or groups. The use of the multiple sorting procedure and systematic analysis of data from it is possible, in part because of developments in non-metric multidimensional scaling procedures, the use of which will also be illustrated later in this chapter.

Sorting as a Focus for an Interview

Many of the explorations of which interviews are a part are aimed at coming to grips with the conceptualizations of the interviewee, whether it is a market research study, such as looking at the corporate image of banks (Frost & Canter, 1982), or a more theoretical exploration of architects' use of stylistic terms (Groat, 1982), and how these concepts develop throughout the training to become an architect (Wilson & Canter, 1992) or even research of a more pragmatic nature, looking at why people move house (Brown & Sime, 1980).

A particularly pertinent study is that by Scott and Canter (1997) in which comparisons of people's experiences of places were compared with their reactions to pictures of those places. In all cases it is the particular categories and concepts people use that is at issue, as well as the way in which they use them. The interview is especially suited to these types of exploration, because the interviewer and the interviewee can explore each other's understandings of the questions being asked and because the one-to-one situation can accommodate a more intensive interaction.

Unfortunately though, the potentials of the interview are frequently its pitfall. Asking open-ended questions in the relaxed way thought to increase rapport is the formula for unanalyzable material. What is needed is a way of providing a focus for the interview to guide and structure the material produced without constraining the interviewee unduly. Bruner et al. (1956) were some of the first to show clearly the possibilities for exploring the nature of the concepts people have by studying how they assign elements to categories. Such a procedure provides a focus for the interview, allowing other related material beyond that generated by the sorting to be noted.

Sorting procedures of various types have been used frequently in the environmental psychology field because they enable researchers to use illustrations and other visual material as well as reference to places and activities, which are difficult to accommodate within other procedures. It is helpful to mention the range of applications; from those used to generate similarity matrices (Horayangkura, 1978; Ward, 1977; Ward & Russell, 1981) to those seeking to integrate the sorting process with the verbal descriptions and explanations inherent in a one-to-one interview situation (Garling, 1976; Groat, 1982; Palmer, 1978). In the case of the latter, the researchers have intentionally used the sorting technique precisely because it is free of the limitations discussed earlier.

Clearly then, in using the sorting procedures as an interview focus, the interviewer's task is to identify the interviewee's salient categories and the pattern of assignments used to relate categories to elements. The more freedom the interviewee can be given in performing this task the more likely that the interviewer will learn something of the interviewee's construct system rather than just clarifying his/her own. Such freedom should extend to the range and structure of the categories, of which the constructs are composed, as well as to constructs and elements sorted.

The Multiple Sorting Procedure

The multiple sorting procedure advocated here asks little of the interviewees other than that they assign elements to categories of their own devising; it differs from other response formats in that no limitations are necessarily placed on how the sorting is to be done. In fact, the respondent is encouraged to sort the elements, using different criteria, a number of times. The rationale for this less restrictive version of the sorting process is the belief that the meanings and explanations associated with an individual's use of categories are as important as the actual distribution of elements into the categories.

The actual act of sorting items is a common activity. For example, in choosing a house, people will literally sort through the particulars sent to them by estate agents.

In many other areas of choice, whether it be clothing, books, partners, or political parties, there is an explicit selection on the basis of a personal categorization scheme. But even when a selection is not overtly involved, such as in evaluating how successful a given setting is likely to be for a given activity the judgment is based on an implicit categorization scheme.

To carry out the multiple sorting, a person is presented with a set of elements and an introduction and instructions as follows:

> I am carrying out a study of what people think and feel about *places where children play* [A] so I am asking a number of people *chosen at random* [B] to look at the following *pictures* [C] and sort them into groups in such a way that all the pictures in any group are similar to each other in some important way and different from those in the other groups. You can put the picture into as many groups as you like and put as many pictures into each group as you like. It is your views that count.
>
> When you have carried out a sorting, I would like you to tell me the *reasons* [D] for your sorting and what it is that the pictures in each group have *in common* [E].
>
> When you have sorted the pictures once I will ask you to *do it again* [F], using any different principles you can think of and we will carry on as many times as you feel able to produce different sorts. Please feel free to tell me whatever occurs to you as you are sorting the pictures.

The items in italics and indicated with letters in [ ] are those components of the instructions that change for different procedures in relation to different research questions. It must be emphasized, however, that these instructions are only a general statement of what is possible. The flexibility of the procedure is such that many different variations of the instructions are possible. Pilot work is always essential in order to discover what particular instructions are appropriate for each study, although typically all components [A] to [F] must be explicitly dealt with.

The elements to be sorted ([C] in the instructions), depending on the research question, may be generated by the interviewee or the interviewer; they may be labels, concepts, objects, pictures, or whatever, as will be illustrated. The person is usually asked to look through the elements to familiarize him/herself with them; also, the purposes of the research enterprise are explained (relating to instructions components [A] and [B]). In particular, it is pointed out that the interviewer is interested in the interviewee's ways of thinking about the elements presented. The interviewee is then asked to sort the elements into groups so that all the elements in any given group have something important in common, which distinguishes them from elements in other groups. Thus, a number of groups are produced which may vary in the number of elements in them. The number of groups may also vary from person to person for the same set of elements.

An individual example

To illustrate how this can work with one person consider a multiple sort carried out with a gambler we will call Ace. I was interested in Ace's views of various casinos, as part of a larger project to study what it was that gamblers enjoyed about gambling. The particular purpose of the sorting procedure was to see the basis on which a gambler selects which casino to visit and to get some understanding of his view of the

Table 8.1   Record of Ace's sorts.

First Sort: Class of Casino
1   Gaming halls: G, H, D, A
2   Middle class: B, C
3   High class: E, F

Second Sort: Type of Frills
1   Just gambling: A
2   Vaudeville: B, G, H
3   Sedate dining: E, D, C, F

Third Sort: Size of the Stake
1   Less than £5: A
2   Between £5 and £25: G, H, B
3   Greater than £25: C, D, E, F

Fourth Sort: Most likely place for me to make money at
1   Most likely: A, G, H
2   Not so much: B
3   Too expensive: C, D, E, F

Fifth Sort: Preference
1   Most preferred: A, G, H, E
2   Solid casinos: C, D
3   Bit quiet: F
4   Did not like at all: B

Casinos: A = Golden Nugget; B = Playboy; C = Park Lane;
D = Palm Beach; E = Hereford; F = Park Tower; G and H =
Las Vegas casinos.

casinos available. I wanted to know what sort of world a gambler is part of; what type of choices he sees as being available to him.

Ace was asked to list on cards all the casinos he knew in any detail and to assign names for his own convenience. For the researcher's convenience, each card was given a letter on the back. On his first sort, Ace chose to divide the cards into three groupings. These groupings were recorded as shown in Table 8.1, with the letters indicating the casinos.

At this stage the researcher has an indication of each category scheme for the respondent. Such information can be very valuable, especially when working with groups of people who are not especially articulate. But there are a number of further developments of the procedure possible within the same framework. The verbal concomitants of the category scheme can be read by asking the interviewees to indicate the basis on which they have carried out the sorting, as in the instructions [D] and [E].

This generates two levels of description. The first is a superordinate description of the principle for the sorting, from instructions [D]. With Ace, for example, "whether the casinos have frills or not" or "the amount of money to play the lowest stake." The second is a set of category labels for each of the groups (instructions [E]), for example, for the "frills" sort, Ace's categories were "places with no frills," "places with sedate dining," and "vaudeville"; for the "stakes" sort, Ace's categories were "less than £5," "between £5 and £25," and "greater than £25."

A useful way of recording this verbal information is shown by reference to Ace's sorting of casinos in Table 8.1. The categories are summarized with a description of the category scheme for the sort as well as labels for each of the groups within this sort. Other comments and points of clarification made by the respondent can easily be accommodated within this format, as well as any order that might be given to the category groupings. Given the value of the procedure as a focus for exploring a content domain, these comments may generate material of considerable value in their own right. Thus, the researcher need not reduce the responses to bipolar scales, which are often ambiguous when considered at some time after the interview.

Unlike the analyses discussed by Schiffman et al. (1981), and used, for example, by Ward and Russell (1981), the multiple sorting data need not be reduced to association matrixes, typically aggregated across groups. Both the superordinate descriptions and the category labels can be subjected to content analysis. No structure or order to these descriptions is initially assumed or implied. This is particularly important for the category labels.

The bipolar dichotomies of rating scales, and traditional Kelly constructs, are not assumed, nor is the order of items from ranking or scaling. If the interviewee specifies a particular order, as in the "amount of the stake" example, then note can be taken of that, but if any order might be more obscure, as in the "frills" example, then that can be utilized as well. Indeed, category schemes frequently emerge that are not simply bipolar. This raises questions about the extent to which such bipolarity, assumed in much research, is an actual feature of psychological processes or an artifact of the structured measuring instruments used.

A comparison of individuals

Individual sortings, such as Ace's, become especially interesting when comparisons can be made between individuals. As part of the same study, a casino manager also went through a sorting procedure using the casino and parts of casinos of which he had direct experience. The results of the casino manager's sortings are given in Table 8.2. The sortings from Ace and the manager, taken together, serve to illustrate the way in which very specific foci can be developed for analysis, dealing directly with the unique, idiosyncratic conceptualizations of particular importance.

Table 8.3 shows the data matrix derived from the sorts illustrated in Table 8.1. This is created by assigning numerical category values to each of the groups in each sort as indicated in the table.

When individuals carry out detailed sorts on elements that are special to themselves, there is always a possibility that over a variety of sorts they repeat similar categories, simply assigning different labels to each categorization. Thus, an individual who is fluent but not especially cognitively complex, may generate a large number of apparently different sorts, which on closer examination are found to have little in the way of variation between the different sortings.

This is relevant if comparison is to be made between individuals, because it is the key aspects of their conceptual systems that we need to understand, not simply how

Table 8.2   Record of casino manager's sorting.

First Sort: Staff Recruitment
1   Career staff: A, B, C, F
2   Recruit from outside: E, D, G

Second Sort: Staff Training:
1   Little training: A, B, C, F
2   More training: E, D, G

Third Sort: Staff Benefits
1   Mainly for senior staff: A, B, C, F
2   Also for lower staff: E, D, G

Fourth Sort: Sex of Staff
1   Male only: A, B, C, E, D
2   Male and female: F, G

Fifth Sort: Staff Contact with Customers
1   None: A
2   Good with company support: G, E, D
3   Good with no company support: F
4   Unclear: B, C

Sixth Sort: Staff Experience
1   Trainee staff: A, B, C
2   Mixed: E, D
3   Inexperienced staff: F, G

Seventh Sort: Whether Takes Checks or Cash
1   Cash: A, B, C
2   Mixed: E, D
3   Checks: F, G

Eighth Sort: Concern for Customer Quality
1   Quantity only: A, B, C, E
2   Quality and quantity: D
3   Quality: F, G

Casinos: A = Golden Nugget; B = Palm Beach; C = International; D = Hereford; E = Park Lane; F = Curzon House; G = Gladbroke.

many words they can string together. Thus, it is necessary to do an analysis for each individual and to reveal the main conceptual structure within which the individual is working.

In regard to the gambler and the manager a separate Multidimensional Scalogram Analysis MSA (described below) for each were carried out and a schematic representation of the computer results prepared to facilitate a comparison of their two conceptual systems a shown in Figure 8.3.

The partitioning of these figures is derived from an examination of the way in which each individual sort contributes to the spatial configuration. Thus, it is clear that the manager divides casinos up on the basis of how they deal with the

Table 8.3 Data matrix derived from Ace's sortings.

Elements (Casinos)	First	Second	Third	Fourth	Fifth
A	1	1	1	1	1
B	2	2	2	2	4
C	2	3	3	3	2
D	1	3	3	3	2
E	3	3	3	3	1
F	3	3	3	3	3
G	1	2	2	1	1
H	1	1	2	2	1

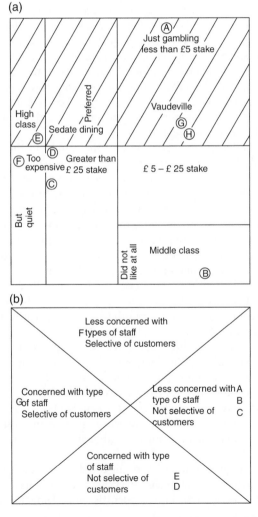

Figure 8.3 Summary MSA of (a) Ace's sortings (see Tables 8.1 and 8.3), and (b) casino manager's sortings (see Table 8.2).

clientele and how the overall casino management deals with its staff. This gives two broad facets. One in terms of those who selecet their staff carefully and those who do not. The second in terms of those who are selective of their clientele and those who are not. This generates a four-way classification of casinos: (i) those that select their staff carefully but are not too selective of their clientele; (ii) those selective about their clientele but not so careful of their staff; (iii) those selective of both staff and clientele; (iv)and those not especially careful about how they chose their staff or their clientele. This reveals the division the manager makes between the staff and the clientele and the way in which his perspective relates to selectivity and overall standards. At first sight, the gambler's MSA reveals a very different sorting.

The analysis here used MSA (available through the software package HUDAP, http://www.ittn.org.il/technology.php?cat=0&Yissum&tech_id=34-2007-1854_Yissum). In this case each of the sortings acted as a separate variable and each individual had a separate matrix. The matrix consisted of the elements as rows and the sortings as columns (as illustrated in Table 8.3). The cells of the matrix are numbers indicating the sorting categories[2] to which the different elements were assigned. Each matrix was put into a separate MSA. The analysis, in this instance, generates a configuration in which each element (in this case, casinos) was a point in the space. The closer together any two casinos are in this spatial representation the more similar they are in terms of the categories that are assigned to them over the number of sorts carried out by each individual.

By looking at the locations in the space of the casinos in the MSA output and checking back with the categories that each place was assigned it is possible to summarize the configuration and produce the schematic representations of the main themes underling the sortings illustrated in Figure 8.3. Essentially, there is a two-way division between those casinos that are very up-market and those casinos that are more general. The gambler makes a more precise distinction within the more general casinos between those that have added frills like the famous Playboy Clubs, or those that are just large gaming halls with little extra, and a group in between. Clearly, the gambler makes much more refined judgments about the nature of the action going on within the casino than does the manager. By contrast the manager considers the quality of the staff, a perspective it would have been difficult to access by any other procedure. However, they both share the superordinate categorization of how selective the casinos are.

This selectivity of casinos throws an interesting light on the whole gambling experience. It shows that an individual, in effect, is playing himself into some sort of exclusive club. These casinos, then, unlike most in the United States, may gain some of their important qualities from the way in which both the management and the gamblers draw lines between who can afford to be in which places. Certainly, further discussion of these conclusions with the respondents here as well as with other management groups would be necessary to test that hypothesis more fully.

It is difficult to see quite how such a result could be derived from a conventional questionnaire procedure. Open-ended interviews could well have revealed the same sort of material, but they might have hidden the underlying structures in people's conceptualizations.

Aggregate of conceptualizations

For Gabriele, the Repertory Grid could be an interesting option to study people's conceptualizations of places for outdoor activity. But it does suffer from being quite a long-winded and demanding procedure for both respondents and researchers. It is also focused on revealing unique aspects of individuals. So although there are many ways of generating aggregate data from groups of people, for Gabriele's purposes a procedure that generates a composite account of the conceptualizations of a sample of respondents is likely to be more useful. The *Multiple Sorting Task* (MST), described above, but first described in detail by Canter, Brown, and Groat (1985) would fit the bill.

The way the MST is used by Gabriele is as follows: Participants are given a set of cards, each showing one of the 33 different places that could be possible areas for outdoor recreation. Each card has a photograph of the location, a map of where it is, and a brief description of the type of location it is and the facilities that it offers. The location is given relative to the area that the proposed housing development would be in, which I will call "Bracknell." The participants are people living near Bracknell who have a similar socio-demographic make-up to those who are likely to live in the proposed development. In the present case I will describe a study that had 31 participants.

Each of the 31 people were independently asked to sort the 33 places into categories using the criteria; "Why do people go to these places/what do people use these different places for?"

It is of course possible to ask people to sort freely on the basis of whatever comes to mind or to give very distinct criteria such as how pleasant the places are, but following the spirit of Kelly's personal construct theory the MST is most interesting when people are given some freedom in how they assign elements to categories. People can also be asked to sort the elements a number of times using different criteria, as illustrated with the study of casinos, which is why it is called a "multiple" sorting task. But for simplicity here I will just deal with one sorting instruction.

Respondents are told that they can use as many different categories as they think necessary but that each location can only feature in one category in each of the sorts.

They are instructed to note the different categories that they use to sort the locations, giving each a clear description. They then list on a sheet which of the locations featured in each of the categories.

Analysis There are a number of different ways of analyzing this material. For instance a matrix can be derived that shows how often each element is put in the same category as each other element. However, this loses the details of each individual's response. In the present case responses to the sorting tasks were pooled across all participants and subjected to the multidimensional analysis technique, the MSA. This is how it's done. Firstly, each category used by each of the participants is given a number. For example, if a person used three categories – Good for Day Out, Local and Convenient, Good for Adult Walk – then any location assigned to the first category (Good for Day Out) would be given a value of 1, any assigned to the second category (Local and Convenient) would be given a value of 2, and any assigned to the third category (Good for Adult Walk) would be given a value of 3. As already indicated the numbers are arbitrary because MSA treats them simply as categories.

Once all locations had been assigned numerical values for each individual's sort, an overall profile was then created for each location. The profile was determined by the 31 scores assigned by the individuals. So, for example, the place called "The Lookout" had the following profile:

$$
\begin{array}{ccccccccccccc}
5 & 1 & 1 & 2 & 4 & 1 & 2 & 2 & 3 & 2 & 1 & 1 & 2 \\
1 & 2 & 2 & 3 & 2 & 5 & 4 & 4 & 1 & 1 & 1 & 3 & 1 \\
1 & 1 & 1 & 2 & 1 & & & & & & & &
\end{array}
$$

Each of these numbers has a different meaning because they relate to a different category as described by each person. Therefore no conventional arithmetic can be applied to these numbers. However, the rather unusual MSA statistical program does allow a very interesting and useful analysis of all the responses in the study.

The MSA software compares the profiles across all respondents of each location with every other location. It produces a plot in which the positioning of the different points (in this instance the 33 locations) is such that the closer they are to one another the more similar the profiles for those points (locations) are, and the further apart they are the less similar the profiles for those points (locations) are. So, for example, if two locations tended to be categorized similarly across most respondents then they would be close together on the plot. If they tended to be categorized very differently, then they would be at opposite ends of the plot. MSA just deals with the numerical categories in the profiles. It takes no account of the words the respondents used. In this sense it is non-verbal and consequently allows comparisons of how people categorized the places without being influenced by the actual words they used. It works with each individual's personal categorizations, but generates a composite picture as shown in Figure 8.4.

The labels in Figure 8.4 are actual locations in the South of England if you wanted to look them up on the Internet. You could then make your own decisions about the basis for people's judgments. That is one of the advantages of this procedure. It allows researchers to consider what underlies respondents' judgments in an objective way even though those judgments are based on the personal views of the respondents

Figure 8.4 can thus be examined to consider groupings of the variables (locations) in the MSA plots in terms of:

1. l the types of locations comprising the different groupings;
2. the attributes or characteristics that they possess;
3. participants' knowledge and actual usage of the locations; and
4. participants' conceptualizations of the locations, as revealed in discussions conducted as part of the sorting task interview.

Classification categories used in sort   Four regions can be distinguished in Figure 8.4 which I have indicated by drawing lines to show the boundaries between those regions. It is rather unusual to have such clear regions, but this does indicate that people do have quite distinct ideas about what sorts of places these are. Generally people sorted places according to what types of activities they thought those places would be used for.

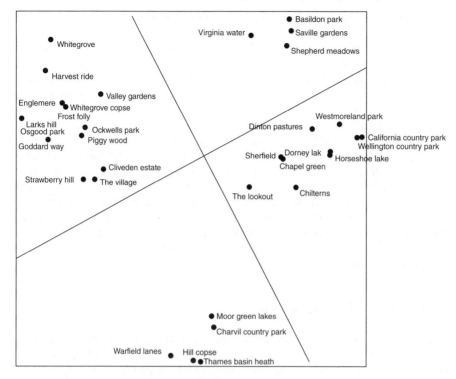

Figure 8.4 MSA results derived from sorting of 33 locations by 31 individuals.

For example, the grouping to the bottom of Figure 8.4 typically have lanes or routes for jogging or hiking, and are seen as being good for bike riding, typically being local and easy to get to with a bicycle, or facilities for water sports with lakes designated for such activities. They include Hill Copse, Warfield Lanes, Thames Basin Heath, Moor Green Lakes, and Charvil Country Park.

The comments that describe these locations give a very clear indication of conceptions of the places, even though each respondent used slightly different words. For example: good for sports/biking, more active time out, local for jogging, weight-loss – exercise (safety in numbers), for hobbies , outdoor activities, sporting day out, fishing, and watching wildlife.

The group to the top left of Figure 8.4 are the local/convenient places. They include places with such charming names as Strawberry Hill, Larks Hill, Whitegrove Copse, Harvest Ride, Goddard Way, Whitegrove, Piggy Wood, and Frost Folly. These tend to be locations on or around the outskirts of towns or urban areas, with few or no facilities, that are seen as being useful and convenient for short walks, possibly with children, and/or dogs.

The group to the top right of Figure 8.4, which included Virginia Water, Saville Gardens, Basildon Park, and Shepherd Meadows, are seen as places with few facilities/amenities, which are viewed as being more tranquil and picturesque. They are consequently regarded as green parks for rambling/walkers, adult hiking, long walks at the weekend, but not for children.

The group to the middle right of Figure 8.4 including The Lookout, Wellington Country Park, California Country Park, Dinton Pastures, Horseshoe Lake, Westmoreland Park, and Dorney Lake were revealed through the descriptions given and the group discussions that were held by presenting subsets of respondents with these results and asking them to discuss. They were revealed as being typically locations for days out with the children and adults to go walking, that are local and convenient for short walks and good for dog walking and sporting activities .

Gabriel therefore has four distinct types of activities to cater for and by looking at the physical characteristics of these places can put forward proposals as to which places are likely to be used in what ways by future residents of the proposed housing development. He can also indicate what changes to the available outdoor places would make them more or less attractive to users for different activities, for example, more facilities for children in certain areas. There is even a hint of possible conflicts between users that may need to be managed, such as those between people fishing and people cycling.

Summary and Conclusions

This chapter has presented a detailed account of multiple sorting procedures, with respect to both their theoretical origins and their numerous applications to open-ended interview situations. As the first section of the chapter has demonstrated, the multiple sorting procedure has roots in both the early clinical object sorting techniques and the paired comparison procedures advocated by multidimensional scaling enthusiasts. But, more importantly, the multiple sorting procedure derives from two parallel concerns in psychology: the significance of the respondents' own view of the world, most clearly articulated by George Kelly; and the recognition that this world view is built around a pattern of categorizations. In this respect, the multiple sorting procedure reveals theoretical links to work in the development of the Repertory Grid and to other research in social and clinical psychology. With respect to the interview process, the second portion of this chapter has provided examples of its adaptability, and ease of administration. However, one of its primary virtues may also be a burden to the researcher. It probably makes even greater demands than the Repertory Grid on the intellectual stamina of the investigator, forcing her or him to clarify exactly what it is that he/she is looking for and why. In this respect it serves as an appropriate complement to other forms of the interview procedure. The multiple sorting task thus takes its place among the family of interviewing procedures.

Glossary

Cognitive complexity   The degree of sophistication of any person's set of conceptualizations in a particular domain. This can be related to the number of terms that the person can apply in the domain as well as the richness of the underlying structure (cf. Bieri, 1971).

Constructs   Ways of conceptualizing or categorizing entities. Used most distinctly in personal construct theory to describe the way in which any two entities are regarded as similar to each other and different from a third. In this context they have two ends or "poles," one derived from the similarities, the other from the differences.

Elements   The term used in personal construct theory to describe the entities that are being construed, for example, people, places, activities.

Method of triads   A procedure for developing bipolar constructs. Three elements are presented to the respondent, who is asked how two are similar and different from the third.

Multidimensional Scaling (MDS)   A statistical procedure that represents entities in a notional space such that the closer together any two entities are the more similar they are on some measure of association or correlation. There are a great many MDS procedures.

Multidimensional Scalogram Analysis (MSA)   A unique MDS procedure (see above) that compares the profiles of categories to represent distances between points in space rather than direct measures of association. This was developed by Lingoes (1973). Described in Zvulun(1978).

Notes

1   This example is based on an actual consultancy project carried out by the author. The project details have been simplified here because the legal and planning consent issues are very complex drawing on UK planning regulations and European Union requirements.
2   The numbers are dealt with as categories by the MSA algorithm not as ordinal values.

References

Adams-Weber, I. R. (1979). *Personal construct theory: Concepts and applications.* Chichester, UK: Wiley.

Allport, G. W. (1937), *Personality: A psychological interpretation.* New York, NY: Holt Saunders.

Argyle, M., Furnham, A., & Graham, I. A. (1981). *Social situations.* Cambridge, UK: Cambridge University Press.

Bieri, I. (1971)., *Cognitive structures in personality.* In H. M. Schroder and P. Suedfeld (Eds.), *Personality theory and information processing.* New York, NY: Ronald Press.

Block, J. (1961). *The Q-sort method in personality assessment and psychiatric research.* Springfield, IL: Charles C. Thomas.

Bonarius, H., Holland, R., & Rosenberg, S. (Eds.). (1981). *Personal construct psychology: Recent advances in theory and practice.* New York, NY: St. Martin's Press.

Brown, I., & Sime, J. (1980). A methodology for accounts. In M. Brenner (Ed.), *Social methods and social life* (pp. 157–188). London, UK: Academic Press.

Bruner, J., Goodnow, I., & Austin, G. (1956). *A study of thinking.* New York, NY: Wiley.

Canter, D. (1977). *The psychology of place.* London, UK: Architectural Press.

Canter, D., Brown, J., & Groat, L. (1996). A multiple sorting procedure for studying conceptual systems. In D. Canter (Ed.), *Psychology in action* (pp. 40–71). Dartmouth, UK: Aldershot.

Douglas, M. (Ed.) (1977). *Rules and meanings.* Harmondsworth, UK: Penguin.

Fransella, F., & Bannister, D. (1977). *A manual for Repertory Grid Technique.* London, UK: Academic Press.

Frost, A., & Canter, D. (1982). Consumer psychology. In S. Canter and D. Canter (Eds.), *Psychology in practice: Perspectives on professional psychology.* Chichester, UK: Wiley.

Garling, T. (1976). The structural analysis of environmental perception and cognition. *Environment and Behavior, 8,* 385–415.

Glaser, B., & Strauss, A. (1967). *The discovery of grounded theory.* Chicago, IL: Aldine.

Groat, L. (1982). Meaning in post-modern architecture: An examination using the multiple sorting task. *Journal of Environmental Psychology, 2,* 3–22.

Hankinson, G. (2004). Repertory Grid analysis: An application to the measurement of destination images. *International Journal of Nonprofit and Voluntary Sector Marketing, 9.*

Honikman, B. (1974) Architectural uses of the Rep Test. In P. Slater (Ed.), *The intrapersonal space* (pp. 96–110). Chichester, UK: Wiley.

Horayangkura, V. (1978). Semantic differential structures. *Environment and Behavior, 10,* 555–584.

James, W. (1890). *Principles of psychology.* New York, NY: Holt Saunders.

Kelly, G. (1955). *The psychology of personal constructs.* New York, NY: Norton.

Lingoes, J. (1973). *The Guttman–Lingoes Nonmetric Program Series,* Ann Arbor, MI: Mathesis Press.

Miller, G. A. (1956). The magical number seven, plus or minus two. *Psychological Review, 43,* 81–114.

Morrison, P., & Lehane, M. (1995). Exploring qualitative data. *Journal of Forensic Psychiatry and Psychology, 6,* 552–563. doi:1080/09585189508410783.

Osgood, G. E. (1962). Studies in the generality of affective meaning systems. *American Psychologist, 17,* 10–28.

Osgood, G. E., Suci, G. I., & Tanenbaum, P. M. (1957). *The measurement of meaning.* Urbana, IL: University of Illinois Press.

Palmer, I. (1978) Citizen assessment of the coastal visual resource, *Coastal Zone 78. II.* San Francisco, CA: American Society of Civil Engineers.

Pitt, D. G., & Zube, E. H. (1979). The Q-sort method: Use in landscape assessment research and landscape planning. In G. H. Eisner (Ed.), *Our national landscape.* Pacific Southwest Forest and Range Experiment Station, Berkeley, CA.

Rosch, E. (1977). Human categorization. In N. Warren (Ed.), *Advances in cross-cultural psychology (Vol. 1).* London, UK: Academic Press.

Schiffman, S. S., Reynolds, L. M., & Young, F. W. (1981). *Introduction to multidimensional scaling.* London, UK: Academic Press.

Scott, M. J., & Canter, D. V. (1997). Picture or place? A multiple sorting study of landscape. *Journal of Environmental Psychology, 17,* 263–281.

Shaw, M. L. G. (1982). The extraction of personal meaning from a Repertory Grid. In E. Shepherd and I. E. Watson (Eds.), *Personal meanings.* Chichester, UK: Wiley.

Smith, A. E., & Medin, D. L. (1981). *Categories and concepts.* London, UK: Harvard University Press.

Stephenson, W. (1953), *The study of behavior: Q-technique and its methodology.* Chicago, IL: University of Chicago Press.

Stringer, P. (1974). Individual differences in Repertory Grid measures for a cross-section of the female population. In D. Canter & T. Lee (Eds.), *Psychology and the built environment* (pp. 96–104). London, UK: Architectural Press.

Vygotsky, L. (1934). *Thought and language.* Boston, MA: MIT Press.

Ward, L. M. (1977). Multidimensional scaling of the molar physical environment. *Multivariate Behavioral Research, 12,* 23–42.

Ward, L. M., & Russell, J. A. (1981). Cognitive set and the perception of place. *Environment and Behavior, 13*, 610–632.

Wilson, M., & Canter, D. (1992). The development of central concepts during professional education. *Applied Psychology: An International Review, 39*, 431–455.

Zvulun, E. (1978). Multidimensional scalogram analysis: The method and its application. In S. Shye (Ed.), *Theory construction and data analysis in the behavioral sciences* (pp. 237–264). San Francisco, CA: Jossey-Bass.

Suggested Sources

A video in which I demonstrate the use of the multiple sorting procedure in an application to new product development for chocolates (!) as a market research project (which has the background music I composed …) is available on YouTube at https://www.youtube.com/watch?v=KKlD6JS8Npk. Or you can get to it via the YouTube channel ProfDVC "Mapping People's Conceptualizations."

For a recent account of MSA with qualitative data see Morrison and Lehane (1995).

A wide-ranging resource on Personal Construct Psychology is www.idiogrid.com.

9

Behavioral Methods for Spatial Cognition Research

Daniel R. Montello

University of California, Santa Barbara, CA, United States

The Seattle Public Library's Central Library building is an impressive glass and steel structure that opened to much fanfare in 2004. Although the building is undeniably striking and attracted glowing attention from architects and critics, not every report from members of the general public has been so positive. Many people have claimed that finding one's way around the building is exceptionally confusing and disorienting. Gabriel (he goes by Gabe) works for the prominent architectural firm in Holland that designed the building. His bosses have asked him to lead an investigation to figure out why their building is disorienting and what can be done about it. Gabe realizes he needs to look into the study of spatial cognition, which concerns how people comprehend and learn the spatial layouts of environments, in order to find their way efficiently while traveling around them and tell others how to find their way in them. Gabe's background in geography and architecture provides excellent preparation for studying spatial cognition in public buildings, because it has taught him about spatiality and about built environments. But he will also need behavioral research methods like those discussed in this chapter.

Spatial cognition is the multi-disciplinary study of perception, thinking, reasoning, and communication that is fundamentally about spatial properties and relations (henceforth, spatial properties) in the environment, whether by humans, non-human animals, or computational entities such as robots (Montello & Raubal, 2012). It therefore includes research from several sub-disciplines of psychology, geography and cartography, architecture and planning, anthropology, linguistics, education, biology, computer science, and more. With such a multi-disciplinary heritage, studying spatial cognition potentially involves a great variety of methodological approaches. In order to constrain this chapter and discuss some specific methods most directly relevant to Gabe's research interests, the focus of this chapter is delimited to the study of human spatial cognition with primary data collected via behavioral methods.

Primary data are data collected for the purpose of answering a researcher's specific research questions, using methods tailored to best address those questions, typically

Research Methods for Environmental Psychology, First Edition. Edited by Robert Gifford.
© 2016 John Wiley & Sons, Ltd. Published 2016 by John Wiley & Sons, Ltd.

by that researcher herself or himself. The use of secondary data to study spatial cognition is not addressed; secondary data are collected for some purpose other than answering a researcher's specific research question and nearly always by someone other than that researcher. However, light could be shed on spatial cognition issues with carefully chosen secondary data, including archival data sources (such as administrative, demographic, or economic records) or physical traces (remnants of human activity such as wear marks on a lawn or the arrangement of chairs left after a meeting). Heth and Cornell (1998) studied the thinking and behavior of lost people using case records from search-and-rescue operations.

Behavioral methods involve recording behavior, including where people travel, where they look or point, and what they say or write. This review will broadly distinguish the observation of behavior from **explicit reports** (tests and surveys). Both non-verbal and verbal behavior can be observed (and coded and interpreted); prominent examples of non-verbal behavior in spatial cognition research include both locomotion and eye movement. Responses to explicit reports can also be distinguished as being non-verbal or verbal, with non-verbal responses comprising either scaling or sketch mapping. Scaling in spatial cognition research comes from either the psychometric or psychophysical traditions of research psychology.

In this chapter, research methods used exclusively to study spatial cognition in non-human animals are not discussed (e.g., Shettleworth & Sutton, 2005), although some behavioral methods are applied to both humans and non-humans. And some spatial cognition researchers are especially interested in computational modeling, perhaps to create navigating robots (e.g., Kuipers, 2000; Yeap & Jefferies, 1999). Computational modeling involves an extensive and very distinct set of methods for studying spatial cognition, of course, and are not considered further here. Finally, there is increasing interest in understanding the neuroscience of spatial cognition, and this also involves extensive and sophisticated methods beyond the scope of this chapter. Especially promising within the last couple decades or so has been the application of brain imaging, especially functional magnetic resonance imaging (fMRI), to understanding human spatial cognition (e.g., Maguire et al., 1998; Wolbers, Hegarty, Büchel, & Loomis, 2008).

As we saw above, scholars are sometimes interested in bridging the gap between basic and applied research. Some people think this is the gap between laboratory and field research, but in fact, basic research, with its focus on general explanations of phenomena for the sake of understanding itself, can be conducted in lab or field settings. Likewise, applied research, with its focus on understanding in order to achieve practical outcomes, can also be conducted in either setting. Laboratories are specialized environments for conducting data collection designed to facilitate physical control of potentially confounding or distracting variables. In the case of behavioral research with humans, such distractions include things like noise, salient objects in the visual field, or people walking by. So researchers should be familiar with methods appropriate in either lab or field settings. This will include existing environments like cities, campuses, and public buildings, and also **virtual environments (virtual realities or VR)** that simulate existing places with varying levels of detail and types of sensorimotor involvement (see Chapter 11 for more discussion of simulating environments for research).

Media for Experiencing Spatiality and Acquiring Spatial Beliefs

All phenomena in the domain of spatial cognition involve research participants' experience of spatial properties and their consequent acquisition of beliefs about the properties. Spatial properties include size, shape, location, distance, direction, connection, containment, and more. Spatial properties of environments can be experienced and acquired in a variety of ways, via one or more different media. Montello and Freundschuh (1995) identified four broad classes of such media (they called them "sources" of experience and knowledge). Spatial properties can be experienced and acquired through direct environmental experience while stationary or moving through the environment itself. The movement might be mechanically aided, such as by automobile, bicycle, or airplane. Spatial properties can also be experienced and acquired through indirect environmental experience, including through static pictorial representations (maps, pictures), dynamic pictorial representations (animations, movies), or natural language (spoken or written). A special case is when people experience and acquire spatiality in VR environments; depending on the type of VR system, this would be more like direct environmental experience or dynamic pictorial experience. Furthermore, people often experience and acquire spatiality via multiple media, such as when people both walk around a city and look at a map of it. Continuing research issues concern whether and how information from multiple media is combined or otherwise coordinated in experience and mind.

Montello and Freundschuh (1995) also discussed various factors that differentiate psychologically relevant ways people experience and acquire environmental spaces through different media. These include which sensorimotor systems are involved (vision, touch, walking, head turning, etc.), whether the medium incorporates static or dynamic information (in content or presentation), whether the medium provides sequential or simultaneous access to information, how abstract the medium's symbol system is, whether and how the medium involves translation of spatial (or temporal) scale, what viewing perspectives the medium allows or requires, and how much precision and detail the medium provides about spatial properties – it can be too much, too little, or appropriate.

Clearly, spatial cognition researchers need to think about the medium through which their participants have experienced and acquired spatial properties. This is true whether the researcher specifically exposes participants to the spatial properties or studies beliefs about the properties the participants bring to the study – properties the participants have experienced and acquired in their own way, some time before taking part in the study. Of course, a researcher gains empirical control over understanding the effects of different media if he or she controls participants' exposure to the spatial properties. Such control is not always possible, but when it is, the researcher will be in a better position to explain participants' spatial experience and learning. These choices about how to expose participants to environmental information then become a critical part of the choices researchers must make as part of their research methods.

Observation of Behavior

Since we are restricting our focus to behavioral methods in this chapter, it makes sense first to consider methods that simply involve observing spatially relevant behavior in environments (see Chapter 2 for more discussion of observational methods in environment-behavior research). Behavior is overt, potentially perceptible actions or activity by people. It is not thoughts, feelings, purposes, or motivations. That is, behavior is what we do, not why we do it or how we experience doing it. Nonetheless, behavior is nearly always goal-directed, and most environment-behavior researchers do not consider aimless movement to be behavior. For example, falling is not behavior but attempting to break your fall is.

When collecting data by observing behavior, the behaviors of individuals or groups are watched or listened to. Often, the behavior is somehow recorded. But these records are not, in themselves, data. The records must be coded to convert them into data, typically by segmenting them into relevant units and categorizing the units into meaningful classes (Boehm & Weinberg, 1997). This is a drawback of behavioral observation; coding is almost always hard and time consuming, and it is often difficult to do reliably, so that different coders segment and categorize the records in about the same way.

When using behavioral observation as a method, environment-behavior researchers can set up contrived situations or bring research participants into artificial settings in order to observe their behaviors. In contrast, they can focus on ongoing behavior as it naturally occurs in its actual settings. Historically, this approach was favored by researchers such as ethnographers, who study humans, and ethologists, who study non-human animals. It can provide the substantial benefit of creating data from behavior that does not change because it is becoming research data. That is, behavioral observation often produces data non-reactively. At least it does this when the observers or recording devices are hidden (observation of public behavior is considered ethically allowable). It may even be non-reactive when not hidden, as long as the people observed have become used to being observed and no longer "perform for the camera." Given enough time, even a participant observer may become an accepted part of a setting and not treated unusually by participants (participant observation may be a problematic data source for other reasons). Even when those being observed are fully aware they are participating in a study, certain behaviors such as eye movements may not be readily influenced by consciously held beliefs. That said, it bears emphasizing that, with any form of data collection, including the explicit reports discussed below, reactance – wherein participants change because they know they are being studied – is possible. But it only possibly occurs, not necessarily.

Observing non-verbal behavior

Observing locomotion. In the context of environment-behavior research, observed behavior will often be locomotion, moving one's body from place to place in a coordinated fashion (Montello, 2005). Coordinated means that people walk (e.g., crawl, hop, bicycle, drive) without colliding into barriers, driving off paths, or meandering randomly. A classic example of behavioral observation in environment-behavior research is the work of Hart (1979). He and his assistants observed a small group of children who lived close to each other in a small town. They observed and coded the behaviors of the children in the natural settings of their ongoing activities in and around their homes, intending to learn about the children's experience and understanding of their local surrounds. Behavioral observations were coded to address questions about the children's spatial activities and use of places, beliefs about places (including spatial properties), and their values and emotions concerning places.

An example of using behavioral observation to study spatial cognition with adults comes from an even earlier study by Yoshioka (1942). He and his assistants surreptitiously followed a large number of visitors, one by one, to the New York World's Fair, recording the locations and times of the exhibits they visited. They analyzed behavior patterns of the initial turning direction, the spatial relationship between each visitor's entrance and exit locations, and the spatial patterns of routes traveled. Although Yoshioka was interested in behavioral patterns in and of themselves, he also tried to explain the behaviors by inferences about internal mental states, including personality, motivation, and spatial knowledge. Valid or not, such inferences tend to be difficult to make with behavioral observations, pointing to one of their chief limitations as a method of studying spatial cognition. It can be difficult or impossible to determine the validity of inferences about mental states made from behaviors that do not directly express mental states; in contrast, explicit reports like surveys are thought to directly express mental states (below).

Observing eye movements. As implied above, observed behaviors are not restricted only to locomotion. An increasingly important technique involves observing and recording the behavior of participants' eyes as they look at something, whether a picture, text, or environmental scene. Researchers may be interested in tracking locations in the visual field where participants focus their gaze for some period of time, or in the spatial patterns of the eyes' scan paths to different parts of the visual field. Either way, researchers assume that the location where people are looking is the feature (object or event) in the world that is holding the person's attention. This logic ties the behavior of the eyes to inferences about mental states; also, patterns of eye movements are later correlated with responses to surveys or tests.

One of the earliest examples of eye-movement recording from environment-behavior research comes from Carr and Schissler (1969), who used fairly intrusive equipment that included a camera lens mounted to a contact lens to record participant eye movements while they rode as a passenger in a car. However, that research was an unusually early example of recording eye movements of traveling people, and it was only feasible for passengers who sat fairly still in a car; there was hardly any duplication of it for decades. The great majority of eye-movement research has examined non-locomoting participants, viewing static images or pictures. One of the potential benefits of studying spatial cognition with VR technology is that it reduces some of the technical difficulties of recording eye movements of locomoting individuals (Loomis, Blascovich, & Beall, 1999). One of the most exciting recent methodological advances for those studying environmental cognition is the development of workable technology for mobile eye-tracking, that can validly record eye movements even for pedestrians looking at their real surrounds (Kiefer, Straub, & Raubal, 2012).

Even with static images in a lab, however, analyzing eye-movement records is usually fairly complex; an enormous amount of data is typically recorded in a short time, and it must be processed in sometimes non-obvious ways in order to make sense of it. The technologies for recording eye movements typically involve costly equipment that can be troublesome to calibrate and touchy to maintain consistently. So far, these technologies do not allow surreptitious recording, so reactance is always possible. However, in many research contexts, participants will not be able to control their eye movements readily or may have no motivation for altering them (anecdotally, some researchers report that eye movements recorded on city streets reveal participants looking inordinately at attractive people walking by).

Observing verbal behavior

Although it was stated above that behaviors are overt actions by people, not directly the mental states that might explain the behaviors, we can still think of listening to or reading people's linguistic expressions as behavioral observation. Of course, the explicit reports considered below often involve verbal expression, and the distinction between verbal expressions as observable behaviors versus reports of beliefs is subtle. Nonetheless, there is an important difference that bears recognizing. When a researcher wants to study verbal expressions as the phenomenon of interest, with a focus (and coding) of what someone says or writes, this is behavioral observation. When a researcher considers the verbal expression to be the medium by which people express their beliefs about something, this is explicit reports in a verbal response format.

This becomes clearer when we consider examples of using records of verbal behavior as the basis for data. In the context of spatial cognition, research on giving verbal route directions is the most common example. Ward, Newcombe, and Overton (1986) coded the verbal directions female and male college students gave for routes determined from maps. Allen (1997) coded a corpus of verbal route descriptions, summarizing the types of features included in the descriptions and how they varied among individual describers. Allen (2003) also coded the non-linguistic gestures which so often accompany verbal route directions. Emmorey, Tversky, and Taylor (2000) have observed and coded sign language, which itself is technically a natural language, in order to examine how it uses spatial patterns to express spatial beliefs.

An intriguing recent use of written language as behavioral data for spatial cognition comes from Louwerse and Benesh (2012). They analyzed a large corpus of words and phrases found in J. R. R. Tolkien's famous novels *The Hobbit* and *The Lord of the Rings*, using automated coding techniques from computational linguistics. Their program carried out a statistical frequency comparison of references to city names in the novel, showing that the frequency of co-occurrence of city names (of fictional places) predicted the latitudes and longitudes of those cities quite accurately, because closer places were more often mentioned closely to each other in the novel. They report the fascinating finding that human research participants (new to the stories) who read the novels could estimate the spatial locations of the cities about as well as those who studied maps of the fictional places.

Case Study: How People Get Lost and Found in the Seattle Public Library

At the beginning of this chapter, we told the story of Gabe's new assignment at his architectural firm to design and conduct research on why people get disoriented in the Seattle Public Library and what can be done about that, if anything, from a design perspective (see Chapter 13 for more discussion of conducting evaluation research on built environments). In fact, human-environment researchers Laura Carlson, Amy Shelton, Ruth Conroy Dalton, Christoph Hölscher, and Saskia Kuliga have been conducting just this research project. After reading about the library building and the ideas that guided its design by the architectural firm in Holland (although Gabe is fictional, this firm is not), these researchers toured the building extensively. These preliminary steps supported the development of their studies incorporating an array of behavioral research methods. In particular, they have had research participants walk around the library, in some cases, with instructions to search for particular target locations (such as a particular room). The researchers collect and record observations of the participants' non-verbal behavior, especially where they walk (their locomotor routes), but also what they look at and who they talk to, if anybody. To efficiently collect this rich data set, the researchers developed an iPad app they call PeopleWatcher™ (Dalton, Conroy-Dalton, Hölscher, & Kuhnmünch, 2012). Records are entered via touchscreen, which supports real-time recording of navigationally relevant behaviors. For this project, the system's display included various buttons and blueprint images for each floor of the library; the system is also Wi-Fi and GPS enabled, and contains a digital compass, still and video camera, and audio recording capability. Thus, the researchers have been able to log precise and detailed information about the locations and times of all events/activities, including their participants' locomotion tracks and other behaviors and events, such as pausing, looking at signs, or asking for or being asked for directions. When they get confused or disoriented, the system can record what participants say about their thoughts or what they find confusing while moving about the library. In addition, the researchers coordinate these detailed logs with explicit-report measures, including psychometric spatial ability scales and sketch maps.

Explicit Reports: Tests and Surveys

Explicit reports are beliefs people express about things – about themselves or other people, about places or events, about activities or objects. They include beliefs people express about spatial properties in the environment. Of course, explicit reports also involve observing and recording human behavior – answering a survey question, whether orally or in writing, is a behavior. But explicit reports are considered to be a distinct type of data collection because data collected this way are determined by research participants' explicit beliefs about something, and they always involve explicit recognition by people that they are being studied by researchers. As we discuss below, the explicitness of explicit reports leads to some of their major strengths as well as their major limitations as a method (see Chapter 5 for more discussion of conducting surveys in environment-behavior research).

Explicit reports, including surveys, interviews, and tests, can ascertain many different types of beliefs: behaviors, knowledge, opinions, attitudes, expectations, intentions, experiences, and demographic characteristics. Explicit reports often request responses that cannot readily be judged as being right or wrong; the responses are personal opinions or preferences that cannot be compared to an objective standard of correctness, although they can be identified as common or unusual, related to other variables such as demographics, and so on. When explicit responses *can* be assessed for correctness, and that is of major interest to the researcher, we call the reports tests. Tests are used to study knowledge rather than opinion, in other words. Clearly, when studying spatial cognition, explicit reports often do constitute tests, as people's expressed beliefs about spatial properties can typically be compared to an objective standard, and such a comparison is frequently (not always) of central interest to the researcher.

Explicit-report instruments and the individual items (questions) that make them up are administered in various formats; likewise, responses are collected in various formats. Responses to explicit-report instruments in the domain of spatial cognition are very often – probably more often – expressed non-verbally rather than verbally, in numbers, gestures (such as pointing), graphics, or manipulable objects. Respondents commonly mark lines, draw pictures (including maps), sketch on or annotate maps, or construct physical models such as city layouts with blocks (Kitchin, 2000). But explicit reports are often administered verbally, and in even in spatial cognition, responses can be expressed verbally.

There are other aspects of how explicit reports are to be administered to consider. They can be self-administered or administered by the researcher. They can be administered individually or to groups of respondents. They can be administered in person (face to face), through the mail, over the telephone, or on the Internet (increasingly popular with researchers). Reports can be done with the help of computer programs that display questions and accept answers through the keyboard and mouse. Interviews may be audio or video recorded.

And there are still more choices for researchers to make about the design of explicit-report instruments and items besides administration and response format. Closed-ended items are those that give respondents a small, finite number of pre-determined options from which to choose a response. Open-ended items do not; they allow respondents to give any response, of any length, that fits within the response format chosen. Standardized items are the same for each respondent, typically administered in the same way and in the same order for each respondent (they may be closed- or open-ended). Non-standardized items are often useful if one wants to ask follow-up questions that will vary depending on earlier answers respondents gave.

A variety of considerations determine the best way to administer and collect responses to explicit reports in a given study. These include the cost of administration, the number and nature of items to be administered, the rate of response one needs to get, whether one needs to do follow-up data collection, and the nature of respondents (such as their age and language skill). Particular interviewer artifacts may result from one's choices, perhaps from ways the appearance of a researcher could distort the honesty or validity of people's responses. Female respondents may under-report their spatial abilities to male research assistants, for example.

Explicit reports are straightforward and among the most flexible types of data collection in human spatial cognition research. If you want to know what people think, just ask them! But this apparent transparency is something of an illusion, and the limitations of explicit reports are substantial. They frequently depend on respondents' memories (such as for where they have traveled), but people sometimes forget or otherwise recall information in a distorted way, given that memory is elaborative and constructed (e.g., Hyman & Loftus, 1998). The emotionality of events can create stronger recall or stronger forgetting. Questions that require a great deal of aggregation ("how many times have you visited that neighborhood in your life"?) are more suspect than those with little aggregation. Truthfulness can be an issue, insofar as people sometimes intentionally give distorted answers in order to make themselves appear more impressive, to support the research or researcher, or to hurt the research or researcher. That is, people lie or practice deception with good or bad intent. Of course, explicit reports in verbal form can be compromised because some beliefs or feelings may be hard to put into words; non-verbal response formats are especially useful in spatial cognition research for this reason. Some beliefs and feelings may not be full accessible to consciousness, being subconscious or unconscious. A case in point, people often do not know how or why they do or do not believe certain things, their common willingness to offer personal lay theories about these things notwithstanding. Finally, most environment-behavior researchers study beliefs and feelings because of their relationship to action or behavior, but this relationship is not very strong in many cases. Behavior is often determined by habits, social or cultural norms, situational constraints and opportunities, and so on (Ajzen, 2001; Stern, 2000).

Scaling in spatial cognition

Scaling refers to a large and diverse set of explicit-report techniques in which respondents directly express their beliefs about quantitative properties of the environment, of objects or events, of themselves, or of others. Quantitative means that properties are not just classified but rated or estimated at a metric level of measurement – interval or ratio. Ordinal ranking is mostly treated in the next section, but it should be recognized that many authors consider rating scales to generate data that are only ordinal (others reasonably argue that such data may be treated as *approximately* metric), and even when using ranking tasks that clearly do generate only ordinal data, various analytic methods allow some metric information to be inferred or "extracted" from ordinal data (e.g., the non-metric MDS we consider below).

Scaling comes from two important methodological traditions within research psychology, **psychophysics** and **psychometrics**. Psychophysics refers to a set of techniques originating in the nineteenth century in which participants systematically estimate quantities of some property that the researcher then relates to the values of the objectively measured quantities (Gescheider, 1997). In spatial cognition, psychophysics has been used to study properties such as distance or size. Psychometrics, originating in the early twentieth century, refers to a set of techniques in which participants systematically estimate quantities of some property that do not correspond in any direct way to an objectively measurable quantity (Borsboom, 2005). In spatial cognition, these might be attitudes, abilities, preferences, or personality traits (see Chapter 6 for more discussion of measuring attitudes in environment-behavior research).

Psychometric scaling   Psychometric rating scales come in a variety of specific forms. Semantic differentials have people rate the degree to which something is described better by one adjective or its opposite (hot–cold, near–far). A second type is a Likert scale, which has people rate the degree to which they agree or disagree with a particular statement. In the area of spatial cognition, Hegarty, Richardson, Montello, Lovelace, and Subbiah (2002) developed and validated a 15-item Likert scale (shown in Box 9.1) to assess people's beliefs about their own "sense-of-direction."

In general, rating scales typically have from 5 to 10 scale values (less with children), with an odd number of values if a middle value of neutrality makes sense for the question ("neither hot nor cold"). People often informally go well beyond this; it is common to hear people say something like, "rate this on a scale from one to a hundred."

Box 9.1   Santa Barbara Sense-of-Direction Scale.

Sex: F M   Today's date:_____
Age:_____

This questionnaire consists of several statements about your spatial and navigational abilities, preferences, and experiences. After each statement, you should circle a number to indicate your level of agreement with the statement. Circle "1" if you strongly agree that the statement applies to you, "7" if you strongly disagree, or some number in between if your agreement is intermediate. Circle "4" if you neither agree nor disagree.

strongly agree 1 2 3 4 5 6 7 strongly disagree

1. I am very good at giving directions.
2. I have a poor memory for where I left things.
3. I am very good at judging distances.
4. My "sense of direction" is very good.
5. I tend to think of my environment in terms of cardinal directions (N, S, E, W).
6. I very easily get lost in a new city.
7. I enjoy reading maps.
8. I have trouble understanding directions.
9. I am very good at reading maps.
10. I don't remember routes very well while riding as a passenger in a car.
11. I don't enjoy giving directions.
12. It's not important to me to know where I am.
13. I usually let someone else do the navigational planning for long trips.
14. I can usually remember a new route after I have traveled it only once.
15. I don't have a very good "mental map" of my environment.

Thinking about quantities on a 100-point scale is probably meaningful for most people in our culture, but it goes well beyond the valid discriminatory abilities of people. That is, it will produce spurious precision.

Psychophysical scaling Montello (1991) reviewed psychophysical scaling and other techniques for collecting estimates of quantities in spatial cognition (his focus was specifically on the cognition of environmental distances). Ratio estimation requires respondents to draw or mark lines or shapes to represent their belief about the amount of some quantity they have experienced, relative to a standard line or shape that represents a standard quantity. For example, "If this line represents the length of the first hallway you walked, draw a line to show the total length of the walk through the building." Jansen-Osmann and Wiedenbauer (2004) used ratio estimation to explore the "route-angularity effect" in spatial cognition, in which people think routes with more turns are longer than routes with fewer turns but of the same actual length (in fact, this and other research studies find the effect to be inconsistent, not found reliably). Battersby and Montello (2009) used ratio estimation to collect estimates of the areas of countries and other world regions, in order to investigate the possibility that exposure to non-equivalent map projections systematically distorts people's beliefs about land areas. Their respondents adjusted an icon of each region on a computer screen so its size was in appropriate ratio to the size of the standard area, the conterminous United States ("lower 48") (Figure 9.1).

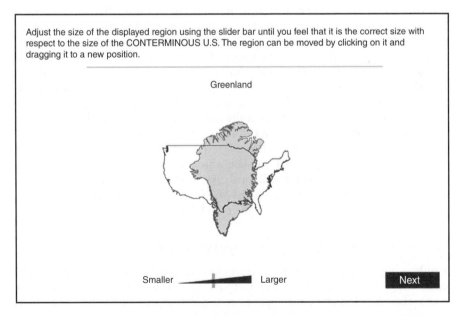

Figure 9.1 Psychophysical scaling technique of ratio estimation. The area of a landmass (Greenland, in this example) is adjusted until the participant believes it is in appropriate ratio to the standard area of the conterminous United States. Adapted from Figure 4 in Battersby and Montello, 2009; used with permission.

In contrast to ratio estimation, magnitude estimation collects responses directly in numerical form; it requires respondents to provide a number to represent their belief about the amount of some quantity they have experienced, relative to some standard quantity given a number. For example, "If the distance from the courthouse to the bus station is 100 units, give a number that equals the distance from the courthouse to the water park." In one of their studies, Battersby and Montello (2009) used magnitude estimation instead of ratio estimation to collect estimates of the areas of world regions. Their respondents gave numbers to represent the areas of world regions, given that the conterminous United States had an area of 1,000 units. In fact, many researchers simply ask respondents to estimate quantities like distances in units they are already familiar with, like miles or meters. One can appreciate this estimation in familiar units as being magnitude estimation with standard units acquired by participants before coming to the study.

Estimates of distances collected by scaling reveal participants' beliefs about distances between places in the environment taken two at a time. Such pairwise estimates are not mutually coordinated and do not directly reveal anything about the participant's conception of the layout of the entire environment. Pairwise distance estimates are often analyzed with a technique called **multi-dimensional scaling (MDS)** (Montello, 1991). For example, Golledge, Briggs, and Demko (1969) created two-dimensional configurations of cognitive maps of Columbus, Ohio, by applying MDS to pairwise estimates of distances in that city. In general, MDS algorithms take as input a matrix of distance estimates (in nonspatial contexts, this is often a matrix of similarity estimates) collected on a pairwise basis and reproduce it in a configuration space of one or more dimensions. The algorithm minimizes the difference, or stress, between the patterns of distances in the matrix and in the solution configuration. The solution can be of any spatial dimensionality, but one tries to minimize stress with a minimal number of dimensions. In environmental spatial cognition research, two-dimensional solutions typically work well (not perfectly).

Scaling techniques collect data efficiently and with apparent quantitative precision; the results can be statistically analyzed directly, without further coding. But psychophysical scaling that measures at the ratio level necessarily involves translating spatial scale (size) between the quantitative property being estimated and the quantitative response. The latter expresses the former at a reduced scale. This requires research participants to translate scale mentally, which is challenging for many people and can introduce additional error in the measurement process. Waller and Haun (2003) developed a version of MDS that reproduces subjective configurations based on direction estimates rather than distance.

Other non-verbal explicit reports in spatial cognition

Besides scaling techniques, researchers can have respondents estimate spatial properties using various other non-verbal methods. Participants may simply indicate the routes they travel in the environment, from which aspects of the person's beliefs about the routes can be inferred (Nasar, 1983); this is an explicit approach to obtaining data that could also be obtained via behavioral observation. Participants can rank order sequences of places along a route or order distances between places instead of rating them with a scaling task. In fact, Golledge et al. (1969) actually performed

MDS on *rankings* of distances between pairs of places, a simple task for participants in which they indicate which of two pairs are further apart; MDS can extract implicit metric spatial structure from such ordinal data.

Montello (1991) discusses the technique of reproduction, in which respondents directly walk or otherwise travel to a place indoors or outdoors, in order to estimate distances or locations. A major benefit of this technique, when it is feasible, is that it does not require any scale translation on the part of research participants. Some researchers also argue that having people travel to locations is a more naturalistic and functionally relevant task for assessing spatial knowledge than indirect tasks such as scaling, pointing, or mapping. Loomis et al. (1993) had respondents with or without visual impairments (wearing blindfolds in the latter case) estimate locations of places in a large room by walking directly to those places. More or less continuous records of these "tracks" were made, which could then be coded to create various specific variables, such as the distance from the walked endpoint to the correct target location (Figure 9.2).

Spatial cognition researchers frequently want to assess beliefs about directions rather than distance. The phenomenon of spatial orientation is, as its name suggests, most centrally about knowing which direction you need to travel to get to a destination (Montello, 2005). Participants can indicate directions by pointing directly with their hand, turning their body, or rotating the dial of a pointing device (Montello, Richardson, Hegarty, & Provenza, 1999). These **judgments of relative**

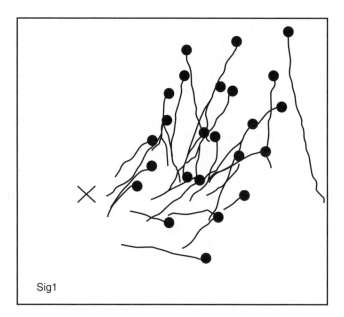

Figure 9.2 Technique of spatial reproduction represented by records of the tracks of a single sighted respondent that captures the respondent's walks to estimated locations in a large room. Circles show the respondent's starting locations on different trials (starting at different places), and X indicates the actual target place to which the respondent is attempting to walk. Adapted from Figure 5 in Loomis et al., 1993; used with permission.

direction (JRD) can be made from the perspective of a participant's current location and heading, or from an imagined location and heading, pointing to a target "as if" standing in a particular place or facing a particular direction. McNamara, Rump, and Werner (2003) used JRDs to study participants' cognitive maps of the layout of a city park, having them indicate directions from various imagined locations and headings.

The performance of different techniques for estimating directions is compared by Montello et al. (1999). These authors also discuss implications of analyzing the accuracy of directional estimates in terms of **absolute error**, which is the absolute value of estimates minus the correct value; **constant error**, which is the signed value of the mean estimate minus the correct value; or **variable error**, which is the variability of the estimates around their mean value. When working with constant and variable errors, it is correct to analyze directions with **circular (directional) statistics**. Unless the direction estimates for a given trial are fairly bunched around their mean value, it is quite misleading not to use circular statistics.

Sketch maps and related formats in spatial cognition

One of the most straightforward ways to find out what people think about the spatial layout of the environment is to ask them to "draw a map." Lynch (1960) is widely credited with introducing the technique of sketch mapping to spatial cognition and environment-behavior research (in fact, he also had respondents describe trips through the city, give verbal directions, and list distinctive places and features). Since then, probably hundreds of studies and countless additional informal data collections and demonstrations have asked people to sketch maps of places at various scales. The study by Jansen-Osmann and Wiedenbauer (2004) discussed above not only used ratio estimation to examine subjective distances but also had participants sketch maps. Baird, Merrill, and Tannenbaum (1979) had college students sketch maps of their campus, and compared them to MDS configurations generated from pairwise distance estimates. Saarinen collected sketch maps at the world scale over many years (e.g., Saarinen, Parton, & Billberg, 1996). He has observed that more familiar places tend to be drawn larger and with more detail, and one's home region is often centered in the sketch (although the influence of particular Western projections that center the Atlantic Ocean are common, too). Similar to map sketching, participants can be asked to construct physical models (Portugali, 1996).

As is so often true of open-ended methods (sometimes called "qualitative" methods), the ease and simplicity of collecting records is not matched by the ease and simplicity of coding and analyzing the records. This point was made above about behavioral coding. Analyzing sketch maps is something of a notorious problem in research. One piece of good advice is that you should figure out what kind of information you want to get from the sketch maps, based on what research questions you want to address. There is no omni-relevant way to analyze them. You can count features or measure spatial properties; you can assess them for accuracy by comparing them to a standard of what is correct; you can code the orientation of the map (what is at the top); you can code their drawing style (linear or survey); you can code the presence or absence of verbal labels; you can assess the relative scale of the map overall or in different parts; and more.

Once you decide what to code on the maps, another common difficulty is that certain variables can be hard to code, if not impossible, depending on how correctly, completely, and clearly the maps were drawn. How can one measure the accuracy of distances if it is not known which road that refers to? How can one tell if that landmark is located correctly, if one can't tell which landmark you thought that was, or you provide a label that is not correct? These thorny issues can be somewhat ameliorated by providing more structure to participants than just a blank page or screen (Kitchin, 2000). You could provide path networks like roads, macro-features such as mountains or water bodies, or indications of the proper scale to draw the map. You could provide a list of features to be located on the map, allowing you to focus on the location of placed features, not whether they are included in the first place. If features on the map can be matched with corresponding features in the world (or on another map), techniques like **bidimensional regression** (Friedman & Kohler, 2003) can quantitatively compare the degree of correspondence (relative accuracy) of the two layouts, giving the amount of rotation, translation, and scaling needed to make them correspond as much as they can.

Verbal explicit reports

As we discussed above, explicit reports are often collected as verbal responses. This method is sometimes used in spatial cognition research, although less than in most areas of research in the social and behavioral sciences, areas that probably use verbal responses most often to collect data. For instance, a marketing researcher might ask you to describe in words what you think about a particular product or a sociologist might ask you to say what you think about people of different racial groups. One can further distinguish verbal expressions themselves as the behavior of interest (behavioral observation) from verbal reports as the medium by which people express their explicit beliefs about something.

Taylor and Tversky and their colleagues (e.g., Taylor & Tversky, 1995) have reported several studies of spatial cognition assessed by people's oral and written responses. They have used verbal responses to study spatial perspectives and other aspects of the reference systems by which people store and recall spatial beliefs stored in memory. In a unique and very interesting study, Bahrick (1983) assessed people's cognitive maps for a small city and college campus after retrieval intervals of as many as several decades. He did this by testing not only current and recent students at the college but also alumni, some of whom had graduated over 40 years earlier and had rarely or never been back to the city. He collected data on their cognitive maps, including the accuracy of their spatial knowledge, by having them recall names of city and campus buildings, spatially ordering them along dimensions of east–west and north–south. He also gave them a structured map-sketching task, providing an outline map of the city with streets and buildings indicated but not labeled; participants were asked to name the streets and buildings.

Hirtle and Jonides (1985) collected verbal recalls of landmark structures (mostly buildings) on a college campus as a clever way to reveal their participants' memory organizations for the campus layout. By having the participants repeatedly recall the names of the campus landmarks, seeding each recall sequence with a different starting landmark, they could apply cluster analysis to reveal persistent tendencies for their participants to recall mentally related landmarks close together in the recall sequence. The researchers could then examine properties of the clustered landmark to show that spatial proximity, for instance, or functional relatedness provided the basis for memory associations.

An important verbal method for collecting data on people's spatial thinking is protocol analysis. Protocol analysis requires people to "think aloud" when they are reasoning about some problem. Their verbal responses are recorded and coded, and in spatial cognition research, behavioral measures such as pointing or looking are frequently recorded as well. For instance, Passini (1992) reported protocol analyses of people wayfinding to a destination inside a public building, having his participants talk about what they were looking at and thinking about while trying to find a destination.

Summary and Conclusions

This chapter contains a discussion of behavioral methods for conducting research studies in spatial cognition. Spatial cognition researchers study perception, thinking, reasoning, and communication that is fundamentally about spatial properties in the environment. This review has focused on the study of human spatial cognition with primary data collected via behavioral methods, probably the most common methods for collecting data by environment-behavior researchers. The review distinguishes behavioral methods based on observation from those based on explicit reports, including tests, surveys, and interviews. Both behavioral observation and explicit reports can be based on either verbal or non-verbal behavior (or a combination). Verbal behavior can be spoken or written, and may include gestures and other para-verbal behavior. Non-verbal behaviors studied in spatial cognition include locomotion, eye movements, psychophysical and psychometric scaling, and map sketching.

The review suggests that environment-behavior researchers have choices to make when designing studies. These choices should be dictated by a reckoning of the benefits different methods offer, and the costs they extract. Different methods tell us more or less about particular behaviors, particular beliefs, particular preferences, and so on. They come with different costs, whether of time, effort, money, or comfort.

Before we end, it is appropriate to remember that environment-behavior researchers basically study the interactions of humans and environments (some would say "transactions," to suggest an integrated, indivisible system of human–environment). That points to the important truth that we cannot understand human–environment by focusing only on human behavior and mind. We must also understand the environment, including its physical and socio-cultural aspects. That is especially fitting to remember for researchers who have training not only in cognitive disciplines such as psychology but also in environmental disciplines such as geography and architecture.

In the context of spatial cognition research, that includes understanding how the layout and appearance of built and natural environments influence spatial learning and wayfinding. A detailed analysis of the environment can help. Factors such as visibility, differentiation of appearance, and layout complexity and shape have been recognized as important (Carlson, Hölscher, Shipley, & Dalton, 2010;

Kelly, McNamara, Bodenheimer, Carr, & Rieser, 2008; Weisman, 1981). Analyzing vistas – the extents of people's lines-of-sight from different places and in different directions – is increasingly recognized as relevant; these have traditionally been called "viewsheds" when outdoors and "isovists" when indoors. A fruitful approach to understanding the complexity of path networks, whether hallways or roads, is provided by the techniques of space syntax analysis (Kim & Penn, 2004).

The social and cultural environment is important, too. Observing people verbally interacting with each other would be a useful way to address the understudied problem of spatial reasoning in groups (Hutchins, 1995). Cultural and regional conventions influence the design of built spaces, of road signs, of guidebooks, and of maps (Koshiro, 2003; Lawton, 2001). Spatial cognition may differ even more fundamentally across cultures as a function of differences in the way spatial languages use reference systems (Levinson, 2003).

Glossary

Absolute error Error in an estimated quantity such as distance, direction, or area, calculated by taking the absolute value of the difference between the estimated value and the correct value. Averaged over estimation trials, it assesses total error of estimation, including both systematic bias and unsystematic variability.

Bidimensional regression Statistical technique for analyzing two-dimensional data, such as estimated locations in a spatial layout. Allows quantitative comparison of the degree of correspondence (relative accuracy) of two layouts (two estimated layouts, or one estimated and one actual layout), giving the amount of rotation, translation, and scaling needed to make them correspond as much as possible.

Circular (directional) statistics Appropriate statistical techniques for analyzing data such as directional estimates that vary across part or all of 360 angular degrees. However, absolute directional errors are linear and do not require circular statistics.

Constant error Error in an estimated quantity such as distance, direction, or area, calculated by taking the signed (directional) difference between the estimated value and the correct value. Averaged over estimation trials, it assesses systematic error of estimation, indicating any bias in one direction or another (e.g., direction estimates in the clockwise direction).

Explicit reports Type of data collection in which people's intentional expression of their beliefs about themselves, other people, places, events, activities, or objects are recorded. Surveys assess beliefs that are not or cannot be scored primarily for accuracy (i.e., not compared to a standard of correctness); tests assess beliefs that are scored primarily for accuracy.

Judgments of relative direction (JRD) Estimates of directions in the environment made from the perspective of a participant's current location and heading, or from an imagined location and heading, pointing to a target "as if" standing in a particular place or facing a particular direction.

Multi-dimensional scaling (MDS) Computational algorithm that generates a spatial configuration of any number of dimensions (most often two-dimensional in environmental spatial cognition research) given as input a matrix of pairwise estimates of distance, similarity, or another property. The algorithm creates a configuration solution by minimizing the difference, or stress, between the patterns of values in the input matrix and in the solution configuration.

Scaling (psychometric)   Set of techniques in which participants systematically estimate quantities of some property that do not correspond in any direct way to objectively measurable quantities; includes rating scales. In spatial cognition, psychometrics can be used to study attitudes, abilities, preferences, or personality traits.

Scaling (psychophysical)   Set of techniques in which participants systematically estimate quantities of some property that the researcher then relates to the values of the objectively measured quantities; includes ratio and magnitude estimation. In spatial cognition, psychophysics can be used to study properties such as subjective distance or size.

Variable error   Error in an estimated quantity such as distance, direction, or area, calculated by taking the absolute value of the difference between the estimated value on one trial and the mean estimate across trials. Averaged over estimation trials, it assesses unsystematic error of estimation, indicating variability or resolution of estimation.

Virtual environments (virtual realities or VR)   Interactive, real-time, three-dimensional graphical computer displays that simulate the experience of moving through real environments, actual or imagined. They display varying levels of detail and invoke different types of sensorimotor involvement, but prototypically present a first-person perspective, appear fairly realistic, and change appropriately in response to user movements (i.e., they incorporate at least partial active control).

References

Ajzen, I. (2001). Nature and operation of attitudes. *Annual Review of Psychology, 52,* 27–58.

Allen, G. L. (1997). From knowledge to words to wayfinding: Issues in the production and comprehension of route directions. In S. C. Hirtle & A. U. Frank (Eds.), *Spatial information theory: A theoretical basis for GIS* (pp. 363–372). Berlin, Germany: Springer.

Allen, G. L. (2003). Gestures accompanying verbal route directions: Do they point to a new avenue for examining spatial representations? *Spatial Cognition and Computation, 3,* 259–268.

Bahrick, H. P. (1983). The cognitive map of a city: Fifty years of learning and memory. In G. H. Bower (Ed.), *The psychology of learning and motivation* (Vol. *17,* pp. 125–163). New York, NY: Academic Press.

Baird, J. C., Merrill, A. A., & Tannenbaum, J. (1979). Cognitive representation of spatial relations: II. A familiar environment. *Journal of Experimental Psychology: General, 108,* 92–98.

Battersby, S. E., & Montello, D. R. (2009). Area estimation of world regions and the projection of the global-scale cognitive map. *Annals of the Association of American Geographers, 99,* 273–291.

Boehm, A. E., & Weinberg, R. A. (1997). *The classroom observer: Developing observation skills in early childhood settings* (3rd ed.). New York, NY: Teachers College Press.

Borsboom, D. (2005). *Measuring the mind: Conceptual issues in contemporary psychometrics.* Cambridge, UK: Cambridge University Press.

Carlson, L. A., Hölscher, C., Shipley, T. F., & Dalton, R. C. (2010). Getting lost in buildings. *Current Directions in Psychological Science, 19,* 284–289.

Carr, S., & Schissler, D. (1969). The city as a trip: Perceptual selection and memory in the view from the road. *Environment and Behavior, 1,* 7–36.

Dalton, N. S., Conroy-Dalton, R., Hölscher, C., & Kuhnmünch, G. (2012). An iPad app for recording movement paths and associated spatial behaviors. In C. Stachniss, K. Schill, & D. Uttal (Eds.), *Spatial cognition VIII* (LNAI 7463, pp. 431–450). Berlin, Germany: Springer-Verlag.

Emmorey, K., Tversky, B., & Taylor, H. A. (2000). Using space to describe space: Perspective in speech, sign, and gesture. *Spatial Cognition and Computation, 2,* 157–180.

Friedman, A., & Kohler, B. (2003). Bidimensional regression: Assessing the configural similarity and accuracy of cognitive maps and other two-dimensional data sets. *Psychological Methods, 8,* 468–491.

Gescheider, G. A. (1997). *Psychophysics: The fundamentals* (3rd ed.). Mahwah, NJ: Erlbaum.

Golledge, R. G., Briggs, R. & Demko, D. (1969). The configuration of distances in intraurban space. *Proceedings of the Association of American Geographers, 1,* 60–65.

Hart, R. (1979). *Children's experience of place.* New York, NY: Irvington.

Hegarty, M., Richardson, A. E., Montello, D. R., Lovelace, K., & Subbiah, I. (2002). Development of a self-report measure of environmental spatial ability. *Intelligence, 30,* 425–447.

Heth, C. D., & Cornell, E. H. (1998). Characteristics of travel by persons lost in Albertan wilderness areas. *Journal of Environmental Psychology, 18,* 223–235.

Hirtle, S. C., & Jonides, J. (1985). Evidence of hierarchies in cognitive maps. *Memory & Cognition, 13,* 208–217.

Hutchins, E. (1995). *Cognition in the wild.* Cambridge, MA: MIT Press.

Hyman, I. E., & Loftus, E. F. (1998). Errors in autobiographical memory. *Clinical Psychology Review, 18,* 933–947.

Jansen-Osmann, P., & Wiedenbauer, G. (2004). The influence of turns on distance cognition: New experimental approaches to clarify the route-angularity effect. *Environment and Behavior, 36,* 790–813.

Kelly, J. W., McNamara, T. P., Bodenheimer, B., Carr, T. H., & Rieser, J. J. (2008). The shape of human navigation: How environmental geometry is used in the maintenance of spatial orientation. *Cognition, 109,* 281–286.

Kiefer, P., Straub, F., & Raubal, M. (2012). Location-aware mobile eye-tracking for the explanation of wayfinding behavior. *15th AGILE International Conference on Geographic Information Science (AGILE 2012),* Avignon, France.

Kim, Y. O., & Penn, A. (2004). Linking the spatial syntax of cognitive maps to the spatial syntax of the environment. *Environment and Behavior, 36,* 483–504.

Kitchin, R. (2000). Collecting and analysing cognitive mapping data. In R. Kitchin & S. Freundschuh (Eds.), *Cognitive mapping: Past, present and future* (pp. 9–23). London, UK: Routledge.

Koshiro, S. (2003). A comparative study of the spatial descriptions in tourist guidebooks. *Geographical Review of Japan, 76,* 249–269.

Kuipers, B. (2000). The spatial semantic hierarchy. *Artificial Intelligence, 119,* 191–233.

Lawton, C. A. (2001). Gender and regional differences in spatial referents used in direction giving. *Sex Roles, 44,* 321–337.

Levinson, S. C. (2003). *Space in language and cognition: Explorations in cognitive diversity.* Cambridge, UK: Cambridge University Press.

Loomis, J. M., Blascovich, J. J., & Beall, A. C. (1999). Immersive virtual environment technology as a basic research tool in psychology. *Behavior Research Methods, Instruments, & Computers, 31,* 557–564.

Loomis, J. M., Klatzky, R. L., Golledge, R. G., Cicinelli, J. G., Pellegrino, J. W., & Fry, P. A. (1993). Nonvisual navigation by blind and sighted: Assessment of path integration ability. *Journal of Experimental Psychology: General, 122,* 73–91.

Louwerse, M. M., & Benesh, N. (2012). Representing spatial structure through maps and language: Lord of the Rings encodes the spatial structure of Middle Earth. *Cognitive Science, 36*(8), 1556–1569.

Lynch, K. (1960). *The image of the city.* Cambridge, MA: MIT Press.

Maguire, E. A., Burgess, N., Donnett, J. G., Frackowiak, R. S. J., Frith, C. D., & O'Keefe, J. (1998). Knowing where and getting there: A human navigation network. *Science, 280* (May 8), 921–924.

McNamara, T. P., Rump, B., & Werner, S. (2003). Egocentric and geocentric frames of reference in memory of large-scale space. *Psychonomic Bulletin & Review, 10,* 589–595.

Montello, D. R. (1991). The measurement of cognitive distance: Methods and construct validity. *Journal of Environmental Psychology, 11,* 101–122.

Montello, D. R. (2005). Navigation. In P. Shah & A. Miyake (Eds.), *The Cambridge handbook of visuospatial thinking* (pp. 257–294). Cambridge, UK: Cambridge University Press.

Montello, D. R., & Freundschuh, S. M. (1995). Sources of spatial knowledge and their implications for GIS: An introduction. *Geographical Systems, 2,* 169–176.

Montello, D. R., & Raubal, M. (2012). Functions and applications of spatial cognition. In D. Waller & L. Nadel (Eds.), *Handbook of spatial cognition* (pp. 249–264). Washington, DC: American Psychological Association.

Montello, D. R., Richardson, A. E., Hegarty, M., & Provenza, M. (1999). A comparison of methods for estimating directions in egocentric space. *Perception, 28,* 981–1000.

Nasar, J. L. (1983). Environmental factors, perceived distance and spatial behavior. *Environment and Planning B, 10,* 275–281.

Passini, R. (1992). *Wayfinding in architecture* (2nd ed.). New York, NY: Van Nostrand Reinhold.

Portugali, J. (1996). Inter-representation networks. In J. Portugali (Ed.), *The construction of cognitive maps* (pp. 11–43). Dordrecht, The Netherlands: Kluwer.

Saarinen, T. F., Parton, M., & Billberg, R. (1996). Relative size of continents on world sketch maps. *Cartographica, 33,* 37–47.

Shettleworth, S. J., & Sutton, J. E. (2005). Multiple systems for spatial learning: Dead reckoning and beacon homing in rats. *Journal of Experimental Psychology: Animal Behavior Processes, 31,* 125–141.

Stern, P. C. (2000). Toward a coherent theory of environmentally significant behavior. *Journal of Social Issues, 56,* 407–424.

Taylor, H. A., & Tversky, B. (1995). Assessing spatial representation using text. *Geographical Systems, 2,* 235–254.

Waller, D., & Haun, D. B. M. (2003). Scaling techniques for modeling directional knowledge. *Behavior Research Methods, Instruments, & Computers, 35,* 285–293.

Ward, S. L., Newcombe, N., & Overton, W. F. (1986). Turn left at the church, or three miles north: A study of direction giving and sex differences. *Environment and Behavior, 18,* 192–213.

Weisman, J. (1981). Evaluating architectural legibility: Way-finding in the built environment. *Environment and Behavior, 13,* 189–204.

Wolbers, T., Hegarty, M., Büchel, C., & Loomis, J. M. (2008). Spatial updating: How the brain keeps track of changing object locations during observer motion. *Nature Neuroscience, 11,* 1223–1230.

Yeap, W. K., & Jefferies, M. E. (1999). Computing a representation of the local environment. *Artificial Intelligence, 107,* 265–301.

Yoshioka, J. G. (1942). A direction-orientation study with visitors at the New York World's Fair. *Journal of General Psychology, 27,* 3–33.

Suggested Readings

Ericsson, K. A., & Simon, H. A. (1993). *Protocol analysis: Verbal reports as data* (Rev. ed.). Cambridge, MA: MIT Press.

Foreman, N., & Gillett, R. (Eds.) (1997). *Handbook of spatial research paradigms and methodologies* (Vol. 1: Spatial cognition in the child and adult). East Sussex, UK: Psychology Press.

Fowler, F. J. (2009). *Survey research methods* (4th ed.). Thousand Oaks, CA: Sage.

Gentry, T. A., & Wakefield, J. A. (1991). Methods for measuring spatial cognition. In D. M. Mark & A. U. Frank (Eds.), *Cognitive and linguistic aspects of geographic space* (pp. 185–217). Dordrecht, The Netherlands: Kluwer.

Gerber, R., & Kwan, T. (1994). A phenomenographical approach to the study of pre-adolescents' use of maps in a wayfinding exercise in a suburban environment. *Journal of Environmental Psychology, 14,* 265–280.

Golledge, R. G. (1976). Methods and methodological issues in environmental cognition research. In G. T. Moore & R. G. Golledge (Eds.), *Environmental knowing* (pp. 300–313). Stroudsburg, PA: Dowden, Hutchinson & Ross.

Krippendorff, K. (2009). *Content analysis: An introduction to its methodology* (2nd ed.). Thousand Oaks, CA: Sage.

Newcombe, N. (1985). Methods for the study of spatial cognition. In R. Cohen (Ed.), *The development of spatial cognition* (pp. 277–330). Hillsdale, NJ: Erlbaum.

Rosenthal, R., & Rosnow, R. L. (2007). *Essentials of behavioral research: Methods and data analysis* (3rd ed.). Boston, MA: McGraw-Hill.

Webb, E. J., Campbell, D. T., Schwartz, R. D., & Sechrest, L. (2000). *Unobtrusive measures* (Rev. ed.). Thousand Oaks, CA: Sage.

Zeisel, J. (2006). *Inquiry by design: Environment/behavior/neuroscience in architecture, interiors, landscape, and planning* (2nd ed.). New York, NY: W.W. Norton.

10

Microworlds
Using Computers to Understand Choices about the Use of Natural Resources

Angel Chen[1] and Paul A. Bell[2]
[1] University of Victoria, BC, Canada
[2] Colorado State University, CO, United States

Maria was fascinated by her research method class while pursuing a graduate degree in psychology. When the time came for her to pick a topic for her research project, she knew right away that she would enjoy investigating the impact of human interactions and activities on natural resources. However, she was struggling with an important decision concerning the setting in which the study would be conducted. Maria felt most comfortable working in the controlled setting of a laboratory. She believed that knowledge advances best when systematic, scientifically valid methods are employed. However, she realized that resource management is best understood when data collection occurs in the "real world." As Maria pondered this issue, she was startled as Gabriel yelled across the room "Holy cow! My cabbages got stolen!!" Maria rolled her eyes and gave him a nasty look. Gabriel responded apologetically, "Sorry, honey. I was playing FarmVille. This is so addictive." "Right. What is FarmVille, anyway?" "It's an online social network game. The goal is to create a virtual farm. Players cultivate, irrigate, fertilize, and harvest different types of vegetables and fruits. Players sell their produce in exchange for virtual money. This is all very time consuming. But there is a short cut: You can steal other people's vegetables, and it becomes a competition when ... Hey, where are you going?" Maria rushed out, with only one thing in her mind: Computer simulation.

The relation between human and environment is two-fold: We depend on its resources to maintain our existence and improve our well-being, yet high levels of industrialization and consumption have stretched and broken the limits of planet Earth as if we were separated from, or even superior to, the ecosystem we rely on. How should we study a phenomenon as complex as decisions and management of natural resources? A major challenge concerns a dilemma between laboratory and field settings. The conflict arises from the trade-off between **internal validity** and

Research Methods for Environmental Psychology, First Edition. Edited by Robert Gifford.
© 2016 John Wiley & Sons, Ltd. Published 2016 by John Wiley & Sons, Ltd.

external validity (Runkel & McGrath, 1972). Internal validity refers to the ability to demonstrate causal relationships between independent and dependent variables. External validity refers to the degree that results can be generalized beyond the limited research setting and participant sample from which the data were obtained. Laboratory experiments allow systematic control over variables, but tend to have some degree of artificiality, that is, they may not reflect the "real-world" setting. In contrast, field research is realistic, but studies conducted in natural environments are often subject to confounds, making any causal interpretation of data difficult. The root of the dilemma lies in the inability to handle complexity (Brehmer & Dörner, 1993): Whereas field studies have too much complexity and uncertainty to establish definite conclusions, laboratory research has too little complexity to comfortably conclude that the outcome applies beyond the lab.

Despite the trade-off, mainstream research in psychology takes place under a constricted setting, giving rise to the perception of the laboratory experiment as "science par excellence." Advocates of laboratory investigation assert that the ability to establish definitive causal inferences is the essence of a scientifically valid research in which findings can be generalized to most behavioral phenomena. However, another crucial challenge for laboratory studies is to develop realistic experimental tasks that not only involve participants (experimental realism) but also instantiate the events that occur in the real world (mundane realism).

The current chapter examines how laboratory simulations – also known as microworlds – serve as a possible resolution to the basic dilemma of laboratory and field settings by allowing experimental investigation of behavior in contexts that represent the dynamic nature of a real-world system while establishing both experimental and mundane realism in the laboratory (Brehmer & Dörner, 1993). Before turning to a detailed description of microworlds, it is worth presenting a brief review of the **commons dilemma** paradigm as a conceptual framework for studying individual choices in resource management and its traditional research methodologies (for further discussion, see Edney & Harper, 1978). Next, we review what a microworld is, the essential characteristics of a microworld, and methodological approaches in using a microworld in research. To illustrate these aspects, we present a computer-based commons dilemma simulation (FISH 4). We will then discuss how microworlds bridge the gap between field and laboratory studies with two major advantages they offer: realism and experimental control.

Commons Dilemma

Many decisions in resource management can be conceptualized as social dilemmas, a class of situations in which individual interests collide with collective interest. A social dilemma has three main properties (Dawes, 1980; Liebrand, 1983): (1) members of a group have the choice between a cooperative and a defective choice; (2) from an individual perspective, defection is rational – by choosing the self-maximization alternative choice the decision maker will receive a better payoff regardless of what others do; and (3) the aggregated outcome of self-interested decisions results in a deficient collective outcome that is worse for all. Two common experimental paradigms of social dilemmas are the resource dilemma and the public goods problem (also known as the "take-some" dilemma and the "give-some" dilemma, respectively). Economists distinguish between "private goods" or items owned by individuals and bought and sold in a market (such as clothes or cell phones), and "public goods" or items not owned by individuals (such as a national park or the fish in the sea). Both social dilemmas pit self-interest against collective group interest. In the commons dilemma (resource dilemma), a shared resource such as water supply or a national forest will replenish over time as long as those sharing it cooperate and do not as individuals take or harvest more of the resource than will be naturally replenished. In the public goods problem, inspired by Olson (1965), individuals must decide how much to voluntarily contribute to a resource (e.g., public television or a charity that serves all) that is freely accessible and non-excludable (i.e., non-paying consumers cannot be excluded from accessing it). The selfish choice of not contributing to the pool that serves all does retain resources for the individual, but if enough potential contributors act selfishly, the common pool does not have enough resources to operate.

The commons (resource) dilemma paradigm (Dawes, 1973; Lloyd, 1837/1968) consists of an opportunity to consume desirable, exhaustible, and renewable resources, such as water and forest. The danger of resource exhaustion arises when a resource is harvested more quickly than it can be generated (e.g., water is used at a higher rate than the reservoirs are replenished). The short supply forces harvesters to confront a dilemma: defection ("get as much as you can" at the expense of the community) or cooperation (exercising restraint in order to preserve the commons). Although it is rational to defect, unrestrictive harvesting – if practiced by enough people – inevitably leads to resource destruction. The tragedy of the commons is illustrated by Hardin (1968) in the collapse of common pastures for herding cattle. The paradigm has been used as a conceptual framework to explain a variety of environmental problems, such as deforestation, global climate change, and the loss of biodiversity, to name but a few.

Simulating Commons Dilemmas

Concern over environmental degradation provoked systematic investigation of factors that may contribute to mismanagement of resources. How can we study a situation that is as complex as the commons dilemma? Although field experiments may seem appealing because of their high ecological validity, it may be difficult to control aspects of the resource and the situation, and it may require multiple seasons or years of observation to observe the consequences of overharvesting on both the resource and the reactions of the participants. Lack of control potentially permits many unmeasured variables to influence behaviors in the commons. Alternatively, laboratory study of commons dilemmas, using simulation techniques to capture the inherent conflict between individual and collective levels, allows for systematic manipulation of many independent variables and measurement of numerous individual differences and outcomes. Early simulations of the commons dilemma typically involved a contrived task engaged by small groups of participants, who could be separated by dividers in the same laboratory room and communicated with through non-verbal means (e.g., writing on a blackboard). One such non-computerized simulation is the "nuts game" (Edney, 1979) in which participants can take any quantities of walnuts or hardware store hex nuts out of a shallow bowl (a resource pool). The nuts are redeemable for something valuable, such as money or food. After each replenishment cycle (10-second interval), the number of nuts remaining in the bowl are doubled (symbolizing regeneration rate). The task continues until the bowl is emptied or a certain number of rounds or a time limit is reached. Another early simulation is the "points game" (Edney & Bell, 1983) in which three participants in each round may individually choose to harvest up to three points from a shared pool of 15 points, with the quantities in the pool and the harvests recorded on a chalk board. The remaining points in the pool are doubled after every two rounds. The simulation ends when the pool is depleted or 15 rounds have run. Examples of a commons depleting outcome and a commons sustaining outcome are shown in Table 10.1. In a typical simulation of commons dilemmas, cooperation is often used as a dependent variable and may be defined in several ways, such as the number of trials elapsed without extinguishing the resource pool (e.g., the number of times the group leaves at least one point), the total harvest (e.g., the total number of points garnered by all participants), or the average amount of resource harvested per individual per trial averaged over trials. These measures can be used to infer defecting (non-cooperative), cooperative, or mixed strategies. With the advent of computer technology, complex experiments can be conducted with interconnected computers and large data sets can be managed. Computers afford accuracy and efficiency and have attracted a variety of

Table 10.1 Examples of a commons depleting outcome and a commons sustaining outcome in the points game.

Round	Player A	B	C	Total harvest	Calculation	Commons value at end of round
Commons depleting outcome						
Start						15
1	1	2	2	5	$15-5=10$	10
2	2	2	2	6	$(10-6)\times2$	8
3	2	2	2	6	$8-6=2$	2
4	1	1	0	2	$2-2=0$	0
Commons sustaining outcome						
Start						15
1	1	1	1	3	$15-3=12$	12
2	2	2	2	6	$(12-6)\times2=12$	12
3	1	0	1	2	$12-2=10$	10
4	1	1	1	3	$(10-3)\times2=14$	14
5	1	2	1	4	$14-4=10$	10
6	1	1	1	3	$(10-3)\times2=14$	14

procedures to study commons dilemma behavior (e.g., Akimov & Soutchankski, 1994; Chapman, Hu, & Mullen, 1987; Fusco, Bell, Jorgenson, & Smith, 1991; Powers, 1987; Summers, 1996).

Microworlds Defined

Microworlds are given various terms, including "virtual environment" and "scaled world," and have different applications, such as recreational video games, interactive educational technology, and training simulations (e.g., a flight simulator). In psychological research of decision making, a microworld is a computer-generated environment that exists in laboratories. It is a simplified, idealized model that adequately simulates the essential elements of a real-world system. Based upon empirical data, a limited set of variables and relations between those variables are formulated. Microworlds provide a rich, dynamic environment in which participants' interaction with or management of a simulated system can be investigated (DiFonzo, Hantula, & Bordia, 1998).

Microworlds can be distinguished from other types of simulation and research instruments. First, microworlds are designed to represent interactive, complex, ever-changing real-world systems (e.g., fisheries) with real human participants. They are distinct from computer simulation of behavioral phenomena that occur in a one-dimensional world where human activity is represented by a computer program rather than by real people. While the former aims to understand strategies inferred from patterns of behavior of real people, the latter focuses on developing and testing mathematical models of behaviors of simulated agents (e.g., Macy, 1996). Second, microworlds provide interactive scenarios of complex problems in which participants are required to act and react repeatedly over time. Therefore, microworlds are different from computerized administration of instruments or manipulation, in which the participants respond in a passive manner.

To be categorized as a microworld, the entity must possess, in varying degree, three essential features: It must be complex (have a goal structure), dynamic (operate in real time), and opaque (the participant must make inferences about the system; Brehmer & Dörner, 1993). First, the complex aspect of microworlds necessitates participants' considerations of several possibly contradictory goals (e.g., self-maximization or conservation). Participants have to prioritize different goals as situational demands may change over time (e.g., when a resource is depleting). They are required to choose multiple courses of actions, yet any given action has possible repercussions, forcing them to make trade-offs.

Second, microworlds involve a dynamic decision-making task (Brehmer, 1992; Gonzalez, Vanyukov, & Martin, 2004), which is characterized by: (1) a sequential nature – a series of decisions must be made to achieve some goals; (2) interdependence – the decisions are not discrete or isolated to one another, as early decisions influence later decisions and mistakes made in previous decisions can be fixed by later decisions; (3) semi-indeterminancy – the decision problem changes at any point of time and depends on both the autonomous system factor and consequences of previous decisions; and (4) time-boundedness – participants have to make decisions in timely responses to changing contingencies. This can be stressful, since participants cannot determine when they have to make their decisions. Taken together, a dynamic decision-making task is characterized by a feedback relation between the participant and the microworld: The current state of the system is dependent upon participants' activities, and the system changes as a function of autonomous system factors and consequences of actions made on it. The dynamic perspective is essential to understanding resource management and other decision phenomena, in which the relation between personal influences (internal states and overt behavior) and the system's internally generated forces are inherently interactive (Vallacher & Nowak, 1994) and time-dependent (Hogarth, 1980). Therefore, traditional methodologies (e.g., questionnaires) may be too static to make inferences about a dynamic system.

Third, opaqueness refers to the "invisibility" of some aspects of the system (Brehmer, 1992). Microworlds are opaque because they require exploration and experimentation. In microworlds, the relations (feedbacks) among variables follow certain rules that are largely unknown to participants. To acquire knowledge about the system, participants must gather information about the microworld and form hypotheses about the hidden structure. As participants interact with the microworld, they might discover its structure through consequences of their decisions.

Methodological Approaches in Microworld Research

Three methodological approaches can be distinguished in microworld research: the individual differences approach, the experimental approach; and the case study approach (Brehmer & Dörner, 1993). In the individual differences approach, experimenters are interested in personal factors (e.g., social orientation) that affect performance. Several measurements are administered to a large sample of participants before they engage in the same microworld. This line of research often employs the false feedback procedure in which participants are deceived into believing they are interacting with other participants who are in fact virtual "people" programmed by the experimenter. The use of the same computerized "people" confronted by all participants permits systematic investigation of individual influences on behavior. In the experimental approach, participants are randomly assigned to different conditions in which properties of the microworld are manipulated (e.g., feedback delays) in order to determine how they affect performance (e.g., Brehmer & Nählinder, 2007; Hine & Gifford, 1996). The purpose of this approach is to study the effect of structural and situational factors that apply to all decision makers. Finally, in the case study approach, each participant's behaviors are closely examined to identify what is typical or atypical. The goal is to generate hypotheses and develop theories about how people handle complexity and uncertainty in a given situation.

FISH 4

Because a fish stock (supply of fish in a body of water) is easy to understand as a renewable, collective resource, several programs use the fish system to study harvesting behavior of real people; examples include the fish-harvesting simulation of Moxnes (1998) and the "individual choice and social effects" model of Summers (1996).

We choose to depict FISH 4 as an example for this chapter because it is relatively new and yields a fine instrument for studying the effects of various system properties on individual harvesting behavior.

FISH 4 and its earlier version FISH 3 (Gifford & Gifford, 2000) are Java-based microworld environments that simulate a fish stock for investigating the resource management decision making of individuals and small groups. FISH 4 allows either standalone mode (running it on a single computer) or networked mode (connects any computers with Internet access). It can be run with all human fishers or a combination of human and computer-simulated fishers.

FISH 4 runs in real time and creates a virtual fishery in which participants play the role of fishers and harvest from an ocean supply. Refer to Figure 10.1, which shows a screenshot of a participant's view during the simulation. Participants experience an ocean-fishing context through graphics (images of colored fish are displayed in an ocean) and text (e.g., "spawning" represents resource replenishment). The tallies of fish caught, money earned, location status, and other information are displayed next to the ocean view. During each season (trial of the experiment), individual fishers decide how much resource to harvest (catch fish). Each fishing season ends when all fishers have caught as many fish as they wish and return to port. Resource regeneration occurs between each season through the spawning of remaining fish after a previous season. The notion that the growth of a fish stock is

This is season 5. There are 66 fish remaining.

Fisher	Location	Fish caught Season	Overall	Profits Season	Overall
You	⚓	0	57	$0.00	$5.70
6224	●	8	40	$0.80	$4.00
1832	●	4	47	$0.40	$4.70
9511	●	2	17	$0.20	$1.70

Figure 10.1 A screenshot during a simulation in FISH 4.

contingent on the available fish from a previous season signifies the commons dilemma. Each fisher may choose to harvest more fish than the fish stock can regenerate itself, at the risk of collapsing the fish stock. In fact, fishers are capable of exhausting the resource within one season. Each fisher may also choose to restrain his or her harvest in the interest of sustaining the fish stock. The simulation continues until all the fish have been caught or a number of seasons (unknown to participants) have been completed.

Many different scenarios may be created, through varying as many as 30 parameters, several of which represent the essential elements of commons dilemmas such as the initial and maximum fish stock (pool size), the number of seasons (replenishment trials), and the regeneration rate of the fish stock. The study investigator may also define the probability of harvest, the degree of uncertainty in the fish stock (by displaying "mystery" fish in the ocean), various income and expense variables (e.g., payment for each fish caught and the operating cost of fuel and labor), the length of time permitted for a cast, awareness of other harvesters (i.e., whether all fishers' identities, status, and profits are displayed), and the level of greediness of computer-generated fishers. In FISH 4, as in many other microworld studies, system complexity is generated with independent variables, in contrast to the manipulation of a single static feature in many traditional psychological experiments.

FISH 4 automatically collects information in ASCII (text) format which can easily be transferred to most statistical packages. These data include fish caught, profits earned, and time spent fishing. In addition, two measures of cooperation are automatically computed by FISH 4: individual restraint (IR) and individual efficiency (IE). These measures reflect two cooperative harvesting strategies: preservationism (taking little or none of a resource) and sustainability (taking just enough of a resource so that the fish stock regenerates to its original amount). IE and IR are proportional measures, in which the regeneration rate and the proportion of the pool harvested by an individual harvester are taken into account (see Gifford & Hine, 1997 for computational formulas for IE and IR). Hence, cooperation measures used by FISH 4 pertain to participants' tactics or strategies. They are considered as more appropriate measures of harvesting pattern as opposed to the absolute number of fish harvested or the number of seasons elapsed (Gifford & Hine, 1997).

Advantages of Microworlds

As mentioned, decision making in the real world is dynamic, time-constrained, and ill-defined (Lipshitz, Klein, Orasanu, & Salas, 2001). Although field methods (e.g., observation and interview) in natural settings seem attractive to collect realistic data, causal claims may be unattainable. In this section, we will discuss how microworld research may bridge the gap between laboratory and field studies by allowing experimental investigation in ecologically valid situations (Brehmer & Dörner, 1993). This is mainly achieved by two significant advantages that a microworld offers: realism and experimental control (DiFonzo, Hantula, & Bordia, 1998).

Realism

Realism is enhanced in microworlds through the simulation of dynamic systems. Two types of realism can be distinguished (Aronson & Carlsmith, 1968). First, experimental realism (or psychological realism) refers to the extent that participants are impacted by and actively involved with the experiment. Second, mundane realism refers to the extent that the activity involved in the experiment is applicable to real-life situations.

Experimental realism is enhanced though the dynamic nature of microworlds for a number of reasons. First, microworlds engage sensory and temporal involvements. By incorporating sounds and videos, a microworld provides vivid and engrossing experiences. Participants are able to experience the passage of time (e.g., days, seasons, years) through temporally related changes in the environment. Second, a microworld creates real stakes by using monetary contingencies. Observations of participants indicate that even a small payoff can evoke hostile responses toward defectors (e.g., Tindall & O'Connor, 1987). Third, microworlds necessitate interaction from active participants. These interactions closely recreate real-life situations in which participants carry out actions and experience events and consequences in the present. This approach is considered far more compelling a mode of involvement than non-dynamic methods in which participants are instructed to imagine scenarios that describe events and behaviors in a distant manner. Microworlds are interactive because they consist of side effects, goal conflicts, feedback delays, and uncertainty. To successfully accomplish the complex task imposed by a microworld, participants must engage in information search and goal analysis, as well as consider time constraint and consequences. All of these demand effortful processing and strategic planning.

High levels of experimental realism are likely to enhance the internal validity of a study (Aronson & Carlsmith, 1968). Internal validity refers to the extent to which an independent variable (IV) causes the changes seen in the dependent variable (DV). When the experimental manipulation involves the participant in the research (i.e., high experimental realism), the outcome behavior is likely due to the manipulation of the IV as opposed to other extraneous factors (such as demand characteristics or boredom).

Mundane realism is the degree to which the experimental setting and task correspond to the real-life circumstances in which the phenomenon of interest occurs naturally. Mundane realism deals with external validity, or generalizability of research findings. Although it is desirable for microworld research to have mundane realism, it is not essential for three reasons. First, in many instances, experimental research is aimed to develop and test a theory, but not necessarily to establish generalizability (Berkowitz & Donnerstein, 1982; Mook, 1983). Most microworld research on the commons dilemma is primarily concerned with investigating psychological mechanisms and processes that lead to resource depletion.

Second, most microworld-based research aims to capture the essential features of field experiences, but not necessarily the surface similarities of a particular field setting. To be validly generalized, a simulation must present the central characteristics (e.g., dynamic, interactive, and complex) embedded in a system, while describing structural relationships among parts of the system in functional terms. Because microworlds replicate the dynamic system inherent in the real world (Omodei & Wearing, 1995), they offer greater mundane realism than traditional experimental research.

Third, the physical resemblance between the experimental setting and the setting to which the study is to be generalized does not necessarily translate to a higher degree of external validity. In fact, apart from the most narrowly investigative foci, excessive preoccupation to mundane realism can hinder generalizability (DiFonzo, Hantula, & Bordia, 1998; Locke, 1986). Dipboye and Flanagan (1979), for example, demonstrated that an external validity problem can actually arise from a detailed simulation of a manufacturing plant setting, because it is too restrictive to be generalized across different settings and populations. Notably, the essential features of a system captured in microworlds provide a robust foundation for broad generalizability.

Experimental control

Microworlds offer a high level of experimental realism to strengthen the inference of causality. **Experimental control** ensures that the observed effects are due to the manipulation of independent variables, rather than extraneous variables. Two major confound problems are **experimenter bias** and **experimental errors**.

Experimenter bias (or the **experimenter expectancy effect**) is introduced by an experimenter whose expected notion of the data subtly communicates to the participants, through body language and verbal messages, subtle indications of hypotheses. In turn, participants who are motivated to determine the purpose of an experiment are attentive to those cues and may alter their behavior to conform to the experimenter's expectations (Adair & Epstein, 1968; Orne, 1962; Rosenthal & Rosnow, 1991). Although many methods have been suggested to minimize the bias, such as following a strict procedural protocol or using a double-blind method, they cannot completely eradicate the effect because human (experimenter–participant) interactions are inevitable to some degree (Rosenthal & Fode 1963). Microworlds employ a mechanized instructional format so that any social cues, such as tone of voice, posture, and facial expression, are prevented. For example, FISH 4 utilizes video tutorial and text messages so that it is possible for participants to use the program without intervention on the part of experimenters. Moreover, microworlds can vary individualized feedback to a participant, while holding other aspects of the message constant to all participants. For example, in FISH 4, the "end of simulation" message is displayed to all participants, on the same part of the screen and at the same time. The message states, "All the fish are now gone. You have caught xxx fish, and you have earned *yyy*," where *xxx* reflects the number of fish caught by an individual participant, and *yyy* represents amount of money he or she has earned.

Experimental error refers to inaccuracy, or imprecision of the results arising from procedural mistakes and human errors in administrative tasks. Experimental error is inevitable in any laboratory experiment, particularly with dynamical methodology that requires repeated, rapid, and multiple data reception, computation, and feedback. With computer technology, microworlds serve as an effective medium for dealing with complex data while offering consistent, standardized procedures free of human errors.

Other advantages

Computerized data management in microworlds maximizes efficiency and accuracy. This speeded-up data-collection process is relatively inexpensive, and eliminates mechanical errors of coding and data entry. In microworlds, data are automatically collected, aggregated, and calculated electronically in real time. For example, FISH 4 computes four cooperation formulae – restraint and efficiency at both the individual and group levels – for each season and over all seasons (Hine & Gifford, 1996). This information provides rates of defection and cooperation that are readily available for data analysis.

Another unique feature of microworlds is that they can simulate a period of years within a couple of minutes, and thus may examine the long-term effects of participants' decisions on real-world systems. In contrast, a field study may require several years, or even decades, to properly investigate real-world negative collective outcomes (e.g., extinction of a resource).

Microworlds can be conducted in a laboratory or over the Internet. With the widespread diffusion of personal computers, the Internet can reach geographically distant participants and decrease the cost of recruiting large, diverse, or specialized samples. For example, FISH 4 supports a fully networked and interactive environment in which any number of oceans can be shared and any number of computers can be connected via the Internet.

Finally, manipulating independent variables and setting up multi-factorial designs is relatively easy compared to conventional laboratory and field experiments. The simulation can be set up in a series of studies that systematically vary several experimental manipulations (e.g., level of computer fisher greediness or uncertainty of stock size) or help explore factors of interest before implementing more expensive field research. In addition, microworlds enable researchers to experiment with more extreme conditions (e.g., natural disasters or oil spills in the ocean) or extremely long time-series that are otherwise impractical, unethical, or illogical to manipulate in the real world.

Summary and Conclusion

Ironically, ecological capital – the very natural resources upon which human survival depends – can easily be degraded by human behavior. The commons dilemma paradigm helps explain mismanagement of resources by confronting individuals with a choice of self-interest and collective interest. Microworlds can be used to study commons dilemmas. Microworlds are computer simulations of a real-world rate characterized by complex, dynamic, and opaque properties. By combining experimental control exhorted by experimental researchers and realism emphasized by naturalistic researchers, microworlds enable systematic investigation of participants' interactions with a system while offering enhanced realism. It is our hope that the introduction of microworlds in this chapter partly addresses the growing interest in ways of studying sustainability and brings a fresh perspective for future research into resource management behavior.

Glossary

Commons dilemma   A situation in which people harvest from a shared, regenerating resource such that overharvesting by enough individuals will deplete the resource before it can regenerate; thus, cooperation to harvest at or below the regeneration rate is necessary to preserve the resource.

Experimenter bias   What happens in an experiment when an experimenter whose expected notion of the data subtly communicates to the participants, through body language and verbal messages, subtle indications of hypotheses and thus triggers actions on the part of participants to confirm hypotheses.

Experimental error   Inaccuracy or imprecision of results in an experiment arising from procedural mistakes and human errors in administrative tasks.

Experimenter expectancy effect   Another term for experimenter bias.

External validity   The degree that results can be generalized beyond the limited research setting and participant sample from which the data were obtained.

Internal validity   The ability to demonstrate causal relationships between independent and dependent variables.

Microworld   A computer simulation in which real human participants interact with each other via computer connections over time without knowing exactly what other participants are choosing to do, such that continual decisions must be made based on whatever information is available, with that information changing over time.

References

Akimov, V., & Soutchankski, M. (1994). Automata simulation of N-person social dilemma games. *Journal of Conflict Resolution, 38*, 138–148.

Aronson, E., & Carlsmith, J. M. (1963). Effect of the severity of threat on the devaluation of forbidden behavior. *Journal of Abnormal and Social Psychology, 66*, 583–588.

Adair, J. G., & Epstein, J. S. (1968). Verbal cues in the mediation of experimenter bias. *Psychological Reports, 22*, 1045–1053.

Berkowitz, L., & Donnerstein, E. (1982). External validity is more than skin deep: Some answers to criticisms of laboratory experiments. *American Psychologist, 37*, 245–257.

Brehmer, B. (1992). Dynamic decision making: Human control of complex systems. *Acta Psychologica, 81*, 211–241.

Brehmer, B., & Dörner, D. (1993). Experiments with computer-simulated microworlds: Escaping both the narrow straits of the laboratory and the deep blue sea of the field study. *Computers in Human Behavior, 9*, 171–184.

Brehmer, B., & Nählinder, S. (2007). Achieving what cannot be done: Coping with the time constants in a dynamic decision task by doing something else. *Scandinavian Journal of Psychology, 48*, 359–365.

Chapman, J., Hu, L., & Mullen, B. (1987). GROUP1 and GROUP2: BASIC programs for laboratory research on the commons dilemma and group persuasion. *Behavior Research Methods, Instruments, and Computers, 18*, 466–467.

Dawes, R. M. (1973). The commons dilemma game: An N-person mixed motive game with a dominating strategy for defection. *Oregon Research Institute Research Bulletin, 13*, 1–12.

Dawes, R. M. (1980). Social dilemmas. *Annual Review of Psychology, 31,* 169–193.

DiFonzo, N., Hantula, D. A., & Bordia, P. (1998). Microworlds for experimental research: Having your (control and collection) cake and realism too. *Behavior Research Methods, Instruments, & Computers, 30,* 278–286.

Dipboye, R. L., & Flanagan, M. F. (1979). Research settings in industrial and organizational psychology: Are findings in the field more generalizable than in the laboratory? *American Psychologist, 34,* 141–150.

Edney, J. J. (1979). The nuts game: A concise commons dilemma analogue. *Environmental Psychology and Nonverbal Behavior, 3,* 252–254.

Edney, J. J., & Bell, P. A. (1983). The commons dilemma: Comparing altruism, the Golden Rule, perfect equality of outcomes, and territoriality. *The Social Science Journal, 20,* 23–33.

Edney, J. J., & Harper, C. S. (1978). The commons dilemma: A review of contributions from psychology. *Environmental Management, 2,* 491–507.

Fusco, M. E., Bell, P. A., Jorgenson, M. D., & Smith, J. M. (1991). Using a computer to study the commons dilemma. *Simulation and Gaming, 22,* 67–74.

Gifford, J., & Gifford, R. (2000). FISH 3: A microworld for studying social dilemmas and resource management. *Behavior Research Methods, Instrumentation, and Computers, 32,* 417–422.

Gifford, R., & Hine, D. W. (1997). Toward cooperation in commons dilemmas. *Canadian Journal of Behavioural Science, 29,* 167–178.

Gonzalez, C., Vanyukov, P., & Martin, M. K. (2005). The use of microworlds to study dynamic decision making. *Computers in Human Behavior, 21,* 273–286.

Hardin, G. (1968). The tragedy of the commons. *Science, 162,* 1243–1248.

Hine, D. W., & Gifford, R. (1996). Individual restraint and group efficiency in commons dilemmas: The effects of uncertainty and risk-seeking. *Journal of Applied Social Psychology, 26,* 993–1009.

Hogarth, R. M. (1980). Beyond discrete biases: Functional and dysfunctional aspects of judgmental heuristics. *Psychological Bulletin, 90,* 197–217.

Liebrand, W. B. G. (1983). Interpersonal differences in social dilemmas: A game theoretical approach. *Dissertation Abstracts, 43,* 2373.

Lipshitz, R., Klein, G., Orasanu, J., & Salas, E. (2001). Taking stock of naturalistic decision making. *Journal of Behavioral Decision Making, 14,* 331–352.

Locke, E. A. (1986). *Generalizing from laboratory to field settings: Research findings from industrial-organizational psychology, organizational behavior, and human resource management.* Lexington, MA; Lexington Books.

Lloyd, W. F. (1837/1968). *Lectures on population, value, poor laws and rent.* New York, NY: August M. Kelly.

Macy, M. (1996). Natural selection and social learning in prisoner's dilemma: Coadaptation with genetic algorithms and artificial neural networks. In W. B. G. Liebrand & D. M. Messick (Eds.), *Frontiers in Social Dilemmas Research.* Berlin, Germany: Springer Verlag.

Mook, D. G. (1983). In defense of external validity. *American Psychologist, 38,* 379–387.

Moxnes, E. (1998). Not only the tragedy of the commons: Misperceptions of bioeconomics. *Management Science, 44,* 1234–1248.

Olson, M. (1965). *The logic of collective action.* Cambridge MA: Harvard University Press.

Omodei, M. M., & Wearing, A. J. (1995). The Fire Chief microworld generating program: An illustration of computer-simulated microworlds as an experimental paradigm for studying complex decision making behavior. *Behavior Research Methods, Instruments, & Computers, 27,* 303–316.

Orne, M. T. (1962). On the social psychology of the psychological experiment: With particular reference to demand characteristics and their implications. *American Psychologist, 17,* 776–783.

Powers, R. B. (1987). Bringing the commons into a large university classroom. *Simulation & Gaming, 18*, 443–457.

Rosenthal, R., & Fode, K. (1963). The effect of experimenter bias on performance of the albino rat. *Behavioral Science, 8*, 183–189.

Rosenthal, R., & Rosnow, R. L. (1991). *Essentials of behavioral research: Methods and data analysis* (2nd ed.). New York, NY: McGraw-Hill.

Runkel, P. J., & McGrath, J. E. (1972). *Research on human behavior: A systematic guide to method*. New York, NY: Holt, Rinehart & Winston.

Summers, C. (1996). Multimedia environmental decision making simulations. *Behavior Research Methods, Instruments and Computers, 24*, 598–602.

Tindall, D. B., & O'Connor, B. (1987). *Attitudes, social identity, social values, and behavior in a commons dilemma*. Paper presented at the Canadian Psychological Association Conference, Vancouver, BC.

Vallacher, R. R., & Nowak, A. (1994). *Dynamical systems in social psychology*. San Diego, CA: Academic.

Suggested Readings

Bell, P. A., Petersen, T. R., & Hautaluoma, J. (1989). The effect of punishment probability on overconsumption and stealing in a simulated commons. *Journal of Applied Social Psychology, 19*, 1483–1495.

Brehmer, B., & Dörner, D. (1993). Experiments with computer-simulated microworlds: Escaping both the narrow straits of the laboratory and the deep blue sea of the field study. *Computers in Human Behavior, 9*, 171–184.

Dawes, R. M. (1980). Social dilemmas. *Annual Review of Psychology, 31*, 169–193.

Gifford, J., & Gifford, R. (2000). FISH 3: A microworld for studying social dilemmas and resource management. *Behavior Research Methods, Instrumentation, and Computers, 32*, 417–422.

Gonzalez, C., Vanyukov, P., & Martin, M. K. (2005). The use of microworlds to study dynamic decision making. *Computers in Human Behavior, 21*, 273–286.

11

Simulating Designed Environments

Arthur E. Stamps III

Institute of Environmental Quality, San Francisco, CA, United States

Once upon a time, an enterprising young researcher, working at a place that might be called, say, Art's Café Américain, set out to unravel the intricacies of environmental aesthetics. The method was simple: get up shortly before moonset, brew a fresh pot of inspiration, drink a couple of cups, and wait for my blonde-over-blue muse to sashay in. Call her, say, Ilsa. With Ilsa's help there was hardly ever a dearth of ideas, but they were all just figments of imagination. To translate imagination into reality requires converting a figment into something perceptible. For vision, that requires a segue from imagination to image. For designed environments, that implies creation of a simulation of an as not-yet-existing place. To a designer, a need to spend time creating images is an invitation to have fun, so the message here is play it, man. Play as time goes by.

More specifically, the topic of this chapter is how simulations can be used to find out how responses such as feelings or behaviors are influenced by properties of physical environments. There is a very substantial amount of available data on this topic. As of May, 2012, a search on the *Science Citation Index* for the term "design simulation" generated 135 million references. With such an abundance of information, a considerable amount of selection was needed to decide what to include in this chapter. The selection criterion used was "What would I have liked to know at the beginning of my career that would make my research be as efficient and productive as possible?". Application of this criterion to the literature suggested that the answers could be divided into three parts: (1) identifying strategic decisions that will assist in deciding what one wants to simulate and viable options for doing the simulations; (2) knowing the empirical data on the validities of various types of simulations; and (3) knowing how to translate the scientific findings into practical applications. Accordingly this chapter is divided into three parts, and here they are.

Research Methods for Environmental Psychology, First Edition. Edited by Robert Gifford.
© 2016 John Wiley & Sons, Ltd. Published 2016 by John Wiley & Sons, Ltd.

Strategic Decisions

Guidance on choosing simulations can be obtained by identifying strategic decisions and their options that will influence choices of what simulation protocols would best suit which research goals. Based on experience covering 30 years, 100+ publications, and somewhere north of 1500 simulations, I would recommend that people who intend to use simulations as an integral part of their work will find it useful to consider making strategic decisions on the following issues: (1) purpose, (2) sensory modality, (3) describing objects in space and time, (4) validity, (5) efficiency, and (6) skills and tools.

Purpose

Purpose matters because choosing the most efficient means (e.g., the medium) will depend on the purpose of the simulations. The key question here is "What kind of result will I need?". Various answers are possible. Perhaps the most common answer is the need to simulate a unique environment. This is the goal when simulations are used for evaluating options during the design process (Collingwood, 1938; Schon, 1983; Xijuan, Yinglin, & Shouwei, 2003, p. 375), for visual impact assessment (Sheppard, 1989), or for participatory planning (Kwartler & Longo, 2008). Another option, and the option that is adopted in this chapter, is that simulations are used to create environments that instantiate scientific concepts. This is a very much a non-trivial choice. Formally this means creating simulations within the scientific protocols of experimental design (Fisher, 1935), random sampling (Deming, 1950), and statistical validity (American Psychological Association, 2009, pp. 30–37). The reason why designing for scientific purposes is non-trivial is the workload. Studies with rigorous experimental designs will require dozens if not hundreds of environments. Contemporary statistical protocols enable researchers to calculate just how large a study has to be by using power analysis (Cohen, 1988). In many cases power analysis will indicate that sample sizes need not be as large as is often reported in the behavioral literatures. It is no longer necessary to round up more than the usual number of suspects.

Each environment must be created to express the stimulus properties under inquiry and either not express or control for properties that will confuse conclusions. These statistical facts, combined with the time required to generate the environments, lead to the unpleasant but inescapable conclusion that there will be a need to generate valid simulations as efficiently as possible. Examples of scientific simulations include Nasar's (1998) studies on different components of a city's image, covering factors such as likability, identity, structure, distinctiveness, visibility, and symbolic significance, and Stamps' (2000) work on design evaluation.

Sensory modality

Sensory modality matters, because, if one is interested in expressing differences in sounds, silent stimuli won't do, or if one is interested in perfumes, visual images probably won't suffice. People, like many animals, can acquire information through many sensory modalities, ranging, in terms of distance, from visual, auditory, olfactory, haptic, and gustatory. People can also obtain information kinesthetically, through movement. Most of the research on environmental simulation has focused on vision because, normally, people look at environments rather than listen to them, smell them, touch them, or eat them. Counter-examples can, of course, be imagined. Relaxing by the soothing sound of a mountain creek entails sound, as would coping with ambient stress in a factory. Flowers convey information in both visual and olfactory modalities, to which anyone with a roadside rose garden can attest after observing legions of pedestrians literally stop and smell the flowers. Touch rather than vision becomes important if one is designing environments for the visually impaired or if one is designing furniture. Examples of environments that convey information through taste are somewhat more difficult to imagine. Aside perhaps from young children, people do not normally put parts of environments in their mouths. One example of important gustatory factors in environmental design that does come to mind is edible gardens. Creasy (2010) provides images of over 300 eye-popping, mouth-watering gardenscapes. For example, a single 1 x 1 m planting bed can express a brilliant mélange of yellows, oranges, purples, and whites while simultaneously expressing a vibrant salad menu of violas, nasturtiums, chives, and arugula (Creasy, 2010, p. 84). Of course, the concept of eating the garden can have its downside if the plants are poisonous. Stewart (2009, p. 1) describes a formal dinner party given in 1865 wherein cook seasoned the roast with shavings of monks-hood instead of horseradish, causing two guests to drop dead before dessert. Take-away message #1: don't listen when someone says "The hemlock looks particularly good today would you like some Dear?". Take-away message #2: inferences based on examples, whether real or fantasized, are very weak because counter-examples can usually be found or imagined. For scientific work, it is much more productive to stay within data obtained with random sampling, controls, and/or formal experimental designs.

Perhaps the strongest theoretical case for the importance of acquiring knowledge through kinesthetics is Gibson's *ecological psychology*, as indicated by the following: "The fact of a moving point of observation is central for the ecological approach to visual perception" (Gibson, 1979, p. 43). A more expansive expression of the centrality of dynamic factors in Gibson's theory is as follows: "A point of observation at rest is only the limiting case of a point of observation in motion ... Observation implies movement" (Gibson, 1979, p. 72). Additional details are given in Gibson (1979, pp. 72–86, 121–126, 197). The relevance of Gibson's theory to the present chapter is this: If movement is required for observation, the environments should be expressed in dynamic media rather than static media.

To summarize this section: the sensory modality discussed here is vision because vision is the most important sense people use at the scales typically covered in this chapter. The issue of whether or not simulations must be dynamic is addressed in the next part of the chapter.

Describing objects in space and time

When creating synthetic environments, one is confronted with the blunt fact that all objects have to be specified as materials located in three-dimensional Euclidian geometry. There is no way around this. No computer program can create an "arousal," or a "complexity," or a "pleasant," or any other of the many items on the many lists of adjectives that have often been used to describe environments.

The only thing a computer can understand is "put that there." The implication for scientific simulations is that the stimuli – for example, the environments – must be expressed in physical terms. The appropriate experimental protocol is a psycho-physical experiment. Responses can be described in verbal terms but the environments have to conform to the math in Euclidean geometry in order to be simulated. The best source I have found for expressing psychological and physical concepts is Krantz, Luce, Supper, and Tversky (1971). For readers who need to create environments to match specific hypotheses, several literatures will be highly useful: computational geometry in general (O'Rourke, 1998); basic concepts such as con-vexity/concavity and visibility in general (O'Rourke, 1987); visibility from individual locations (Davis & Benedikt, 1979); and pattern recognition (Russ, 1995). The work covered in this chapter uses psycho-physical research protocols with stimuli created as specified in three-dimensional Euclidean math and as formalized with computational geometry.

When expressing objects in time and space visually another issue needs to be con-sidered: selection of viewpoint. While the adage "give me a camera and a place to stand and I will show the world" may work as rhetoric, it is of no help whatsoever when deciding upon a location from which something should be visualized. For example, in 1876 the faculty of the École des Beaux Arts forbad the use of perspec-tives in their annual architectural jury on the grounds that perspectives would change the visual appeal of the project (Silvergold, 1974). This idea – the effect of the medium is so large that it matters more than what is being simulated – has been called the Beaux-Arts Hypothesis. When phrased as "the medium is the massage," this idea has become known as the McLuhan Syndrome (McLuhan & Fiore, 1967). In the Beaux-Arts tradition, this may have made a great deal of sense. After all, one knock-off of a Roman temple looks pretty much like the next knock-off of a Roman temple, so the only discernible difference between the two could well be the view-point effect. However, even in the context of a museum exhibit, the viewpoint effect may be non-existent or trivial. No one would think of evaluating the Mona Lisa on the criterion of where one stood (after all, her eyes follow you around regardless of where you are in the gallery). Nor would one evaluate Ms. Lisa based on the appear-ance of the frame. For sculpture, though, it's a different story. Although one can obtain some comprehension of Michelangelo's David from a single view, different impressions are obtained as one walks around it. For sculpture, multiple views are desirable but valuable information can also be obtained from a single view. For environments such as rooms or streetscapes or planetariums or being swallowed by a leviathan, where one is inside of the stimulus rather than viewing it as an object, it is a matter of empirical inquiry to find out how many viewpoints are needed. The third section of this chapter presents data relevant to this topic.

Validity

Over the last 40 years the most common objection I've received regarding simula-tions is concern about validity. More specifically the objection is that results obtained from simulations do not predict responses obtained in actual environments. Many justifications of this objection can be found. One is that simulations are different from actual environments because the simulations are restricted in properties such as size or sensory modality. That is perfectly true: a postcard of a mountain is smaller than the actual mountain and the aroma of the wild flowers is usually (thank heavens!) not printed on the card. However, in rigorous scientific work, the pattern of inference is more subtle. Typically, results are reported as contrasts. Instead of claiming that a mountain is large, the claim would be if, in reality, a real mountain is larger than a real molehill, then, given valid simulations, the simulation of the mountain will be larger than the simulation of the molehill. Other factors, such as smell, will be the same for both images and so the smell effect, if any, cancels out. This is the principle of scientific control. Scientific control sounds like a frightfully Orwellian concept, but a kinder, gentler and actually more faithful interpretation would be that extraneous effects balance each other out and so permit clean inferences. Experimental design is one answer to the question "How do you compensate for the brontosaurus in the living room?", and the answer is "Put an equal but opposite brontosaurus in the dining room." Factors that require control for scientific simulations include location of viewpoint, camera lens, color depth, and lighting. For example, if one is attempting to study the effect of room height on spaciousness, and then locates the viewpoint for some rooms at eye level but locates the viewpoint in other rooms just below the ceiling, then the conclusions will be incorrect. The same caveat applies to camera lenses. If some images are expressed with a wide angle lens (24 mm lens, horizontal angle 74 degrees horizontal angle, 1.29 radians) while other images are visualized with a normal angle lens (50 mm lens, 39.6 degrees horizontal angle, .69 radians), then any subsequent contrasts between the two sets of images will be invalid. Control of lighting is also required. Drawing valid comparisons is not possible between images created or photographed with 16 million colors and images shown with 256 colors, or lighting (designed or actual) with different values of intensity, direction, and reflections. These factors have to be the same for both sets of images (e.g., controlled), or any subsequent conclusions will not be valid. For this paragraph, the message is that when contemplating which simulation protocol to use, think about how well it can control for factors such as viewpoint, angle of view, and lighting. If it does support those controls, it is worth including in one's visualization toolkit. If it does not support those controls ... Useful references for experimental design include Fisher (1935), Cox (1992) and Montgomery (1997).

The other scientific solution, applicable to those contemplating using photographs of existing environments rather than creating synthetic scenes, is random sampling. Two common alternatives are photographing anything that happens to be at hand (such as one's college campus) or picking out images that seem "typical" or "best illustrate" some idea (using garages to represent built environments and flower gardens to represent natural environments when trying to establish differences between built and natural environments). Neither of these two alternates will support valid conclusions, so it is worthwhile to know about sampling before collecting images of existing environments. Useful references for random sampling include Deming (1950, 1960) and Sudman (1976).

Another aspect of the validity issue is how to measure it? One method is to ask people to rate simulations on scales such as "How realistic does this scene seem?", or "To what degree does this scene capture presence?". Another way is to obtain responses of any type in actual environments, make simulations of those environments, obtain the same responses to the simulations, and see how well the responses obtained with the simulations compare against the responses obtained in the field. The work cited in this chapter uses the latter definition of validity.

So, when making choices that involve validity, it is important to realize that scientifically valid simulations involve considerably more than point-and-shoot. Careful attention to experimental protocols are not only recommended but also required.

Efficiency

Efficiency may not, at first blush, seem like an important issue, but, as time goes by, it becomes more and more important. In the long run, a typical academic career might span 30 years from PhD to retirement, which, with a research cycle of 5 years, leaves time for 6 ideas. With a research cycle of 2 years, there is time for 15 ideas. If one has any of the knowledge junkie gene at all, 15 is better than 5, so efficiency becomes really important, in the long run. For simulations, efficiency is also important in the very short run, which means, in computer terms, running time. Running time is very strongly connected to computer power. For example, with a computer running with 32 bits, one cpu at 2.3 GZ and a production load of 150 simulations, the total rendering time was about 1800 hours. After the most recent upgrade to a 64-bit machine with 6 cpu's at 3.3 GZ, the rendering time was reduced by 95% (no, not a misprint, rendering time was reduced by a factor of 20), and so it was possible to reduce the amount of time spent throwing pixels at the screen from 1800 hours/ year to 90 hours/year. This was a substantial and most welcome addition to the research protocol. The reduction in processing time made it possible to create simulations with anatomically correct people (e.g., synthetic people created with algorithms based on human anatomy) and botanically correct vegetation (created in algorithms that model how various species of plants actually grow), as rendered in real amounts of light (as lux) from intended directions and with specified color temperatures. Much better!

However, this level of realism was possible only for a single image. A typical rendering time with this machine for a single image of two people in a small garden is about 10 minutes. Creation of a virtual reality simulation at the same level of fidelity would require the ability to calculate simulations at the rate of 24 frames per second, or an efficiency increase factor of 14,400. If computing power continues to increase according to Moore's Law (computer capacity doubles every 18 months), then it will be about 20 years before dynamic simulations provide the same information as do present-day static simulations. So, for the medium range future, it seems that static simulations might be more efficient than dynamic simulations, barring empirical evidence to the effect that dynamic simulations better represent responses obtained on-site.

So, for efficiency, the most important things apply as time goes by, and efficiency is one of those most important things. Sigh.

Skills and tools

There are many excellent overviews of how different types of environments can be simulated with different tools. Burden (1985) describes media such a drawings models, computer graphics, and sequential simulations. Marans and Stokols (1993) cover topics such as simulating for planning and design, multimedia, color arousal and comfort, synthetic landscapes, and dynamic simulations. Andrews (2003) focuses on technical aspects of capturing all the environment visible from one location. The technical aspects include use of digital photography, varieties of equipment and software, printing, creating interactive panoramas and virtual reality models. Hanzl (2007) reviews many new formats for presenting visual information, including three-dimensional models, VRML, XML, GIS, planning support systems, and computer games. Both capital and run-time costs for these different formats will vary widely so it will probably be wise to choose the simplest format that will provide the abilities to address the purposes of the simulations.

The overviews listed in the preceding paragraph tend to focus on equipment and examples of renderings. Since I need to do a considerable amount of design and simulating for my research, I have a suite of hardware and software that permits creation of 120–180 scenes per year. The current hardware list is the fastest computer and biggest screen I could afford for the design work, and, for the field work, a high-end 35 mm camera with a perspective-correcting lens, ambient and spot light meters, a compass, a clinometer, a meter stick, and a gps device. The light meters, compass, clinometer, a meter stick and the gps device are included in the camera toolkit because of the scientific criterion of being able to specify, and thus replicate, the location and direction of view. Scientific photography requires both photographic and surveying skills. For the computer software, the main program is a professional CAD package, supplemented with other specialized programs for people, plants, landscapes, textures, and number-crunching. These programs are neither cheap nor easy to learn (the standard method for learning computer programs is (a) grab hair firmly, (b) YANK!, (c) repeat a thousand times), so, when choosing one's kit, it will be worth the time to make sure that firepower is really needed or whether the research can be done with simpler tools. Recommendations for specific brands of equipment are not given here because the technology is changing so quickly that any advice regarding specific equipment would be obsolete before this book is published let alone purchased. Consequently only strategic guidance is included in this section. Criteria I typically use when purchasing programs are (a) Will it do the job? (b) Is the program open to many formats or will it only support its own internal format? (c) Are the formats stable over time or are they changed every year or so, and, if so, are they backwards-compatible? (d) Does the program have a reputation for stability or is it error-prone? (e) When you need service, do you get help or do you get voicemail? Using software that does the job over many formats with files that remain usable over decades, don't have many bugs, and, when there are bugs there are experts who can fix them, will be make one's research much more productive than any of the alternatives and so is very much worth the extra cost. These choices also become more and more important, as time goes by.

Another strategic decision is whether to choose professional or consumer simulations. The professional option will entail not only the types of equipment given in the previous paragraph but professional design skills as well. The only way to design synthetic environments is well … to design them. The skills required to design synthetic environments are pretty much the same skills needed to design real environments, so the required skill set is a background in architecture or a related design field such as landscape architecture (for natural scenes) or interior design (for interior scenes). For a long time, high-end CAD programs were the only way to produce accurate simulations. However, there are now off-the-shelf do-it-yourself consumer software programs for designing environments, so, if any of those have been tested for validity, then they would be viable options for non-designers who wish to create simulations for scientific work. Photoshop or Sketchup might work, if validation data are available. Another source of design skills for non-designers is the gaming industry. Due to the amount of money in gaming, there are now plug-ins for professional game engines that enable non-designers to create synthetic environments. A key point in choosing these consumer programs is whether they support real (e.g. SI) units. If so, they might be able to generate scientifically valid simulations. If, on the other hand, the units are from 0 to 100 or 0 to 255 or 0 to 80 or any other arbitrary measure, then the program may be suitable for artistic effect but not for scientific conclusions. Again, before using these games engines to create stimuli, the validity of the games vis-à-vis on-site data should be demonstrated.

Summary of strategic decisions

When choosing protocols for the creation of stimuli, it may be worthwhile to consider: (1) whether the intended use will be to express scientific concepts or a unique environment; (2) whether the simulation can be only visual or must express other sensory modalities; (3) whether the operational definitions of causes and effects are expressed verbally or mathematically; (4) whether the medium is valid; (5) whether the medium is efficient;, and (6) whether the medium is within the available skill sets. Many options are available for each of these six issues. The options taken in this chapter are: (1) the purpose is scientific knowledge; (2) the only sensory modality considered is vision; (3) effects are human responses such as feelings measured with semantic differential scales and causes expressed as materials located in three-dimensional Euclidean space, the properties of which are measured in mathematical concepts; (4) these choices appear to generate experiments that are highly valid (the data behind this claim are given in the next part of the chapter); (5) these choices support a highly efficient production schedule (over 100 simulations per year); and (6) the author happens to have both a PhD and is a licensed architect and so has access to both skill sets.

Using more than one skill set has advantages and disadvantages. The advantage is that it enables cross-fertilization of concepts from widely different sources. The disadvantage is that it sometimes causes cognitive dissonance which makes communication difficult and leads to questions such as "Who are you really and what did you do before?". Academic reviewers seem to be particularly prone to fits of cognitive dissonance which, given the importance of publications in scientific careers, is something to consider. In my experience the advantages of having multiple skill sets outweigh the disadvantages, but the choice regarding single or multiple skill sets will be important and so it is useful to think about the implications before becoming locked into either option. This issue will not go away. After all, it's still the same old story, the quest for fame and glory, a case of write or die … as time goes by.

Simulation Validity The first part of this chapter provided overviews of general issues and some options for choosing simulation protocols. In this section the focus is narrowed to reporting data on the validities and efficiencies of different simulation media, where validity is indicated by correlations against responses obtained on-site and efficiency is indicated by cost-benefit analysis. In this day and age, when people are accustomed to experiencing feelings through dynamic media such as a classic movie (like, say, *Casablanca*), it might be supposed that environments have to be represented dynamically. Maybe ... maybe not. In general terms, the hypotheses for dynamic simulations are:

H1. Environments cannot be simulated but must be experienced, live, in living color, dynamically, and in person. You have to be there to get it. This implies an effect size of $r_{\text{on-site, simulated}} = 0.0$ for responses obtained on-site vis-à-vis responses obtained from simulations.

H2: People move about when in real environments, therefore simulations must be dynamic. This implies that the correlation of responses obtained in the field and also obtained with dynamic simulations will be greater than the correlation of responses obtained in the field and with static simulations, or $r_{\text{on-site, dynamic}} > r_{\text{on-site, static}}$.

Thus, this section considers two hypotheses: (H1) how well responses obtained in actual environments correspond to responses obtained in simulations, and (H2) whether dynamic simulations are more valid than static simulations. The literature now contains sufficient data to test H1 and H2. Data relevant to H1 (simulations cannot be used to represent environments) were reported in a literature review covering 1215 stimuli and over 4200 respondents (Stamps, 2000, pp. 101–113). At that time, there were not sufficient data in the public record to make claims regarding dynamic simulations, so the focus was on the efficacies of various static media. Media covered in that review included on-site, slides, black and white slides, tinted sketches, digitized slides, black and white sketches in low, medium, and high abstraction, computer sketches, verbal descriptions, black and white photographs, color photographs, models, full-size mock-ups, 140-degree color photographs, 63-degree color photographs, unframed photographs, working drawings, pen and ink line drawings, and photomontages. A meta-analytic summary of the main results is shown in Table 11.1. (For readers new to meta-analysis, a short synopsis with emphasis on environmental research is given in Stamps, 2002.)

Table 11.1 Summary of major findings from literature review of 2000.

				.05 ci	
Medium	*Medium*	*r*	*n*	lo	hi
On-site	Slides/color photos	.83	185	.79	.87
Slides	Digitized slides	.84	309	.80	.87
Slides	B&W sketches	.69	23	.50	.81
On-site	B&W sketches	.56	18	.06	.83
Color photos	B&W photos	.41	18	−.12	.73

Perhaps the most important implication of the data in Table 11.1 is that preferences obtained from slides or colored photographs correlated at $r = .83$ with preferences obtained on-site. The .05 confidence interval (ci) on the correlation of $r = .83$ for $n = 185$ was [.79, .87]. This ci does not include 0.0, so the null hypothesis (H1: static images cannot be used to represent environments) was refuted. (In terms of the "p-level" paradigm, the statistics were $r = .83$ on $n = 185$, $t(183) = 20.13$, $p < .0001$). A second important implication is that some media performed better than other media. In particular, it appears that color is a necessary requirement for a valid visual simulation protocol. With color, the correlation with on-site preferences was $r = .83$; without color, the correlation decreased to the 40s and 50s.

By 2010 there were sufficient data in the public record to update the review to include dynamic simulations (Stamps, 2010b). That review covered 6323 participants and 967 environments. Responses included ratings of pleasure, naturalness, familiarity, order, inertia, arousal, threat, disliking, liking of the environment, nice area to walk through, good area to live in, appreciation of the area, visual appeal, evaluation, ambience, arousal, privacy, security, pleasant, interest, comfortable, excited, playful, water, built, water flow, sun, sound, strolling, resting, talking, observing, preference, and spaciousness. Some studies reporting findings for physical properties such as distance, height, width, and length. Other studies reported behaviors such as path choice and exploration. The meta-analytic summary of the main results is given in Table 11.2. The sources for Table 11.2 are given in the Appendix.

Here is how to interpret Table 11.2. Three comparisons were evaluated: on-site vs. static color, on-site vs. dynamic simulations, and static color vs. dynamic simulations. Each comparison was based on findings listed in the Appendix. For example, "1–17" means the calculations for on-site vs. static media were calculated from data obtained from the references in rows 1–17 of the Appendix. $\hat{r}$ is the estimate of the correlation between the two media. It is also the measure of the effect size for its respective comparison. Σn is the number of stimuli over which the correlation was calculated. The ".05 ci" is the confidence interval for the correlation. If it includes 0.0, the comparison meets the standard "$p < .05$" level for distinguishing the results from random chance. The values of χ^2 and its associated df express the heterogeneity of the data used to test a comparison. If the ci does not include 0.0 and if this χ^2 is significant, the interpretation is that there is a solid overall finding for the claim in question but there is also a lot of variety in the data and so further, more focused research would probably be worth doing. If the respective ci does not include 0 and respective χ^2 is not significant, more detailed work would probably not be worth doing. Stick a fork in it: it's done. Move on to another topic that is not already so firmly established.

Table 11.2 Main results from meta-analysis of static and dynamic media, 2010.

Comparisons	Findings	$\hat{r}$	Σn	.05 ci	χ^2 (df)	α	n_{over}
On-site/static	1–17	.87	205	.84, .90	32.0 (16)	.01	28,252
On-site/ dynamic	18–26	.83	171	.78, .87	35.2 (8)	2e-5	15,007
Static/dynamic	27–33	.82	135	.76, .86	6.1 (6)	.41	8,446

The last column (n_{over}) provides even more specific guidance for planning research. It is the number of data points (in this case, the number of scenes of environments) that would switch the significance of a comparison from significant to non-significant or vice versa. If a current finding is significant, n_{over} will be positive and indicates the amount of new data, with a finding of $r = 0.0$, which would be needed to impeach the respective claim on empirical grounds. On the other hand, if the current correlation is not significant, n_{over} will be negative and indicates the amount of data, with a finding of the current estimated correlation, which would be needed to bring it up to the .05 standard. Or, in short, n_{over} provides estimates of the workloads needed to justify current criticisms or future studies on a particular comparison. The connection of n_{over} to the concept of efficiency in choosing a visual simulation medium or, for that matter, in planning a scientific career, should be obvious.

Thus, in plain language, the interpretations of Table 11.2 are these: For the comparison of responses obtained on-site or from static color images, there is a very strong correlation and it would take a criticism with about 28,000 environments to deny the efficacy of static color simulations based on empirical evidence. Of course, some people will be Shocked! Shocked! to find out science has been going on here, and so they will continue to object to the use of simulations on non-scientific grounds. The solution is to present the facts and hope they eventually come around, as time goes by.

Returning to the connection between responses obtained on-site or from static color images, there is substantial variation in the relevant data, suggesting that, before using any particular medium, make sure that any particular medium works. The relevance of this point to the concept of validity should be obvious: don't assume validity, test for it. For the comparison between on-site and dynamic media, n_{over} drops to about $n = 15,000$, which is still a rather daunting amount of work. Again, there is a lot of variation in the data for on-site vs. dynamic media, so, again, validation before utilization seems like good advice. The third comparison was between static and dynamic simulations. Overall these two protocols produced very nearly the same results ($r = .82$), but now there was no detectable heterogeneity in the data ($\alpha = .41$). This suggests that future research would probably be more rewarding if spent on another topic.

Finally, the correlations from Table 11.2 provide a direct test of H2. Which performs better: static or dynamic simulations? The envelope please .... drum roll ... and the answer is ... neither! It's a statistical tie. The difference between $r = .87$ on $n = 205$ and $r = .83$ on $n = 171$ was not detectable ($Z = 1.39$, $\alpha = .16$). Perhaps to belabor the point: with equal demonstrated validity, efficiency becomes important in selecting a visual medium.

Summary of simulation validity

To our thinking, the empirical data in the collective record clearly indicates that H1 (visual images cannot be used to represent environments) is not now, nor has it been for the last 25 years, scientifically tenable. The data also indicate that static color and dynamic simulations are equally effective for the purposes of researching static stimuli such as rooms, buildings, plants, or landscapes. Given the much higher costs of dynamic simulations, efficiency suggests that static color images are more efficient and will enable researchers to investigate far more ideas during their careers than would be possible if they were committed to using the more expensive dynamic simulations.

Examples

Some examples might help clarify the conditions under which different simulation protocols might be the more appropriate medium in different types of environments. The types of environments were taken from basic concepts in geometry: convexity and degrees of freedom of movement. The first example addresses the theoretical question of whether people do actually use visual kinesthesis when evaluating convex environments. The second example addresses the question of whether viewpoint location makes a non-trivial difference in concave environments. The third example describes a practical application when the environment is convex and the degrees of freedom of movement are linear ($df = 1$), such as movement along a streetscape. The immediate application of this example is contextual design review.

Example 1: Use of kinesthesis in convex environments

The first hypothesis of visual kinesthesis is that, when evaluating environments, people actually do move direction of vision (with eyes or head) and location (with feet). Relevant data, covering 65 participants and 38 environments, were reported in Stamps (2010a). Environments were expressed in virtual reality worlds of galleries, the walls of which featured works of Art. (Given the author's name, anything he does is automatically a work of Art. It's very convenient.) The task was to explore the environment and evaluate it in terms of visual appeal, on a scale of 1 to 8. The virtual reality engine collected responses of visual preference and, at one second intervals, also the participant's location and angle of direction of view. This time and motion data enabled a direct test of the concept of visual kinesthesis. If someone moved, a plot of location vs. time would result in an arrow. If someone stopped and turned their eyes/head, the resulting plot would show a cartwheel. The top of Figure 11.1 shows the plots of all the participants for the simplest possible geometry: a convex space in which everything is visible without any locomotion at all. The bottom of Figure 11.1 shows the whole room as captured from two station points. The plot of paths taken clearly support the first concept of visual kinesthesis. A few people stopped and swiveled around; most just moved about. In fact, in all the scenes in all the studies in all the virtual worlds, everyone walked in mine. To my thinking, these results clearly support the first hypothesis of visual kinesthesis.

Example 2: Locations of viewpoints in concave environments

This example focused on finding out how many viewpoints would be needed to evaluate how spacious a room seems to be. One hypothesis was that, since people move around, no number of viewpoints will do but rather the environments have to be represented dynamically. Another hypothesis is that a small number of viewpoints, such as the locations showing the maximum area, the average area, and the

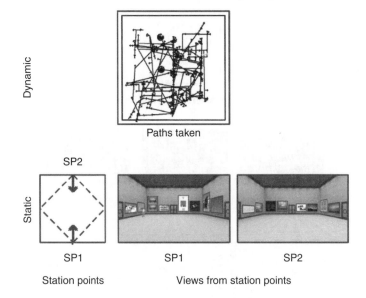

Figure 11.1   (Top) Paths taken by all participants. (Bottom) Two static images that show the entire environment.

least area in the room, would suffice. Accordingly, two sets of stimuli were created. The original data for this example, covering 44 participants and 32 stimuli, are described in Stamps (2007). The venue consisted of, again, Art galleries. One set of galleries was created as virtual reality models. The other set of galleries was created, using computational geometry, to represent each gallery with viewpoints showing the most, average, and least floor area. All scenes, whether in dynamic or static media, had the same geometry, materials, lighting, camera angle, height of camera above floor, and response (spaciousness rated on a scale of 1 to 8). The correlation of rated spaciousness, calculated between environments expressed in a virtual reality model and with three static color images, was $r = .79$. To my thinking, this result was not compatible with the second assertion of visual kinesthesis (it is necessary to preserve motion in order for a simulation to be valid). Static images from a few locations expressed spaciousness just as well as did an immersive virtual reality experience, even in concave environments. See Figure 11.2.

Example 3: Contextual design review

This last example was motivated by the overlap between the practical application of design review and a body of relevant scientific knowledge. Design review is widely enforced. In the United States, for example, a study of 371 cities indicated that over 90% of the larger cities use design review (Lightner, 1993). The importance of contextual fit stems from the fact that it is a major evaluation criterion in design review. Lightner (1993) found that 77% of US planning departments evaluated new buildings using the general criterion of how well the building would fit into its context. Contextual fit is also an important criterion for evaluating building projects

Path taken by one person

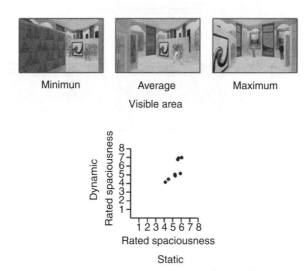

Minimun   Average   Maximum

Visible area

Static

Figure 11.2   (Top) Paths taken by one person. (Middle) Views from locations with the minimum, average, and maximum area of view. (Bottom) Spaciousness as evaluated in static or dynamic media.

in other countries, including the UK (Uzzell & Jones, 1996), France (Loew, 1994), Germany (Pantel, 1994), Sweden (Nystrom, 1994), Italy (Vignozzi, 1994), the Netherlands (Nelissen & de Vocht, 1994), Spain (Calderon, 1994), and Japan (Hohn, 1997). Evaluation of contextual fit requires valid pre-construction simulations, which, in turn, requires knowledge of how people actually perceive environments. For example, in the legal literature on design review (Rathkopf & Rathkopf, 1987, pp. 14–19; Williams, 1974, p. 265; Ziegler, 1986, p. 245), a major theme is that aesthetic evaluations of environments should be based on the environment as seen in the street rather than as it might be seen as a museum exhibit. Implementation of the theme to contextual design review requires a selection of presentation medium. Should one be thinking Mona Lisa, David, or Leviathan? One solution, proposed by Mullins (2006) in the context of an international architectural competition, was that dynamic visualizations of the project were required (e.g., David). It was suggested that, in the future, dynamic simulations should be required for public competition juries. Is that necessary? Is it efficient?

Since the choice of simulations depends on how people perceive environments, effective design review would seem to require knowledge about things such as "How long does it take?", "Is it a matter of detailed scrutiny or a snap decision?", "Are judgments made when one is moving or when one is standing still?", "Are

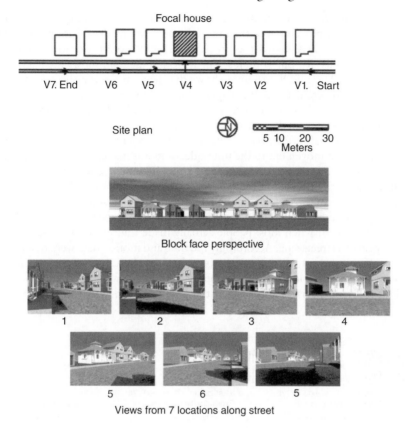

Figure 11.3 Site plan, static color elevation, and seven views along a street.

multiple viewpoints needed or can the information required for judgment be obtained from one or two views?". In order to address these questions, two experiments were done (Stamps, 2011, 2012). In the first experiment the streets were shown as static color images. In the second experiment the streets were shown as a movie clip with 512 frames. By moving a slider, the participants could move up or down the street, thus providing a dynamic simulation. Figure 11.3 shows a street as expressed in both types of simulations. The top of Figure 11.3 shows the site plan. The middle of Figure 11.3 shows the street in what is known as a block face elevation. The bottom of Figure 11.3 shows the street as seen from 7 of the 512 frames in the dynamic simulation. View one is the focal house as seen from the end of the street. Views two and three show closer views. Scene four shows an elevation of the individual focal house.

Twelve synthetic streets were created using the scientific protocols described above. In the static condition, responses were recorded for visual appeal. In the dynamic condition, visual appeal was recorded but so were the locations of the participants at one second intervals. These time and motion data were used to find out what goes on when people evaluate streetscapes. There were two spatial variables: total path length and number of times a participant turned to obtain a different view.

There were three temporal variables: total time, time spent standing still, and time spent from the last movement to the time a decision was made (decision time). The top row of Figure 11.4 shows the time (x axis) and motion (location along the street, on the y axis) for one stimulus. The left-hand diagram shows the data for all 25 participants. The middle diagram shows the diagram for the shortest decision time. The right diagram shows the diagram for the longest decision time. It can be seen that there was a large difference in the paths taken by different people.

For researchers interested in personal differences in exploratory behavior, behavior analyses of individual differences in total time, time spent standing still, and time spent from the last movement to the time a decision was made, would be of interest. However, for decision makers who need to know how people in general view projects from the commons (public regions, access to which cannot be denied under the applicable social contract), the required knowledge is the amount of each factor (path length, number of different views, total time, time spent standing still, and decision time) spent when most people actually made their decisions regarding the visual appeal of a streetscape. Accordingly the time and motion data were re-analyzed in terms of the percentage of participants (y axis) by the values of each of the five spatial/temporal variables (length, number of different views, total time, time spent standing still, and decision time) when the final judgment was recorded (x axis).

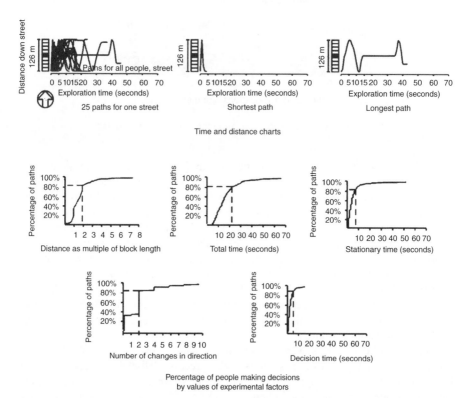

Figure 11.4   Paths taken. (Top) Distances along street by time. (Bottom) Percentages of people who made their judgments by the value of the exploratory factor at decision time.

The middle and bottom rows of Figure 11.4 show the plots of this analysis. Overall it can clearly be seen that, for all five spatial/temporal variables, there was a quick rise in percentages of paths ending at low levels of the variables, followed by a kink in the charts and a gradual leveling-off of increases in paths. The kinks all seemed to fall at about 80% of the paths, so those values were interpreted as representing the perceptive process used by the typical person in the street. Thus, for distance, the 80% cut-point was twice the block length: once all the way up, once all the way back. For total time, the cut-point was 22 seconds. For time spent stopping and staring the cut-point was 6 seconds. For number of multiple looks the cut-point was 2. For decision time after all information had been gathered the cut-point was 5.4 seconds. In short, most of the people took about 15 seconds to get information and another 5 seconds to make a decision. Looking at the infill project once from each side sufficed. Thus, if a decision maker asked for evidence-based advice on how ordinary people evaluated the visual appeal of ordinary streetscapes, the take-away message would be:

> How long did it take to evaluate a streetscape? About 22 seconds.
> Is it a matter of detailed scrutiny or a snap decision? At 5 seconds, the answer to that is a snap.
> Are judgments made when one is moving or when one is standing still?. Standing still.
> Are multiple viewpoints needed or can the information required for aesthetic judgment be obtained from one or two views? Two views were sufficient.

The comparison of visual appeal obtained from static colored blockfaces and the dynamic medium of walking down the street was $r = .81$ ($t(14) = 4.78$, $\alpha = .0003$). The relevant data are shown in Figure 11.5. This finding indicates that a simpler, cheaper simulation protocol worked just as well as a much more complex, expensive simulation protocol. Of the 512 frames in the dynamic simulation, 510 frames were not necessary. For readers interested in this line of inquiry, additional data for stimulating streetscapes are described in Stamps (1993), in which evaluations of one-point and two-point simulations were compared, and for nature scenes (Meitner, 2004), in which dynamic panoramas were compared to four static images.

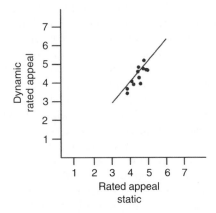

Figure 11.5 Visual appeal as rated from static color blockfaces and by walking down the street.

Results from the streetscape study indicated that two views of a proposed new project in a streetscape would suffice, while results from the nature scenes indicated that four views would work just as well as dynamic interactive panoramas for expressing all 360 degrees of vision from a single location.

Summary of examples

The intent of this section was to illustrate, through examples, how the theoretical concepts of kinesthesis, convexity, and degrees of freedom of movement will influence choices of simulation medium. The examples suggest that effects due to kinesthesis can be expressed just about as well in a few static images (one for convex environments such as rectangular rooms, two for convex environments with one degree of locomotion, such as streetscapes, three for concave environments such as art galleries with partitions, and four for the general case of expressing effects due to all 360 degrees (2π radians) of horizontal view) as compared to more costly dynamic simulations.

Of course, more work could still be done. It's still a story without an ending. But ... to be efficient, let the data and meta-analyses guide you in selecting which topics will most reward your future efforts. Solid commands of the skill sets presented above could be the beginnings of a beautiful relationship.

Summary and Conclusion

This chapter contained three parts. Part 1 lists some major issues and options for selecting simulation protocols. The basic message from Part 1 is that the creation of scientifically valid and efficient simulations requires much more than applying pencil to paper, brush to canvas, or keystrokes to computer programs. Scientific validity requires solid knowledge of experimental design, random sampling, and the need for a large number (scores or hundreds) of simulations. The requirement of a large number of simulations puts a premium on efficiency, whether efficiency is measured in the nanoseconds of computer time or over the 30-year span of a research career. Part 2 presents the empirical data on the respective validities of various simulation media, with the overall results that both static color and dynamic color simulations were quite valid vis-à-vis on-site responses and were both equally valid vis-à-vis each other, so the choice of static or dynamic media is a question of efficiency rather than validity. Part 3 illustrates some examples to show how the ideas in this chapter actually work. Overall, in my view, simple simulations appear to work just as well as fancy simulations, so, in terms of efficiency, if simple simulations will suffice for the purposes of any given experiment, it will be in the researcher's best interest to go with the simplest medium. Besides which, if one does a lot of clean, simple experiments, and one of them does not come out as it was supposed to, it's not a big deal. Neither first job nor tenure nor merit promotion nor professional reputation is hostage to any one study, so that means one can focus on finding out rather than advocating a particular viewpoint. After all, you must remember this: a miss is just a miss, a try is but a try, the world will always welcome learners, as time goes by...

Here's looking at you, kid.

Appendix

Parameters and Sources of Experimental Data on Simulation Validity. Listings of articles included in meta-analysis of static and dynamic media, 2010.

	Venue	Medium1	Medium2	Responses	n_{subj}	n_{stim}	n^*	r	Reference
1	Landscape	On-site	Static color	Visual appeal	193	10	10	Stim	0.67	Brush (1979, p. 504)
2	Landscape	On-site	Static color	Visual appeal	n/a	6	6	Stim	0.99	Daniel & Boster (1976, p. 50)
3	Landscape	On-site	Static color	Visual appeal	n/a	18	18	Stim	0.82	Daniel & Boster (1976, p. 50)
4	Landscape	On-site	Static color	Visual appeal	164	34	34	Stim	0.79	Dearinger (1979, p. 77)
5	Landscape	On-site	Static color	Visual appeal	797	6	6	Stim	0.77	Dunn (1976, p. 6)
6	Landscape	On-site	Static color	Visual appeal	25	15	15	Stim	0.68	Gimblett (1990, p. 198)
7	Landscape	On-site	Static color	Visual appeal	n/a	10	10	Stim	0.72	Howard, Mlynarski, & Sauer (1972)
8	Landscape	On-site	Static color	Visual appeal	122	12	12	Stim	0.91	Hull & Stewart (1992, p. 108)
9	Landscape	On-site	Static color	Visual appeal	na	10	10	Stim	0.96	Kane (1981, p. 87)
10	Landscape	On-site	Static color	Visual appeal	58	34	34	Stim	0.95	Kellomaki & Savolainen (1984, p. 101)
11	Landscape	On-site	Static color	Visual appeal	91	12	12	Stim	0.80	Palmer & Hoffman (2001, p. 157)
12	Landscape	On-site	Static color	Visual appeal	190	8	8	Stim	0.80	Seaton & Collins (1972. p. 6–10–7)
13	Landscape	On-site	Static color	Visual appeal	74	8	8	Stim	0.98	Shafer & Richards (1974, pp. 2–22)
14	Landscape	On-site	Static color	Visual appeal	427	20	20	Stim	0.74	Shelby & Harris (1985, p. 62)
15	Landscape	On-site	Static color	Visual appeal	46	6	6	Stim	0.74	Shuttleworth (1984, p. 74)
16	Landscape	On-site	Static color	Visual appeal	47	6	6	Stim	0.91	Shuttleworth (1984, p. 74)
17	Landscape	On-site	Static color	Visual appeal	307	8	8	Stim	0.92	Zube, Pitt & Anderson (1974, p. 50)
18	Street	On-site	Virtual reality	12 affective scales x 2 rooms	84	1	24	Scales	0.54	Bishop & Rohrman (2003, p. 259)
19	Rooms	On-site	Virtual reality	5 affective scales x 2 rooms	101	2	10	Scales	0.80	Slangen - de Kort et al. (2001, Table 4, p. 20)
20	Museum	On-site	Virtual reality	Height, width, length	24	3	54	Scales	0.85	Henry (1992, pp. 81–82)
21	Outdoor path	On-site	Video	15 affective and behavioral scales	103	1	15	Scales	0.93	Huang (2009, Tables 1, 2, 3, pp. 330–332)
22	Room	On-site	Virtual reality	9 behavior measures	32	1	9	Scales	0.90	Lessels & Ruddle (2005, Tables 1–2, pp. 588, 592)

(continued)

(continued)

	Venue	Medium1	Medium2	Responses	n_{subj}	n_{stim}	n^*		r	Reference
23	Subway station	On-site	Quicktime movie	Choice of paths	78	36	36	Stim	0.67	Zacharias (2006, p. 7)
24	plazas and rooms	On-site	Virtual reality	Distance estimate	10	2	14	Stim	0.98	Hayashibe (2002, figures 3–4, p. 579)
25	Hallway	On-site	Virtual reality	Distance estimate	24	2	6	Stim	0.99	Witmer & Kline (1998, figure 3, p. 155)
26	Hallway	On-site	Virtual reality	Distance	48	3	3	Stim	0.99	Thompson et al. (2004, p.567)
27	Outdoor path	Video	Frames from video	15 affective scales	51	23	15	Scales	0.94	Heft & Nasar (2000, Table 3, p. 312)
28	Outdoor path	Video	Slides	15 affective and behavioral scales	106	12	15	Scales	0.77	Huang (2009, Tables 1, 2, 3, pp. 330–332)
29	Landscapes	360 degree rotation	4 static images/site	Scenic beauty	118	47	47	Stim	0.80	Meitner (2004, Table 2, p. 10)
30	Rooms	Virtual reality	3 static images/virtual reality	Spaciousness	39	32	12	Stim	0.79	Stamps (2007, p. 553)
31	Streets	Virtual reality	3 static images/virtual reality	Spaciousness	109	30	14	Stim	0.87	Stamps (2009)
32	Rooms	Virtual reality	Static images	How many non-target cubes were visited before the target cube was visited	18	3	18	Subjects	0.70	Peruch, Vercher, & Gauthier (1995, p. 10)
33	Streets	Virtual reality	Static images	Visual appeal	25	30	14	Stim	0.81	Stamps (2012)

References

American Psychological Association. (2009). *Publication manual of the American Psychological Association.* Washington, DC: American Psychological Association.

Andrews, P. (2003). *360 degree imaging: The photographer's panoramic virtual reality manual.* Mies, Switzerland: Rotovision.

Bishop, I. D., & Rohrmann, B. (2003). Subjective responses to simulated and real environments: A comparison. *Landscape and Urban Planning, 65,* 261–277.

Brush, R. O. (1979). The attractiveness of woodlands: Perceptions of forest landowners in Massachusetts. *Forest Science, 25*(3), 495–506.

Burden, E. (1985). *Design simulation.* New York, NY: Wiley.

Calderon, E. (1994). Design control in the Spanish planning system. *Built Environment, 20*(2), 157–168.

Cohen, J. (1988a). *Statistical power analysis for the behavioral sciences.* Hillsdale, NJ: Erlbaum.

Collingwood, R. G. (1938). *The principles of art.* Oxford, UK: Oxford University Press.

Cox, D. R. (1992). *Planning of experiments.* New York, NY: Wiley.

Creasy, R. (2010). *Edible landscaping: Now you can have your gorgeous garden and eat it too!* San Francisco, CA: Sierra Club Books.

Daniel, T. C., & Boster, R. S. (1976). Measuring landscape aesthetics: The scenic beauty estimation method. Fort Collins, CO: USDA Forest Service.

Davis, L. S., & Benedikt, M. L. (1979). Computational models of space: Isovists and isovist fields. *Computer Graphics and Image Processing, 11,* 49–72.

Dearinger, J. A. (1979). Measuring preferences for natural landscapes. *Journal of the Urban Planning and Development Division, Proceedings of the American Society of Civil Engineers, 105*(UP1), 63–80.

Deming, W. E. (1950a). *Some theory of sampling.* New York, NY: Dover.

Deming, W. E. (1960). *Sample design in business research.* New York, NY: McGraw-Hill.

Dunn, M. C. (1976). Landscape with photographs: Testing the preference approach to landscape evaluation. *Journal of Environmental Management, 4,* 15–26.

Fisher, R. A. (1935a). *The design of experiments* (1971 ed.). New York, NY: Hafner.

Gibson, J. J. (1979). *The ecological approach to visual perception* (1986 ed.). Hillsdale, NJ: Erlbaum.

Gimblett, H. R. (1990). Environmental cognition: The prediction of preference in rural Indiana. *Journal of Architectural and Planning Research, 7*(3), 222–324.

Hanzl, M. (2007). Information technology as a tool for public participation in urban planning: A review of experiments and potentials. *Design Studies, 28,* 289–307.

Hayashibe, K. (2002). Apparent distance in actual, three-dimensional video-recorded, and virtual reality. *Perceptual and Motor Skills, 95,* 573–582.

Heft, H., & Nasar, J. L. (2000). Evaluating environmental scenes using dynamic versus static displays. *Environment & Behavior, 32*(3), 301–322.

Henry, D. (1992). *Spatial perception in virtual environments: Evaluating an architectural application.* MSc, University of Washington, Seattle.

Hohn, U. (1997). Townscape preservation in Japanese urban planning. *Town Planning Review, 68*(2), 213–255.

Howard, R. B., Mlynarski, F. G., & Sauer, G. C. (1972). A comparative analysis of affective responses to real and represented environments. In W. Mitchell (Ed.), *Environment and cognition* (pp. 6–66). New York, NY: Seminar Press.

Huang, S.-C. L. (2009). The validity of visual surrogates for representing waterscapes. *Landscape Research, 34*(3), 323–335.

Hull, R. B., & Stewart, W. P. (1992). Validity of photo-based scenic beauty judgments. *Journal of Environmental Psychology, 12,* 101–114.

Kane, P. S. (1981). Assessing landscape attractiveness: A comparative test of two new methods. *Applied Geography, 1,* 77–96.

Kellomaki, S., & Savolainen, R. (1984). The scenic value of the forest-landscape as assessed in the field and the laboratory. *Landscape Planning, 11,* 97–107.

Krantz, D. H., Luce, R. D., Supper, P., & Tversky, A. (1971). *Foundations of measurement I: Additive and polynomial representations.* Mineola, NY: Dover.

Kwartler, M., & Longo, G. (2008). *Visioning and visualization: people, pixels and plans.* Cambridge, MA: Lincoln Institute of Land Policy.

Lessels, S., & Ruddle, R. L. (2005). Movement around real and virtual environments. *Presence, 14*(5), 580–596.

Lightner, B. C. (1993). Survey of design review practices. *Planning Advisory Services Memo.* Chicago, IL: American Planning Association.

Loew, S. (1994). Design control in France. *Built Environment, 20*(2), 88–103.

Marans, R. W., & Stokols, D. (Eds.). (1993). *Environmental simulation: Research and policy issues.* New York, NY: Plenum.

McLuhan, M., & Fiore, Q. (1967). *The medium is the massage.* New York, NY: Bantam.

Meitner, M. J. (2004). Scenic beauty of river views in Grand Canyon: Relating perceptual judgments to locations. *Landscape and Urban Planning, 68,* 3–13.

Montgomery, D. C. (1997). *Design and analysis of experiments.* New York, NY: Wiley.

Mullins, M. (2006). Interpretation of simulations in interactive VR environments: Depth perception in cave and panorama. *Journal of Architectural and Planning Research, 23*(4), 328–340.

Nasar, J. L. (1998). *The evaluative image of the city.* Thousand Oaks, CA: Sage.

Nelissen, N., & de Vocht, C. L. (1994). Design control in the Netherlands. *Built Environment, 20*(2), 142–156.

Nystrom, L. (1994). Design control in planning: The Swedish case. *Built Environment, 20*(2), 113–126.

O'Rourke, J. (1987). *Art gallery theorems and algorithms.* Oxford, UK: Oxford University Press.

O'Rourke, J. (1998). *Computational geometry in C* (2nd ed.). Cambridge, UK: Cambridge University Press.

Palmer, J. F., & Hoffman, R. E. (2001). Rating reliability and representation validity in scenic landscape assessments. *Landscape and Urban Planning, 54,* 149–161.

Pantel, G. (1994). Design control in German planning. *Built Environment, 20*(2), 104–112.

Peruch, P., Vercher, J., & Gauthier, G. M. (1995). Acquisition of spatial knowledge through visual exploration of simulated environments. *Ecological Psychology, 7*(1), 1–20.

Rathkopf, A. H., & Rathkopf, D. A. (Eds.). (1987). *The law of zoning and planning.* New York, NY: Clark Boardman.

Russ, J. C. (1995). *The image processing handbook.* Boca Raton, FL: CRC Press.

Schon, D. A. (1983). *The reflective practitioner: how professionals think in action.* New York, NY: Basic Books.

Seaton, R. W., & Collins, J. B. (1972). Validity and reliability of ratings of simulated buildings. In W. S. Mitchell (Ed.), *Environmental design: Research and practice.* Los Angeles, CA: University of California Press.

Shafer, E. L., & Richards, T. A. (1974). A comparison of viewer reactions to outdoor scenes and photographs of those scenes. *US Forest Service Research Paper, NE-302.*

Shelby, B., & Harris, R. (1985). Comparing methods for determining visitor evaluations of ecological impacts: Site visits, photographs, and written descriptions. *Journal of Leisure Research, 17*(1), 57–67.

Sheppard, S. R. (1989). *Visual simulation: A user's guide for architects, engineers, and planners.* New York, NY: Van Nostrand Reinhold.

Shuttleworth, S. (1984). Consensus and the perception of landscape quality. *Landscape Research, 9*(1).

Silvergold, B. (1974). *Richard Morris Hunt and the importation of Beaux-Arts architecture to the United States.* Ph.D. dissertation, University of California, Berkeley.

Slangen - de Kort, Y. A., Ijsselsteijn, W. A., Kooijman, J., & Schuurmans, Y. (2001). Virtual environments as research tools for environmental psychology: A study of the comparability of real and virtual environments Retrieved from http://www.temple.edu/presence2001/part-present.htm

Stamps, A. E. (1993). Validating contextual urban design photoprotocols: Replication and generalization from single residences to block faces. *Environment and Planning B: Planning and Design, 20,* 693–707.

Stamps, A. E. (2000). *Psychology and the aesthetics of the built environment.* Norwell, MA: Kluwer.

Stamps, A. E. (2002). Meta analysis. In R. Bechtel & A. Churchman (Eds.), *The handbook of environmental psychology* (pp. 222–232). New York, NY: Wiley.

Stamps, A. E. (2007). Evaluating spaciousness in static and dynamic media. *Design Studies, 28,* 535–557.

Stamps, A. E. (2009). On shape and spaciousness. *Environment & Behavior, 41*(4), 526–548.

Stamps, A. E. (2010a). Slines, entropy and exploration. *Environment and Planning B: Planning and Design, 37,* 704–722.

Stamps, A. E. (2010b). Use of static and dynamic media to simulate environments: A meta-analysis. *Perceptual and Motor Skills, 111*(2), 1–12.

Stamps, A. E. (2011). Parameters of contextual fit: Diversity, matching, individual style, responses. *Journal of Urbanism, 4*(1), 7–24.

Stamps, A. E. (2012). A walk down the block: Spatial and temporal parameters of aesthetic judgments about ordinary streetscapes. *Perceptual and Motor Skills, 114*(2), 1–10.

Stewart, A. (2009). *Wicked plants: The weed that killed Lincoln's mother & other botanical atrocities.* Chapel Hill, NC: Algonquin.

Sudman, S. (1976). *Applied sampling.* New York, NY: Academic Press.

Thompson, W. B., Willemsen, P., Gooch, A. A., Creem-Regehr, S. H., Loomis, J. M., & Beall, A. C. (2004). Does the quality of the computer graphics matter when judging distances in visually immersive environments? *Presence, 13*(5), 560–571.

Uzzell, D. L., & Jones, E. M. (1996). Incorporating the visual impact of buildings into BREEAM: A study for the Building Research Establishment. Guilford, UK: University of Surrey.

Vignozzi, A. (1994). Design control in Italian planning. *Built Environment, 20*(2), 127–141.

Williams, N. (1974). *American planning law: Land use and the police power.* Chicago, IL: Callaghan.

Witmer, B. G., & Kline, P. B. (1998). Judging perceived and traversed distance in virtual environments. *Presence, 7*(2).

Xijuan, L., Yinglin, W., & Shouwei, J. (2003). A metrics based task analysis model for design review planning. *Design Studies, 24,* 375–390.

Zacharias, J. (2006). Exploratory spatial behavior in real and virtual environments. *Landscape and Urban Planning, 78,* 1–13.

Ziegler, E. H. (1986). Aesthetic controls and derivative human values: The emerging basis for regulation. In J. B. Gailey (Ed.), *1986 zoning and planning law handbook* (Vol. *1,* pp. 239–253). New York, NY: Clark Boardman.

Zube, E. H., Pitt, D. G., & Anderson, T. V. (1974). *Perception and measurement of scenic resources in the Southern Connecticut river valley.* Amhurst, MA: Institute for Man and His Environment, University of Massachusetts.

Suggested Readings

For background on how to do science:

Bacon, F. (1605). *Advancement of learning* (1952 ed.). New York, NY: Collier.

Cohen, J. (1988). *Statistical power analysis for the behavioral sciences.* Hillsdale, NJ: Erlbaum.

Collingwood, R. (1945). *The idea of nature.* Oxford, UK: Clarendon Press.

Cummings, G. (2012). *Understanding the new statistics: Effect sizes, confidence intervals, and meta-analysis.* New York, NY: Routledge.

Deming, W. E. (1950). *Some theory of sampling.* New York, NY: Dover.

Fisher, R. A. (1935). *The design of experiments* (1971 ed.). New York, NY: Hafner.

12

Planning the Built Environment
Programming

Jay Farbstein[1], Richard E. Wener[2], and
Lindsay J. McCunn[3]
[1] *Jay Farbstein & Associates, Los Angeles, CA, United States*
[2] *New York University, NY, United States*
[3] *University of Victoria, BC, Canada*

Gabriel sat down at his desk, coffee in hand, ready to begin a new week in his "hole." At least, that's what Maria called it when she stopped by his office last month. She was right: his cubicle did not face a window. In fact, very little light penetrated from the windows on the other side of the building because of the tall partitions separating him from his co-workers. He was always cold and the number of days he was absent because of illness was starting to bother him. It was only a matter of time before he heard from his supervisor.

During his short enrollment in architecture school, Gabriel learned that the physical environment of the workplace could affect employee engagement and satisfaction – even health. He wondered why the higher-ups didn't hire an architectural programmer when the office was renovated three years ago. If they had, employees surely would have had more direct involvement in the planning process, and at least would have been sure that their needs and concerns had been considered. That way, the office might have been designed better – there might not have been so much wasted space. The heat distribution might be more efficient and a better layout would certainly have been planned to maximize the view from the southwest facing windows.

Gabriel realized that the reason these things were not considered before the remodel was because of an ongoing debate around the office about whether academic studies concerning the built environment could be utilized in the "real world." Secretly, he'd been trying to understand the balance between theory and practice since he began his job with the regional government. Gabriel finished his coffee and began to look up local programming firms online. Perhaps he could persuade his director to hire one of them to show his colleagues the value of applying environment-behavior research.

Research Methods for Environmental Psychology, First Edition. Edited by Robert Gifford.
© 2016 John Wiley & Sons, Ltd. Published 2016 by John Wiley & Sons, Ltd.

Built environments should support the current and future functions and needs of **users** and organizations. Including **programming** as an early step in a design project can help to ensure this support. This is because programmers systematically gather, analyze, interpret, and summarize behavioral information about a setting before design and construction phases occur.

As organizations become larger, a distinction emerges between building user and owner, and the distance between users and the designers hired by an owner can become more profound. The likelihood that an owner understands the detailed concerns and needs of building users is reduced, leading to the need for a distinct process to identify this information. A programmer will compile information concerning spaces, how they are used, and the people who use them. Environmental problems and challenges specific to the setting being created or altered will be defined during programming; solutions to those problems can be crafted and formally recommended. Along the way, interactions between paying **clients**, occupants, and architects can be facilitated.

The origins of programming can be traced back to two major movements. Cherry (1999) suggests that programming arose after the Second World War in response to the development of systems analysis and identification of the need to more systematically gather information to support the design process. Programming also sprang from growing concern in the design community for integrating participatory processes into architecture in the 1970s and 1980s, as well as the emergence of the field of **environment-behavior research** linking social science methodologies with design issues. Over the subsequent years, programming has become fully integrated into the design process and recognized as a standard part of professional practice by architects, interior designers, landscape architects, and planners (e.g., The American Institute of Architects, 2009).

This chapter defines programming, its goals, the range of roles a programmer may play during a project, and some of the challenges associated with its practice. It also provides an overview of methods used by programmers together with suggestions about how a programmer can select among them, and tailor them to a particular project's requirements. These aspects are illustrated in a detailed case study about a programming project carried out by one of the authors.

Programming Defined

By definition, programming is the initial phase of the design process where information that serves as a basis for making good design decisions – ones that support the needs of the project's owners and users – is developed and documented. The focus here is on behavioral-based programming as it addresses the functional, organizational, and psychological needs of these groups, rather than on technical requirements. For example, a behavioral-based program would not include an assessment of a building's plumbing or electrical systems, but might address related issues, such as privacy needs in bathrooms.

Successful buildings support efficient operations, respond to important cultural needs, engender user satisfaction and comfort that, in turn, support job performance, minimize absenteeism, illness, or even – in some settings – reduce violence. A well-developed behavioral program can contribute to a building's success by tapping into the experience of clients and users concerning information about features that are important to them, and critical to their optimal use of the building – and by bringing to bear lessons learned from the research literature (so-called "evidence-based design").

Methods used in programming are focused on a particular place, population, and set of functions, while addressing the range of building features needed to support them. Thus, a thoughtfully produced program will identify the key challenges and opportunities posed by the unique circumstances of the project and offer insight into user needs. The programmer can and should challenge potentially preconceived notions about what the design should be like. This is one advantage of the programming phase being independent of the design phase. A programmer may ask an organization whether it really needs a new facility - something a designer might not be willing to do.

On the other hand, although programming may be a distinct phase in the process, the issues uncovered and the decisions made during programming are typically revisited as the project progresses and as more is learned about the space in question, its possibilities, and constraints (refer to Figure 12.1 showing programming as part of a cyclical activity where the five phases of the **design cycle** connect to, and build

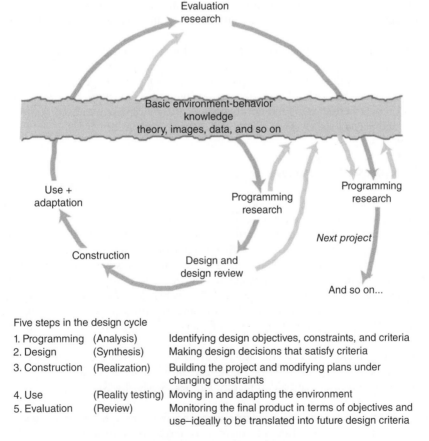

Five steps in the design cycle

1. Programming	(Analysis)	Identifying design objectives, constraints, and criteria
2. Design	(Synthesis)	Making design decisions that satisfy criteria
3. Construction	(Realization)	Building the project and modifying plans under changing constraints
4. Use	(Reality testing)	Moving in and adapting the environment
5. Evaluation	(Review)	Monitoring the final product in terms of objectives and use–ideally to be translated into future design criteria

Figure 12.1 The five steps of the design cycle (Zeisel, 2006).

upon, each other). The programming phase feeds information to the design phase, while **post-occupancy evaluation** (POE) informs future iterations of programming. POE involves the final phase of the design process where strengths and weaknesses of a building's form and function are examined (Chapter 13 provides in-depth information about POE).

Clients and Users

Let us elaborate on the differing relationships clients and users of a building can have in the programming process. Users of a building represent a host of occupants who live or work in, visit or spend time in the building, including, for example, line staff or supervisors, sales personnel, patrons, apartment tenants, and patients. Clients typically own or control the building (or represent the entity who does). An owner could be a developer, government agency, or business that leases out retail or office space. In almost all cases, the owner contracts with the programming professional directly or through a subcontract with another member of the design team. In addition, the client holds ultimate decision-making authority over a project and, to a large extent, decides how extensive the program will be and how much access the programmer can have to occupants, staff, clients of the organization, and affected or interested members of the public.

That said, a programmer may well advocate for more extensive user involvement, justifying the time and expense in terms of increased quality of information and, ultimately, a building that better meets their needs. On some larger and more complex projects, a higher level decision-making committee (to whom the programmer would report periodically) and another more broadly representative committee of interested parties, stakeholders, and the like, may be involved.

The Goals of Programming

In general, the main goal of programming is to provide guidelines that will ensure good fit between a design and the needs of users and the organization operating in the building. Programmers aim to identify important needs and issues that ought to be considered during subsequent phases of the design process. In some instances, a client will not have an exhaustive understanding of the needs of building users, especially in large, complex projects such as prisons, hospitals, or airports (Hershberger, 2002). In this case, a goal of the programming phase is to positively affect the outcome of a project by ensuring input is received from a wide variety of types of users and visitors about their activities and needs.

The programmer will need to gather information about many different aspects of the proposed environment. Fritz Steele, a pioneer of social design, has outlined some of the most frequently identified categories (Steele, 1973):

1. Shelter and security: Users desire access to fresh air and daylight, adequate space, freedom from threats to their safety, territorial control, etc.

2. Social contact: Users want privacy balanced with opportunity for communication with others.
3. Task instrumentality: Work performance and user satisfaction is often enhanced when specific microspatial arrangements are accommodated.
4. Symbolic identification: The environment is more understandable and satisfying when appropriate symbols are in place to convey user status or space use.
5. Growth: Users typically want opportunities to explore and learn. The organization wants to be sure the building will support future development.
6. Pleasure: Controllability, comfort, convenience, and aesthetic appeal are variables that assist users in having positive experiences.

In the next section, we outline the range of roles the programmer may play in facilitating effective communication among parties involved the design process.

Programmer Roles

By personal style, inclination, or necessity, a programmer may be required to serve as a liaison between clients, users, and perhaps the public. It can be challenging to keep the conversation constructive among people with these differing perspectives, who may have conflicting ideas about elements of the design. Kent Spreckelmeyer (1987) describes four possible roles for the programmer: facilitator; information collector; information interpreter; and, information manager. A programmer may play all these roles – or switch among them – depending on the demands of the project.

As a facilitator, the programmer helps clients and users negotiate the design process as they make decisions. A facilitator helps to ensure that those who will be directly affected by the project are adequately represented and considered. This may take place in workshops or other participatory sessions where input from all parties can be collected, synthesized, and discussed.

A programmer acting as a collector of information is primarily interested in finding or creating data-gathering techniques and instruments that address the topics of interest, and assuring the precision of data-gathering methods (e.g., sampling and field procedures, instrument testing, statistics). Methods used by a programmer in this role typically range from observing and recording user behavior to interviewing users in order to obtain detailed descriptions of their thoughts and feelings about a specific environmental feature in a space.

The role of information interpreter has been described as processing raw data into useful information (Pena & Parshall, 2001). Here, the programmer translates the complex information gathered in the previous step into meaningful concepts that will aid in the design of a supportive, comfortable, and useful space. The data and analysis are packaged as a clear and thorough report for the client, users, and architect – often including graphic illustrations of the programming concepts.

Finally, in the manager role, the programmer focuses on decision making, as well as the resolution of conflicting viewpoints between the client and users. In arbitrative circumstances, a programmer is typically expected to arrange environmental information in well-defined, hierarchical categories so that issues can be identified and resolved at each stage of the process.

Programming Methods

As in any research endeavor, a key part of the programming process is choosing the right data-collection methods to meet the demands of the situation. Since it is inappropriate to apply a one-size-fits-all, standardized process to diverse projects, a programmer's first step is to identify the kind of information needed, and the resources available, taking into account time, money, and personnel.

In addition, some of the methods outlined below are similar to those used in a POE (see Chapter 13). In fact, one use of a POE may be to gather information to support programming (e.g., how is an existing site perceived and used? Which building attributes are worth retaining or repeating? Which improvements would make the space more satisfying, comfortable, and productive for users and visitors?

Literature review

By building on available knowledge, the researcher does not have to start from scratch or reinvent the wheel. Thus, familiarity with what has been learned before in the form of theory, models, and findings relevant to a project is essential. The purpose of a literature review is to identify what is known about the type of facility or user based on previous projects and research.

A literature review can uncover a variety of useful information: findings about general features or issues that may apply across types of settings (e.g., lighting, noise, wayfinding), or about user groups (elderly, children, disabled), or about particular kinds of settings (open offices, hospitals, institutions). For professionals who regularly work in the same kinds of settings, a literature review will be portable from job to job, only needing to be periodically updated.

The accessibility of digital information has revolutionized this method, collapsing time and distance in finding and obtaining information, especially if one has access to licensed, fee-for-view databases, as available in most universities and many public libraries. Search engines can turn up an abundance of sources, uncovering information that no traditional search through a paper library card catalogue could ever find. Sources such as Google Scholar, that searches scientific sources, and Google Books, that finds and often displays entire volumes, can be invaluable to practitioners who do not have access to scholarly databases. In addition, some sources collect information about facilities on a variety of issues. These databases sometimes compare sites on specific issues, such as the Commercial Buildings Energy Consumption Survey (CBECS) from the US Department of Energy (http://www.buildingbenchmarks.com/), or provide more general information, such as the American Institute of Architects' Building Research Information Knowledgebase (http://www.brikbase.org/), and online newsletters Research Design Connections (https://researchdesignconnections.com/), and Informe Design (http://www.informedesign.org/).

Although a search engine may allow a programmer to quickly identify books, journals, and articles that are of relevance, determining the quality of found literature remains a responsibility of the programmer, since a search engine does not discriminate among newspaper articles, blog posts, and non-peer-reviewed articles on the one hand, and higher quality academic, refereed research papers on the other.

Also, a literature review is scalable, in the sense that it can range from the quick and inexpensive to the extensive and time consuming, depending on available time and need. Studies can be found in traditional ways (e.g., published and peer-reviewed sources) but often, especially for design studies, information exists in the "gray literature" of unpublished reports.

Gathering information about user perceptions, preferences, needs, and desires

The choice of methods to use and how to use them depends on the kind of data needed and the time and resources available. Three broad categories of data-gathering techniques are available, including self-reports (surveys and interviews), observations of how occupants use spaces, and responses to simulations of what the proposed facility might look like. These vary in time, effort, and cost involved, and in the kind of questions addressed and the type of data yielded. Although each method has its strengths and weaknesses, they are often used in combination to "triangulate" and improve the level of confidence in findings and programming recommendations.

Self-report methods Self-report methods are, to a large extent, systematic and sophisticated ways of asking a setting's users: "what do you think about 'x'?" These methods seek to glean from users what they think about space needs from their use of existing environments, and how they perceive the setting based on their own experiences, desires, and goals. Gathering this information in a way that yields rich data from a broad and representative sample, and in a way that reduces biases and addresses critical issues, is where skill and craft come in.

Questions and responses may be tailored to a particular place or situation or to a single issue or concept (such as stress or job satisfaction). In some cases, pre-existing survey forms may be available, though more usually the questions must be crafted by the programmer. Among the advantages of using existing surveys are that they provide comparability (how one group responds compared to others), reliability (consistency or replicability of responses), and validity (the degree to which the questions address the intended concept). However, the programmer would not want to sacrifice relevance to the subject project just to use a well-tested survey form.

An open-ended item poses a question without demanding selection from a limited set of responses. Participants are able to shape their own response; their answers can provide information that is rich in context and ideas. Responses to closed-ended surveys are limited to a set of options offered by the researcher, making statistical tabulation easier. The trade-off relates to the time and cost of each piece of data. In the hours a programmer may need to conduct individual interviews with a small number of people, many surveys can be distributed and completed. Similarly, content analysis of interviews or open-ended survey questions is time consuming, while closed-ended surveys can be analyzed much more quickly.

Information technology has made surveys even more time efficient. Many are now conducted on computers, often through web-based systems that eliminate the cost and time for printing, copying, distribution, collection, and data entry. Portable technologies (e.g., smart phones or tablets) broaden options for responses (Raento,

Oulasvirta, & Eagle, 2009). Users can be queried weekly, daily, or hourly at their workplace via smart phone apps for real-time information gathering that can be related to changing environmental conditions. Using automated data entry and pre-defined scripts for analysis in statistical programs, a set of tables and figures can be available, moments after the last survey is completed.

Interviews   Interviews can be considered as a variation on self-report surveys – where the researcher asks the questions in person. Again, responses can be open-ended or require selection from fixed categories (the latter are, of course, much easier for the interviewer to record). A set of interviews with open-ended questions conducted early in the process can help the researcher understand what issues need to be addressed and what response sets should be offered. The depth provided by interview responses can help interpret answers to closed-ended, scaled items.

Moreover, individual interviews need not always be lengthy. Intercept interviews attempt to "grab" users as they enter or leave a space, and are typically limited to just a few short items. In programming a new landscape for a park, for instance, park users may be asked how often they come, what the primary reason was for visiting the park, how they got there, and where they visited. Interviews can also be made more time efficient by conducting them with groups (Bickman & Rog, 2009), that might entail interviewing 6 to 12 people at a time. Although participants are not anonymous (making this method inappropriate for some highly sensitive issues) the interaction among subjects can provide added value to information obtained.

Gathering information about how space is used

Learning about how an existing space is used can contribute substantially to planning for new ones. Formal or designated uses (e.g., those indicated by room names) may represent only part of the spectrum of behaviors that actually occur in a setting. For example, a conference room is used for formal, pre-planned meetings, the library for reading, and the kitchen for preparing food. But conference rooms can also serve as places to take private phone calls, libraries for meetings, and kitchens for parties – or many other functions. In fact, learning that the kitchen served as dining room, childcare space, and family room in an apartment (while the living room and dining room often remained unused except to greet formal company) (Gans, 1962) helped architects re-shape these spaces to better meet the needs of residents.

Gaining access to information about how spaces are used tends to be time consuming – both in gathering and analyzing the data. Thus, some of the methods described below are highly labor-intensive.

User diaries   Users can be asked to keep diaries of what they do, where they do it, and how they feel about the level of support the setting provides. This method can range from providing users with a blank notebook, software document, or online entry space with instructions for use. Diaries can be made more systematic by structuring the times responses are made. Some researchers have used computer or tele-communication systems to prompt responses. For instance, participants have been given pagers with instructions to respond (e.g., "Where am I now? What am I doing now?") when paged, with computer programs randomizing the times their beepers are called (Soupourmas, Ironmonger, Brown, & Warner-Smith, 2005). Programs on smart phones can do all of this as well as provide the online survey.

Walk-through interviews Design researchers in New Zealand have developed walk-through – or touring – interviews as a rapid information-gathering technique for existing sites (Daish, Gray, Kernohan, & Salmond, 1982). The method starts with a briefing to discuss the building and the process, followed by a walking tour of each space within the site with a group that includes researchers and members of user interest groups. Often, the tour includes intercept interviews with users as they are encountered along with photo-documentation. Some common questions are: "What happens here/what is this for?" "What works/is successful?" "What doesn't work/isn't successful?" "What should be kept or changed?" and "What makes a space like this good?" (Daish et al., 1982, p. 81). The walk-through is capped by a debriefing review session where findings are summarized and agreed upon.

Observation Observations can be valuable in understanding which aspects of an existing space or design work well (and should be retained or strengthened in the new one) and which work poorly or inhibit activities (and should be eliminated). Observations can be informal and unstructured, or more systematic.

Informal observations provide anecdotal information about the use – or misuse – of spaces. Examples might include noting where employees use portable electrical heaters to address thermal comfort, or how users place plants or coats at a desk to reduce visual exposure and increase privacy. The quality of information gathered can depend on the observer's sensitivities, the choice of spaces to visit, and even the time of day or season of the year. Formal observations, such as behavioral mapping or tracking, allow the programmer to obtain a more complete and unbiased picture of how and where users spend their time (Ittelson, Rivlin, & Proshansky, 1970; Sommer & Sommer, 1992). A map represents user locations at a moment in time, while tracking shows how they move through the space.

A behavioral map is essentially a detailed snapshot of who is where and doing what in an entire space at a point in time, with repeated snapshots (e.g., every 20 or 60 minutes) over a number of days. The number and duration of the observations would be determined to provide an accurate picture of use. Tracking, rather than producing a static picture, follows the movement of one person at a time, noting what they do and where they go as they move through a space. As the "tracks" of multiple users are overlaid, a pattern may emerge that indicates desired destinations and pathways. Tracking can be especially useful in understanding movement and wayfinding issues as was demonstrated in studies of US post offices (Kantrowitz & Farbstein, 1996) where they contributed to redesign of the retail areas to better accommodate desired patterns of use.

Mapping and tracking can be very time consuming, but their use has been much aided by the development of telecommunication devices for support. In the example mentioned above, observations of multiple post office sites were conducted using BMAP (Wener, 2002), a program run on a handheld personal digital assistant (PDA). Significant technological advances have resulted in People Watcher, an Apple iPad-based program for mapping and tracking (Dalton, Conroy Dalton, & Hoelscher, 2013; Dalton, Dalton, Hölscher, & Kuhnmünch, 2012). With People

Watcher, an onscreen plan of the space is available and an observer merely needs to run a finger along the screen, tracing a user's path to record both time and place of movement.

Photo/video documentation   Still and video photography provide other useful means of recording information on space use (within the ethical bounds of consideration for occupant privacy). Still photography is especially useful for noting, and later presenting, examples of use and space issues, while video recording in real time or by time-lapse imagery can provide unparalleled sources of information on use of space over time. Whyte's (1980) use of time-lapse film to understand the use of public plazas, for instance, led to critical changes in New York City's zoning laws for the design of these kinds of spaces.

The omnipresent use of security systems in many modern buildings also provides opportunities for collecting information. These may include utilizing the video feed from security cameras, databases storing information on the movement of employees and visitors in, out, and through spaces using scanned bar-coded tags, or recordings from radio-frequency identification (RFID) cards. These methods are limited only by future technology, the imagination of the researcher, and reasonable expectations of privacy.

Simulation

Programmers (and designers) may choose to simulate potential characteristics of a planned space as a way to elicit user reactions to alternate configurations. Architectural plans and models are common types of simulations, but many lay people have difficulty reading plans or imagining use from scaled-down models. In response, designers have developed systems for full-scale simulations (or mockups), using inexpensive and quickly altered materials, including the equivalent of foam sheets or blocks. Generally, these mockups are effective at modeling spatial dimensions and relationships, but do not accurately reproduce surface texture or colors, lighting, views, and the like. Even such limited systems require extensive space, time, and funds.

By contrast, digital technologies provide the possibility of more affordable simulations of spaces that can allow the user to walk through or "fly" over the posited space. These simulations can be relatively realistic in capturing surface effects and their digital nature makes it fairly easy to modify designs so users can "experience" the impacts of proposed changes.

One example of such a simulation program at an urban scale is Betaville (Skelton, Koplin, & Cipolla, 2011). This is an "open-source multiplayer environment in which ideas for new works of public art, architecture, urban design, and development can be shared, discussed, tweaked, and brought to maturity in context, and with the kind of broad participation people take for granted in open source software development."

Agent-based models are simulations of the actions and interactions of individuals or groups to assess their effects on a system as a whole. These models make use of experience and existing data sets (often from previous POEs) to create computer-based models of how people may act in new situations (Andrews, Yi, Krogmann, Senick, & Wener, 2011). Thus, an agent-based model used for design programming purposes might assess the use of a variety of lighting schemes (such as changing window sizes and treatments, task lighting, or kind and size of overhead lighting) and generate data indicating the kind of illumination that results, and how energy bills are likely to be affected, as well as how variously profiled user groups are likely to respond in terms of satisfaction and perceived comfort.

Needs assessment

A needs assessment can be considered either as an early phase of, or precursor to, programming. At this stage, very basic questions are asked concerning the likely future direction of an organization operating in a particular building or set of buildings. How will the organization grow or change over time? Will it continue to pursue its mission in the ways that it has in the past, or will it reconsider how it could do things more effectively – or even modify its very mission? Will there be forces in its environment (locally or globally defined) to which it must respond? To answer these questions, a programmer might employ techniques such as visioning (described in the Group Process Methods section of this chapter), benchmarking, or system performance modeling as part of an exercise in projecting future patterns of activity and space needs. Sometimes, through engaging in this process, an organization that intended to conduct a limited architectural effort finds itself rethinking broader aspects of organizational design.

Benchmarking   Part of understanding where an organization needs to go is knowing how it is currently doing. One way of doing this is to compare it to the "state-of-the-art" or best practices in its field. There are a number of ways to achieve this, but all methods generally begin by assembling comparative information about the organization and its peers. For example, a justice agency may require a programmer to collect data that compares rates of arrests, incarcerations, convictions, or recidivism in similar jurisdictions. A programmer might try to understand whether the agency is more or less effective than its peers by comparing the types of rehabilitative programs offered, and their outcomes.

For other organizations, measures might be time to market for new products, sales, staff performance or turnover, cost per unit of output, or a host of other variables chosen for their relevance to the organization's goals. In some cases, programmers may check whether industry standards or governmental mandates are being met or exceeded. More environmental measures can also be developed, such as square feet provided per staff or patient, operating costs per square foot, and the like.

When it comes to benchmarking facilities and their operations, an excellent approach is to take a group of clients on tours of buildings considered to be state-of-the-art. Similar to the touring interviews described above, clients can meet and exchange ideas with building users as they walk through the spaces, learning about how and why design decisions were made and what is working well and not so well. Clients may identify aspects of the planning process, and features that they would like to incorporate, as well as undesirable features (e.g., "we wouldn't want that in our building!"). Ideally, the programmer would prepare specific questions and formally process the results. Photo documentation is essential for pinpointing desirable features and sharing them with participants who were not able to join the tour.

Tours that involve travel to other locales can be invaluable opportunities for developing group cohesion through the range of formal and informal shared experience (e.g., riding a bus or taking meals together).

System modeling   System modeling entails building a statistical model of factors concerning an organization's past performance that could reasonably be thought to generate need for facilities (e.g., number of employees, number of items produced or sold, number of bookings into a jail, or length of stay prior to release). The model must include variables that may drive future changes (e.g., projected population growth or decline, changes in demographics that indicate number of children of school age).

Some models test hypotheses about the degree to which change in one variable explains another. Many times, a variety of scenarios are developed that reflect possible ranges or rates of change. Clients and decision makers select the most likely scenario to use as a basis for facility planning. This scenario becomes the basis for quantifying future states of the organization and, thus, its demand for facilities.

An alternative way of thinking about projected future states is called "backcasting." Differentiated from the kinds of statistical forecasting described in the preceding paragraphs, backcasting is "a method in which the future desired conditions are envisioned and steps are then defined to attain those conditions, rather than taking steps that are merely a continuation of present methods extrapolated into the future" (Holmberg & Robèrt, 2000, p. 294).

To summarize, a formal needs assessment typically includes projections of future levels of demand and activity that will need to be accommodated in a new facility. Such projections may even demonstrate that a new facility is not needed – perhaps the problem can be solved in another way, or at another location.

Focus groups

A focus group represents a highly structured technique borrowed from market research where it is used extensively to test or refine concepts and products before they are released. Conducting focus groups as part of programming is more unusual, but they may be justified under certain circumstances. For example, Kantrowitz and Farbstein (1996) used focus groups for the US Postal Service when developing design guidelines for a new concept in retail lobbies (the place where a customer can buy a stamp or mail a letter). Since the Postal Service is a national enterprise, focus groups were conducted in several locations around the country. For each group, a number of interested customers were recruited by randomly approaching individuals who visited certain post offices. Focus group participants are often offered an honorarium for participation, since they are required to come to a special facility and give an hour or more of their time.

Questions for focus groups are always prepared in advance. The group is led by a facilitator trained to carefully present discussion topics and ensure the group stays on track, including following up with probing questions in response to initial answers. Generally, a facilitator gives every participant the opportunity to respond. Often, images that represent alternative approaches to planning or design are shown to participants who are asked to respond to them.

A focus group facility (often in a market research company's office) is equipped with audio and video recording equipment so that a complete record of the proceedings can be made. Among other uses, this frees a facilitator from having to take notes. Many facilities are also set up for live observation of the group through one-way glass from a second room, allowing the client or owner to see and hear responses first-hand. Participants are informed in advance, and again at the session, that they are being recorded and may be observed.

A primary benefit of the focus group method is the considerable depth of the responses and the real-life, spontaneous quality of participant reactions that are often very rich (as compared to the dry statistics from a survey). Drawbacks include the cost and effort of organizing a focus group, renting a facility, and recruiting and paying the participants. The qualitative analysis and interpretation of results are also very time consuming.

Group process methods

This section addresses methods intended to assist a group in generating concepts, discovering the range of its members' responses to options and, ultimately, moving toward a consensus decision, if one is achievable. Such methods should be viewed as a means of helping a group surface issues and ideas, and work toward consensus by discovering the level of convergence (or divergence) of opinions. Despite the use of voting, group process methods should not be seen as a way of enforcing "majority rules."

Nominal group technique (NGT)   This is a well-known and widely used method adapted and updated from Delbecq, Van de Ven, and Gustafson (1975). NGT proceeds through a formal series of steps and can be applied to many types of questions or issues. A group of participants is selected based on the type of issue being dealt with, for example, as Delbecq and Van de Ven (1971) point out, problem exploration, knowledge exploration, priority development, or proposal or option development. The structure of the process remains essentially the same and can be used as needed with a programming task force, depending on the issue at hand, as outlined below.

1. A focal question is developed and communicated to the group. This could be very broad or quite focused. For example, "What are the important challenges the new facility will have to address?" or "Which is the best site/location for our new building," or "How can we best plan the nurses' stations in the new hospital?" In the first case, the group might be quite broadly representative, while in the third, nurses, aides, and supervisors might be included.
2. Six to twelve participants generally take part. Conducting NGT with more than 12 people becomes challenging and time consuming. However, the technique can be adapted to larger groups that may or may not be subdivided and taken through the process separately before coming together to review and integrate the results. Participants are seated in a non-hierarchical arrangement, perhaps at a U-shaped table, with the facilitator and one or more flipcharts at the front. In response to a specific question, each participant writes as many ideas as they can think of on a sheet of paper, cards, or even large Post-it™ notes.

3. In round-robin fashion, each participant proposes one idea at a time. Then, the next participant proposes an idea, and so forth. The facilitator either records ideas on a flipchart or posts the card on the wall. This process is repeated until all ideas are listed. Participants pass when they have exhausted their list. There is no need to duplicate ideas, but if an important variation is offered, it should be listed. The ideas are assigned numbers for easy reference during subsequent steps. They are not attributed to their proposer, as the point is to encourage the group to take ownership in ones they support.

4. A brief discussion of each idea takes place to clarify intent, develop an understanding of its importance, or to defend it. Any participant can provide comments and contribute their understanding of the idea.

5. Each individual votes in private to prioritize the ideas. They may be given a set number of votes (e.g., to state their top 5 or 10 depending on the number of ideas and participants), or rank ideas sequentially, from best to worst. Participants can also be given adhesive dots to stick next to say their top 5 ideas. Votes are tallied and the ideas with the greatest support are identified and ranked. The process can stop there, or the top ranked ideas can be further discussed to flesh out their meanings and implications.

NGT is a generic planning process, not limited to facility programming. It is, however, particularly well suited to generating ideas and ensuring that all members of the group participate without regard to their place in the organizational hierarchy. It is also quite useful for selecting the most promising options and for setting priorities among them. NGT is, in some ways, a more recent incarnation of "brainstorming," a technique widely used to stimulate group creativity, though brainstorming's effectiveness has been challenged by Delbecq and Van de Ven (1971), and more recently by Lehrer (2012), who refers to research showing that NGT produces more ideas and creative solutions than brainstorming. On the other hand, NGT is highly structured and may appear overly rigid to some participants.

Visioning   One way NGT (or other less formal methods) can be applied is through visioning. The visioning process is oriented toward the creative imagining of a future state – one that would seek to improve upon current conditions. While the focus of visioning is on generating new ideas, the process begins with a review and agreement about current conditions and their precedents. Consideration of how a client organization has evolved, together with recognition of trends, provides the background for considering how situations might develop and, more importantly, how the organization might want them to be in the future (recall the discussion of "backcasting" above). Thus, visioning is a structured process that might proceed along the following steps (borrowed from a project by Farbstein):

1. **Outline past and current situations and identifiable trends:** Review demographic, social, economic, and technological factors that might impact the organization. For example, in a city hall planning process, the programmers prepared a briefing paper and discussed:
    *   city demographics and population projections;

- base assumptions about anticipated growth and resource availability or limits;
- trends in law enforcement, technology, office work, and design.

2. **State goals and directions:** If an organization has a mission statement and formalized goals, they should be reviewed. For the same city hall plan, programmers asked participants to consider:
   - demand for and provision of services;
   - types and numbers of staff (given this city's staffing model and anticipated build-out of its urban land area);
   - use of current and new technologies;
   - legal mandates;
   - environmental performance goals;
   - resources and limitations.

   To help them in this exercise, programmers provided sample goals:
   - Be a great place to work.
   - Have facilities that support efficient and effective work.
   - Have facilities that support evolving technologies and new forms of work (e.g., "new officing," telecommuting, hotelling, paperless workplace).

3. **Create alternative visions of the future:** Programmers divided participants into small groups of 6 to 10 and asked them to imagine a day at city hall 10 or 20 years in the future when some or all of the goals are realized. Participants were asked "what would you be doing, who would be there, what technologies would be in use, what would the place look like?"

4. **Note challenges that need to be overcome:** Often, obstacles can stand in the way of achieving a new vision. In order to make the vision a reality, it is worthwhile to review potential problems and talk about possible solutions. This exercise is also helpful in determining the feasibility of a particular vision (e.g., obstacles may be too great to overcome). For the city hall example, programmers explored the following:
   - What limiting features of the current situation need to be recognized, overcome, or accepted in order to achieve the visions? (e.g., demographics, resources, geography, politics, attitudes)
   - Should the visions be modified to be more practical, or should constraints be removed?

The resulting vision in this example was arrived at with creativity and supported by consensus. Often, visioning can provide an outstanding basis for more detailed programming work.

Facilitation For many projects, much of the work of eliciting information and working toward programming recommendations is done in groups of decision makers (clients) or information providers (users) as discussed in the section on Clients and Users, above. It is the responsibility of the programmer to ensure that group discussions proceed in a productive direction. One will want to avoid having one or more participants begin with a "manifesto" about what they think the new building should look like, running the risk of polarizing or alienating the group. Thus, to start things off in a positive direction, the programmer may ask participants to explain what they do now and the extent to which current activities are likely to continue to be relevant to the organization (or their building) in the future. This can also reinforce the notion that design decisions must support functional and operational goals. The programmer guides discussion toward broad operational goals, the users who will be accommodated in the facility, and what will be done there. Once these aspects are understood, spatial implications can be brought up. The programmer would ask about the types of spaces needed, how big they need to be, how they are related in terms of location, what furnishings they will have, what ambient conditions will be needed, and what technological supports are required.

Sometimes keeping a group on track can pose challenges to a programmer, particularly when strong divergence in opinion emerges, for example, over objectives or directions. This is why the guiding principles for structuring and facilitating group processes are openness and inclusion. These qualities may not make it possible to avoid conflict but provide the means to resolve it. When there is a wide variety of participants whose values, concerns, and objectives may not be identical, only an open, inclusive, and interactive process can provide the possibility for real resolution, without resorting to authoritarian decision making and the imposition of a direction that may not garner wide support.

Certain facilitation principles consistently contribute to success. The facilitator should set an appropriate tone for the group. This tone should demonstrate mutual respect (e.g., allowing divergent opinions) and democratic equality (e.g., everyone may express their thoughts, regardless of status). Making these expectations clear at the start of the process is helpful. As discussions progress, the facilitator may pose certain topics, ensuring that everyone gets an opportunity to state their ideas, calling on those who tend to hold back to make sure they have an opportunity to speak. While not all members of the group will be equally knowledgeable or artful in expressing themselves, the facilitator must actively listen and respond to each participant. Each viewpoint should be documented with equal emphasis until a shared direction becomes apparent.

This process does not always work easily; not infrequently there are strong-willed (or even impolite) participants. When one member attempts to dominate a group, the facilitator is obligated to handle the situation with respect and firmness. This kind of situation can become more challenging with a person of greater power. For this reason, composing a group of individuals with widely divergent degrees of power or influence is generally not recommended.

Another important attribute for a facilitator is to remain neutral and objective at all times. Participants may stake out positions early in the process, but a facilitator must not be seen to take sides. Since the facilitator may also be the programming consultant – and be expected to render a recommendation at the appropriate time – all facts and analysis should be considered before a final position is taken. Thus, a facilitator should reserve any professional judgment until the point in the project where it is appropriate.

One final observation: some disputes may require policy formation or resolution at the highest levels within an organization. When this is the case, the programmer is responsible for ensuring that the client is aware of the need for such involvement. The programmer should be prepared to provide an analysis of the issues and options to be considered and direction that needs to be adopted, while a project manager for the client (or appropriate upper manager) arranges for the information to be put on the agenda of a decision-making body.

How to Choose and Adapt Methods

We have introduced a wide range of programming methods that can be used to develop information and aid in making decisions. In preparing a program for a particular project, however, one would not consider using all of these available methods. So, the questions are: how to choose among them and, once chosen, how to adapt them to effectively serve a project's needs?

As mentioned earlier, the issue of available time and resources is central. Does the programming effort need to be very efficient and find answers quickly – or is there time to explore and gradually work toward consensus decisions? If the former, the programmer is likely to use fewer and more efficient methods. If the latter, the programmer can review the literature, take participants on facility tours, conduct broad surveys, and facilitate many cycles of exploration and review meetings involving both users and decision makers.

Table 12.1 arrays all of the programming methods we have introduced and indicates the level of effort and expertise they require, as well as the nature of the information they develop (general versus highly project-specific).

The Challenges of Programming

The programming process faces a number of limitations and challenges. Temporal limitations relate to the timing of programming (when it is completed compared to when the project is built and occupied – and the many changes that can occur in technology or the organization's environment in the interim), the length of the programming phase, the commitment of resources, and the difficulty in general of visualizing (let alone predicting) the future.

Other challenges result from roles and relationships among the affected parties. Owner-clients generally commission the program, but may or may not want building users to be involved in the process. This may pose a dilemma for a programmer who feels a commitment to such engagement. Even if a client supports programming, actual users (or even the client organization itself) may be unfamiliar operationally or culturally to the programmer who must find ways to ensure he or she is not imposing inappropriate values on the project. All of these challenges must be considered when selecting programming methods.

In addition, accomplishing all of the needed programming tasks can be time consuming. Planning the work, making arrangements for workshops, interviews and surveys, and analyzing large amounts of collected data are major undertakings. One may need to justify to a client that systematically gathering programming data about user needs is money well spent.

It can also be risky for a program to be too highly specified in terms of prescribing requirements for a building. This is especially the case when an organization is subject to substantial change in its markets, environment, or technologies. The possibility exists that staff, or the nature of a business, might change and invalidate the recommendations of the program report. A partial response to this situation is to devote considerable effort to understanding the likelihood – and perhaps the possible directions – of change an organization may face. Examining best practices in its field,

Table 12.1 Comparison of programming methods.

Method	Time/Cost	Special expertise	Specificity of information
Literature review	Low	None	General
Databases of facility information	Low	Data mining	General
Self-report			
Individual interviews	High	Interviewing	Specific
Focus group	Very high	Facilitation	Specific
Questionnaires	Moderate –low	Statistics	General to specific
Behavior observation			
Self-diaries, prompting	Moderate		Focused
Instrumented (cameras, existing databases, etc.)	Moderate –low	Tech-savvy	Focused
Photo-video documentation			
Formal observations (coding)	High	Reliable coding & statistics	Focused
Informal observations (notes)	Moderate		Focused
Simulation			
Physical	High		Very specific, relevant
Digital	Moderate–high		Very specific, relevant
Agent-based models	Moderate –low		Specific, if valid
Needs assessments			
Benchmarking	Low	None	General
System modeling	High	Statistical modeling	Specific
Group process			
Nominal group technique	Moderate	Facilitation	Very specific
Visioning	Moderate	Facilitation	General to specific
Facility tours	High	None	General to specific

and developing scenarios to which the building might need to respond, could be effective ways to mitigate this risk. In fact, a program might specify the range of possible futures for a building – perhaps with a probability or level of likelihood attached to each one. Decisions can then be made about how a building could respond. Another approach is to express programmatic requirements in terms of needed performance rather than specifying particular attributes. These approaches are not mutually exclusive and can be combined.

An additional limitation may be the independence of the design team from the programming phase. While it can be argued that it is beneficial for the programmers to remain independent of the design team in order to be free of their influence, one can also argue the opposite. Architects who will execute the design phase can provide an understanding of the implications and challenges that a particular program requirement may pose. They may also benefit from the detailed anecdotal comments received during programming that generally cannot be included in a program report.

Case Study: Juvenile and Family Court Project

This section will illustrate some of the methods – and the process for choosing and adapting them – from a project carried out by one of the authors. This case study outlines the planning and programming process for the juvenile and family courts in a large, urban county. The county is considered to be quite progressive regarding the legal and social issues addressed by these courts. Indeed, the primary impetus for the project was the court's desire to improve coordination and delivery of services to families engaged in proceedings, and greater integration (perhaps even unification) of two otherwise independent sets of court functions (a goal that poses many challenges to justice administration, as well as for facilities).

In order to understand the way the project was organized, one must know something about the roles and powers of the various agencies involved in the court. The Superior Court is, by statute, responsible for adjudicating cases in these areas. The court (in the form of judges and staff) was the primary client of the project. The court, however, is a function of county government that provides both its operating budget and facilities. Thus, the county was the paying client who contracted for the consultant's programming and planning services and provided project management, oversight, and ultimate decision authority.

It is worth noting that while common interests exist between the courts and the county, such as ensuring public safety and providing excellent public services, divergent ones also remain. County government has an obligation to provide adequate and safe facilities for the court but must balance the allocation of resources against all the other demands on its budget. The court must demonstrate fiscal responsibility to the public, but must also advocate for facilities that allow it to provide excellent public services in an efficient and effective manner.

In addition to these primary actors, there are a myriad of other county, state, and non-government agencies (e.g., prosecutors, defense attorneys, social workers, probation officers, counselors, drug and alcohol specialists) who are important users of the facilities, not to mention the actual parties – the juveniles who may be in court facing the consequences of delinquent activities or may be the victims of abuse, or up for adoption or placement in a foster home – and the family members who are divorcing and dealing with property division, child custody, and sometimes domestic violence. In addition, there are the attorneys who specialize in these fields of law. Finally, members of the general public may also be interested in the project or concerned in one way or another with the facility's location or structure. Probably, this is about as complex and multi-layered a set of clients and users as one is likely to come across. So, how does a programmer organize a process to successfully navigate through all these interests?

Local government in this county is dedicated to extensive participation and had already set up two broadly representative planning committees before the consultants were hired – a steering committee and a working group. At the apex of the project was the steering committee with a mandate to make recommendations to county government. It consisted of the presiding judge of the Superior Court, a member of the city council, and high-level representatives of the principal county and non-county agencies involved with the project, as well as a member of the bar and other related entities. The steering committee, which met less frequently, was supported by a working group composed of representatives of the same types of entities, but more of them. Its role was to provide hands-on knowledge of the workings of each entity that would likely be accommodated in the facility. In fact, there were 18 members of the steering committee and approximately 48 members of the working group. As would be expected, not all members attended all meetings though some were able to join by video conference.

The county also organized public input in the form of occasional presentations to the family law bar association and general public. It was clear, however, that these meetings were for the purpose of sharing information about the project's status and gathering responses; they did not delegate authority to the public. Input would be considered but not necessarily incorporated.

The project proceeded through two main phases. The first was a master planning exercise intended to help the county decide the overall scope and location for the courts by projecting needs and examining options for where services might be offered. The second entailed a more detailed design program focused on one set of options for a particular location. During master planning, the principal methods used were group process, needs assessment, decision exercises, and observations of their space.

Group process (for both phases) entailed facilitating and presenting to the steering committee and working group. The needs assessment involved quantitative analysis of judicial (and related) workload projections and provided a basis for estimating space needs under the various options. A qualitative assessment was also conducted seeking to better understand the cases that involved both juvenile court and family court matters. These were the candidates for the integrated or unified family and juvenile court, though other benefits of collocation were also identified, including increased efficiency of support functions.

Figure 12.2   Participants voting on Master Plan options. Photo Credit: Jay Farbstein.

Once options were identified, special workshops were organized to evaluate and rank them. Here, decision exercises were used. For example, participants were given a certain number of adhesive dots and asked to place them on the options they found most appealing (Figure 12.2). This provided an instant measure of the more favored options and stimulated an open-ended discussion of the reasons for and against each choice. The discussion made it possible to prepare a list of planning objectives based on criteria that were mentioned. The criteria were then ranked through a similar voting process and discussed until consensus was achieved.

The planning phase culminated with a number of options for location, scale, and composition of the project. Negotiations between the court and the county led to the selection of a particular site that would serve a major portion of the county with all juvenile and family court functions. It was, in fact, a site that already housed the outmoded court facilities and allowed a direct connection to a juvenile detention center. The programming phase fleshed out this option, providing enough information for a subsequent team to take the project through the design phase. As this phase progressed, the steering and working groups continued to meet to receive status reports and provide direction.

The programming process entailed two main methods: facility tours and structured small group interviews. Tours were conducted in three states at recently built courts that represented state-of-the-art designs for this type of facility – especially ones that had integrated family and juvenile functions. The tours were of great value in opening participants' eyes to different ways of achieving desired outcomes.

Structured, open-ended interviews were conducted with small groups representing each of the dozens of functions that would be housed in the new facility. Generally, participants were managers and supervisors who were very familiar with operations. Interviews started with questions about operations, asking participants

---

Box 12.1   Programming interview topics.

For each included area, participants should come prepared to discuss the following topics:

- Space needs – review the space list (rooms included and size of each room).
- Design standards and guidelines – as applicable to each area.
- Design objectives and image – for function, aesthetics, cost, time, energy efficiency, and "message" to users.
- Layout and relationships – location of the area within the building and internal relationships ("bubble" diagrams will be developed if appropriate).
- Security concerns, objectives, and design requirements (for materials and systems).
- Furniture and equipment – requirements for built-in (e.g., clerk counters) and moveable furniture (types of workstations, etc.).
- Special ambient environment requirements (light, acoustics, air quality, comfort).
- Special building system requirements (heating, ventilation, air conditioning, etc.).
- Special material and finish requirements (floors, walls, ceilings).

to describe their main operational objectives, who would be involved, what they would do, the movement of people and things, security concerns, and the like.

Only after operations were described were participants asked about spatial and environmental requirements. This part of the discussion began by enumerating the spaces that might be needed to accommodate people and activities, followed by sketching a diagram of how spaces ought to interrelate so that flows and interactions were supported. Sketches were done on flipcharts or white boards and recorded photographically (and later translated into an electronic drawing program). Finally, participants were asked about needed attributes of the spaces – from furnishings and equipment, to ambient environmental qualities. Responses were recorded as text that was edited into a report chapter for each function. After the information was documented and reviewed, a follow-up meeting was held to receive comments and make modifications. This program provided the basis for the county to move forward with design – and gave the participants the means to assess design proposals in terms of the degree to which they met user needs. See Figures 12.3 and 12.4.

Box 12.2   Overview of functions and operations – Design requirements.

- Design objectives.
- Space requirements.
- Flexibility.
- Location and spatial relationships.
- Safety and security.
- Finishes – performance requirements or suggested materials for floors, walls, ceilings.
- Furnishings and fixtures (moveable versus fixed).
- Ambient environment – heating, cooling, ventilation, lighting, and acoustics.
- Types and volumes of items stored.
- Equipment and systems – power, plumbing, telecommunications and audio-visual.
- Display.
- Site requirements.

Other:

- Future trends
- Days and hours of operation.
- Occupants/users (by type and their special requirements).
- Psychological or socio-cultural issues.
- Policies and procedures.
- Activities.
- Circulation patterns – for people, information, and things.

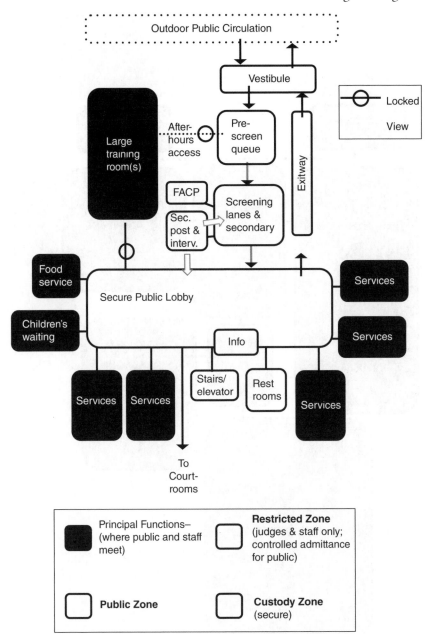

Figure 12.3 Entry, security screening, & lobby relationships diagram.

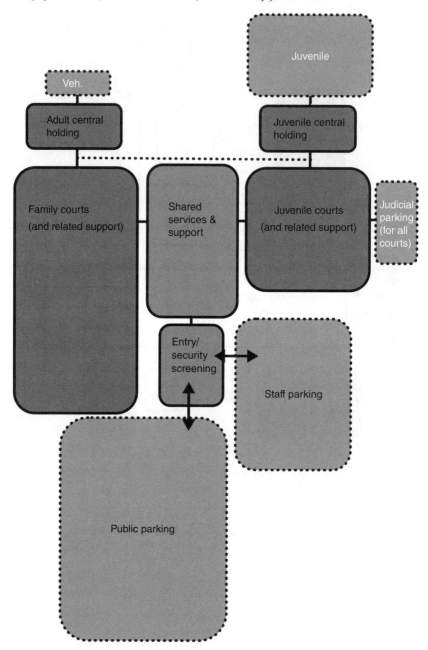

Figure 12.4   Overall functional relationship diagram for the project.

Summary and Conclusions

A design program develops and documents client and user needs that define the basis for subsequent phases of the design process. Several methods are used in a typical programming project. Ranging from surveys and observational techniques, to interviews, site tours, and group processes, the programmer has a wide range of options to choose from, depending on the nature and constraints of the project. Through the use of appropriate methods, a project can be expected to be more successful when information about users is systematically developed and clearly documented before design begins.

Glossary

Clients   Clients typically own or control (or represent the entity who controls) the building.

Design cycle   The process of building design whereby five phases (programming, design, construction, use, and evaluation) connect to, and build upon, each other.

Environment-behavior research   A field of study that merges social science methodologies with design issues.

Post-occupancy evaluation (POE)   The final phase of the design process where strengths and weaknesses of a building's form and function are examined.

Programming   A phase of the design cycle whereby information about a space is systematically gathered, analyzed, and summarized before the design and construction phases occur.

Users   Building users are a host of occupants who visit or spend time in the building but typically do not own or control it.

References

American Institute of Architects (2009). "Programming", *B202™–2009, Standard Form of Architect's Services*, Washington, DC: AIA.

Andrews, C. J., Yi, D., Krogmann, U., Senick, J. A., & Wener, R. E. (2011). Designing buildings for real occupants: An agent-based approach. *Systems, Man and Cybernetics, Part A: Systems and Humans*, 41(6), 1077–1091.

Bickman, L., & Rog, D. J. (2009). *The Sage handbook of applied social research methods*. New York, NY: Sage.

Cherry, E. (1999). *Programming for design*. New York, NY: Wiley.

Daish, J., Gray, J., Kernohan, D., & Salmond, A. (1982). Post occupancy evaluation in New Zealand. *Design Studies*, 3(2), 77–83.

Dalton, N., Conroy Dalton, R., & Hoelscher, C. (2015). People Watcher: An app to assist in recording and analyzing spatial behavior of ubiquitous interaction technologies. *4th International Symposium on Pervasive Displays*, 10-12 June, Saarbrücken, Germany.

Dalton, N., Dalton, R., Hölscher, C., & Kuhnmünch, G. (2012). An iPad app for recording movement paths and associated spatial behaviors. In C. Stachniss, K. Schill, & D. Uttal (Eds.), *Spatial Cognition VIII: International Conference, Spatial Cognition 2012*, August 31–September 3, Kloster Seeon, Germany.

Delbecq, A. L., & Van de Ven, A. H. (1971). A group process model for problem identification and program planning. *Journal of Applied Behavioral Science, 7*(4), 466–492.

Delbecq, A. L., Van de Ven, A. H., & Gustafson, D. H. (1975). *Group techniques for program planning: A guide to nominal group and Delphi processes.* Glenview, IL: Scott, Foresman.

Gans, H. (1962). *The urban villagers: Group and class in the life of Italian-Americans.* New York, NY: Free Press.

Hershberger, R. (2002). Behavioral-based architectural programming. In R. Bechtel & A. Churchman (Eds.), *Handbook of environmental psychology* (pp. 292–305). New York, NY: Wiley.

Holmberg, J., & Robèrt, K.-H. (2000). Backcasting – A framework for strategic planning. *International Journal of Sustainable Development & World Ecology, 7*(4), 291–308.

Ittelson, W. H., Rivlin, L. G., & Proshansky, H. M. (1970). The use of behavioral maps in environmental psychology. In H. M. Proshansky, W. H. Ittelson, & L. G. Rivlin (Eds.), *Environmental psychology* (pp. 658–668). New York, NY: Holt, Rinehart, & Winston.

Kantrowitz, M., & Farbstein, J. (1996). POE delivers for the post office. In G. Baird (Ed.), *Building evaluation techniques.* New York, NY: McGraw-Hill.

Lehrer, J. (2012). Groupthink: The brainstorming myth. *The New Yorker, 30,* 12.

Pena, W. M., & Parshall, S. A. (2001). *Problem seeking: An architectural programming primer.* New York, NY: Wiley.

Raento, M., Oulasvirta, A., & Eagle, N. (2009). Smartphones: An emerging tool for social scientists. *Sociological Methods & Research, 37*(3), 426–454.

Skelton, C., Koplin, M., & Cipolla, V. (2011). *Massively participatory urban planning and design tools and process: the Betaville project.* Paper presented at the Proceedings of the 12th Annual International Digital Government Research Conference: Digital Government Innovation in Challenging Times.

Sommer, R., & Sommer, B. B. (1992). *A practical guide to behavioral research.* Oxford, UK: Oxford University Press.

Soupourmas, F., Ironmonger, D., Brown, P., & Warner-Smith, P. (2005). Testing the practicality of a personal digital assistant questionnaire versus a beeper and booklet questionnaire in a random-time experience-sampling method context. *Annals of Leisure Research, 8*(2–3), 142–152.

Spreckelmeyer, K. (1987). Environmental programming. In R. B. Betchel & R. W. Marans (Eds.), *Methods in environmental and behavioral research* (pp. 247–269). New York, NY: Van Nostrand Reinhold.

Steele, F. I. (1973). *Physical settings and organization development.* Reading, MA: Addison-Wesley.

Wener, R. E. (2002, May 22-26, 2002). *BMAP 3.0: Handheld Software to Support Behavior Observations.* Paper presented at the 33rd Annual Conference of The Environmental Design Research Association, Philadelphia, PA.

Whyte, W. H. (1980). *The social life of small urban spaces.* Washington, DC: The Conservation Foundation.

Zeisel, J. (2006). *Inquiry by design: Environment/behavior/neuroscience in architecture, interiors, landscape, and planning.* New York, NY: W.W. Norton.

Suggested Readings

Duerk, D. P. (1993). *Architectural programming: Information management for design.* New York, NY: Wiley.

Hershberger, R. (1999). *Architectural programming and predesign manager.* New York, NY: McGraw Hill.

Kemper, A. M. (Ed.). (1979). *Architectural handbook: Environmental analysis, architectural programming, design and technology and construction.* New York, NY: Wiley.

Kumlin, R. (1995). *Architectural programming: Creative techniques for design professionals.* New York, NY: McGraw-Hill.

Sanoff, H. (1980). *Methods of architectural programming.* New York, NY: Van Nostrand Reinhold.

13

Did that Plan Work? Post-occupancy Evaluation

Richard E. Wener[1], Lindsay J. McCunn[2], and Jennifer Senick[3]

[1] New York University, NY, United States
[2] University of Victoria, BC, Canada
[3] Rutgers University, NJ, United States

Gabriel sat down in his newly renovated office. He had successfully lobbied the executive team at his workplace to hire a programmer to inform the renovation of the building's interior. After much discussion about the costs and benefits, management agreed and, 10 months later, the dust had settled. Gabriel found himself broadly satisfied with the changes. The air quality seemed better, more employees had desks near windows, and the functional areas of the office made sense for each department. But some lingering issues remained: thermostats were covered in plastic cases so people couldn't adjust the temperature. This meant that previous complaints about controllability and thermal comfort were not totally alleviated by the renovation.

Gabe also noticed that some of his colleagues who often made conference calls ended up in an open-plan layout and complained about privacy since others (Gabriel included) could overhear conversations. Gabriel wondered if he should suggest to the executive that a follow-up investigation of the office design be done. Perhaps there were some simple fixes a professional could recommend, or improvements that could be made to the next space the company occupied. He recalled from his university days the term "post-occupancy evaluation" as being a kind of check-up after a building has been used for a while – to see how the design really "worked" for occupants. Even though the process would cost more money, it seemed to make sense to Gabriel. After all, why not make a renovation as informative, complete, and comfortable for users as possible?

Post-occupancy evaluation (POE) is exactly what it sounds like: an evaluation of a physically defined space after users have occupied it. POEs advance a series of questions, such as whether the ideas and recommendations put forward in the programming phase of the design process have been working as intended? Have

Research Methods for Environmental Psychology, First Edition. Edited by Robert Gifford.
© 2016 John Wiley & Sons, Ltd. Published 2016 by John Wiley & Sons, Ltd.

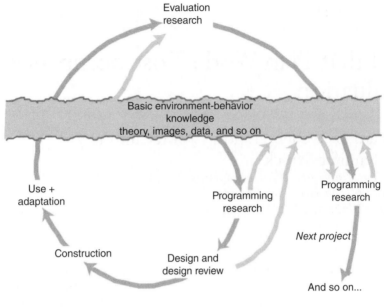

Five steps in the design cycle

1. Programming (Analysis)   Identifying design objectives, constraints, and criteria
2. Design   (Synthesis)   Making design decisions that satisfy criteria
3. Construction   (Realization)   Building the project and modifying plans under
                                   changing constraints
4. Use   (Reality testing) Moving in and adapting the environment
5. Evaluation   (Review)   Monitoring the final product in terms of objectives and
                                   use–ideally to be translated into future design criteria

Figure 13.1   The five steps of the design cycle.

the goals and intentions of clients and occupants been implemented after the dust of construction or renovation has settled? What specific behavioral responses to the structure have occupants shown?

In practice, most POEs are of individual buildings or landscapes, although broader assessments at the scale of the neighborhood or community can also fit this approach. POEs are not the same as architectural reviews or criticisms, or informal walkthroughs by design professionals of completed buildings or renovations. These other approaches have existed as long as professionals have created spaces for **clients** and they play useful, even critical, roles in the **design cycle** (see Figure 13.1). But they are as different from POE as a political essay is from public polling. That is, an essay is highly individual, idiosyncratic, subjective, and only as useful as the author's judgment. POE does not replace critique in the overall design process, but rather seeks to provide a base of evidence that describes the outcomes of a particular design project. Essentially, a POE uses data about what worked and what did not, and how people function in, and respond to, the space and its various features and technologies.

Post-occupancy Evaluation Defined

POE is a systematic assessment of one or more (and usually recently) designed, occupied spaces. Professionals make use of established quantitative and qualitative social science research methods to describe the nature of a site and the quality of its operation and function for various user groups. POEs often compare and contrast data against certain criteria that may be theoretically constructed, client- or designer-driven, longitudinal (measuring the same site at many points in time, or against predecessor sites), or cross-sectional (measuring a space against other sites involved in the same project, or to those evaluated in other studies or existing databases at roughly the same points in time).

The term "post-occupancy evaluation" stems from the use of the word "occupancy" in building-related professions to mean the point in time when people move into a space, often after an occupancy permit has been obtained. Hence, post-occupancy evaluation refers to studies that commence after the move-in process has been completed. A number of definitions for POE have been offered, usually having in common a focus on the intensely practical nature of this form of research, in that they identify the use of the results for improving sites. Most definitions also note that POE is a systematic assessment, to differentiate it from more casual reviews (e.g., Preiser, Rabinowitz, & White, 1988; Wener, 2003; Zimring, 2002; Zimring & Wener, 1985).

POEs are typically conducted for those interested in improving past designs and prototypes, and in establishing baselines and standards of quality and operation. Stripped down to its most basic elements, a POE can provide clear, objective, and quick feedback on the results of a process for which no naturally occurring feedback exists. For example, for many of the physical elements of building systems, feedback is inherent to the system. It can be obvious when structural elements fail or when there are failures in broadly experienced aspects, such as lighting and heating, ventilation, and air conditioning (HVAC) systems. Metered feedback is often provided about energy use (a high electric bill may trigger investigation). There are no such natural feedback mechanisms that make behavioral problems visible, except in extreme conditions. Most often, behavioral impacts concerning occupant health, comfort, satisfaction, and productivity are subtle. Thus, POE represents a mechanism for providing the feedback necessary for occupant growth and development, and corresponding achievement of organizational objectives in applicable situations. Indeed, feedback is a critical part of the growth process: without timely and accurate feedback it is difficult to fix mistakes and improve design quality associated with building operations.

The parts of POE definitions commonly include: (1) a methodological note (e.g., "the systematic assessment of ...") (Carthey, 2006; Royal Institute of British Architects, 1998; Turpin-Brooks & Viccars, 2006; Zimring, 2002) sometimes prescribing specific techniques, such as the use of surveys, or observations (Preiser, 1995); (2) a mention of what can be evaluated (e.g., buildings, facilities, designed space); and (3) a purpose for which the results will be used (e.g., "with the intention of improving the process or settings," Zimring, 2002, p. 307; "tool for ... continuously improving the quality and performance of ... facilities," Preiser, 1995, p. 1;

"to modify a specific building or setting type, ... [and] to improve design practice," Wener, 2003, p. 732). There may also be a note about the consumers of this information (e.g., architects, owners, users) or the kinds of issues commonly addressed (e.g., health and safety, wayfinding, thermal comfort, privacy, and confidentiality, Preiser, 1995).

Some past definitions also refer to the use of specific criteria to which outcomes will be compared. Where specific criteria cannot be found, implicit ones may be developed, even though these may sometimes be vague (e.g., "the extent to which a building meets the needs of its end-users," Riley, Kokkarinen, & Pitt, 2010, p. 202). Others note that POEs should address not only designer criteria and occupant suggestions but also, in a more basic manner, occupant needs (Friedmann, Zimring, & Zube, 1978; Hadjri & Crozier, 2009) and that benefits can be immediate or long term. Many recent POEs also make explicit reference to the contribution of building occupant behavior to building performance (e.g., Gill et al.'s (2010) study of low-energy dwellings).

Concern has been raised over the decades that POE is an infelicitous term – not readily clear to a layperson. Although a better term is hard to come by, "evidence-based design" is gaining considerable currency with similar, though not completely overlapping, meaning (Hamilton & Watkins, 2008; Ulrich, Berry, Quan, & Turner Parish, 2010; Ulrich et al., 2008; Zimring & Bosch, 2008). Wolfgang Preiser, who has written extensively on post-occupancy evaluation, has suggested another term: building performance evaluation (BPE; Preiser, 2001b). BPE is a form of POE that "emphasizes a holistic, process-oriented approach to evaluation" (p. 9) that includes assessment of the various political forces, as well as economic and social forces, that shape a building.

Drawing from the descriptions outlined above, our definition of POE is that it represents a formal way to review and reflect on the outcomes of the design process. As Shibley (1982, p. 64) notes, design without evaluation is like "action without reflection." POEs ought to be thoughtful and systematic, using valid and reliable social science methods to assess the use and performance of a designed environment for one or several user groups and purposes. POE clients may be workers or residents concerned with comfort, satisfaction, or health. Clients may also be owners or managers who care about building performance, productivity, or costs. In the same vein, designers may seek to understand the success of programs, features, aesthetics, and quality of design practices, while future users and members of the public may want to know about reduced energy consumption, water pollution, or carbon emissions in relation to the assessed environment.

A Brief History of POE

There is no thorough written history of post-occupancy evaluation to trace the early precedents and critical influences leading to its development. However, several authors place POE's inception in the 1960s as part of the growth of environmental psychology and **environment-behavior research** in general (Bechtel, 1997; Preiser, 1995; Preiser et al., 1988; Wener, 2008). As designers increasingly sought the help of social scientists to better understand issues with buildings and find approaches to improve the behavioral impacts of design, particularly for special populations, the kind of research that is now known as POE became a logical tool to employ.

Similar to the history of programming (discussed in Chapter 12), POEs were less necessary in an earlier time when design was often a personal experience and a direct relationship existed between one person (owner/client) and another (architect/designer). In such situations it was relatively easy for these individuals to translate past experience into future improvements. POE as a formal and systematized process was made more critical by the nature of modern design and organizational systems that often separates owners, users, and designers in place and time.

Early POEs conducted in the 1960s were commonly one-off case studies (Preiser, 1999). Approaches to POE research advanced over the next several decades to become more systematic, employing standardized instruments in multiple facilities. Often completed for university spaces, such as dormitories, where researchers had easy access (Wheeler, 1967), subsequent POEs were conducted in places like psychiatric hospitals, jails, and public housing where findings could support people who otherwise might have little impact on, or control over, design decisions (Friedmann et al., 1978; Preiser et al., 1988; Shibley, 1982; Wener & Olsen, 1980; Zimring, 2002). As POE grew as a specialty, and its benefits became more obvious, projects were taken up by large US government agencies (e.g., General Services Administration, US Postal Service, and the US Federal Bureau of Prisons), as well as by private corporations. POEs make particular sense for any operation that is responsible for a great deal of space and for creating multiple iterations of similar designs.

POE makes the most impact when repeatedly used as part of a cycle (e.g., Figure 13.1). That is, ideally a POE should assess an existing facility, feed the results into the design process for a replacement facility, re-evaluate the new building, present results again, modify recommendations for the building type, and so on. But this kind of longitudinal and iterative procedure is rare, at least as seen in publically available studies.

One recent example includes an evaluation by a research team at Carnegie Mellon University of over 400 workstations in 20 Federal office buildings across the United States between the years 2005–2008 as a basis for future indoor environmental quality standards and guidelines (Choi, Loftness, & Aziz, 2012). Another example is a recent two-year cross-sectional longitudinal POE in 10 office buildings by a research team at Rutgers University. The team gauged occupant responses to energy retrofits and voluntary shedding of electricity load during times of peak usage as a means to refine future retrofit designs and determine suitability for enrolling in a mandatory energy reduction program (Senick et al., 2013).

Even fewer published examples of POEs have followed the same building type through multiple generations to describe progress and changes over time. One example of a multigenerational POE was done on three generations of jails (Wener, Frazier, & Farbstein, 1985). An earlier example by Ladd Wheeler and Ewing Miller (Wheeler, 1967) included evaluations over four generations of dormitories at an Indiana university. Both studies clearly demonstrated the ability of research data to support significant modifications of critical design decisions.

The green building movement has also brought with it a renewed focus on both building performance relative to environmental impacts, and on how buildings can detract from, or promote, occupant satisfaction, productivity, and health. POE may help substantiate or refute the "better building" claims of the green building movement while providing an evidence base for continuous improvement toward green building objectives. At a larger scale, POE provides a basis to help interpret "big data" about buildings, transportation, waste, and other urban systems. These kinds of data – archival data sets of very large systems enabled by sensors that measure minute-by-minute infrastructure performance – are being assembled in a number of sizable urban centers to improve material sustainability. Another emerging area in which POE may prove helpful is the changing nature of workspace itself, and the modern paradox of mobile occupants in a "non-territorial" setting where they may be assigned a space when they arrive at the office, rather than having a regular place to sit (Brill, 1994; Volker & Van der Voordt, 2005).

The next section outlines the types of POE and further explains its unique benefits and changes in the design process.

Types of Post-Occupancy Evaluation

The distinctions noted earlier among different forms of POEs (e.g., one-off case studies versus studies of multiple sites using standardized instruments) are descriptive but do not fully address differences in purpose and use. Wener (1989) has suggested that POEs can be classified into two types: comparative POEs and generative POEs. Comparative POEs make comparisons among spaces for the purpose of creating norms or for understanding changes in operation before and after a new design is implemented. Generative POEs identify problems and foster ideas for solutions and improvements (as is likely to be useful as part of a future programming process). The former type is more likely to require objective methods, such as in standardized questionnaire scales, while the later often necessitates more open-ended techniques.

Another way of understanding POE types is to categorize them as one of three levels that represent different kinds of studies and can be viewed as stages of research that may logically follow one another in a full and complete assessment (Preiser, 1988). Level 1 POEs (or Indicative POEs) tend to be brief, broad, and shallow benchmarking studies that use objective instruments capable of quick and relatively inexpensive assessments and comparisons of many facilities on a number of dimensions. Indicative POEs can identify trouble spots (or flag highly positive aspects) in an environment. This may lead to higher level POEs conducted to clarify findings.

Level 2 POEs (Investigative POEs) are often detailed case studies of an individual site to understand how it functions, often with a combination of quantitative and qualitative research instruments. Last, Level 3 POEs (Diagnostic POEs) typically address a particular issue (e.g., lighting, privacy) or type of space (e.g., office cubicles, conference rooms, nursing stations) across a number of facilities to better understand, address, and improve design. The following section outlines the methods used in these types of POEs.

Post-Occupancy Evaluation Methods

Assessing attitudes and behaviors in a setting

There is considerable overlap between the methods and instruments used in collecting data for post-occupancy evaluation and for architectural programming. Many data-gathering techniques are the same as those used in programming research, of which POE is often a part. Thus, detailed discussions of many of these methods can be found in Chapter 12.

Standardized methods   As noted by Zimring (2002), approaches to POE have matured beyond one-off methodologies toward the development of set, standardized packages of instruments created for specific settings. These standardized scales have several advantages (Wener, 1982). First, they save on the time and costs involved in creating new instruments and approaches for a particular study, while building a base of instruments that have some degree of reliability and validity. In addition, they increase the chance that data gathered from many sites will be comparable using the same items and scales, so that each case becomes part of a large database of information. As Zimring (2002) notes, packages of instruments have been developed and used for a variety of facility types, including, offices, health care settings, correctional buildings, children's environments, and post offices.

Walkthrough interviews   Walkthrough interviews allow researchers to quickly understand how a facility functions via a running commentary from users, and informal observations and photo documentation (again, see Chapter 12).

Structured interviews   Structured interviews allow researchers to gain the depth, detail, and context that may be missing from closed-ended surveys. This may be especially critical to generative POEs (see Chapter 12).

Surveys   Surveys conducted on paper, computers, or on smart mobile devices, provide a means of collecting a great deal of data quickly, and in a more standardized and quantitative fashion, than interviews. However, there can sometimes be a loss of the depth and richness of information than can arise during interviews with users.

Surveys also allow for the repeated administration of scales. Such systematic repetition in data collection can allow researchers to note changes over time, before and after design interventions, or as related to variations in conditions (see Chapter 12).

Observation of activity   Observation of actual behavior, either directly (with an observer present) or unobtrusively (perhaps with a hidden observer or camera), can provide information on the amount, type, timing, and flow of user behavior. One systematic kind of observation is **behavioral mapping** as a way of recording users' activity. Self-reports of space use can be an efficient and useful means of gathering data through surveys or interviews, as noted above. However, the behaviors people report may not always be accurate. Self-reports can vary from reality because of people's desires to meet expectations or social norms, motivation to "look good" (Fowler, 2009; Krosnick, 1999), or simply because people are not always aware of where and how they use space.

Observation of behavior using instrumentation or human observers can address this problem by providing objective measurements of space use. This is typically done by compiling behavioral data on where people go, what behaviors they engage in, with whom they engage with, and how behaviors vary over time. Ittelson, Rivlin, and Proshansky (1970) provided an early discussion of how these techniques can provide useful pictures of spatial issues in psychiatric settings. Subsequent studies have used these techniques in spaces as varied as children's settings, gardens for seniors, and jails (Coates & Sanoff, 1971; Cosco, Moore, & Islam, 2010; Hernandez, 2007; Ittelson, Rivlin, & Proshansky, 1970; Milke, Beck, Danes, & Leask, 2009; Zimring & Wener, 1985).

There is always a concern that the act of observing people will be obtrusive and will consequently change behaviors being studied (Webb, Campbell, Schwartz, & Sechrest, 1966; Zeisel, 2006). Observations of inmates during POEs of jails, for instance, Wener and Olsen (1980), never directly recorded an incident of intimidation, harassment, or aggression. This occurred, in part, because the jails in question were relatively safe. However, it may have also been related to the fact that inmates knew they were being observed.

Overcoming this challenge can be difficult depending on the aims of a particular POE. Sometimes logistics and ethical considerations leave little choice but to conduct observations in the open, but not always. For example, Bechtel used instrumentation of a museum floor to record footpaths of visitors (Bechtel, 1967) and William H. Whyte (1980) famously used hidden, time-lapse cameras to observe use of urban plazas for evaluating features that were more successful than others. His findings became part of the New York City Zoning Code.

Traditionally, behavioral observations have been done in person with a pen, a clipboard, and a stopwatch in hand. This method can be laborious for data collection, data entry, and analysis. Not surprisingly, there have been a number of attempts since the mid-1980s to utilize mobile smart devices to support observations for mapping or tracking individuals in indoor or outdoor spaces (Dalton, Dalton, Hölscher, & Kuhnmünch, 2012; Kahng & Iwata, 1998, 2000; Noldus, Trienes, Hendriksen, Jansen, & Jansen, 2000; Wener, 2002). For example, "People Watcher" is a sophisticated program for handheld tablet devices that allows an observer to track subjects by moving a finger on a floor plan imported to the device (Dalton et al., 2012). The program provides instant analysis of the data and has been largely used in studies of wayfinding behavior in buildings.

Conceptual approaches in assessing the physical setting

Usability, effectiveness, and efficiency Whether building designs and particular building attributes function properly and well is an important consideration of post-occupancy evaluation. In particular, the green building movement has been heavily promoted for its potential to mitigate the negative impacts of buildings on the environment, and to affect increases in human satisfaction and productivity (e.g., by improving thermal comfort, indoor air quality, and so on). However, positive attitudinal and behavioral outcomes are not consistently found in green buildings (McCunn & Gifford, 2012), and green buildings are not always easy to use. Because usability is critical to success (Blumstein, Krieg, Schipper, & York, 1980; Case, 1984; Völlink, Meertens, & Midden, 2002; Wener, 1984) it should be a central measurement included in the POEs of these facilities.

Broadly, **usability** refers to how easily people can use systems and devices. The case study outlined later in the chapter demonstrates formalized usability metrics in a POE of several buildings retrofitted with newer lighting technologies and advanced HVAC control strategies. This POE was done to evaluate the effectiveness and efficiency of advanced energy retrofits, along with user satisfaction and related objectives. These characteristics are central to the International Standards Organization (ISO) 9241-11, 1993c definition of usability, which derives from studies of ergonomic principles as applied to the design of human–information system interactions, but which can apply to building scale systems as well.

As characterized in Andrews et al. (2011), **effectiveness** refers to the extent to which design goals for intended uses of a system (such as lighting, temperature set points, or overall energy use) are achieved. Whereas, **efficiency** is a function of the expenditure of resources and user effort needed to achieve intended design goals.

The extent to which users find a building system to be acceptable (and usable) can be understood by measuring user satisfaction. The level of human effort (efficiency) needed for a system to be effective may also affect user satisfaction, especially as it relates to control over key functions of the building system. In turn, measuring efficiency may provide evidence of user behavior impacting the performance of the overall building system.

Controllability, satisfaction, and comfort   POE practitioners often measure occupants' perceived level of control through self-report methods or by observing how often they adjust attributes of their surroundings. Theory and research have shown that environmental control is important to satisfaction and stress reduction (Evans & Stecker, 2004). Perhaps there are physical barriers to controlling the temperature of a space (e.g., inaccessible thermostats) or the lighting (artificial light sources too high to easily reach).

Although POE methods of gathering data on user **controllability** usually involve interviews and surveys, more objective options are becoming available (Zimring, 2002). Instruments that record how many times a window is opened or when a thermostat is manually altered, or lighting logs of how often a user adjusts an IP-addressable dimmable ballast can provide important data about users' control behaviors in a space.

Occupant satisfaction and comfort are other subjective variables that can be investigated in a POE. Indeed, these data can relay much about how building users perceive a finished space, and whether changes have been well received. Numerous studies exist on the ways satisfaction and comfort form for people in a building and, not surprisingly, the determinants of human satisfaction and comfort in a space are complex. For example, Cole and Lorch (2002), and Bordass and Leaman (2001) note that stable thermal conditions, usability of ventilation and lighting controls, operable windows, and views out of the building help office workers feel satisfied and comfortable.

As with measuring the aforementioned factors, it makes sense to employ more than one collection method during a POE to ensure validity. Use of multiple methods, also called triangulation, compensates for imperfections or inherent biases in any one method (Johnson, Onwuegbuzie, & Turner, 2007; Webb et al., 1966). For example, users might complete a questionnaire about their levels of satisfaction and comfort with a building, as well as be interviewed about how they feel about various areas in the building. These data can be merged to form a more comprehensive understanding of where in a setting users feel most (and least) satisfied and comfortable. Similarly, information about user privacy could be collected by observing occupants' behaviors and by asking them how private they feel in specific areas of the building. Because post-occupancy evaluations are often done to assess (to subsequently fix) design functionality for users, and to inform future architectural programs, accurate and comprehensive data are critical.

For POEs to be most effective, it is important to have rigorous measurement to the physical setting to which users are responding. Obtaining objective measures of aspects of the physical setting that are likely to affect occupant comfort, satisfaction, and controllability (e.g., lighting levels, thermal conditions, and acoustical qualities of the setting, such as decibel levels and reverberation) can be valuable. For instance, some studies have sought to find connections between measures of productivity and quality control (e.g., sales calls completed, accidents) and wellness (e.g., absence, sickness records) and physical building conditions. For example, Choi et al. (2012) measured temperature, relative humidity, carbon dioxide and carbon monoxide concentrations, total particulates, volatile organic compounds, light levels, radiant temperature, and air velocity, in addition to occupant satisfaction. And, sick leave rates were used to assess productivity in an office-based study of energy performance and occupant satisfaction (Agha-Hossein, El-Jouzi, Elmualim, Ellis, & Williams, 2013), as well as in an earlier study associating outdoor air supply rate, humidification, and occupant complaints (Milton, Glencross, & Walters, 2000).

Building on a methodology developed by the PROBE project in the United Kingdom known as "TM22 (2006)," Menezes, Cripps, Bouchlaghem, and Buswell (2012) used POE to closely monitor small energy loads and occupancy patterns and behavior to improve the accuracy of building energy model predictions. Other work has related light, thermal comfort, noise levels, and air quality to occupant perceptions of the setting in hospitals and elementary schools (e.g., De Giuli, Da Pos, & De Carli, 2012; De Giuli, Zecchin, Salmaso, Corain, & De Carli, 2012). Andrews et al. (2011) took this approach one step further in joining data from POEs to computer models of human behavior in order to validate and re-calibrate models of how building occupants behave.

The Challenges of Post-occupancy Evaluation

This chapter has focused on the advantages of post-occupancy evaluation as a method of informing building users, stakeholders, and the overall design cycle of the strengths and weaknesses of a space. However, several challenges exist in undertaking an assessment of a building after users have had an opportunity to interact with its design and experience how it functions in relation to their needs. It is not always clear to whom the cost of doing a POE should fall. Despite the benefits of the POE process, the question of "who will pay?" is typically the first to be asked. As summarized by Turpin-Brooks and Viccars (2006), clients may perceive their payment for the building construction, renovation, or interior design to already include a final assessment component to ensure functionality. Sometimes, design firms do cede evaluation as part of their scope of services and as a cost that cannot be recovered or billed.

To better explain this resistance, imagine that a POE is performed in a building and major problems are uncovered – perhaps severe enough to reduce the building's value for the client. Who, then, among clients, programmers, designers and contractors, is to blame for the problems, and is liable for the costs to fix them? Can the POE be used to ascertain or fix liability (Meir, Garb, Jiao, & Cicelsky, 2009)? Such questions are typically not the intent of the social scientist, but still might arise. Challenges like this are project-specific and require clear communication between everyone involved.

Another challenge of POE is a lack of dissemination of knowledge about its methods, outcomes, and practical considerations (Cooper, 2001; Preiser, 2001a). Often, designers, clients, and users are not educated about what POE is or how it is accomplished (Zimmerman and Martin, 2001). As Turpin-Brooks and Viccars (2006) state, unless POE becomes part of the standard suite of design procurement, the full range of potential benefits of post-occupancy evaluation may not be realized.

Case Study: Usability Assessment of Lighting and Heating, Ventilation, and Air Conditioning (HVAC) Conditions in Three Tenanted Buildings

This case study is drawn from a larger study of three commercial office buildings in the greater Philadelphia region that underwent advanced energy retrofits (Senick et al., 2013). The POEs were designed to do four things: (1) Enhance understanding of the roles occupant behaviors play in building energy performance, particularly as they relate to the usability of the advanced energy retrofits; (2) Test methodologies and metrics to support usability-based evaluations of energy use and design strategies in office settings; (3) Collect baseline and post-retrofit behavioral and observational data concerning HVAC and lighting energy-saving technologies to test the impact of the retrofits, and; (4) Offer improvements to the design and implementation of advanced retrofits.

Although the changes varied slightly by building, the energy retrofits to these buildings included the following elements:

- Installation of advanced lighting controls with upgrades to fully dimmable, network addressable electronic ballasts and low wattage bulbs.
- Web-accessible open protocol intelligent energy management systems to monitor power use, lighting and HVAC systems.

- Smart metering and real-time monitoring of energy usage, with control integration of major building systems.
- Retro-commissioning of building HVAC system.

Research design and methods

The three POEs included longitudinal data collection to investigate differences in buildings over time, as well as cross-sectional comparisons across buildings. The research team conducted a baseline evaluation of existing conditions and occupant satisfaction with respect to lighting and HVAC systems in two of the buildings in February 2012. Follow-ups to the baseline evaluations of these two buildings were made in December 2012. At this time, a POE was also conducted at the third property after retrofits had already taken place and included a detailed baseline survey and daily surveys.

Initial visits at all three sites began with a walkthrough with the property manager. Approximately 125 individual workspaces were visited along with common areas in the three buildings. Lighting measurements were obtained in a variety of occupied and common spaces during the initial visits, as well as the post-retrofit visits, to assess the effectiveness of the retrofit and compare observations with occupant self-reports. Temperature and humidity readings were also taken during the follow-up visits.

Observations and interviews were recorded on prepared forms as well as on floor plans provided by the building owner. Comments from interviews and observations were aggregated for each building based on themes or topics that emerged during the analysis, and focused on efficiency, satisfaction levels, and adaptive responses to unsatisfactory conditions. Building-level data, including those noted above as well as researcher observations of adaptive behavior to adverse thermal or lighting conditions (e.g., use of space heaters, opening or closing of blinds, use of task lights), were then evaluated for broader themes that inform building usability-behavioral research. These themes include human–machine interface (HMI) challenges and the extent to which the design of some building systems fail to take into account complex organizational structures and the role of social mediation in building condition outcomes.

Summary of pre-retrofit evaluation

Concerns about thermal comfort dominated the pre-retrofit visits. Occupants reported that thermostats were limited in their usefulness, and workers had developed adaptive behaviors that ranged from personal strategies (e.g., dressing in layers) to using blinds that were available to control light and heat discomfort, as well as contacting management and using energy-intensive appliances (e.g., portable heaters and fans). In addition, occupants often reported some areas as being too bright (mostly common and circulation areas, but also workspaces), although the placement of cubicle walls were sometimes not well coordinated with lighting fixtures, reducing the level of direct lighting on work surfaces (see Figure 13.2).

Figure 13.2 Misalignment of workspace and lights. Source: Rutgers Center for Green Building Archive.

Summary of post-retrofit evaluation

Post-retrofit findings were generally more positive, with some interviewees in the buildings reporting that temperatures had felt "better." However, occupants continued to identify:

- The need to dress in layers to accommodate temperature fluctuations throughout the day.
- Inconsistent heating in colder months in all buildings.
- Use of heaters and fans in both summer and winter seasons.
- Continuing lack of control over thermostats.
- Occupants also perceived facility managers as responsive, and felt positively about the results when managers adjusted conditions in response to complaints.

Figure 13.3 depicts occupants' perceived versus preferred temperature in one of the buildings. If the gap is large, more occupant effort is required to achieve satisfaction (a measure of efficiency) and satisfaction with the current condition is likely to be lower. The measurements taken by the research team indicated a fairly wide variation, correlating with occupants' self-reports see Table 13.1.

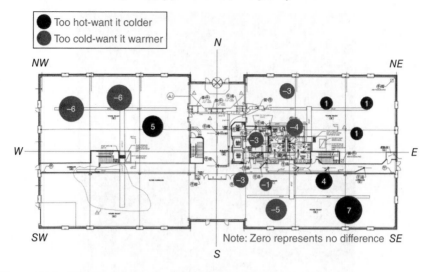

Figure 13.3 First-floor respondents reported temperature preferences (perceived vs. ideal. *n* = 14 (a sample of first-floor occupants); each circle represents a respondent. Source: Rutgers Center for Green Building Archive.

Table 13.1 Actual temperature ranges of floors 1–3, Occupants *n* = 57.

	Temperature ranges (°F) Post-retrofit
Office	70.5–79.3
Circulation	72–80
Common	71.5–78.9
Cubicle	73.1–77.7

Source: Rutgers Center for Green Building Archive.

Although occupants in all three buildings indicated that lighting levels were currently adequate, many occupants in all of the buildings described frustrations with the newly installed sensors:

- Sensors close to higher foot-traffic areas would be triggered even when the room was empty (such as conference rooms).
- Conversely, lights would go out in occupied rooms, forcing workers to move around to activate the sensors.

- Safety and security concerns were expressed because of delays in brightening that sometimes left people in the dark in labs or other potentially hazardous areas or in a common spaces (e.g. restroom, reception area).
- Users reported closing their window blinds in order to increase privacy (from pedestrians) and the amount of artificial light received – an example of an adaptive action to benefit comfort at the expense of building performance (e.g., daylighting).

Occupants were comfortable with lighting levels but concerned about their inability to turn off or otherwise adjust overhead lights. Figure 13.4 shows the difference between perceived and desired lighting for one of the buildings. If the gap is large, more occupant effort is required to achieve a satisfactory lighting level. Illumination levels in these spaces varied widely. However, this was not unexpected given the different spatial contexts, such as directional exposure (north, south, east, west), proximity to windows, partition heights, and so on see Table 13.2.

Lighting control and variation

Task lighting used as a response to insufficient illumination can be useful as a way of adding to occupant control of available light, while simultaneously conserving energy use. However, this POE found that task lighting was an underused resource. There were few task lights available to (or being used by) occupants,

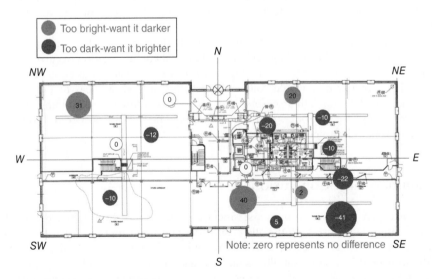

Figure 13.4 First-floor respondents reported lighting preferences (perceived vs. ideal). *n* = 14 (a sample of first-floor occupants); each circle represents a respondent. Source: Rutgers Center for Green Building Archive.

Table 13.2   Actual lighting ranges.

	Lighting ranges (lux) Post-retrofit
Office	470–2350
Circulation	130–555
Common	195–1825
Cubicle	415–480

Source: Rutgers Center for Green Building Archive.

either because individual occupants had not integrated task lighting into their workspace, or the lighting was not present as an option. In addition, occupants typically relied upon overhead lighting that, in many cases, could not be turned off and created excess lighting.

Providing greater control over lighting can provide opportunities for occupants to reduce brightness. But, customizable/controllable lighting may also affect occupant satisfaction and create new social dynamics within workspaces concerning control (e.g., how should the lighting be controlled, and who ought to do it?). Indeed, building technologies often have complex and multi-faceted controls that need careful adjustment to provide user comfort while maintaining efficient use of energy. If the person–system interface for these controls is difficult or obscure (e.g., Norman, 1988), they can be ignored or set incorrectly, making users dissatisfied and unproductive, as well as force adaptive responses that waste time and energy.

In sum, lessons learned in this three-building POE were successfully incorporated into the final phase of building retrofits. Additional communication occurred with the building occupants in advance of the retrofits to set expectations about a "trial-and-error" period that would follow the retrofits, as well as help to determine optimal locations for lights sensors, and so on. Accordingly, the building owner ensured that service providers of the retrofits would make more post-retrofit on-site visits to make adjustments as needed.

Summary and Conclusions

Post-occupancy evaluation is an assessment tool to examine how effective a building's design is for users. POEs allow both designers and users to learn from the strengths and weaknesses of a design to inform future architectural programs. Methods used in a POE should include as many user groups and data-gathering techniques as possible. Surveys, interviews, site walkthroughs, direct and instrumented observations are some common ways of collecting data about how users function in a building they have occupied for a period of time, including satisfaction and comfort. Information about physical aspects of a space can also be gathered during the POE process, such as functionality and assessments of user controllability.

POE offers many advantages to those directly involved, as well as to others who may encounter the findings at different stages of the design cycle. However, the process has specific challenges and resolution often depends on the particular details of the project. Questions of cost and liability are common issues for stakeholders. Design researchers urge for better availability of POE education concerning its role in the design process, and how it can assist designers and users in attaining optimal spaces in the short and long term.

Glossary

Clients   Clients typically own or control (or represent the entity who controls) the building.

Controllability   The degree to which building occupants can control (or perceive themselves to control) environmental attributes.

Design cycle   The process of building design whereby five phases (programming, design, construction, use, and evaluation) connect to, and build upon, each other.

Effectiveness   The extent to which design goals for intended uses of a system (such as lighting, temperature set points, or overall energy use) are achieved.

Efficiency   A function of the expenditure of resources and user effort needed to achieve intended design goals.

Environment-behavior research   A field of study that merges social science methodologies with design issues.

Post-occupancy evaluation (POE)   The final phase of the design process where strengths and weaknesses of a building's form and function are examined after users have moved in.

Programming   A phase of the design cycle whereby information about a space is systematically gathered, analyzed, and summarized before the design and construction phases occur.

Usability   The degree to which the physical building functions properly for users.

Users   Building users are a host of occupants who visit or spend time in the building but do not own or control it.

References

Agha-Hossein, M., El-Jouzi, S., Elmualim, A., Ellis, J., & Williams, M. (2013). Post-occupancy studies of an office environment: Energy performance and occupants' satisfaction. *Building and Environment, 69*, 121–130.

Andrews, C. J., Yi, D., Krogmann, U., Senick, J. A., & Wener, R. E. (2011). Designing buildings for real occupants: An agent-based approach. *Systems, Management and Cybernetics, Part A: Systems and Humans, 41*, 1077–1091.

Bechtel, R. B. (1967). Hodometer research in museums. *Museum News, 45*, 23–26.

Bechtel, R. B. (1997). *Environment and behavior.* Thousand Oaks, CA: Sage.

Blumstein, C., Krieg, B., Schipper, L., & York, C. (1980). Overcoming social and institutional barriers to energy conservation. *Energy, 5*, 355–372.

Bordass, W., & Leaman, A. (2001). Assessing building performance in use 4: The probe occupant surveys and their implications. *Building Research & Information, 29*, 129–43.

Brill, M. (1994). Checking-in: The office as hotel. *Design Management Journal, 5,* 24–29.

Carthey, J. (2006). Post-occupancy evaluation: Development of a standardized methodology for Australian health projects. *International Journal of Construction Management, 1,* 63–80.

Case, F. D. (1984). Design implications of living with passive solar homes. *Journal of Architectural and Planning Research, 1,* 85–104.

Choi, J.-H., Loftness, V., & Aziz, A. (2012). Post-occupancy evaluation of 20 office buildings as basis for future IEQ standards and guidelines. *Energy and Buildings, 46,* 167–175.

Coates, G., & Sanoff, H. P. (1971). Behavioral mapping: The ecology of child behavior in a planned residential setting. *International Journal of Environment Studies, 2,* 227–235.

Cole, R., & Lorch, R. (2002). *Building culture and environment.* Oxford, UK: Blackwell.

Cooper, I. (2001). Post-occupancy evaluation – Where are you? *Building Research & Information, 29,* 158–163.

Cosco, N. G., Moore, R. C., & Islam, M. Z. (2010). Behavior mapping: A method for linking preschool physical activity and outdoor design. *Medicine & Science in Sports & Exercise, 42,* 513–519.

Dalton, N., Dalton, R., Hölscher, C., & Kuhnmünch, G. (2012). An iPad app for recording movement paths and associated spatial behaviors. In C. Stachniss, K. Schill, & D. Uttal (Eds.), *Spatial Cognition VIII: International Conference, Spatial Cognition 2012,* August 31–September 3, Kloster Seeon, Germany.

De Giuli, V., Da Pos, O., & De Carli, M. (2012a). Indoor environmental quality and pupil perception in Italian primary schools. *Building and Environment, 56,* 335–345.

De Giuli, V., Zecchin, R., Salmaso, L., Corain, L., & De Carli, M. (2012b). Measured and perceived indoor environmental quality: Padua Hospital case study. *Building and Environment, 59,* 211–226.

Evans, G. W., & Stecker, R. (2004). The motivational consequences of environmental stress. *Journal of Environmental Psychology, 24,* 143–165.

Fowler, F. J. (2009). *Survey research methods* (Vol. 1). Thousand Oaks, CA: Sage.

Friedmann, A., Zimring, C., & Zube, E. H. (1978). *Environmental design evaluation.* New York, NY: Plenum.

Gill, Z., Tierney, M., Pegg, I., & Allan, N. (2010). Low-energy dwellings: The contribution of behaviors to actual performance. *Building Research & Information, 38,* 491–508.

Hamilton, D. K., & Watkins, D. H. (2008). *Evidence-based design for multiple building types.* New York, NY: Wiley.

Hadjri, K., & Crozier, C. (2009). Post-occupancy evaluation: Purpose, benefits and barriers. *Facilities, 27,* 21–33.

Hernandez, R. O. (2007). Effects of therapeutic gardens in special care units for people with dementia. *Journal of Housing for the Elderly, 21,* 117–152.

International Organization for Standardization (ISO). (1998). ISO Standard 9241-11, 1998: *Ergonomic requirements for office work with visual display terminals (VDTs), Part 11: Guidance on usability.* Geneva, Switzerland: ISO.

Ittelson, W. H., Rivlin, L. G., & Proshansky, H. M. (1970). The use of behavioral maps in environmental psychology. In H. M. Proshansky, W. H. Ittelson, & L. G. Rivlin (Eds.), *Environmental psychology: Man and his physical setting* (pp. 658–668). New York, NY: Holt, Rinehart & Winston.

Johnson, R. B., Onwuegbuzie, A. J., & Turner, L. A. (2007). Toward a definition of mixed methods research. *Journal of Mixed Methods Research, 1*(2), 112–133.

Kahng, S., & Iwata, B. A. (1998). Computerized systems for collecting real-time observational data. *Journal of Applied Behavior Analysis, 31,* 253–261.

Kahng, S., & Iwata, B. A. (2000). Computer systems for collecting real-time observational data. In T. Thompson, D. Felce, & F. J. Symons (Eds.), *Behavioral observation: Technology and applications in developmental disabilities* (pp. 35–45). Baltimore: Brookes.

Krosnick, J. A. (1999). Survey research. *Annual Review of Psychology, 50*, 537–567.

McCunn, L. J., & Gifford, R. (2012). Do green offices affect employee engagement and environmental motivation? *Architectural Science Review, 55*, 128–134.

Meir, I. A., Garb, Y., Jiao, D., & Cicelsky, A. (2009). Post-occupancy evaluation: An inevitable step toward sustainability. *Advances in Building Energy Research, 3*, 189–219.

Menezes, A. C., Cripps, A., Bouchlaghem, D., & Buswell, R. (2012). Predicted vs. actual energy performance of non-domestic buildings: Using post-occupancy evaluation data to reduce the performance gap. *Applied Energy, 97*, 355–364.

Milke, D. L., Beck, C. H. M., Danes, S., & Leask, J. (2009). Behavioral mapping of residents' activity in five residential style care centers for elderly persons diagnosed with dementia: Small differences in sites can affect behaviors. *Journal of Housing for the Elderly, 23*, 335–367.

Milton, D. K., Glencross, P. M., & Walters, M. D. (2000). Risk of sick leave associated with outdoor air supply rate, humidification, and occupant complaints. *Indoor Air, 10*, 212–221.

New Jersey Green Building Manual. (2011). *Building Performance Evaluation*. Retrieved from http://greenmanual.rutgers.edu/newresidential/strategies/bpe.php

Noldus, L. P. J. J., Trienes, R. J. H., Hendriksen, A. H. M., Jansen, H., & Jansen, R. G. (2000). The Observer Video-Pro: New software for the collection, management, and presentation of time-structured data from videotapes and digital media files. *Behavior Research Methods, Instruments, & Computers*, 197–206.

Norman, D. A. (1988). *The psychology of everyday things*. New York, NY: Basic.

Preiser, W. F. E. (1995). Post-occupancy evaluation: How to make buildings work better. *Facilities, 13*, 19–28.

Preiser, W. F. E. (2001a). Feedback, feedforward and control: Post-occupancy evaluation to the rescue. *Building Research & Information, 29*, 456–459.

Preiser, W. F. E. (2001b). *The evolution of post-occupancy evaluation: Toward building performance and universal design evaluation*. Federal Facilities Council: Learning from our buildings – a state-of-the-practice summary of post-occupancy evaluation, pp. 9–22.

Preiser, W. F. E., Rabinowitz, H. Z., & White, E. T. (1988). *Post-occupancy evaluation*. New York, NY: Van Nostrand Reinhold.

Riley, M., Kokkarinen, N., & Pitt, M. (2010). Assessing post-occupancy evaluation in higher education facilities. *Journal of Facilities Management, 8*, 202–213.

Royal Institute of British Architects. (1998). A research policy for the architectural profession. In F. Duffy & L. Hutton (Eds.), *Architectural knowledge: The idea of a profession* (pp. 166–169). London, UK: Taylor & Francis.

Senick, J. A., Sorensen Allacci, M., Wener, R. E., Andrews, C. J., Plotnik, D., Shinde, P., & Malenchak, S. (2013). *Post-retrofit assessment of lighting and HVAC conditions in three tenanted buildings*. Liberty Property Trust – PECO Smart Grid Investment Grant Program. Prepared by the Center for Green Building at Rutgers University for the U.S. Department of Energy, Energy Efficient Buildings Hub, Philadelphia, PA.

Shibley, R. (1982). Building evaluations services. *Progressive Architecture, 63*, 64–67.

The Chartered Institution of Building Services Engineers. (2006). Energy assessment and reporting method. Retrieved from http://www.cibse.org/content/100_Days/TM22.pdf

Turpin-Brooks, S., & Viccars, G. (2006). The development of robust methods of post-occupancy evaluation. *Facilities, 24*, 177–196.

Ulrich, R. S., Berry, L. L., Quan, X., & Parrish, J. (2010). A conceptual framework for the domain of evidence-based design. *Health Environments Research and Design, 4,* 95–114.

Ulrich, R. S., Zimring, C. M., Zhu, X., DuBose, J., Seo, H., & Choi, Y. (2008). A review of the research literature on evidence-based healthcare design. *Health Environments Research & Design Journal, 1,* 61–125.

Usable Buildings Trust. PROBE Archive. Retrieved from http://www.usablebuildings.co.uk/Pages/UBProbePublications1.html

Völlink, T., Meertens, R. E. E., & Midden, C. J. H. (2002). Innovating "diffusion of innovation" theory: Innovation characteristics and the intention of utility companies to adopt energy conservation interventions. *Journal of Environmental Psychology, 22,* 333–344.

Volker, L., & Van der Voordt, D. (2005). An integral tool for the diagnostic evaluation of non-territorial offices. In B. Martens & A.G. Keul (Eds.), *Designing social innovation: Planning, building, evaluating* (pp. 241–250). Göttingen: Hogrefe & Huber.

Webb, E., Campbell, D. T., Schwartz, R., & Sechrest, L. (1966). *Unobtrusive measures: Nonreactive research in the social sciences.* Chicago, IL: Rand McNally.

Wener, R. E. (1982). Standardization of testing in post-occupancy evaluations. In A. C. P. Bart, G. Francescato (Eds.), *Proceedings of the 13th Annual Conference of the Environmental Design Research Association.* (pp. 77–84). College Park, MD: EDRA.

Wener, R. E. (1984). Review of "Behavioral and Design Implications of Living With a Passive Solar and Wood Burning: Integrated Design Research for Household Energy Conservation: Clothing, Interiors, and Housing." *Journal of Architectural and Planning Research,* 73–76.

Wener, R. E. (1989). Advances in evaluation of the built environment. In E. H. Zube & G. T. Moore (Eds.), *Advances in environment, behavior, and design, Vol. 2* (pp. 287–313). New York, NY: Plenum.

Wener, R. E. (2002). BMAP 3.0: *Handheld software to support behavior observations.* Paper presented at the 33rd Annual Conference of the Environmental Design Research Association, Philadelphia, PA.

Wener, R. E. (2003). Post-occupancy evaluation for the built environment. In R. Fernandez-Ballesteros (Ed.), *The encyclopedia of psychological assessment* (pp. 732–736). London, UK: Sage.

Wener, R. E. (2008). History and trends in environmental design research. *Journal of Architectural and Planning Research, 25,* 282–297.

Wener, R. E., Frazier, W., & Farbstein, J. (1985). Three generations of evaluation and design of correctional facilities. *Environment and Behavior, 17,* 71–95.

Wener, R. E., & Olsen, R. (1980). Innovative correctional environments: A user assessment. *Environment & Behavior, 12,* 478–493.

Wheeler, L. P. (1967). *Behavioral research for architectural planning.* Ewing Miller Associates, Architects.

Whyte, W. H. (1980). *The social life of small urban spaces.* Washington, DC: The Conservation Foundation.

Zeisel, J. (2006). *Inquiry by design.* New York, NY: Norton.

Zimmerman, A., & Martin, M. (2001). Post-occupancy evaluation: Benefits and barriers. *Building Research & Information, 29,* 168–174.

Zimring, C. (2002). Post-occupancy evaluation: Issues and implementation. In R. Bechtel & A. Churchman (Eds.), *Handbook of environmental psychology* (pp. 306–319). New York, NY: Wiley.

Zimring, C., & Bosch, S. (2008). Building the evidence base for evidence-based design: Editors' introduction. *Environment and Behavior, 40,* 147–150.

Zimring, C., Weitzer, W. H., & Knight, R. C. (1982). Opportunity for control and the designed environment: The case of an institution for the developmentally disabled. In A. Baum & J. Singer (Eds.), *Advances in environmental psychology, Vol. 4: Environment and health.* Hillsdale, NJ: Erlbaum.

Zimring, C., & Wener, R. E. (1985). Evaluating evaluation. *Environment & Behavior, 17,* 97–117.

Suggested Readings

Preiser, W. F. E. (2001). Feedback, feedforward and control: Post-occupancy evaluation to the rescue. *Building Research & Information, 29,* 456–459.

Turpin-Brooks, S., & Viccars, G. (2006). The development of robust methods of post-occupancy evaluation. *Facilities, 24,* 177–196.

Zimring, C. (2002). Post-occupancy evaluation: Issues and implementation. In R. Bechtel & A. Churchman (Eds.), *Handbook of environmental psychology* (pp. 306–319). New York, NY: Wiley.

14

Action Research
Enhancing Application

Valeria Cortés[1] and Robert Sommer[2]

[1] *University of Victoria, BC, Canada*
[2] *University of California, Davis, CA, United States*

Environment-behavior researchers face an *application gap* because designers, planners, or facilities managers, the presumed users of environment-behavior research, do not access academic journals, because "they would find them laden with jargon, over-detailed, too much concerned with theory and methodology ..." (Spencer, 2007, p. 5). Too often researchers study problems of little interest to practitioners and when they do investigate applied issues, the path to application is not clearly marked (Russell & Ward, 1982; Seidel, 1985). Environmental psychologists have produced large amounts of scientific research useful to decision-making processes but it is generally available in research libraries that practitioners do not access.

Now that interest in sustainability is on the rise, one would think that there is more applied environmental psychology being undertaken in this area, but that is not the case (Spencer, 2007, p. 13). The need for putting environmental psychology research into policy and architectural and urban design practice exists and it is important that practitioners and researchers communicate better and review existing research to find its practical applications.

Some scholars (Nickerson, 2003; Seidel, 1985; Spencer, 2007) suggest that application can be enhanced by using better clarification and dissemination strategies: making reports accessible and readable to different target audiences or considering linkage strategies – having a connector who can communicate with both researchers and potential users of research information.

Although these strategies can help address the existing divide between research and application, it is desirable to go even further. It is possible to engage in a process in which researchers and stakeholders together conduct and apply research designed to solve actual problems experienced by the stakeholders and in that way bring about change and development. One way researchers can ensure that real problems and real people are always front and center in their studies is to engage in *action research* (AR). This is not business as usual for the researcher but a different kind of business because AR is concerned with "undertaking action and studying that action as it is taking place" (Coghlan & Shani, 2005, p. 533). Instead of the researcher

Research Methods for Environmental Psychology, First Edition. Edited by Robert Gifford.
© 2016 John Wiley & Sons, Ltd. Published 2016 by John Wiley & Sons, Ltd.

doing a study and publishing the results in a scientific journal or delivering a written report to an organization, the researcher assists a group to do its own research on a problem of interest to them. This shifts authority and responsibility from the researcher to the group.

What is Action Research?

Action research is a reflective process of actively engaging with an organization or group with the purpose of addressing a real-life issue and effecting change, while conducting research and post-research evaluation. It is *reflective* because it includes a retrospective and cyclical analysis of the group's performance and process in order to gain knowledge from experience (Leitch & Day, 2000), thus enhancing individual and group learning, as well as improving AR practice. It is a *process of active engagement* because all involved have shared accountability, commitment, and power, and because it involves the stakeholders. It *addresses a real-life issue,* bridging the gap between research and application. It *effects change* because those involved in a successful AR project should be better off as a result of it. It is *research* because it uses a range of research methods, tools, and techniques. The process includes *evaluation* using post-research analysis to examine the relevance of the intervention.

Social psychologist Kurt Lewin was one of the first researchers to conceptualize action research. He conceived of AR as a cyclical process of analysis, fact finding, conceptualization, planning, implementation, and evaluation to simultaneously solve problems and generate new knowledge (Lewin, 1946). More recent definitions state that AR is a set of systematic research and intervention activities that emphasize reflection in action and on action (Leitch & Day, 2000), and "a joint venture between external researchers with [organization] members over ... a matter of genuine concern to them" (Eden & Huxham, 1996, p. 75).

AR has been applied in various contexts worldwide; given the different contexts, many traditions have emerged, variously described as **participatory action research**, **community-based research, action science**, or **action learning** (see Glossary); all related to AR's goals and emphasis on applicability and relevance. These terms are not the same as applied research, as AR rejects a separation between basic and applied studies, in the belief that the advancement of knowledge and practical utility can be accomplished within a single study, providing that the potential users of the information have helped to formulate the problem, chosen the methods, and assisted in data collection and analysis. For example, in a program to improve working conditions in a factory, if the employees have not been directly involved throughout the research, it is not AR, regardless of the researcher's good intentions or success in improving the work environment.

Boog (2003) suggests that action research can be seen as a continuum: at one end is a strong focus on mobilizing people, and at the other, the emphasis lies entirely on thorough investigation of a problem. In practice, one need not emphasize either goal exclusively. Instead, AR rewards flexibility: the ability and willingness to adapt to the situation, always maintaining the push toward involving participants in real-world problem solving.

Before delving into this chapter's case study, a word of warning. AR is not as neat and straightforward as presented here. It can be a messy process including many detours and re-evaluations. The purpose of the following case study is to provide a general understanding of the action research process. There are eight phases identified in this scenario:

1. A community identifies an issue as a potential AR project.
2. Relationship building and setting the ground for effective group learning.
3. Develop the research plan; select and train a research team.
4. Conduct research that includes the stakeholders, tabulate results, and write a report circulated for comments to the stakeholders.
5. Discuss implementation strategies and proceed to take action.
6. Post-research evaluation and reflection.
7. Dissemination.
8. Celebration.

Case Study: The Commons Tree-Planting Project

A community identifies an issue as a potential AR project

Annabelle, an environmental psychologist, nature lover, and behavioral researcher with a keen interest in community development, is a volunteer with The Commons, a grassroots organization that aims to strengthen community resilience and environmental sustainability. Recently, food security advocates in the community approached The Commons to discuss the feasibility of planting trees with edible fruits or nuts in their neighborhood. The neighborhood currently has many mature trees that do not bear edible fruit. From a food security perspective, this is a wasted opportunity. With a fairly modest long-term effort, the neighborhood streets could be lined with trees producing nutritious and edible nuts and fruits. Food security advocates also argued the project would encourage community building and promote healthy living.

At the last Commons meeting, members and food security advocates discussed how to proceed. Some members were enthusiastic, but others questioned the feasibility of the project and its expected outcomes. In the past they had butted heads with the city council in trying to change its policies on tree planting; even trying to remove a tree adjacent to their property to plant another species proved to be a challenge. Furthermore, young trees may not bear sufficient fruit or nuts for years. Skeptics argued that the neighborhood would lose interest much earlier than that. Ultimately, it all came down to a question of whether the relationship of the neighbors to their urban environments could be changed – whether they could be convinced to join forces on a long-term project, advocate for it at city council, invest the time and effort necessary to make this happen, and whether this joint effort could also increase the social resilience of the residents and their relationship to their environment.

Some members suggested AR as a way of analyzing the situation and getting the facts, along with informing the neighborhood of the issues. Annabelle supported this

Box 14.1   Excerpt from Annabelle's journal (April 22).

Did they choose me as a facilitator because I am a researcher? I know about AR
but have never implemented it. I feel uneasy, I think that an important part of
this project is to negotiate my role as a researcher and facilitator. I think it will
be difficult to engage in a participatory process and consider all stakeholders
but I look forward to this challenge.

Box 14.2   Excerpt from Annabelle's journal (April 28).

Today we had a particularly challenging meeting. I had to bite my tongue to
restrain myself from assuming control! I felt frustrated at the lack of understanding of research and upset by the terribly inaccurate opinions of some
group members.

My role in this process is so important and influential! I am realizing the
extent of it. Starting by being flexible and changing the schedule according to
the team's needs and being receptive to what is said and why (and to not
immediately argue the point). I need to meet them where they are, not where
I want them to be. I need to remember that they are not researchers and that
this is not about me ...

idea and discussed the possibility of developing the research capacity of the organization, so that it could tackle the issue of food sustainability in the neighborhood and
have the skills to address future issues. After some deliberation The Commons members decided to try AR. They established a research team and appointed Annabelle as
facilitator. Box 14.1 contains an extract from Annabelle's diary.

Annabelle searched for theories and past studies of urban tree planting and resident involvement, in order to have the appropriate background to make informed
decisions and to design the best possible AR plan. This literature review helped set
the context for the AR project. The action researcher should have knowledge of
previous work in order to increase the understanding of the problem and, if needed,
translate it into a lay vocabulary. Drawing on theory and past practice is essential to
ground the research.

At the next meeting, Annabelle experienced the first of many frustrations. After
the ramblings of some peers and the negativity of others, she felt compelled to take
control. She restrained herself: she knew the importance of having a participatory,
inclusive, and democratic process where everyone's voices are heard, regardless of
their knowledge or experience. She knew that detaching the research from the group
would diminish their involvement with the project, so she worked hard at remaining
in the facilitator role instead of being the decision maker. Box 14.2 indicates
Annabelle's thoughts.

Point to ponder: Paradigm shift and the new role of the researcher
According to Boog (2003, p. 5) "action researchers must be ready to cross the traditional disciplinary boundaries and draw from the theories and techniques of the various disciplines of social science;" they not only do research, but they become facilitators of the group process and students of group dynamics.

Annabelle's challenges are, first, to conduct research that produces benefits for the stakeholders. This can only be achieved if she helps the group elicit and voice people's desired outcomes. Second, she needs to make sure the process can be maintained by the organization afterwards. In other words, the action researcher needs to nurture members to take responsibility for the proceedings, to help them understand the research methods so that they are able to carry on when the action researcher is no longer present. Box 14.3 illustrates Annabelle's decisions.

Point to ponder: Values in action research
Instead of the researcher doing a study and giving the results to a group or organization, the researcher assists the group in doing its own research. For the research process, this represents a major shift in authority and approach. Traditionally, the researcher does not have the participants peeking behind the stage or making decisions about the study, and publications are generally the hoped-for tangible product of an academic study. Therefore, participatory action research represents a shift in authority. Instead of being controlled and autocratic, it is collaborative and inclusive. Koch and Kralik (2001) describe action research as based on democratic, equitable, liberating, and life-enhancing principles. AR is not only about research and action, but also about shared learning and empowerment.

The AR group process should be inclusive and promote mutual understanding with shared responsibility (Kaner, 1996). It needs to integrate stakeholders' perspectives and ensure that power is shared. The AR group process pursues mutual understanding and the need to accept the legitimacy of others' needs and perspectives. See Box 14.4 for an excerpt from Annabelle's journal.

Box 14.3   Excerpt from Annabelle's journal (April 28).

I will follow these guidelines, as I enter this new world of action research:

- I'm there as a catalyst.
- Stimulate people to change and to enable them to examine various courses of action and the potential consequences.
- The essence of the work is process (the way things are done).
- The key is to enable people to develop their own analysis of the issues.
- Start where people are, not where I think they ought to be.
- Focus on both the problem and on human relations (Stringer, 1996).

Box 14.4   Excerpt from Annabelle's journal (May 6).

Last week I reflected on my role and how I need to be careful about not imposing my own perspective. But I think it is equally important that I keep in check the impositions from the quick, assertive, articulate, powerful and influential members of the group.

Point to ponder: Ethical considerations

Because AR is carried out in real-life circumstances, action researchers must pay close attention to ethical considerations. O'Brien (1998) suggests a number of principles that should be taken into account when conducting AR:

- Make sure all relevant stakeholders are consulted.
- Decision making regarding the direction of research and outcomes is collective.
- Researchers are explicit and transparent about the nature of the research process from the beginning, including all personal biases and interests. All members must understand these principles.
- There is equal access to information generated by the process for all participants.
- The researcher and the research team must create a process that maximizes the opportunities for involvement of all participants.
- The process must remain transparent and open to suggestions and change.

Other standard ethical considerations might be required depending on the study: withdrawal of participants at any time; maintaining anonymity and confidentiality; becoming aware of power relationships; being careful not to identify individuals in publications; requesting consent from participants when needed; and so on. If the action researcher is associated with a university or government agency he/she must receive human subjects approval before embarking on a study.

Relationship building and setting the ground for effective group learning

Because Annabelle was already volunteering with The Commons, the relationship-building aspect of the study was smooth. It was easier to facilitate the group process, to develop trust, and to get buy-in from the research team that was formed. Nevertheless, the research team wanted to lay the groundwork for effective collaboration, so they allotted time to discuss the team's expectations and roles, and to thoroughly describe the process and the tools they could use. See Box 14.5 for an update of Annabelle's thoughts.

Point to ponder: Reaching consensus

The task of the action researcher is to develop a setting in which individuals with divergent ideas and perceptions can reach a mutual understanding and share decision making. Although it may require time and multiple meetings, dialogue is the basis

Box 14.5   Excerpt from Annabelle's journal (May 6).

We had a very productive meeting today.

I described the action research process in detail. (To some members of the group the idea of becoming researchers came as a surprise, they thought I was going to do all the work.)

We engaged in a conversation regarding the group process. I have never allotted this much time thinking about or planning the group process, roles, expectations, etc. At the end my brain hurt, but we had a plan and a sense of cohesion and accomplishment! After the meeting everyone was clear about the process and roles, and "S" volunteered to provide basic training on conflict resolution skills at the next meeting (that's a bonus since she is a mediator). These are our group agreements:

The Commons Action Research Team
Group Agreements

- We will listen actively to all ideas
- Everyone's opinions matter
- Anyone can call "time out" if they need a break
- All team discussions will remain confidential
- We will respect and embrace differences
- We will be supportive rather than judgmental
- All team members will contribute their ideas and resources
- We will stay focused and acknowledge when we are sidetracked
- When we have a difference of opinion we will discuss facts and not personalities
- We will have process checks to evaluate how the process is going
- We will all work to make sure there are not hidden agendas, and that all issues and concerns can be addressed openly
- We will have fun doing the project

of reaching **consensus** or at least of increasing the ownership of the decision-making process (Stringer, 2007). While consensus may be difficult to achieve, it is a powerful tool for generating agreement and ownership of the process.

With the support of a skilled facilitator, the process starts with the group identifying the underlying concerns of all stakeholders in order to depolarize opposing views and set the ground for collaboration. Table 14.1 shows a seven-step process of consensus-oriented decision making (Hartnett, 2010).

Develop the research plan; select and train a research team

After the problem has been identified, the research team needs to find the facts in order to provide context to the situation, prepare a research plan, and implement solutions based on the data collected. Here is where the action researcher's skills and

Table 14.1 Steps for reaching consensus.

1. Frame the topic	The discussion starts with someone suggesting a problem or idea they think the group should address
2. Open discussion	Group members identify different solutions/proposals to address the issue
3. Identify underlying concerns	The group identifies the underlying needs that drive the proposed ideas
4. Collaborative proposal development	Each proposal is developed to its full potential by the whole group
5. Choose a direction	The group engages in a comparative analysis of pros and cons of each option and uses a preference gradient vote; e.g., rating each proposal 1–5 with 1 showing most support
6. Draft a final proposal	The group agrees on a final proposal based on the result of the analysis/voting and having reviewed any unsatisfied concerns
7. Closure	Members agree to cooperate to implement the solution or review feelings about the outcome (this is no time to change the proposal)

knowledge are most relevant, as she will guide the creation of the research plan and train the team in the research methods to be used.

Based on a framework of *look, think, act* (Stringer, 1996), the research team developed a series of guiding questions as a way to constructing their research plan, making sure they considered the total context and the interconnectedness of the environment and everyone in it (see Figure 14.1).

As mentioned before, action research is not an orderly linear activity but a cyclical one. Annabelle and the research team will find themselves revisiting information and processes, and sometimes making radical changes in the plan. "Although there may be many routes to a destination, and although destinations may change, travelers on the journey will be able to maintain a clear idea of their location and the direction in which they are heading" (Stringer, 1996, p. 9). Therefore, the researcher will allow for flexibility and adaptability depending on the situation.

Using the framework in Figure 14.1, Annabelle helped the research team define a series of questions and converted them into questionnaire items that were easy to score. See Box 14.6.

Point to ponder: Developing an effective survey (For more information read Chapter 5)
The research team agreed to distribute the survey in two different ways: through email, using The Commons database, and door-to-door, with the purpose of meeting residents, generating rapport, and building community. Annabelle pre-tested the survey with other organization members and friends to see if the items were clear. She instructed the group on how to conduct door-to-door interviews and tabulate responses.

LOOK

Gather relevant information

- What do we know so far?
- What do we need to know?
- What are our assets and resources?

Data gathering:

- What are the best methods for gathering information?
- How will data be organized and stored?
- How are we going to analyze data

Think

Understanding the situation and its interconnections
Interpret data and analyze:

- What is happening here?
- Why are things as they are?

Act

Plan the intervention/solution/action. Set goals:

- Who will be involved in action planning and implementation?
- What resources will be needed?

S.M.A.R.T. agreements (specific, measurable, accountable, realistic, within a timeline)

Implement

Evaluate

- When will we conduct the post-research evaluation?
- What are we looking for after implementing the actions?

Other questions

- Who should be involved?
- What are the connections to other contexts?
- How do we ensure change?
- How do we ensure reflection on each step?
- How will findings be reported and presented?

What are we missing?

Figure 14.1   The action research process (based on Craig, 2009, and Stringer, 1996).

Box 14.6   Excerpt from Annabelle's journal (June 27).

We have been working on developing a survey for the past month It has been a challenging process because each of the team members proposed their own questions so we had to narrow them down while maintaining a good group dynamic (and avoid conflict).

Here are some of the questions that the group initially brainstormed:

- Do neighbors want to be part of a community tree-planting program?
- Would the tree planting increase community involvement?
- Do neighbors believe the tree planting would raise awareness of food security issues?
- Would the tree planting promote other pro-environmental behaviors?
- How many households want trees in their front yards?
- What species of trees do people want?
- Are people interested in planting edible nut trees as a future source of food?
- What do people know about food security in the city?
- Are neighbors interested in advocating at city council?
- Do people know the neighbors in their block?
- Do people know which trees around them bear edible fruits or nuts?
- What is people's relationship to their environment in this neighborhood?

Some of these questions are too vague. I look forward to sharing my expertise on how to develop effective surveys.

Annabelle noticed a change in the group dynamic. The research team seemed motivated to take action. She realized that the training was empowering for people who had never done research, or at least not on behalf of an organization they cared about. The research team had reached a new level of competence. See Box 14.7 for Annabelle's thoughts on progress.

Point to ponder: The emancipatory power of action research
Since action research is an approach aimed at social change, at emancipation and empowerment, it may pose a challenge to the existing social order. It allows those in a less privileged position to increase power and consciousness over their situation. This is especially true for studies with a focus on social justice issues in community-based research (Boog, 2003). Nevertheless, increasing people's awareness and actively engaging them in reflective research, such as AR, can lead to organizational change and in the way people participate in society.

A key step in AR involves encouraging and teaching local groups to do their own research in the future. The researcher may still be available as a consultant but a group may choose to conduct surveys or use other procedures on its own. To this end, group members are given training (as in an introductory methods course)

Box 14.7 Excerpt from Annabelle's journal (July 18).

The training with the research team was a success. During and after the training I could sense the team's excitement and an increase in knowledge and ability. Regardless of the outcome, these people are ready to do research by themselves and that gives me a sense of accomplishment!

OK, I have to be objective. Some folks questioned their roles as researchers, because they were not trained scientists and were not confident in their ability. I fear they will continue to question themselves for a while, and I need to help them trust their skills.

in interviewing, questionnaire construction, sampling, and data analysis. Those who want to become AR facilitators and assist groups to conduct their own research, must learn conventional research methods and more. "More" in this instance is learning group processes and adapting conventional research methods to less than ideal conditions, when lay people have an equal say as to research methodology and it is not possible to achieve random samples, standardized conditions, or to check interviewer reliability. Although this loss of control can be frustrating to a researcher, it can also be rewarding when lay people take ownership, contribute their ideas, talents, and knowledge of local conditions, become advocates for the results, and are empowered to conduct their own research in the future. This helps ensure that the results will not be filed and forgotten as happens in so many studies.

Conducting research

The research team conducted door-to-door interviews with the residents on one of the main avenues in the neighborhood and sent out an online survey to those who were registered with The Commons and the neighborhood community association. The team collected responses from 170 residents. See Figure 14.2.

Point to ponder: Tools for conducting research
Action research is a holistic approach to problem solving and effecting change rather than a single method for collecting and analyzing data. For this reason, it allows for different research tools depending on the situation. Qualitative methods might include a research journal (Craig, 2009), search conferences (O'Brien, 2001), case studies, mapping, role-play, semi-structured interviews, simulations, or art-based methods. In the quantitative approach, the most frequently used method is the self-survey, in which the research team works with the community to create a survey and provides assistance to them at all stages of the research process. It is called a self-survey because members of the organization develop the survey questions with the assistance of the research consultant and administer it to other stakeholders.

Keeping a journal is an important tool of the AR approach. Projects are fluid, with shifting roles and relationships, and stakeholders make decisions that must be recorded promptly lest they are forgotten when the study is written for a

(All of the following are answered on a Likert-type scale, from 1 = Definitely do not agree, to 5 =

Definitely agree.)

- Food security is an issue I care about.
- I am usually on the lookout for edible plants in my environment.
- I know and have a friendly relationship with most of the neighbors in my block.
- I see myself residing in this neighborhood for the foreseeable future.
- I am willing to lend my support to a tree-planting project.
- I would like to volunteer on environmental and resilience-related projects in my community.

Figure 14.2   Sample questions from The Commons survey.

Box 14.8   Excerpt from Annabelle's journal (July 9).

I would have done a very different questionnaire, focusing on different issues (more on the effects of tree-planting programs and less on food security).

Analyzing the data was very interesting; I could see the team jumping to the wrong conclusions based on their wishes and gut feelings. But we had to look at the data with objectivity and respect what the neighborhood really wants.

wider audience. The researcher's field journal is also a tool for recording details such as delays and refusals, interpersonal conflict, problems related to the situation, information about the process, ideas, and so on. The journal guides the process because the act of writing encourages the researcher to think through issues. According to Craig (2009), the journal usually contains three types of information: ideas and comments, reflecting the thought process of the researcher; general research information, consisting of notes and other ideas related to the study; and environment and participant-based material, usually information about participants, the setting, and the group process. See Box 14.8 for an excerpt from Annabelle's journal.

Data analysis

After the surveys and door-to-door interviews were completed, Annabelle helped the research team tabulate the results and analyze the data. The team then moved on to the next stage, the *think* part. Their findings are summarized in Figure 14.3.

Point to ponder: Rigor

Donald Schön (1983) asks rhetorically whether researchers should stay in the tower, set on the hard, high ground of rigorous research or descend into the swamp to deal with the most important and challenging problems that require trade-offs in technical rigor. Swamps are uncomfortable places, sticky, and full of unknown creatures.

Findings of The Commons Research Project

The survey results presented several pieces of good news to The Commons team, although not everything was positive. Among the most encouraging findings, a large majority of respondents (64%) somewhat or definitely agreed to lend their support and volunteer in the tree-planting project. In conversations with respondents, Commons members found that people were willing to collaborate not so much for the fruit itself, but because they wanted to better connect with their neighbors (only 13% agreed or definitely agreed that they knew and had friendly relations with most of their block neighbors).

Most people felt positively toward environmental issues (72%), even if they had not desired edible fruits and nuts in their urban environments until then. Many door-to-door respondents seemed enlightened by the possibility of starting to forage for fruits and nuts that they did not know were already present in their environment.

Among the negatives, Commons researchers found a vocal minority that strongly disliked the idea of any food security or environmental projects. Actually, a few people stopped answering the survey as soon as its subject became clear. (When this phenomenon arose, it led to a discussion among the Commons research team on what to do to avoid self-selection bias in sampling. Annabelle explained the standard methods to deal with this, and also role-played with her peers on how to keep wary respondents involved in the survey, and on how to avoid identifying themselves as environmentalists.) Furthermore, the neighborhood had a large population of students who did not see themselves becoming long-term residents. This did not rule out their participation in the project (which, again, presented an opportunity for community socialization as well as environmental action), but it did suggest to Commons researchers that there would need to be continuing community building.

Figure 14.3 Excerpt from findings of The Commons research project.

Fortunately the choice between tower and swamp is not irrevocable. Botany and geology provide ample precedent of university researchers making scheduled forays into swamps, jungles, and polar regions where data are collected under difficult conditions and brought back to the university for analysis. The crucial point is that researchers should adopt the research model appropriate to their circumstances. There are times for the twentieth permutation of a laboratory experiment with college students, times for contract studies designed to answer practical questions for a client, and times for collaborative studies with groups and organizations set within an AR framework.

AR emphasizes the importance of local knowledge. Lewin (1948) declared that lawfulness in science means an if-so linkage between hypothetical laws and hypothetical effects but this does not tell us what conditions exist locally, do the job of diagnosis, or prescribe a strategy for change. Lewin maintained that these activities must be performed at the local level where circumstances are always unique. Honadle (1996) notes that when a community is faced with an important decision about a local problem, people require specific, timely information to help them make decisions. They need answers to their questions, not information about a subject area.

Effecting change – Taking action

Finally the research team reached the stage of taking action. This does not mean that they were not acting before, but now it was their chance to implement what they had learned. They engaged The Commons membership, the neighborhood, and other interested members of the community in their action planning. See Figure 14.4 for an action plan.

One thing that the research team emphasized when preparing their action plan was the continuing nature of this project. The short-term actions, such as the initial meeting, petition, and tree-planting party, could only be conceived as first steps toward building community and resiliency in the neighborhood. The transient nature of many residents, as well as the resistance of a few neighbors, suggested the need for constant reaching-out efforts, as well as for a celebratory and socializing tone for the tree-planting events.

Point to ponder: Change in small groups
According to Bargal (2012), the small group is one of the most effective means to effect social change. Lewin (1946) suggested that behavior patterns are anchored in norms and interpersonal relations originating in the groups to which one belongs, hence the potential for change residing in small groups.

Community Building

Goal: To increase resident involvement and to generate community buy-in

Actions

1.   Organize a community meeting to share the results of study and proposed actions. Take their suggestions as input and for future programming

2.   Organize a free educational workshop on the topic of the impact of planting fruit and nut trees. Reflect, evaluate, and make changes if needed

3.   Sign a petition to plant fruit and nut trees. Reflect, evaluate, and make changes if needed

4.   After petition is signed, approach city parks, city hall, and local arborists and nurseries to ask for their support. Reflect, evaluate, and make changes if needed

Tree planting
Goal: To plant a minimum of 20 fruit and nut trees in the neighborhood

1.   Mobilize the neighbors to plan a tree-planting party
2.   Organize tree-planting party at local coffee shop
3.   Reflect, evaluate, and make changes if needed.

Education: Tree-planting program
Goal: To create a sustainable tree-planting program in collaboration with The Commons and the neighbors based on previous actions and feedback

---

Figure 14.4   Proposed action plan.

> **What? So What? Now What?**
>
> <u>What?</u> (Describe objectively)
> What happened? What issue is been addressed? What did I observe? What did I do?
> Report the facts of the experience.
>
> <u>So What?</u> (Include feelings)
> Why this is important to me? What did I learn or notice? Analyze the experience.
>
> <u>Now What?</u>
> Description of next steps. How can I apply what I learned? What follow-up can I do?
> What am I going to do differently next time?

Figure 14.5 Reflection protocol (adapted from Thompson-Grove, 2004).

Post-research evaluation and reflection

A main component of AR is the reflection implemented throughout the project cycle and not only done as an afterthought at the end.

Point to ponder: Critical reflection

Critical reflection is at the core of action research and it is essential to promote group learning. Putting reflection at the center of the change process acknowledges the cognitive dimension and the emotional dimension of those involved. Acknowledging the relationships between thinking, feeling, and behaving are central to developing effective approaches to change (Leitch & Day, 2000). Figure 14.5 describes a protocol for engaging in intentional reflection, and enhancing participants' cognitive, affective, and behavioral connections to the work.

The Commons research team engaged in intentional reflection through journal writing. They reflected while acting, modifying their actions as needed and engaging in a retrospective analysis of the situation in order to gain insight (Schön, 1983).

Post-research evaluation

Post-research evaluation is a key component of the action research process because it is the way to assess whether the intervention or solution was satisfactory and effected positive changes. Post-research evaluation provides input regarding the issue, and it allows the organization to take a step back and reflect on its work. It allows the team to document the process and the outcomes and to justify their practice. The success of action research lies not just on whether change can be measured but on what is learned from the experience. Finally, the methods used and the data generated can inform other AR projects.

According to Riel and Lepori (2011), a practical way to evaluate the AR project is to measure whether the project has achieved three main outcomes – on the personal level, assessing individual growth; on the organizational level, focusing on the increased competency and betterment of the organization and the community; and on the scholarly level, assessing whether the project is contributing to the AR field and generating new knowledge.

The research team administered a survey six months after the tree-planting party with the purpose of measuring the project's effects. It focused on whether the neighborhood had modified its perceptions on food security and influenced community relations. The results from that survey led to the team to reassess their approach, to overcome the barriers that prevented people joining the effort, and to encourage residents to invite others to join the project.

Dissemination

Action researchers need to disseminate the knowledge generated in an accessible and multi-modal manner. This represents a major shift for the academic researcher accustomed to thinking of academic journals as the only legitimate dissemination method. Not only must they find other outlets, but also they must use the language and format required by each type of dissemination.

Academic behavioral sciences depend heavily upon a trickle-down model for disseminating their findings. Researchers conduct studies which are published in technical journals with the hope that the results will somehow filter down to policy makers and the public. Deficiencies in this dissemination model, at least from the standpoint of influencing practice, include the following:

1. Issues deemed important by the researcher may not be important or relevant to others.
2. The methods and conditions used to study the problem are often so artificial as to distort the situation studied, thus precluding generalization to the outside world.
3. Practitioners and the public are not likely to see an article published in a technical journal.
4. Practitioners and the public will not be able to understand an article written in technical jargon and employing complex statistical procedures.
5. If they happen to read and understand the article, the implications for action may not be clear. The translation from lab to life needs to be made.
6. Assuming that policy makers, practitioners, or the public read and understand the article, grasp the implications for action, and actually do change policy or practice on the basis of the research, this may occur without the researcher's knowledge. Even when the trickle-down model succeeds, the researcher may be unaware of it. The lack of feedback reduces opportunities for refining and improving research practice.

Studies done in collaboration with lay groups typically require the use of outlets other than technical journals. When lay individuals are full partners in the research, they are likely to choose methods less rigorous and reliable than those preferred by professionals. Studies designed to meet the information needs of a lay organization will lack theoretical significance. For the most part, they will not want a sophisticated statistical analysis their membership cannot understand. For these and other reasons, articles using an AR approach are not likely to be accepted by basic research journals. Those who use AR must seek other outlets for disseminating their studies.

When working with grassroots organizations, it is efficient to use their newsletters, blogs, and social media to reach the membership and beyond to a wider audience. Many topical areas have trade magazines and professional newsletters to reach their membership. This does not rule out scientific journals, which are essential for reaching the research community, but requires other types of outlets to reach other audiences. More so than other approaches, AR lends itself to multiple dissemination.

Annabelle and her research team presented the results in three different ways. First, they discussed the findings with the rest of The Commons members and to interested residents in a meeting organized in collaboration with the community association. In addition, one of the team members and Annabelle wrote articles for The Commons newsletter and blog; later on, the community newspaper editor asked to publish the article, spreading the word about the project to others. Finally, Annabelle prepared a technical paper for an action research journal.

Celebration

The first celebration was the tree-planting party. The Commons was subsequently successful in getting support from the city. The post-research evaluation found residents believed that the trees improved the neighborhood and provided a food source for future generations; it increased the sense of community, neighbors became better acquainted with one another; there was increased knowledge of food security; and among the residents, increased awareness of tree maintenance needs.

Strengths and Limitations

Although AR can generate community enthusiasm and tangible improvement for the residents, it also has drawbacks. First, it takes more time than mainstream research; consultation can be a tedious process; and training lay people requires additional effort (Sommer & Sommer, 2001). Furthermore, the action researcher has less control, and it allows for changes during the process, as the organization might decide to alter the procedures or drop out midway. The action researcher has to facilitate group learning. Certainly, this should not restrain researchers from engaging in AR; it should be an invitation to develop skills that will be useful not only in this type of study but also in other fluid situations.

Conclusion

According to Parlee (1983), "Psychological knowledge would be dramatically changed if it were consistently developed through interaction with its 'subjects' and intended audiences instead of being developed with professional colleagues in mind and 'given away'" (p. 1). Instead of the researcher doing a study and publishing the results in a scientific journal or delivering a written report to an organization, the researcher assists a group to do its own research on a problem of interest to them. This shifts authority and responsibility from the researcher to the group.

Figure 14.6 Sequential steps in AR. The figure in the striped shirt is ART, standing for Action Research Trainer.

In this chapter, eight implementation phases were suggested (for a variant, see Figure 14.6):

1. A community identifies an issue as a potential AR project.
2. Relationship building and setting the ground for effective group learning.
3. Develop the research plan; select and train a research team.
4. Conduct research that includes the stakeholders, tabulate results, and write a report circulated for comments to the stakeholders.
5. Discuss implementation strategies and proceed to take action.
6. Post-research evaluation and reflection.
7. Dissemination.
8. Celebration.

AR is not a neat and orderly approach where every step is planned in advance. It has three goals which hopefully can be achieved within a single study: the advancement of knowledge; the improvement of a local situation; and the refinement and improvement of action research.

Glossary

Action learning A method focusing on learning and action (Pedler, 2011).
Action science Focusing on individual and organizational change and double-loop learning cycles (Smith, 2001).

Community-based research A collaborative enterprise between academic researchers and community members, with a focus on democratization of knowledge (Strand et al., 2003).

Consensus A group decision-making process consisting of participants having explored all available suggestions. Everyone agrees and supports the decision and understands the rationale behind it.

Participatory action research An integrated activity that combines social research with education and action. Generally conducted in developing countries and mainly with a focus on adult education (Brown & Tandon, 1983).

References

Bargal, D. (2012). Action research. *Small Group Research, 39*, 17–27.

Boog, B. (2003). The emancipatory character of action research, its history and the present state of the art. *Journal of Community and Applied Social Psychology, 13*, 426–438.

Brown, L. D., & Tandon, R. (1983). Ideology and political economy in inquiry: Action research and participatory research. *Journal of Applied Behavioral Science, 19*(3), 277–294.

Coghlan, D. & Shani, A. (2005). Roles, politics and ethics in action research design. *Systematic Practice and Action Research, 18*, 533–546.

Craig, D. V. (2009). *Action research essentials*. San Francisco, CA: Jossey-Bass.

Eden, C., & Huxham, C. (1996). Action research for the study of organizations. In S. Clegg, C. Hardy, & W. Nord (Eds.), *Handbook of organizational studies* (pp. 526–542). London, UK: Sage.

Hartnett, T. (2010). Consensus-oriented decision-making: The CODM model for facilitating groups to widespread agreement. Gabriola Island, BC: New Society Publishers.

Honadle, B. W. (1996). Participatory research for public issues education. *Journal of the Community Development Society, 27*, 56–77.

Kaner, S. (1996). *Facilitator's guide to participatory decision-making*. Gabriola, BC: New Society.

Koch T. & Kralik D. (2001). Chronic illness: Reflections on a community-based action research program. *Journal of Advanced Nursing, 36*, 23–31.

Leitch, R., & Day, C. (2000). Action research and reflective practice: Towards a holistic view. *Educational Action Research, 8*, 179–193.

Lewin, K. (1946). Action research and minority problems. In G. W. Lewin (Ed.), *Resolving social conflicts* (pp. 201–216). New York, NY: Harper & Row.

Nickerson, R. (2003). *Psychology and environmental change*. Hillsdale, NJ: Erlbaum.

O'Brien, R. (2001). An overview of the methodological approach of action research. In R. Richardson (Ed.), *Theory and practice of action research*. João Pessoa, Brazil: Universidade Federal da Paraíba. (English version) Retrieved from http://www.web.ca/~robrien/papers/arfinal.html

Parlee, M. B. (1983). President's letter. *Division 35 Newsletter, 10*(1), p. 1.

Pedler, M. (2011). *Action learning in practice* (4th ed.). Aldershot, UK: Gower.

Riel, M., & Lepori, K. (2011). *A meta-analysis of the outcomes of action research*. American Educational Research Association Conference, New Orleans.

Russell, J. A., & Ward, L. M. (1982). Environmental psychology. *Annual Review of Psychology, 33*, 651–688.

Schön, D. (1983). *The reflective practitioner*. New York, NY: Basic Books.

Seidel, D. (1985). What is success in E&B research utilization? *Environment and Behavior, 17*(47), 47–70.

Smith, M. K. (2001). Chris Argyris: Theories of action, double-loop learning and organizational learning. Retrieved from www.infed.org/thinkers/argyris.htm

Sommer, B. & Sommer, R. (2001). *A practical guide to behavioral research: Tools and techniques* (5th ed.). New York, NY: Oxford University Press.

Spencer, C. (2007). Environmental psychology is eminently applicable, but is it being applied? In. E. Edgerton, O. Romice, & C. Spencer (Eds.), *Environmental psychology. Putting research into practice*. Cambridge, UK: Cambridge Scholars Publishing.

Strand, K., Marullo, S., Cutforth, N., Stoecker, R., & Donohue, P. (2003). Principles of best practices for community-based research. *Michigan Journal of Community Service Learning, 9*, 5–15.

Stringer, E. (1996). *Action research. A handbook for practitioners*. Thousand Oaks, CA: Sage.

Stringer, E. (2007). *Action research* (3rd ed.). London, UK: Sage.

Thompson-Grove, G. (2004). *What? So what?* Now what? School Reform Initiative. Retrieved from *schoolreforminitiative.org/doc/what_so_what.pdf*

Suggested Readings

Argyris, C., Putman, R., McLain, D. (1985). *Action science: Concepts, methods, and skills for research and intervention*. San Francisco, CA: Jossey-Bass.

Edgerton, E., & Romice, O. (2007). *Environmental psychology. Putting research into practice*. Cambridge, UK: Cambridge Scholars Publishing.

Stringer, E. (2007). *Action research* (3rd ed.). London, UK: Sage.

Whyte, W. F. (1991). *Participatory action research*. London, UK: Sage.

15

Research Designs for Measuring the Effectiveness of Interventions

Wokje Abrahamse
Victoria University of Wellington, New Zealand

Gabriel and Ethan are sitting in the campus library. Gabriel is working on an assignment for his environmental psychology course. The assignment entails designing a study that examines the effectiveness of online pledges to change an environmental behavior of his choosing. He has decided to look at the effectiveness of online pledges as part of the Meatless Monday campaign to try and reduce meat consumption. He discusses his idea with Ethan.

"We learned in our course that meat consumption has a large environmental impact and so I have signed this online pledge, committing myself to no longer eat meat on Mondays. Now I need to figure out how to measure its effectiveness." "How are you going to do that?" "I would need a group of people who sign the pledge and then monitor their meat consumption before and after they sign the pledge. I also need a control group of people who do not sign the pledge." *He looks at Ethan. "Sure – I'll be in your control group. But doesn't that pose a problem right there? You already eat less meat than I do. Couldn't it be that your pledge group consists of people who are already eating less meat than people in your control group? That could affect your results." Gabriel is leafing through his textbook. "Good point. However, if I measured meat consumption in both groups beforehand, I could check to make sure that the groups are not too different from each other." "Great idea." "Hey, do you want to go get a burger? All this talk about food has made me hungry." "I thought you signed a pledge…?"*

Interventions to encourage pro-environmental behaviors (PEBs) are aimed at improving environmental quality and sustainability. It is therefore important to gather empirical evidence (an "evidence base") to establish the effectiveness of interventions in encouraging behavior change. This chapter provides an overview of research designs that can be used to test the effectiveness of interventions, namely experimental, quasi-experimental, and non-experimental designs. Then, the main

Research Methods for Environmental Psychology, First Edition. Edited by Robert Gifford.
© 2016 John Wiley & Sons, Ltd. Published 2016 by John Wiley & Sons, Ltd.

threats to validity will be discussed. Finally, some recommendations will be provided regarding the different phases of doing intervention research, including some of the practicalities of doing field research.

For the purpose of this chapter, interventions are defined as any approach that has the intent to change or alter pro-environmental behavior. An overview of some of the most frequently used interventions is provided in Chapter 16. The effectiveness of interventions to encourage pro-environmental behaviors are usually evaluated by means of field experiments, which are aimed at measuring the extent to which an intervention results in changes in behavior in everyday circumstances. For example, field studies can help answer questions such as: Did the media campaign on climate change result in increased awareness of this issue? Did the provision of information encourage households to save energy?

In intervention studies, participants are typically assigned to either an intervention group or a no-intervention group. The intervention group is also referred to as a **treatment group,** which is the group of participants who receive the intervention. The no-intervention group is referred to as the control group and these participants generally do not receive any intervention. Most intervention studies will include measurement of the variables of interest before and after implementation of the intervention, such as knowledge, attitudes, or behavior. These so-called **pre-test measures** yield quantifiable measures of levels of engagement in the behavior (or attitudes, knowledge) before any intervention takes place. The measurement after implementation of the intervention, the **post-test measure,** provides information about any changes in the outcome measure following implementation of an intervention.

Research Designs

Generally, three types of research designs can be used to assess the effectiveness of interventions in applied settings: experimental, quasi-experimental, and non-experimental designs. Experimental and quasi-experimental designs are examples of a between-subjects design, and non-experimental designs are examples of a within-subjects design (see Chapter 16). In this section, experimental, quasi-experimental, and non-experimental designs are discussed, and using examples, advantages and disadvantages of each design are discussed.

Experimental designs

How do we know that an intervention caused any observed changes in behavior? Experimental studies have a number of important characteristics that can help determine causation (Shadish, Cook, & Campbell, 2002). In experimental studies, the intervention (cause) is systematically varied and the effect on behavior is observed. Experimental studies can help determine whether this systematic variation in the cause (intervention) is related to variation in the effect (behavior). Further, various steps can be taken to reduce the plausibility that other explanations can account for the effect. One of the key characteristics of experimental designs is randomization. In **randomized experiments**, participants are assigned to either an experimental or a control group. This helps create groups of participants that are similar to one another. Any differences in behavior that are observed between groups after the experiment are likely to be a result of the intervention and not the result of differences between the groups that existed before the intervention. In Ethan's study on the effect of online pledges on reducing meat consumption, for example, ideally he would randomly assign participants to either a pledge group or a no-pledge group to ensure there are no systematic differences between the groups to begin with. Randomized experiments are generally considered the gold standard for demonstrating causality, that is, in helping determine that the intervention is responsible for the change in the outcome measure (e.g., Creswell, 2012; Fisher & Foreit, 2002; Shadish et al., 2002).

In a **pre-test–post-test control group design** (Campbell & Stanley, 1963) participants are randomly assigned to either an experimental group or a control group and an initial measurement takes place of the variables of interest (pre-test). The experimental group then receives the intervention, while the control group does not receive this intervention. After the intervention period is completed, a second measurement of the variables of interest takes place (post-test). For example, this experimental design could be used to examine the effectiveness of energy-saving tips to encourage households to reduce their energy use (see Figure 15.1). If these researchers find that households in the intervention group saved significantly more energy than households in the control group, because of manipulation of the intervention and random assignment, they could feel confident that the differences in energy savings can be attributed to the intervention.

This research design can also be expanded with additional experimental groups, referred to as a **multiple treatment design**. These designs include more than one intervention (or treatment) group in addition to a control group. This can be useful when researchers want to compare different interventions to find out which intervention is more effective. Returning to our hypothetical energy conservation example, the study could be expanded by adding an experimental group of households that receives a financial incentive for buying energy-efficient light bulbs. The researchers could then examine whether providing a financial incentive is more effective than providing energy-saving advice.

A multiple treatment design can also be used to examine whether a combination of interventions is more effective than the use of a single intervention. For example,

Time			
	Pre-test measure of energy use		Post-test measure of energy use
Random assignment of participants to:			
Experimental group	No intervention	Information	No intervention
Control group	No intervention	No intervention	No intervention

Figure 15.1 Example of a (hypothetical) pre-test–post-test control group design used to measure the effect of information in encouraging energy conservation (adapted from Campbell & Stanley, 1963).

a study can be set up (see Figure 15.2) to examine the effect of combining energy-saving advice with a financial incentive in encouraging energy conservation. In this case, one group of households would be given information only, a second group would only be given a financial incentive, a third group would receive the combination of energy-saving advice and an incentive, and a fourth group would serve as a control group and not receive any information or an incentive. The advantage of multiple treatment designs is that it allows researchers to examine more than one intervention or combination of interventions to encourage behavior change. At the same time, the addition of more experimental groups also means that more participants are needed. In field studies, this can be an important trade-off between the number of experimental groups included and the need to recruit a sufficient number of participants for each group.

Randomized experiments have been employed in environmental psychology to establish the effectiveness of interventions (for an example, see Box 15.1). However,

Random assignment of participants to:	Pre-test measure of energy use	Time →	Post-test measure of energy use
Experimental group 1	No intervention	Information	No intervention
Experimental group 2	No intervention	Financial incentive	No intervention
Experimental group 3	No intervention	Information + financial incentive	No intervention
Control group	No intervention	No intervention	No intervention

Figure 15.2 Example of a (hypothetical) pre-test–post-test control group design with multiple treatments used to measure the effect of information and incentives to encourage energy conservation (adapted from Campbell & Stanley, 1963).

Box 15.1 Example of a randomized experiment.

Bamberg (2006) examined the effect of personalized travel information and a free day-pass in encouraging public transport (PT) use among people who had just moved house. When people move house, they generally need to reconsider travel options and this posed an opportunity to encourage the use of PT. Using a randomized experiment, residents who had recently moved house were randomly assigned to the experimental (information + free ticket) or control group (no intervention).

PT use and car use were measured via a postal survey six months prior to the intervention and three months after the intervention. Before the intervention, there were no significant differences between intervention and control group in PT use and car use, indicating that randomization had been successful. After the intervention, participants in the intervention group had significantly increased PT use, from 18% to 47%, while PT use in the control group did not change significantly.

Car use decreased in the intervention group, suggesting that car trips were being replaced by PT trips. These results indicate that information and a free PT pass were effective in increasing PT use and reducing car use (see Figure 15.3).

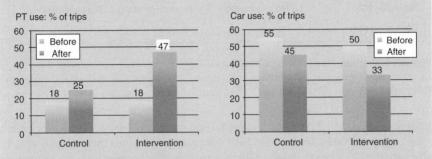

Figure 15.3 The percentage of PT trips (left) and car trips (right) before and after the intervention for the experimental and control group (based on data reported in Bamberg, 2006).

in applied settings and field studies, random assignment of participants to groups is often not feasible. For example, researchers wanting to examine the effect of information to reduce energy use in campus residences would have difficulty randomly assigning students to different residences. In this case, a cluster-randomized trial can be employed (for an example, see Carrico & Riemer, 2011). In a cluster-randomized trial, clusters of participants are randomly assigned to the experimental and control group. For example, students in one residence building could be randomly assigned to be the group receiving information, whereas students in a second campus building would not receive any information.

Quasi-experimental designs

Quasi-experimental designs are often used in environmental psychology research. **Quasi-experimental designs**, like experimental designs, are characterized by systematic variation of one variable (e.g., information or no information) and participants are assigned to either an intervention group or a control group (see Figure 15.4). Pre-test and post-test measures of the behavior of interest can also be taken. When a pre-test is not feasible, because of time or resource constraints for example, researchers can employ a post-test-only design.

In contrast to randomized experiments, quasi-experimental studies do not include random assignment of participants to groups. Random assignment is often not possible in field studies because of availability of participants, or because of the

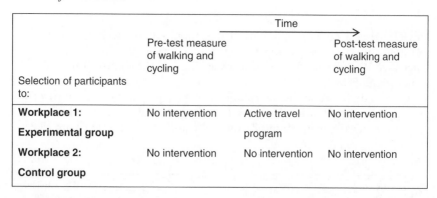

Figure 15.4 Example of a (hypothetical) quasi-experimental design to measure the effect of an active travel program to encourage the uptake of walking and cycling (adapted from Campbell & Stanley, 1963).

setting. Instead, participants are assigned to groups based on some form of selection (Shadish et al., 2002). In the case of self-selection, participants themselves choose to take part in the intervention group. In the case of researcher selection, the researchers assign participants to receive an intervention. To illustrate, if one assumes that the participants in Ethan's study who signed a Meatless Monday pledge volunteered to do so, this is an illustration of self-selection to the intervention group.

Quasi-experimental designs are often employed to evaluate the effectiveness of interventions, especially when behavior change initiatives rely on voluntary participation. Imagine a local council is interested in the effect of their workplace travel plan to encourage the uptake of walking and cycling to work. Signing up to the scheme is voluntary and because of this, it would be difficult to randomly assign employees to either the intervention group (i.e., active travel program) or a control group. In this case, a quasi-experimental design would be suitable. Employees who work at workplaces without active travel plans could be used as a comparison group.

In quasi-experimental studies, it may be more difficult to attribute any changes in behavior to the intervention. Because random assignment does not occur in quasi-experimental studies, systematic differences may exist between the groups at the outset (e.g., the intervention group already walked to work more than the control group before the active travel program was implemented). However, researchers employing quasi-experimental designs still have a relatively large amount of control over other aspects of the experiment, such as the inclusion of more than one comparison group, or the inclusion of other variables (covariates) that may affect the intervention (e.g., environmental concern or socio-demographic characteristics).

For example, the researcher can examine any differences in active travel or socio-demographic variables at pre-test to examine if there are any systematic differences between the two groups prior to implementation of the scheme. Because of this level of control, the researcher can be more confident that any differences in the uptake of active travel modes between groups after the intervention may be attributable to the active travel program (for an example of a quasi-experimental study, see Box 15.2).

Another example of a quasi-experimental design is a **factorial design**. In a factorial design, one variable is systematically varied and the other variable is examined at

Box 15.2 Example of a quasi-experimental design.

Poortinga, Whitmarsh, and Suffolk (2013) examined the effect of the introduction of a charge on single-use carrier bags in encouraging shoppers to use their own bags instead of disposable plastic ones. A quasi-experimental field study was conducted with two independent samples: one from Wales (where the charge was introduced) and one from England (where no charge existed). Telephone surveys were conducted among participants two weeks before the introduction of the charge and again six months after introduction of the charge.

The two samples were compared at pre-test and there appeared to be no systematic difference in bag use or in socio-demographic characteristics. Results indicate that following the introduction of the charge participants in the Wales sample were more likely to use their own bags (see Figure 15.5). In England, there was a slight increase in bag use, but this was not statistically significant. This study suggests that the introduction of the single-use carrier bag charge appeared to encourage shoppers to use their own bags.

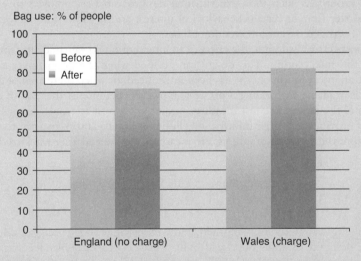

Figure 15.5 Changes in bag use (i.e., percentage of people bringing own bags) before and after introduction of the single-use carrier bag charge in Wales (Poortinga et al., 2013).

two or more levels. The advantage of this design is that it allows researchers to examine the independent and combined effects of an intervention on an outcome (Creswell, 2012). This design allows for the testing of interaction effects (see also Chapter 4).

For example, in our earlier energy conservation study, researchers may be interested in finding out whether the effectiveness of providing energy conservation advice in encouraging energy savings depends on people's levels of environmental concern. In this case, the intervention is either administered or not (information: yes or no) and participants are classified as being either high or low in environmental concern (concern: high or low). This is called a 2 x 2 factorial design: both variables have two levels of measurement or variation.

These researchers may well find that information about energy-saving tips has a stronger effect for people who have high levels of environmental concern, and that it does not seem very effective for people with lower levels of environmental concern. Factorial designs can be useful, because they provide insight into the boundary conditions of the effectiveness of interventions. In this case, based on these findings it would appear that information campaigns could be targeted differently to different people, depending on levels of environmental concern (for an example of a factorial design, see Box 15.3).

Non-experimental designs

Non-experimental designs can also be used to examine the effectiveness of interventions. These types of designs do not include random assignment, nor is there a control group. As such, non-experimental designs can be employed to examine changes over time in certain behaviors of interest and it allows for changes to be observed across different intervention phases.

In a post-test-only design, the effect of an intervention is evaluated after introduction of this intervention. This design can be used when the opportunity arises to evaluate an intervention once it has been introduced, or when there are not enough resources available to conduct a pre-test. However, because of the lack of control group and the lack of pre-test measure, studies using post-test-only designs generally only provide descriptive information (Fisher & Foreit, 2002). In a pre-test–post-test design, the variables of interest are measured before and after the introduction

Box 15.3   Example of a factorial design.

Schultz, Nolan, Cialdini, Goldstein, and Griskevicius (2007) used a 2 x 2 factorial design to examine the effect of the provision of social norm feedback on household energy use. Households were divided into two groups: those with energy use above or below the neighborhood usage. Then, households received descriptive norm feedback about how they were doing compared to this average. In addition, some households also received injunctive social norm feedback, conveying approval or disapproval of their energy usage.

Households who used less energy than average received a happy face on their feedback report, while households above the neighborhood average received a sad face. The use of a factorial design allowed the researchers to examine the effect of feedback for low and high energy users separately. When given descriptive norm feedback, high energy users decreased energy use, while low energy users increased usage (see Figure 15.6).

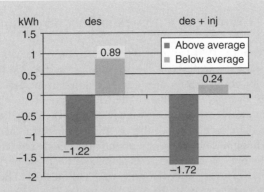

Figure 15.6 Changes in electricity use (in kWh) for the four feedback groups (based on data reported in Schultz et al., 2007). des = descriptive norm feedback, inj = injunctive norm feedback.

When given descriptive and injunctive norms feedback, high energy users saved energy, while low energy users did not appear to change their energy use much (the increase was not statistically significant). It would appear that the effect of normative feedback depends on whether energy use is above or below the neighborhood average.

	Pre-test measure of energy use	Time →	Post-test measure of energy use
Intervention group	No intervention	Information	No intervention

Figure 15.7 Example of a (hypothetical) pre-test-post-test non-experimental design to measure the effect of information to encourage energy conservation.

of an intervention (see Figure 15.7). This allows for changes to be monitored over time. This design is useful when it is not possible to assign participants to a control group. For example, imagine that a group of researchers is interested in the effectiveness of information to encourage household energy conservation, but they do not have sufficient resources to recruit households for a control group. In this case, the researchers could survey the same group of participants before and after the information provision to examine any changes in energy use over time (for an example of a non-experimental study, see Box 15.4).

One of the main advantages of non-experimental designs is that fewer participants are needed, because each participant serves as their own control. This also reduces the amount of variation that could exist between groups as a result of systematic differences between individuals before an intervention (e.g., one group already has

Box 15.4   Example of a non-experimental design.

Staats and colleagues (1996) examined the effectiveness of a nationwide media campaign to raise awareness of climate change in the Netherlands. The campaign ran for about 2.5 months and was aimed at increasing knowledge about climate change, with the underlying assumption that increased knowledge and awareness would encourage people to change behavior.

To examine the effectiveness of the campaign, the researchers used a pre-test–post-test design. They recruited about 900 Dutch residents who filled out a survey before the campaign was launched. Of those participants, 700 filled out the same survey after the campaign had finished. The survey measured people's awareness of global warming and willingness to engage in a number of pro-environmental behaviors.

After the campaign, knowledge of global warming was higher compared to pre-test. However, there was no difference in willingness to engage in pro-environmental behaviors after the campaign, compared to before the campaign. Based on the results of this study, it would appear that following the campaign, changes in knowledge were noted, but no changes in behavior were observed.

a higher awareness of climate change than another group). A disadvantage of non-experimental designs is that because of the lack of control group, it is difficult to tease out the influence of potential confounding variables that may have affected the intervention's effectiveness. In our hypothetical example, it may well be that while households were provided with energy-saving advice as part of this study, a nation-wide awareness campaign about energy conservation was also running. Because of the set up of the study, it would be difficult to conclude whether it was the provision of energy-saving advice, the awareness campaign, or a combination of both that affected energy conservation.

Threats to Validity

Let's return to our earlier question: How do we know that an intervention caused any observed changes in behavior? A number of factors can compromise one's ability to claim that the intervention resulted in changes in the outcome variable (i.e., internal validity). Here, a number of common threats to validity are discussed as well as the extent to which each research design deals with these threats (see Creswell, 2012, for a more detailed discussion of threats to validity).

History refers to events that occur between the pre-test and the post-test that may influence the outcome measure, independent of the intervention. For example, imagine that the researchers in the energy conservation study discussed earlier in the chapter discover that during their study on the effect of energy-saving advice on energy conservation, the government launched a national energy conservation awareness campaign. As this governmental campaign may have also affected energy conservation, the researchers would not be able to distinguish the effect of their intervention from that of the government campaign.

Maturation refers to the observation that participants themselves change (mature) while taking part in a study, especially when a study takes place over longer periods of time. Participants become older, wiser, more experienced, and this may result in changes that are independent of the intervention.

Selection occurs when the participants selected for the experimental group systematically differ from those in the control group prior to the start of the intervention. For example, let's assume that a study finds that the provision of information about climate change is effective in increasing awareness about climate change, compared to a control group. Now imagine that for some reason, participants in the information group had significantly higher levels of environmental concern compared to the control group to begin with. In this case, the effect of the information cannot be distinguished from the initial differences in the groups that were selected.

Mortality (or attrition) refers to the drop out of participants during the course of a study. This can be problematic when drop out of participants is selective, for example, there is a systematic difference between participants who drop out and participants who remain in the study. Let's return to the study that examines the effect of an active travel program to encourage walking and cycling to work. As it turns out, during the study a substantial number of participants drop out. A comparison between these groups reveals that especially those participants who never walked or cycled to work at pre-test dropped out of the study, while participants who were already walking or cycling to work remained in the study. This means that the sample of participants at post-test is different from the initial sample of participants at pre-test and this may affect the researchers' ability to attribute any changes in walking and cycling to the active travel program.

Testing refers to practice gained in filling out a survey. When participants fill out a pre-test survey, this may affect how they fill out the post-test survey. For example, if a survey is examining the effect of an information campaign on awareness about climate change, participants may do slightly better on post-test questions because they remember the questions or the answers from the pre-test. The increase in knowledge or awareness may simply be a result of practice gained on the pre-test. One way to address this issue is to ensure the time between pre-test and post-test is not too short, or to employ a post-test-only design.

Regression to the mean is a phenomenon that occurs when participants who score highly on a measure at pre-test have a tendency to score lower at post-test. In contrast, participants who score low on a pre-test tend to score more highly on a post-test. In other words, over time, participants tend to regress toward the mean. This could be an issue when researchers are interested in examining the effect of a intervention on participants with extreme scores on some measure (e.g., high environmental concern compared to those with low environmental concern). A possible solution would be to also include a group of participants who do not have very high scores on either side of the spectrum (e.g., average scores on environmental concern).

Diffusion of treatments may occur when the participants in the experimental and control group can communicate with one another. It can create a threat to internal validity when participants in the different groups learn what intervention the other groups are receiving. This could be a potential issue when the experimental and control groups are in close proximity, for example, when students in one campus residence receive an intervention, while students in another residence on the same campus do not. If students in the intervention group communicate about this intervention with students in the control group, this may influence the results. Where possible, it is important to try and separate the intervention and control groups so as to minimize the possibility for participants in different groups to learn about the intervention.

Resentful demoralization refers to the fact that participants in the control group may become resentful and demoralized when they realize they are not receiving any intervention, while others are receiving an intervention. One possible solution is to make use of a staggered intervention, whereby participants in the control group receive the intervention after the study is concluded.

The three different research designs are susceptible to different threats to validity (see also Creswell, 2012). Because of random assignment of participants, experimental designs largely control for threats to internal validity. If successful, randomization of participants means the groups are similar and this minimizes the possibility of history, maturation, and selection. When using a pre-test and post-test, testing may be a threat to validity in experimental designs. This could be minimized by using a post-test-only design. Diffusion of treatments and resentful demoralization are also possible in experimental studies, but procedures could be put in place to minimize contact between the experimental and control groups.

Quasi-experimental designs do not use random assignment and they are therefore more susceptible to the possibility of history, maturation, and selection. Selection may be addressed by examining any differences between the intervention and control groups at pre-test. Testing may also be a threat to validity in quasi-experimental designs, but this can be minimized when a post-test-only design is used. Diffusion of treatments and resentful demoralization are also possible threats to validity in quasi-experimental designs, but procedures could be put in place to minimize contact between the two groups.

Non-experimental studies are generally susceptible to the possibility of history and testing. History could be an issue when other events occur during the intervention period, which may affect the outcome measure. Because only one group is studied, selection is not relevant. Diffusion of treatments may be an issue if researchers use interventions sequentially and the use of one intervention may influence a subsequent intervention (Creswell, 2012). Resentful demoralization does not pose threats to validity in non-experimental designs, because each participant in the study receives the same interventions.

Practical Considerations

Conducting intervention research in field settings comes with its own challenges. Sometimes a trade-off needs to be made between what is desirable and what is feasible. In this concluding section, some guidelines are provided for conducting intervention research in applied settings.

1. Choosing a research design. Ultimately, the choice of research design will depend on the research question one wishes to answer. A non-experimental

design such as a pre-test–post-test design is suitable for answering research questions that aim to gain insight into changes over time (within a group of individuals or a geographical location), because this design allows changes to be observed across different intervention phases. A quasi-experimental design is appropriate for research questions that focus on examining the effectiveness of one or more interventions compared to a no-treatment control group. It can be used when there is no opportunity to randomly assign participants to groups. While experimental designs would be the preferred option in view of their ability to deal with threats to internal validity, in applied settings, this is not always feasible.

2. Choosing outcome measures. Ideally, intervention studies examine multiple outcome measures, such as behaviors, attitudes, and awareness. These outcome measures can be collected through observation (e.g., electricity meter readings) or via surveys (e.g., self-reported energy-saving behaviors). It is important to select outcome measures that are reliable and valid, that is, measures that have good construct validity. It is also important to assess the outcome measure with precision. For example, to assess whether employees have started walking to work as a result of an active travel program, a question like "did you walk to work in the past week?" only gives information about whether or not people walked to work, not how often they did so. In this case, it might be more useful to ask "for each day of the past week, indicate which travel mode you used for traveling to and from work." That way, the researcher can assess changes in walking as well as changes in other travel modes as a result of the intervention. When using pre-test and post-test questions, it is important to be aware of the potential for testing effects to occur, that is, that participants score better on the post-test because they have become familiar with the survey questions. Testing is usually less of a problem when a longer time period has elapsed between pre-test and post-test. It is also important to include any known covariates that may affect the influence of the intervention (e.g., gender, environmental concern).

3. Recruiting participants. Recruitment of participants in intervention studies can occur in a number of different ways. The location of the research will in part inform how recruitment will take place. Participants may be recruited via random sampling (e.g., letters of invitation sent to randomly selected addresses). Another approach is recruitment through convenience sampling, whereby existing address lists or existing networks are used. Recruitment and retention of participants can be time consuming. Some participants will drop out during the course of an intervention study, that is, between pre-test and post-test. In that case, it is important to examine this mortality and compare the participants who remained in the study and those who dropped out, to examine any systematic differences between the two. If there are differences, this may affect one's ability to draw firm conclusions about the effectiveness of an intervention.

4. Analyzing and interpreting the results. There are different analytical tools to examine differences between groups statistically (e.g., t-tests, ANOVA, ANCOVA, repeated measures analysis). A discussion of each of these falls beyond the scope of this chapter (see for example, Field, 2013). An important

thing to bear in mind when interpreting the findings is that the chosen research design will guide one's ability to infer causality. Here, it would also be important to include any known covariates that may influence the findings. Ultimately, it is important to rule out alternative explanations that may account for the findings.

Summary and Conclusion

In environmental psychology, intervention research focuses on evaluating the effectiveness of interventions to encourage pro-environmental behaviors. It is important to gather empirical evidence regarding the extent to which interventions such as information provision, online pledges, and active travel programs are effective in encouraging the desired behavior changes. Intervention researchers use experimental design, quasi-experimental designs, and non-experimental designs to assess whether an intervention has been effective in encouraging behavior change.

Let's return to Ethan's Meatless Monday project. In an experimental study, Ethan would randomly assign participants to a control group (who do not sign a pledge) and an experimental group (who do sign a pledge). The treatment manipulation (pledge, no pledge) and the random assignment is a powerful combination to help Ethan establish the causal effect of signing an online pledge in reducing meat consumption. Because of these two features, experimental studies have a high internal validity, that is, the ability to infer cause and effect. However, in field settings random assignment is not always feasible. The pledge in Ethan's example is a voluntary initiative, which could make random assignment of people to a pledge group rather difficult. In that case, Ethan can employ a quasi-experimental design. While quasi-experimental studies do not include random assignment, the researcher still has a substantial amount of control over the treatment manipulation and outcome variables (the inclusion of covariates for example). Ethan could also employ a non-experimental design and examine meat consumption before and after people sign the Meatless Monday pledge. This design has the advantage that Ethan can recruit fewer participants and it allows him to monitor changes over time. However, non-experimental designs are vulnerable to threats to validity such as history and testing. In field settings, sometimes trade-offs need to be made between what is desirable from a research design point of view and what is feasible.

Glossary

Experimental design   A research design characterized by random assignment of participants to groups and systematic variation of the treatment (intervention).

Diffusion of treatments   Occurs when the participants in the experimental and control group learn which intervention the other groups are receiving.

Factorial design   A research design in which one variable is systematically varied and the other variable is examined at two or more levels.

History   Refers to events that occur between pre-test and post-test that may influence behavior, independent of the intervention.

Maturation Participants become older, wiser, more experienced (i.e., they mature) and this may result in changes that are independent of the intervention.

Mortality (or attrition) Refers to drop out of participants; this can be problematic when drop out of participants is selective.

Multiple treatment design A research design that includes more than one treatment group in order to assess the effect of more than one intervention or the effect of a combination of interventions.

Non-experimental design A research design suitable for monitoring changes over time; there is no random assignment of participants and no systematic variation of a treatment.

Post-test measure Provides a measure of the levels of engagement in behavior after the intervention has taken place.

Pre-test–post-test control group design A type of experimental design whereby participants are randomly assigned to either a treatment or a control group and measurements of behavior take place before and after the intervention

Pre-test–post-test design A type of non-experimental research design in which variables of interest are measured before and after the introduction of an intervention, allowing for changes to be monitored over time.

Pre-test measure Provides a measure of the levels of engagement in behavior before any intervention has taken place.

Quasi-experimental design A research design whereby a treatment is systematically varied, but there is no random assignment of participants.

Randomized experiment A type of study that uses a true experimental design; considered the gold standard for demonstrating causality.

Regression to the mean A phenomenon that occurs when participants who score highly on a measure at pre-test have a tendency to score lower at post-test and participants who score low on a pre-test to score more highly on a post-test.

Resentful demoralization The observation that participants in the control group may become resentful and demoralized when they realize they are not receiving any intervention, while others are receiving an intervention.

Testing The observation that participants may do better in the post-test survey because they have gained practice in filling out the survey during the pre-test.

Treatment group In intervention research, this refers to the group of participants who received the treatment, or intervention (e.g. information).

Selection Occurs when participants selected for the treatment group differ systematically from those in the control group prior to the start of the intervention.

References

Bamberg, S. (2006). Is a residential relocation a good opportunity to change people's travel behavior? Results from a theory-driven intervention study. *Environment and Behavior*, *38*, 820–840.

Carrico, A. R., & Riemer, M. (2011). Motivating energy conservation in the workplace: An evaluation of the use of group-level feedback and peer education. *Journal of Environmental Psychology*, *31*, 1–13.

Campbell, D. T., & Stanley, J. C. (1963). *Experimental and quasi-experimental designs for research*. Chicago, IL: Rand McNally.

Creswell, J. W. (2012). *Educational research: Planning, conducting, and evaluating quantitative and qualitative research* (4th ed.). Boston, MA: Pearson.

Field, A. (2013). *Discovering statistics using IBM SPSS statistics*. London, UK: Sage.

Fisher, A., & Foreit, J. (2002). *Designing HIV/AIDS intervention studies: An operations research handbook*. Washington, DC: Population Council.

Poortinga, W., Whitmarsh, L., & Suffolk, C. (2013). The introduction of a single-use carrier bag charge in Wales: Attitude change and behavioral spillover effects. *Journal of Environmental Psychology, 36*, 240–247.

Schultz, P. W., Nolan, J. M., Cialdini, R. B., Goldstein, N. J., & Griskevicius, V. (2007). The constructive, destructive, and reconstructive power of social norms. *Psychological Science, 18*(5), 429–434.

Shadish, W. R., Cook, T. D., & Campbell, D. T. (2002). *Experimental and quasi-experimental designs for generalized causal inference*. Boston, MA: Houghton Mifflin.

Staats, H. J., Wit, A. P., & Midden, C. Y. H. (1999). Communicating the greenhouse effect to the public: Evaluation of a mass media campaign from a social dilemma perspective. *Journal of Environmental Management, 46*, 189–203.

Suggested Readings

Creswell, J. W. (2012). *Educational research: Planning, conducting, and evaluating quantitative and qualitative research* (4th ed.) Boston, MA: Pearson.

Shadish, W. R., Cook, T. D., & Campbell, D. T. (2002). *Experimental and quasi-experimental designs for generalized causal inference*. Boston, MA: Houghton Mifflin.

16

Applying Behavioral Science for Environmental Sustainability

E. Scott Geller[1], Wokje Abrahamse[2], Branda Guan[3], and Reuven Sussman[3]

[1] Virginia Polytechnic Institute and State University, VA, United States
[2] Victoria University of Wellington, New Zealand
[3] University of Victoria, BC, Canada

Gabriel has just come home from his monthly meeting with the campus sustainability committee. He's a little grumpy. He does not like meetings, especially those that seem to go on and on without defining a meaningful action plan. But one of the issues raised at the meeting intrigued him. "How can we reduce the excessive amount of water students use, especially when taking showers?", asks Gabriel. The committee seemed divided about what the most effective approach would be.

"Hmm, I don't know," replies Ethan, "Maybe some signs would help, asking students to save water." "I don't think signs are going to help much," Maria responds. "After a while you just don't notice them anymore. Besides, what if students don't know how to save water? What about a penalty for using more than a certain amount of water? Or, better yet, could we give students some kind of reward if they reduce water consumption?"

"But how would you know which technique would be more effective: a sign or an incentive?", Gabriel asks. "What if one group of students gets a 'save water' sign, another group of students receives an incentive, and a third group gets no water-saving intervention?", Ethan proposes. "And then you assess whether the groups are different in how much water they use." "I guess so … But, if the signs are on campus, everybody can see them."

"How about we first measure the amount of water used per residence hall, then we put up signs, and a little while later we add the incentive and then later we take away the incentive intervention to see if water usage returns to baseline," Ethan responds. "You record the water-meter results per each residence hall, and see if it changes when the conditions change." "I like it, Ethan," Gabriel says, "Actually, I was thinking… would you like to present your idea to the ERB committee? Maybe you could go to the next meeting instead of me?"

Research Methods for Environmental Psychology, First Edition. Edited by Robert Gifford.
© 2016 John Wiley & Sons, Ltd. Published 2016 by John Wiley & Sons, Ltd.

Much applied behavioral science research addresses societal problems. Environmental issues, such as the growing impact of climate change and the gradual decline of many of the earth's ecosystems are examples of these problems. Humans play a pivotal role in both the cause and the solution to most environmental issues. Intervention research in environmental psychology focuses on increasing the frequency of environmentally responsible behavior (ERB), and decreasing the occurrence of environmentally harmful behavior (EHB). But how effective is a particular intervention approach? What works well, what doesn't influence a target behavior, and how can an intervention be changed to be more effective?

In this chapter, we first provide a brief overview of the most common interventions used to promote ERB and discourage EHB. Then we outline two main research designs employed by researchers to evaluate the effectiveness of an intervention, namely a within-subjects design and a between-subjects design (for related chapters on research designs see Chapter 1; for survey research see Chapter 5). We highlight advantages and disadvantages of each design, and then discuss some general issues in conducting intervention-based research, including issues related to intervention planning and implementation.

Behavior Change: Antecedents and Consequences

How can householders be encouraged to reduce their energy consumption? How can commuters be influenced to travel to work on public transport instead of in their personal vehicles? A practical problem-solving approach to answering these critical environmental sustainability questions is called applied behavior analysis or applied behavioral science. **Applied behavioral science** (ABS) is an approach to intervention development and evaluation initially conceptualized and researched by B. F. Skinner (Geller, 2008, 2014a; Lehman & Geller, 2008). According to Skinner, people engage in behavior to gain positive or pleasant consequences and to avoid negative or unpleasant consequences (Skinner, 1974).

In other words, people do things because of the consequences following their actions. For example, people may commute to work by car instead of the train because it gives them flexibility and a sense of personal control or freedom. Applied behavioral scientists focus on the use of positive rather than negative consequences to encourage behavior change (see Geller, 2002, 2008, 2014a).

With ABS, the development of a behavior-change intervention begins with defining an observable behavior to target (e.g., how people commute to work: personal vehicle vs. mass transit); then by considering the motivating consequences for the EHB mode of travel (e.g., convenience, personal control, cost), and then developing an intervention that provides positive consequences for commuting that reflects ERB (e.g., provide commuters with a free voucher to try out public transit for a week).

The assumption here is that people will choose public transit if the positive consequences (i.e., saving money) outweigh the negative consequences (e.g., inconvenience and loss of personal control). After a week of using public transport, it's hoped some natural consequences will support the ERB choice. For example, some participants might find public transit more convenient and comfortable than expected; some might experience advantages in having an opportunity to read or review papers for work; or others might develop a social connection with other users of mass transit.

While consequences motivate behavior, activators direct behavior. More specifically, **activators** or behavioral antecedents are stimuli in the environment that tell people what to do, and sometimes point out the availability of a reward or positive consequence or a penalty or negative consequence if the target behavior is performed. **Incentives** specify a reward (e.g., a lottery coupon per each reusable bag for groceries), whereas **disincentives** indicate a penalty for designated behavior (e.g., $100 fine for littering). These behavior-change interventions reflect the sequence of Activator – Behavior – Consequence, referred to as the ABC model. This model is the foundation for many interventions designed and implemented to encourage ERB or discourage EHB (Bolderdijk, Lehman, & Geller, 2013).

In line with the distinction between activators and consequences, behavior-change interventions are generally classified as either activator or consequence interventions (Geller, 2014a; Lehman & Geller, 2008). Activators provide knowledge or awareness, and are incentives or disincentives if they indicate a behavioral consequence. For instance, providing householders with information about the financial savings (incentive) or financial costs (disincentive) of certain energy-use behaviors will likely have more impact than an activator that does not specify consequences for performing the target behavior (Geller, Winett, & Everett, 1982).

Consequence interventions influence ERB by providing a positive consequence contingent on the occurrence of a desired target behavior. For instance, giving householders a lottery coupon for correctly classifying their recyclables as paper, glass, or plastic may encourage them to continue such recycling behavior in order to receive another chance to win the lottery. In this section, we provide a brief overview of the most commonly used interventions developed to promote ERB and discourage EHB. (For more extensive reviews of the behavior-focused intervention literature, see Abrahamse & Steg, 2013; Abrahamse, Steg, Vlek, & Rothengatter, 2005: Dwyer, Leeming, Cobern, & Porter, 1993; Geller, Winett, & Everett, 1982; Lehman & Geller, 2004; Lokhorst, Werner, Staats, van Dijk, & Gale, 2013; Schultz, Oskamp, & Mainieri, 1995.)

Activator interventions

A number of ERB intervention strategies are classified as activator strategies. These include information, prompts, goal setting, modeling, and behavioral commitment.

Information provision serves to inform people about the importance and the benefits of engaging in certain ERBs. Examples of these are information campaigns and workshops. However, information alone is often not very effective at encouraging behavior change, especially when the target behavior is inconvenient to perform (Abrahamse et al., 2005; Geller, 1992; Staats, Midden, & Wit, 1999). Information is more effective when it is **tailored** for the target group in question (e.g., Abrahamse, Steg, Vlek, & Rothengatter, 2007; Daamen, Staats, Wilke, & Engelen, 2000). Also, the use of social influence can improve the impact of information provision.

Social influence occurs when behaviors are influenced by the behavior of others (Cialdini, 2001). For example, information delivered by **block leaders** (or ERB champions) can be an effective approach to increase the occurrence of ERB (Hopper & Nielsen, 1991). Furthermore, the behavioral influence of information is enhanced when it refers to **social norms** by making it salient that other people are performing the desired behavior (e.g., "A majority of your colleagues are using public transport to get to work"; Goldstein, Cialdini, & Griskevicius, 2008; Schultz, Nolan, Cialdini, Goldstein, & Griskevicius, 2007).

Verbal and written **prompts** inform people of a desired behavior in a particular setting. For example, a "Do not litter" sign in a park, or a "Please switch off" sticker above a light switch in a classroom activates people to engage in these ERBs. Prompts are most effective when they are given in close proximity to the designated target behavior and this target is easy to perform (Abrahamse & Matthies, 2013; Geller et al., 1982).

Goal setting provides participants with a target to hit. It's assumed people will be motivated to change their behavior when they have a particular reference point to work toward, such as an energy-saving goal of 10% (an *outcome goal*), or a goal to take the bus to work three times a week (a process or *behavioral goal*). Goal setting is often used in combination with other interventions, such as behavioral commitment and feedback (Becker, 1978).

The most effective goals are SMARTS, for Specific, Motivational, Achievable, Relevant, Trackable, and Shared (Geller, 2014b). More specifically, the goal should: (1) *specify* the target ERB frequency or sustainability outcome to accomplish within a certain time; (2) indicate natural or extrinsic *motivational* consequences obtained when the goal is attained; (3) be perceived as *achievable* by the participant(s); (4) be viewed as *relevant* for environmental sustainability; (5) specify a scheme for measuring and *tracking* the target ERB en route to achieving the goal; and (6) be *shared* with relevant others for social support.

Modeling employs other people (i.e., "models") to demonstrate the desired behaviors to an audience. Sometimes a positive consequence following the target behavior is shown. It's hoped the example will be followed when the target behavior is understandable, relevant, meaningful, and rewarding to those viewing the modeled ERB (e.g., Winett, Leckliter, Chinn, Stahl, & Love, 1985; see Box 16.1).

Another activator is behavioral **commitment**, which involves asking for a formal agreement to perform a particular behavior. Behavioral commitments are most influential when they are public, active, and voluntary (Cialdini, 2001). For example, volunteering to sign a petition (active) in front of a peer group (public) to start conserving electricity, evokes a sense of personal obligation to fulfill the commitment (Pallak & Cummings, 1976; see Lokhorst et al., 2013 for a meta-analysis of commitment strategies to increase the frequency of ERBs).

Consequence strategies

Two consequence interventions are typically used to increase the frequency of ERB: rewards and feedback.

Rewards are introduced following desirable ERBs to encourage their recurrence. Rewards can be very effective at encouraging the performance of ERBs (Bolderdijk et al., 2013), but the effects tend to be short-lived. When the reward is removed, the frequency of the rewarded behavior typically decreases (Abrahamse et al., 2005), unless intrinsic (or natural) consequences support the behavior and/or certain psychological states or expectancies affect the propensity for participants to actively care for the environment (Geller, 1995, 2002).

Feedback informs individuals of the consequences of their behavior, enabling them to recognize the benefits of desirable behavior or the liabilities of undesirable behavior. *Supportive feedback* acknowledges the occurrence of an ERB and may influence recurrence of this desirable behavior. In contrast, *corrective feedback* designates the occurrence of an EHB and aims to decrease the frequency of this undesirable behavior. For example, the provision of feedback about energy use supports relevant ERB when it displays energy savings, but it's corrective for relevant EHB when it shows an increase in financial cost. Behavioral feedback is particularly effective at encouraging behavior change when it is soon, certain, and frequent (Abrahamse et al., 2005; Geller, 2002).

Evaluating the Effectiveness of Interventions

Now let's consider ways to assess the impact of interventions to encourage ERBs. We first describe two research designs that have been used to test the effectiveness of behavior-focused intervention. Afterwards, we outline some basic principles of intervention research, including issues related to **intervention planning** and implementation, as well as evaluating the long-term impact of an intervention.

Research designs to evaluate intervention impact

Interventions to encourage ERB aim to save environmental resources, and improve and sustain environmental quality. Therefore, it's important to demonstrate empirically the extent to which an intervention designed to increase the frequency of ERB or decrease the occurrence of EHB meets this aim. The effectiveness of an intervention is usually evaluated with a field study that assesses systematically the extent to which a particular intervention results in desirable changes in the target behavior or in the outcome of one or more behaviors.

Generally, two types of research designs are used to assess the behavioral impact of an intervention. In a **within-subjects design**, every participant contributes to every phase, including the baseline or no-intervention phase. For this type of design, the effectiveness of an intervention is assessed by monitoring changes in behavior over consecutive observation sessions during baseline, intervention, and post-intervention withdrawal phases among the same participants (or the same location, such as a neighborhood). Imagine, for example, a group of researchers uses a within-subjects design to determine whether information provision and financial incentives increase the use of public transport from suburbs into the city center. Thus, they recruit participants in one of the city's suburbs and systematically observe their public transport use for days before, during, and after the intervention.

After establishing a baseline measure of the number of participants using public transport, the researchers administer the information and incentive interventions in sequence. First, they give participants information about public transport routes, followed by a period of no intervention. Then, they give the same participants an incentive to use public transportation (e.g., a voucher to try out public transit for a week). After discontinuing the incentive phase, the researchers keep monitoring public transport use during a post-intervention follow-up phase (see Figure 16.1).

Figure 16.1 Example of a hypothetical within-subjects design used to assess the independent impact of information and an incentive on the use of public transport (Hopper & Nielsen, 1991).

One of the major advantages of within-subject designs is that relatively few participants are needed, as each participant serves as its own control. This reduces the amount of variation that may occur from individual differences (e.g., age, gender, socio-economic status, education). One of the disadvantages of within-subjects designs are **carry-over effects** which generally refer to the possibility that taking one test may influence performance on the next test (e.g., improved results because of practice or impaired results because of fatigue or boredom).

For intervention researchers, carry-over effects imply that exposure to the first intervention may have influenced effects of the subsequent intervention. For example, in our hypothetical example, participants first receive information about public transport routes, followed by an incentive. So when participants receive the free voucher, they may be likely to try out public transport because they had been informed by the activator: the information provision.

This design makes it difficult to evaluate the independent effect of each intervention (i.e., information vs. incentive). **Counterbalancing** is one way to address this issue. Specifically, one group of participants receives information first, followed by incentives, and a second group first receives incentives, followed by information. But, of course, other factors could influence the number of participants using the transport system. For example, it may well be that some public transport users experience delays because of network upgrades, which may affect their subsequent transportation decisions. Or perhaps the rail network ran a promotional campaign of its own, making it difficult to attribute any observed increases in public transit use to the researchers' intervention.

A **between-subjects design** examines the effect of an intervention by randomly assigning participants to one or more intervention groups and a control group, and thereby addresses some of the disadvantages of a within-subjects design. In a between-subjects study, participants are either part of a treatment group (receiving the intervention) or part of a control group (not exposed to the intervention). In contrast to within-subjects studies, participants experience only one intervention condition or no intervention (i.e., the control group).

In a **longitudinal study**, the ERB, EHB, or a relevant outcome measure is assessed at two or more time points. Longitudinal designs are among the most powerful designs available because they evaluate long-term behavioral impact of an intervention, but they are also the most costly and cumbersome to implement.

Let's return to our hypothetical public transport study. For a between-subjects design, the research team could select three suburbs of the same city. The researchers would then assign residents living in one suburb to the control group; these participants would not receive information or incentives. Residents in a second suburb would receive information about public transport routes, and residents of a third suburb (i.e., the reward group) would receive a free transit voucher.

Box 16.1 Example of a within-subjects design.

Sussman and colleagues (2013) examined the effectiveness of prompts and modeling to encourage food composting in a university setting. They used a within-subjects design, whereby the interventions were sequentially introduced in the same university cafeteria. During a period of five weeks, the use of composting bins in the cafeteria was monitored by trained observers who checked the percentage of appropriate composting behavior.

In Week 1, baseline measures of composting behavior were taken and no intervention was implemented. In Week 2, signs encouraging composting were placed on all tables in the cafeteria as well as near the composting bins. In Week 3, modeling (see below) was introduced. One model demonstrated appropriate trash separation by composting ahead of the patron. In Week 4, two models demonstrated appropriate trash separation. In Week 5, the models were no longer present and only the signs remained in place. The results indicate that composting increased significantly from baseline when the signs were introduced (see Figure 16.2). There was no significant change when the model was introduced. When two models were used to demonstrate composting, composting significantly increased again.

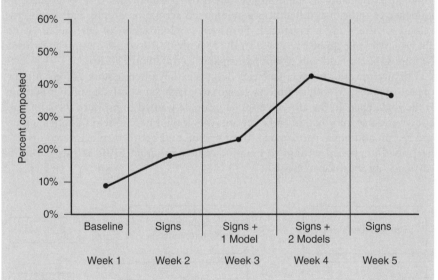

Figure 16.2 Percentage of patrons who composted during each phase of the study (Sussman et al., 2013).

The researchers would then monitor public transport use among participants from these three suburbs before and after the intervention. Hence, changes in public transport use between the control group and the other two suburbs may be attributable to the interventions. Of course, it's not possible to rule out completely that factors other than the intervention may influence the use of public transport (e.g., prolonged delays, weather conditions, gasoline costs). However, the inclusion of a control group enables more confidence that changes between groups can be attributable to the intervention.

With a between-subjects design, more than one intervention can be tested simultaneously, as well as combinations of intervention components. For example, researchers could evaluate the combined effect of providing both information and an incentive by adding a fourth suburb that receives both information and an incentive. This design allows for a comparison of the separate effects of various intervention strategies, because each participant receives only one intervention at a given time (see Figure 16.3).

It's important to ensure that prior to implementation of the intervention, the control group and intervention groups are not too different from each other on the ERB or EHB of interest (e.g., one group is not already using public transit significantly more than the other groups prior to the study) or on some other relevant characteristic (e.g., socio-demographic characteristics). This can be addressed by randomly assigning participants to the intervention groups and the control group (for more on randomization, see Chapter 3). This is called a randomized controlled trial (RCT), which is considered the "gold standard" for assessing the effectiveness of an intervention (for an example see Howden-Chapman et al., 2008).

When participants are randomly assigned to treatment and control groups, the influence of individual differences is minimized across the groups and the internal validity of the study is enhanced. However, randomization of participants is not always feasible in applied settings. In the hypothetical study, for example, it would be impossible to randomly assign participants to the suburb groups.

A disadvantage of between-subjects designs is they often require a larger number of participants than within-subjects designs to enable statistically significant findings. If the researchers in the aforementioned example wanted to measure the combined effectiveness of information and a reward, they would have to select another suburb and recruit additional participants. Both within- and between-subjects designs have been used in applied settings to examine change in target ERBs as a function of a particular intervention strategy.

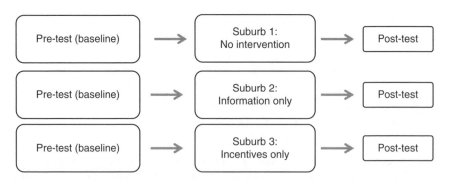

Figure 16.3 Example of a (hypothetical) between-subjects design to examine the relative effectiveness of information and a reward on use of public transportation.

Ultimately, the choice of a research design depends on the empirical question addressed. A within-subjects design can evaluate the variation of behavior over time within a group of individuals, because this design allows the behavior of the same individuals to be tracked across different intervention phases. A between-subjects design is more appropriate for examining differential behavioral effects of one or more intervention procedures as compared with a no-treatment control group.

Box 16.2   Example of a between-subjects design.

Hopper and Nielsen (1991) used the block-leader approach to promote participation in a community-wide recycling program. The block-leader approach involves the recruitment of volunteers to act as opinion leaders to encourage the adoption of a certain ERB. Participating households were given information about recycling and reminders about recycling pick-up dates. For one group of households, information and reminders were delivered in person by block leaders. For a second group, the information and reminders were delivered by the researchers. A third group of households received only an informational leaflet. Recycling was measured over a period of seven months by observing whether or not households had put out their recycling bin.

Both behavior and social norms were measured before and after implementation of the block-leader approach. Compared to information and prompts, the block-leader approach was the most effective at encouraging recycling. Moreover, social norms related to recycling were more strongly endorsed by householders who had been exposed to the block-leader approach, presumably because block leaders were part of the same neighborhood in which recycling was encouraged. As depicted in Figure 16.4, block leaders had the most impact on the ERB; but compared to the no-intervention control group, prompts and information were also influential.

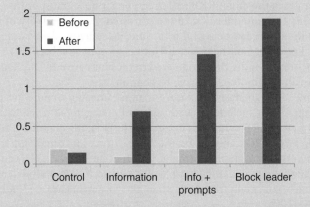

Figure 16.4   The average number of times participants recycled before and after implementation of the intervention as a function of the intervention group (Hopper & Nielsen, 1991).

Measurement

Once an appropriate research design is chosen, a method for measuring the dependent variable(s) is determined. Most intervention studies include an assessment of the dependent variable(s) before and after implementation of the intervention. Assessment before the intervention provides information about the current quantity and/or quality of the target ERB(s) or outcome of an ERB (e.g., electricity or water usage). This is called a **baseline measure**. Measurement after implementation of the intervention, considered a post-test measure, provides information about any changes in the target ERB(s) or outcome(s) of the ERB(s).

Sometimes, follow-up measures are included, which assess behavior change when the intervention is discontinued. As indicated above, periodic assessments over an extended period of time are considered longitudinal studies (Abrahamse et al., 2005; Dwyer et al., 1993), providing insight into the long-term effectiveness of an intervention. Unfortunately, follow-up measurements over long periods of time are rare because of response cost and limited resources, as well as attrition or drop out of participants. However, longitudinal studies are critical to assessing whether the behavioral impact of an intervention is durable or maintained.

Researchers often use a survey to measure some dependent variables, such as attitudes, awareness, and intentions; ERBs are observed in field settings, such as recycling (see Box 16.1; and Chapter 4), carrying groceries in reusable bags, riding mass transit, depositing food waste in a composting bin, or picking up litter. Often the impact of a behavior-change intervention is assessed by measuring the outcome of ERB (e.g., by weighing recycled materials, reading electricity or water meters, counting the litter collected). When ERB or the outcome of ERB cannot be observed directly, researchers rely on self-reported ERB on a survey. For example, a survey might ask participants how often they commute to work by public transport, or what items they recycle and how often. Surveys are necessarily used to assess ERB-related attitudes and awareness (see Chapter 5).

To evaluate the effectiveness of a behavior-focused intervention, it's critical to measure changes in the target ERB (e.g., recycling, public transport use, energy use) over time. This gives an indication of the consistency and durability of intervention impact. In addition, it can be useful to include an analysis of the context, from the participants' knowledge of the target ERB to environmental barriers (e.g., inconvenience or discomfort of the ERB compared to the alternative EHB). This can inform the development of a more effective intervention.

For example, an evaluation of an information campaign to raise awareness about climate change might include an assessment of engagement in climate mitigation behaviors as well as ERB awareness before and after an information campaign (e.g., Staats et al., 1999). It may well be that an information campaign is effective at raising awareness about global warming, but does not result in relevant changes in ERB. Such findings would suggest information alone is not sufficient to change behavior, which is actually the case when the target behavior is not convenient (Geller, 1992, 2002).

As another example, let's assume the group of researchers in our earlier example found the reward was not sufficient to increase the use of public transport among the participants. Then the comparative use of mass transit during baseline vs.

intervention phases would provide no information relevant to designing a more effective intervention. It may be some people consider use of public transport use to be a low-class means of travel and is actually demeaning. Or perhaps some potential participants fear an assault or robbery when using the mass transport system. A survey implemented before and after an intervention could explore the potential barriers to use of public transport, and determines if a negative opinion or attitude about this ERB improves after the intervention (see Box 16.2).

Planning and Implementing an Intervention

Obviously, an intervention designed to influence ERB needs to be carefully planned before implementation (Geller, 2002; Steg & Vlek, 2007). An acronym that defines the application of behavioral science to increase the frequency or improve the quality of ERB is DO IT, for the four sequential processes of Define, Observe, Intervene, and Test (Geller, 2002, 2008). When developing a behavior-change intervention, it's important to define precisely the ERB or the EHB outcome one wishes to change. Researchers may be interested in encouraging electricity conservation among households and thus monitor the electric meters of particular households over time. Or, the intervention might focus on the efficient use of certain electronic appliances. Residents could be asked about their use of these appliances via a survey and/or the actual electricity use of certain appliances could be monitored directly as an outcome of relevant ERB.

It's also important to specify the target group for the intervention, such as house-holders, employees, or students. Why? Because the impact of a particular intervention can be influenced dramatically by dispositions of the participants, as well as the target ERB (see Abrahamse & Steg, 2013). If the intervention is aimed at individual households, information or feedback may be useful. Alternatively, if the intervention targets a group of householders in the same neighborhood, researchers may want to consider using a social influence techniques. Thus, it's important to define both the target ERB and the target participants, as this will guide the choice of intervention technique and the method for testing intervention impact.

Further, intervention programs are more effective when they address specific barriers to the relevant ERB. It's recommended to first identify those barriers to performing the target ERB and then design an intervention program that removes or minimizes these barriers (McKenzie-Mohr, 2000). Barriers vary as a function of the targeted individuals and the target ERB. Hence, the planning phase should include a careful examination of the ERB barriers to change. Research suggests that a combination of intervention techniques is generally more effective than a single intervention process, because various intervention components can address multiple ERB barriers to remove or minimize (Abrahamse et al., 2005; Gardner & Stern, 2002).

Finally, it's important to consider environmental problems and solutions from an interdisciplinary perspective. In particular, interventions to encourage the performance of a particular EBR could draw from a variety of relevant academic disciplines, such as sociology, environmental sciences, and geography. For example, which type of grocery bag is really more detrimental to the environment: paper or plastic? Environmental

Box 16.3   Example of an interdisciplinary study.

A study by Abrahamse and colleagues (2007) examined the effects of tailored information, goal setting, and feedback to encourage energy conservation. For this interdisciplinary study, households were provided with customized information about energy-saving techniques via a website. The interdisciplinary team consisted of environmental psychologists, environmental scientists, and computer engineers. The environmental psychologists selected a combination of intervention components, and developed a survey to assess the effectiveness of the intervention.

The environmental scientists developed a tool that calculated energy savings associated with the adoption of certain energy-saving measures per each individual household. In this way, households only received energy-saving options relevant for them (i.e., tailored information, see above). The computer engineers developed a website through which the customized energy-saving advice was communicated to individual households.

Households were randomly assigned to one of three groups in a between-subjects design. For one group, households received a combination of information, goal setting, and individual feedback about their energy savings. Households in a second group received the same combination of interventions, as well as group feedback that revealed the energy savings of all participating households. A control group did not receive any of these interventions. After five months, households exposed to the combination of interventions had saved more energy than the control group, but no differences emerged between the two intervention groups.

sciences can help provide insight into the environmental impact of different ERBs, such as comparing the carbon footprint of different travel modes.

Ideally, interventions should target ERBs with relatively high environmental impact (Gardner & Stern, 2002). Environmental scientists could help indicate which ERBs should be the target of an intervention process, and behavioral scientists can help indicate which intervention approach would likely have the most long-term and cost-effective impact on a particular ERB within a particular context and under designated circumstances or contingencies. Thus, it seems an interdisciplinary approach will optimize the cost-effectiveness and the environmental benefits of a plan to target the occurrence of a certain ERB and/or EHB. Actually, interdisciplinary studies are increasingly being used to evaluate the effectiveness of interventions (e.g., Matthies, Kastner, Klesse, & Wagner, 2011; see also Box 16.3).

Summary and Conclusion

In environmental psychology, intervention research focuses on evaluating the impact of interventions designed to encourage the performance of ERB rather than EHB. Empirical evidence regarding ERB impact of various intervention components such as information provision, commitment, and feedback informs the development and application of increasingly more cost-effective interventions. Intervention researchers use within-subjects designs and between-subjects designs to assess the effectiveness of an intervention program. With a within-subjects design, researchers monitor changes in behavior over time among the same group of participants. Fewer participants are needed in a within-subjects design, because all participants contribute to each phase of the study.

For a between-subjects design, participants are randomly assigned to different groups, allowing researchers to compare the effectiveness of different intervention strategies with a no-intervention control group. Generally, more participants are needed for between-subjects designs. Interventions need to be carefully planned before they are implemented.

It's also important to assess the effectiveness of interventions in terms of changes in behavioral antecedents, such as attitudes and social norms, as well as changes in actual behavior. The assessment of long-term effects is important in this respect. Finally, environmental problems are multi-faceted in nature. Insights from different disciplines should be used to inform the planning and implementation of interventions to encourage long-term behavior change.

Glossary

Activators Environmental stimuli that direct behavior and sometimes announce the availability of a consequence.

Applied behavioral science An intervention approach that targets observable behaviors and alters activators and/or consequences to encourage behavior change.

Attrition: Drop out of participants, which may affect the findings, particularly common in longitudinal studies.

Baseline measure A measure of the levels of engagement in the target behavior before any intervention has taken place.

Between-subjects design A design used to examine the effect of an intervention by assigning participants to one or more intervention groups or a control group.

Block-leader approach An approach whereby volunteers are recruited and asked to talk to members of their community about environmental issues and/or encourage them to start engaging in specific behaviors.

Carry-over effects The observation that taking one test may influence performance on the next one (e.g., improved results because of practice or impaired results because of fatigue or boredom).

Commitment A technique whereby individuals or groups are asked to sign a pledge (commitment) to change their behavior, often connected to a specific goal.

Counterbalancing A technique to address the issue of carry-over effects by including a group of participants who receive the intervention components in reverse order.

Disincentive An activator that announces a penalty following a designated behavior.

Feedback An intervention that gives people information about their performance (usually in relation to a behavioral or outcome goal), and thereby makes the consequence(s) of a certain behavior salient.

Goal setting   An intervention that establishes clear performance targets, often combined with feedback or commitment.

Incentive   An activator that announces the availability of a reward following a certain behavior.

Intervention planning   The process of selecting interventions, based on a thorough diagnosis of the problem (e.g., Who is the target group? What are barriers to change?).

Information provision   An intervention that provides people with information about a particular environmental problem and/or information relevant to ERB that helps to alleviate the problem.

Longitudinal study   A study that measures the effectiveness of an intervention at two or more time points.

Modeling   An intervention whereby one or more persons demonstrate a desired behavior.

Prompt   An activator that entails a brief verbal or written message or pictogram, drawing attention to a desirable behavior.

Reward   A positive consequence following the occurrence of a desirable behavior.

Social norms   Standards of behavior that inform members of a social group how to act.

Tailoring   Customizing an intervention approach to meet unique needs or desires of an individual or designated group.

Within-subjects design   A research design that assesses the effectiveness of an intervention by monitoring changes in behavior over time among the same participants during baseline, intervention, and withdrawal phases.

References

Abrahamse, W., & Matthies, E. (2013). Informational strategies to promote pro-environmental behaviors: Changing knowledge, awareness, and attitudes. In L. Steg, A. E. van den Berg, & J. I. M. de Groot (Eds.), *Environmental psychology: An introduction* (pp. 223–232). New York, NY: Wiley-Blackwell.

Abrahamse, W., & Steg, L (2013). Social influence approaches to encourage resource conservation: A meta-analysis. *Global Environmental Change, 23*, 1773–1785.

Abrahamse, W., Steg, L., Vlek, C., & Rothengatter, T. (2005). A review of intervention studies aimed at household energy conservation. *Journal of Environmental Psychology, 25*, 273–291.

Abrahamse, W., Steg, L., Vlek, C., & Rothengatter, T. (2007). The effect of tailored information, goal setting, and tailored feedback on household energy use, energy-related behaviors and behavioral antecedents. *Journal of Environmental Psychology, 27*, 265–276.

Becker, L. J. (1978). Joint effect of feedback and goal setting on performance: A field study of residential energy conservation. *Journal of Applied Psychology, 63*, 428–433.

Bolderdijk, J. W., Lehman, P. K., & Geller, E. S. (2013). Encouraging pro-environmental behavior with rewards and penalties. In L. Steg, A. E. van den Berg, & J. I. M. de Groot (Eds.), *Environmental psychology: An introduction* (pp. 233–242). New York, NY: Wiley.

Cialdini, R. B. (2001). *Influence: Science and practice*. Boston, MA: Allyn & Bacon.

Daamen, D. D. L., Staats, H., Wilke, H. A. M., & Engelen, M. (2001). Improving environmental behavior in companies. The effectiveness of tailored versus non-tailored interventions. *Environment and Behavior, 33*, 229–248.

Dwyer, W. O., Leeming, F. C., Cobern, M. K., Porter, B. E., & Jackson, J. M. (1993). Critical review of behavioral interventions to preserve the environment: Research since 1980. *Environment and Behavior, 25,* 275–321.

Gardner, G. T., & Stern, P. C. (2002). *Environmental problems and human behavior.* Boston, MA: Allyn & Bacon.

Geller, E. S. (1992). It takes more than information to save energy. *American Psychologist, 47,* 814–815.

Geller, E. S. (1995). Integrating behaviorism and humanism for environmental protection. *Journal of Social Issues, 51,* 179–195.

Geller, E. S. (2002).The challenge of increasing proenvironment behavior. In R. G. Bechtel & A. Churchman, (Eds.), *Handbook of environmental psychology* (pp. 525–540). New York, NY: Wiley.

Geller, E. S. (2008). Applied behavior analysis. In S.F. Davis & W. Buskist (Eds.), *21st Century psychology: A reference handbook. Vol. 2* (pp. 435–447). Thousand Oaks, CA: Sage.

Geller, E. S. (2014a). The foundation: Applied behavioral science. In E.S. Geller (Ed.), *Actively caring for people: Cultivating a culture of compassion* (4th ed.). (pp. 5–34). Newport, VA: Make-A-Difference.

Geller, E.S. (2014b). The psychology of self-motivation. In E. S. Geller (Ed.), *Actively caring for people: Cultivating a culture of compassion* (4th ed.) (pp. 63–90). Newport, VA: Make-A-Difference.

Geller, E. S., Winett, R. A., & Everett, P. B. (1982). *Preserving the environment: New strategies for behavior change* (pp. 113–157). New York, NY: Pergamon.

Goldstein, N. J., Cialdini, R. B., & Griskevicius, V. (2008). A room with a viewpoint: Using social norms to motivate environmental conservation in hotels. *Journal of Consumer Research, 35,* 472–482.

Hopper, J. H., & Nielsen, J. M. (1991). Recycling as altruistic behavior: Normative and behavioral strategies to expand participation in a community recycling program. *Environment and Behavior, 23,* 195–220.

Howden-Chapman, P., Pierse, N., Nicholls, S., Gillespie-Bennett, J., Viggers, H., Cunningham, M., Phipps, R., Boulic, M., et al. (2008). Effects of improved home heating on asthma in community dwelling children: Randomized controlled trial. *British Medical Journal, 377,* a1411.

Lehman, P. K., & Geller, E. S. (2004). Behavior analysis and environmental protection: Accomplishments and potential for more. *Behavior & Social Issues, 13*(1), 12–32.

Lehman, P. K., & Geller, E. S. (2008). Applications of social psychology to increase the impact of behavior-based interventions. In L. Steg, A. P. Buunk, & T. Rothengatter (Eds.), *Applied social psychology: Understanding and managing social problems* (pp. 57–86). Cambridge, UK: Cambridge University Press.

Lokhorst, A. M., Werner, C., Staats, H., van Dijk, E., & Gale, J. L. (2013). Commitment and behavior change: A meta-analysis and critical review of commitment-making strategies in environmental research. *Environment and Behavior, 45,* 3–34.

Matthies, E., Kastner, I., Klesse, A., & Wagner, H. J. (2011). High reduction potentials for energy user behavior in public buildings: How much can psychology-based interventions achieve? *Journal of Environmental Studies and Sciences, 1,* 241–255.

McKenzie-Mohr, D. (2000). Promoting sustainable behavior: An introduction to community-based social marketing. *Journal of Social Issues, 56,* 543–554.

Nolan, J. M., Schultz, P. W., Cialdini, R. B., Goldstein, N. J., & Griskevicius, V. (2008). Normative social influence is underdetected. *Personality and Social Psychology Bulletin, 34,* 913–923.

Pallak, M. S., & Cummings, N. (1976). Commitment and voluntary energy conservation. *Personality and Social Psychology Bulletin, 2,* 27–31.

Schultz, P. W., Nolan, J. M., Cialdini, R. B., Goldstein, N. J., & Griskevicius, V. (2007). The constructive, destructive, and reconstructive power of social norms. *Psychological Science, 18*, 429–434.

Schultz, P. W., Oskamp, S., & Mainieri, T. (1995). Who recycles and when? A review of personal and situational factors. *Journal of Environmental Psychology, 15*, 105–121.

Skinner, B. F. (1974). *About behaviorism*. New York, NY: Random House.

Staats, H. J., Wit, A. P., & Midden, C. Y. H. (1999). Communicating the greenhouse effect to the public: Evaluation of a mass media campaign from a social dilemma perspective. *Journal of Environmental Management, 46*, 189–203.

Steg, L., & Vlek, C. (2009). Encouraging pro-environmental behavior: An integrative review and research agenda. *Journal of Environmental Psychology, 29*, 309–317.

Sussman, R. Greeno, M., Gifford, R., & Scannell, L. (2013). The effectiveness of models and prompts on waste diversion: A field experiment on composting by cafeteria patrons. *Journal of Applied Social Psychology, 43*, 24–34.

Winett, R. A., Leckliter, I. N., Chinn, D. E., Stahl, B. N., & Love, S. Q. (1985). The effects of videotape modeling via cable television on residential energy conservation. *Journal of Applied Behavior Analysis, 18*, 33–44.

Suggested Readings

Gardner, G.T., & Stern, P.C. (2002). *Environmental problems and human behavior*. Boston, MA: Allyn & Bacon.

Geller, E.S. (2014). (Ed). *Actively caring for people: Cultivating a culture of compassion* (4th ed.). Newport, VA: Make-A-Difference.

Geller, E. S., Winett, R. A., & Everett, P. B. (1982). *Environmental preservation: New strategies for behavior change*. New York, NY: Pergamon.

McKenzie-Mohr, D., & Smith, W. (1999). *Fostering sustainable behavior: An introduction to community-based social marketing* (2nd ed.). Gabriola Island, BC, Canada: New Society.

17

Improving Human Functioning
Ecotherapy and Environmental Health Approaches

Thomas Doherty[1] and Angel Chen[2]
[1] *Lewis and Clark Graduate School, OR, United States*
[2] *University of Victoria, BC, Canada*

When Annabelle did her undergraduate degree in psychology, she took as many courses on therapy as she could. In fact, if she were not primarily interested in environmental psychology, she would probably be studying counseling or social work. Annabelle's minor was environmental studies and she goes outdoors almost every weekend, whether to a park, garden, or the woods. She knows from personal experience that spending time outdoors in a beautiful, natural setting feels healthy for her. She is interested in how spending time in nature influences other people's well-being and helps them to cope with personal difficulties.

Annabelle sees research as a way to solve immediate problems for people. She has heard about counselors using ecotherapy and wilderness therapy and wonders what the research says about this. She also wonders how something so personal and intangible as "connecting with nature" can be studied in a scientific way. Annabelle described her interests in nature and ecotherapy to Maria, Ethan, and Gabriel and received positive feedback. Although her colleagues shared her love of the outdoors and desire to help others, they wondered what an ecotherapy program would look like and how to demonstrate its evidence base. They brainstormed about ways that Annabelle could begin testing her own hypotheses about ecotherapy and decided it would be best to see what programs already existed. This was a helpful first step for Annabelle, who wants to manifest her environmental identity and values in a useful way.

We will begin with an anecdote from one of the author's experience on studying outcomes at a wilderness therapy program using the Youth Outcome Questionnaire (Y-OQ), a well-known measure used to study the effectiveness of youth therapy (Burlingame, Wells, & Lambert, 1995). Outcomes evaluation is a particular kind of research methodology used to objectively validate the effectiveness of specific programs (Cone, 2001). This anecdote will highlight some common issues and

Research Methods for Environmental Psychology, First Edition. Edited by Robert Gifford.
© 2016 John Wiley & Sons, Ltd. Published 2016 by John Wiley & Sons, Ltd.

dilemmas you may encounter while conducting environmental psychology research on therapeutic outcomes. They include problems resulting from **single method bias** and working with small sample sizes, balancing differing views about the goals of the research, and dealing with varying levels of buy-in from stakeholders regarding the research process itself. Also, it may take a few attempts to clarify and operationalize the most important dependent variables to study.

> When I (Thomas) was working as a clinical supervisor at a wilderness therapy program, we began utilizing outcome measures in our work with small groups of youth that were undertaking 21-day backcountry therapy treks. Inspired by the outcomes work being done in the field, we decided to use the Y-OQ measure. Initial results were confusing, however. Our small program's results seemed scattered and difficult to interpret. They did not mirror the clear trends seen in larger studies with hundreds of participants. Further, within the small wilderness trek groups of seven youths, some clients scored higher (i.e., endorsing more symptoms) at the end of the trek. This was counter to our observations of the youths' improvement. Everyone was busy and certainly did not want to spend time collecting data that wasn't useful, or even worse that made the program look bad!
>
> However, when we looked closer at the data and compared the Y-OQ scores to the observations of the counselors and verbal self-reports of the youth themselves (i.e., adding other kinds of qualitative and corroborating data) we found that, in some cases, a youth's report of more problems was a sign of improvement. Many had minimized their problems at the outset. Thus, more open endorsement of symptoms (such as feelings of depression) was indicative of a positive outcome. Since these young people were involved in a long-term therapy process, this expressiveness was a good thing. They were more open and willing to talk about themselves, possibly more insightful, and presumably better able to make use of therapy going forward. These experiences led to additional questions: Was it most important to assess overall program outcomes as the directors wanted or individual client improvements that the counselors were interested in, and what about the more basic research questions (e.g., on therapeutic mechanisms of wilderness therapy)?

This story illustrates some of the complexities involved in validating programs and interventions. Any kind of outcome study is, we must remember, a research project, and the more "data points" (i.e., information to work with) available, the more informative a research is. A basic tenant of research is avoiding "single method bias," that is, basing conclusions on only one type of measurement. Our attempt to rely on the Y-OQ data alone was a great example. (You can find a better example of a study using the Y-OQ later in the chapter.)

In hindsight, we could have also predicted that our program's outcomes would have more variability than the larger studies we sought to emulate. A basic tenet of statistics is the "law of large numbers," that is, it is easier to see trends in larger data sets (whether in client outcome scores or any other kind of data). When data sets are small, they are more likely to demonstrate diversity – the individual differences are highlighted. Nobel prize-winning psychologist Daniel Kahneman (2011) describes this "law," as well as other common cognitive biases and mental shortcuts that are important for investigators to be aware of.

Thomas's example also highlighted the differences between "nomothetic" research – investigating large groups of people in order to generate findings that apply to everyone, often conducted with quantitative methods, versus "ideographic" research – investigating a few individuals in-depth in order to achieve a unique understanding of them, often conducted with qualitative methods (Cone, 2001, p. 13). Finally, the example also highlights the need to use clinical judgment in therapeutic contexts – that is, attention to biases, willingness to revise one's theories or hypotheses in the light of new information, and consideration of interpersonal, cultural, and contextual factors (see APA Presidential Task Force on Evidence-Based Practice, 2006).

Given a variety of potential treatments and outcomes in **ecotherapy** and environmental health approaches, and the dynamic nature of health, it's important to carefully consider your choice of research methods. In this chapter we will discuss three research programs that provide excellent role models:

- Forestry Scotland's "Branching Out" program
- The Outdoor Behavioral Healthcare Industry Research Council (OBHIRC)
- University of Illinois Landscape and Human Health Laboratory (LHHL)

As the programs highlight, prospective researchers will find that attention to the basics of good research design and selecting practically useful research objectives will serve them well, along with flexibility and willingness to innovate (see Kuo, 2002). But, before proceeding to details about research programs, it is worth addressing the linkages between environmental psychology and human health and well-being. This reveals the basis for ecotherapy and environmental health approaches and alerts us to factors involved in our research designs, including how to operationalize "nature" as a therapeutic mechanism.

Environmental Psychology and Human Health

A robust literature exists on the environmental determinants of human psychological well-being – in terms of stress reduction, improved cognitive and emotional functioning, and the development of identity, efficacy and meaning – and how these are influenced by the design of buildings and other living spaces, contact with domestic and nearby nature (e.g., house plants, gardens, and parks), and experiences in more wild places (see Bechtel & Churchman, 2002; Clayton & Myers, 2009; Clayton & Opotow, 2003; Gifford, 2007; Kaplan & Kaplan, 1989; Kaplan, Kaplan & Ryan, 1998). Natural settings, outdoor activities, and contacts with other species have been utilized in therapeutic ways, with a variety of client groups, in the fields of ecotherapy, environmental social work, wilderness and adventure therapy, horticultural therapy, and in animal-assisted therapies (Blazina, Boyraz, & Shen-Miller, 2011; Gass, Gillis & Russell, 2012; Gray, Coates & Hetherington, 2012; Haller & Kramer, 2006; Hasbach, 2012).

In addition, these findings parallel initiatives in the fields of medicine and environmental health on the influence of nature-based methods and nature views on physical health outcomes, including the use of healing gardens in hospitals and creation of community-wide greening programs (e.g., Frumkin, 2005, 2012; Hartig & Marcus, 2006; Ulrich et al., 2008). Knowledge of the therapeutic effects of experience in nearby and wild nature can be seen as a promising, potential component of Jorm's (2012) concept of "mental health literacy" – both in terms of self-help strategies and potential psychological treatments.

Further, once these benefits are documented they provide valid reasons for preserving and creating green space and for the support of environmental conservation initiatives. The natural, health-promoting processes described above draw people to the outdoors. At the same time, the challenge for researchers is to experience these processes while evaluating them critically and empirically.

Choosing Research Methods

The studies we will highlight demonstrate the importance of a clear and compelling research agenda that answers questions important to stakeholders (Kuo, 2002). They also illustrate the effective use of quantitative and qualitative methods to study treatment outcomes and evaluate new programs (for detailed information on how to conduct studies using quantitative and qualitative methods, see Chapters 3 and 7, respectively). The study of ecotherapy and environmental health can be approached in a number of ways, ranging from positivist/biomedical approaches (e.g., quantitative symptom reduction and physiological measures) to post-positivist/biopsychosocial approaches (i.e., these include the personal meaning of treatment and roles of interpersonal support systems), to interpretive/humanistic approaches (e.g., in-depth qualitative interviews), and constructivist/critical approaches (i.e., these recognize the roles of cultural discourses, power, and equity in the research process) (Marks & Yardley, 2004).

In terms of the restorative effects of nature contacts, qualitative methods are generally most suitable for inquiring into the personal meanings of these experiences (e.g., through focus groups, journals, or using a video diary). These case studies can provide a solid foundation for developing satisfying and effective therapeutic techniques. However, policymakers and funders are more likely to be persuaded about a treatment's utility by the evidence of quantitative data, such as precise information on the prevalence and impacts of the issue and the pay-offs of nature-based treatment. As you will see, we describe research outcomes in qualitative and quantitative terms, to harness the benefits of both methodologies.

Reflection about Your Personal Beliefs and Motivations

Like all research, investigations of environmental psychology and health take place in a cultural context. In our case, this context is marked by changing attitudes about what is often referred to in the popular literature as "nature connection" (see Louv, 2005), as well as enduring questions about the role and value of other-than-human-nature in our lives (e.g., Kahn, 2011; Kellert, 1997; Merchant, 1980). A number of paradoxical trends make this topic a fascinating area of study, such as evidence of lower participation in nature-based recreation in the United States and worldwide (Pergams & Zaradic, 2008), even as the recognition of the health-promoting properties of green contacts increases (e.g., Alter, 2013).

Environmental topics arouse emotions; they are politicized, and ultimately involve personal values and attitudes (Leiserowitz, Maibach, Roser-Renouf, Feinberg, & Howe, 2013; McCright & Dunlap, 2011; Stokols, Misra, Runnerstrom, & Hipp, 2009). Also, as a rule, "environmental issues" – including reduced access to health-promoting green spaces – tend to disproportionately impact people who are least privileged, leading to questions of justice and equity (for a discussion, see Agyeman, Bullard, & Evans, 2003). Thus, new researchers may find it helpful to refer to findings on the development of environmental awareness and advocacy to clarify their motivations and increase their sense of efficacy (see Kempton & Holland, 2003; Stern, 2000).

As a potential researcher, self-reflection will have numerous pay-offs. Clarifying your personal motivations will help you identify which study topic most deserves the many hours you will devote to it – hopefully leading to more perseverance and satisfaction in your work. **Reflexivity** about research methods can help identify which approaches you are best suited for and increase your awareness of blind spots and biases that may impact your findings. Finally, attention to a larger vision of values and ethics can challenge you to see where your research may have practical policy implications – how it can help to change the world.

Operationalizing Nature: Domestic, Nearby and Wild

As the totality of material phenomena, nature is all encompassing. All human cultural objects and technologies are in some sense natural. For the purposes of our chapter, we will approach the concept of nature as it is commonly used in environmental psychology: as the natural world, a counter to the built world, and a proxy for places, processes, objects, or beings that are in some measure outside of human artifice or control, or that manifest organic processes. In environmental psychology research contexts, it is also necessary to distinguish the type or quality of "nature" we are describing. For example, researchers (e.g., Clayton & Myers, 2009) may characterize nature and natural settings as:

- **Domestic nature**: examples include living plants in homes or offices, indoor gardens, aquariums, pets.
- **Nearby nature**: parks, gardens, urban greenery, waterways, beaches.
- **Managed nature**: forests, zoos, farmlands, fisheries, wildlife refuges.
- **Wild nature**: places, beings, or processes that are objectively, or perceived to be, beyond human control, including remote areas (e.g., high alpine settings, the open ocean), designated wilderness areas, weather and climactic phenomena, and free-roaming creatures.

For the purposes of research methodology, it is important to be clear about what aspects of "nature" you intend to investigate, and how these are to be operationalized and measured. In terms of wilderness therapy, for example, the sense of a setting as "wild" can be subjective (e.g., a place that feels far away, requires self-reliance, and has presence of large predators). Further, in the United States, wilderness areas have specific attributes and are protected by a legal designation based on the 1964

Wilderness Act (http://www.wilderness.net/). Thus, the status of a backcountry setting as wilderness can be objectively verified by its legal designation; quantitatively assessed by its size, scale, or number of visitors; or qualitatively assessed through investigations of visitors' perceptions.

The Research Programs and Their Methods

In this section, we'll take an in-depth look at three innovative research programs that focus on human well-being and the natural environment. We will provide a brief summary of the programs and their aims, examine their methodologies, and provide some advice from the researchers of these programs. These studies highlight the importance of a clear and compelling research agenda that answers questions of significance to stakeholders (Kuo, 2002). They also illustrate the effective use of quantitative and qualitative methods to study treatment outcomes and evaluate new programs.

Ecotherapy in the community: Forestry Scotland and Branching Out

On a grassroots level, many people partake of activities in nearby and wild nature for recreation and well-being. At the level of professional practice, ecotherapy provides resources and techniques for mental health counselors and health care providers to utilize nature-based activities, topics, and metaphors in their therapeutic work (Hasbach, 2012). Therapeutically, this includes prescribing time spent in a restorative natural setting as a treatment itself (e.g., Jordan & Marshall, 2010) or using an eco-therapy frame to harness individuals' values about ecology or sustainability to foster general health or therapeutic goals (see Doherty, 2012; Reese & Myers, 2012).

Ecotherapy is also used to address concerns about environmental issues that arise in counseling, such as anxiety or despair at the scope of the problems (Randall, 2005). Some ecotherapy approaches seek to go deeper and resolve a cultural-level split from wild nature in developed societies that is seen to manifest on personal and cultural levels and impact health, identity, and tendency to ecologically destructive behaviors (e.g., Buzzell & Chalquist, 2009; Fisher, 2012; Macy & Brown, 1989).

All of these approaches have merits and appropriate research methodologies. To date, the use of nature-based activities in community-based counseling has shown one of the most promising research literatures (e.g., MIND UK, 2007). In our chapter, we will focus on such a community-level initiative: Forestry Scotland's "Branching Out" program.

Branching Out (http://www.forestry.gov.uk/branchingout) is a government-funded program offering ecotherapy on referral for mental health patients by engaging them in activities in woodland settings. The service consists of 3-hour sessions of activities per week for a 12-week period. During each session, clients in small groups of up to 15 take part in a variety of activities, including physical activity, conservation activities, bushcraft, and environmental arts.

These activities were selected based on the criteria that they were enjoyable, beneficial to the area, could be completed using hand tools, and allowed moderate physical exercise (see Table 17.1 for a list of activities). Evaluation of the program,

Table 17.1   Forestry Scotland's Branching Out activities.

Program Activities			
Conservation	Invasive species removal	Construction	Bird boxes
	Seed Collection & planting		Platters/baskets
	Planting & harvesting Willow		Wreaths
	Orchard maintenance		Benches
	Litter collection		Fences
	Bluebell survey		Shelter
Bushcraft	Map reading	Exercise	Health walk
	Orienteering		Tai Chi
	Shelter building		(All construction and conservation activities)
	Fire building		
	Campfire cooking		
	Knot work		
	Tool use & maintenance		
	Tree identification		
Environmental Art	Photography	Other	Visit to Scottish Museum of Rural Life/Bullwood Woodwork Project/ Hardwood Sawmill
	Wreath making		
	Nature postcards		
	Tree wrapping		
	Work in clay		
	Willow sculptures		

Adapted from Wilson, N. W., Jones, R., Fleming, S., Lafferty, K., Knifton, L., Cathrine, K., & McNish, H. (2011). Branching out: The impact of a mental health ecotherapy program. *Ecopsychology, 3*, 51–57.

utilizing both quantitative (Wilson et al., 2011) and qualitative methodologies (Wilson et al., 2010), was based on one-year results of four 12-week blocks.

Quantitative outcome measures. Pre- and post-measures of general health, mental well-being, and physical activity were assessed by standardized questionnaires completed by clients. General health was measured using the 12-item SF-12v2 Health Survey (Ware, Kosinski, Turner-Bower, & Gandeck, 2007). Mental well-being was measured by the Warwick-Edinburgh Mental Well-Being Scale (WEMWBS; Parkinson, 2007). Physical activity was measured by the Scottish Physical Activity Questionnaire (SPAQ; Lowther, Mutrie, Loughlan, & McFarlane, 1999). In SPAQ, respondents recall the number of minutes spent performing leisure and occupational physical activities.

A sample t-test was conducted to determine if there was a significant difference between baseline and post-intervention scores on the SF-12v2, WEMWBAS, and SPAQ. Initial results indicated that attendance in the program led to significantly improved physical activity levels, but were inconclusive regarding general health and mental well-being. The authors concluded that a longer program may be necessary to determine the impact on these parameters.

Qualitative interviews. A qualitative approach was adopted to assess clients' perceptions of program elements that facilitated change. Semi-structured interviews with clients ($n = 28$) and two focus groups with clinicians ($n = 5$ and $n = 3$) were conducted. Individual interviews with clients were conducted on site and lasted approximately 20 minutes. Interviewees were randomly selected by the drawing of lots using willow herb stalks. Interviewees were informed that participation was voluntary and that their anonymity and confidentially were assured. The interview schedule consisted of 10 sequential questions; prompts were included for further direction.

Focus groups with clinicians. A facilitator led the discussion and ensured all respondents had equal opportunity to respond. In order to ensure clients' confidentiality, referring to individuals' names was not permitted. Verbatim transcription of interview data was analyzed thematically by interpretive **phenomenological analysis** (IPA; Smith, Harre, & Langenhove, 1995). Meaning, rather than frequency, was central in the process and the transcript was read several times to document emergent themes.

Eight themes emerged from the data: five master themes pertaining to client outcomes and three themes pertaining to the service logistics. This result indicated that: (1) by providing meaningful activity and recognition (e.g., tasks that demonstrate competency and contribution to the community) and (2) opportunity for team building (e.g., social networking facilitated by small group sizes) in a (3) dynamic environment (i.e., contrasted with hospital and household routines), Branching Out improved physical health, daily structures, socialization skills, transferable knowledge, and a sense of achievement/self-esteem.

Future directions. The second phase of program evaluation will involve probing the costs and potential health benefits to the participants. The evaluation process will involve three stages of data collection: baseline before starting on Branching Out; at the end of the 12-week project- and a 3-month follow-up. Measures used for the evaluation will include the SF-12 Health Survey, the International Physical Activity Questionnaire, and the Stage of Change Questionnaire for Physical Activity. This project is currently in the data-collection process.

Advice to new researchers

"As soon as you've got enough information to make a start, get something on paper. Once that is done there is a long process of consultation and refinement. Speak to everyone involved, get to know them and spend time talking through the ideas and problems." – Neil Wilson, Researcher, Branching Out Program.

Wilderness and adventure therapy: the outdoor behavioral healthcare industry research council

Although closely related to ecotherapy in concept and practice, the wilderness and adventure therapy (WT/AT) traditions have developed along separate lines, in the context of outdoor education and leadership programs; resource, recreation and tourism studies; and in rehabilitation programs for young people with behavioral or substance abuse issues (e.g., Manning, 2010; Norton & Holguin, 2011; Priest & Gass, 2005). Present-day programs have origins in the nineteenth- and early twentieth-century summer camp and scouting movements in North America and Europe. They further evolved and became specialized with the introductions of "Outward Bound" style wilderness adventure, outdoor survival training, and more sophisticated theories of therapy (e.g., Walsh & Gollins, 1976). For a history and introduction to WT/AT, see Davis-Berman and Berman (2008), Gass, Gillis and Russell (2012), and White (2012).

Assessing treatment outcomes of wilderness programs. Longitudinal outcome studies completed by the Outdoor Behavioral Healthcare Industry Research Council (OBHIRC) (http://www.obhrc.org/; http://obhic.com/research.html) are illustrated here. The research cooperative is sponsored by professional wilderness therapy programs in the United States and Canada and housed at the University of New Hampshire. The first major OBHIRC study, entitled "Assessing treatment outcomes in **outdoor behavioral healthcare** (OBH) using the Youth Outcome Questionnaire" (Russell, 2003), reported outcomes for a sample of adolescents (the majority male, aged 16–18) who attended seven wilderness therapy programs that averaged 45 days in length during the period May 1, 2000 to December 1, 2000. Adolescent well-being was evaluated utilizing the Youth Outcome Questionnaire (Y-OQ) and the Youth Outcome Questionnaire-Self Report (Y-OQ-SR) (Burlingame et al., 1995). Complete sets of admission and discharge data were collected for 523 client self-assessments and 372 parent assessments.

Research questions and design. A time-series research design with a single base-line assessment was used in the study (e.g., Graziano & Raulin, 1997) and the following research questions were addressed: (a) To what extent did positive outcomes result from wilderness therapy treatment, as measured by Y-OQ and Y-OQ-SR score differences between admission and discharge? (b) How did treatment outcome vary according to age, gender, and psychiatric diagnosis? (c) How did treatment outcome vary according to program length? (d) To what extent did clients maintain improvements at 12-months post treatment? Furthermore, the study discussed the rationale for using the Y-OQ as well as metrics to determine clinically significant change (i.e., a decrease of 13 points or more on the Y-OQ measure indicated significant symptom reduction or meaningful change).

Results. On average, both clients and their parents reported that symptoms were significantly reduced at discharge. The actual score reduction on the Y-OQ measures exceeded 13 points from admission to discharge (i.e., a meaningful change) for 55% of youth self-reports and 85% of parent reports. The average Y-OQ total scores at discharge for youth self-reports and parent assessment scores were 48.95 and 48.33, respectively, close to the normal functioning cut-off score of 46, while 43% of client self-reports and 46% of parent assessment scores at discharge were clearly within the normal range (at 46 or lower; See Table 17.2).

Table 17.2   OBHRIC wilderness therapy outcomes – Y-OQ scores.

Mean Y-OQ Scores at Admission, Discharge for Client Self-Reports and Parent Assessments

N	Period	M	SD[1]	Mean Difference
Client Report SR Y-OQ				
523	Admission			
	Y-OQ Score	70.53	32.85	20.07*
523	Discharge			
	Y-OQ Score	48.95	32.23	
Parent Assessment Y-OQ				
372	Admission			
	Y-OQ Score	100.19	28.35	51.64*
372	Discharge			
	Y-OQ Score	48.55	37.47	

Note. Y-OQ – Youth Outcome Questionnaire (Burlingame, Wells, & Lambert, 1995).
* Indicates clinically significant changes was demonstrated as a result of treatment.
Source: Russell, K. C. (2003). Assessing treatment outcomes in outdoor behavioral health-care using the Youth Outcome Questionnaire. *Child and Youth Care Forum, 32,* 355–381. Reproduced with permission.

Significance of the findings. The study found that participating in wilderness therapy treatment reduced behavioral and emotional symptoms of young people. It was notable that parents or caregivers rated their children as having significant psychological and behavioral symptoms at intake (i.e., at levels associated with inpatient hospital treatment) and that both participants and their parents reported significant improvements. A significant gap in the reports of parents and the children at intake was notable, and provided validation for anecdotal observations of counselors who witnessed parent–child disagreement on the severity of the youths' problems. The finding that parent and child scores were compatible at discharge provided empirical support for observations that these young people and their families were more likely to agree about the issues at discharge. Youths randomly sampled at 12 months maintained outcomes, and according to self-reports, had continued to improve. This was an important finding because the degree to which clients can apply skills and lessons learned in wilderness environments to their everyday lives had not been well documented in the literature (Russell, 2003).

Two-year qualitative follow-up. In 2005, a follow-up study, entitled "Two years later: A qualitative assessment of youth well-being and the role of aftercare in outdoor behavioral healthcare treatment" (Russell, 2005), was conducted with the initial OBHIRC sample of clients. This study used interviews of parents and youths to assess youth well-being at 24 months post-treatment, perceptions about the effectiveness of wilderness therapy, and utilization of aftercare services (e.g., outpatient therapy).

The follow-up study included a qualitative case study approach (Erlandson, Harris, Skipper & Allen, 1993). Responses were analyzed using the theory-building program for qualitative data, Non-numerical Unstructured Data Indexing, Searching and Theorizing (NUD-IST; Richards & Richards, 1994).

About 80% of parents and 95% of youths perceived outdoor behavioral healthcare treatment as beneficial, that the majority of clients reported good academic performance, and that family communication had improved. Aftercare services such as outpatient or residential treatment were utilized by 85% of the youth. These services were perceived as important in facilitating the transition from an intensive wilderness therapy experience to family, peer, and school environments.

Qualitative methods allowed for rich description of single case studies using evocative participant responses (e.g., "I am grateful to the program for giving me sensibility, like I can do it you know" and "Opened my eyes to what I had in life and taught me to appreciate things, my family, even little things"). Results also revealed qualitative aspects of the wilderness therapy experience (e.g., get away, out in open, no stress or worries, time reflect, confidence and esteem) (Russell, 2005).

Advice to new researchers

"It is important to note that there are a variety of journals from various disciplines publishing articles on adventure therapy (AT), including medical, mental health, social work, and education journals. This interdisciplinarity suggests a growing interest in the use of AT as an intervention to facilitate change in individuals, but requires looking beyond specific disciplines and being well versed in a variety of literature." – Keith Russell, Western Washington University.

Public health approaches: The Landscape and Human Health Laboratory

Work in the areas of environmental and public health includes the study of community-wide, epidemiological, and other large-scale therapeutic approaches to the use of green spaces and outdoor activities (e.g., Frumkin, 2010, 2012; Kuo, 2010, Largo-Wright, 2011; Maller et al., 2008; U.S. Environmental Protection Agency, 2012). These approaches address whole communities and combine individualized and population-level studies to seek patterns in well-being associated with the design of urban and residential spaces and to influence healthcare policy and urban planning. Studies typically target self-reported benefits as well as physiological indicators of stress such as blood pressure and cortisol concentrations (Bowler, Buyung-Ali, Knight, & Pullin, 2010). Research by the University of Illinois' Landscape and Human Health Laboratory (LHHL) on the beneficial effects of "green time" for children with attention issues is focused on here (http://lhhl.illinois.edu/)

Using both correlational studies and online nationwide survey and field experiments, research at the LHHL demonstrated that exposure to a relatively natural setting can help relieve children's attention deficit-hyperactivity disorder (ADHD) symptoms. ADHD is a neurobehavioral disorder primarily characterized by a deficit in directed attention. Children diagnosed with ADHD experience significant functional impairment in academics and socialization (Loe & Feldman, 2007; Nijmeijer et al., 2008). A nature-based intervention for ADHD is based on **attention restoration theory** (Kaplan, 1995), which predicts that natural environments, drawing predominately on involuntary attention, ameliorate attention fatigue and restore children's' ability to concentrate.

Correlational studies. Data from an initial Midwestern sample (Faber Taylor, Kuo, & Sullivan, 2001), and a subsequent, online nationwide sample (Kuo & Faber Taylor, 2004) were collected by surveys of parents of children with ADHD. Participants were presented with a list of after-school and weekend activities conducted in three settings – indoor, built outdoor (e.g., downtown), and green outdoor (e.g., parks). For each activity, post-activity attentional functioning of their child was made on a 5-point Likert scale (1 = Much worse, to 3 = Same as usual, to 5 = Much better). The after-effects of activities taking place in green outdoor setting were better than those activities taking place in either indoor or built outdoor settings (see Figure 17.1) The correlational nature of these studies helped to determine the existence of a relationship between nature and ADHD symptom reduction.

To address the causal role of green settings, a controlled field experiment was conducted (Faber Taylor & Kuo, 2009). The study utilized a within-subjects design (crossover trials) in which the same participant received a sequence of different treatments and control. This design controlled for individual factors (e.g., age) and case characteristics (e.g., multiple diagnoses). Seventeen children (ages 7 to 12 years old) diagnosed with ADHD were recruited through newspaper advertisements, electronic newsletter, and flyers.

Upon completing a series of puzzles designed to induce attention fatigue, children without medication completed 20 minutes of guided walks in three settings differing in the extent to which natural or urban elements predominated (an urban park, a downtown area, and a residential area) but of relatively equivalent terrain, noise, and

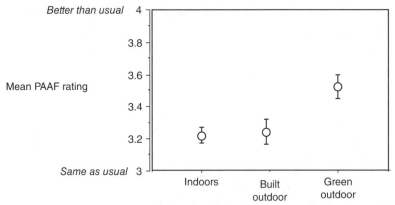

Mean postactivity attentional functioning ratings for indoor, built outdoor, and green outdoor activities

Figure 17.1 Research findings on children, green settings and attention. Adapted from Faber Taylor, A., Kuo, F. E., & Sullivan, W. C. (2001). Coping with ADD: The surprising connection to green play settings. *Environment and Behavior, 33*, 65. Copyright 2001.

pedestrian density. Children were randomly assigned to the three sessions (settings) separately in a counterbalanced order, with each session scheduled one week apart at a similar time of day. To control for social influences across environments, each child was accompanied by the same guide who kept conversation at a minimum.

After each walk, the Digit Span Backwards (DSB) test (Wechsler, 1955) a standard measure of concentration, was administered by an evaluator blind to children's walking conditions. DSB requires listening to a sequence of numbers and reciting those items in reverse order. Results indicated significant improvement on concentration after walking through the "greenest" setting (city park) than through either of the two other settings.

Combined approaches from the field experiment and the correlational studies had complementary strengths and non-overlapping weaknesses that compensated for each other's limitations and established convergent findings. The use of the controlled comparison across settings and the objective test of concentration help to address the issue of causality and subjectivity in the survey-based work. The use of a national sample with a wider range of age, geographic regions, and activities account for generalizability in the experimental study. Thus, the multi-method perspective adopted by the LHHL helped to increase the validity and reliability of its research findings.

Advice to new researchers

"In essence, high-impact research is **decision-oriented research**. Decision-oriented research compares the impacts of different real-world choices that decision-makers routinely confront – for example, between spending more or less on landscaping, between different kinds of artwork in hospital rooms, or between retaining versus removing green space in your schools." – Francis Kuo, Landscape and Human Health Laboratory (Kuo, 2002, p. 341).

Research in Environmental Psychology and Health: Reflection on Practical and Ethical Issues

Berger (2008) provides several practical research tips. She notes "every researcher begins not only by formulating a hypothesis but also by learning what other scientists have discovered about the topic in question and what methods might be useful and ethical in designing research" (p. B-5). She advises students to become familiar with professional journals in their area of interest and to read original studies, and not simply rely on media accounts, which can be biased, simplified, or misleading. She adds: "Make it personal. Think about your life and experience and observe things that interest you; this will make you more reflective."

Consult the ethics code in your discipline

Most healthcare disciplines have a well-articulated **ethics code** and it is important to consult these for guidance on ethical issues that arise throughout the research process. For example, the APA Ethics Code (APA, 2010) has sections that span topics from Boundaries of Competence and Bases for Scientific and Professional Judgments, to Informed Consent and Maintaining Confidentiality, Test Scoring and Interpretation and Explaining Assessment Results, Maintenance of Records, and on to Debriefing Research Studies and Reporting Research Results.

In addition, there are now frameworks set up to guide adventure therapy. The Association for Experiential Education has a set of accreditation standards for adventure, experiential, and therapeutic adventure programs that addresses issues such as competence, technical standards for conducting outdoor activities, and **risk management** and oversight (http://www.aee.org/accreditation-manual). A key APA Ethics Standard to note when designing new or innovative programs is 2.01 (e) "In those emerging areas in which generally recognized standards for preparatory training do not yet exist, psychologists nevertheless take reasonable steps to ensure the competence of their work and to protect clients/patients, students, supervisees, research participants, organizational clients, and others from harm" (APA, 2010, p. 5).

Risk management

In all therapeutic endeavors, and in research that addresses people and their well-being, it is crucial to identify possible **iatrogenic effects**, commonly known as "side effects" (e.g., injury or discomfort). It is also critical to prevent or mitigate risks in therapeutic activities and to clearly address potential risks so clients can provide their "informed consent" for the study before it begins. Although there is the potential for injury when being active in outdoor adventure activities (particularly those that involve water-based or high altitude sports), it is notable that wilderness and adventure therapy programs have been found to be safer in terms of injury rates for adolescents aged 15–19 years than more common activities like downhill skiing, driving, and high school football (Gass, Gillis & Russell, 2012).

Multicultural competency

Cultural competence in research is the ability of researchers and staff to take into account the culture and diversity of a population when developing research ideas, conducting research, and exploring applicability of findings (Program for Cultural Competence in Research, 2010). **Multicultural competency** in environmental health related research can be promoted and ensured in several ways. They all begin with being mindful of the cultural differences between you as an investigator and the people in your potential research setting.

For example, even though outcome assessment is likely to be welcomed in most programs (and possibly mandated by funding sources), some settings may be wary of outside "researchers," particularly those serving persons of color, indigenous groups, or any group that perceives itself to be a victim of injustice, racism, or objectifying by western science. In these cases, the use of **participatory research design** (e.g., Walter, 2009) and holistic/indigenous methods (e.g., Denzin, Lincoln, & Tuhiwai Smith, 2008; Wilson, 2009) may be most appropriate. They include efforts to address ethnocentric assumptions on researchers' part and in the research design; use of dialogue, consensus, and participatory methods to formulate research questions and determine relevant outcomes; and honoring culture-specific rituals and ceremonies.

Therapeutic mechanisms, satisfaction and the placebo effect

In addition to cultural competency, new researchers need to become sophisticated about the differences between satisfaction and outcomes, and the role of expectations when assessing a treatment and its effectiveness (including controlling for their own expectations). As Gass, Gillis, and Russell (2012, p. 286) note, it is important for researchers in innovative areas such as adventure therapy to ask the "hard questions" about their programs if they are aspiring to evidence-based practice.

For example, it is necessary to acknowledge the difference between client satisfaction and objective problem change, and that these variables are not highly correlated (Pekarik & Guidry, 1999). For example, a person can be very satisfied with a treatment (e.g., in terms of the therapeutic modality or their relationship with their health provider) in the absence of significant effects of the treatment (e.g., reductions in symptoms or functional improvements in health).

Promising therapies can be rejected if not presented in a satisfying way; satisfying therapies may not ultimately be shown to be effective. It is also important to recognize and attempt to control for placebo effects – therapeutic effects associated with contextual factors including a person's expectations about a treatment's effectiveness (see Price, Finniss, & Benedetti, 2008). To address these issues, studies must develop sufficient rigor, including scientific methods, such as randomized assignment to treatments, use of comparison or control groups, large samples, or stating limitations of their methodologies (Gass, Gillis & Russell, 2012).

Summary and Conclusions

In reviewing the programs for this chapter, it was necessary to move across a number of disciplines and dig into the separate "silos" where the needed information could be found on: (1) theories of well-being vis-à-vis humans and nature; (2) basic findings on therapeutic mechanisms; (3) applied studies with specific groups; (4) fully fledged intervention programs; and (5) appropriate research methods and examples. A pressure toward specialization is experienced by practitioners and researchers (and often demanded by training programs). However, there are pragmatic benefits of looking beyond your field of study to find allied approaches and findings (El-Ghoroury, 2011). By taking a wider view – for example, expanding your literature review to include databases in mental health counseling *and* social work *and* education *and* public health – you will find that research and intervention in these areas often proceeds on separate but parallel lines.

The essence of interdisciplinary work is to find the "right tool for the job" (Doherty, 2011). As our research examples show, it is important to integrate qualitative, quantitative, and culture sensitive approaches to maximize the validity and usefulness of your investigations. This includes looking across academic and healthcare specialties and recognizing their associated organizational and cultural contexts.

The authors would like to thank the researchers from the programs we highlighted for sharing their time and insights. We hope that you can also appreciate the importance of clearly operationalizing constructs like "nature" and "wilderness" in your study. Highlighting the therapeutic effects of green spaces from nearby nature to wilderness areas demonstrates their conservation value in a tangible way. Knowledge of how individuals can utilize experience in nearby and wild nature to promote health and well-being can be seen as a component of mental health literacy – both in terms of self-help strategies and as potential psychological treatments. From both a human and an environmental ethics perspective, our research methods do matter.

Annabelle felt empowered when she reported back to Maria, Ethan, and Gabriel. After exploring some basics of environmental psychology, she was clearer about the benefits of natural spaces and processes for human health. After surveying innovative programs, she was aware of an eco-therapeutic spectrum that ranged from backyard gardens to wilderness areas. She was able to recognize the moral and ethical aspects of her interest in environmental health as well as the practical and technical considerations about what treatments worked best for who, how to investigate this, and how to communicate her findings. She felt more able in her research methods to approach perceptions about the environment and health in a scholarly and empirical way that could also account for the role of culture and socio-economic status. She was more conscious of sources of bias in her research work, and thus was able to design and plan her methodology systematically. Finally, with the knowledge of testing real-world outcomes, she felt more confident in articulating the benefits of ecotherapy and environmental health approaches in a way that demonstrated their value for human health and as a compelling rationale for environmental conservation.

Glossary

Attention restoration theory   Exposure to natural environments restores individuals' ability to concentrate on tasks, like schoolwork, that demand effortful attention.

Decision-oriented research   A study that compares the impacts of different real-world choices that decision makers routinely confront.

Domestic nature   Examples include living plants in homes or offices, indoor gardens, aquariums, and other species kept as pets.

Ecotherapy   Mental health approaches that address environmental topics or use natural objects, other species, or activities in the outdoors as part of the therapeutic process.

Ethics code   Written guidelines used by healthcare and other disciplines to define best practices and to address potential risks and dilemmas encountered in practice, such as rules for confidentiality and informed consent.

Iatrogenic effects   Unintentional injury or discomfort associated with a health treatment, commonly known as "side effects."

Managed nature   Examples include forests, zoos, farmlands, fisheries, wildlife refuges.

Multicultural competency   The ability of researchers to take into account the culture and diversity of a group when developing research ideas, conducting research, and applying findings.

Nearby nature   Spaces adjacent to buildings that afford access to greenery, wildlife, and varied landscapes, such as parks, gardens, and beaches.

Outdoor behavioral healthcare A term for wilderness therapy used by professional programs to better coordinate their services with other forms of healthcare treatment such as hospitals or outpatient therapy.

Participatory research design Design that empowers research participants through dialogue, selects outcomes that are practically useful to them, and honors culture-specific values, beliefs, and rituals.

Phenomenological analysis A qualitative research method that focuses on clarifying the meaning of an event or an experience for research participants, in their own words, rather than testing a pre-existing hypothesis.

Reflexivity Awareness on the part of researchers regarding their personal beliefs, attitudes, and experiences as they relate to the research process.

Risk management Efforts and practices to identify potential dangers or harms associated with therapeutic or research activities and to minimize their likelihood or impacts.

Single method bias Flawed research findings associated with using only one measure or data source, such as a verbal self-report or a symptom checklist, rather than incorporating multiple, externally verifiable sources.

Wild nature Places or processes that are objectively, or perceived to be, beyond human control due to their remoteness and level of challenge, legal designation as a wilderness area, extreme weather or climate, or activities of free-roaming creatures.

Youth Outcome Questionnaire (Y-OQ) A standardized set of questions used to determine the effectiveness of therapies for adolescents, for example, used for program evaluation or to compare effects of different programs or techniques.

References

Agyeman, J., Bullard, R. D., & Evans, B. (2003). *Just sustainabilities.* Cambridge, MA: MIT Press.

Alter, A. (2013). How nature resets our minds and bodies. *The Atlantic.* http://www.theatlantic.com/health/archive/2013/03/how-nature-resets-our-minds-and-bodies/274455/

American Psychological Association. (2010). *American Psychological Association ethical principles of psychologists and code of conduct.* Retrieved from http://www.apa.org/ethics/code2002.html

APA Presidential Task Force on Evidence-Based Practice. (2006). Evidence-based practice in psychology. *American Psychologist, 61,* 271–285.

Bechtel, R. B., & Churchman, A (2002). (Eds.). *Handbook of environmental psychology.* New York, NY: Wiley.

Berger, K. S. (2008). *The developing person* (7th ed.) New York, NY: Worth.

Blazina, C., Boyraz, G., & Shen-Miller, D. (2011). (Eds.). *The psychology of the human-animal bond: A resource for clinicians and researchers.* New York, NY: Springer.

Bowler, D. E., Buyung-Ali, L. M., Knight, T. M., & Pullin, A. S. (2010). A systematic review of evidence for the added benefits to health of exposure to natural environments. *BMC Public Health, 10,* 456–.

Burlingame, G. M., Wells, M. G., & Lambert, M. J. (1995). *The Youth Outcome Questionnaire.* Stevenson, MD: American Professional Credentialing Services.

Buzzell, L., & Chalquist, C. (2009). (Eds.). *Ecotherapy.* San Francisco, CA: Sierra Club Press.

Clayton, S., & Myers, G (2009). *Conservation psychology.* New York, NY: Wiley-Blackwell.

Clayton, S., & Opotow, S. (2003). (Eds.), *Identity and the natural environment: The psychological significance of nature.* Cambridge, MA: MIT Press.

Cone, J. D. (2001). *Evaluating outcomes.* Washington, DC: American Psychological Association.

Davis-Berman, J., & Berman, D. (2008). *The promise of wilderness therapy.* Boulder, CO: Association for Experiential Education.

Denzin, N., Lincoln, Y., & Tuhiwai Smith, L. (2008) *Handbook of critical and indigenous methodologies.* Thousand Oaks, CA: Sage.

Doherty, T. J. (2011, October) Ecopsychology and environmentally-focused psychologies. *Environmental, Population, and Conservation Psychology Bulletin.* Retrieved from http://www.apadivisions.org/division-34/publications/newsletters/epc/2011/10/ecopsychology.aspx

Doherty, T. J. (2012, August). *Nature-based stress reduction: Linking research on mindfulness and restorative natural environments.* Paper presented at the American Psychological Association Annual Convention, Orlando, Florida.

El-Ghoroury, N. H. (2011) Looking beyond our silos. *gradPSYCH.* Retrieved from http://www.apa.org/gradpsych/2011/11/matters.aspx

Erlandson, D. A., Harris, B. L., Skipper D. L., & Allen, S. D. (1993). *Doing naturalistic inquiry: A guide to methods.* Newberry Park, CA: Sage.

Faber Taylor, A., & Kuo, F. E. (2009). Children with attention deficits concentrate better after walk in the park. *Journal of Attention Disorders, 12,* 402–409.

Faber Taylor, A., Kuo, F. E., & Sullivan, W. C. (2001). Coping with ADD: The surprising connection to green play settings. *Environment and Behavior, 33,* 54–77.

Fisher, A. (2012). *Radical ecopsychology* (2nd ed.). Albany, NY: State University of New York Press.

Frumkin, H. (2010). (Ed.). *Environmental health: From global to local.* San Francisco, CA: Jossey-Bass.

Frumkin, H. (2012). Building the science base: Ecopsychology meets clinical epidemiology. In P. H. Kahn Jr. & P. H. Hasbach (Eds.), *Ecopsychology: Science, totems, and the technological species* (pp. 141–172). Cambridge, MA: MIT Press.

Gass, M. A., Gillis, H. L., & Russell, K. C. (2012). *Adventure therapy: Theory, research, and practice.* New York, NY: Routledge.

Gifford, R. (2007). *Environmental psychology.* Colville, WA: Optimal Books

Graziano, A. M., & Raulin, M. L. (1997). *Research methods: A process of inquiry* (3rd ed.). New York, NY: Addison Wesley Longman.

Gray, M., Coates, J., & Hetherington, T. (2012). *Environmental social work.* New York, NY: Routledge.

Haller, R. L. & Kramer, C. L. (2006). *Horticultural therapy methods: Making connections in health care, human service, and community programs.* Philadelphia, PA: Haworth Press.

Hartig, T., & Marcus, C. C. (2006). Healing gardens: Places for nature in health care. *Lancet, 368,* S36–37.

Hasbach, P. H. (2012). Ecotherapy. In P. H. Kahn & P. H. Hasbach (Eds.), *Ecopsychology: Science, totems, and the technological species* (p9. 115–140). Cambridge, MA: MIT Press.

Jordan, M., & Marshall, H. (2010). Taking counselling and psychotherapy outside: Destruction or enrichment of the therapeutic frame? *European Journal of Psychotherapy and Counselling, 12,* 345–359.

Jorm, A. F. (2012) Mental health literacy: Empowering the community to take action for better mental health. *American Psychologist, 67,* 231–243.

Kahn, P. H., Jr. (2011). *Technological nature, adaptation and the future of human life.* Cambridge, MA: MIT Press.

Kempton, W., & Holland, D. C. (2003). Identity and sustained environmental practice. In S. Clayton & S. Opotow (Eds.), *Identity and the natural environment: The psychological significance of nature* (pp. 317–341). Cambridge, MA: MIT Press.

Kahneman, D. (2011). *Thinking, fast and slow.* New York, NY: Farrar, Straus and Giroux.

Kaplan, R., & Kaplan, S. (1989). *The experience of nature: A psychological perspective.* Cambridge, MA: Cambridge University Press.

Kaplan, R., Kaplan, S., & Ryan, R. L. (1998). *With people in mind: Design and management of everyday nature.* Washington, DC: Island Press.

Kaplan, S. (1995). The restorative benefits of nature: Toward an integrative framework. *Journal of Environmental Psychology, 15,* 169–182.

Kellert, S. R. (1997). *Kinship to mastery: Biophilia in human evolution and development.* Washington, DC: Island Press.

Kuo, F. E. (2002). Bridging the gap: How scientists can make a difference. In R. B. Bechtel & A. Churchman (Eds.), *Handbook of environmental psychology* (pp. 517–533). New York, NY: Wiley.

Kuo, F. E., & Faber Taylor, A. (2004). A potential natural treatment for attention deficit/hyperactivity disorder: Evidence from a national study. *American Journal of Public Health, 94,* 1580–1586.

Kuo, F. E. (2010). Parks and other green environments: Essential components of a healthy human habitat: National Recreation and Park Association. Retrieved from http://www.nrpa.org/uploadedFiles/Explore_Parks_and_Recreation/Research/Ming%20(Kuo)%20Reserach%20Paper-Final-150dpi.pdf

Largo-Wright, E. (2011). Cultivating healthy places and communities: Evidence-based nature contact recommendations. *International Journal of Environmental Health Research, 21,* 41–61. doi:10.1080/09603123.2010.499452

Leiserowitz, A., Maibach, E., Roser-Renouf, C., Feinberg, G., & Howe, P. (2013). *Global warming's six Americas, September 2012.* New Haven, CT: Yale Project on Climate Change Communication. http://environment.yale.edu/climate/publications/Six-Americas-September-2012

Loe, I. M., & Feldman, H. M. (2007). Academic and educational outcomes of children with ADHD. *Journal of Pediatric Psychology, 32,* 643–665.

Louv, R. (2005). *Last child in the woods.* Chapel Hill, NC: Algonquin.

Lowther, M., Mutrie, N., Loughlan, C., & McFarlane, C. (1999). Development of a Scottish physical activity questionnaire: A tool for use in physical activity interventions. *British Journal of Sports Medicine, 33,* 244–249.

Macy, J., & Brown, M. Y. (1989). *Coming back to life: Practices to reconnect our lives, our world.* Gabriola Island, BC: New Society Publishing.

Maller, C., Townsend, M., St. Ledger, L., Henderson-Wilson, C., Pryor, A., Prosser, L. et al. (2008). *Healthy parks, healthy people: The health benefits of contact with nature in a park context: A review of current literature* (2nd ed.). In Social and Mental Health Priority Area, Occasional Paper Series. Melbourne, Australia: Faculty of Health and Behavioural Sciences. Retrieved from http://parkweb.vic.gov.au/__data/assets/pdf_file/0018/313821/HPHP-deakin-literature-review.pdf

Manning, R. E. (2010) *Studies in outdoor recreation* (3rd ed.). Corvallis, OR: Oregon State University Press.

Marks, D. F., & Yardley, L. (2004). *Research methods for clinical and health psychology.* London, UK: Sage.

McCright, A. M., & Dunlap, R. E. (2011). The politicization of climate change and polarization in the American public's views of global warming, 2001–2010. *The Sociological Quarterly, 52,* 155–194. doi:10.1111/j.1533-8525.2011.01198.x

Merchant, C. (1980). *The death of nature: Women, ecology, and the scientific revolution.* San Francisco, CA: Harper.

MIND UK (2007). *Report: Ecotherapy – The green agenda for mental health.* http://www. mind.org.uk/media/273470/ecotherapy.pdf

National Council on Measurement in Education (NCME, 1999). *Standards for educational and psychological testing.* Washington, DC: American Psychological Association. Retrieved from http://www.apa.org/science/programs/testing/standards.aspx#overview

Nijmeijer, J. S., Minderaa, R. B., Buitelaar, J. K., Mulligan, A., Hartman, C. A., & Hoekstra, P. J. (2008). Attention-deficit/hyperactivity disorder and social dysfunctioning. *Clinical Psychology Review, 28,* 692–708.

Norton, C. L., & Holguin, B. (2011). Restoration not incarceration: Preliminary evaluation of an eco-social work intervention for formerly incarcerated young adults. *Ecopsychology, 3,* 205–212.

Parkinson, J. (2007). Establishing national mental health and well-being indicators for Scotland. *Journal of Public Mental Health, 5,* 42–48.

Pekarik, G. & Guidry, L. (1999). Relationship of satisfaction to symptom change, follow-up adjustment, and clinical significance in private practice. *Professional Psychology: Research and Practice, 5,* 474–478.

Pergams, O. R. W., & Zaradic, P. A. (2008). *Evidence for a fundamental and pervasive shift away from nature-based recreation.* http://www.pnas.org/content/105/7/2295.abstract

Price, D. D., Finnis, D. B., & Benedetti, F. (2008). A comprehensive review of the placebo effect: Recent advances and current thought. *Annual Review of Psychology, 59,* 565–590.

Priest, S., & Gass, M. (2005) *Effective leadership in adventure programming* (2nd ed.). Danvers, MA: Human Kinetics Publishing.

Program for Cultural Competence in Research (2010). *Cultural competence in research annotated bibliography.* Harvard Catalyst Program for Faculty Development & Diversity. https://catalyst.harvard.edu/pdf/diversity/CCR-annotated-bibliography-10-12-10ver2-FINAL.pdf

Randall, R. (2005). A new climate for psychotherapy? *Psychotherapy & Politics International, 3,* 165–179.

Reese, R. F., & Myers, J. E. (2012). Ecowellness: The missing factor in holistic wellness models. *Journal of Counseling & Development, 90,* 400–406.

Richards, T. J., & Richards, L. (1994). Using computers in qualitative research. In N. D. Denzin & Y. S. Lincoln (Eds.), *Handbook of qualitative research.* London, UK: Sage.

Russell, K. C. (2003). Assessing treatment outcomes in outdoor behavioral healthcare using the Youth Outcome Questionnaire. *Child and Youth Care Forum, 32,* 355–381.

Russell, K. C. (2005). Two years later: A qualitative assessment of youth well-being in the role of aftercare in outdoor behavioral healthcare treatment. *Child and Youth Care Forum, 34,* 209–239.

Smith J. A., Harre, R., & Langenhove, L. V. (1995). *Rethinking methods in psychology.* London, UK: Sage.

Stern, P. C. (2000). Toward a coherent theory of environmentally significant behavior. *Journal of Social Issues, 56,* 407–424.

Stokols, D., Misra, S., Runnerstrom, M. G., & Hipp, J. A. (2009). Psychology in an age of ecological crisis: From personal angst to collective action. *American Psychologist, 64,* 181–193. doi:10.1037/a0014717

Ulrich, R. S., Zimring, C., Zhu, X., DuBose, J., Seo, H., Choi, Y., Quan, X., & Joseph, A. (2008). *A review of the research literature on evidence-based healthcare design.* http://edinnovation.com.au/documents/attachments/58-hcleader-5-litreviewwp.pdf

U.S. Environmental Protection Agency (2012). *Sustainable and Healthy Communities Strategic Research Action Plan 2012–2016.* Retrieved from http://www2.epa.gov/ research/sustainable-and-healthy-communities-strategic-research-action-plan-2012-2016

Walsh, V., & Gollins, G. (1976). *An exploration of the Outward Bound process.* Denver, CO: Outward Bound Publications.

Walter, M. (2009). Participatory action research. In M. Walter (Ed.), *Social research methods* (2nd ed.). Oxford, UK: Oxford University Press.

Ware, J. E., Kosinski, M., Turner-Bower, D. M., & Gandeck, B. (2007). *User's manual for the SF-12v2™ health survey.* Lincoln, NB: Quality Metric Inc.

Wechsler, D. (1955). *Wechsler Adult Intelligence Scale manual.* New York, NY: Psychological Corporation.

White, W. (2012). A history of adventure therapy. In M. A. Gass, H. L. Gillis, & K. C. Russell (Eds.), *Adventure therapy: Theory, research, and practice* (pp. 19–46). New York, NY: Routledge.

Wilson, N. W., Fleming, S., Jones, R., Lafferty, K., Catherine, K., Seaman, P., & Knifton, L. (2010). Green shoots of recovery: The impact of a mental health ecotherapy program. *Mental Health Review Journal, 15*, 4–14.

Wilson, N. W., Jones, R., Fleming, S., Lafferty, K., Knifton, L., Cathrine, K., & McNish, H. (2011). Branching out: The impact of a mental health ecotherapy program. *Ecopsychology, 3*, 51–57.

Wilson, S. (2009). *Research is ceremony: Indigenous research methods.* Winnipeg, CA: Fernwood.

Suggested Readings

American Horticultural Therapy Association: http://ahta.org/

Children & Nature Network – Research Page: http://www.childrenandnature.org/documents/C118/

Forestry Scotland Branching Out program: http://www.forestry.gov.uk/branchingout

University of Illinois Landscape and Human Health Laboratory (LHHL): http://lhhl.illinois.edu

Outdoor Behavioral Healthcare Industry Research Council: http://www.obhrc.org/

UK Mind Program: http://www.mind.org.uk/media/273470/ecotherapy.pdf

18

Research and Design for Special Populations

John Zeisel[1], Robert Gifford[2], Mark Martin[3], and
Lindsay J. McCunn[2]

[1] Hearthstone Alzheimer Care, United States
[2] University of Victoria, BC, Canada
[3] Optimal Environments, Inc., FL, United States

Ethan's grandmother lives a short bike ride away, in the bungalow she had spent all her adult life. They had been packing boxes together for days. Her dementia was worsening and everyone in the family thought it best that she move into a care home before it got worse. As the transition drew nearer, Ethan naturally thought about the challenges she would face with new people and routines in an unfamiliar environment. He also wondered how she would find her way around the care home and how she would figure out how to bring the comforts of her life at home into an institutional setting. He wondered how an environmental psychologist might sensitively research building design for the special group of individuals living in the care home. What would a research project be like with participants in a therapeutic setting who sometimes do not fully grasp where they are, or have a wide variety of physical problems? More than when he was an undergraduate, Ethan began to appreciate the practical and ethical difficulties in conducting environment-behavior research among persons living with cognitive or physical deficits. He planned to pay close attention to the physical environment at the care home, once his grandmother had settled in.

Designing physical environments for persons with different mental and physical needs and abilities requires understanding both the needs and people's capacities, and how these interact with built environments. People–place research affords such understanding, enabling designers to create built settings that better meet whatever special needs users of an environment might have. However, specialized research methods are required when designing for vulnerable individuals.

Research Methods for Environmental Psychology, First Edition. Edited by Robert Gifford.
© 2016 John Wiley & Sons, Ltd. Published 2016 by John Wiley & Sons, Ltd.

To address the difficult issues (and rewarding outcomes) surrounding designs for special populations, this chapter discusses research methods for studying the preferences, attitudes, and behaviors of persons who live with cognitive decline (e.g., dementia) and physical challenges (e.g., multiple sclerosis).

Dementia and Environmental Design

The likelihood of developing **dementia** increases linearly with age. In 2011, the oldest baby boomers turned 65. This is one indication that the need for environment-behavior research that serves older people with cognitive challenges will increase. Such research is essential to ensure that residential and therapeutic settings are accessible, comfortable, safe, and support as full and rewarding a life as possible for persons who live with cognitive decline such as dementia.

To select the most effective research methods for this purpose requires understanding the nature of cognitive decline and its implications for design. The term "dementia" means cognitive decline. Alzheimer's disease includes a group of dementia causes that are linked by a common brain pathology characterized by fibrillary plaques and neuronal tangles.

Linked to reduced function in the brain's frontal lobe, people who live with dementia typically find it increasingly challenging to negotiate new physical settings by themselves. This brain region supports executive function, the ability to make sense of and organize complex processes, in this particular case, complexity in the physical environment. Executive function is the ability to mentally combine separate elements into a whole, to organize steps in a process into a coherent sequence, and to make sense of seemingly random events, such as the many steps required to make a cup of tea or brush one's teeth. Think about how many there are and you will understand how essential executive function is for everyday life.

Persons with dementia, faced with a high degree of complexity without assistance of others, often exhibit secondary symptoms, such as apathy, anxiety, agitation, or aggression – the four "A's" of Alzheimer's. These behaviors are not directly caused by changes to the brain, but result from the fact that the person cannot easily accomplish what she or he wants. Environments that are difficult to navigate often cause these secondary symptoms because people become frustrated; environments that indicate the intended use of a space with no ambiguity can reduce these reactions. This clearly highlights the importance of appropriate building design for people with dementia.

Another consideration when designing for people with dementia is that many have difficulty navigating a building from entry to destination or remembering where places in the building are, even when the place would be very familiar to the ordinary person after a few visits. Ordinarily, **cognitive mapping** enables us to figure out, and then remember, landmarks and paths connecting the places we travel to and from. Cognitive mapping – related both to short-term memory and executive function – often is significantly impaired for those living with dementia. Successful cognitive mapping employs physical and symbolic landmarks as navigational guides. Therefore, the more a physical environment can provide such landmarks as cues to where a person has been, is, and is going to, the longer they will be able to function independently in a setting.

Another manifestation of dementia of the Alzheimer's type is reduced impulse control, which rests in three parts of the brain: the hippocampus (helps with the allocation, storing, and recall of memories), the orbitofrontal cortex (decision making), and the thalamus (sensory perception and motor function regulation). Persons with impaired impulse control due to impacts on these brain areas, who find themselves in an emotional situation, are likely to express strong feelings of attraction, anger, fear, or joy. While others with greater impulse control might feel these emotions, they pay more attention to consideration of politeness, appropriateness, and how others will be affected by their behavior. Persons with Alzheimer's with impaired impulse control are likely to say what they feel without reservation. Over time, as impulse control structures in the brain are progressively damaged during the process of dementia, people may increasingly "act out" when confronting frustrating environmental elements. For example, if such a person encounters a door they expect to be open but is locked instead, he or she might strike the door or shout out.

Research methods: General considerations

Conducting environmental design research on perceptions, behaviors, and attitudes of those with cognitive deficits can be a challenge if the researcher merely employs standard methods he or she might employ in others situations or even methods appropriate to other special needs groups. Each such group is different, with its own specifications, limitations, and idiosyncrasies. Nevertheless, most environment-behavior research studies share the broad goal of maximizing the fit between people and their environments. These studies often examine whether a physical setting matches what people intend to do in it and whether the setting is supportive, comfortable, and safe. In addition, as mentioned earlier, for special populations, environment–behavior mismatches can have significant negative consequences, meaning the contribution of design and the built environment to their well-being is that much more important.

Environment-behavior research methods used to study the needs of those with cognitive decline living at home should consider at least two things. First, those who still live at home are more likely to be at an earlier stage of dementia than those who reside in an assisted living facility. Thus, they will generally be more able to answer questions directly and be more familiar with their immediate surroundings. Second, a spouse or child living with a study participant at home is likely to be able to contribute knowledge about a participant's needs and preferences whereas, in an assisted living facility, professional caregivers are more likely to know the person only in the context of that setting. Depending on the effort made to share a resident's lifestyle experience and history, assisted living personnel may be more or less knowledgeable about those aspects of a participant's life.

Because one of the most important problems that persons with dementia encounter in the built environment is finding their way around, we focus on that next.

Methods for studying wayfinding strategies for people with dementia

Wayfinding is the mental and physical act of navigating through an environment. For most of us, finding our way around a place is an unconscious process involving procedural memory and learning. The same is true for those with dementia: the more self-evident a pathway is and the more cues along the path are multi-sensory, the easier wayfinding will be. Because those with dementia often have difficulty generating cognitive maps to follow, as discussed earlier, they often appear to "wander" aimlessly, although they themselves feel they have a purpose and destination.

Behavioral research can help discover the ways in which those with memory and cognitive impairments find their way; this knowledge can in turn be used to design environments that assist people to find their way rather than to wander. As discussed elsewhere in this book (see Chapters 2 and 9), observational methods employed to study non-specialized populations can also be appropriate for use with special populations.

A study conducted by one of this chapter's authors and his colleagues can serve as a practical example of this kind of observational method (Zeisel et al., 2003). The researchers followed and observed with a behavioral checklist persons with Alzheimer's disease who walked past a certain point in a special care unit at a randomly selected time every hour. The researchers then identified each item in the environment a person looked at (e.g., painting or photograph), stopped in front of (e.g., a table or window) or passed through, (e.g., doorway), and where the participant ended up.

To collect data for this study, the researchers used a "post-it note" method of environmental tagging. Just below the ceiling, where people do not usually look (approximately 8 feet up a wall), they stuck a yellow post-it note with a large black number representing whatever object was directly below. As someone with Alzheimer's walked by the object, raised their eyes to look at it, walked through it, or stopped in front of it, the object's number was recorded, as well as how much time the person was engaged in the particular behavior.

A special pen was used to swipe a barcode on a plasticized code sheet on which every post-it note number and each behavior was listed in advance. When a researcher observed a behavior and swiped the appropriate barcode associated with that object, an automatic timer started. The timer stopped when the barcode was swiped again, thereby recording not only which object was part of the person's natural wayfinding, but also how long the behavior lasted.

Passini et al. (1998) employed another research method used in studying wayfinding for people with dementia. Researchers followed and observed patients as they walked through a hospital. They recorded and described "on-the-spot" where participants lost their way, often where signs stated too much information (e.g., a sign indicating where the dining room was, along with the entire lunch menu and times when the dining room was open).

One critique of this method for observing wayfinding behavior is that, depending on the physical characteristics of the setting and the role the observer takes, it can be quite intrusive, influencing the data. If they become aware they are being followed and observed, participants may alter their behavior. Employing this research approach requires that investigators select an unobtrusive role (e.g., wearing a white coat in a hospital), and position themselves appropriately.

Methods for studying environmental familiarity for people with dementia

Researchers may elect to employ other approaches to study how familiarity of a setting influences the way people think, feel, and behave. Three methods are readily available for this. The first is to simply ask the person what she or he perceives and experiences in familiar versus strange settings. The second is to systematically observe details about the physical space inhabited by persons with dementia. The third is to observe behavior in the environments occupied by people living with dementia.

When simply asking persons with dementia about environmental attributes they think are familiar, one effective method is the sorting task. Sorting is a hard-wired skill in all humans and therefore is less affected by dementia (Zeisel, 2009). Asking participants to sort visually instead of using only words optimizes the quality of sorting task data. For example, a researcher might prepare a set of cards with drawings or photos of various objects and places and ask the person to sort them into two boxes, one labeled "familiar" and the other "unfamiliar." A pre-test to establish word meanings can be useful in selecting which pair of words works best. For example, the boxes might be labeled "relaxes me" and "makes me nervous" rather than "familiar" and "unfamiliar," which can be too abstract a concept for some people with dementia.

Another strategy for using the sorting method is to slowly go through a deck of cards with each person, showing the cards one at a time and asking whether the image on the card is familiar or unfamiliar, then encouraging the person to independently place the card in the appropriate box. Before starting this process, a pilot phase is essential in which the researcher demonstrates the correct behavior using cards that will not be included in the main part of the study, so the person clearly understands the task.

The second method often used to learn how those with dementia conceptualize familiarity is to observe and record the physical environments they inhabit. This method requires the researcher to list and categorize each object these persons choose to keep in spaces they spend considerable amounts of time (e.g., sitting room, bedroom, and so on). One challenge with this method is the difficulty in determining whether people placed an object in a particular spot because its familiarity made them feel relaxed, or whether someone else – a caring spouse or adult child, for instance – put the object in a certain place because he or she thought it would be functional or calming for the participant. Obviously, one way to overcome this challenge is to interview caregivers about this.

The third method involves systematically observing the behavior of persons with dementia to glean information about familiar objects and spaces. This method requires an analytic leap on the part of the researcher, who must decide whether an observed behavior reflects a participant's response to familiarity, or to a lack of familiarity, of an object or setting. For example, a researcher may define behaviors such as lower agitation, aggression, and apathy as positive responses to familiar objects and surroundings when they are actually defensive responses to an unfamiliar setting. One way to ensure that such observations are valid is to ask the person to talk about the objects in their personal space after observations have been recorded.

Case Study: A Multiple Sclerosis Center Program and Post-Occupancy Evaluation

This case study describes the **programming** and **post-occupancy evaluation** (see earlier chapters) of a building designed to provide an envelope for three groups of people who deal with **multiple sclerosis (MS)**: those afflicted with the disease; staff members who help them; and friends and family who visit. Under one roof, it houses spaces for physiotherapy, social interaction, teaching and learning, administration, storage, leisure (crafts and exercises), and counseling. The design had to recognize that users would be engaged in many diverse activities. The goal was to create a facility that successfully combined a clinic, an office, and a home away from home.

Multiple sclerosis is a debilitating and poorly understood disease that affects thousands of people around the world in a broad variety of ways. The condition often leads to reductions in muscle function that confine its victims to wheelchairs. MS is not steadily progressive, but rather follows unpredictable cycles. In many cases, the severity of MS changes spontaneously and individuals often recover for a time, which can improve their mobility and other abilities.

MS poses special challenges when designing whole buildings for those with the condition. First, individuals with MS are often diagnosed in their 20s but usually live a near-normal lifespan, so MS facilities must be planned for all adult age groups. Second, MS affects a variety of physiological systems, from vision to fine motor coordination, overall strength, and bladder control. These effects can vary in any individual both in terms of severity and the physiological system affected. Third, at any given time, people with no visible disability, others with a wide range of disabilities, as well as staff who do not have MS use the same building.

The story

One spring day, the executive director of the local Multiple Sclerosis Society phoned to ask another one of the chapter's authors to give a talk to the Society's board of directors. He was told the Society was facing a number of design challenges with the buildings they occupied. The Society was housed in three separate buildings in three different neighborhoods. One held its administrative offices, another the physiotherapy clinic, and a third its storage facilities (see Figures 18.1 and 18.3 for facades and Figure 18.2 for the interior retail area of the electronics building). Transportation and communication between the buildings were difficult and the environments of the offices and clinic were clearly inadequate.

The researcher outlined to the board the social design process by which a building could be created that incorporates the needs and preferences of building users, and

Figure 18.1 The building exterior before the renovation.

Figure 18.2   The retail area before the renovation.

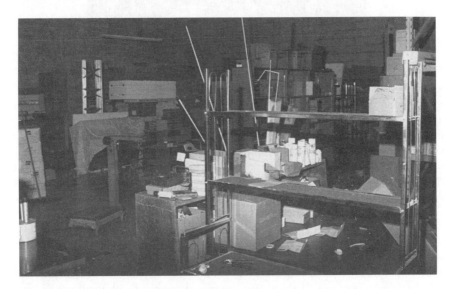

Figure 18.3   The warehouse before the renovation.

illustrated the process with examples. A few days later, the chair of the board called to negotiate a contract for programming the renovation of a retail electronics building the Society was already in the process of acquiring.

The board chair's call was welcome first because the opportunity to help design a building for a group of people with special needs was more of a challenge and thus more interesting than designing a building for a group of able-bodied persons. This project called for clear design recommendations for a group with uncommon requirements, which was a pleasant challenge.

Figure 18.4   The building exterior after the renovation.

The second reason the call was welcome was that the researcher experienced positive acceptance of the process by the board chair and his team. During the question and discussion period after the invited talk, the chair, feeling that it was his duty to take charge of the situation, rolled out a large sketchpad on a movable stand. He began offering potential design solutions to problems he thought the Society would face in the renovation. He seemed unaware that the research and design process would lead to firm design recommendations, and these speculations were too early and presumptuous.

Eventually, the executive director courageously interrupted the chair and said, "Isn't the purpose of this meeting to listen to our speaker's views on the process by which the design decisions might be made, rather than to make the decisions right now?" The talk had emphasized that the most fruitful design discussions needed to reflect the views of individuals who use the building every day – in this case MS patients, their families, staff members, and volunteers. As the project progressed, the chair enthusiastically adopted the idea that building users must be consulted in the design process.

The old and new premises

The Society's existing premises included a clinic in a local building shared with several other social service organizations, a storefront suite of offices about half a mile away, and rented storage space in a building a couple of miles from both the clinic and the offices.

The new building acquired by the Society was an L-shaped structure with two stories on the longer side and a single story warehouse on the shorter side. In moving

Figure 18.5 The physiotherapy and offices after the renovation.

Figure 18.6 The atrium after the renovation.

from three spaces to one much larger building, the Society was integrating its operations into a single building triple its present size.

The design cycle

The **design cycle** employed in the project, including detailed programming and a post-occupancy evaluation, has been described earlier in this book. In this chapter, we focus on methods used when the clients have special needs. Even if architects try to imagine how building users might function in a new space, they will have very different life experiences and perspectives from those who use the building.

Setting out

The preliminary discussions the researchers held with staff and patients indicated three overriding themes. First, there was near total consensus that the new building must be made as accessible as possible to individuals with MS who walk with difficulty or use wheelchairs. There is a great difference, the future users stressed, between saying that a building should be accessible and creating one that is actually accessible. Respondents stressed that many buildings that were supposedly accessible, were not accessible for many of those for whom it was designed. Accessibility remains an empty concept if it is not specifically defined for each type of disability, each type of activity, and each type of setting. Recommendations were requested to be based on specific definitions of disability rather than generic ones.

A second theme and goal that emerged was the significance of creating a setting that draws people together and welcomes them to a homelike place. Every effort, they emphasized, should be made to avoid institutional characteristics. A third theme the users raised was the necessity to upgrade the decor and equipment in the office and clinic areas to be more modern and professional. More specifically, this meant brightening the space by painting it, acquiring new and more functional chairs and filing cabinets, removing unrelated equipment and clutter, and rearranging the space to better reflect the flow of activities.

Charting a course

The team set about creating a list of building "domains" – that is, facets of the structure that deserved attention in the programming process. "Domain" means not only the usual functional areas of the facility (e.g., lounge, kitchen), but also design elements (e.g., lighting, ventilation) and miscellaneous design concerns (e.g., flexibility of arrangements, the approach to the building). Twenty-three domains were identified which will be described later.

The two primary methods of gathering data for the program were interviews and observations. Interviews were selected in favor of questionnaires, although questionnaires would have been more economical, because many of the respondents had difficulty writing which questionnaires would require, while interviewing left the recording of the structured dialogue to researchers.

Observation was also selected as a method to overcome the fact building users (able-bodied as well as others) are sometimes "out of touch" with their own behavior (see also Chapter 2), making self-report unreliable. When we are involved in an activity, we often unconsciously and automatically overcome and thus pay little attention to mild or moderate obstacles in the physical setting. Watching and recording how individuals actually interact with their surroundings can therefore be a valuable supplement to interviews. Observations of staff and client use of the old clinic and offices were structured to attend to all 23 domains.

Interviews

Everyone connected with the MS Society was invited to be interviewed, either through a personal invitation or through notices in the Society newsletter. While a few individual interviews were conducted, including patients, office staff, physiotherapy clinic staff, volunteers who helped in the office and clinic, the board of directors, and several groups of persons with MS from other districts, family members, and friends. Over 20 formal interviews of groups ranging in size from 1 to 25 people were conducted lasting from 1 to 3 hours. Over 80 individuals participated in interviews.

Each interview was structured to cover the 23 domains and ended with a question about whether anything pertaining to the design of the new building had been missed. Thus, the interviews were both structured, so that everyone was queried about every major domain, and unstructured, in that comments were solicited on topics important to the respondent that were omitted from the basic interview. As expected, the interviews produced a very large mass of information that had to be sorted, compared, reconciled, and integrated.

Observations

Behavioral observations of the clinic and the offices supplemented the interviews and uncovered numerous behavior patterns that no one thought to mention in the interviews. Observations also identified behavior patterns that were different from the impression given in the interviews, as well as behavior patterns that confirmed interview responses. Many hours were spent observing the workings of the office and clinic to identify typical activity patterns.

During the data collection phase, several interim meetings with board members and the executive director were held to report preliminary findings. Often, a trend in preference or behavior that we spotted was confirmed or further explained by Society officials.

Goals and recommendations

Over 150 recommendations were made. With the executive director, the architect, and the board, the researchers had to decide which would actually be beneficial, which were feasible given financial and design constraints (e.g., the shell of the building could not be substantially altered), and which the data showed would be welcomed by different individuals sharing the same part of the building. For each domain, an overall goal and a set of specific recommendations that would facilitate that goal were prepared.

Many specific recommendations were of concern only in this particular building, so not all are listed. The interested reader may, however, see brief versions of the recommendation in Tables 18.1 to 18.4. While specific design solutions must be found within the constraints of each project, the tables of domains and goals may

Table 18.1 Priority 4 (Highest) Program Recommendations.

Adopted	Partially adopted	Not adopted	No longer a concern
More, accessible washrooms	Smooth floors and sills*	Door with mail slot	Bell, for receptionist
Separate reception area	Two accessible washrooms*	Nonisolated receptionist*	Offices in showroom space
Private counseling room	Clinic shielded from foyer	Enclosed foyer	Centrally located elevator*
Automatic opening door	Coatracks in all main rooms	Handrails in all halls	
Reception desk and waiting area			
Telephone in reception			
Parking visible tram reception			
Coatracks in foyer			
Noninstitutional foyer			
Remove boards on windows			
Building mostly nonsmoking			
Smoking room			
Expand clinic by 3,000 sq. ft.			
Open-space clinic			
Staff lunchroom			
Direct passage to clinic/office			
New telephone system			
Wire for more phones			
Mirrors in clinic			
Screen clinic from parking			
Accessible clinic coat rack			
Review tire alarms			
Fire Department Examination			

* Item recommended in the POE study for adoption or completion when funds become available.

Table 18.2 Priority 3 Program Recommendation.

Adopted	Partially adopted	Not adopted	No longer a concern
Social lounge	Ramped curbs	Separate handicraft area*	Elevator for two wheelchairs*
Equipment repair area	Illuminated durable sign	Street signs	Diffusers on clinic lamps
More, closed office space	Accessible and flexible clinic tables	Entry overhang	Ceiling fans
More storage space	Separate craft and physiotherapy storage*	Grid system for clinic equipment	Upstairs office space*
Kitchen	Easy-opening doors*	Resting bed	Inventory control
Handy DART parking spots	Accessible and non central smoking room*	Separate painting and physiotherapy*	
Well-lit parking			
Improve landscaping			
Increased natural light			
Full-spectrum and indirect light			
Rheostat controls			
Incandescent lighting in lounge			
Smooth flooring			
Shelves for ultrasound			
Equipment and sink			
Plants in main rooms			
Lockable clinic			
Locking storage and offices			

* Item recommended in the POE study for adoption or completion when funds become available.

Table 18.3   Priority 2 & 1 Program Recommendations.

Adopted	Partially adopted	Not adopted	No longer a concern
Educational space	Wider parking spots	Two meeting rooms*	Tuck and/or gift shop
Blackboard	Disability parking signs	Games and exercise space	Hot-water heating
More electrical outlets	Electrical outlets higher than usual	Hydrotherapy pool	
	Light and heat controls lower than usual	Fireplace	
		Overnight accommodation*	
		Eight ambulatory parking spots	
		No concrete parking barriers	
		Repave parking lot	
		Snow grating	
		Double glazed windows	
		Cafe tables for lounge	

*Item recommended in the POE study for adoption or completion when funds become available.

alert designers and facility managers to important considerations in the design of any building for the disabled.

The 23 domains are presented here in the order that a typical user or visitor might experience them in the process of finding the place, entering, engaging in various activities, and leaving:

- **Approaching the building.** The building is in an odd corner of town, not on a main street. GOAL: The building must be easy for visitors and new members to find. Signage must begin at nearby main streets.
- **Parking.** The current parking lot contains 20 spaces. The width of these is normal to slightly narrow for retail parking. The lot is flat and paved asphalt. At busy times the parking lot may not hold all the vehicles of those using the building. GOAL: Parking must be close and plentiful, and arranged so that patients, staff, volunteers, and visitors (in that order) have easy access to the main entrance.
- **Building exterior.** Part of the building is clad in wood and stone, and the rest is clad in stucco. The small boulevard area is an untended jumble of shrubs and weeds. GOAL: The outside of the building must be attractive and non-institutional in appearance.
- **Entry.** Three small glass doors currently serve as entries to the retail part of the building. One small wooden door and a large vertically-opening metal door serve as entries to the warehouse area. GOAL: Provide maximum accessibility to the building with minimum exposure to the elements. Smooth and sheltered passage from vehicles to the interior is desirable.
- **Foyer.** The present building has no real foyer. GOAL: Provide an area inside the entrance for orientation, information, and waiting for transportation.

Table 18.4   Program Recommendations Not Given a Priority.

Adopted	Partially adopted	Not adopted	No longer a concern
Break up "warehouse" look	Textured and lower lounge ceiling	Umbrella rack in foyer	Staff parking in nearby offsite lot
Operable windows	Stackable clinic chairs	Art on clinic ceiling	Parking on road
Heat pump	Full-size kitchen	"You-Are-Here-Map"	Two-hour street parking
Locally controlled heating	Accessible washrooms*	Door handle near hinges*	Parking-lot sign
Ventilate to ASHRAE standards	"Occupied" washroom signs*	Shallow sink	Clinic staff door
Avoid dry air	Adequate space below sinks*	Single control taps	Assessment area by reception
Quiet HVAC system	Side toilet paper*	Zero-gap toilets	Office partitions
Carpeted office	Easy-reach soap dispenser*	Wall-hung toilets	Office carpet
Desk for clinic	Plants in every room	Various-height toilets*	Noninstitutional maps
Desk chairs for office	Smooth floors and sills*	Side toilet handle	Fund-raisers' plaques
Clinic color—not white or green	Doors with lever-type handles	Off-track washrooms	Marked volunteer area
Kitchen equipment	Clinic sound absorbers*	Bell in washrooms*	Emulate good local signs
Retain and upgrade washrooms	Art in major areas	"Century" tub	New kitchen cups
Wide washroom doors	TV, stereo, and cable	Sound system	Social lounge kitchen
Lever-type door handles		Mat fixed to bed	Smooth tile flooring
Smooth flooring		Wheelchair scale	Upstairs shower
No privacy screens		Longer parallel bars	Educational washroom
Storage cabinets		Recreational equipment	One computer
Towel dispenser			Office display space
Adequate floorspace			Two-wheelchair elevator*
Wheelchair-height counters			Stair use restrictions
Adequate hallway widths			Elevator*
Washer and dryer			Adequate burglar alarm

(continued)

Table 18.4   (continued)

Adopted	Partially adopted	Not adopted	No longer a concern
Adequate phones			
Photocopy machine			
Quiet typewriters			
Janitorial equipment			
VCR			
Nonsmoking zone			
Preserve natural light			
Private ultrasound area			
Soundproof meeting rooms			
Review keying and control			

*Item recommended in the POE study tor adoption or completion when funds become available.

- **Lighting.** The building currently is lit with banks of fluorescent ceiling fixtures. Some, but not all, MS patients report difficulties with fluorescent lighting. GOAL: Reduce irritation and headaches that might be caused by lighting. Do so without significantly increasing lighting costs.
- **Windows.** Fenestration in the electronics building was limited to the parking lot side of the building and the south side, facing the street. The latter windows are boarded up because of recurrent vandalism. Other parts of the building have no windows. Windows on the second story can be opened, but those facing the parking lot on the first floor cannot. GOAL: Provide as much natural light and individual control of ventilation as possible within current energy conservation standards.
- **Heating.** MS patients are sensitive to coolness and complain that they cannot adjust the temperature. GOAL: Provide heating that is not too drying and is subject to personal control.
- **Ventilation.** Some MS patients are particularly sensitive to air pollutants. Many are strongly opposed to smoking, but others are dedicated smokers. Some valuable volunteers are smokers and should not be driven away by a total ban on smoking. Certain stressful occasions, such as counseling for newly diagnosed patients, may make smoking an acute need even for casual smokers. Activities such as painting produce fumes that require extra ventilation. GOAL: An excellent supply of clean air is necessary and a place in the building for smokers.
- **Clinic ceilings.** Physiotherapy often requires patients to lie on their backs for up to 45 minutes. Most ceilings are dull. Some heavy clinic equipment needs to be suspended from the ceiling. GOAL: Provide visual interest (e.g., art) on the ceiling for patients who lie on their backs for long periods in the clinic. Ensure that the clinic ceiling is strong enough to support equipment.

- **Floors.** The first floor of the electronics building is covered with tiles; the second with carpeting. Underneath, it is pitted and uneven in places. GOALS: Provide maximum ease of movement for ambulatory and chair-bound patients. Reduce noise and meet the aesthetic concerns of office staff. Smooth the floor as much as possible (more so than for an able-bodied population) to avoid painful bumps for wheelchair users and unnecessary lifting of legs for those who walk with difficulty.
- **Space.** The newly developed space will triple the old space, so there should be plenty of room to design for each different activity. GOAL: Provide adequate space for all activities in the building.
- **Furniture.** Some furniture will be moved from the old buildings, but some will need to be acquired. GOAL: Specify tables, chairs, and other furnishings that are comfortable and efficient.
- **Decor.** The most common opinion expressed was that the new building avoid an institutional look. The terms "pleasant" and "homelike" were mentioned often. Naturally, a variety of opinions about specific colors that would create the desired effect were expressed. GOAL: Decorate the clinic area in warm but not garish tones and the office area to look professional.
- **Signs.** Signs may be inadequate in number or in information, they may be over-done and institutional, or they may serve as aids that help people find their way and prevent accidental intrusions (e.g., salespeople in the clinic). GOAL: Use a system of signs that informs without being overbearing.
- **Lunchroom.** The electronics building has a staff lunchroom on the second floor containing seating and basic kitchen facilities. MS office staff currently takes coffee breaks and are on call if needed during these breaks while staff on lunch breaks are supposed to be off duty. In the new location, staff may leave the building for lunch more often than they have in the past. Since the second floor as a whole is not intended at present to be developed, first-floor space for staff lunches is needed. GOAL: Provide an indoor "getaway" for staff when they choose not to leave the building for lunch.
- **Kitchen.** Current kitchen facilities are limited to the kitchenette in the lunchroom. GOAL: Provide space for basic kitchen functions in the office, clinic, social area, and future occupational therapy area.
- **Bathrooms.** The electronics building has two washrooms upstairs and one downstairs. All three are typical (not very accessible) washrooms. One upstairs washroom has a standard shower. Accessible washrooms are near the top of most MS clients' list of priorities and are essential to a successful MS facility. GOAL: Provide washrooms that are fully accessible to wheelchair and ambulatory clients located near each major center of activity.
- **Flexibility of spatial arrangements.** The increased space available in the new building should reduce the need for flexibility and a separate space therefore might be dedicated to some activities that formerly occurred in the same place. However, flexibility is still needed in some spaces. For example, the office computer needs to be easily available to multiple users. GOAL: Use separate spaces for incompatible activities but provide spatial arrangements that promote cooperation where activities should be or must be well coordinated.
- **Machines and equipment.** Some machines and equipment will be brought from the current buildings and some will have to be acquired. GOAL: Provide machines

and equipment that promote efficiency, professionalism, and pleasantness in these three settings.

- **Adjacencies.** Activities from two buildings will be combined in one new building, but the new building was not designed for physiotherapy. Careful consideration must be given to possible clashes between individuals involved in office work, physiotherapy, crafts, socializing, counseling, and meeting. Patients undergoing physiotherapy must not be exposed to the view of passersby. GOAL: Design the building so that it promotes a sense of unity in the Society as a whole, but arrange activities so that noise and visual access do not cause privacy problems.
- **Personal possessions.** Staff, clients, and visitors carry personal items into the building. GOAL: Provide space for these items that maximizes convenience of access and security.
- **Building security.** While security is important, so is homelike quality. GOAL: Provide a secure environment for all building users, but not at the expense of the homelike quality of the spaces.

Ranking and wrangling

As noted earlier, over 150 specific recommendations in 23 domains were reported to the board. While each one is important, the board felt that some recommendations were more important than others. The Society's board therefore made the final decision about the relative importance of each recommendation.

The board graded each recommendation into one of the following categories:

- Priority 4: Recommendations judged essential.
- Priority 3: Recommendations judged very desirable.
- Priorities 2 and 1: Recommendations judged desirable, but less so than the foregoing.

Generally, the board agreed with the final recommendation rankings. A few notable exceptions occurred in which the research team tried to convince the board that a particular recommendation needed a higher priority. For example, whether windows should be operable sparked debate. Some board members believed any windows that *can* be opened *will* be left open at inappropriate times (such as all night), leading to vast increases in energy costs. The research team argued that building users have an educable and responsible nature and that giving them that seemingly small sense of control is valuable. The research team won that debate, but lost others.

Design and construction

As often happens, the project became deadline-oriented. The architect, who had been selected from a short list of those with experience in designing facilities for the disabled, hurried to translate as many of the recommendations as possible into a formal design. Perhaps because of the rush, there was less communication between the research team and the architect in this period than might be desirable. Little communication took place either because the 36 pages of specific, ranked recommendations was an entirely adequate basis for the formal design or the architect was unaccustomed to interacting with program consultants.

The post-occupancy evaluation

There were casual reports that most building users were very happy with the building. However, occupants of new buildings usually undergo a "honeymoon" period during which their satisfaction is based more on the newness of the building than on its day-to-day performance in the longer run. Therefore, the research team waited 18 months to perform a post-occupancy evaluation not influenced by the honeymoon effect.

Responsible environmental psychologists are not interested in POEs that merely make their work look good; they want to know the truth about how a building is performing. The POE often takes the form of a new set of recommendations because of: (a) slips between the program and construction; (b) program elements that were not quite functional; and (c) naturally evolving occupant needs and patterns of use. A four-part evaluation was conducted: audit, interviews, observations, and new recommendations.

Audit.   No building is constructed with every recommendation fulfilled. Some recommendations fall victim to shortages of funds, some are not as urgent as others, and some conflict with other more important recommendations. We began our POE by conducting an audit. Which recommendations from the original program were incorporated into the new building, and which were not? Each recommendation was placed into one of four categories:

- Adopted (fully incorporated into the building).
- Partially adopted (done partly or in some locations only).
- Not adopted (no sign of the recommendation).
- No longer a concern (N/A) (the recommendation is now irrelevant because of other changes, or there is no evidence that anyone cares anymore).

Not all of even the highest priority recommendations were adopted. This is not particularly surprising, given the large number of recommendations that were made (and followed). An estimate of the fulfillment rate of the recommendations was made. Why bother counting them up at all? First, the board should carefully examine all the recommendations that were not fully adopted as part of the basis for planning the next round of changes to the building. All the recommendations that were not already adopted should be reconsidered. Second, a measure of the fulfillment rate might be related to the satisfaction of building users. For example, to obtain a 90% approval rate, must one fulfill 90% of all recommendations, or will 70% or less do? Next the team set out to determine how satisfied the users were.

Interviews.   The goal was to discuss the new building with as many building users as possible. About 80 clients, staff, board members, and others had been inter-viewed in the programming phase. To interview the same number of users within the constraints of a smaller POE budget, the interview was designed to focus on the respondent's salient satisfactions and dissatisfactions, rather than systematically covering every domain of the building. Interviews were conducted with all 9 staff members, 38 clients, 6 volunteers, 8 spouses, and 16 board members, for a total of 77 individuals.

Respondents were asked, "What do you like most about the new building?" The interviewer repeated the question once in order to elicit any further building "likes." The interviewer then asked, "What do you like least about the building?" and repeated the question as before. Next, the question was asked, "Overall, how satisfied are you with the building?" Finally, respondents were asked how often, if ever, they participate in the organized programs that occur in the afternoon and whether and how often they informally drop into the center.

The natural turnover in Society membership, combined with some differences in respondent availability and willingness to discuss the building's design, resulted in the POE interviews being divided about equally between those who were involved in the programming phase and those who were not. The most-liked features of the new building are listed in Table 18.5.

Table 18.5   Most-Liked Building Features in the POE, with Sample Comments (number of mentions follows each item)

Frequently mentioned features	*Less-often-mentioned features (under five mentions)*
Light (sunny and bright) 20*	Parking (convenient)
Spacious (openness) 20* "Gives psychological uplift"	[not mentioned by physio. or office staff]
Everything (the whole building) 16* "It's like the Ritz-Carlton compared to before"	Our own building "Equals positive in change of attitudes"
Accessibility (client friendly) 16* "Building has TOTAL accessibility"	"Even clients who don't regularly visit take pride in the facility"
[not mentioned by physio, or office staff]	One level (no stairs)
Integrated facility (proximity of staff) 15 "Not scattered, feels whole"	[only mentioned by once/week clients and board]
Atrium (and the plants) 12 "Enjoy the area, even it I don't spend much time in there"	Equipment (amount and proximity) Windows
Layout (convenience) 11 "I know where everything is" Number of washrooms 11	Colors [only mentioned by volunteers and physio. staff]
[only mentioned by clients and volunteers]	Smoke room
Indirect lighting It "If it was bad, we'd notice"	[only mentioned by once/week clients and office staff]
Lounge 9 "A nice place, and comfortable"	
Library 7	
[only mentioned by clients and volunteers]	
Sliding doors 6	
Decor and furniture (attractive) 6 "Quality of furniture gives message that clients are important"	
Kitchen 5	
Atmosphere 5	

* mentioned by more than 20 percent of respondents

The 77 respondents mentioned a total of 195 most-liked features, about 2.5 items per respondent. The features mentioned by at least 20% of those we interviewed were:

- the light, sunny, bright atmosphere;
- the openness and spaciousness;
- "everything" (the whole building); and
- accessibility.

These four features account for 72 of the 195 mentions. These features and the remaining, less-often mentioned features are listed in Table 18.5. Nearly half of the respondents (36) could not think of anything they disliked about the building. The entire group of 77 respondents mentioned a total of 71 least-liked features, about .9 items per respondent. Thus, one indication of overall satisfaction is that the average respondent ventured 2.5 times as many "most-liked" features as "least-liked" features. The two domains that received the most "least-liked" mentions were bathrooms and storage. The details of these concerns are listed in Table 18.6, along with the other "least-liked" features mentioned in the interviews.

Table 18.6   Least-Liked Building Features (number of mentions follows each item).

Frequently mentioned features	*Less-often-mentioned concerns (under five mentions)*
Nothing (so far) 36	Temperature (clinic and assessment area too hot)
Numerous problems were cited with the bathrooms 18	Noise in clinic waiting area
Bathroom rails are shaky and some would like to have rails mounted on the walls	Front door (closes too quickly)
Some found the height of the toilet to be a problem	Smoking room (entry difficult, not used, fumes come into bathroom, no sand in ashtrays)
Bathroom doors were hard to close from the inside and the locks were difficult	Parking (not enough)
Counters were too low for some chairs to get under and not all visitors found the sinks accessible	Facade (too much cement)
	Atmosphere (still a little too institutional)
People found the soap dispenser and the toilet paper hard to reach	Handrails (too few)
The placement of the light switches was seen as awkward and the bathroom towels were cited as hard to use	Lounge (purpose mixed up, carpet hard to wheel on)
	Atrium (floor sills, not used much)
Storage was the next largest concern 9	Kitchen (colors are too institutional, no space for dishwasher)
Amount of storage space	Clinic (pillars present obstacles, space becoming too tight, hanging lights hard to maintain)
Blocked access to the clinic storage	
Use of the elevator shaft for storage	Office (circulation bottleneck, chair glide-pad too small)
Painting storage not being separate from the clinic (as recommended)	Second floor (not being used)
Type and height of shelving	

Next, respondents were asked for their overall level of satisfaction with the new building, offering the alternatives "very unsatisfied," "somewhat unsatisfied," "neutral," "somewhat satisfied," and "very satisfied." About 95% of the respondents said they were "very satisfied" and the other 5% pronounced themselves "somewhat satisfied."

The next interview question asked respondents to mention changes they would like to see in the building. A large number and varied range of suggestions were made. These were evaluated and many were incorporated into the new POE recommendations.

Observations.   Interviews allow building users to report their satisfactions and their beliefs about what is right and wrong about the building. Several hours were also spent observing normal building activities in the office, clinic, and during some programs (bridge, Tai Chi, and painting). Notes on these sessions fill several pages, but two examples were that card-playing (and similar activities) could be improved by the addition of larger tables, and too much time was spent adjusting and jockeying furniture in preparation.

When the new building was being planned, some speculated that a new, larger, attractive building would draw more people. Over the first year, this speculation was confirmed. The clinic now saw about 20% more clients than one year ago. The office staff reported an increase in the number of visitors (both patients and outsiders). The number of staff hours also increased, and a new occupational therapist was hired.

New recommendations.   The changes recommended in the POE were based on several sources: the inventory of original recommendations (i.e., those that were not adopted or not fully adopted in the construction phase); suggestions made by respondents in the POE study; and changes based on observations of the building in action.

The recommended changes fall into several distinct categories. The first category echoes a major theme from the programming phase, bathrooms. The MS Society has already begun to remedy the problems with the bathrooms, but some of the changes to be recommended have not yet been dealt with. Probably a few concentrated hours spent with clients who prefer different configurations would result in an array of bathroom plans that would meet the needs of nearly everyone and might prevent a long series of separate alterations.

The second category includes a collection of items that would improve accessibility to clients in other areas of the building. The third category includes items that would cost relatively little but would affect a fair number of clients or staff. Clearly, as usual, some features are more desirable than others. After estimating desirability quantitatively, each item's desirability was qualitatively scored according to the following formula:

$$\text{Desirability} = \left(\text{Urgency} \times \text{Number of Building Users Affected}\right) / \text{Cost}$$

The fourth category of changes related to the acquisition of an elevator and development of the upper floor. The fifth and last category of recommended changes included items that are not particularly urgent. They were suggestions for the board to consider when some of the more immediate concerns are met.

Conclusions

Almost everyone was very satisfied with the new building. The original three goals were to create an accessible building, a true center, and a professional image. The second and third of these seem clearly present. Accessibility is very adequate in most areas of the new building, but is still not ideal. Finding the perfect bathroom (or, more accurately, the perfect *array* of bathrooms for persons whose affliction affects different parts of their bodies) is an intriguing and challenging task.

The executive director of the Society and others were convinced that the programming and post-occupancy evaluation process produced a much better facility than the normal design process would have. The difference lies in many small but important design elements that even sensitive architects would not notice, mainly because they do not experience buildings the way those afflicted with multiple sclerosis experience them.

A Note on the Ethics of Researching Special Populations

Ethical considerations are paramount when studying people with differing needs, abilities, and levels. Persons with impairments may not understand the purpose of a research project or how its results will be used. For this reason, among others, researchers need to obtain signed consent not only from family members but also from participants whenever possible. During the course of the research, observers must also be aware of implied indications of consent – called "assent." If at any time participants indicate that they do not want to take part in a study, researchers must accept this inclination immediately.

Summary and Conclusion

This chapter outlines some of the ways people with special needs can be helped by environmental psychology research methods. Observational research methods, interviews, programming, and post-occupancy evaluation are among the techniques that can be used. A take-home message for conducting environment-behavior research with special populations is that someone with a mental or physical impairment is a person first, and a study participant second. Every individual has numerous capabilities that can be employed to gather useful and valid information about their attitudes, behaviors, preferences, and feelings. Researchers who do not underestimate the capacity of participants will be most likely to discover new and exciting solutions, and make important contributions to the well-being and quality of life of special populations.

Glossary

Cognitive mapping   The mental representation of a place or space which allows an individual to acquire, code, store, recall, and decode information about it.

Dementia   A severe loss of cognitive ability in a previously unimpaired person, beyond what might be expected from normal aging.

Design cycle   The process of building design in which five phases (programming, design, construction, use, and evaluation) connect to, and build upon, each other.

Multiple sclerosis (MS)   An inflammatory disease in which the insulating covers of nerve cells in the brain and spinal cord are damaged, resulting in a wide range of physical, mental, and sometimes psychiatric symptoms.

Post-occupancy evaluation (POE)   The final phase of the design process, in which the strengths and weaknesses of a building's form and function are examined.

Programming   A phase of the design cycle in which information about a space to be built or renovated is systematically gathered, analyzed, and summarized before the formal design and construction phases occur.

References

Gifford, R., & Martin, M. (1991). A multiple sclerosis centre program and post-occupancy evaluation. In W. F. E. Preiser, J. Vischer, & E. T. White (Eds.), *Design innovation: The challenge of cultural change*. New York, NY: Van Nostrand Reinhold.

Passini, R., Rainville., C., Marchand, N., & Yves, J. (1998). Wayfinding and dementia: Some recent research findings and a look at design. *Journal of Architectural and Planning Research, 15*, 133–151.

Zeisel, J. (2009). *I'm still here: A breakthrough approach to understanding someone living with Alzheimer's*. New York: NY. Avery/Penguin.

Zeisel, J., Silverstein, N. M., Hyde, J., Levkoff, S. M., Lawton, P., & Holmes, W. (2003). Environmental correlates to behavioral outcomes in Alzheimer's special care units. *The Gerontologist, 43*, 697–711.

Suggested Readings

Day, K., & Calkins, M. P. (2002). Design and dementia. In R. B. Bechtel, & A. Churchman (Eds.), *Handbook of environmental psychology* (pp. 374–393). New York, NY: Wiley.

Preiser, W. F. E., Vischer, J. C., & White, E. T. (Eds.) (1991). *Design intervention: Toward a more humane architecture*. New York, NY:. Van Nostrand Reinhold.

Zeisel, J. (2006). *Inquiry by design: Environment, behavior, and neuroscience in architecture, interiors, landscape and planning*. New York, NY: Norton.

Zeisel, J. (2009). *I'm still here: A breakthrough approach to understanding someone living with Alzheimer's*. New York, NY: Avery/Penguin.

19

Advanced Statistics for Environment-Behavior Research
Multi-level Modeling and Structural Equation Modeling

Donald W. Hine[1], Victor Corral-Verdugo[2],
Navjot Bhullar[1], and Martha Frias-Armenta[2*]
[1] University of New England, NSW, Australia
[2] Universidad de Sonora, Mexico

Ethan stands dejectedly in the corner of the student lounge sucking the life out of his third beer. "Ugh – I was really happy to be admitted into this program for postgraduate study in environmental psychology, until I discovered that I need to enroll in advanced statistics. I thought I was through with all that crap."

Maria, an outstanding PhD candidate and wise beyond her years, gives Ethan a sympathetic look. "I feel your pain, postgraduate statistics is one tough unit. But, like they say, if it doesn't kill you …." Ethan interrupts. "Maybe it won't kill me – but it certainly depresses the hell out of me."

"Look … you need to be philosophical about these types of things. Think of advanced statistics as a door that opens to a new universe of research possibilities. Before I took the postgraduate statistics unit, I was pretty firmly stuck in the land of t-tests. Every time I came up with a new research question, it was always framed in terms of a two-group comparison on whatever dependent variable my supervisor had suggested during our last meeting."

Ethan nods to be polite, but is far from convinced that this conversation will have a happy ending. Maria persists. "But when I started learning about multilevel and structural equation modeling, my life changed. I gave up drinking to keep my mind clear, and all of a sudden I was seeing latent variables and hierarchical data structures wherever I looked. I even started writing songs about matrix algebra and getting into some engrossing discussions with my housemates about the advantages and disadvantages of different fit indices."

---

*Hine and Bhullar wrote the sections on multi-level modeling and integrated the chapter. Corral-Verdugo and Frias-Armenta wrote the section on structural equation modeling.

Research Methods for Environmental Psychology, First Edition. Edited by Robert Gifford.

Ethan looks perplexed, "You gave up drinking?"

"But the best thing ..." Maria continues, "I started thinking about my research area in a fundamentally different and much more sophisticated way. I started recognizing embarrassing flaws in my past research, and discovered that my supervisor could benefit from a few statistics tutorials himself. But most important, I finally started getting some really promising new ideas for my own research program. I had escaped t-test land, and like a liberal arts graduate, I had discovered that the world of research was far more captivating and exciting than anything I had ever encountered in the past!"

Ethan holds his hands up in surrender. "OK... you've convinced me. Maybe multivariate statistics won't be so bad after all. But I'm still not giving up beer."

This chapter serves as a conceptual introduction to two advanced statistical procedures that are becoming increasingly influential in environment-behavior research: multi-level modeling and structural equation modeling. The chapter is intended for researchers and graduate students who have a basic background in statistics but are not familiar with more advanced approaches to multivariate modeling. The chapter is organized into two parts. The first part focuses on multi-level modeling, introducing basic principles and highlighting practical issues associated with designing studies and conducting analyses. The second part focuses on structural equation modeling and follows a similar format.

Multi-level Modeling

Multi-level modeling (MLM) refers to a powerful and highly flexible set of statistical techniques designed for data that have a hierarchical or nested structure (Hox, 2010; Raudenbush & Bryk, 2002). Common examples of nested data include: (1) students sampled from classrooms, which, in turn, are sampled from schools; (2) respondents sampled from several different countries or geographical locations; and (3) multiple observations sampled over time from the same set of survey respondents. Observations collected at the lowest level of the hierarchy are typically referred to as Level 1 data, whereas data collected at higher levels are referred to as Level 2, Level 3, and so on.

Traditional approaches for dealing with nested data structures

Prior to the introduction of MLM, two analytic strategies were commonly applied to **nested data**. The first strategy, disaggregation, involves ignoring the higher levels of the nested structure and treating all data as being situated at Level 1 in the hierarchy (e.g., using students as the main unit of analysis, disregarding that some students in the sample were selected from the same classroom). The main problem with this strategy is that variance due to higher level group effects are not partitioned from the data. This results in a violation of the **independent errors assumption** that underlies most standard parametric statistical tests, resulting in inflated Type 1 error rates – that is, increasing the probability of falsely concluding variables are significantly related, when they are not. Later in the chapter, we will discuss the independent errors assumption in more depth, and explain how to assess it.

Whereas disaggregation involves ignoring higher level group differences and focusing on individual observations, aggregation involves an opposite strategy: individual observations are ignored and attention is directed to higher levels in the data hierarchy. For example, rather than using the individual respondent as the primary unit of the analysis, data are averaged to create a single data point at the level of classroom, neighborhood, nation, etc. The main problem with this approach is that much of the variability in the data is lost, fundamentally changing the research question from something about individuals to something about groups (Osborne, 2000). This can prevent researchers from investigating theoretically important questions about individual-level cognitions, affective responses, and behaviors, which traditionally have been of great interest within psychology. Aggregation to the group level can also result in substantial reductions in statistical power given that typically there are far fewer data points at Levels 2 and 3 than at Level 1 (Hox, 2010).

MLM represents an attractive alternative to disaggregation and aggregation by providing a mechanism for partitioning individual and group level variance, and then simultaneously investigating effects across multiple levels of nested data. In doing so, it helps researchers disentangle individual and group level effects, avoid the dependent errors problem arising from disaggregation, and overcome the loss in individual level variability and power associated with aggregation.

Types of research questions addressed by MLM

MLM is perhaps best conceptualized as a multi-level form of multiple regression. At the lowest level of analysis (Level 1), one or more predictor variables are arranged in a linear equation to predict a dependent variable. Generally, separate regression analyses are run for each Level 2 group (e.g., each classroom, nation), producing a set of Level 1 intercepts and beta coefficients for each group. As explained in more detail below, the Level 1 intercepts and beta coefficients are used as dependent variables in subsequent Level 2 analyses to answer a broad range of research questions. In this brief introduction, we will focus on three types of questions commonly evaluated in MLM studies.

Group differences in intercepts (means) An initial question addressed in almost all MLM studies is whether there are mean differences on a Level 1 dependent variable across a Level 2 grouping variable. For example, to determine whether concern about climate change differed across nations, one could test whether the intercepts of the Level 1 linear model (which reflect group means) differ across the countries included in the analyses.

In ANOVA terms, this would be equivalent to a one-way analysis assessing the ratio of between-group and within-group variability. This initial model is often referred to as a "null" or "baseline" model. This model is often compared with other more complex models (i.e., models including additional Level 1 and/or Level 2 predictors) using a likelihood ratio test. More complex models are only interpreted if they fit the data significantly better than the baseline model (Garson, 2012).

Group differences in slope MLM can also be used to assess whether slopes, reflecting the linear relationship between a Level 1 predictor and a Level 1 dependent variable, vary as a function of a higher level grouping variable. Building on our previous example, if a group of researchers were interested in the extent to which participants' concern about climate change is predicted by direct experience with extreme weather events (e.g., droughts, floods, bushfires), they could assess this by testing if the slopes (beta coefficients) for the weather experience predictor from the Level 1 analyses vary significantly as a function of the Level 2 grouping variable (nation). This model is sometimes referred to as a random slopes or random coefficients model, given that the beta coefficients from the Level 1 equations are computed separately for each group, and then these slopes are used as dependent variables for the Level 2 analysis.

Cross-level interactions MLM also enables researchers to investigate potential interactions across different levels of data. For example, to determine whether gross domestic product (GDP, a Level 2 variable that may reflect a nation's capacity to effectively respond and adapt to climate change effects) interacts with experience with extreme weather events (a Level 1 variable tied to participants) to predict climate change concern, one could assess this through a Level 2 model in which GDP predicts the Level 1 beta coefficients (slopes) associated with weather experiences. A significant effect for GDP would indicate that the magnitude (and possibly also the direction) of the predictive effect of weather experiences on climate change concern varies as a function of (i.e., is moderated by) nations' GDP.

For discussions about how MLM can be applied to answer more advanced questions (e.g., applications related to meta-analysis, multi-level path analysis, and growth curve analysis), we refer the interested reader to Garson (2012), Hox (2010), Raudenbush and Bryk (2002), and Tabachnick and Fidell (2012).

Selected examples from environment-behavior research

To date, MLM has not been used extensively in environment and behavior research. However, interest appears to be growing. For example, Schultz and his colleagues (2012) used MLM to investigate spatial biases in perceiving the severity of environmental problems across countries. They found that individuals who were happier, younger, and living in smaller communities tended to rate environmental problems as more severe at the global as opposed to local level. Across two samples, they found that between 13–20% of the variability in spatial bias could be attributable to country level effects, suggesting that individual level, as opposed to cultural, differences were more important in understanding this bias.

Hine, Gifford, Heath, Cooksey, and Quain (2009) applied MLM to identify which feedback cues guided harvest decisions in a computerized commons dilemma simulation. In this study, participants had to decide how many fish to harvest from a common pool each season. The simulation lasted for 60 seasons. Thus, the study involved a repeated measures design in which seasonal harvest decisions were nested within individuals. Level 1 analyses revealed that harvesters took significantly more fish during seasons when feedback suggested fish stocks, fish value, and fishing expenses were high; and when non-cooperative and cooperative others had taken more fish and fewer fish, respectively, in the previous season.

The Level 2 analyses revealed several cross-level interactions, indicating that harvesters' responses to feedback varied as a function of their social values and environmental attitudes.

Brown, Perkins, and Brown (2004a, 2004b) applied MLM to assess the whether physical incivilities (e.g., the presence of unkempt lawns and litter) predict crime in neighborhood blocks with varying levels of social cohesion. Thus, in this study, households (Level 1) were nested within neighborhood blocks (Level 2). They reported a significant cross-level interaction in which incivilities predicted less crime in blocks characterized by higher levels of social cohesion. They interpreted this finding as suggesting that social cohesion among neighbors can attenuate possible negative effects of a deteriorating physical environment.

Considerations related to non-independent errors and statistical power

Non-independent errors. One important challenge associated with nested research designs is that they often produce data that violate the assumption of independent errors, which is critically important for many statistical analyses based on the general linear model, including multiple regression. For example, if, as in our previous examples, a researcher is interested in whether direct experience with extreme weather predicts concern about climate change in a multi-national sample, one might expect respondents from the same nation to be more similar to each other in terms of climate change concern (e.g., due to shared culture and media) than to respondents from other nations. As noted earlier, failure to control for such class-level dependencies can result in inflated Type 1 error rates and inaccurate statistical tests (Hox, 2010; Raudenbush & Bryk, 2002).

The **intraclass correlation coefficient** (ICC, ρ) can be used to assess the degree to which dependencies are present due to hierarchical data structures. The ICC represents the ratio of between-group differences on a variable with individual differences within groups, and is equivalent to η^2 from a one-way ANOVA with group (e.g., classroom, nation) as the independent variable (Tabachnick & Fidell, 2012). Higher ICC values indicate that the independence of errors assumption has been violated. If the ICC is very small, there may be no need to conduct MLM and traditional approaches such as multiple regression or ANOVA may be appropriate (Garson, 2012).

Given that the impact of group dependencies on alpha inflation varies as function of sample size, there are no fixed guidelines about what constitutes the lower bound for a problematic ICC. With smaller sample sizes (e.g., 10 participants per Level 2 group), an ICC of .01 increases the nominal Type 1 error rate from .05 to .06, an increase that is unlikely to prevent most researchers from having a good night's sleep. However, with larger groups (e.g., 100 participants per Level 2 group) the same ICC value increases the Type 1 error rate to .17, and an ICC of .20 can push the rate as high as .70 (Barcikowski, 1981). See Table 19.1 for a more complete summary.

Statistical power. In MLM, statistical power (the probability of detecting an effect given that the effect is present) is determined by a myriad of factors including effect size, the number of observations at each level of analysis (Level 1, 2, etc.), the size of the ICC, whether the effects being tested are fixed or variable, and the extent

Table 19.1   Intraclass correlation and Type 1 error rate inflation.

N	.01	.05	.20
		ICC (ρ)	
10	.06	.11	.28
25	.08	.19	.46
50	.11	.30	.59
100	.17	.43	.70

N = number of observations per group. Values in each cell of the table are Type 1 error rates (α). Adapted from Barcikowski, 1981, p. 270.

to which predictors are correlated (Tabachnick & Fidell, 2012). Importantly, simulation studies indicate that adding Level 2 units to a sample tends to result in greater increases in power than in adding Level 1 units (Hofmann, 1997). Thus, in our hypothetical study on experience of extreme weather events on climate change concern, researchers would get more "power bang" for their buck by sampling a large number of nations, as opposed to sampling a large number of respondents from a smaller number of nations.

The presence of highly correlated predictors can also have a detrimental effect on power. When researchers incorporate correlated predictors in a regression model, it is not uncommon for the predictors as a group to explain a substantial amount of variance in a dependent variable, but for none of the individual predictors to be statistically significant. This occurs because the significance tests for individual predictors correspond to the amount of unique variance each predictor explains in the dependent variable after controlling for all the other predictors in the model. This problem is accentuated in MLM given that correlations between predictors at all levels of the model are taken into account when models are run, making it even more difficult for any single predictor to be statistically significant. To address this problem, Tabachnick and Fidell (2012) recommend that researchers use a small number of relatively uncorrelated predictors in their models, guided by theory wherever possible.

A more detailed consideration of issues related to statistical power in MLM can be found in Hox (2010). Free software for determining power and optimum sample sizes for MLM can be obtained from Scientific Software International's *HLM resources* page: http://www.ssicentral.com/hlm/resources.html

MLM software and online sources of information

Most standard statistics software packages, including IBM SPSS, SAS, STATA, and Mplus now include modules for conducting MLM. There are also several specialist programs available, the most notable being MLWin (Rasbash, Charton, Browne, Healy, & Cameron, 2005) and HLM (Raudenbush et al., 2011). Tabachnick and Fidell (2012) provide a useful table comparing the features of these programs in their chapter on MLM. In addition, there are several excellent online sources of worked examples and general advice about performing MLM. Several of these sources are presented in Table 19.2.

Table 19.2   Online sources for MLM worked examples and advice.

Source	*URL*
The Centre for Multilevel Modelling	http://www.bristol.ac.uk/cmm/
UCLA HLM software resources	http://www.ats.ucla.edu/stat/hlm/
Mplus software website	http://www.statmodel.com/
HLM software website	http://www.ssicentral.com/hlm/examples.html

Structural Equation Modeling

Structural equation modeling (SEM) is a statistical technique that allows the testing and estimation of causal relations between variables, through the combination of causal assumptions and the use of data and statistical operations (Pearl, 2012). SEM has a rich multi-disciplinary history which has been thoroughly documented by Matsueda (2012). It combines elements of factor analysis (initially developed in psychology to assess the structure of intelligence), path analysis (used by geneticists to model inheritance in populations and by sociologists to model status attainment), and simultaneous equation models (used by economists to model supply and demand).

The 1970s were characterized by substantial interdisciplinary integration culminating in Goldberger and Duncan's (1973) edited volume *Structural Equation Modeling in the Social Sciences*, and Jöreskog and Sörbom's (1974) hugely influential LISREL (LInear Structural RELations) software, which has played a dominant role in the social sciences for many years. The procedure is now widely used across psychology to analyze data produced as part of experimental and correlational research projects (MacCallum & Austin, 2000).

The use of SEM in the environment-behavior field is increasing, especially within the last decade. A review of papers published in *Environment and Behavior* (E&B) and the *Journal of Environmental Psychology* (JEP) indicates so. In E&B, six studies reporting the use of SEM were published since the journal's foundation (1969) up to 2001. From 2002 and upwards the number increased up to 48. In the JEP, five reports appeared from 1981 to 2001; while the number escalated up to 15 in the 2002–2012 period. Nevertheless, an underuse of SEM procedures in the environmental psychology field is detected, especially in those cases where its application (e.g., latent variable assessment, psychometric assessment, causal modeling) is recommended.

SEM's capability to *simultaneously* solve multiple equations within a single model represents an attractive feature for researchers interested in testing realistic explanatory models of environment–behavior interactions (Corral-Verdugo, 2002). The contrast between the classical single-equation regression model and a multiple-equation SEM model is illustrated in Figure 19.1, with a hypothetical example of relationships between five types of pro-ecological behaviors (v1–v5).

SEM as a path analysis

In the regression model example (Figure 19.1(a)), the set of four independent variables (IV, v1–v4) describing pro-environmental behaviors predicts a dependent variable (DV, v5: encouraging friends to recycle objects); no relation is assumed to exist

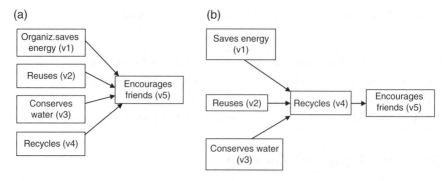

Figure 19.1 Contrast between (a) multiple regression and (b) multi-equation SEM models.

between the IVs. The resulting regression equation is: v5 = v1 + v2 + v3 + v4 + e5 (where e5 means the error or unexplained component of the variance in the v5 variable or DV in this case).

Alternatively, in the SEM model (Figure 19.1(b)), two simultaneously specified multiple-regression equations appear, using the same variables that the regression model considered. In the first equation, v4 is predicted by v1, v2 and v3 (v4 = v1 + v2 + v3 + e4) and in the second equation, v5 is directly predicted by v4 (v5 = v4 + e5). Finally, v5 is *directly* predicted by v4, but also *indirectly* affected by v1, v2, and v3 through v4.

Therefore, in an SEM model an independent variable (v4) can also be a dependent variable at the same time, and *direct* and *indirect effects* can be estimated. In environment–behavior interactions of real life, a variable that is part of a group of predictors influencing a dependent variable can also be affected by one or more of those other predictors. In the above example, level of recycling might be influenced by an individual's effort in saving energy, conserving water, and reuse of objects.

This situation generates multi-step causal paths, which explains why the SEM model in Figure 19.1 is tested as a **path analysis** (PA), one instance of SEM. A PA is performed estimating the coefficients of a multiple-equation model involving hypothesized causal flows between **manifest variables** (i.e., variables that can be directly registered or observed).

SEM includes **exogenous variables** and **endogenous variables**; the distinction between the two being whether the variable is predicted (or influenced) by another variable or not. Within a SEM, other variables are predicted by exogenous variables, but exogenous variables are never predicted by other variables. In the SEM model (b) of Figure 19.1, v1, v2, and v3 are exogenous variables, while v4 and v5 are endogenous variables.

SEM as a confirmatory technique

SEM also assumes a *confirmatory approach*, which implies a previous knowledge (based upon a theory) of the relationships between the studied variables (Bentler, 2006). This contrasts with the exploratory approach used in some regression and factor analyses. Any theory presumes that, in most cases, the association between variables is causal.

In Figure 19.1, the direction of the causal flow is represented by arrows departing from the independent (exogenous) variables toward the dependent (endogenous) variables. Yet, in the context of SEM, assuming causality does not necessarily validate conclusions of causal relationships between variables (Pearl, 2012); these conclusions should emerge from characteristics of the research design (for instance, an internally valid experimental design) or the logic of causal order (such as one variable preceding another in time).

A confirmatory model begins with one or more hypotheses that are represented in a causal model. Such a model is then tested against the obtained data. If a correspondence results between the hypothesized relationships and the observed data, then the model is assumed to exhibit **goodness of fit**. The data represent the whole set of interrelations between all the measured variables. In the SEM context, this is called the **saturated model** (sometimes referred to as the "inclusive model").

This model has no degrees of freedom, and, of course, explains all the variance of the assessed variables. Although powerful, this model is unpractical and unscientific because it lacks parsimony. Alternatively, the **restricted model** (sometimes referred to as the "theoretical" model) is practical and scientific because it is aimed at explaining as much variability as possible in a phenomenon using a limited number of relationships extracted from the entire set of interrelations contained in the saturated model.

SEM also allows the possibility of constructing **latent variables**: hypothetical constructs that cannot be measured directly, but are estimated from observed indicators. Those observed or manifest variables are assumed to "load" into the hypothetical constructs in the same way observed variables load into their latent variables in a factor analysis. Figure 19.2 illustrates the construction of the latent variable "pro-ecological behavior" from a series of four observed indicators. The observed indicators are represented in squares or quadrangles, while the latent variable is represented as an oval. The direction of the arrow implies that the latent variable "causes" their manifest indicators. Those indicators are also caused or affected by un-modeled measure error (i.e., the variance in the indicators not explained by the latent variable).

SEM as a hybrid approach

A special feature of SEM involves the combination of the two illustrated approaches in Figures 19.1 and 19.2. Such combination permits the specification

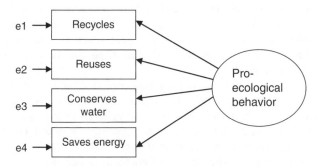

Figure 19.2 The latent variable "pro-ecological behavior" and its observed indicators.

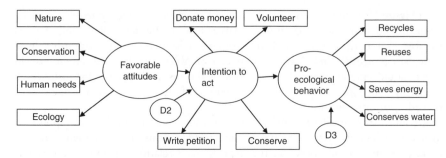

Figure 19.3   Full latent variable model of pro-ecological behavior predicted by intention to act and favorable attitudes toward natural resources conservation.

and testing of a path analysis of latent variables, also called a full latent variable model. In this model, a number of latent variables are constructed from their corresponding indicators and, then, a model of causal relations between those hypothetical constructs is specified and tested. The SEM component in which a latent variable is constructed from its manifest indicators is called the *measurement model*, while the *structural model* is the one showing the potential causal dependencies between the latent variables.

Figure 19.3 illustrates a full latent variable model. In the model, three hypothetical constructs are assumed to emerge from the interrelations among their corresponding observed indicators. These confirmatory factor analyses constitute the measurement model. There is a causal path departing from "favorable attitudes," which influence the intention to act, and finishes in pro-ecological behavior, directly predicted by intention to act. This path constitutes the structural model. Notice that "favorable attitudes" is the only exogenous factor; therefore, the "intention to act" and "pro-ecological behavior" latent endogenous variables generate *disturbances* (D2 and D3). These are equivalent to the errors of manifest variables, which are not shown in Figure 19.3.

SEM testing

A structural model considers three elements or phases: model specification; estimation; and the evaluation of goodness of fit. Model specification is the exercise of formally stating a model (Hoyle, 2012); this can be done in a diagram as in Figures 19.1, 19.2, and 19.3. Direct and indirect relations are declared as well as variances of independent variables and errors. Causal relations, variances, and covariances are parameters that are specified as either fixed (by the researcher) or free (estimated from the data).

Estimation, in turn, implies obtaining the numerical values for the unknown parameters (Chou & Bentler, 1995). Estimation methods such as single-stage least squares, or the iterative maximum likelihood or generalized least squares, are used to obtain estimates (beta coefficients, factor loadings, standard error estimates, variances, covariances) and their significance tests.

Goodness of fit indicates the degree of correspondence between the specified model and the data. Chi-squared (χ^2) is one of the used indicators of goodness of fit.

A χ^2 value of zero means a perfect fit; therefore low and non-significant χ^2 values are expected for good models. Since χ^2 is sensitive to sample size (large sample sizes produce a significant $\chi^{2)}$ and violations to SEM assumptions (i.e., normal distribution of data, correct specification of models), alternative practical indices of fit are used, such as non-normed fit index (NNFI) and the comparative fit index (CFI) (Bentler, 2006).

Values equal to or higher than .90 are expected in order to accept a model's consistency with the data. An additional fit index is the root mean square error of approximation (RMSEA); values of RMSEA approaching zero are desired, and a value of .05 or less indicates a reasonable error of approximation (Browne & Cudeck, 1993).

SEM worked examples

Three SEM applications (path analysis, confirmatory factor analysis, and full latent-variable modeling) are illustrated from hereon with actual data from a study examining predictors of pro-environmental behavior. The correlation matrix used to generate the analyses is presented in Table 19.3.

The first set of variables (INT1–INT4) includes items regarding the respondents' intention to act pro-environmentally (volunteer in conservationist actions, cooperate with pro-ecological organizations, use energy efficiently, conserve water); PEB1–PEB4 considers the self-report of pro-ecological actions (recycling, pointing out non-ecological actions, reading about environmental topics, and encouraging friends to conserve); IND1–IND4 refer to items assessing feelings of indignation due to environmental deterioration (cut trees, contaminating factories, polluted streets, wasted water); finally AFF1–AFF4 assess feelings of affinity for nature, manifested in feeling happy in nature, good mood because of contact with plants, well-being produced by open places, and feeling good by staying in natural patios.

A superficial analysis of this matrix (see Table 19.3) reveals that the highest correlations are concentrated within those subsets of items (in bold). Yet, other salient correlations also appear between items that are not part of the same subset. This suggests the specification of four different factors, but also potential associations between the latent variables that will be constructed later as part of this example.

A *path analysis* is specified using the following equations:

$$PEB4 = * INT1 + * AFF1 + ePEB4$$
$$INT1 = * IND3 + * AFF1 + eINT1$$
$$/COVARIANCES$$
$$IND3, AFF1 = *$$

Where * means a free parameter to estimate.

These equations specify three hypotheses: (1) the act of encouraging friends to conserve the environment will be directly influenced by the intention to volunteer in conservationist actions and by feeling happy in nature; (2) such intention to act will be affected by feelings of indignation due to contamination of streets and by feeling happy in nature; and (3) these two exogenous variables will covariate significantly.

Table 19.3 Correlation matrix of analyzed variables*.

	INT1	INT2	INT3	INT4	PEB1	PEB2	PEB3	PEB4	IND1	IND2	IND3	IND4	AFF1	AAF2	AFF3
INT2	**.74**														
INT3	**.34**	**.26**													
INT4	**.45**	**.28**	**.33**												
PEB1	.25	.19	.23	.20											
PEB2	.30	.26	.20	.27	**.42**										
PEB3	.25	.28	.30	.24	**.33**	**.37**									
PEB4	.29	.26	.28	.27	**.54**	**.40**	**.47**								
IND1	.32	.34	.33	.22	.30	.17	.26	.26							
IND2	.32	.33	.20	.12	.25	.13	.22	.25	.25						
IND3	.24	.20	.13	.13	.13	.13	.12	.03	.08	**.39**					
IND4	.33	.30	.30	.26	.36	.15	.31	.26	.11	**.22**	**.43**				
AFF1	.20	.21	.21	.16	.19	.23	.25	.31	.33	.35	.14	.04			
AFF2	.21	.16	.16	.20	.25	.28	.30	.25	.22	.22	.14	.14	**.68**		
AFF3	.28	.23	.23	.23	.14	.27	.23	.23	.22	.29	.10	.18	**.54**	**.52**	
AFF4	.19	.21	.21	.20	.18	.18	.21	.30	.25	.24	.16	.14	**.57**	**.63**	**.65**

* Variables explained in text.

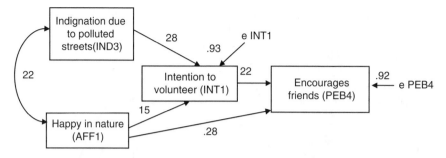

Figure 19.4 Path analysis of four observed indicators of conservationism factors: Reporting indignation due to polluted streets (IND3) and feeling happy in nature (AFF1) influence intention to volunteer in a conservationist enterprise (INT1), which, in turn, affects encouraging friends to conserve (PEB4). All structural coefficients and the covariance are significant ($p < .05$). Goodness of fit: $\chi^2 = .58$ (1 df), $p = .44$; NNFI = .99, CFI = 1.04; RMSEA =.00. PEB4's R^2 =.15.

Results of the model estimation are presented in Figure 19.4. All hypotheses were confirmed by significant ($p < .05$) path coefficients and covariance between the exogenous variables. The model revealed both statistical and practical goodness of fit. The model explains 15% of the variance ($R^2 = .15$) in the PEB4 dependent variable.

Because previous knowledge of the researchers indicated the presence of a four-factor structure subjacent to the interrelations among variables, a *confirmatory factor analysis* (CFA) was specified. The following equations produced the specified representation:

IND1 =* F1 + eIND1; IND2 =* F1 + eIND2; IND3 =* F1 + eIND3; IND4 =* F1 + eIND4
AFF1 =* F2 + eAFF1; AFF2 =* F2 + eAFF2; AFF3 =* F2 + eAFF3; AFF4 =* F2 + eAFF4
INT1 =* F3 + eINT1; INT2 =* F3 + eINT2; INT3 =* F3 + eINT3; INT4 =* F3 + eINT4
PEB1 =* F4 + ePEB1; PEB2 =* F4 + ePEB2; PEB3 =* F4 + ePEB3; PEB4 =* F4 + ePEB4
/COVARIANCES
F1 to F4 =*

These equations specify that IND1–IND4 are part of a "Feelings of indignation" factor (Factor 1), while items AFF1–AFF4 constitute the "Feelings of affinity for nature" factor (Factor 2). In turn, "Environmental intention" is the factor (Factor 3) emerging from interrelations between INT1–INT4, and "Pro-ecological behavior" is the factor (Factor 4) to be constructed from the PEB1–PEB4 indicators.

Figure 19.5 confirms the hypothesized four-dimensional structure. All loadings from every factor on its corresponding manifest variables are significant ($p < .05$). This can be considered evidence of convergent construct validity (Bentler, 2006). Although χ^2 resulted significant, the NNFI and CFI produced values higher than .93, and the RMSEA (value = .05) indicated an appropriate goodness of fit.

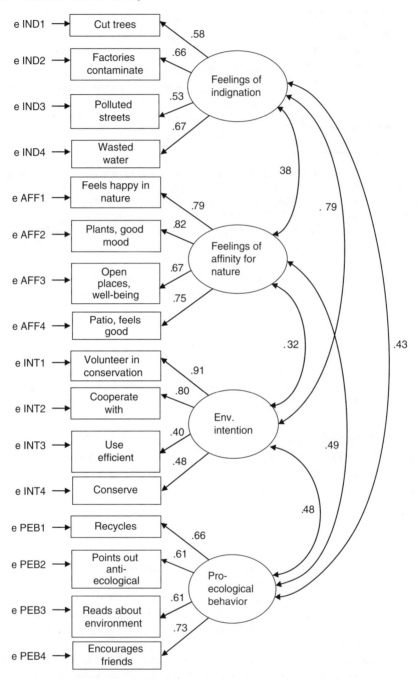

Figure 19.5 Confirmatory factor analysis of negative and positive environmental emotions, intention to act, and pro-ecological behavior. All factor loadings and covariances between factors are significant ($p < .05$). Values of errors are not reported. Goodness of fit: $\chi^2 = 149.10$ (98 *df*), = .0006; NNFI = .93, CFI = .95; RMSEA = .05.

Subsequently, those four factors were included in a *full latent variable model*, as follows:

IND1 =* F1 + eIND1; IND2 =* F1 + eIND2; IND3 =* F1 + eIND3; IND4 =* F1 + eIND4
AFF1 =* F2 + eAFF1; AFF2 =* F2 + eAFF2; AFF3 =* F2 + eAFF3; AFF4 =* F2 + eAFF4
INT1 =* F3 + eINT1; INT2 =* F3 + eINT2; INT3 =* F3 + eINT3; INT4 =* F3 + eINT4
PEB1 =* F4 + ePEB1; PEB2 =* F4 + ePEB2; PEB3 =* F4 + ePEB3; PEB4 =* F4 + ePEB4
F3 = *f1 +* f2 + d3; F4 = *f2 +* f3 + d4
/COVARIANCES
F1, F2 =*

The measurement model of this representation repeats the equations of the above-described CFA, and adds the structural component in which "Environmental intention" (Factor 3) is predicted by "Feelings of indignation" (Factor 1) and "Affinity for nature" (Factor 2); while "Pro-ecological behavior" (Factor 4) is predicted by "Affinity for nature" (Factor 2) and "Environmental intention" (Factor 3).

The results of this SEM are represented in Figure 19.6. In addition to confirming the emergence of the four factors, the parameter estimation shows that the paths of relations between latent variables resulted as expected. All factor loadings, structural coefficients, and the covariance were salient and significant.

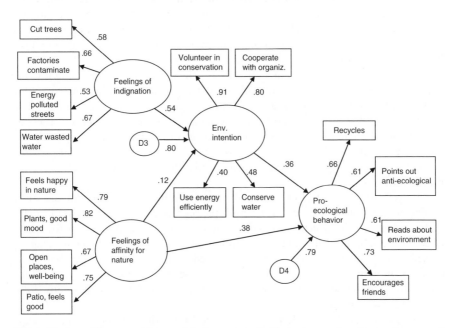

Figure 19.6 Full latent variable model of pro-ecological behavior predicted by environmental emotions and intention to act. Errors for observed variables are not reported. All factor loadings and the covariance between exogenous factors are significant ($p < .05$). Goodness of fit: $\chi^2 = 150.29$ (99 df), $p = .0007$; NNFI = .93, CFI = .94; RMSEA= .05. Intention to act $R^2 = .35$; Pro-ecological behavior $R^2 = .36$.

The model explains 36% of the variance in pro-ecological behavior. The goodness of fit indicators were similar to those obtained in the CFA; thus, it is presumed that the model indicates an appropriate correspondence with the data.

Further applications of SEM

The previous examples illustrated three basic SEM applications to the study of environment–behavior topics. Yet, the reader should be aware that SEM has additional uses and adaptations including latent growth models for longitudinal data, the application of Bayesian methods, the integration of generalized linear methods and multi-level models within SEM, and the formal treatment of causality, among many others (Matsueda, 2012). Those applications are potentially utilizable for the analysis of data in environmental psychology studies.

Considerations related to sample size and power analysis

SEM is a large sample analysis strategy (Kline, 2011). Ad hoc rules of thumb requiring 10 observations per indicator in SEM were originally suggested by Nunnally (1967). However, complexities of information requirements in structural model estimation increase with the number of potential combinations of latent variables, whereas the information supplied for estimation increases with the number of measured parameters times the number of observations in the sample size. Therefore, sample size in SEM can be alternatively computed through two methods: the first as a function of the ratio of indicator variables to latent variables; and the second as a function of minimum effect, power, and significance. Software and methods for computing both have been developed by Westland (2010).

In the SEM context, power analysis assesses the probability of rejecting the null hypothesis given that the null hypothesis is false. The covariance matrix, along with a vector of means, relating to the alternative hypothesis is generated. This represents the hypothesized population effects. A model (representing the null hypothesis) is then tested in a structural equation model, using the population parameters as input. An analysis based on the chi-square of this model provides estimates of the sample size required for different levels of power to reject the null hypothesis.

A power analysis in SEM can be conducted for individual paths or for the entire model. In the first case, a method for multiple regression is sometimes used; such a method requires the specification of the unique variance explained by the direct effect of a variable on other. This is the amount by which the proportion of explained variance in the dependent variable is supposed to increase by adding that direct effect into the model. The level of alpha is also specified, the non-centrality parameter for the appropriate F distribution is calculated and special tables (Cohen, 1988) are used to estimate power.

Saris and Satorra (1993) developed a method for estimating power that is more specific to SEM. The process starts with the assumption of the size of a direct effect of X (IV) on Y (DV). Using this value and the other a priori values of parameters in the model, a predicted covariance matrix is produced using methods based on matrix algebra. This covariance matrix is specified as input data to an SEM program.

Table 19.4 Online sources for SEM worked examples and advice.

Source	URL
AMOS Development Corporation	http://www.amosdevelopment.com/download/
EQS Multivariate Software	http://www.mvsoft.com/demos.htm
Mplus software website	http://www.statmodel.com/
LISREL software website	http://www.ssicentral.com/
Statistical Analysis Software	http://www.sas.com/technologies/analytics/statistics/stat/index.html

MacCallum, Browne, and Sugawara (1996) presented an approach to power analysis at the model level, which is based on the RMSEA and non-central chi-square distributions for three different types of null hypotheses: (1) $H0$: $\varepsilon 0 \leq .05$ (the model has *close fit* in the population); (2) $H0$: $\varepsilon 0 \geq .05$ (a *not close fit*); and (3) $H0$: $\varepsilon 0 = 0$ (an *exact fit*). The exact-fit hypothesis is tested, but because this hypothesis is not typically plausible, only the close-fit and not-close-fit hypotheses are taken into account.

Higher power for a test of the close-fit hypothesis indicates the plausibility to reject an incorrect model. Alternatively, higher power for a test of the not-close-fit hypothesis implies better certainty to detect a correct model. Estimated power or minimum sample sizes can be obtained by consulting special tables in MacCallum et al. (1996).

SEM software and online sources of information

LISREL, EQS, AMOS, and MPlus are specialized software programs that can be used to specify and test structural equation models. These programs are user-friendly and include tutorials for the learning of SEM applications. In addition, there are a number of online sources of worked examples and general advice about performing SEM. Some of these sources are presented in Table 19.4.

Summary and Conclusions

Multi-level modeling and structural equation modeling are two sophisticated and highly flexible procedures for investigating environment–behavior relations. Although often not formally acknowledged, many environment-behavior studies involve nested data (e.g., responses nested within individuals, individuals nested within communities). This creates data dependency problems that undermine the traditional analysis strategies. MLM provides an elegant solution to dependency issues, while providing researchers with a tool to address a broad range of new research questions. SEM includes a broad array of statistical techniques that includes path analysis, confirmatory factor analysis, and hybrid models that combine both approaches. It is particularly useful for assessing how well specified models fit observed data, and under certain conditions can be used to draw inferences about the causal pathways through which psychological and situational factors exert their influence on behavior. We hope that our introduction to these topics inspires researchers and students, like Ethan and Maria, to conceptualize their research questions, study designs and data analysis strategies in new and exciting ways.

Glossary

Endogenous variables   In SEM, variables that have causal arrows leading to them. These variables can be thought of as dependent variables, or variables that are explained by other variables in the model.

Exogenous variables   In SEM, variables that have causal arrows leading away from them. These variables can be thought of as independent or predictor variables. Exogenous variables explain variance in endogenous variables.

Goodness of fit   How well a statistical model fits a set of observations. In SEM, there are many different indices that describe goodness of fit.

Independent errors assumption   In many traditional statistical procedures (e.g., multiple regression and ANOVA) errors are assumed to be normally distributed and independent. This assumption is often violated in research designs involving nested data. MLM represents one possible strategy for dealing with this problem.

Intraclass correlation coefficient   A descriptive statistic that describes how strongly units within a group resembles each other. Commonly used in MLM studies to determine the extent that data dependencies are present in nested data. High values indicate that the independent errors assumption has been violated, making traditional statistical analyses such as multiple regression or ANOVA inappropriate.

Latent variables   Variables that are not directly observed, but are based on patterns of responses to observed variables. In factor analysis, latent variables are often referred to as "factors."

Manifest variables   Variables that can be directly measured or observed.

Nested data   Data with a hierarchical structure in which one level of data is organized within one or more other levels. Common examples are responses nested within individuals (repeated measures) or individuals nested within communities or nations.

Path analysis   A statistical method for testing causal hypotheses. It represents one type of SEM than involves no latent variables.

Restricted model   In SEM, a model that specifies a limited number of associations between measured variables, often based on a theory or clear set of hypotheses. If this model fits the data well, this provides evidence in favor of the theory.

Saturated model   In SEM, a model that includes all possible associations between measured variables. This model has no degrees of freedom, and necessarily explains all the variation in the data. Sometimes referred to as the "inclusive model."

References

Barcikowski, R. S. (1981). Statistical power with group mean as the unit of analysis. *Journal of Educational Statistics, 6,* 267–285.

Bentler, P. M. (2006). *EQS. Structural equation program manual.* Encino, CA: Multivariate Software.

Brown, B. B., Perkins, D. D., & Brown, G. (2004a). Incivilities, place attachment and crime: Block and individual effects. *Journal of Environmental Psychology, 24*, 359–371.

Brown, B., Perkins, D. D., & Brown, G. (2004b). Erratum to "Place attachment in a revitalizing neighborhood: Individual and block levels of analysis." *Journal of Environmental Psychology, 24*, 141.

Browne, M., & Cudeck, R. (1993). Alternative ways of assessing model fit. In K. A. Bollen & J. S. Long (Eds.), *Testing structural equation models* (pp. 136–162). Thousand Oaks, CA: Sage.

Chou C. P., & Bentler, P. M. (1995). Estimates and tests in structural equation modeling. In R. H. Hoyle (Ed.), *Structural equation modeling: Issues and application* (pp. 37–55). Newbury, CA: Sage.

Cohen J. (1988). *Statistical power analysis for the behavioral sciences*. Hillsdale, NJ: Erlbaum.

Corral-Verdugo, V. (2002). Structural equation modeling. In R. B. Bechtel & A. Churchman (Eds.), *Handbook of environmental psychology* (pp. 256–270). New York, NY: Wiley.

Garson, G. D. (2012). *Hierarchical linear modeling: Guide and applications*. Thousand Oaks, CA: Sage.

Goldberger, A. S., & Duncan, O. D. (1973). *Structural equation models in the social sciences*. New York, NY: Academic.

Hine, D. W., Gifford, R., Heath, Y., Cooksey, R., & Quain, P. (2009). A cue utilization approach for investigating harvest decisions in commons dilemmas. *Journal of Applied Social Psychology, 39*, 564–588.

Hofmann, D. A. (1997). An overview of the logic and rationale of hierarchical linear models. *Journal of Management, 23*, 723–744.

Hox, J. (2010). *Multilevel analysis: Techniques and applications* (2nd ed.). New York, NY: Routledge.

Hoyle, R. H. (2012). Model specification in structural equation modeling. In R. H. Hoyle (Ed.), *Handbook of structural equation modeling* (pp. 126–144). New York, NY: Guilford.

Jöreskog, K. G. & Sörbom, D. (1974). *LISREL III* [Computer software]. Chicago, IL: Scientific Software International.

Kline, R. (2011). *Principles and practice of structural equation modeling* (3rd ed.). New York, NY: Guilford.

MacCallum, R. C., & Austin, J. T. (2000). Applications of structural equation modeling in psychological research. *Annual Review of Psychology, 51*, 201–226.

MacCallum R. C., Browne M. W., & Sugawara H. M. (1996). Power analysis and determination of sample size for covariance structure modelling. *Psychological Methods, 1*, 130–149.

Matsueda, R. L. (2012). Key advances in the history of structural equation modeling. In R. H. Hoyle (Ed.), *Structural equation modeling: Issues and application* (pp. 17–42). Newbury, CA: Sage.

Nunnally, J. C. (1967). *Psychometric theory*. New York, NY: McGraw-Hill.

Osborne, J. (2000). The advantages of hierarchical linear modeling. *Practical Assessment, Research, and Evaluation, 7*, 1–3.

Pearl, J. (2012). The causal foundations of structural equation modeling. In R. H. Hoyle (Ed.), *Handbook of structural equation modeling* (pp. 68–91). New York, NY: Guilford.

Rasbash, J., Charlton, C., Browne, W. J., Healy, M., & Cameron, B. (2009) *MLwiN Version 2.1*. Centre for Multilevel Modelling, University of Bristol.

Raudenbush, S. W., & Bryk, A. S. (2002). *Hierarchical linear models: Applications and data analysis methods* (2nd ed.). Thousand Oaks, CA: Sage.

Raudenbush, S. W., Bryk, A. S., Cheong, A. S., Fai, Y. F., Congdon, R. T., & du Toit, M. (2011). HLM 7: Hierarchical linear and nonlinear modeling. Lincolnwood, IL: Scientific Software International.

Saris, W. E., & Satorra, A. (1993). Power evaluations in structural equation models. In K. A. Bollen & J. S. Long (Eds.), *Testing structural equation models* (pp. 181–204). Newbury Park, CA: Sage.

Schultz, P. W., Milfont, T. L., Chance, R. C., Tronu, G., Luis, S., Ando, K., Rasool, F. et al. (2012). Cross-cultural evidence for spatial bias in beliefs about the severity of environmental problems. *Environment and Behavior.* doi:10.1177/0013916512458579

Tabachnick, B. G., & Fidell, L. S. (2012). *Using multivariate statistics* (6th ed.). Boston, MA: Pearson.

Westland, J. C. (2010). Lower bounds on sample size in structural equation modeling. *Electronic Commerce Research and Applications, 9,* 476–487.

Suggested Readings

Garson, G. D. (2012). *Hierarchical linear modeling: Guide and applications.* Thousand Oaks, CA: Sage.

Hox, J. (2010). *Multilevel analysis: Techniques and applications* (2nd ed.). New York, NY: Routledge.

Hoyle, R.H. (2012). *Handbook of structural equation modeling.* New York, NY: Guilford.

Kline, R. (2011). *Principles and practice of structural equation modeling* (3rd ed.). New York, NY: Guilford.

Tabachnick, B. G., & Fidell, L. S. (2012). *Using multivariate statistics* (6th ed.). Boston, MA: Pearson.

20

Meta-analysis
An Analysis of Analyses

Christine Kormos
University of Victoria, BC, Canada

It was a beautiful weekend day and Maria, Ethan, and Gabriel decided to take advantage of the nice weather by heading down to the taco stand at the wharf to enjoy some delicious food and soak up some rays sea-side. On arriving at the wharf, they realized that many others had had a similar idea; the wharf was busy and there was a lengthy line-up at the taco stand. But the sun was shining, making the prospect of a long wait seem not so bad.

"I'm going to get in line before it gets any longer," stated Gabriel. "Plus, I'm starving!"

Distracted by the harbor seals nearby – who were being fed fish by children in the crowd – Maria wandered off to get a better look at the local "wildlife."

"I'm going to hold off on the tacos until the line dies down," said Ethan. "Maybe I'll go sit with Maria and make sure that she doesn't fall in and accidentally become seal-food." Ethan then joined Maria, who was lying down on a bench with her hat pulled over her face to help block the sun.

"I feel so relaxed," Maria said dreamily, "I just love being around animals and by the water; being in nature just makes my stress melt away. If I could, I would stay in the outdoors all the time."

"Really?" asked Ethan, "I'm totally the opposite. The seals are great and all, but I'd much prefer to be downtown, exploring some old buildings or checking out that new development that's being built. Those kinds of urban environments are much more interesting and exciting than sitting out here getting sunburnt."

"You've got to be kidding," replied Maria, pushing her hat aside to stare at Ethan in disbelief. "Pretty much everybody prefers being outdoors compared to urban environments. It's kind of a fact."

"Well, I bet that I'm not alone and that there are a lot of people who prefer urban settings over natural ones," stated Ethan flatly, trying to conceal his growing frustration.

"Yeah, maybe strange people," replied Maria with a sly smile.

At this point, Gabriel returned, happily eating his taco, and unwittingly sat down on the bench in between the debating duo.

Research Methods for Environmental Psychology, First Edition. Edited by Robert Gifford.
© 2016 John Wiley & Sons, Ltd. Published 2016 by John Wiley & Sons, Ltd.

"But what does it mean if you find some studies that show that most people prefer natural settings and I find some studies that show that most people prefer urban settings; how does that tell us anything about the 'truth' across all of these different studies?" continued Ethan. "There have probably been many studies done on this topic, and so it's likely that some may support each of our viewpoints. Also, maybe different types of people – perhaps people who grew up in the city versus rural places – are more likely to prefer urban versus natural environments. For example, I grew up in a big city and so maybe that's why I don't find nature to be as exciting as the city."

Suddenly a seal popped its head up right near their bench, enticed by the prospect of Gabriel's taco. Gabriel jumped, but managed to hold on to his taco.

"I don't know guys, I'm going to have to side with Maria on this one," stated a breathless Gabriel. "Nature can be pretty darn exciting ... But if you really want to figure out which of you is more like the majority of other people in terms of preference for natural environments versus built environments, and if you want to explore various individual-level differences that may account for preference, why don't you just do a meta-analysis of all of the research in this area, and then you'll have your answer?"

"Fine, maybe I'll do that just that," stated Maria, sliding the hat back over her eyes and re-assuming her comfortable position on the bench.

"I'll be curious to hear the results of your meta-analysis," said Ethan wryly, "but in the meantime, how about we call it a truce and celebrate over our shared preference for tacos?"

Overview and Brief History of Meta-analysis

Overview

Meta-analysis refers to the "statistical synthesis of results from a series of studies" (Borenstein, Hedges, Higgins, & Rothstein, 2009, p. xxi). Rather than considering individual studies in isolation, meta-analytic procedures enable researchers to examine the entire body of evidence related to one question or topic. These procedures allow the researcher to estimate the mean magnitude, or strength, of the combined effect size across all related studies – with more weight given to more precise studies with larger sample sizes – as well as to evaluate the statistical significance of this summary effect size. For instance, meta-analysis has been used to address whether or not the intervention strategy of commitment-making leads to short- and long-term behavior change, compared to control conditions (Lokhorst, Werner, Staats, van Dijk, & Gale, 2013). Furthermore, these procedures allow us to quantify the degree of variance (or heterogeneity) across study effect sizes to determine whether the effect size is consistent, and thus robust, across the series of studies sampled, or whether it varies considerably across studies. If found to vary, these procedures then permit us to explore study-level covariates (or moderators) that account for the differences in the observed effect sizes across the studies and populations sampled. For example, these procedures may be used to explore whether the effectiveness of commitment-making is, in general, increased in studies that have combined this intervention strategy with other types of interventions (Lokhorst et al., 2013).

Important to note, however, is that meta-analytic procedures are merely statistical tools that can (theoretically) be used to combine and evaluate any set of data; for instance, a series of disparate studies could be synthesized to yield a statistically accurate but conceptually meaningless overall effect size. Thus, the meaningfulness of the synthesis hinges on the degree to which the included studies are comparable and the extent to which the process has been systematically conducted and transparently reported. As a result, two defining characteristics of meta-analyses is that they are systematic and transparent (i.e., replicable).

This chapter will first provide a brief history of the meta-analytic approach, followed by a discussion of the advantages and disadvantages of narrative reviews versus meta-analysis and a description of the underlying assumptions of the two statistical models used in meta-analyses. Next, this chapter will outline the steps involved in systematically identifying, evaluating, and synthesizing data from a group of studies, and then it will list key meta-analytic statistics as well as guidelines for reporting results. For further reference, there are several excellent textbooks that summarize meta-analytic approaches. Borenstein, Hedges, Higgins, and Rothstein's (2009) textbook is excellent, but many other great references exist (e.g., Card, 2011; Cooper, 2010). Additional references and guidelines for conducting and reporting meta-analyses include the PRISMA website (www. prisma-statement.org), as well as the *Cochrane Handbook for Systematic Reviews of Interventions* (Higgins & Green, 2011), although this latter reference focuses on health care and health policy.

Brief history

The term "meta-analysis" was coined and formalized by the statistician Gene Glass in 1976. Although Glass is widely recognized as the modern founder of this method, meta-analytic methodology pre-dates his work by several decades (e.g., Cochran, 1937), with the first true meta-analysis consisting of a review of 145 extra-sensory perception experiments published from 1882 to 1939, conducted by Pratt and Rhine and colleagues (see Bösch, 2004). More recently, evidence-based medicine has increasingly relied on this technique, and its popularity has grown among policy-makers and scholars in far-reaching disciplines, including environmental psychology. In an age of ever-proliferating knowledge, meta-analytic procedures offer an efficient means to assess the "overall" state of knowledge on a particular topic, as well as the potential to resolve inconsistencies among individual studies. Furthermore, meta-analyses can be helpful for designing interventions and guiding future research given that these procedures allow researchers to consider the current state of knowledge in an area through a broad lens. Researchers have even gone so far as to meta-analyze meta-analyses, such as Richard, Bond, and Stokes-Zoota's (2003) analysis of 322 meta-analyses of social psychological phenomena – resulting in an exceptionally broad lens! In short, meta-analysis is truly a tool with many applications.

Narrative Reviews versus Meta-Analyses

Narrative reviews

Before the 1990s, narrative reviews were the primary approach used to synthesize data from multiple, related studies. A **narrative review** is a non-statistical summary of findings; the researcher combines findings from related studies by counting the number of statistically significant studies compared to the number of statistically non-significant studies (in a process known as *vote counting*) and thus arrives at conclusions about a given research area. For instance, similar to meta-analysis, the narrative review approach can be used to address whether or not a certain pro-environmental intervention is successful.

Advantages of narrative reviews   Narrative reviews have several advantages, one of which being that oftentimes the primary studies (especially earlier ones) do not report the statistics necessary to conduct a meta-analysis, whereas given their qualitative nature, narrative reviews are not hindered by this lack of available statistics. For instance, an informative and well-cited narrative review was conducted on intervention studies for household energy conservation even though a meta-analysis was deemed impossible because of a lack of available statistics (Abrahamse, Steg, Vlek, & Rothengatter, 2005). Another relative advantage of narrative reviews is that under-developed research areas may not yet contain enough literature to result in sufficient power to conduct a meta-analysis; however, narrative reviews can often still be conducted even in these cases where a meta-analysis would be premature. (Of course, a narrative review can always be followed up by a meta-analysis at a later date as more studies are conducted.) A final key advantage of narrative reviews is that they can provide a qualitative overview of the state of knowledge in a research area as well as an in-depth analysis of included studies. In contrast, the more quantitative meta-analytic approach may not allow, as readily, this more nuanced discussion. The narrative review approach is not, however, without its limitations.

Disadvantages of narrative reviews   One of the main disadvantages of the narrative review approach is that it relies solely on statistical significance (or p-values) for vote counting. Vote counting can be misleading in terms of interpretations about effect size. p-values merely convey that the effect size is not zero, they do not, however, reflect the strength of the association. As such, although it is tempting to assume that different p-values reflect different effect sizes, that similar p-values reflect similar effect sizes, and that a more significant p-value indicates a larger effect size and vice versa, this is not necessarily the case. The **power** of a given study – the probability that its statistical tests will detect a significant finding, if one exists – is directly influenced by its sample size. Therefore, a significant p-value may indicate either (1) a large effect size or (2) a small or medium effect size in a large sample. (In fact, given a large enough sample size, a statistical comparison will show a significant difference unless the population effect is exactly zero.) Furthermore, a non-significant p-value may indicate either (1) a small effect size or (2) a medium or large effect size in a small sample. Studies with very small sample sizes are often under-powered and so may have difficulty detecting significance. Therefore, vote counting assumes that a non-significant *p*-value indicates a lack of an effect, whereas, in fact, small, moderate, and even large effect sizes can result in non-significant *p*-values because of low statistical power. Problematically, errors in interpretation stemming from vote counting tend to worsen as the number of studies considered increases.

For example, imagine that you conducted a narrative review on a series of small-sized intervention studies aimed at increasing recycling, and that 50 percent of the included studies yielded significant results. You may conclude that the findings are inconsistent, and subsequently explore why the effectiveness of the intervention differed across studies. In reality, however, the true effect sizes may be positive and consistent across all studies, but some of the studies failed to detect significance because they were under-powered. Thus, misinterpretations about *p*-values resulting from vote counting, which focuses on *p*-values and not effect sizes, can present serious problems in narrative reviews.

Second, the narrative review process is prone to subjectivity, which may cause two researchers to arrive at different conclusions about the same research question. For instance, given that researchers weight each study according to an implicitly assigned level of importance, one researcher may assign more subjective weight to larger studies whereas another researcher may assign more weight to higher quality studies (Borenstein et al., 2009). Also, researchers may differ in the threshold of evidence they require before concluding that an intervention, for example, is successful. To complicate matters, narrative reviews do not typically provide detailed explanations of the process by which they identify and synthesize studies and arrive at conclusions. This lack of a systematic process and transparency in reporting can pose considerable problems.

Last, narrative reviews become less feasible as the number of included studies increases. Although a reviewer may be able to synthesize data from a handful of studies in his/her head, the process becomes less feasible as the number of included studies increases, until it eventually becomes impossible to yield a valid synthesis. This difficulty in considering a larger number of studies becomes especially pronounced when it comes to evaluating how the summary effect varies according to study-level covariates; as such, narrative reviews are not well suited for assessing moderators.

Meta-analyses

As a result of the above-outlined limitations of narrative reviews, the meta-analytic approach has increasingly gained in popularity since the 1990s.

Advantages of meta-analyses   The meta-analytic technique is relatively objective, given that it relies on a statistical synthesis of results, and it is also systematic, given that one key goal is to minimize possible subjectivity involved in the study screening and selection phase. Another main advantage of meta-analysis is that it has as a central tenet transparent reporting of all phases of the decision-making process during study selection and synthesis.

An additional key advantage of meta-analysis is that it offers a statistical, quantitative synthesis of the data, whereby the relative contribution of each study's effect size is objectively weighted according to its sample size, with larger studies contributing more heavily to the overall effect size compared to studies with smaller sample sizes (Borenstein et al., 2009). As outlined above, meta-analysis works with effect sizes and yields an estimate of the magnitude of the overall effect. By working with effect sizes, as opposed to *p*-values, meta-analyses avoid problems associated with misinterpreting a non-significant *p*-value to reflect a trivial effect or a significant *p*-value to reflect an important effect. Meta-analysis also allows us to compare effect sizes across studies.

Another advantage of meta-analysis is that it incorporates all of the study effect sizes into a single statistical analysis, whereas narrative reviews treat each study as discrete, with the synthesis occurring in the researcher's head. Furthermore, with meta-analysis, established statistical techniques can be used to identify the true dispersion among study effect sizes and evaluate moderators. In the case of narrative reviews, even if the *p*-value directly reflected the effect size (e.g., if all studies had an identical sample size), it is still not possible to assess the dispersion in effect sizes across studies. Last, meta-analytic procedures allow researchers to assess and adjust for publication bias, as discussed below.

Disadvantages of meta-analyses   Despite the above advantages of meta-analyses, these procedures are not without their criticisms, such as those outlined in several creatively titled articles, including Eysenck's (1978), "An exercise in mega-silliness" and Shapiro's (1994), "Meta-analysis/shmeta-analysis." These criticisms focus mostly on the application of the meta-analytic method, as opposed to the method itself, and many of the criticisms could also apply to narrative reviews (Borenstein et al., 2009).

One such criticism is that meta-analysis mixes apples and oranges by combining different kinds of studies in the same analysis. The concern is that summary effects may conceal important differences across studies. Indeed, the studies combined in a meta-analysis will differ (to varying degrees) from one another in terms of their characteristics, such as study design. Reviewers must exercise their best judgment in determining how similar the studies must be to be appropriate to combine and yet different enough to illuminate study-level covariates at play. By virtue of their nature, meta-analyses will nearly always consider broader questions than individual studies. Thus, ultimately it comes back to the goal of the analysis and a judgment call on behalf of the reviewer. Also, the meta-analysis can be used to empirically address questions about how differences in the studies influence differences in their effect sizes.

Another popular criticism is the notion of "garbage in, garbage out," where the concern is that a meta-analysis of low-quality primary studies runs the risk of masking these errors in the original studies once their results are synthesized. In response to this criticism, proponents of meta-analysis argue that study quality can be added as an inclusion criterion to eliminate poor-quality studies from the analysis. Additionally, study quality can be assessed as a moderator variable to quantify the influence of quality on effect size, or to compare effect sizes of lower-quality studies to those of higher-quality studies.

Last, one of the key advantages of meta-analytic procedures (namely, their rigor) can also be a disadvantage in that it can render these procedures inappropriate, or impossible to conduct, for certain under-developed areas of research. Therefore, with meta-analysis, the researcher is limited by what can be quantified, based on what has specifically been examined in each study. For example, many intervention studies examine the effectiveness of the intervention but they vary widely in terms of the other covariates (e.g., attitudes and social norms) that they include, and this can make it difficult or impossible to apply meta-analytic techniques across certain subsets of studies.

Underlying Assumptions of Statistical Models

Fixed-effect versus random-effects models

A summary effect can be computed using the fixed-effect model or the random-effects model. With the **fixed-effect model**, the assumption is that all studies in the analysis share one true (i.e., fixed) effect size, and thus that the summary effect is the estimate of this common effect size of the underlying population. Given this, an assumption of this model is that all variables that could influence the effect size are identical across all studies. Another assumption of this model is that all of the observed differences in effects are the result of sampling error and, as such, the study weights are assigned to minimize within-study error. Although it is reasonable to anticipate that the effect sizes will be similar across included studies – given that studies must be similar enough to reasonably synthesize their findings – it is often unrealistic to expect that they all have an identical effect size, and thus the fixed-effect model is not commonly used in the social sciences.

In contrast, with the **random-effects model** the true effect is allowed to vary across studies. Effect sizes may vary across studies for a variety of reasons, including mixes of participants (e.g., gender, socio-economic status, and level of education) and other differences, such as study design. These moderators can influence the magnitude of the effect size in each study and, although we may not have information about the specific influence of all the possible moderators in each study, in most cases it is logical to assume that these factors exist and result in variations in the observed effect sizes. Hypothetically, if an infinite number of studies were performed within the parameters of your inclusion criteria, the true effect sizes of these studies would be normally distributed about a mean, and observed study effect sizes are assumed to reflect a random sample of these effect sizes. Under the random-effects model, the goal is to estimate the mean of this distribution, and therefore there are two sources of variance: within-study error in estimating the effect size of each study, and variation in the true effects across studies. Thus, study weights are assigned to minimize these two sources of variance. The random-effects model is more plausible than the fixed-effect model for the majority of meta-analyses based on published literature, including those in environmental psychology, and thus is more commonly used.

Method for Conducting a Meta-analysis

This section provides step-by-step guidelines for how to conduct a basic meta-analysis. Readers may also wish to consult the following meta-analyses for reference: Hines, Hungerford, and Tomera (1986-1987); Gifford, Hine, and Veitch (1997);

Bamberg and Moser (2007); Osbaldiston and Schott (2012); Abrahamse and Steg (2013); Lokhorst et al. (2013); and Kormos and Gifford (2014). Likely there are also many other meta-analyses that have been published since the printing of this textbook.

Study selection

The study selection phase is the most important part of the meta-analysis; as mentioned above, the quality and meaningfulness of your synthesis depends on the extent to which you are thorough and systematic at this phase. Figure 20.1 depicts the flow diagram for the study selection process (Moher, Liberati, Tetzlaff, & Altman, The Prisma Group, 2009).

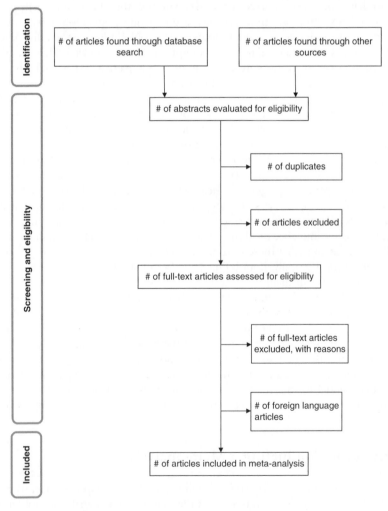

Figure 20.1   Flow diagram for study selection process.

First, clearly articulate your **eligibility criteria**. Readers should know exactly which criteria studies had to meet to be eligible for inclusion in your meta-analysis. Of course, these criteria will vary broadly, but two common criteria are that full-text articles have to be accessible in English (or another language of your choice), unless the appropriate information can be obtained through email from the authors; and also that studies have to provide primary, quantitative data, containing the information necessary to calculate the effect size. (If an article meets all of your inclusion criteria except the last one, authors can be emailed in an attempt to procure this information, but be clear to report this in your analysis.) Second, describe how the studies were identified and whether you searched for relevant published and unpublished studies, or just published studies. Indicate which online databases you used for your search (e.g., PsycINFO and ProQuest Dissertations and Theses) and include the date up until which the search is current. Mention key truncated search terms, taking into consideration multiple spellings (e.g., Canadian and American) as well as which field you searched in (which is typically the Abstract field). Record how many articles you identified from each database through this search strategy, and also indicate if you identified articles that may have been inadvertently missed through some additional means, such as reference lists of relevant articles or subject listerves. Third, indicate whether one or two members of the research team (two is preferable) screened all article titles and abstracts to determine whether or not they met the basic eligibility criteria. If insufficient information is available in the abstract to determine eligibility, then retrieve and evaluate the full-text article. Record how many initial exclusions were made based on the eligibility criteria, and thus the size of the remaining pool of potentially useful articles. Fourth, thoroughly evaluate the full-text versions of each article and make further exclusions, based on the eligibility criteria, as necessary. Record the final number of studies and total number of participants to be included in your analysis.

Data extraction

Indicate which statistics you extracted from each study to compute effect sizes (e.g., means, standard deviations, and sample size). In addition, if necessary, indicate which values were coded from each study for the moderation analyses, such as participant characteristics (e.g., mean age and socio-economic status) and methodological characteristics (e.g., the type of pro-environmental behavior and year of publication).

Data synthesis and analysis

Describe the software that you used to calculate effect sizes for each study and the overall effect size. Note that three different types of software can be used to conduct a meta-analysis (see Borenstein et al., 2009). The first option is to use a spreadsheet, such as Microsoft Excel. Although this approach allows the researcher to understand the formulas that underlie meta-analytic procedures, it is not ideal because these spreadsheets do not allow for a full array of options and are error-prone. Another option is to use a general-purpose statistical package, such as SPSS or SAS. However, these packages are designed for the analysis of primary studies, not meta-analyses, and as such it is very difficult to assign weights to each study and to perform sub-group analyses or meta-regression. The third option is to use a software package designed specifically for meta-analysis. This is the most convenient option because it allows for the greatest ease of assigning weights and carrying out more complicated moderator analyses. There are a variety of computer programs available for meta-analysis, including Comprehensive Meta-analysis (CMA) 2.0 (developed by Borenstein, Hedges, Higgins, & Rothstein; see www.meta-analysis.com), RevMan 5.0 (developed by The Cochrane Collaboration; see www.cc-ims.net/RevMan), as well as a set of macros developed for use with the general-purpose statistical package called Stata 10.0 (developed by Rosenberg, Adams, & Gurevitch; see www.metawinsoft.com). (Note, however, that only CMA and the Stata macros support subgroup analyses and meta-regression, and have the capability to fully assess publication bias.)

Next, indicate the type of data formats used to compute effect sizes for each study. Perhaps all of the studies in your analysis used a common design and reported the same type of data (e.g., means, standard deviations, and sample size for two independent groups). Or, perhaps the studies in your analysis used a variety of designs (e.g., some independent groups and some matched groups) or reported data in different formats. For example, some of your studies may report *p*-values and sample sizes, whereas others may provide data that requires the computation of an odds ratio or a chi-square value. The CMA program can handle data in a wide variety of formats, and RevMan and the Stata macros can also accept a variety of the most common data formats. However, you need to mention which types of data formats were included in your analysis. The beauty of specialized software packages, such as CMA, is that you can enter data in a wide variety of formats to mix and match in the same meta-analysis, and the program calculates individual effect sizes for all studies. This is also the case for more complex data structures, such as hierarchical structures with multiple outcomes within studies.

Following this, indicate the type of effect size that you selected for the overall summary effect, and also mention whether or not any transformations occurred prior to the analysis of the combined effect, such as the *z*-transformation that is necessary with *r*-values. Last, record whether the data were synthesized using a random-effects model or fixed-effect model. As mentioned above, the majority of meta-analyses in the social sciences employ the random-effects model.

Important Meta-analysis Statistics

Effect size

This section will focus on common measures of effect size used in social science meta-analyses, which are effect sizes from correlational data (*r*), and effect sizes from standardized mean differences (*d* or *g*) or unstandardized mean differences (*D*). More detailed descriptions of the other types of effect size, employed mostly in medical interventions include effect sizes from binary data, for example, risk ratios (*RR*), odds ratios (*OR*), or risk differences (*RD*) can be seen in other meta-analysis textbooks.

A single meta-analysis may contain studies that use any one of these measures of effect size, or values from which a measure of effect size may be computed by the researcher. The researcher must decide which effect size to use as the estimate of the overall effect size – typically this is the effect size that is used in the majority of the individual studies included in the analysis. In cases where the primary studies present different effect sizes, you can convert from one type to another to standardize the type of effect size for the overall estimate. Statistically speaking, it does not matter if the studies used independent groups or matched groups, and so the effect size can be calculated regardless of variations in study design and then all of the studies can be included in the same synthesis. (Note, however, that it is the researcher's responsibility to ensure that studies with different designs do not also differ in more substantive ways that could threaten the meaningfulness of the synthesis.)

Effect sizes from correlations   When the primary studies use a correlation to assess the strength of the association between two continuous variables, the correlation coefficient (i.e., Pearson's *r*) can be used as a measure of effect size. This is an intuitive measure that is already standardized to take into consideration differences in the original scales. In meta-analyses, the correlations are first converted into Fisher's *z* scale, the analysis is conducted using the transformed values, and then the summary effect is converted back into Pearson's *r* for presentation.

Effect sizes from means   When the primary studies report means and standard deviations in two groups, the unstandardized mean difference (D) or standardized mean difference (Cohen's *d*) are the most appropriate effect size measures.

If all studies in the analysis used the same scale and if that scale is known or inherently meaningful, then the meta-analysis can be performed on the unstandardized, or raw, difference in means (D). The benefit with D is that it is intuitively meaningful because the difference is in the same metric as the scale itself. D can either be calculated from studies that use either independent groups, matched groups, or pre-post test scores (see Borenstein et al., 2009, pp. 22–24). Meta-analysis software programs do the calculations for D if the researcher enters the mean, standard deviation, and sample size for each group.

If, however, the included studies use a variety of measures to evaluate the outcome, then it is not meaningful to combine raw mean differences. In these cases it is necessary to divide the mean difference in each study by that study's standard deviation to create the standardized mean difference (Cohen's *d*). The benefit with *d* is that all effect sizes are now comparable across studies, which allows for the comparison of different outcome measures within the same meta-analysis. The unbiased estimate of *d* is represented by Hedges' *g* (Hedges, 1981), and *d* can be converted to *g* using a correction factor called *J* (see Borenstein et al., 2009, pp. 27–28). Again, these values can be computed by software programs from studies that include two independent groups, matched groups, or pre-post scores in one group.

Heterogeneity

Estimating heterogeneity   Aside from merely quantifying summary effect sizes, another goal of meta-analysis is to estimate variation in effects across studies (**heterogeneity**) and to explain patterns in these effect sizes. For example, if a meta-analysis reveals that the effectiveness of an intervention varies across different types of pro-environmental behavior, the next step is to quantify this dispersion and

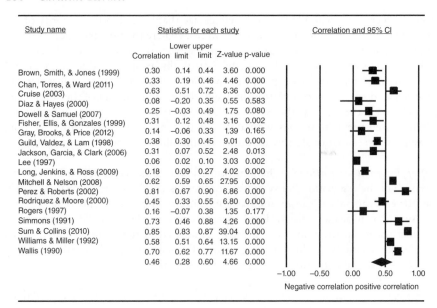

Figure 20.2   Example of a forest plot depicting the effect size measure and additional statistics for each study. This mock meta-analysis examines the correlation between environmental concern and pro-environmental behavior (note: not based on real data).

identify variables that explain it. As a crude measure of heterogeneity, the researcher can "eye-ball" the dispersion present in the effect sizes, as shown in a forest plot (Figure 20.2). The problem, however, is that the variation we observe is partly spurious because it contains true variation in effect sizes (i.e., in the underlying population) as well as random error; thus, before searching for moderators to explain heterogeneity, we must evaluate how much (if any) of the observed variance in effect sizes is real.

Q is the most basic measure of heterogeneity, and it is standardized. It is computed by comparing the observed variation (i.e., weighted sum of squares; WSS) to the amount of variation, or WSS, that would be expected if all studies shared a common effect size, and the excess is thought to reflect true differences among studies. This ratio can be used to generate several other measures of heterogeneity, such as I^2, T^2, and T. In general, all of these indices will be low (or zero) if the total variation is low compared to within-study error, and vice versa if the total variation is high compared to within-study error. This section will focus on two of these measures that are most important to report in a meta-analysis; specifically, the statistical test of the Q-value, which conveys a measure of uncertainty about whether or not the observed heterogeneity is real, and the I^2 ratio, which conveys a measure of the magnitude of heterogeneity.

The statistical test of Q addresses the question of whether the excess variance, or heterogeneity, is statistically significant. If the associated p-value is < 0.05, we reject the null hypothesis (i.e., that the true dispersion is exactly zero) and conclude that all of the studies do not have a common effect size.

The proportion of the observed variance that reflects real, rather than spurious, differences in effect size is represented by I^2. This is the ratio of true heterogeneity to total observed variation across observed effect estimates, expressed with a range of 0% to 100% (Higgins, Thompson, Deeks, & Altman, 2003). As such, I^2 is a measure of inconsistency across the studies. If I^2 is close to zero, then nearly all of the observed variance is spurious and so it is not necessary to examine moderators. However, if I^2 is large, then a large proportion of the observed variance is real and so you may wish to explore possible factors that might explain this variance, such as through subgroup analysis or meta-regression. As a rule of thumb, values of 25%, 50%, and 75% may be considered low, moderate, and high (Higgins et al., 2003). Note, however, that this value refers to the proportion of variance that is real, but does not refer to the amount of absolute variance. Therefore, a high I^2 value does not necessarily mean that the effects are spread across a wide range; it may merely mean that they were estimated precisely.

Two other measures of heterogeneity, T^2 (an estimate of the variance of the true effects, on the same scale as the effects themselves, but squared) and T (the standard deviation of the true effect sizes), which this chapter will not discuss in detail, refer to the amount of true heterogeneity. Whereas I^2 refers to the proportion of variance that is real but does not represent the absolute value of this variance, T^2 reflects the absolute value of the true variance but does not reflect the proportion of observed variance that is true.

Subgroup analyses If you find that significant heterogeneity exists among study effect sizes, then you are justified in exploring possible factors that may account for that dispersion. **Subgroup analyses** are appropriate when you wish to compare the mean effect sizes of two or more subgroups of studies; as such, these analyses can be thought of as analogous to an analysis of variance (ANOVA) in a primary study. In subgroup analyses, each study is coded and classified on the basis of a categorical moderator, and these analyses may be performed using either the fixed-effect or the random-effects model, although the latter is typically more appropriate. The Q-test of homogeneity is used to compare the statistical significance of the mean effect across subgroups to determine if it differs between or across the groups. For example, subgroup analyses may be used to determine whether or not the inclusion of a goal-setting intervention to a social norm message intervention has any additional influence on effect size compared to the base intervention.

Meta-regression **Meta-regression** can be used to evaluate the relationship between one or more study-level covariates and effect size. Therefore, each study is typically coded for continuous moderator(s), although categorical variables may also be used if they are dummy-coded. Using this technique, you can assess the influence of the covariates and predict effect sizes in studies with certain characteristics. As such, meta-regression is roughly analogous to multiple regression in a primary study (see Figure 20.3). For instance, meta-regression can be used to assess whether the descriptive social norms of participants in the samples included in the meta-analysis significantly influences the observed effect sizes. Note, however, that the use of meta-regression, particularly with multiple covariates, is only recommended when you have approximately 10 studies per covariate. Again, the Q-test is used to assess

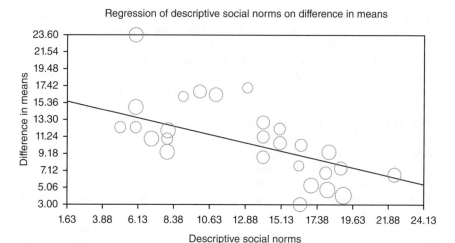

Figure 20.3 Example of meta-regression figure depicting the influence of participants' descriptive social norms on observed effect sizes, as represented by the difference in means (note: not based on real data).

statistical significance, typically employing the random-effects model. In addition, the magnitude of the relationship can be quantified using an index based on the percent reduction in true variance that is similar to R^2 among primary studies.

One final note of caution is that the association between effect size and subgroup membership or between effect size and covariates is observational and thus cannot be used to prove causality (even if all of the studies in the meta-analysis have used random assignment).

Publication bias

Publication bias refers to a bias in the articles that are likely to be published compared to those that are available to be published. One type of publication bias, the **positive results bias**, refers to the increased likelihood for researchers to submit, and for editors to accept, significant results rather than those that support the null hypothesis, resulting in an over-representation of significant findings in the published literature (Sackett, 1979). In fact, research has shown that significant results are three times more likely to be published compared to those that support the null hypothesis (Dickersin et al., 1987). The related "file drawer problem" refers to the tendency for non-significant results to remain unpublished by researchers (i.e., to stay in their file drawers or, nowadays, on their hard drives) (Rosenthal, 1979). Problematically, these unreported studies may, on average, suggest different results from those that are published, given that even a small number of such "file drawer" studies can lead to significant bias (Scargle, 2000). Understandably, if published studies do not accurately represent all studies on a particular topic/question, then meta-analytic results can be seriously flawed unless proper precautions are taken to adjust for this bias.

One important technique that can be undertaken during the study selection phase to minimize the effects of publication bias is to conduct a search that includes the "gray" literature (i.e., unpublished literature, such as government reports, conference papers, and dissertations); for example, one source for gray literature is the ProQuest Dissertations and Theses database. Although a meta-analysis *should* include a thorough search of all related articles, it can be difficult to identify articles in the gray literature and many reviews contain a small proportion of unpublished studies. Therefore, it is difficult to know the extent to which the bias has been avoided. Luckily, however, several analyses can be performed during the data analysis phase to assess the potential influence of publication bias on your results. The aim of a publication bias analysis is to categorize your results into one of three categories: (1) trivial impact of publication bias; (2) non-trivial impact, but where the major finding is still valid; and (3) considerable impact of publication bias, enough to call the major finding into question (see Borenstein et al., 2009).

First we want to see if there is evidence that publication bias impacted the observed effect. One tool for displaying the association between study sample size and effect size is the **funnel plot**. Here, effect size is on the X axis and the variance or standard error (indicative of sample size) is on the Y axis. A visual analysis of this plot should be based on the assumption that studies with small sample sizes (and thus often large variance) are more susceptible to publication bias because only the largest effects will be significant, whereas studies with larger sample sizes are more likely to be published irrespective of whether or not their results are significant. In general, therefore, we expect bias to increase as sample size decreases. When the effect size estimates are plotted against variance, a symmetrical funnel is observed when publication bias is not present (because then the sampling error is random), whereas an asymmetrical funnel is formed when potential publication bias is present. That is, a gap near the bottom left of the plot indicates where we would expect non-significant studies to be had we been able to find them. However, the funnel plot interpretation is largely subjective, and so several additional tests of publication bias have been proposed.

One test created to assess whether or not the overall effect is robust (i.e., how confident we can be that the effect is not merely an artifact of bias) is **Rosenthal's (1979) classic fail-safe N**. This test provides the number of studies with a mean effect size of zero that would be necessary before the overall effect found in the meta-analysis would become statistically non-significant. If only a small number of studies are needed to negate the effect, then there is cause for concern; in contrast, if a large number of studies would be needed to negate the effect, then there is less cause for concern. Thus, this value can provide an estimate of the robustness of the finding and how likely it is that the true effect is non-zero.

As an extension of the funnel plot, the **Trim and Fill procedure** (Duval & Tweedie, 2000a, 2000b), has been proposed to estimate the impact of the publication bias as well as what the effect size would have been in the absence of bias. This procedure can be used to infer the existence of unpublished studies and subsequently adjust the meta-analysis by imputing these missing studies to result in an unbiased estimate of the combined effect size. Specifically, it is an iterative procedure that selectively removes extreme effect sizes from small studies from the positive side of the funnel plot, and replaces them with imputed scores to produce a more symmetrical funnel plot about the newly derived overall effect size (see Figure 20.4), resulting in a less-biased estimate

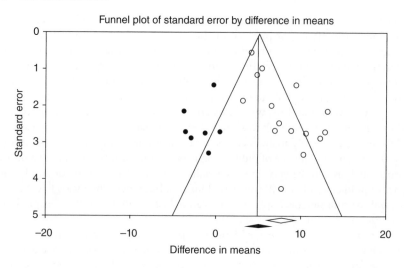

Figure 20.4   Example of a funnel plot depicting standard error by difference in means (note: not based on real data).

of the overall effect size. If either no or few studies need to be trimmed, and therefore if the adjusted point estimate is similar to the observed point estimate, then it is unlikely that publication bias substantially contributed to the observed effect size.

Reporting Meta-analysis Results

Table 20.1 displays an outline of the typical results reported in a meta-analysis. (Note, of course, that the empirical findings and thus necessary statistics to report will vary according to the specifics of the questions investigated in your analysis.)

Summary and Conclusions

The meta-analytic approach offers many advantages over pre-existing approaches. These procedures allow the researcher to estimate and evaluate the combined effect size across all related studies, to quantify heterogeneity across effect sizes, and to explore study-level covariates. However, this approach is not always appropriate or possible and, in some cases, a narrative review is better suited to the research question at hand. The decision about which synthesis technique is more appropriate to use is at the discretion of the researcher. As noted, meta-analytic procedures are merely statistical tools that can be used to combine and evaluate any set of data, and so it is up to researchers to ensure that this technique is used to synthesize appropriate studies, and also that this synthesis is conducted systematically and transparently. Insofar as this occurs, meta-analysis offers the potential to help researchers make sense of ever-proliferating knowledge as they strive to conduct and apply their research most efficiently and effectively.

Table 20.1 The typical outline for statistics that are generally reported in meta-analytic results.

Reporting meta-analytic results

Descriptive statistics
Number of included studies and total participants
Table with descriptive statistics for each study (e.g., group means, sample sizes, participant age, and gender)

Overall effect size
State whether employed random-effects or fixed-effect model
Overall summary effect significant?
    Summary effect (e.g., r, d, D, and g), confidence interval, and p-value
    Associated magnitude of effect size
Forest plot (effect size, *SEM* and *CI* statistics for each study) – provides intuitive sense of the data (see Figure 20.2)

Heterogeneity
Significant heterogeneity detected among effect sizes? (If so, estimate dispersion. If not, effect is consistent across all studies)
    Include $Q(df)$ value and associated p-value
I^2 value and percent of variance explained by true systematic effect size differences between studies (i.e., $I^2 \times 100$)
Heterogeneity analyses suggest need to explore possible moderating variables (yes/no)?

Moderator analyses
Which moderators emerged as significant and non-significant?
Categorical moderators: subgroup comparison results (Qvalue (df) value and p-value)
    Which had the greatest effect sizes (report average effect sizes for subgroups)
    Continuous moderators: meta-regression results (Qmodel (df) value and p-value)
    How was the covariate related to the summary effect size (i.e., negatively or positively, and describe relationship)?
    Can include figure, if desired (see Figure 20.3)

Publication bias
Rosenthal's (1979) fail-safe N value, and implications
Results of Duval and Tweedie's (2000a, 2000b) Trim and Fill procedure (i.e., how many studies needed to be trimmed and what was the adjusted point estimate?)
    Can include figure, if desired (see Figure 20.4)
    What do these analyses suggest about the potential influence of publication bias on the observed effect size?

Glossary

Eligibility criteria The criteria that studies had to meet to be eligible for inclusion in the meta-analysis (e.g., full-text articles have to be accessible in a language of your choice).

Fixed-effect model The assumption with this model is that all studies in the analysis share one true effect size, and thus that the summary effect is the estimate of this common effect size of the underlying population (i.e., that all variables that could influence the effect size are identical across all studies).

Another assumption is that all of the observed differences in effects are the result of sampling error.

Funnel plot   A subjective tool to assist in evaluating potential publication bias. This plot displays the association between study sample size or standard error (Y axis) and effect size (X axis). A symmetrical funnel is observed when publication bias is not present (because then the sampling error is random), whereas an asymmetrical funnel is formed when potential publication bias is present.

Heterogeneity   Variation in effect sizes across studies.

Meta-analysis   A statistical approach that enables researchers to examine an entire body of evidence related to one question or topic, and to estimate and evaluate the mean strength of the combined effect size across all related studies, with more weight given to more precise studies with larger samples sizes.

Meta-regression   A statistical technique used to evaluate the relationship between one or more study-level covariates (i.e., either continuous moderators or categorical moderators that are dummy-coded) and effect size.

Narrative review   A non-statistical summary of findings whereby the researcher combines findings from related studies by counting the number of statistically significant studies compared to the number of statistically non-significant studies, and thus arrives at conclusions about a given research area.

Positive results bias   One type of publication bias, which refers to the increased likelihood for researchers to submit, and for editors to accept, significant results rather than those that support the null hypothesis, leading to an over-representation of significant findings in the published literature.

Power   The probability that a statistical test will detect a significant finding if one exists.

Publication bias   Bias in the articles that are likely to be published compared to those that are available to be published.

Random-effects model   According to this model, the true effect is allowed (and assumed) to vary across studies according to a variety of moderators, such as socio-demographic characteristics of participants and other differences among studies (e.g., design).

Rosenthal's classic fail-safe *N*   A test created to assess the robustness of the overall effect (i.e., how confident we can be that the effect is not merely an artifact of bias) as well as how likely it is that the true effect is non-zero. This test provides the number of studies with a mean effect size of zero that would be necessary before the overall effect found in the meta-analysis would become statistically non-significant.

Subgroup analyses   A statistical technique that can be used to compare the mean effect sizes of two or more subgroups of studies (often classified on the basis of a categorical moderator); as such, these analyses can be thought of as analogous to an analysis of variance (ANOVA) in a primary study.

Trim and Fill procedure   An extension of the funnel plot, proposed by Duval and Tweedie (2000a, 2000b) to estimate the impact of the publication bias. This procedure can be used to infer the existence of unpublished studies and subsequently adjust the meta-analysis by imputing these missing studies to result in an adjusted, unbiased estimate of the combined effect size.

References

Abrahamse, W., Steg, L., Vlek, C., & Rothengatter, T. (2005). A review of intervention studies aimed at household energy conservation. *Journal of Environmental Psychology*, 25, 273–291.

Abrahamse, W., & Steg., L. (2013). Social influence approaches to encourage resource conservation: A meta-analysis. *Global Environmental Change*, 23, 1773–1785.

Bamberg, S., & Moser, G. (2007). Twenty years after Hines, Hungerford, and Tomera: A new meta-analysis of psycho-social determinants of pro-environmental behaviour. *Journal of Environmental Psychology*, 27, 14–25.

Borenstein, M., Hedges, L., Higgins, J., & Rothstein, H. (2009). *Introduction to meta-analysis*. Chichester, UK: Wiley.

Bösch, H. (2004). Reanalyzing a meta-analysis on extra-sensory perception dating from 1940, the first comprehensive meta-analysis in the history of science. In S. Schmidt (Ed.), *Proceedings of the 47th Annual Convention of the Parapsychological Association* (pp. 1–13). University of Vienna, Austria.

Card, N. A. (2011). *Applied meta-analysis for social science research*. New York, NY: Guilford Press.

Cooper, H. (2010). *Research synthesis and meta-analysis: A step-by-step approach* (3rd ed.). Thousand Oaks, CA: Sage.

Cochran, W. G. (1937). Problems arising in the analysis of a series of similar experiments. *Journal of the Royal Statistical Society*, 4, 102–118.

Dickersin, K., Chan, S., Chalmers, T. C., et al. (1987). Publication bias and clinical trials. *Controlled Clinical Trials*, 8, 343–353.

Duval, S., & Tweedie, R. (2000a). A nonparametric "trim and fill" method of accounting for publication bias in meta-analysis. *Journal of the American Statistical Association*, 95, 89–98.

Duval, S., & Tweedie, R. (2000b). Trim and fill: A simple funnel-plot-based method of testing and adjusting for publication bias in meta-analysis. *Biometrics*, 56, 455–463.

Eysenck, H. J. (1978). An exercise in mega-silliness. *American Psychologist*, 33, 517–519.

Gifford, R., Hine, D. W., & Veitch, J. A. (1997). Meta-analysis for environment-behavior research, illuminated with a study of lighting level effects on office task performance. In G. T. Moore & R. W. Marans (Eds.), *Advances in environment, behavior, and design* (vol. 4). New York, NY: Plenum.

Glass, G. V. (1976). Primary, secondary, and meta-analysis of research. *Educational Researcher*, 5, 3–8.

Hedges, L. (1981). Distribution theory for Glass's estimator of effect size and related estimators. *Journal of Educational Statistics*, 6, 107–128.

Higgins, J. P. T., & Green, S. (Eds.). (2011). *Cochrane handbook for systematic reviews of interventions*. http://handbook.cochrane.org/

Higgins, J., Thompson, S. G., Deeks, J. J., & Altman, D. G. (2003). Measuring inconsistency in meta-analyses. *British Medical Journal*, 327, 557–560.

Hines, J. M., Hungerford, H. R., & Tomera, A. N. (1986–1987). Analysis and synthesis of research on responsible environmental behavior: A meta-analysis. *Journal of Environmental Education*, 18, 1–8.

Kormos, C., & Gifford, R. (2014). The validity of self-report measures of proenvironmental behavior: A meta-analytic review. *Journal of Environmental Psychology*, 40, 359–371.

Lokhorst, A. M., Werner, C., Staats, H., van Dijk, E., & Gale, J. L. (2013). Review of commitment-making strategies in environmental commitment and behavior change: A meta-analysis and critical research. *Environment and Behavior*, 45, 3–34.

Moher, D., Liberati, A., Tetzlaff, J., & Altman, D. G., The PRISMA Group (2009). Preferred reporting items for systematic reviews and meta-analyses: The PRISMA statement. *PLoS Med 6* (6): e1000097. doi:10.1371/journal.pmed1000097

Osbaldiston, R., & J. P. Schott. (2012). Environmental sustainability and behavioral science: Meta-Analysis of proenvironmental behavior experiments. *Environment and Behavior*, *44*, 257–299.

Rosenthal, R. (1979). The "file drawer problem" and tolerance for null results. *Psychological Bulletin*, *86*, 638–641.

Richard, F. D., Bond Jr., C. F., & Stokes-Zoota, J. J. (2003). One hundred years of social psychology quantitatively described. *Review of General Psychology*, *7*, 331–363.

Sackett, D. L. (1979). Bias in analytic research. *Journal of Chronic Disease*, *32*, 51–63.

Scargle, J. D. (2000). Publication bias: The "file-drawer problem" in scientific inference. *Journal of Scientific Exploration*, *14*, 94–106.

Shapiro, S. (1994). Meta-analysis/shmeta-analysis. *American Journal of Epidemiology*, *140*, 771–778.

Suggested Readings

Borenstein, M., Hedges, L., Higgins, J., & Rothstein, H. (2009). *Introduction to meta-analysis*. Chichester, UK: Wiley.

Card, N. A. (2011). *Applied meta-analysis for social science research*. New York, NY: Guilford Press.

Cooper, H. (2010). *Research synthesis and meta-analysis: A step-by-step approach* (3rd ed.). Thousand Oaks, CA: Sage.

Higgins, J., & Green, S. (Eds.). (2011). *Cochrane handbook for systematic reviews of interventions*. http://handbook.cochrane.org/

PRISMA website (www.prisma-statement.org).

Author Index

Research Methods for Environmental Psychology, First Edition. Edited by Robert Gifford.
© 2016 John Wiley & Sons, Ltd. Published 2016 by John Wiley & Sons, Ltd.

Subject Index

Research Methods for Environmental Psychology, First Edition. Edited by Robert Gifford.
© 2016 John Wiley & Sons, Ltd. Published 2016 by John Wiley & Sons, Ltd.